T0212695

Lecture Notes in Computer Science 8905

Commenced Publication in 1973
Founding and Former Series Editors:
Gerhard Goos, Juris Hartmanis, and Jan van Leeuwen

Editorial Board

More information about this series at http://www.springer.com/series/7409

Mitsuko Aramaki · Olivier Derrien
Richard Kronland-Martinet · Sølvi Ystad (Eds.)

Sound, Music, and Motion

10th International Symposium, CMMR 2013
Marseille, France, October 15–18, 2013
Revised Selected Papers

 Springer

Editors

Mitsuko Aramaki
CNRS - LMA
Marseille
France

Richard Kronland-Martinet
CNRS - LMA
Marseille
France

Olivier Derrien
Toulon-Var University and CNRS - LMA
Marseille
France

Sølvi Ystad
CNRS - LMA
Marseille
France

ISSN 0302-9743   ISSN 1611-3349 (electronic)
Lecture Notes in Computer Science
ISBN 978-3-319-12975-4   ISBN 978-3-319-12976-1   (eBook)
DOI 10.1007/978-3-319-12976-1

Library of Congress Control Number: 2014957858

LNCS Sublibrary: SL3 – Information Systems and Applications, incl. Internet/Web, and HCI

Springer Cham Heidelberg New York Dordrecht London

Printed on acid-free paper

Springer International Publishing AG Switzerland is part of Springer Science+Business Media
(www.springer.com)

Preface

The 10th International Symposium on Computer Music Multidisciplinary Research CMMR 2013 "Sound, Music and Motion" (http://www.cmmr2013.cnrs-mrs.fr/) took place in Marseille, the European Capital of Culture 2013, during October 15–18, 2013 and was organized by the Laboratoire de Mécanique et d'Acoustique (LMA). This 10th anniversary was the opportunity to federate strong forces from Marseille's region on both the scientific and artistic sides by associating on the one hand renowned French laboratories and universities: LMA, Institut des Sciences du Mouvement (ISM), Laboratoire de Neurosciences Cognitives (LNC), Laboratoire d'Analyse, Topologie, Probabilities (LATP), Sciences, Arts et Techniques de l'Image et du Son (SATIS), and on the other hand renowned music and dance associations: Ubris Studio, n+n corsino, which took care of the artistic program of the conference.

This 10th CMMR event gathered around 170 delegates from 21 countries during 4 days including 11 oral sessions, 2 poster and demo sessions that covered traditional topics of previous CMMR events and specific topics related to the theme of the conference. In addition, 5 installations were exposed around the campus during the whole conference. Five renowned keynote speakers were invited to present their respective works: Jean-Claude Risset from the LMA (France), Marcelo M. Wanderley from the Centre for Interdisciplinary Research in Music Media and Technology (Canada), Cathy Craig from the Movement Innovation Lab (Northern Ireland), Norbert Corsino (artist choreographer, France), and Daniel Deshays (sound director and engineer, France). Their presentations are available at: http://www.cmmr2013.cnrs-mrs.fr/Keynotes.html. Concerts related to the music festival associated to the conference took place each evening after the scientific sessions in partnership with the Bernardines theater which hosted two concerts. A satellite workshop on the theme "Music, Movement and Brain" was also organized by Cynthia M. Grund and her "Nordic Network for the Integration of Music Informatics, Performance and Aesthetics" the day before the conference, featuring paper presentations, a panel, and tutorials.

This symposium was initiated in 2003 and has been organized in several countries (Europe and India in 2011). The CMMR acronym originally symbolized Computer Music Modeling and Retrieval and the first CMMR gatherings mainly focused on information retrieval, programming, digital libraries, hypermedia, artificial intelligence, acoustics, and signal processing. Little by little CMMR has moved toward more interdisciplinary aspects related to the role of human interaction in musical practice, perceptual and cognitive aspects linked to sound modeling, and how sense or meaning can be transmitted either from isolated sounds or musical structure as a whole. During CMMR 2012, the Steering Committee therefore decided to slightly change the significance of the acronym from Computer Music Modeling and Retrieval to Computer Music Multidisciplinary Research. This means that new research communities now are welcome to the conference in addition to the traditional ones.

The CMMR 2013 post-proceedings edition is the 10th book published by Springer Verlag in the Lecture Notes in Computer Sciences Series (LNCS 2771, LNCS 3310, LNCS 3902, LNCS 4969, LNCS 5493, LNCS 5954, LNCS 6684, LNCS 7172, LNCS 7900). The book is divided into 10 chapters containing the peer-reviewed and revised versions of 38 selected conference papers and 2 keynote papers for this post-proceedings edition. The chapters reflect the interdisciplinary nature of this conference, which welcome any sound-related topic. This year particular emphasis was placed on the conference theme "Sound, Music and Motion", including topics on musical gestures and new interfaces (Chapter 1) as well as multimodal relations between sounds and gestures (Chapter 4) and between sounds and images (Chapter 8). More sound-specific topics were presented from varied standpoints including analysis and mathematical representations of sounds (Chapter 7), sound synthesis (Chapter 6), sonification (Chapter 3), and auditory perception and cognition (Chapter 9). Finally, music information retrieval (MIR) contributions that have always been an important part of the CMMR conference are presented in three different chapters dealing with classification (Chapter 2), data mining (Chapter 5), and recognition (Chapter 10).

We would like to thank all the participants of CMMR 2013 who strongly contributed to make this 10th anniversary an unforgettable event. We would also like to thank the Program Committee members for their indispensable paper reports and the Music Committee for the difficult task of selecting the artistic contributions. We are truly grateful to the Local Organizing Committee at the LMA that handled all the practical issues and ensured effcient and harmonious coordination between the different actors of the conference. Finally, we would like to thank Springer for accepting to publish the CMMR 2013 post-proceedings in their LNCS series.

September 2014

Mitsuko Aramaki
Olivier Derrien
Richard Kronland-Martinet
Sølvi Ystad

Organization

The 10th International Symposium on Computer Music Multidisciplinary Research CMMR 2013 "Sound, Music and Motion" was organized by the Laboratoire de Mécanique et d'Acoustique, Marseille (France).

Symposium Chair

Richard Kronland-Martinet   CNRS-LMA, France

Paper, Program, and Proceedings Chairs

Richard Kronland-Martinet	CNRS-LMA, France
Mitsuko Aramaki	CNRS-LMA, France
Sølvi Ystad	CNRS-LMA, France
Olivier Derrien	Toulon-Var University and CNRS-LMA, France

Special Sessions Chairs

Rémi Adjiman	SATIS, France
Mathieu Barthet	Queen Mary University of London, UK
Christophe Bourdin	ISM and Aix-Marseille University, France
Lionel Bringoux	ISM and Aix-Marseille University, France
Kristoffer Jensen	Aalborg University, Denmark
Peter Sinclair	Ecole Supérieure d'art d'Aix-en-Provence and Locus Sonus - audio in art, France
Diemo Schwarz	IRCAM, France
Bruno Torrésani	LATP and Aix-Marseille University, France

Demonstration and Installation Chairs

Charles Gondre	CNRS-LMA, France
Gaëtan Parseihian	CNRS-LMA, France

Communication and Sponsoring Chairs

Simon Conan	CNRS-LMA, France
Etienne Thoret	CNRS-LMA, France

Committees

Local Organizing Committee

Jessica Bouanane	CNRS-LMA, France
Jacques Chatron	CNRS-LMA, France
Simon Conan	CNRS-LMA, France
Charles Gondre	CNRS-LMA, France
Antoine Gonot	SATIS and CNRS-LMA, France
Gaëtan Parseihian	CNRS-LMA, France
Alain Rimeymeille	CNRS-LMA, France
Etienne Thoret	CNRS-LMA, France
Thierry Voinier	CNRS-LMA, France

Program Committee

Rémi Adjiman	ASTRAM-SATIS, France
Mitsuko Aramaki	CNRS-LMA, France
Federico Avanzini	University of Padova, Italy
Peter Balazs	Acoustics Research Institute, Austria
Mathieu Barthet	Queen Mary University of London, UK
Frédéric Bevilacqua	IRCAM, France
Stefan Bilbao	University of Edinburgh, Scotland
Christophe Bourdin	ISM and Aix-Marseille University, France
Lionel Bringoux	ISM and Aix-Marseille University, France
John Ashley Burgoyne	University of Amsterdam, The Netherlands
Marcelo Caetano	Institute of Computer Science, Greece
Philippe Depalle	McGill University, Canada
Olivier Derrien	Toulon-Var University and CNRS-LMA, France
Myriam Desainte-Catherine	LaBRI, University of Bordeaux, France
Barry Eaglestone	University of Sheffield, UK
Gianpaolo Evangelista	Linköping Institute of Technology, Sweden
Bruno Giordano	University of Glasgow, Scotland
Rolf Inge Gødoy	University of Oslo, Norway
Antoine Gonot	SATIS and CNRS-LMA, France
Fabien Gouyon	INESC Porto, Portugal
Brian Gygi	National Biomedical Unit for Hearing Research, UK
Goffredo Haus	University of Milan, Italy
Kristoffer Jensen	Aalborg University, Denmark
Brian Katz	LIMSI, France
Richard Kronland-Martinet	CNRS-LMA, France
Sylvain Marchand	Université de Bretagne Occidentale, France
Sabine Meunier	CNRS-LMA, France
Eduardo Miranda	University of Plymouth, UK
Emery Schubert	University of New South Wales, Australia

Diemo Schwarz	IRCAM, France
Peter Sinclair	Ecole Supérieure d'art d'Aix-en-Provence
	and Locus Sonus - audio in art, France
Julius O. Smith	Stanford University, USA
Bruno Torrésani	LATP and Aix-Marseille University, France
George Tzanetakis	University of Victoria, Canada
Marcelo M. Wanderley	CIRMMT, Canada
Sølvi Ystad	CNRS-LMA, France

Additional Reviewers

Charles Bascou
Mattia Bergomi
Eric Boyer
Yinan Cao
Baptiste Caramiaux
Simon Conan
Luke Dahl
Alastair Disley
Sebastian Ewert
György Fazekas
Nicholas Gillian
Marcello Giordano
Mailis Gomes Rodrigues
Charles Gondre
Jens Hjortkjær
Hyung-Suk Kim

Luca Andrea Ludovico
Davide Andrea Mauro
Jean-Arthur Micoulaud-Franchi
Oriol Nieto
Gaëtan Parseihian
Rui Penha
Lise Regnier
Pasi Saari
Stephen Sinclair
Guillaume Stempfel
Etienne Thoret
Giovanna Varni
Charles Verron
Thierry Voinier
Michael Winters

Contents

Augmented Musical Instruments
and Gesture Recognition

Investigation of the Harpist/Harp Interaction

Delphine Chadefaux[1,2]([✉]), Jean-Loïc Le Carrou[1,2], Benoît Fabre[1,2],
and Laurent Daudet[3]

[1] LAM / Institut Jean Le Rond D'Alembert, Sorbonne Universités,
UPMC Univ Paris 06, UMR 7190, 75005 Paris, France
[2] LAM / Institut Jean Le Rond D'Alembert,
UMR CNRS 7190, 75005 Paris, France
delphine.chadefaux@univ-amu.fr,
{jean-loic.le_carrou,benoit.fabre}@upmc.fr
[3] Institut Langevin, Paris Diderot University,
ESPCI, UMR CNRS 7587, Paris, France
laurent.daudet@espci.fr

Abstract. This paper presents a contribution to the field of the musician/instrument interaction analysis. This study aims at investigating the mechanical parameters that govern the harp plucking action as well as the gestural strategies set up by harpists to control a musical performance. Two specific experimental procedures have been designed to accurately describe the harpist motion in realistic playing contexts. They consist in filming the plucking action and the harpists gestures using a high-speed camera and a motion capture system, respectively. Simultaneously, acoustical measurements are performed to relate the kinematic investigation to sound features. Results describe the musical gesture characteristics. Mechanical parameters governing the finger/string interaction are highlighted and their influence on the produced sound are discussed. Besides, the relationship between non sound-producing gestures and musical intent is pointed out. Finally, the way energy is shared between harpist arm joints according to various playing techniques is analyzed.

Keywords: Harp · High-speed video analysis · Motion capture · Acoustics · Data mining

1 Introduction

A musical performance can be split into several processes (see Fig. 1) requiring expertise in many research fields to achieve its complete proper analysis. The musician has first to interpret the played score before setting the instrument into vibrations. Then, the latter produces the sound which is radiated in the room and perceived by the audience. Eventually, while playing, the musician adjusts his performance based on tactile and acoustical feedbacks as well as conveys his musical intent to the audience through corporal expression. Based on this

© Springer International Publishing Switzerland 2014
M. Aramaki et al. (Eds.): CMMR 2013, LNCS 8905, pp. 3–19, 2014.
DOI: 10.1007/978-3-319-12976-1_1

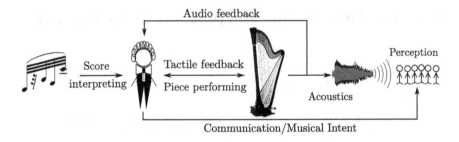

Fig. 1. Block diagram of a musical piece performance.

statement, we choose to focus the present paper on the musician's actions on the instrument in a harp performance. Stringed instruments are well-investigated at the mechanical and acoustical levels [7] and can now be satisfyingly synthesized [8,14,18]. However, the way to control these sound-synthesis are still lacking of realism at a mechanical level since parameters controlled by musicians while playing are not taken into account. Investigations of musician control parameters in musical contexts are thus required to propose improvements in this field and provide an understanding of the sound differences between musicians [4,15].

A skilled musician develops the ability to control his sound production during many years of practice until reaching the capability to precisely define the whole set of acoustical features that govern the produced note. This notion is directly related to the *acoustical signature* of each musician which depends on the control parameters he owns to play a given instrument (e.g. bow force, bow velocity and bow-bridge distance for the violin [16]). In the present case of plucked string instruments, the control parameters consist in the initial conditions of the string vibrations provided by the musician (string's shape, velocity, rotation around its axis, as well as its angle of polarization at the release instant [5]). The control of such highly-precise movements cannot be only governed at the hand level. The control parameters that define the sound production result from complex mechanisms combining musician motion, audio and proprioceptive feedback. Hence, improving the understanding of these mechanisms through gestural analysis of musicians in realistic musical context is valuable to perform relevant gesture-based sound synthesis through virtual character animation [2].

The current paper relates the main experimental contributions of a general study of harp performance [3]. The first section aims at investigating the sound producing gestures, i.e. the plucking action. The experimental procedure is presented in Sect. 2.1. Then acoustical and kinematic descriptors are defined and computed to discuss the range of value as well as the impact of the harpist control parameters on the string vibration in Sect. 2.3. The second part deals with an experimentally-based analysis of the gestural strategies in harp performance. We successively present the experimental setup and the data processing method carried out in Sects. 3.1 and 3.2, respectively. Finally, the descriptors are computed to point out underlying gestural strategies in different musical context in Sect. 3.3.

2   Plucking Analysis

A detailed description of the harp plucking action has been provided in [5] from an acoustical point of view. Further kinematics analyses of the collected database are proposed in the following section and discussed relatively to musical considerations.

2.1   Experimental Procedure

Ten harpists have participated in a set of measurements carried out to study the harp plucking. They have been asked to perform proposed *arpeggio* and chords sequences involving only the left hand on an Atlantide Prestige Camac concert harp. The scores of these musical excerpts are presented in Fig. 3. Measurements mostly consist in accurately capturing the finger and string trajectories in the 3D-space through a high-speed camera set at 5167 fps and fixed to the instrument to let harpists tilt the harp at their convenience. The spatial range allowed by the latter sample rate induces to film only one harp string (the 30th string, D♭3 at about 140 Hz) from the entire set of strings involved in the proposed musical excerpts. Thus the performed analyses focus on the 30th string plucked with annular and forefinger in *arpeggio* and chord sequences contexts. The high-speed camera directly provides displacements in the (e_x, e_y) plane defined in Fig. 2 while a mirror is required to estimate the trajectories' component along the e_z-axis. Figure 2 shows an image captured with the high-speed camera. The left part of the image presents the direct framing while the right part shows the associated mirror view. The black markers disposed on the finger and the string are then automatically tracked throughout the film based on an image processing procedure described in [5]. Simultaneously, resulting acoustical signals and soundboard vibrations have been measured with two standard microphones placed at about one meter of the harp's column and an accelerometer fixed at the bottom of the studied string, respectively.

2.2   Data Processing

As high-speed camera films of harp plucking reveal that finger motion mainly takes place in the plane perpendicular to the strings-plane, finger/string interaction is investigated in the grayed (e_x, e_z)-plane in Fig. 2. A sample of the collected finger/string trajectories database is proposed in Fig. 2. Instants t_c and t_r mark the beginning and the end of the plucking action, respectively. At t_c the finger starts to touch the string while t_r corresponds to the instant the finger releases the string, i.e. the beginning of the string's free oscillations. Between these two instants, two plucking phases exist: the sticking (when finger and string move in parallel) and the slipping (when the string slips on the finger surface with opposite direction) phases. The former lasts about 200 ms while the latter's duration is about 3 ms [5]. Under the classical assumptions that the

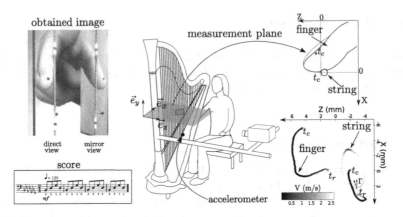

Fig. 2. Scheme of the experimental setup carried out to analyze the harp plucking action. An image obtained through the high-speed camera is presented as well as an example of finger and string trajectories in the measurement frame of reference (grayed plane).

string is flexible, of uniform linear density ρ_l, stretched to a tension T and fixed at its ends, its transverse vibrations are

$$r(y,t) = \sum_{n=1}^{\infty} \Phi_n(y)(x_n(t)\cos\Gamma e_x + z_n(t)\sin\Gamma e_z), \qquad (1)$$

where $x_n(t)$ and $z_n(t)$ are the generalized displacements [7], $\Phi_n(y)$ is the modal deflection [7], and the angle of polarization Γ is defined in Fig. 2 as the angle between e_x and the major axis of the ellipse shaped by the vibrating string. As the harp strings are attached at the soundboard through a simple knot, we assume this fixation system will favour the transmission of the e_x component of the vibrations to the soundboard. Thus, the previous expression can be simplified as

$$r(y,t) = \sum_{n=1}^{\infty} \Phi_n(y)x_n(t)\cos\Gamma e_x, \qquad (2)$$

$$= \sum_{n=1}^{\infty} \Phi_n(y)\left(A_n\cos\omega_n t + B_n\sin\omega_n t\right)\cos\Gamma e_x, \qquad (3)$$

where the damping is supposed to be negligible on the early oscillations, ω_n are the eigen-frequencies and A_n and B_n are the modal amplitudes depending from the initial displacement D_{t_r} and velocity V_{t_r} of the string at the plucking position y_0, both assumed to be triangular-shaped along the string length:

$$A_n = \frac{2D_{t_r}\sin(k_n y_0)}{k_n^2 y_0(L - y_0)}, \text{ and } B_n = \frac{2V_{t_r}\sin(k_n y_0)}{k_n^3 y_0(L - y_0)c}, \qquad (4)$$

with $c = \sqrt{T/\rho_l}$ the wave velocity. Finally, we obtain

$$r(y,t) = \sum_{n=1}^{\infty} \Phi_n(y) \frac{2 \sin(k_n y_0) \cos \Gamma}{k_n^2 y_0 (L - y_0)} \left(D_{t_r} \cos \omega_n t + \frac{V_{t_r}}{\omega_n} \sin \omega_n t \right) e_x. \quad (5)$$

A harpist disposes of the four following parameters to control his sound production: D_{t_r}, V_{t_r}, Γ and y_0. In spite of its strong influence on the spectral content of the played note, it has been shown that the plucking position is not a discriminating feature between harpists [5]. Further, it has been measured that the 30th string is plucked at about the third of its length. This is why this parameter is not discussed in the present study. At a temporal level, control parameters influence the instant, when the maximal amplitude of the vibrations is reached:

$$t_M = \frac{1}{\omega_0} \arctan \frac{V_{t_r}}{D_{t_r} \omega_0}, \quad (6)$$

as well as the maximal amplitude at t_M:

$$|r|_{max} = \sum_{n=1}^{\infty} \Phi_n(y) \frac{2 \sin(k_n y_0) \cos \Gamma}{k_n^2 y_0 (L - y_0)} \sqrt{D_{t_r}^2 + \frac{V_{t_r}^2}{\omega_n^2}}. \quad (7)$$

Further, control parameters influence also the spectral content of the produced sound. As it is expected to show a good correlation with the sensation of brightness of the sound produced [10], we choose to express the spectral centroid relatively to the harpist control parameters:

$$CGS = \frac{\sum_{n=1}^{\infty} f_n |\tilde{R}_n(f)|}{\sum_{n=1}^{\infty} |\tilde{R}_n(f)|}, \quad (8)$$

$$= \frac{\sum_{n=1}^{\infty} f_n |\Phi_n(y)| \sin(k_n y_0) k_n^{-2} \sqrt{D_{t_r}^2 + V_{t_r}^2/\omega_n^2}}{\sum_{n=1}^{\infty} |\Phi_n(y)| \sin(k_n y_0) k_n^{-2} \sqrt{D_{t_r}^2 + V_{t_r}^2/\omega_n^2}}. \quad (9)$$

where $\tilde{R}_n(f)$ is the Fourier transform of the string's transverse motion $r(y,t)$. This spectral descriptor is often computed on the radiated sound rather than on the string vibrations to characterize the sound production. However, even if the relationship between the vibrations of the string and the radiated sound is not straightforward and requires the knowledge of the soundboard mobility as well as the harp radiation properties, we expect the spectral centroid computed on the string vibrations to give an insight on the influence of the plucking conditions.

2.3   Results

Figure 3 presents an example of finger movements in the (e_x, e_z)-plane for two harpists plucking the 30th string in the four configurations we analyze in this paper, i.e. Db2 played with the forefinger or the annular (referred as to 2 and 4 in the fingering of the proposed scores) in *arpeggio* or chord sequences. The main conveyed result is that the pattern drawn by the harpist finger while plucking a string is a gestural signature of the player in a given musical context. Harp plucking is hence an expert gesture which is characterized by a high repeatability and specificity to the performer. Besides, it is interesting to note that the finger motion give us some insight on the underlying musical structure of the played excerpt. Indeed, second and fourth beats of each repeated sequence show various shapes and thus various emphases. Even if this phenomena is noticeable for chords, it notably occurs in *arpeggio* contexts. Further, whatever the considered finger, we widely observe that the finger motion is more straightforward while playing a chord than an *arpeggio*. This directly results from the implied technique and the duration of the finger/string interaction: in average 140 ms vs. 263 ms for chord and *arpeggio*, respectively. Unlike to *arpeggio* sequence where the interaction lasts the entire duration between two notes, the harpist hand is not positioned on the strings to play a chord and the interaction lasts about a quarter of the amount of time available. The harpist has therefore more time to control his *arpeggio* gesture, which explains the more sinuous patterns. This result also implies that the specificity of the finger trajectory is less obvious for a chord performance.

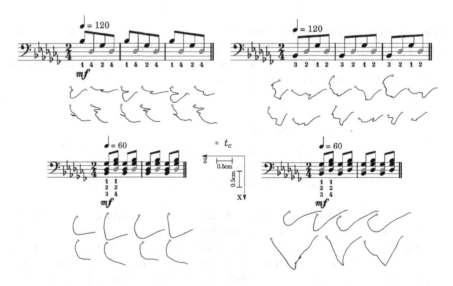

Fig. 3. Finger movement for two harpists performing arpeggio and chord sequences with the annular (referred to as 4) and the forefinger (referred to as 2). The analyzed notes are the grayed ones (D♭2 at about 140 Hz).

Figure 4 presents the maximum soundboard acceleration with respect to the initial conditions of the string vibrations for each harpist. Each of the four graphs corresponds to a playing configuration. The control parameters D_{t_r}, V_{t_r} and Γ

appears to be highly-dependent on the harpist as well as on the plucking context. This result is confirmed by the reasonable uncertainties we estimate. However, no obvious trend can be highlighted between the investigated finger or technique. Besides, the soundboard acceleration results from the combined vibrations of the strings the harpist plucked as well as the strings' vibrations due to the sympathetic phenomena [12]. Regarding the chord sequence, the maximum of acceleration is difficult to interpret since it is a combination of the three plucked strings vibrations. Thus, there is no meaningful trend between the maximum soundboard acceleration and the parameters D_{t_r}, V_{t_r} and Γ for the chord case but the expected globally higher maximum soundboard acceleration. This observation is confirmed by the measured sound pressure level averaged for each playing configuration which is 3 dB to 5 dB higher when performing a chord. As expected based on Eq. 7, the evolution of the maximum soundboard vibrations for the *arpeggio* sequence is related to the initial conditions plane: the more the initial displacement, the higher the maximum soundboard vibrations.

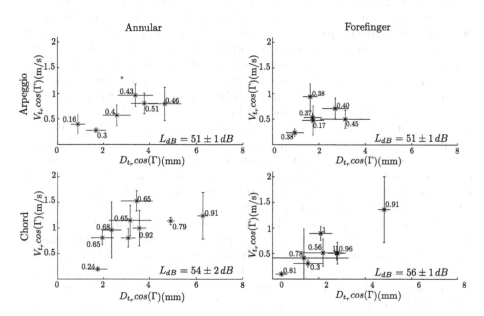

Fig. 4. Initial conditions of the string vibrations for ten different harpists in two musical contexts, and two fingerings associated to the maximum soundboard acceleration (m/s^2) averaged for each musician. For each playing configuration, the averaged sound level computed with a reference sound pressure level of $20\,\mu Pa$ is displayed. The reported uncertainty represents a 95 % confidence interval.

It has previously been underlined that, unlike usually admitted, the initial conditions of a plucked string are a complex mix of displacement, velocity and rotation [5]. In order to control their sound level, harpists adjust the initial displacement they provide to the string. Figure 4 indicates that it is necessarily

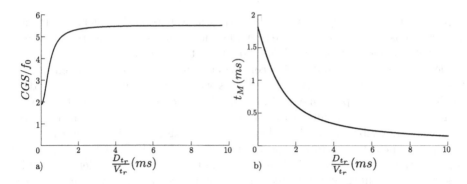

Fig. 5. Influence of the initial conditions of the string vibrations on the spectral centroid (a) and on the instant of the maximal vibrations t_M (b).

related to the initial string's velocity. The bigger the initial string's displacement, the more important the initial string's velocity. Although the latter parameter could only be a control parameter harpists use to precisely govern their sound production, it could also influence the string vibrations features, i.e. the produced sound. In order to get some insight on this question, Fig. 5 shows the evolution of the dimensionless spectral centroid CGS/f_0 and the instant the maximal amplitude of the vibrations is reached t_M with respect to the measured ratio D_{t_r}/V_{t_r}, computed as written in Eqs. 9 and 6, respectively. Figure 5(a) indicates that the dimensionless spectral centroid rapidly rises with D_{t_r}/V_{t_r} and converges toward the limit 5.5 which corresponds to the case $V_{t_r} = 0$. Moreover, 67 % of the collected data corresponds to $D_{t_r}/V_{t_r} < 2$ ms, indicating that the control parameter V_{t_r} conveys to significant variations in the spectral content of the sound production. Besides, Fig. 5(b) indicates that variations in the instant where the maximum of vibration is expected are up to $\Delta t_M = 1.8$ ms at the current fundamental frequency. Most of the ratio D_{t_r}/V_{t_r} computed from the collected database corresponds to $\Delta t_M \in [0.5\,\text{ms}; 1\,\text{ms}]$. Although this order of magnitude seems to be non negligible, further investigation would be required to clearly conclude on the perceptual meaning of these variations in harp playing.

The harp plucking is an expert gesture, highly-repeatable and specific to the player and the musical context. This gesture finely defines the mechanical parameters that governed the string's free oscillations: string's shape, velocity, and angle at the release instant. These parameters controlled by the player directly influence the sound features. However, such skilled gestures cannot be only govern at the hand level, and a more global investigation of harp playing, such as gestural and postural analyses, are required to enhance the current study.

3   Gestural Analysis

In the present section, we present a gestural and postural analysis of harp performance. For this purpose, two approaches are proposed. The first one consists in a kinematic description of the upper-limb motion, especially the hand, accordingly to the musical context. This approach is worthy to improve knowledge on musical gesture and to feed gesture based sound synthesis. The second is an ongoing exploratory analysis of the energetic strategy musicians set up to play harp. This kind of study, as for instance [13], is valuable to propose, in collaboration with musical and medical specialists, optimizations of the musician posture or of the instrument itself (materials, shapes, stringing, ...) to avoid injuries.

3.1   Experimental Procedure

A specific experimental procedure presented in Fig. 6 has been designed in order to investigate the gestural strategies underlying a harp performance. A motion capture system composed of six infrared cameras set at 250 fps has been used to accurately measure the harpist skeleton motion over time as shown in Fig. 7. The skeleton is defined by reflective markers disposed on the harpist according to the Plug-In-Gait model (Vicon Oxford Metrics Ltd, Oxford, UK). As the harp would have obstructed them, the head as well as the chest of the harpist were not captured. Besides, acoustical signals have been measured with two microphones and two standard digital video cameras were placed in the room to control the motion capture reconstruction and to record harpist discussion. The combination of these audio, video and motion signals allows the synchronization of the collected database. Three harpists have been asked to interpret the Debussy's *Danse Profane* three times on an Aoyama Orpheus concert harp for repeatability and adaptation issues. The investigation we propose in the following sections concentrates on two parts of the musical piece which are separated by an animated sequence. They are constituted of octaves and harmonics, respectively. The associated scores are proposed in Fig. 10. These excerpts have been selected because they both are performed with the left upper-limb only and with no change in the pedal configuration and that the repetition of the played note is valuable for variability considerations.

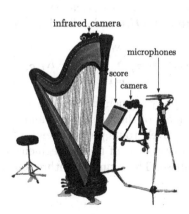

Fig. 6. Scheme of the experimental setup carried out to analyze harpist global posture and gestures.

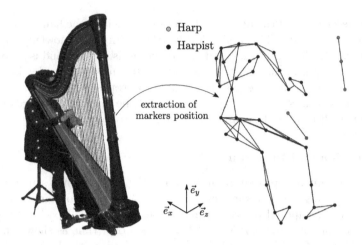

Fig. 7. A harpist during the measurement session and the extracted position of body segments.

3.2 Data Processing

Segmentation. In order to investigate the gestural strategies underlying each selected excerpt, musical gestures associated to notes have to be pointed out. This segmentation is performed according to the sound producing gesture definition proposed in [11]: the harpist fingers are first positioned on the strings, then they pluck the strings and leave them until getting in touch again to play the next note. Experimentally, the onset of each acoustical signal is first determined [1,9] and the instant the fingers are touching the string is highlighted through the hand trajectories in the (e_x, e_z)-plane.

Harpist's Center of Mass. One useful descriptor in the assessment of gestural and postural strategies in a human performance is the center of mass position. It is classically referred to as COM and defined as [17]

$$COM(t) = \frac{1}{M} \sum_{i=1}^{N_l} m_i(s_i^p + K_i(s_i^d - s_i^p)) \qquad (10)$$

where N_l is the number of body segment considered in the reconstructed skeleton of total mass M, m_i the mass of the i_{th} segment and K_i the distance of the i_{th} segment center of mass relatively to its proximal end. s_i^p and s_i^d are the positions of the proximal and the distal ends of the i_{th} segment, directly known through the motion capture database. The required anthropometric data are extracted from [17].

Joint Mechanical Work. Figure 8 presents the computational process set up to analyze the way energy is shared between joints while harp playing. It is mostly based on inverse dynamics method. Knowing forces and moments occurring at the distal end of a segment as well as its center of mass position, a link-segment model [17] allows to estimate forces and moments at the proximal end. For a multi-segment body, this method is applied recursively to estimate forces F and moments M at each arm joints. The mechanical power is then deduced from F and M through the standard relationship $P = M.\omega$ (ω is the angular velocity estimate through Euler's equations of motion). Finally, the mechanical work is obtained from time-integrating the power curve within the gesture duration. Experimentally, as the more distal forces and moments are not directly reachable, we assumed moments to be negligible and forces to be between 2 N and 8 N according to the sound level of each note [5].

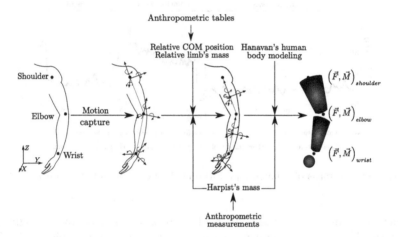

Fig. 8. Retrieval process of forces and moments occurring at a harpist's arm joints.

3.3 Results

Kinematic Analysis. Figure 9 presents the evolution of the center of mass COM of one harpist associated to the acoustical waveform along the beginning of the Debussy's *Danse Profane* which is composed of the investigated octave intervals and harmonics sequences surrounding an animated sequence. The COM is computed according to two harpists skeleton definitions: with and without the harpist's arms represented in black and in gray, respectively. During the octave intervals sequence, unlike the smooth grayed curve, the black one presents regular oscillations revealing the 14 played notes and the 14 left arm gestures. It means that the musician posture is stable in the position shown in the first picture above the waveform. Then, performing the animated sequence required the right hand which is lifted toward the strings at the highlighted (a) instant (see picture 2 and 3). Again, the center of mass computed on the harpist body without arms do not present important variation except a slight rise due to the back bending. At the (b) instant, the harpist muffles the string

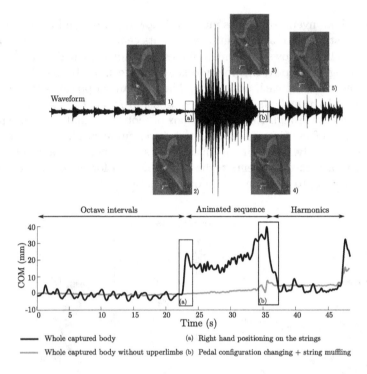

Fig. 9. Center of mass of a harpist performing the beginning of the *Danse Profane*.

(see picture 4) and change the pedal configuration before lowering his right arm to perform the harmonics sequence with the left hand only (see picture 5). The change in the pedal configuration is the only action noticeable on the evolution of the center of mass computed without the arms. The same pattern occurs during the harmonics sequence than during the octave interval one. The harpist body center of mass is almost constant without taking the arms into account. Finally, as we investigate the octave intervals and the harmonics sequences, it is relevant to assume the body posture almost constant and to focus the present analysis on the left arm gestures. A kinematic description of the left hand gestures provided by the three harpists along the two studied musical context is proposed in Fig. 10. For each player referred to as $H_{1,2,3}$ the three takes $T_{1,2,3}$ are presented in the (e_x, e_z)-plane because it is the most emphasized one when harp playing. As at the smaller scale of the plucking action, hand gestures appears to be highly repeatable and specific to a bar and a harpist. Likewise, considering the octave intervals sequence in Fig. 10(a), hand gestures give us insight on the underlying musical construction proposed by the player. For instance, H_3 performs two various gestures while playing a $D\flat$ accordingly to its position in the musical phrase. It seems that this player proposes a 4-time structure. Moreover, harpists emphasize differently the last note of each sequence. Indeed, the associated hand gestures own a specific shape and a higher magnitude than the other notes.

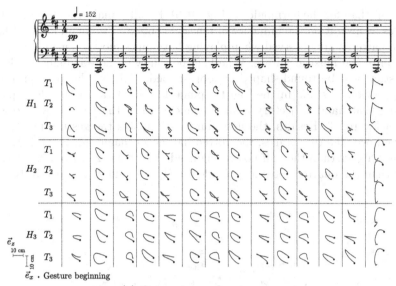

(a) Octave intervals sequence.

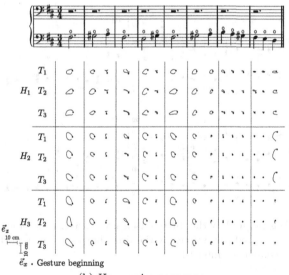

(b) Harmonics sequence.

Fig. 10. Repeatability and characteristics of the three harpists' left hand movement in the (x0y)-plane related to each performance of the *Danse Profane* referred as to $T_{1,2,3}$.

This phenomenon is obviously related to the anticipation of the following musical sequence, as for instance the string muffling, the change in the pedal configuration as well as the hands repositioning. Note that this result is highly noticeable for the octave intervals case in Fig. 10(a) for which the gesture magnitude is more important than for the harmonics in Fig. 10(b). Finally, analysis of the Fig. 10(b) provides us insight on the influence of musical context. Two main kinds of hand gesture patterns are observed when playing harmonics mostly depending on the direction of the musical phrase. Whether the following note is higher or lower, the gesture will be round-shaped or loop-shaped. This is related to an observation previously made in the sagittal plane for the octave intervals sequence assessing that hand trajectory is more sinuous when the hand moves forward than backward [6]. Besides, the note duration impacts the gesture magnitude. Averaged over the three takes, the dotted half notes magnitude are 1.2, 1.2 and 1.8 times higher than the half notes magnitude which are 2.1, 1.5 and 2.1 times higher than the quarter notes magnitude for H_1, H_2 and H_3, respectively.

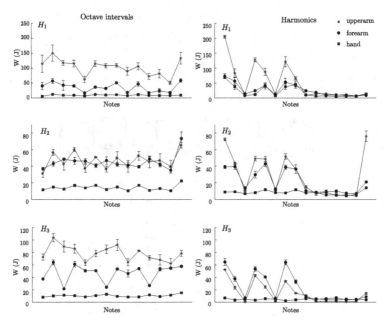

Fig. 11. Work (J) generated by the three muscle groups averaged for each octave interval and harmonic repeated three times by the three harpists. The reported uncertainty represents a 95 % confidence interval.

Dynamic Analysis. Figure 11 presents the work generated by each of the three limb-segments of the harpists left-upperarm in the two musical contexts investigated. The process carried out to estimate this descriptor is explained in Sect. 3.2. The first noteworthy result is that the uncertainties estimated for the three takes are rather small, which allow to pertinently analyze these curves. Then, as expected because of its relative mass, the hand is the limb-segment that generates the less work in the three harpist arms in both octave intervals and harmonics contexts. Considering the former context, an interesting trend is that, although the work generated by the upperarm-segment is always higher than the one generated by the forearm-segment for H_1 and H_3, these two segments appears to contribute equally to the energy generation for H_2. A potential explanation is that, unlike the two others, the last musician is a skilled but non professional harpist. Although a thorough investigation is required to conclude, we assume that a professional harpist try to optimize the energy sharing into his upperlimb to avoid injury. This observation is not confirmed for the harmonics context because of the different playing technique involved. Playing octave intervals conveys to a arm gesture controlled as a block [6], while playing harmonics mostly involves a hand motion with stable elbow and shoulder position. Besides, theoretically, the work generated is directly related on the note duration, which is clearly noticeable in harmonics sequences. Even if each octave interval played is a dotted half note, variations occur in the work curves. H_1 and H_3 present similar patterns in a 4-note structure while H_2 presents a 2-note structure along the octave intervals sequence. This results in slight temporal deviations in the note durations suggesting the musical structure harpist aims at transmitting through up and down beats.

4 Conclusion

This paper has presented a contribution to the musician/instrument analysis in the case of the concert harp at an experimental level. Investigations have focused on characterizing this interaction at the plucking action and at the gestural strategies scales in the most realistic and non invasive contexts. For this purpose, high-speed camera and motion capture system have been used to precisely determinate harpist's fingers and body motion along musical performances. Simultaneously, vibratory and acoustical signals have been measured to enhance the kinematic analysis in the light of the sound production context.

Musical gestures are characterized by their repeatability and their specificity to the player and the context. This result has been verified at the finger temporal and spatial scales as well as at the larger ones of the hand. Performing such a skilled gesture, harpists precisely control the mechanical parameters they provide to the strings, defining their free oscillations and thus, the produced sound features. These plucking parameters are the string's shape, velocity, rotation as well as its angle at the release instant. Besides, gesture analysis give insight on the musical intent. The pattern the finger or the hand draws is typical of the importance given to the considered beat. The way players organize the energy generation between their limbs reveals also the excerpt structure through slight variations in the note duration to emphasize it.

A detailed analysis of the plucking action along the harp *tessitura* would be necessary to generalize the highlighted trends on one gut string. Further, coupling these measurements with arm motion capture will be valuable to estimate absolute order of magnitude of the energy generated or absorbed by each muscle groups. Such an experimental procedure would be interesting to investigate the learning process of a musical piece. It would be a helpful teaching tool to visualize and better understand the relationship between a given gesture or posture and the produced sound, as well as to develop strategies against joints and muscle injury.

Acknowledgments. The authors would like to thank C. Brum Medeiros, M. Ghamsari-Esfahani, L. Quartier, M.-A. Vitrani and M. M. Wanderley for their help during measurements, the harpists who participated in this study: M. Denizot, P. Didier, E. Grégoire-Rousseau, M. Klein, S. Le Conte, C. Levecque, C. Lieby-Muller, A. Malette-Chénier, M. Monod-Cotte, B. Pigaglio, M. Rochut, M.-E. Sutherland and C. Vincent; and R. Martin for her interest and fruitful discussions.

References

1. Bello, J.P., Daudet, L., Abdallah, S., Duxbury, C., Davies, M., Sandler, M.: A tutorial on onset detection in music signals. IEEE Trans. Speech Audio Process. **13**, 1035–1047 (2005)
2. Bouënard, A., Wanderley, M.M., Gibet, S.: Gesture control of sound synthesis: analysis and classification of percussion gestures. Acta Acust. United Acust. **96**(4), 668–677 (2010)
3. Chadefaux, D.: Interaction musicien/instrument: Le cas de la harpe de concert (Musician/Instrument interaction: the case of the concert harp), Ph.D. thesis, Université Pierre et Marie Curie, Paris, France (2012)
4. Chadefaux, D., Le Carrou, J.-L., Fabre, B.: A model of harp plucking. J. Acoust. Soc. Am. **133**(4), 2444–2455 (2013)
5. Chadefaux, D., Le Carrou, J.-L., Fabre, B., Daudet, L.: Experimentally based description of harp plucking. J. Acoust. Soc. Am. **131**(1), 844–855 (2012)
6. Chadefaux, D., Le Carrou, J.-L., Fabre, B., Wanderley, M.M., Daudet, L.: Experimental study of gestural strategies in a harp performance. Acta Acust. United Acust. **99**(6), 986–996 (2013)
7. Chaigne, A., Kergomard, J.: Acoustique des instruments de musique, p. 704. Belin, Paris (2008)
8. Derveaux, G., Chaigne, A., Joly, P., Bécache, E.: Time-domain simulation of a guitar: model and method. J. Acoust. Soc. Am. **114**, 3368–3383 (2003)
9. Duxbury, C., Bello, J.P., Davies, M., Sandler, M.: Complex domain onset detection for musical signals. In: Proceedings of the 6th International Conference on Digital Audio Effects (DAFx), vol. 1, pp. 90–94 (2003)
10. Grey, J.M., Gordon, J.W.: Perceptual effects of spectral modification on musical timbres. J. Acoust. Soc. Am. **63**(5), 1493–1500 (1978)
11. Jensenius, A.R., Wanderley, M.M., Godøy, R.I., Leman, M.: Musical gestures: sound movement and meaning. In: Godøy, R., Leman, M. (eds.) Musical Gestures: Concepts and Methods in Research, 1st edn. Routledge, New York (2009)
12. Le Carrou, J.-L., Gautier, F., Badeau, R.: Sympathetic string modes in the concert harp. Acta Acust. United Acust. **95**, 744–752 (2009)
13. Martin, R.: Tension/détente de la posture du harpiste en Europe occidentale. Travaux de recherche de l'Institut Médecine des arts, Paris, France (2011)
14. Penttinen, H., Pakarinen, J., Välimäki, V.: Model-based sound synthesis of the guqin. J. Acoust. Soc. Am. **120**, 4052–4063 (2006)

15. Schoonderwaldt, E.: The player and the bowed string: coordination of bowing parameters in violin and viola performance. J. Acoust. Soc. Am. **126**(5), 2709–2720 (2009)
16. Schoonderwaldt, E., Demoucron, M.: Extraction of bowing parameters from violin performance combining motion capture and sensors. J. Acoust. Soc. Am. **126**(5), 2595–2708 (2009)
17. Winter, D.A.: Biomechanics and Motor Control of Human Movement, 4th edn, p. 370. Wiley, Hoboken (2009)
18. Woodhouse, J.: On the synthesis of guitar plucks. Acta Acust. United Acust. **90**, 928–944 (2004)

Sonically Augmented Artifacts: Design Methodology Through Participatory Workshops

Olivier Houix[(✉)], Nicolas Misdariis, Patrick Susini, Frédéric Bevilacqua, and Florestan Gutierrez

STMS IRCAM-CNRS-UPMC, 1 place Igor Stravinsky, 75004 Paris, France
{olivier.houix,nicolas.misdariis,
patrick.susini,frederic.bevilacqua}@ircam.fr,
gutierrezflorestan@gmail.com

Abstract. Participatory workshops have been organized within the framework of the ANR project Legos that concerns gesture-sound interactive systems. These workshops addressed both theoretical issues and experimentation with prototypes. The first goal was to stimulate new ideas related to the control of everyday objects using sound feedback, and then, to create and experiment with new sonic augmented objects. The second aim was educational. We investigated how sonic interaction design can be introduced to people without backgrounds in sound and music. We present in this article an overview of three workshops. The first workshop focused on the analysis and the possible sonification of everyday objects. New usage scenarios were obtained and tested. The second workshop focused on sound metaphor, questioning the relationship between sound and gesture. The last one was a workshop organized during a summer school for students. During these workshops, we experimented a cycle of design process: analysis, creation and testing.

Keywords: Workshop · Design · Sound synthesis · Interaction · Rehabilitation

1 Introduction

The ANR project Legos[1] aims at studying how users learn gesture-sound interactive systems, and modify their movement and action over time with sound feedback. Three areas of application are considered: new digital musical interfaces (DMI), rehabilitation and sonic interaction design (SID).

Through these three areas, the action-sound relationship is assessed on different levels: expressiveness and sound control (DMI), movement control and movement quality when guided by an audio feedback (rehabilitation) and quality of the object manipulation by a user in an interactive context (SID). The project is based on experimental approaches and workshops in order to generate an interdisciplinary expertise in design, motor control, sound synthesis and cognitive sciences.

---

[1] http://legos.ircam.fr.

M. Aramaki et al. (Eds.): CMMR 2013, LNCS 8905, pp. 20–40, 2014.
DOI: 10.1007/978-3-319-12976-1_2

We seek to develop novel methodologies for the gestural interfaces design by analyzing and comparing the experimental results of the three mentioned areas. Concerning sonic interaction design, we wanted to study experimentally how a dynamic sound interaction may improve the manipulation of everyday objects in terms of control, learning and user experience.

In this paper, we will first introduce the field of sonic interaction design. Then, the goal of the workshops and the methodology will be presented. Finally, the three different workshops will be detailed.

2 Sonic Interaction Design: A New Play-Ground for Designers and Researchers

Sonic Interaction Design is an active field that "emerged from the desire to challenge these prevalent design approaches by considering sound as an active medium that can enable novel phenomenological and social experiences with and through interactive technology." [8, p. 1]. The idea is to think about the design of sonic feedback, especially continuous interaction, to extend classical human computer interfaces HCI or digitally augmented devices. Interactive Sound Design or Sonic Interaction Design as it is named in the network of reference European COST Action SID IC0601 focuses on the relationship between a user and a system in an active and dynamic process.

Different interactive objects have been developed integrating a dynamic sonic component which allows for facilitating and guiding gestures and actions. Thus, this should allow for improving performance, promoting learning and strengthening the emotional dimension of an object *a priori* silent. These objects have been developed for experimental setups (for design and/or artistic performances) but also to study sound perception in an active process in terms of performance, learning, emotional and aesthetic dimensions.

2.1 Sonic Interactive Objects

The Shoogle [31] proposes new ways of interacting with a mobile device through sound by shaking, tiling or wobbling it. With these explicit actions, different scenarios have been proposed: when the user shakes the mobile device, long messages are associated with metallic sounding balls and short messages with glassy sounding objects.

Grosshauser et al. [9] developed a prototype to study the interaction loop between a human user and a tool in operation like a drilling machine. The authors worked on the sonification with pulsing sounds to make audible when the drilling machine is in the right position either horizontally or vertically, generally at a 90° angle to the wall while drilling and screwing[2].

O'modrhrain et al. [3,20,21] have worked on the integration between sound and touch through three different prototypes: the Pebble Box, the Crumble-Bag and the Scrubber. The PebbleBox is constructed as a wooden box, which

---

[2] A demo S.5.4 Chap. 5 is available at http://sonification.de/handbook/.

contains a layer of polished stones. When the users manipulate the stones, granular synthesis of natural sound recordings provide different collision sounds that change the relationship between action and sound but retaining the core physical dynamics of the original link.

Sonically augmented objects have been also used to test the hypothesis that a gesture can be intuitively and spontaneously adjusted when an associated sound recall the action (i.e. the sound appears as resulting from the action) For example, Rath et al. [25,26] have developed the Balancer corresponding to a very simple interface consisting of a wooden fence that participants could tilt. The manipulation of the interface controlled a synthesis model simulating rolling a ball along a guide. Using a model of virtual ball, users were informed of its position and velocity as a visual or audible feedback, and were able to control the virtual ball.

Another object is the Spinotron, which consists in a vertical pump [14]. The pumping action rotates a virtual gear, which is synthesized by the clicking of a physical impact model. Then, we investigated whether the sound of the gear can guide the handling of the device to perform a specific task. The task was to achieve a given rotation rate by pressing the device with and without audio feedback. The influence of the feedback was examined by assessing learning in twelve successive tasks. Results show that, while participants have said they were not helped by the sound, the performance significantly improved by the presence of sound.

All these results highlight the positive influence of the sound feedback during an interactive process with a tangible object, and show that sonic interaction design is a relevant exploration field to develop.

2.2 From Human Computer Interface to Sonic Interaction Design

Traditional Human Computer Interaction deals generally with the interaction of graphical objects on a screen via a mouse or directly in the case of touch screens.

The use of tangible objects/interfaces induces different paradigms by shifting the attention to the action operated on the physical objects.

In particular, new interactive devices enable the use of sound feedback to inform users on their gestures. Typically, objects are instrumented with sensors and micro controllers for controlling real-time sound synthesis that reacts to the manipulation of the object. The objective is then to establish a dynamic interaction between a user and the object, taking into account the sound dimension. The manipulation of the object produces sounds, which in turn influence the handling of the object.

Our claim in the context of sound design is that the necessary information is in part "available" in our environment, and in addition, exploration of our environment allows to revealing questions and problems about everyday objects: "Attention to what constitutes daily life and a dynamic exploration of the immediate environment, not only enable a better understanding of the world, but enrich the perception, construct logical meaning and sharpen critical thinking" [16].

3   Goals of the Workshops and Methodology

By organizing workshops, we wanted to create case studies in order to frame the project for the three areas of applications (Sonic interaction design, the digital musical interfaces and rehabilitation) by brainstorming and experimenting. Two workshops were addressed to the different members of the project and the last one to students from the "Human computer confluence" summer school[3].

3.1   Goal of the Workshops

The schedule and the content of these workshops correspond to an approach that summarizes the design process cycle of a new product (artifact or service) that we often find in industrial design [23].

The different steps of a new product creation can be divided into four stages: requirements/analysis, design/creation, development, and testing [15]. During the first steps, requirements and analysis are provided by experience or by more formalized approaches (usability testing, user feedback, ...). During the design/creation part, requirements are integrated to propose new ideas during sessions of brainstorming, prototyping, and analysis of existing solutions. This part has been formalized as the conceptualization of ideas (sketches) and the embodiment of the concept (prototypes) [13]. Generally the different solutions are tested in a context of use. It is an iterative process. The development part is the transfer of design requirements and specifications in the formalization of the product. The product is tested with target users to ensure that the product is in line with expectations. All these process could be linear or iterative depending on the project.

During these workshops, we focused on the three stages: analysis, creation and testing for specific usages. The idea was not to develop a final product (the development and testing phases with target users), but to develop experimental prototypes that can be share across the three different fields.

This general approach was used to organized the three following workshops:

1. Usage scenario analysis. Scenario development of the use of everyday objects incorporating a reflection on sound design.
2. Sound metaphor creation. Work on sound metaphors, questioning the relationship between sound and gesture, using the concept of basic actions and the work on the sound synthesis engines.
3. Embodied Interaction and Sound: Object Sonic Interaction. "Human computer confluence" summer school.

For the first workshop, the goal was to analyze usage scenarios integrating dynamic sound design, with the "objects" as the starting point. The second workshop was focused on sonic interaction design, with the "sound" as the starting point. The first workshop allowed us to concentrate on how the sound can contribute to the user experience of an everyday object and the second workshop

---

[3] http://hcsquared.eu/summer-school-2013/lectures-workshops.

to think about the sound gesture relationship within the context of interaction with objects. With the last workshop organized during the summer school HC2, we formalized a framework for participatory workshops that addresses these different topics.

Before presenting a summary of these different workshops, we introduce the participatory workshops.

3.2   What Can We Learn from Participatory Workshops

The theoretical framework of these workshops stems from our participation to the European CLOSED project[4] and the COST Action SID Sonic Interaction Design [8]. Under these projects, different workshops [6,7,29], were organized and have helped to develop a framework, in the spirit of participatory workshops [30] to generate creative, new ideas in interactive sound design context.

A methodology has been established to help the designer generate new scenarios from everyday objects by analyzing them in terms of functionality, contexts of use, associated actions, and existing sounds. Participants are encouraged to hybridize different features, associated actions and contexts of use taken from different everyday objects. The aim is to stimulate the creation of new scenarios of sonic interaction design. During these sessions, participants think together and share experiences during practical exercises.

Practical exercises are diversified, including "speed dating" [2] (generation of ideas in pairs over very short time periods regularly changing partners to promote stimulation), "body storming" [22] (playing active situations with objects to test scenarios), or "sound drama" [12] (the scenarios are staged with objects using audio post-production). This approach can be complemented by prototyping through sensors associated with micro controllers (such as Arduino[5] or Modular Musical Objects[6]).

For our workshops, we used this framework by integrating the different skills of the project members: theoretical background on sound-gesture relationship, hardware and software for motion capture, different approaches to sound synthesis (physical modeling, synthesis based on acoustical descriptors, ...). These different skills gave us the opportunity to prototype the different ideas and to confront them. The workshop organized with external participants (HC2 summer school) represented the opportunity to apply our methodology (analysis, ideation, prototyping and testing).

4   Usage Scenarios of Everyday Objects

4.1   Bring an Object with You!

The aim was to create experimental prototypes to explore how sound can change the interaction experience with everyday objects. Our work was based on the

---

[4] http://closed.ircam.fr.

[5] http://www.arduino.cc/.

[6] http://interlude.ircam.fr/.

analysis of everyday objects [18, 23] in order to propose new user experiences integrating dynamic sound design. The workshop goal was to discuss and propose user cases of everyday objects augmented with sonic interaction that can be applied in different applications, from digital musical instruments and to rehabilitation.

This workshop was held at Ircam[7] in June 2012. The first day was dedicated to the generation of scenarios and the second day to the prototyping of these scenarios with augmented objects. Before the workshop, participants were asked to bring one or two small objects. The choice of the object was set to follow the following rules: simple manipulation with one or two hands, in contact (or not) with another object or support, associated to a specific function and purpose. The first object is supposed to give satisfaction to the user in terms of use. The second object is on the contrary supposed to represent some difficulties (difficult to hold and with a difficult task to achieve).

We introduced the first day to participants the different goals of the workshop. After this introduction, each participant presented their objects and explained their choices.

Grid for Analyzing Objects. We built an analysis grid, in order to analyze everyday products, and propose an extension of the user experience with sound design. This grid reflects part of the analysis of aesthetic components of a product in industrial design (harmonic, functional, cultural, technological and social factors) [23] but also more general approaches concerning the analysis of a product: the function of a product; the form of a product and the use of the product [18].

Participants were grouped in pairs to analyze the different objects using a grid:

- Object description: form, size, material, grip.
- Use: context, primary and secondary functions.
- Action on the object: descriptions, interaction with a support or with an object.
- Experience with the object: positive and negative.

Then, we selected a few objects to build scenarios that integrates sound feedback. The second day, we prototyped the selected scenarios with augmented objects, separating participants into two groups of five participants. At the end of the day, each group presented their works.

4.2 Analysis and Selection of the Objects

Participants brought several objects following the instructions given to prepare the workshop. Each participant explained the objects they brought. This first

---

[7] Participants: Sara Adhitya, Frédéric Bevilacqua, Eric Boyer, Florestan Gutierrez, Sylvain Hanneton, Olivier Houix, Jules Françoise, Nicolas Misdariis, Alexandre Panizzoli, Quentin Pyanet, Nicolas Rasamimanana, Agnès Roby-Brami, Patrick Susini, Isabelle Viaud-Delmon.

round was also intended to involve participants in a participatory framework. These objects were varied: a screwdriver, wooden and plastic citrus presses, a tea infuser, a razor, an apple corer, a rechargeable lamp, keys, a squeegee, a spinning gyroscope with its launcher, matches, a spirit level, a saw, make-up, a sponge, a clothespin, an alarm clock, a lighter, a jam jar, a coffee plunger and a measuring tape. Some objects were difficult to use or manipulate or had a baffling design. Other objects were acceptable, often used in our everyday context and elicited positive emotions during their use.

Participants were then placed in pairs in order to describe the selected objects using the analytical grid (Sect. 4.1). We asked them to highlight the negative and positive aspects of the objects both in terms of ergonomics, design, use and manipulation.

Finally, we focused on the negatives aspects highlighted by the participants. For example, the jam jar was difficult to open and manipulate, the regular movements of the spinning gyroscope were difficult to master, and the spirit level required difficult control which needed visual feedback difficult to maintain.

After this step, participants selected objects to generate scenarios focusing on usage problems. Thus, the different problems encountered were organized when using objects to sample our selection. These categories were: problems of grasping, problems of coordination or adjustment of the action, problems of design, manual or bi manual manipulation, manipulation without visual feedback, signage problems without interaction, reversed tools (for example, pressing the infuser tea to open it). The selected objects and the associated problems were:

- The jam jar and the measuring tape (Bi manual manipulation).
- The spinning gyroscope, the sponge and the squeegee (Adjustment of the action).
- The rechargeable lamp (Signage problem of the charge level).
- The spirit level (Need of visual feedback).

4.3   Imagine New Scenarios of Use

Participants worked in parallel in two groups. While one group worked on a set of objects for 30 min to provide usage scenarios, the other group proceeded in the same way on the other objects. Then the two groups exchanged objects and continued brainstorming for 30 min in the same way. The participants used simple ways to illustrate their scenarios (gestures, vocalizations, paper - pencil, ...). In a second phase, the two groups met in the same room and shared scenarios. The participants presented their ideas that were analyzed and discussed. The main ideas concerning the four objects were then summarized. A selection of scenarios are presented below.

The Jam Jar. One group proposed the sonification of the closing sound of the jam jar in order to be optimal, i.e. not too strong and not too loose.

This idea was related to the work done by Rocchesso et al. [27, 28] on the moka[8]. Another proposition was the use of two beating sounds, like the tuning of a guitar, to prevent strong closing. Other ideas were related to the idea of giving a relationship between the container and contents.

The Spirit Level. The general idea was to enable the "reading" without visual feedback in the case of the user not being in front of the spirit level. The sound could give the necessary information about the direction of the inclination. The natural metaphor of the rain stick was proposed, in reference to the sound installation "GrainStick - 2.0" by Pierre Jodlowski[9]. A possible extension was the hybridization between the spirit level and the measuring tape (rattle sound for giving information about the measured distance).

The Spinning Gyroscope. The participants struggled to run the spinning gyroscope. Its use was not particularly intuitive when starting the rotation of the spinning. Two proposals were made for its use: for relaxation and meditation like the Chinese health balls without launching and for triggering different sound worlds depending on the type of movement. The other group studied the manual mechanism to launch the spinning gyroscope. They noted two main movements: the movement of the wrist in order to move the launcher and the rotational movement of the spinning gyroscope on its axis. The movement of the launcher could be two points instrumented to retrieve information on the move. Two different sounds may be associated with the wrist and spinning gyroscope. The idea was to phase these two parameters for the gesture and action when they were optimal.

The Squeegee. Analyzing the use of the squeegee sheet glass, various control parameters are listed: the inclination of the head of the squeegee, the normal pressure on the surface, the path and the flow velocity. These parameters can also be similar to the use of a razor. Another track is to explore the sonification of the error in the control of the squeegee (the following parameters) rather than the whole gesture. For example, if we consider the pressure on the surface, too much pressure may be associated with a squeaky violin sound. The object does not present special problems of manipulation, but the goal of sonification in this case is to be aware of the movement.

Summary. During this step, participants have created scenarios for these objects by integrating a reflection on the use of sound to improve or expand their uses. Following the discussion about the different scenarios and discussions, we selected two objects (The squeegee and the spinning gyroscope) to deal with the scenarios in depth and make them interactive.

---

[8] http://vimeo.com/898836.

[9] http://brahms.ircam.fr/works/work/27276/.

4.4   Prototypes

Two groups were formed to work specifically on scenarios using the spinning
gyroscope and the squeegee window. The goal is to prototype the scenarios
by instrumenting these objects using sensors associated with sound synthesis
softwares.

Fig. 1. Working group on the spinning gyroscope (1). Participants instrumented the
launcher (2) and the wrist of the user (4) using sensors MO [24] to sonify the movement (3).

The Augmented Spinning Top. At first, the participants discussed how to
obtain the best movement with a minimum of effort. The optimal motion was
identified to be to a small dry tilting of the spinning top in order to begin
the rotation mechanism. This movement gives enough energy to the spinning,
allowing a first cycle and rotation. They observed that participants who were
unable to produce a rotational movement, produced more erratic movements of
the wrist. An imagined solution was to optimize the gesture by sonifying two
parameters: the movement of the wrist (as a fixed angle), and the frequency of the
spinning top due to its frequency rotation. The group was able to demonstrate
a prototype of the spinning top accompanied by sensors placed on the wrist
and the spinning top (see Fig. 1). When the user plays with the spinning top,
he/she received a sound related to his/her gesture with the sound becoming

more "rough" when the movement deviated from the optimal movement. An extension of this work could be the sonification of the phase difference between the movement of the wrist and the spinning top rotation so that the user can correct his/her gesture.

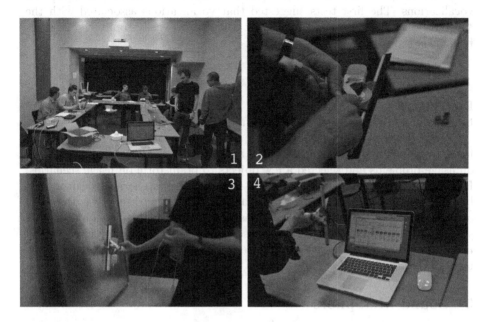

Fig. 2. Working group on the squeegee window (1). Participants instrumented the squeegee using sensors MO [24] (2), and have tested different movements (3) and different sound engines to sonify movement (4).

The Augmented Squeegee. First, participants observed different window cleaning techniques to understand the different movements. By testing themselves this technique on a surface (see Fig. 2), the sequence could be broken down into a succession of repetitive actions (a linear trajectory followed by a rapid rotation to change direction). A first observation was made: it is difficult to keep a fluid gesture during the successions of the linear path followed by the rotation and that this requires training.

To better understand the various successive actions, the idea was to sonify the different parameters such as the angle of the squeegee, the pressure exerted on the surface, and the rotation. The idea was to make fluid changes of direction and regular trajectories. The augmented squeegee with sensors should control a sound synthesis software that suggests an optimal trajectory and movement with a sound metaphor.

For example, considering the angle of the squeegee, if the user kept the race too close to the surface, a sound like "wind" or "white noise" indicates that the squeegee does not adhere enough to the surface, otherwise a grating sound is produced. Finally, between these two non-optimal situations (angles too low or too high), the right movement is sonified with the metaphor of a finger sliding on a glass.

Different types of sounds were tested: earcons or auditory icons [17] and vocalizations. The first tests suggested that vocalizations associated with the "gesture follower"[10] allowed, in the first attempt, to easily sonify the gestures being closest to the movement.

4.5 Summary

During this first workshop, we proposed a methodology to help participants to brainstorm and generate new scenarios from everyday objects.

Participants have analyzed everyday objects in terms of use, function and form. Instead of hybridizing new features and associated actions, we have focused on usage problems and selected a few objects to brainstorm on usage scenarios. Participants used different approaches to illustrate their scenarios: vocalizations, body storming and sound drama. The last part of the workshop was the work on prototyping. We selected two use cases and built augmented objects with sensors and sound synthesis to test our scenarios. During this workshop we did not particularly focus on the relation between sound and action, which is the topic of the next workshop.

5   Sound Metaphors

5.1   Introduction

The objective of this second workshop was to study sound gesture relationship. A first proposition was to work on the decomposition of the movement with basic gestures. The second one was to work on the type of relationship between gesture and sound production through sound metaphors. We also wanted to do further work on the synthesis engines (sound synthesis, physical models of behavior). This workshop was held at Ircam[11] in October 2012. A video summarized this workshop[12].

5.2   Basic Gestures and Sound-Gesture Relationship

Basic Gestures. The analysis of a complex action into elementary actions is derived from work done in the CLOSED project[13]. The aim of these studies

---

[10] http://imtr.ircam.fr/imtr/Gesture_Follower/.

[11] Participants: Sara Adhitya, Frédéric Bevilacqua, Eric Boyer, Jules Françoise, Sylvain Hanneton, Olivier Houix, Fivos Maniatakos, Nicolas Misdariis, Robert Piechaud, Nicolas Rasamimanana, Agnès Roby-Brami, Norbet Schnell, Patrick Susini, Isabelle Viaud-Delmon.

[12] https://www.youtube.com/watch?v=2aPsN0XC4Mo.

[13] http://actionanalysis.wikispaces.com/.

was to break down the basic tasks of daily life, especially in the kitchen and to see if they were associated to a sound resulting, or not, from the actions. We completed this analysis [10] to extend this framework by integrating the results of studies that analyze the manual gesture. For example, studies [19,32] have proposed a taxonomy of manual gesture differentiating a gesture requiring power and another requiring precision. We felt that this approach could help structure our thinking.

Sound-Gesture Relationship. We introduced different types of relationship between gesture and sound production:

– Arbitrary relationships: when a noise parameter varies as a function of arbitrarily gesture, such as when an object is moved upwards and its sonic roughness is increased;
– Metaphorical relationships: when a user pumps a device faster and faster, a virtual sound click is repeated more quickly (it uses the metaphor of a spinning top) [14].

We asked the participants to think about these two types of sound-gesture relationships applied to basic gestures using synthesis techniques (vocalizations, Foley or sound synthesis softwares).

5.3   Examples of Sound-Gesture Relationships

Each participant presented an example of a sound-gesture relationship based on elementary actions. This presentation showed that this exercise could be difficult, for example in imagining the metaphorical relation. Some participants gave examples of case studies related to an object rather than elementary gestures. Nevertheless, all participants attempted to answer it by offering reflections and proposals. Participants gave examples like the ones described below:

– Arbitrary relationship: the cinematic of a ping pong was sonified with simple oscillators depending on the direction. This example can be related to the artistic performance of Robert Rauschenberg "open scores"[14] in 1966. Another example: when there is no movement, there is silence. When the gesture is amplified, a noise becoming a granular texture sonifies the amplitude of the movement. Accidental gesture (with snap) is associated with a percussive sound. This example is inspired by "light music" of Thierry de Mey[15].
– Metaphorical relationship: when a spirit level is inclined, the movement is related to a bubble sound. A torsional movement could be associated with a liquid sound when wringing a cloth. A last example: when a drawer is opened, a sound world unfolds, giving information on its contents.

After these discussions, we defined three case studies that challenge different types of feedback (about the position or about the movement).

---

[14] http://www.fondation-langlois.org/html/f/page.php?NumPage=642.
[15] http://brahms.ircam.fr/works/work/22063/.

5.4   Development of the Case Studies

The participants were separated into three groups to work specifically on these three case studies. We did not use the use cases developed during the first workshop to stimulate new ideas and diversify the scenarios. We have selected the best scenarios that can be applied in the three application areas after the workshops. At the end of the day, each group gave a demonstration of its augmented object.

The Sonic Level. The idea developed with the "sonic level" was to sonify the angle relative to the horizontal axis using a virtual orchestra (an accordion, a guitar and drums). Thus, when the level is flat, the orchestra plays all the instruments (drums, guitar, accordion) and when the angle to the horizontal plane increases, conversely number of instruments decreases until the accordion was played alone (Fig. 3).

Fig. 3. The sonic level.

The eRhombe. A physical model of interaction was developed initially, producing no sound. Indeed, the objective was to first model the behavior of a virtual rhombus which is driven by the rotation of a physical sensor (gyroscope). The user rotates the sensor (MO) and must be consistent with the model when the virtual rhombus starts running and running. The next step is to sonify the virtual rhombus with an abstract or metaphorical relationship.

The Augmented Ping Pong. At the beginning, participants wanted to sonify the position and the acceleration of the racket for the gestures "forehand" and "backhand". They encountered difficulties of motion capture, e.g. to distinguish "forehand" and "backhand". The sounds used in the demonstration were based on the principles of classical sound synthesis. This work was extended after the workshop with a functional prototype and presented to ping pong players [1] (Fig. 4).

Fig. 4. The augmented Ping Pong.

5.5   Summary

The first part of the workshop was focused on sound-gesture relationships based on elementary actions. The different participants found this exercise difficult. A possible explanation is the decontextualization of this exercise. Thus, we asked participants to relate elementary actions to sounds. For participants it was hard to choose a type of sound (arbitrary or metaphorical sounds) in relation with an action without giving a context of production or a situation. This first part was a more theoretical thought on sound gesture relationships. The second part of the workshop was dedicated to the development of three different scenarios based on sonically augmented objects. The different scenarios were not necessarily related to the fist part of the workshop, but the theoretical formalization helped us to propose different types of feedback (about the position or about the movement).

6   Human Computer Confluence Summer School

We organized a workshop with students during the Human Computer Confluence HC2 Summer school from the 17th to the 19th of July 2013 at Ircam. This workshop about "Embodied Interaction and Sound" had two main topics: "Body Sonic interaction"[16] and "Object Sonic Interaction" and involved two student groups. The introduction part of the workshop was common to the two workshops. We present here the results of the "Object Sonic Interaction" part. Five students[17] participated to the workshop.

---

[16] Organized by the Department of Computing, Goldsmiths, University of London.

[17] Participants: Lauren Hayes - PhD student in creative music practice, Emmanouil Giannisakis - Master student in digital media engineering, Jaime Arias Almeida - PhD student in informatics, Alberto Betella - PhD student in communication, information and audiovisual media, David Hofmann - Phd student in theoretical neuroscience.

6.1   Framework

For this workshop, we refined the framework in three parts, summarized in Fig. 5, analysis of different objects brought by participants, generation of basic scenarios using constraints of basic sound and actions categories and development of two scenarios by prototyping objects with sensors and sound synthesis.

Object Analysis. First we asked participants to bring one or two items for the workshop. We gave some constraints: the object should be compact, be

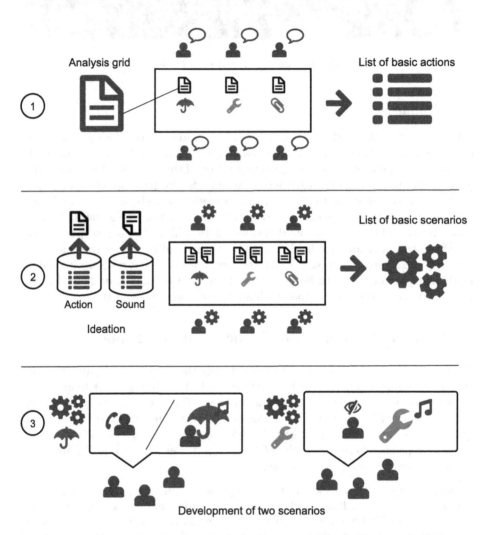

Fig. 5. Framework of the workshop: first objects were analyzed using a grid. Different basic actions were associated with each objects. We used a set of basic actions and sound categories to stimulate scenarios. We selected two scenarios and prototyped them.

manipulated by one or two hands in contact or not with another object or surface. The main function of the object should not be to produce sound (for example: musical instrument). We emphasized that the object should not be necessarily common and should stimulate their imagination. We also indicated that the different objects will be analyzed, hybridized, ..., in order to offer new user experiences with these objects through sound. They brought: a puppet, toothpicks, a dodecahedron wood block, clothespins, an infinite torus, a bracelet and a flag Poi for jugglery.

The different objects were presented by each participant and analyzed by different participant pairs, with permutations. We used the same analysis grid as it was presented before (see Sect. 4.1). We examined the different basic actions associated with these different objects and classified them as sustained, discrete or composed actions, see Fig. 6.

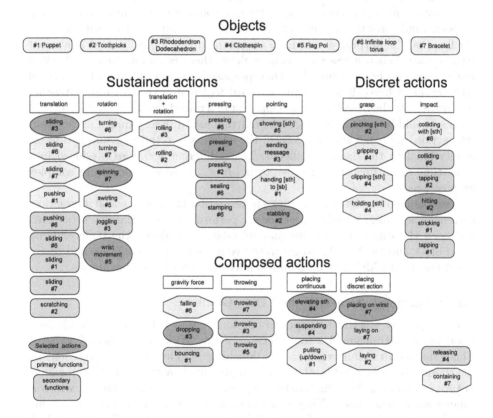

Fig. 6. The different objects (1 to 7) were analyzed with a grid. The different basic actions corresponding to primary and secondary functions are summarized and classified.

Ideation. We selected with participants ten actions among the different categories of actions (Fig. 6): sliding, pressing, hitting, spinning, stabbing, pinching, dropping, wrist movement, elevating something, placing on wrist. We proposed different categories of basic physical interactions (solid, liquid and gas interactions) that produce sound taken from the literature [11]. Ten physical interactions were also given: multiple impacts, rotation, shake, crumple, flow (gas), explosion (gas), bubble, drop/water movement, water shoot and draining. The objects were placed on the table and participants were seated on each side of the table. We randomized and selected for each object one interaction and one sound categories. We asked participants to propose sonic interaction design of new usages for each object.

After this stimulating exercise, the participants presented the 18 different scenarios. The scenarios were all different depending on the combination of sounds and actions. For example the clothespin can be used as a controller for a diving game, by spinning (the action) the clothespin you control the diver and the bubble sound indicates the oxygen lost. A scenario was proposed to learn the use of the flag Poi, the purpose was to have a smooth and periodically wrist movement (the action). When a less movement is done, there is an auditory feedback of water shooting. For the bracelet, they proposed a safety device, when pressed (the action) a hard shaking sound is heard to frighten the aggressor. Another proposition for the bracelet is a development of a mixed reality fighting game, the bracelet could be used as a controller of virtual sword. Every time a player stabs (the action) someone with the sword, the speed of a rotation sound is directly proportional to the damage inflicted. These different scenarios produced in a short time are a first step in order to hybridize these ideas for more complex propositions.

We classified the different scenarios in terms of use: gaming, social interaction, movement learning, tangible interface for performance and alarm. Participants discussed the different scenarios and selected two objects: the dodecahedron wood block and the flag Poi to generate two more complex scenarios and prototyped them with MO controller and sonified them with sound synthesis.

6.2   Slug, Snail, Toad: Sonified Dice Game

The first project was the development of a sonic game. It used the dodecahedron wood block and imagined a sonic version of the "rock-paper-scissors" game[18]. This game as an Asian origin called "Mushi-ken". The "frog" (represented by the thumb) is superseded by the "slug" (represented by the little finger), which, in turn is superseded by the "snake" (represented by the index finger), which is superseded by the "frog". They transposed a sonic version of this game, using sounds of "snake", "frog" and a sound that referred to "Slug". The wood block was instrumented with a wireless MO module [24] (Modular Musical Object) that contains a 3D accelerometer and 3 axis gyroscope). When a player rolls the dice, a sound is produced corresponding to "snake", "slug" or "frog"[19].

---

[18] https://en.wikipedia.org/wiki/Stone_Paper_Scissor.
[19] See the demonstration video: http://youtu.be/EULyOxyNEE4.

In order to recognize which side of the dice is played and to map the side with a specific sound, we used a software using machine learning functions based on Multimodal Hidden Markov Models (MHMMs) [4] implemented as a Max/MSP external [5].

6.3   Flash Mob

The second project was called "Flash Mob" in reference to a group of people that are regrouping suddenly in a public space to perform something atypical or artistic. They used two flags Poi instrumented with a wireless MO module at each flag end. The objective was twofold, the first one was a sonification of the movement in order to learn how to rotate the flag. The second one was the development of new musical interface for artistic performance, see Fig. 7. Two different actions were recognized with the same Max/MSP external: rotational and swinging movements. These two different movements were sonified with sound synthesis based on Buchla[20] sounds recorded previously by one student.

Fig. 7. The two scenarios developed during the workshop HC2. On the left the sonic version of the "slug, snail, toad" game. On the right a demonstration of the sonic flag Poi.

6.4   Summary

The different steps of the workshop and the two final prototypes were demonstrated by the students to the other students and organizers attending at the HC2 summer school. The different students who participated in the workshop were not necessarily familiar with sound, except a student, but they were very active.

A possible limit of our approach was its dependency to technologies of capture and to the Max/msp programming that limit students' autonomy to develop the prototype. But our idea was to develop participants' awareness of this new field of sonic interaction design.

From our point of view, this workshop was an application of the different concepts and issues that we introduced during the previous workshops.

---

[20] http://buchla.com/.

7 Summary and Perspectives

The workshop on "Usage Scenarios of Everyday Objects" was very challenging and participants appreciated this framework highly developed in the design community but less used in our respective disciplines. Participants were able to identify issues related to objects found in the remaining part of the LEGOS project and proposed answers in the form of prototyped augmented objects.

At the time, we did not test different approaches of sound synthesis to refine the sound design of the interactive objects. For example, we have not been able to fully exploit the expressive possibilities of sound synthesis by physical modeling. It was difficult to be closer to the movement. An approach of sound synthesis by physical modeling needs a finer setting in order to make audible the different gestures.

This work will be continued in order to test hypotheses concerning the role of sonic feedback in sensory-motor learning and the type of sound-gesture relationship (metaphorical or abstract).

For the workshop on "Sound metaphors", the use of sound metaphors to sonify gestures showed that beyond the issue of choosing the type of sound, it is paramount to make audible the information associated with different actions that composed the movement. The development of an interaction model as an intermediate structure between the motion capture and sound synthesis engine seems a particularly promising work.

The workshop with external participants during the HC2 summer school allowed us to test our approach and develop thought on our project. An extension of this work could be the development of educational tools for prototyping sonically augmented objects. This is a challenging objective.

These workshops have been beneficial for the LEGOS project because we developed different prototypes to test experimental situations, always questioning the three fields: sonic interaction design, rehabilitation and digital musical interfaces. Following these workshops, we have developed an object with multiple sonic affordances to explore gestural interactions and that will be used for psychological experiments.

These workshops also helped to generate more theoretical questions, especially regarding the distinction between sound metaphor and interaction metaphor.

The theoretical contribution of these workshops is on one hand an extension of a framework to propose a creative process for sonic interaction design. On the other hand we introduced a more theoretical reflection on sound gesture metaphors. It will extend the concept of auditory icons and earcons introduced in human computer interaction to the context of sound-gesture interactions involved in new tangible interface. The development of the experimental device will allow us to study these theoretical issues.

Acknowledgments. This work was supported by ANR French National Research Agency, under the ANR-Blanc program 2011 (Legos project ANR-11-BS02-012) and additional support from Cap Digital. Part of this research was performed within Florian Gutierrez's internship at Ircam as a student of School of Fine Arts TALM Le Mans. We thank the participants of the different workshops.

References

1. Boyer, E.O., Babayan, B.M., Bevilacqua, F., Noisternig, M., Warusfel, O., Roby-Brami, A., Hanneton, S., Viaud-Delmon, I.: From ear to hand: the role of the auditory-motor loop in pointing to an auditory source. Front. Comput. Neurosci. **7**(26) (2013). doi:10.3389/fncom.2013.00026, ISSN 1662-5188
2. Davidoff, S., Lee, M.K., Dey, A.K., Zimmerman, J.: Rapidly exploring application design through speed dating. In: Krumm, J., Abowd, G.D., Seneviratne, A., Strang, T. (eds.) UbiComp 2007. LNCS, vol. 4717, pp. 429–446. Springer, Heidelberg (2007)
3. Essl, G., O'Modhrain, S.: Scrubber: an interface for friction-induced sounds. In: Proceedings of the 2005 Conference on New Interfaces for Musical Expression, pp. 70–75. National University of Singapore (2005)
4. Françoise, J., Schnell, N., Bevilacqua, F.: A multimodal probabilistic model for gesture-based control of sound synthesis. In: Proceedings of the 21st ACM International Conference on Multimedia (MM'13), Barcelona, Spain, pp. 705–708 (2013)
5. Françoise, J., Schnell, N., Borghesi, R., Bevilacqua, F.: Probabilistic models for designing motion and sound relationships. In: Proceedings of the 2014 International Conference on New Interfaces for Musical Expression, NIME'14, London, UK (2014)
6. Franinovic, K., Hug, D., Visell, Y.: Sound embodied: explorations of sonic interaction design for everyday objects in a workshop setting. In: Scavone, G.P. (ed.) Proceedings of the 13th International Conference on Auditory Display (ICAD2007), pp. 334–341. Schulich School of Music, McGill University, Montreal, Canada (2007)
7. Franinovic, K., Gaye, L., Behrendt, F.: Exploring sonic interaction with artifacts in everyday contexts. In: Proceedings of the 14th International Conference on Auditory Display, Paris, France (2008)
8. Franinovic, K., Serafin, S.: Sonic Interaction Design. MIT Press, Cambridge (2013)
9. Grosshauser, T., Hermann, T.: Multimodal closed-loop human machine interaction. In: Proceedings of the 3rd International Workshop on Interactive Sonification (2010)
10. Gutierrez, F.: Développement de scénarios d'usage d'objet du quotidien à travers le design sonore interactif. Ecole des Beaux Arts TALM site le Mans (2012)
11. Houix, O., Lemaitre, G., Misdariis, N., Susini, P., Urdapilleta, I.: A lexical analysis of environmental sound categories. J. Exp. Psychol. Appl. **18**(1), 52–80 (2012)
12. Hug, D.: Investigating narrative and performative sound design strategies for interactive commodities. In: Ystad, S., Aramaki, M., Kronland-Martinet, R., Jensen, K. (eds.) CMMR/ICAD 2009. LNCS, vol. 5954, pp. 12–40. Springer, Heidelberg (2010)
13. Langeveld, L., van Egmond, R., Jansen, R., Özcan, E.: Product sound design: intentional and consequential sounds. In: Coelho, D.A. (ed.) Advances in Industrial Design Engineering, p. 47. InTech, Rijeka (2013)
14. Lemaitre, G., Houix, O., Visell, Y., Franinovic, K., Misdariis, N., Susini, P.: Toward the design and evaluation of continuous sound in tangible interfaces: the spinotron. Int. J. Hum. Comput. Stud. **27**, 976–993 (2009)

15. Lidwell, W., Holden, K., Butler, J.: Universal Principles of Design: 125 Ways to Enhance Usability, Influence Perception, Increase Appeal, Make Better Design Decisions, and Tech Through Design [25 Additional Design Principles]. Rockport Publishers, Beverly (2010)
16. Meyer, A.: Le design. TDC (874) (2004)
17. Misdariis, N., Tardieu, J., Langlois, S., Loiseau, S.: Menu sonification in an automotive media center: design and evaluation. In: Kolski, C. (ed.) Human-Computer Interactions in Transport, pp. 233–281. ISTE Ltd - John Wiley & Sons Inc, Grande-Bretagne (2011)
18. Muller, W., Pasman, G.: Typology and the organization of design knowledge. Des. Stud. **17**(2), 111–130 (1996)
19. Napier, J.R.: The prehensile movements of the human hand. J. Bone Joint Surg. **38**(4), 902–913 (1956)
20. O'Modhrain, S., Essl, G.: PebbleBox and CrumbleBag: tactile interfaces for granular synthesis. In: Proceedings of the 2004 Conference on New Interfaces for Musical Expression, pp. 74–79. National University of Singapore (2004)
21. O'Modhrain, S., Essl, G.: 6 perceptual integration of audio and touch: a case study of PebbleBox. In: Franinovic, K., Serafin, S. (eds.) Sonic Interaction Design, pp. 203–2011. MIT Press, Cambridge (2013)
22. Oulasvirta, A., Kurvinen, E., Kankainen, T.: Understanding contexts by being there: case studies in bodystorming. Pers. Ubiquit. Comput. **7**(2), 125–134 (2003)
23. Quarante, D.: Eléments de design industriel, 3rd edn. Polytechnica, Paris (2001)
24. Rasamimanana, N., Bevilacqua, F., Schnell, N., Guedy, F., Flety, E., Maestracci, C., Zamborlin, B., Frechin, J.L., Petrevski, U.: Modular musical objects towards embodied control of digital music. In: Proceedings of the Fifth International Conference on Tangible, Embedded, and Embodied Interaction, TEI '11, pp. 9–12. ACM, New York (2011)
25. Rath, M.: Auditory velocity information in a balancing task. In: Scavone, G.P. (ed.) Proceedings of the 13th International Conference on Auditory Displays ICAD, Montreal, Canada, pp. 372–379 (2007)
26. Rath, M., Rocchesso, D.: Continuous sonic feedback from a rollling ball. IEEE Multimedia **12**(2), 60–69 (2005)
27. Rocchesso, D., Polotti, P.: Designing continuous multisensory interaction. In: CHI Workshop - Sonic Interaction Design, Firenze, Italy (2008)
28. Rocchesso, D., Polotti, P.: Designing continuous sonic interaction. Int. J. Des. **3**(3), 13–25 (2009)
29. Rocchesso, D., Serafin, S., Rinott, M.: Pedagogical approaches and methods. In: Franinovic, K., Serafin, S. (eds.) Sonic Interaction Design, pp. 125–150. MIT Press, Massachusetts (2013)
30. Soini, K., Pirinen, A.: Workshops-collaborative arena for generative research. In: Proceedings of DPPI (2005)
31. Williamson, J., Murray-Smith, R., Hughes, S.: Shoogle: excitatory multimodal interaction on mobile devices. In: CHI '07 Proceedings of the SIGCHI Conference on Human Factors in Computing Systems, pp. 121–124. ACM, New York (2007)
32. Zheng, J.Z., De La Rosa, S., Dollar, A.M.: An investigation of grasp type and frequency in daily household and machine shop tasks. In: 2011 IEEE International Conference on Robotics and Automation (ICRA), pp. 4169–4175. IEEE (2011)

Vibrotactile Feedback for an Open Air Music Controller

Håkon Knutzen[1,2]([✉]), Tellef Kvifte[3], and Marcelo M. Wanderley[2]

[1] FourMs Lab, Department of Musicology, University of Oslo, Oslo, Norway
hakon.knutzen@gmail.com
[2] IDMIL, CIRMMT, McGill University, Montreal, Canada
marcelo.wanderley@mcgill.ca
[3] Telemark University College, Rauland, Norway
tellef.kvifte@hit.no

Abstract. In this paper we describe an approach for providing vibrotactile feedback for digital musical instruments (DMIs) that are controlled with open air hand motion. The hand motion was captured with infrared marker based motion capture technology. The marker position data was mapped to the control parameters of both sound and vibrotactile signal synthesis. Vibrotactile feedback was provided to the fingertips of the performer by sending the synthesized signals to voice coils actuators that were embedded in a glove. Vibrotactile strategies were developed for two DMI prototypes that focus on different ways of controlling musical sound. Results of an informal evaluation indicate that the synthesized vibrotactile stimuli can provide useful feedback on how the performer is playing the instrument, as well as enhancing the experience of playing the given DMIs.

Keywords: Haptic feedback · Vibrotactile feedback · Open air motion · Open air music controller · Motion capture · Digital musical instrument · DMI · Mapping

1 Introduction

With feedback from musical instruments, we mean that the performer is provided stimuli that varies in accordance with the way the instrument is being played. While auditory feedback is an obvious feedback modality, the performer may also benefit from other feedback modalities, often in combination. *Haptic* feedback encapsulates both *kinesthetic* and *tactile* stimuli [35]. In a musical context, such stimuli provide feedback on musical parameters. Musical kinesthetic feedback involves perception of forces exerted on muscles and joints that can be experienced as feedback on the subject's manipulation of the instrument. The primary focus in this article is feedback involving tactile stimuli, that is, kinesthetic feedback will not be elaborated on.

Perceived tactile feedback involves the perception of texture, vibration, pain, and temperature. The distinction *vibrotactile* feedback involves the perception of

© Springer International Publishing Switzerland 2014
M. Aramaki et al. (Eds.): CMMR 2013, LNCS 8905, pp. 41–57, 2014.
DOI: 10.1007/978-3-319-12976-1_3

musically related vibrations that provide the performer with information on how the instrument is being played. Musical vibrotactile feedback has been pointed out as a feedback modality that performers may benefit from, for instance with regards to playing accuracy and precision [1,24]. Digital musical instruments (DMIs) do not inherit the ability to provide vibrotactile feedback since the sound is not produced by a mechanical system, as in acoustic instruments. DMIs that are controlled with an open air controller are particularly prone to the issues related to lack of vibrotactile feedback since the performer may not even be in touch with a physical control surface when performing. While this introduces several problems, we focused on addressing the issues of how:

– vibrotactile feedback can be provided in a DMI controller design where open air motion is used to control sound.
– vibrotactile signals can be synthesized and how these signals can provide meaningful information on the manipulation of musical parameters of the DMI.
– the vibrotactile feedback is experienced by the performer.

The implementation and experiment in Sects. 3 and 4, was part of the master's thesis work of the first author [23]. First, we explain musical vibrotactile feedback, the concept of open air controllers, and vibrotactile feedback for DMIs. Secondly, we explain the two DMI prototypes and the vibrotactile feedback strategies that were developed with basis in previous research on haptics. Finally, an informal evaluation with five participants was conducted to provide an assessment of the feedback strategies within the scope of the above mentioned problems.

2   Background

2.1   Vibrotactile Feedback

Acoustic instruments are mechanical systems, for instance a membrane coupled to a resonator, that vibrate in order to produce sound. Since the controller is, sometimes inseparably, coupled to the sound generating part of an acoustic instrument, vibrotactile feedback is inherently present. In DMIs the sound is most often created with a computer that eventually converts the digital sound signal into an analog one that in turn can be fed to loudspeakers [21]. Unless the performer is in contact with the loudspeakers, no vibrotactile feedback will be provided.

As mentioned above, vibrotactile feedback has been pointed out as an important feedback modality for the performer. Askenfelt and Jansson explained how string players may benefit from having tactile feedback in ensemble performance [1]. Kvifte explained how a guitarist may benefit from tactile sensing when navigating on the fretboard [24]. Tactile sensing may influence the perception of the "feel" of the instrument as well, that is, the lack of vibrotactile feedback has an impact on the "feel" of DMIs [8,9].

While the perception of vibrotactile sensation may occur on different parts of the body, the hands are natural focal points when dealing with musical vibrotactile feedback [51]. One reason for this is the high concentration of *mechanorecep-tors* in the hands [16,50]. These are the organs to which vibrotactile perception is attributed. Since we are addressing the issue of creating vibrotactile feedback for a DMI controller that uses open air hand motion, we focus on vibrotactile feedback for the hands in this article. The most sensitive frequency range for vibrotactile stimuli is often considered to be 40–1000 Hz [51].

One may distinguish between the *temporal* and the *spatial* domain when referring to vibrotactile feedback stimuli [15]. The former entails that the stimuli parameters evolve over time, e.g. varying amplitude. The latter case involves the perceived notion of stimuli that are distributed along the body [13]. The vibrotactile feedback that is described in this article is in the temporal domain. In the temporal domain, the following signal parameters may be used to convey musical information: *pitch, amplitude, rhythm, roughness,* and *timbre*. The feedback strategies presented in Sect. 3 involved the use of these parameters to convey information.

Pitch and amplitude perception is poor in tactile sensing [3,44]. Nevertheless, one may perceive variance with respect to these parameters. Brown et al. used rhythmic sequences to create tactons (tactile icons) [6]. While *roughness* is not uniformly defined in the literature [15], one explanation of degree of roughness is related to the modulation frequency of an amplitude modulated signal [6,39]. A low modulation frequency corresponds to a low degree of roughness, while a higher modulation frequency corresponds to a higher degree of roughness. Thus, degree of roughness can be used to convey musical information. Okazaki et al. found that harmonic relationships between auditory and vibrotactile stimuli can be perceived [36]. Picinali et al. showed that subjects are able to distinguish between differences in spectral properties of vibrotactile stimuli [42], and Russo et al. showed that subjects may distinguish between instrument timbre with tactile perception [45]. Therefore, spectral variance of the feedback signals was implemented in some of the feedback strategies in Sect. 3.

2.2 Open Air Controllers

A well known problem of the decoupling of the sound controller and the sound generator in DMIs is the fact that the *mapping*, i.e. the coupling of sensor data and sound synthesis parameters, is deemed arbitrary. This means that input from any sensor can control any parameter of the sound. Approaches for developing mapping strategies for the control of sound have been discussed extensively [17–19,25]. However, the issue of mapping to feedback other than auditory has little been discussed, except for [24,26]. This is an issue that is addressed in Sect. 3.

We define *motion* as displacement of an object, such as the limb of a performer, in time. *Gestures* are defined as the meaning bearing component of motion [20]. While the discussion of gesture and motion in music is a long one, an elaboration of this discussion is beyond the scope of this paper. By *open air* motion we mean motion that is executed in open air. Rovan and Hayward used the term open air controller to denote input devices that control musical sound with open air motion [44].

The well known Theremin exemplifies complete touchless control of musical sound. When playing the Theremin, the performer utilizes open air motion of the hands to control amplitude and frequency continuously [38]. While open air motion implies that the performer is not necessarily manipulating the physical control surface of the instrument, the performer may still hold on to a physical object. Rather than creating a sharp distinction between control of musical sound that on the one hand involves complete touchless control of the instrument, and on the other hand control of musical sound that involves touch, we believe it is more fruitful to regard these as extremes of a continuum. Consider for instance how shakers are played in open air. A well known example of DMI controllers, is the Radio Baton [32]. With this controller the performer can control musical parameters by waving two batons in open air above an array of antennas that is sensing the position of the batons. Other examples of open air motion controlled DMIs can be found in [30, 34, 43, 44, 47].

Rovan and Hayward pointed out central problems related to performance with open air controllers [44]. For instance, the performer often needs to rely heavily on proprioception and egolocation. This may introduce imprecision with respect to the performer's perceived absolute position, which in turn may introduce imprecise control of the DMI. Visual stimuli is one way of providing feedback for DMIs with open air controllers. This may be distracting for the performer. Rovan and Hayward pointed out that, with respect to psychology and physiology, vibrotactile perception is more "tightly looped" than visual perception. These mentioned problems illustrate how vibrotactile feedback may prove to be useful for DMIs that are controlled with an open air controller.

2.3   Vibrotactile Feedback for DMIs

DMIs can provide vibrotactile feedback by embedding *actuators*, i.e. devices that produce vibration, in the controller. There exist a wide range of different vibrotactile actuators to choose from [10]. In [22, 46, 49], vibrotactile displays for the hands were made by embedding vibrations motors in glove designs. In this article we will focus on voice coil actuators and how they can provide vibrotactile stimuli to the hands. Since voice coils are devices that in some cases act as loudspeakers, they are capable of producing vibration stimuli that vary in accordance with a synthesized sound signal. For instance, Chafe pointed out how an actuator that vibrates in accordance with the sound signal produced by a DMI can be embedded in the DMI controller surface [8]. The *Breakflute* [4] provides vibrotactile feedback to the fingertips of the performer by embedding actuators in the toneholes of the flute. In the *Haptic Drum*, the *Cellombo*, the *Viblotar*, and the *Vibloslide* vibrotactile feedback is a byproduct of the sound production since the speakers are embedded in the instruments themselves [2, 31]. Egloff used surface-mount speakers as vibrotactile actuators to create a vibrotactile display for sensory substitution [12]. In the context of performing with an open air controller, Rovan and Hayward presented the *tactile ring* which is capable of providing complex synthesized vibration signals to the finger via a ring shaped actuator [44].

3   Implementation: The Vibrotactile Glove and Vibrotactile Feedback Strategies

Four Hiwave 11 mm low profile voice coil actuators [41] were fitted inside four of the fingers of a right handed utility glove, respectively the index, middle, ring, and little finger (Fig. 1). These actuators are similar to the ones Egloff used [12]. A utility glove was chosen since it would likely fit different subjects. A Vicon V460 infrared marker based motion capture system with six M2 cameras (100 fps) was chosen for capturing the motion of the hand. The camera setup resides in the IDMIL (Input Devices and Music Interaction Laboratory) at McGill University.

The utility glove was fitted with a marker configuration (Fig. 1). The position data of the marker on the middle finger was mapped to the signal synthesis in SuperCollider. Both the sound signals and the vibrotactile signals were synthesized in the SuperCollider environment. The sound signals were routed to a headset and the vibrotactile signals were routed to the glove (the signal was amplified by a Sparkfun class D audio amplifier [48]) via a 3.5 mm jack. Although a wireless design would be less obtrusive, low latency was considered to be more crucial. To establish and toggle mappings between the synths in SuperCollider and the marker position data, *libmapper* was used [27,29]. Thus, both position to sound and position to vibrotactile feedback mappings were created using libmapper and the *webMapper* GUI [53].

The DMI prototypes exemplify two different ways in which one may control sound with open air controllers, both on a relatively low and high level. All the vibrotactile signals with varying frequency content were filtered in SuperCollider by two cascaded biquad filters. The filter coefficients were obtained from the Max MSP patch used in [4]. This was an attempt to compensate for the nonlinear frequency response of human tactile perception, as described in [51]. Some of the vibrotactile signals were low pass filtered at 800 Hz to attenuate audible sound coming from the actuators. This has little effect on the perceived outcome of the vibrotactile stimuli since the upper range of perceivable frequencies in the hands is, as explained, often considered to be at 1000 Hz.

Similar to the issue of mapping in DMIs, there is no immediate answer to what the vibrotactile feedback should be like. One obvious approach would be to provide stimuli that resemble the sound signal, such as in [4]. However, there are other ways of providing feedback, cf. the explanation in Sect. 2.1. Using the mentioned parameters, one may create signals that provide feedback on the desired parameters of the sound producing algorithm. In the following sections specific approaches are shown. While some of the vibrotactile strategies are directly linked to the sound signal coming from the DMIs, others were more arbitrarily defined.

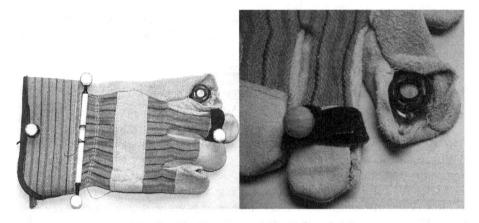

Fig. 1. Glove with fixed marker configuration and index finger actuator exposed (left). Closeup of marker and index finger actuator (right).

3.1 Prototype 1

The mappings of position to sound are described in Table 1. By dividing the marker x-position by a scalar, rounding to the nearest integer and taking modulus 8, the marker x-position was mapped to eight discrete values that in turn were mapped to eight discrete notes of a minor pentatonic scale (passing through one octave). By adjusting the scalar that divides the x-position, this note "grid" spread could be adjusted. The sound synthesis was based on Cottle's code (see [11, p. 24]). This synthesis algorithm is capable of producing a sound with a percussive-like temporal amplitude envelope. Also, the timbre can be varied from "bright" to "dull". The y-position of the marker was mapped to control note triggering such that when the performer crossed a given point, a note would be triggered with a maximum amplitude scaled in accordance with the first difference of the y-position. The z-position was mapped to the timbral parameters of the sound synthesis.

Table 1. Position to sound mapping of DMI Prototype 1.

Input	Mapped to	How
x-pos	frequency (f_0)	one of 8 pentatonic notes
y-pos	amplitude	scaled first difference
	note trigger	crossing given point
z-pos	timbre	low–high→ "dull"–"bright"

The mappings of position to vibrotactile feedback and the signals for the feedback strategies are shown in Table 2. For every newly selected note, a pulse was triggered such that the performer could get feedback on whether or not a new note was selected. This feedback approach was inspired by the way frets on a guitar provide the performer with note selection feedback. Another inspiration for the note selection feedback was found in [33].

Table 2. Mappings of the feedback strategies of DMI Prototype 1.

FS	Signal		
1.1	Sinusoidal		
1.2	Burst		
1.3	Amplitude modulation		
1.4	Filtered sound signal		
FS	Input	Mapped to	How
1.1–1.4	x-pos	note selection feedback frequency (f_0)	for every new note one of 8 pentatonic notes
1.1–1.4	y-pos	amplitude feedback trigger	scaled first difference crossing given point
1.1	z-pos	—	—
1.2	z-pos	burst length	low–high→short–long
1.3	z-pos	modulation frequency	low–high→7–20 Hz
1.4	z-pos	timbre	low–high→ "dull"–"bright"

Four different feedback strategies were developed (Table 2). Like in the position to sound mapping, the y-position was mapped to the trigger of the vibrotactile signal synthesis, while the scaled first difference of the y-position was mapped to the amplitude, and the x-position to f_0. As Table 2 shows, four different signals were used in the feedback strategies (FS):

- A sinusoidal signal with a temporal amplitude envelope that shared the characteristics with the temporal envelope of the sound (FS 1.1).
- A burst of impulses that were filtered by a resonant low pass filter (FS 1.2).
- A sinusoidally amplitude modulated signal (FS 1.3).
- The filtered sound signal produced by Cottle's algorithm (FS 1.4).

FS 1.1 did not provide feedback on the timbre of the sound. Here f_0 of the vibrotactile signal was half the frequency of the sound signal, to keep the tactile signal within the most sensitive range of perceivable frequencies, while also maintaining a harmonic coupling to the sound signal (cf. [36]). With FS 1.2, a burst of pulses that were fed to a resonant low pass filter (filter freq = f_0 of the sound signal) was triggered with every note trigger. While this vibrotactile signal is different from the sound signal produced by the synth, the burst length was controlled in to convey information on the timbre of the sound. FS 1.3 involved amplitude modulation, where the carrier frequency was half the frequency of the sound signal (same reason as FS 1.1). The modulation frequency was controlled by the marker z-position, i.e. varied in accordance with the timbre [6]. FS 1.4 involved feeding the actuators with the filtered sound signal.

To exemplify different outcomes of the vibrotactile feedback, consider first a rapid hand motion executed with the hand raised high: (1) a sinusoidal signal with a high maximum amplitude; (2) a long burst with a high maximum amplitude; (3) a signal with a high degree of roughness and a high maximum amplitude; and (4) the "bright" filtered sound signal with a high maximum amplitude. Second, consider a slow hand motion executed with the hand held low: (1) a sinusoidal signal with a low maximum amplitude; (2) a short burst with a low maximum amplitude; (3) a sinusoidal signal with a low degree of roughness and a low maximum amplitude; and (4) the "dull" filtered sound signal with a low maximum amplitude.

Figure 2 illustrates, in more detail, an example of the first author's interaction with Prototype 1 and FS 1.3. Here one can see a change in spectral spread of the vibrotactile feedback signal as the z-position value increases, meaning that the degree of roughness is increasing. Note selection feedback is also shown (vertical lines in the spectrogram). Notice that whenever the marker y-position crosses the constant line at 0 from a positive value to a negative value, a note is triggered.

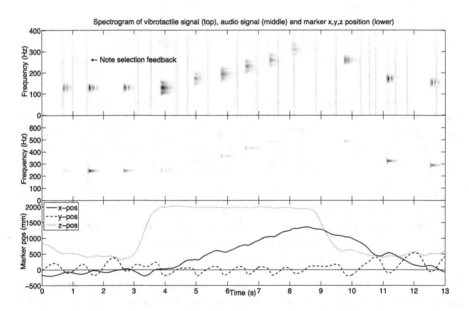

Fig. 2. Example excerpt of the first author playing with FS 1.3 and Prototype 1. Based on [23, p. 58]

3.2   Prototype 2

The position to sound and position to vibrotactile feedback mappings are shown in Tables 3 and 4. Here, a drum loop could be played back by keeping the marker y-position at a value less than zero (Fig. 3). The drum loop was filtered by a resonant low pass filter in SuperCollider, where the marker x-position was mapped to the filter frequency. The marker z-position was mapped to the playback rate of the drum loop. This gave the performer the opportunity to control the mentioned parameters continuously.

Table 3. Position to sound mapping of DMI Prototype 2

Input	Mapped to	How
x-pos	filter frequency	low–high→low–high
y-pos	trigger loop	crossing given point
z-pos	playback rate	low–high→backwards–twice the original speed

As Table 4 shows, FS 2.1 had the same mapping as the mapping of position to sound. This is because the feedback signal is in fact the filtered sound signal. FS 2.2 involved extracting onsets from the drum loop and using these to trigger an amplitude modulated signal with an exponentially decaying temporal envelope, that is, for every new onset the envelope was triggered. A higher playback rate would therefore result in more frequent iterations of the amplitude modulated signal. Degree of roughness was used to convey information on the playback rate as well, i.e. z-position to modulation frequency [6]. The x-position was mapped to an arbitrarily defined range of frequencies to provide feedback on the selected filter frequency.

Table 4. Mappings of the feedback strategies of Prototype 2.

Strategy	Signal		
2.1	Filtered sound		
2.2	Amplitude modulation		
FS	Input	Mapped to	How
2.1	x-pos	filter frequency	low–high→low–high
2.1	y-pos	trigger loop	crossing given point
2.1	z-pos	playback rate	low–high→backwards–2x
2.2	x-pos	carrier frequency	low–high→15–500 Hz
2.2	onsets	trigger feedback	extracted from sound
2.2	z-pos	modulation frequency	low–high→1–30 Hz

When holding the hand high and to the right of the origin of the Vicon coordinate system (negative x-position values), the filter frequency would be low and the playback rate would be close to twice the original. While this would yield a vibrotactile feedback signal similar to the sound signal with FS 2.1, a rapidly iterated signal with a high degree of roughness could be felt with FS 2.2. The latter can be seen in Fig. 3 between time 7–11 s. Here one can see how the z-position value increases as the spectral spread of the vibrotactile signal increases (higher degree of roughness). One can also see how the carrier frequency decreases in the same fashion as the x-position between time 6–10 s.

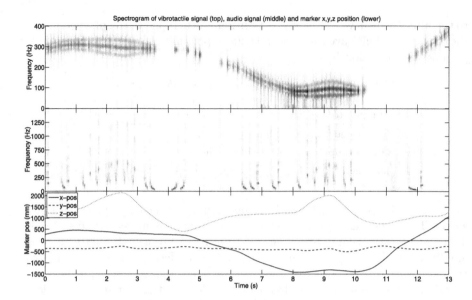

Fig. 3. Example excerpt of the first author playing with 2.2 and Prototype 2. Based on [23, p. 63]

4 Informal Evaluation

An informal evaluation was conducted with five graduate students in the IDMIL at McGill University (Fig. 4). The participants were all familiar with musical practice, as well as DMIs. Here the participants played with the DMI in five separate trials, each lasting no longer than three minutes — one for each feedback strategy, and one without any vibrotactile feedback so that they could give their opinion on whether or not they preferred having any feedback at all. While none of the feedback strategies were explained, the mappings of position to sound were. For both DMI prototypes the participants were instructed to explore the instrument, that is, no formal musical task was given. The participants were also asked if they experienced the glove design to be obtrusive. No quantitative or qualitative analysis of the motion of the participants was performed. With Prototype 1, since absolute frequency discrimination in tactile sensing is poor, the participants were not asked if they could perceive a coupling between the fundamental frequencies of the vibrotactile signals and the sound signals.

4.1 Prototype 1

The participants tried Prototype 1 first. The feedback strategies were provided in different orders for each participant. The note grid spread was also varied between the trials. Here the focus was on finding out if the participants could feel a coupling between the variance in amplitude and timbre of the sound produced by the DMI and the vibrotactile feedback. Another aim was to investigate

Fig. 4. One of the participants during a trial

Table 5. Evaluation summary for Prototype 1

FS	Perceived coupling	Participants
1.1	amplitude:	3/5
	timbre:	1/5
1.2	amplitude:	2/5
	timbre:	1/5
1.3	amplitude:	5/5
	timbre:	3/5
1.4	amplitude:	4/5
	timbre:	4/5
Question	Answer	Participants
Was the note selection feedback useful?	yes:	4
	no:	1
Preferred feedback over no feedback?	yes:	5
	no:	0
Was the glove design obtrusive?	yes:	1
	no:	4

whether or not the participants found the note selection feedback to be useful. The evaluation summary for Prototype 1 is shown in Table 5.

As seen in Table 5, most of the participants found the note selection feedback to be useful. The participant that did not find the note selection feedback to be useful commented that proprioception was a more important for note selection. One participant stated that the perceived effort that was put into the motion when triggering the note felt more important than vibrotactile feedback on amplitude. Conversely, another participant stated that such feedback was useful for understanding the velocity of the hand. With FS 1.1, a participant reported perceived variance in the feedback according to timbral changes. However, this feedback strategy does not vary in accordance with the spectral changes of the sound. The coupling of the parameters of the sound signal and FS 1.2 was hardest for the participants to perceive. This is perhaps not surprising since the vibrotactile signal is different from the audio signal. Couplings between the sound and FS 1.3 and 1.4 seemed to be easier to understand.

4.2   Prototype 2

With Prototype 2, the focus was on finding out if the participants could feel that the feedback varied with the parameters of the sound (Table 6). The participants were asked to explore the DMI with no other instructions than the explanation of the mapping of position to sound. Some participants explained that they found the feedback provided with both feedback strategies to be useful for understanding the rhythm in the drumloop, getting more immersed and getting a better understanding of the space where the motion is used to control the sound. Here FS 2.2 seemed to be more understandable with respect to conveyance of variance in the filter frequency. One may also suggest that extracted onsets are efficient for conveying information related to the playback tempo. In the case of Prototype 2, the participants also preferred having feedback over no feedback.

Table 6. Evaluation summary for Prototype 2

FS	Perceived coupling	Participants
2.1	filter frequency:	1/5
	playback tempo:	4/5
2.2	filter frequency:	4/5
	playback tempo:	5/5
Question	Answer	Participants
Preferred feedback over no feedback?	yes:	5
	no:	0
Was the glove design obtrusive?	yes:	1
	no:	4

5   Summary

We have in this article explained the problems related to vibrotactile feedback and musical performance. While all DMIs are subjected to lack of vibrotactile feedback, we focused on two specific DMI prototypes where sound is controlled using open air motion, i.e. with an open air controller. Such controllers are especially prone to the issues of lack of vibrotactile feedback since the performer may not even touch a physical control surface. We proposed a way of providing complex vibration stimuli in the temporal domain to the fingertips via voice coil actuators, both with signals that are related to the sound coming from the DMI, and with synthesized stimuli signals that are based on previous research on tactile stimuli.

While the informal evaluation only provides a preliminary assessment of the vibrotactile glove and the vibrotactile feedback strategies, some tendencies are shown. Vibrotactile feedback was generally preferred, as opposed to no vibrotactile feedback. This was related to the performer's experience of the "feel" of the DMI. Also, one may argue from the evaluation that the vibrotactile feedback was considered to be useful, e.g for locating notes. Thus, as demonstrated, one may convey information on the manipulation of parameters of a DMI through vibrotactile stimuli. While filtered sound signals can be used to provide vibrotactile feedback, synthesized signals that do not originate from the DMI's sound generator may also convey information on manipulation of DMI parameters.

6   Discussion and Future Work

As explained, one participant reported perceived variance with timbre and FS 1.1. Perhaps is the perceived outcome for this participant related to the fact that one inevitably perceives the vibrotactile feedback and sound simultaneously, that is, through *multimodal perception* [40]. For future work, the relation between vibrotactile feedback and sound may be studied in the scope of multimodal perception.

Albeit demonstrated in a specific context, we believe the described vibrotactile feedback strategies may be an efficient feedback modality for conveying information on musical parameters and events. A formal study with more participants would be necessary for further investigation of the mentioned tendencies. There are different methodologies to choose from. For instance, one could investigate feedback strategies with respect to given musical tasks [52]. Thus, one may for instance with more defined tasks, evaluate what feedback strategies are more efficient than others. Another approach is to, more thoroughly, investigate the performer's experience with the DMI and the vibrotactile feedback [14].

Since one of the participants remarked that the glove was too big, the glove design can be improved. Another participant remarked that although the glove itself was not obtrusive, the wires were. An obvious technical improvement to the mentioned design would be to make it wireless. This would for instance entail that synthesized signals are transmitted wirelessly to a device attached to the glove, or that vibrotactile signals are synthesized on a device that can be worn by the performer [5, 7].

Having tested a set of different vibrotactile feedback strategies, new approaches can be made. New feedback strategies can be founded on existing principles found in acoustic instruments, e.g. physical properties. Also, more arbitrarily related vibrotactile strategies can be defined. Consider for instance how note selection feedback could be more gradual, that is, if the performer could sense the proximity to the notes before selecting them. In some cases the participants could not feel significant variance in amplitude with Prototype 1. The vibrotactile synths are capable of delivering an adequate dynamic range for the participants to perceive noticeable change, however, a different mapping might make such dynamics more pronounced.

An aspect that has not been discussed in the this article is that of longevity in pedagogy. This is a matter that could be targeted in future work. One might argue that the vibrotactile feedback may become increasingly discernible as the participants acquire more skills with the DMI. Also, O'Modhrain highlighted the importance of feedback modalities (other than auditory) in the early stages when learning to play a new instrument [37]. With respect to music therapy, Magee and Burland pointed out that lack of tactile feedback can be problematic when using open air controllers [28]. This may also be a focal point for future work.

Acknowledgments. Marcello Giordano, Clayton Mamedes, Mark Zadel, Joseph Malloch, Stephen Sinclair, Aaron Krajeski, Darryl Cameron and Avrum Hollinger at McGill University for helping out with various technical issues. Also, thanks to the IDMIL students that participated in the evaluation.

References

1. Askenfelt, A., Jansson, E.V.: On vibration sensation and finger touch in stringed instrument playing. Music Percept. Interdisc. J. **9**(3), 311–349 (1992)
2. Berdahl, E., Steiner, H.C., Oldham, C.: Practical hardware and algorithms for creating haptic musical instruments. In: Proceedings of the International Conference on New Inferfaces for Musical Expression, Genova, pp. 61–66 (2008)
3. Birnbaum, D.M.: Musical vibrotactile feedback. Master's thesis, McGill University, Montréal (2007)
4. Birnbaum, D.M., Wanderley, M.M.: A systematic approach to musical vibrotactile feedback. In: Proceedings of the International Computer Music Conference, Copenhagen, vol. 2, pp. 397–404 (2007)
5. Brinkmann, P.: Making Musical Apps: Real-time audio synthesis on Android and iOS. O'Reilly Media Inc, Sebastopol (2012)
6. Brown, L., Brewster, S., Purchase, H.: A first investigation into the effectiveness of tactons. In: Eurohaptics Conference and Symposium on Haptic Interfaces for Virtual Environment and Teleoperator Systems, pp. 167–176 (2005)
7. Bryan, N.J., Herrera, J., Oh, J., Wang, G.: MoMu: a mobile music toolkit. In: Proceedings of the International Conference on New Inferfaces for Musical Expression, Sydney (2010)
8. Chafe, C.: Tactile audio feedback. In: Proceedings of the International Computer Music Conference, Japan, pp. 76–79 (1993)

9. Chafe, C., OModhrain, S.: Musical muscle memory and the haptic display of performance nuance. In: Proceedings of the International Computer Music Conference, Hong Kong, pp. 429–431 (1996)
10. Choi, S., Kuchenbecker, K.: Vibrotactile display: Perception, technology, and applications. In: Proceedings of the IEEE, pp. 1–12. IEEE (2012)
11. Cottle, D.M.: Beginner's tutorial. In: Wilson, S., Cottle, D., Collins, N. (eds.) The SuperCollider Book, pp. 3–54. MIT Press, London (2011)
12. Egloff, D.C.: A vibrotactile music system based on sensory substitution. Master's thesis, Rensselaer Polytechnic Institute, Troy (2011)
13. Geldard, F.A., Sherrick, C.E.: The cutaneous "rabbit": a perceptual illusion. Science **178**(4057), 178–179 (1972)
14. Ghamsari, M., Pras, A., Wanderley, M.M.: Combining musical tasks and improvisation in evaluating novel digital musical instruments. In: Proceedings of the 10th International Symposium on Computer Music Multidisciplinary Research, Marseille, pp. 506–515 (2013)
15. Giordano, M., Wanderley, M.M.: Perceptual and technological issues in the design of vibrotactile-augmented interfaces for music technology and media. In: Oakley, I., Brewster, S. (eds.) HAID 2013. LNCS, vol. 7989, pp. 89–98. Springer, Heidelberg (2013)
16. Halata, Z., Baumann, K.I.: Anatomy of receptors. In: Grunwald, M. (ed.) Human Haptic Perception: Basics and Applications, pp. 85–92. Birkhuser, Basel (2008)
17. Hunt, A., Kirk, R.: Mapping strategies for musical performance (reprint). In: Wanderley, M.M., Battier, M. (eds.) Trends in Gestural Control of Music, pp. 231–258. IRCAM, Centre Pompidou, Paris (2000)
18. Hunt, A., Wanderley, M.M., Kirk, R.: Towards a model for instrumental mapping in expert musical interaction. In: Proceedings of the International Computer Music Conference, Berlin, pp. 209–212 (2000)
19. Hunt, A., Wanderley, M.M., Paradis, M.: The importance of parameter mapping in electronic instrument design. J. New Music Res. **32**, 429–440 (2003)
20. Jensenius, A.R., Wanderley, M.M., Godøy, R.I., Leman, M.: Musical gestures: concepts and methods in research. In: Godøy, R.I., Leman, M. (eds.) Musical Gestures: Sound, Movement, and Meaning, pp. 12–35. Routledge, New York (2010)
21. Jordà, S.: Instruments and players: some thoughts on digital lutherie. J. New Music Res. **3**, 321–341 (2004)
22. Kim, Y., Cha, J., Ryu, J., Oakley, I.: A tactile glove design and authoring system for immersive multimedia. IEEE MultiMed. **17**(3), 34–45 (2010)
23. Knutzen, H.: Haptics in the Air - Exploring vibrotactile feedback for digital musical instruments with open air controllers. Master's thesis, University of Oslo (2013)
24. Kvifte, T.: On images and representations. In: Instruments and the Electronic Age. Taragot Sounds, Oslo (2007)
25. Kvifte, T.: On the description of mapping structures. J. New Music Res. **37**(4), 353–362 (2008)
26. Kvifte, T., Jensenius, A.R.: Towards a coherent terminology and model of instrument description and design. In: Proceedings of the International Conference on New Inferfaces for Musical Expression, Paris, pp. 220–225 (2006)
27. Libmapper. http://libmapper.github.io/. Accessed 4 July 2014
28. Magee, W.L., Burland, K.: An exploratory study of the use of electronic music technologies in clinical music therapy. Nord. J. Music Ther. **17**(2), 124–141 (2008)
29. Malloch, J., Sinclair, S., Wanderley, M.M.: Libmapper: (a library for connecting things). In: Extended Abstracts on Human Factors in Computing Systems, Paris, pp. 3087–3090 (2013)

30. Mamedes, C.R., Wanderley, M.M., Manzolli, J., Garcia, D.H.L.: Strategies for mapping control in interactive audiovisual installations. In: 10th International Symposium on Computer Music Multidisciplinary Research, Marseille, pp. 766–778 (2013)

31. Marshall, M.T., Wanderley, M.M.: Vibrotactile feedback in digital musical instruments. In: Proceedings of the International Conference on New Inferfaces for Musical Expression, Paris, pp. 226–229 (2006)

32. Mathews, M.V.: The radio baton and conductor program, or: pitch, the most important and least expressive part of music. Comput. Music J. 15(4), 37–46 (1991)

33. Moss, W., Cunitz, B.: Haptic theremin: developing a haptic musical controller using the sensable phantom omni. In: Proceedings of the International Computer Music Conference, Barcelona, pp. 275–277 (2005)

34. Nymoen, K., Skogstad, S.A., Jensenius, A.R.: SoundSaber - a motion capture instrument. In: Proceedings of the International Conference on New Inferfaces for Musical Expression, Oslo, pp. 312–315 (2011)

35. Oakley, I., McGee, M.R., Brewster, S., Gray, P.: Putting the feel in "look and feel". In: Proceedings of the Conference on Human Factors in Computing Systems, pp. 415–422, New York (2000)

36. Okazaki, R., Hachisu, T., Sato, M., Fukushima, S., Hayward, V., Kajimoto, H.: Judged consonance of tactile and auditory frequencies. In: Proceedings of the IEEE World Haptics Conference, pp. 663–666, Daejeon (2013)

37. O'Modhrain, M.S.: Playing by feel: incorporating haptic feedback into computer-based musical instruments. Ph.D. thesis, Stanford University, Stanford (2001)

38. Paradiso, J.A., Gershenfeld, N.: Musical applications of electric field sensing. Comput. Music J. 21(2), 69–89 (1997)

39. Park, G., Choi, S.: Perceptual space of amplitude-modulated vibrotactile stimuli. In: IEEE World Haptics Conference, pp. 59–64 (2011)

40. Partan, S., Marler, P.: Communication goes multimodal. Science 283(5406), 1272–1273 (1999)

41. Parts Express: Hiwave tactile actuator. http://www.parts-express.com/pe/showdetl.cfm?partnumber=297-228. Accessed 4 July 2014

42. Picinali, L., Feakes, C., Mauro, D.A., Katz, B.F.G.: Spectral discrimination thresholds comparing audio and haptics for complex stimuli. In: Magnusson, C., Szymczak, D., Brewster, S. (eds.) HAID 2012. LNCS, vol. 7468, pp. 131–140. Springer, Heidelberg (2012)

43. de Quay, Y., Skogstad, S., Jensenius, A.: Dance jockey: performing electronic music by dancing. Leonardo Music J. 21, 11–12 (2011)

44. Rovan, J., Hayward, V.: Typology of tactile sounds and their synthesis in gesture-driven computer music performance. In: Wanderley, M.M., Battier, M. (eds.) Trends in Gestural Control of Music, pp. 355–368. IRCAM, Centre Pompidou, Paris (2000)

45. Russo, F.A., Ammirante, P., Fels, D.I.: Vibrotactile discrimination of musical timbre. J. Exp. Psychol. Hum. Percept. Perform. 38(4), 822–826 (2012)

46. Sachs, D.M.: A forearm controller and tactile display. Master's thesis, Massachusetts Institute of Technology, Cambridge (2005)

47. Schacher, J.C.: Gesture control of sounds in 3D space. In: Proceedings of the International Conference on New Inferfaces for Musical Expression, New York, pp. 358–362 (2007)

48. Sparkfun: Class D mono audio amplifier. https://www.sparkfun.com/products/11044. Accessed 4 July 2014

49. Sziebig, G., Solvang, B., Kiss, C., Korondi, P.: Vibro-tactile feedback for VR systems. In: 2nd Conference on Human System Interactions, pp. 406–410. IEEE, Catania (2009)
50. Vallbo, Å.B., Johansson, R.S.: Properties of cutaneous mechanoreceptors in the human hand related to touch sensation. Hum. Neurobiol. 3(1), 3–14 (1984)
51. Verrillo, R.T.: Vibration sensation in humans. Music Percept. 2(3), 281–302 (1992)
52. Wanderley, M.M., Orio, N.: Evaluation of input devices for musical expression: borrowing tools from HCI. Comput. Music J. 26(3), 62–76 (2002)
53. WebMapper. http://libmapper.github.io/ecosystem/user_interfaces.html. Accessed 4 July 2014

Automatic Classification of Guitar Playing Modes

Raphael Foulon[(✉)], Pierre Roy, and François Pachet

Sony Computer Science Laboratory, Paris, France
{raphael.foulon, pachetcsl}@gmail.com

Abstract. When they improvise, musicians typically alternate between several playing modes on their instruments. Guitarists in particular, alternate between modes such as octave playing, mixed chords and bass, chord comping, solo melodies, walking bass, etc. Robust musical interactive systems call for a precise detection of these playing modes in real-time. In this context, the accuracy of mode classification is critical because it underlies the design of the whole interaction taking place. In this paper, we present an accurate and robust playing mode classifier for guitar audio signals. Our classifier distinguishes between three modes routinely used in jazz improvisation: bass, solo melodic improvisation, and chords. Our method uses a supervised classification technique applied to a large corpus of training data, recorded with different guitars (electric, jazz, nylon-strings, electro-acoustic). We detail our method and experimental results over various data sets. We show in particular that the performance of our classifier is comparable to that of a MIDI-based classifier. We describe the application of the classifier to live interactive musical systems and discuss the limitations and possible extensions of this approach.

Keywords: Audio classification · Playing mode · Guitar · Interactive musical systems

1 Introduction

An ideal interactive musical system should allow users to play as if they were performing with fellow musicians. To achieve this, the behavior of such an ideal system must be predictable and consistent. One way to achieve this is to provide explicit controls such as manual switches, pedals, knobs, or sliding faders. However, some musical intentions cannot be given explicitly because it creates a cognitive overhead that interferes with the performance.

Musicians typically alternate between several *playing modes* when they improvise. A guitarist, for instance may alternate between chord comping, solo melodic improvisation, or walking bass. Each mode calls for a specific reaction from the other musicians. For instance, in a guitar duo, if one musician improvises a solo melody, the other will usually complement with chord comping.

In this paper, we address the problem of automatically classifying the audio input of a guitar improviser into three musical modes (melody, chords, and bass). We show that

© Springer International Publishing Switzerland 2014
M. Aramaki et al. (Eds.): CMMR 2013, LNCS 8905, pp. 58–71, 2014.
DOI: 10.1007/978-3-319-12976-1_4

recognizing these modes automatically and in real-time opens the way to musically aware interactive applications such as VirtualBand [14] or augmented instruments.

Research developed in the MIR community has focused mainly on expressivity parameters and on the classification of playing techniques for various musical instruments. Lähdeoja et al. proposed a system that classifies in real time different playing techniques used by a guitarist [12, 15]. These techniques include up and down legatos, slides, slapped/muted notes, as well as the position of the pick on the neck with regards to the bridge. The system relies on the analysis of both the incoming audio signal and/ or gesture capture data. Similar topics have been investigated with the goal of modeling *expressivity*, such as the articulation in nylon guitar [13]. Abesser et al. present a feature-based approach to classify several plucking styles of bass guitar isolated notes, and describes an automatic classifier of guitar strings for isolated notes using a feature-based approach [1] and a two-step analysis process [2]. Barbancho et al. study the retrieval of played notes and finger positions from guitar audio signals [3]. Instrumental technique classification methods have been investigated for beatboxing [17, 19] and for snare drums [20] with some success.

Stein et al. [18] describe an approach to analyze automatically audio *effects* applied to an electric guitar or bass, and Fohl et al. [6] studied the automatic classification of guitar tones. As we will see below, their objective is in some sense opposite to ours, since we aim at extracting information from the guitar signal that is precisely timbre-independent.

We propose a method to extract information about the musical content that is played, regardless of expressive parameters and of the technique used. For instance, jazz guitarists use various *playing modes*: octave playing (typical of Georges Benson or Wes Montgomery), chord comping, bass lines, mix of chords and bass (as in bossa nova). Our aim is precisely to detect these playing modes in real time for interactive applications. Each mode may be played in many different ways using different techniques and with different expressivity parameters. We do not aim at extracting information about *how* something is played, *e.g.*, staccato, legato, slapped, but rather about *what* is played, *e.g.*, melodies, octaves, single notes, bass, chords.

Playing modes would be in principle easy to analyze from a score of the performance. However, score-related symbolic data (pitches, durations) are available only from MIDI instruments. Furthermore, the accuracy of MIDI guitars is far from perfect and requires specific, expensive hardware. The accuracy of automatic score transcription from audio [10, 16] is not high enough to build robust live systems. More specifically, Hartquist [8] addresses the problem of automatic transcription of guitar recordings, but this approach is only evaluated on a pre-recorded note template library for a nylon string acoustic guitar, therefore, it is unclear whether it can cope with the dynamic variation that can occur in live recordings and with other types of guitars.

One key problem is to detect accurately and robustly polyphony from the guitar signal. The classification of monophony *versus* polyphony has been investigated [11] using the YIN pitch estimation algorithm [4] with bivariate Weibull models. This method is practical since it only requires short training sets (about two minutes of audio signal is enough) and works for many instruments with good performance (6.3 % global error rate). Most importantly, this work shows that YIN is an accurate descriptor for polyphony detection.

In this paper, we describe a mode classifier that classifies guitar audio signals into three basic playing modes described above: bass, chords and melody. Following the approach of Abesser [2], the classifier is based on a two-step analysis process (single frames then smoothing on larger windows), based on YIN-derived features, pitch and inharmonicity indicator [3, 11].

Our classifier is largely timbre-independent, *i.e.*, it performs well on the four types of guitar we tested. We describe the training data in the next section. The classifier is described in Sect. 3 and its performance is discussed in Sect. 4. Section 5 describes applications of the classifier for interactive music systems.

2 Datasets

Although all guitars exploit the sound of vibrating strings, there are different types of guitars and guitar sounds. In order to avoid biases or overfitting due to the use of a single guitar for training data, we built an audio dataset recorded with four guitars of different types:

- Godin LGX-SA solid-body guitar (*God*) – which has also a MIDI output – which output has been fed to a AER Compact 30 jazz amplifier,
- Cort LCS-1 jazz guitar (*Cort*),
- Ovation Electric Legend (model Al Di Meola) electro-acoustic guitar (*Ovat*) and
- Godin Nylon SA nylon string guitar (*Nyl*) (see Fig. 1).

For each guitar, we created a dataset that consists of the recordings of seven jazz standards: *Bluesette*, *The Days of Wine and Roses*, *LadyBird*, *Nardis*, *Ornithology*, *Solar*, and *Tune Up*. Each song has been recorded three times, one for each playing mode: *melody*, *bass*, and *chords*. The database contains therefore 84 files – 4 guitars × 7 songs × 3 modes – for a total audio duration of 1 h 39 min. The audio datasets may be downloaded at http://flow-machines.com/mode_classification_sets.

Fig. 1. The four guitars used to record the dataset. *From left to right*: pure solid-body Godin LGX, hollow-body Cort jazz archtop, Ovation electro-acoustic, and nylon-string guitar Godin Classic.

3 The Mode Classifier

Our method uses a two-phase analysis: first, short signal frames (50 ms) are classified with a supervised classification algorithm, which determines the playing mode over short-time windows, with an imperfect accuracy. Then, information obtained over the 50 ms frames is aggregated to classify a whole audio chunk. The scheme of the algorithm is shown in Fig. 3.

3.1 Feature Selection

We use a training set that consists of jazz guitar recordings corresponding to the three playing modes "bass", "melody" and "chords". The training sets described in this article are all extracted from the guitar recordings presented in Sect. 2.

We performed feature selection to determine which features are the most relevant for our problem. We used the Information Gain algorithm [7] of Weka [9], set with the lowest possible threshold (-1.8×10^{308}) to obtain a list of features ranked by information gain, and ran it on a set of 37 features divided in two sets:

(1) Basic audio features: MFCC (13), harmonic-to-noise ratio, spectral centroid, spectral flatness, spectral kurtosis, spectral decrease, spectral spread, spectral rolloff, spectral skewness, chroma (12), RMS.
(2) YIN features [8]: YIN pitch, YIN inharmonicity indicator and YIN variance.

Feature selection yields the six following features: harmonic-to-noise ratio, YIN pitch and YIN inharmonicity, spectral spread, spectral centroid and spectral kurtosis. This confirms that YIN features are indeed interesting for our task. To further reduce the feature set, we retained only the four following features:

(1) YIN pitch, which was quantized to avoid overfitting (this point is explained below), computed with an absolute threshold of 0.2 for aperiodic/total ratio,
(2) YIN inharmonicity coefficient, computed in the same manner,
(3) Harmonic-to-noise ratio (HNR) of the signal, computed with a fundamental frequency of 185 Hz (which is the lowest frequency possible with 50 ms frames, we would have to work with larger frame lengths to decrease the fundamental),
(4) Spectral spread.

3.2 Frame Selection and Training

The audio signals in the training set are normalized and then sliced into 50 ms frames, with a 75 % overlap. We chose 50 ms to ensure that each frame contains at most one musical event, even when dealing with fast tempos or virtuoso solos.

Preliminary empirical results show that, given our feature set, common statistical classifiers (SVM, decision trees, and Bayesian networks) fail to classify correctly the frames that contain transients. We remove silent frames and frames that contain transients from the training set, and train the classifier on the frames that contain the steady part of the signal.

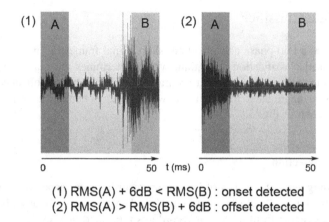

(1) RMS(A) + 6dB < RMS(B) : onset detected
(2) RMS(A) > RMS(B) + 6dB : offset detected

Fig. 2. Simple onset/offset detection procedure. The output of the algorithm is positive if there is a difference of 6 dB or more between the two RMS values.

To do so, we first use a noise gate with a −13 dB threshold to remove silent frames. To detect quickly transient frames, we use a simple onset/offset detection algorithm, presented in Fig. 2, which computes the difference between the RMS values of the first 10 and last 10 milliseconds of the signal, and applies a 6 dB threshold on it. More sophisticated techniques such as frequency domain-based onset detection [5] can be used, but the proposed solution is fast and works well enough for our goals.

Eventually, we extract the four features (YIN Pitch, YIN Inharmonicity Factor, Spectral Spread, and HNR) from the remaining frames (i.e., the frames that contain steady parts of the signal). We use this data to train classifiers using various machine learning algorithms: a Support Vector Machine with linear, radial and polynomial kernels, a Bayesian network and a J48 tree. The best classifier turns out to be a Bayesian network (Weka's *BayesNet* with a "GeneticSearch" algorithm with the default parameters).

3.3   Performance on Frame Classification

To evaluate the performance of the Bayesian network, we train the classifier on one song, *The Days of Wine and Roses* (the longest song of the database), taken from the Godin guitar (*God*) subset, and test it on the six other songs. When we classify the selected audio frames (discarding silent frames and transients) with our feature set and the Bayesian network, we obtain an average F-measure of 0.87. This result is not sufficient for a robust, real-time classifier. In the next section we add an aggregation, or smoothing step to our method to further improve the classifier performance, following the approach of Abesser [2].

3.4   Aggregation

In order to improve the classification performance, we aggregate the results of individual frame classification within a given time window (called thereafter chunk) and

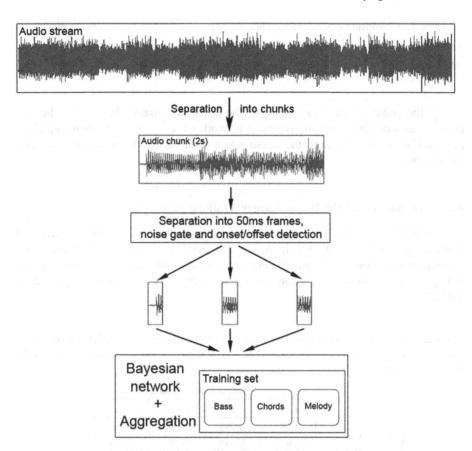

Fig. 3. General scheme of the classification algorithm.

apply a winner-takes-all strategy to identify the mode of the chunk. For interactive musical applications, a typical chunk size is one bar at reasonable tempos (1 s at 240 bpm, 4 s at 60 bpm). For extremely fast tempos, chunks of more than one bar should be considered to avoid performance decrease due to small numbers of frames.

4   Results

This section describes various evaluations of the classifier (including aggregation), highlighting the impact of using different guitars on classification robustness.

4.1   Evaluation on a One-Song Training Set

First, we train the classifier on one single song, "The Days of Wine and Roses", taken from the Godin guitar (*God*) subset. Then, we test it on the six other songs, for each guitar subset, with a chunk duration of 1.5 sec. (the duration of one 4/4 bar at 160 bpm). The results are displayed on Table 1.

Table 1. Classification performance obtained over six songs, for various guitar models

Guitar dataset	God	Cort	Ovat	Nyl
Mean F-measure	**0.96**	**0.941**	**0.854**	**0.839**

For the guitar subsets *Cort* and *God*, the results are slightly better than the pre-liminary ones obtained with the Bayesian network without the aggregation step (0.87 average F-measure). However, the classification results are poor for the *Ovat* and *Nyl* guitar subsets.

4.2   Evaluation with the Use of Larger Training Sets

To improve the performance, we increase the size of the training set: we train and evaluate the classifier with the leave-one-out procedure. Hence, each training set contains now six songs. To study the influence of the guitar type used for training and testing, we repeat this procedure for each guitar subset. The results are displayed on Table 2.

Table 2. Classification performance obtained with the leave-one-out procedure on the whole dataset. The first number is the minimum F-measure over the six tested songs, the second is the average F-measure

		Tested guitar dataset			
		God	Cort	Ovat	Nyl
Training guitar dataset	God	0.956	0.933	0.654	0.71
		0.971	0.968	0.90	0.901
	Cort	0.94.3	0.974	0.753	0.922
		0.963	0. 984	0.94	0.972
	Ovat	0.885	0.917	0.964	0.956
		0.92	0.955	0.978	0.978
	Nyl	0.92	0.961	0.961	0.981
		0.943	0.975	0.975	0.992
	Avg. F-measure	**0.949**	**0.971**	**0.948**	**0.961**

These results show that while a larger training set increases the accuracy, the classification performance depends on the guitar used for training and testing: more specifically, the pairs *God/Cort* and *Ovat/Nyl* seem to give better results when used together (one for training and the other for testing). This can be explained by the fact that the guitars used to record *Ovat* and *Nyl* subsets produce more high-frequency content than the other ones: a feature such as spectral spread is sensitive to timbre.

4.3 Evaluation with a Mixed Training Set

In order to make the classifier more independent of the guitar type, or more generally of timbral variations, we pick tracks from each of the four subsets to build a new training set. We use the recordings of *The Days of Wine and Roses* and *Ladybird* from each subset to train the classifier and test the performance on the five remaining tracks. Results are shown on Table 3.

Table 3. Classification performance obtained with the use of a mixed training set. We compare the minimal F-measures over the four guitars in order to evaluate the timbral sensitivity of the classifier.

<table>
<tr><td></td><td></td><td colspan="5" align="center">Tested guitar dataset</td></tr>
<tr><td></td><td></td><td>*God*</td><td>*Cort*</td><td>*Ovat*</td><td>*Nyl*</td><td>Min.
F-measure</td></tr>
<tr><td rowspan="5">Test song</td><td>Bluesette</td><td>0.971</td><td>0.988</td><td>0.989</td><td>0.995</td><td>**0.971**</td></tr>
<tr><td>Nardis</td><td>0.941</td><td>0.966</td><td>0.973</td><td>0.99</td><td>**0.941**</td></tr>
<tr><td>Ornithology</td><td>0.99</td><td>0.988</td><td>0.99</td><td>0.999</td><td>**0.988**</td></tr>
<tr><td>Solar</td><td>0.977</td><td>0.965</td><td>0.985</td><td>0.997</td><td>**0.965**</td></tr>
<tr><td>Tune Up</td><td>0.968</td><td>0.984</td><td>0.962</td><td>0.952</td><td>**0.952**</td></tr>
<tr><td></td><td>**Min.
F-measure**</td><td>**0.968**</td><td>**0.978**</td><td>**0.98**</td><td>**0.987**</td><td>**0.968**</td></tr>
</table>

Here, we can see that the use of a mixed training set, containing two songs (or a total 31 min of audio), increases the overall performance. We evaluated the classifier with larger training sets, but larger sets do not increase classification accuracy in a significant way. This last training set will be used in the rest of this article.

4.4 Influence of the Analysis Window Length

Since the algorithm includes an aggregation step, we can assume that the accuracy of the classifier depends on the length of the analyzed audio chunks. Figure 4 displays the classification performance obtained over the five tracks which are not included in the training set, for various analysis windows. As a comparison, we added, for each guitar subset, the F-measures obtained without performing the aggregation over the 50 ms frames.

We can see that the classification improves when increasing the analysis window length, reaching a plateau at about .98.

4.5 Real-Time

Since the algorithm consists in feature extraction and simple Bayesian classification, the overall complexity of the algorithm is linear with the analyzed audio window length (other computation such as the aggregation is negligible). The average classification

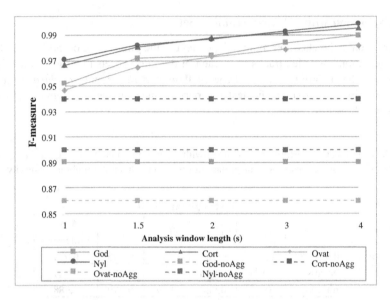

Fig. 4. Classification performance obtained with different analysis window lengths. The series followed by the mention *noAgg (dotted lines)* show the results obtained without the aggregation step.

CPU is 2 % of real-time, with a Java implementation running on an Intel i7 2.67 GHz quad-core, Windows laptop (e.g. the experienced latency obtained for the analysis of a 4/4 bar at 120 bpm is 20 ms). This clearly enables interactive musical applications on commonly available hardware.

4.6   Comparison with MIDI-Based Classification

We compared our algorithm with the performance of a MIDI-based mode classifier described in [14], using the Godin guitar subset (this guitar has a MIDI output). The MIDI-based classifier trains a Support Vector Machine classifier on 8 MIDI features, related to pitch, duration, velocity, and more advanced ones, aggregated over one bar. This classifier is been trained on the song *Bluesette*, and tested on the six other songs. In order to work with the same experimental settings, we adapted the analysis window of our audio-based algorithm on each song, to match the length of a bar. The results are displayed in Tables 4 and 5.

The results we obtain are still reasonable, but weaker than with the preceding training sets. This is due to the fact that audio analysis requires larger training sets than MIDI to reach the same performance. To illustrate this point, we increase slightly our training set and train our classifier with two songs: *Bluesette* and *The Days of Wine and Roses*. We repeat the testing procedure on the five remaining tracks. The confusion matrix is displayed on Table 6.

These results show that our method provides results which are comparable to the ones obtained with the MIDI output of the guitar. This result enables us to integrate our algorithm in actual interactive live applications, without any MIDI support.

Table 4. Classification results obtained with the MIDI-based SVM classifier

		Predicted class			
		Bass	Chords	Melody	F-measure
Actual class	Bass	1314	6	2	0.98
	Chords	24	1294	13	0.97
	Melody	1	12	1318	0.99

Table 5. Classification results obtained with our classifier

		Predicted class			
		Bass	Chords	Melody	F-measure
Actual class	Bass	1118	1	3	0.947
	Chords	85	1017	11	0.936
	Melody	25	31	1065	0.968

Table 6. Classification results obtained with our classifier, with a larger training set

		Predicted class			
		Bass	Chords	Melody	F-measure
Actual class	Bass	811	30	10	0.965
	Chords	0	852	3	0.969
	Melody	18	21	817	0.969

5 Interactive Applications

VirtualBand [14] is an interactive musical engine that enables one or several musicians to control virtual instruments. The virtual instruments interact with the users but also with one another in real time, thus creating possibly complex interactive performance. VirtualBand allows to build bebop-style improvisations by constraining the virtual instruments to follow a predefined harmonic sequence.

VirtualBand was used to create a *reflexive loop pedal* for guitar. This application is based on the mode classifier described here. The goal is to allow guitarists to play a trio with themselves.

Two virtual instruments are instantiated by the system: a *virtual bass player* and a *virtual chord player*. The virtual instruments are silent at the beginning of the session. When the user starts improvising on the predefined chord sequence, its musical production is analyzed by the classifier and used to feed the virtual instruments: when the user plays a bar of bass, the corresponding signal is stored in an audio database accessible to the virtual bass player. Similarly, when the user plays a bar of chords, it is stored in a database that is accessible to the virtual chord player. Each bar in the virtual instrument's databases are labeled with the harmony specified by the predefined chord sequence.

Once the virtual databases are not empty anymore, the virtual instruments start to play along with the user. They follow the "two-other-guys" principle: when the user plays melody, the two virtual instruments play, thus producing the output of a typical jazz guitar trio; when the user plays bass, the virtual chord player plays along; and when the user plays chords, the virtual bass player plays along.

VirtualBand features a real-time pitch-shifting algorithm that enables the virtual instruments to transpose the recorded audio chunks in the virtual databases. For instance, if the user played a bar of chords in C7 (the harmony specified by the chord sequence at a certain point in time), the virtual chord player will be able to play back this bar, after transposition, when the chord sequence specifies a harmony of D7. This is particularly useful if the user never played chords on a D7 harmony. This mechanism reduces the *feeding* phase, i.e., the phase during which the user is playing chords and bass lines to feed the virtual instruments.

VirtualBand also uses harmonic substitution rules enabling the virtual instruments to play back music in a context it was not recorded in. For instance, a bar of chords that was recorded in a C major context may be played back on an A minor context, using the "relative minor" substitution rule, which states that A minor and C major are somehow musically equivalent.

The combination of the transposition and substitution mechanisms allows to reduce the feeding phase to a minimum, typically a few bars for a jazz standard, thus creating lively and entertaining performance.

A detailed version of this example is given in Pachet et al. [14]. This application allows the user to control the musical process while not using physical control devices such as loop pedals, which would interfere with his creative flow. Hybrid modes, such as the "bossa nova" mode (see the next section) can be added to this setup to enable more sophisticated interactions, thanks to the addition of a new virtual instrument.

Another application of the mode classifier, implemented in the VirtualBand engine, is to automatically process the input sound according to the playing mode. Depending on the current playing mode, various audio effects are applied to the audio signal. For instance, the system can add a specific reverberation effect to monophonic melody, tube distortion to chords, and, say, apply dynamic compression and enhance the low end of the bass. The effect chain is applied with a latency that corresponds to the chunk size needed to perform mode classification, *i.e.*, about 1 s.

6 Discussion

We have shown that YIN features, that represent half of our feature set, are efficient to classify guitar playing modes: our classifier is accurate, robust to variations in guitar type, and able to cope with real-time computational constraints, thanks to a small feature set. We also showed that although the accuracy depends on the size of the analyzed audio, this classifier can be used with realistic window sizes. Three points can be improved, to further extend its applicability.

6.1 Features

The method raises issues when dealing with long chord decays (say, more than 5 sec.), when only one note keeps sounding. This case falls off the boundaries of our algorithm and feature set. One solution would be to add a robust onset detector to our algorithm, and restrict the mode computation on the first seconds that follow an onset (we did no implement such a solution).

Another limitation comes from the feature set: we work with a feature set that answers a specific problem, but it may not be efficient to distinguish efficiently yet other playing modes, such as strums or octaves. The algorithm is also somewhat specific to the guitar: the YIN inharmonicity factor may not behave the same with less harmonic instruments, such as the piano.

6.2 Hybrid Playing Modes

In our method, we perform an aggregation step because the frame classifier alone is not accurate enough. Nevertheless, it provides a good hint about the rate of chords, melody and bass, within audio chunks that contain a mixture of different playing modes. For instance, we can consider an extra "bossa nova" playing mode which consists in alternative bass/chords patterns. In order to recognize such a mode, we add an extra rule to the aggregation step of the algorithm: before applying the winner-takes-all strategy to our frames classes, we compute the weight of each class, without taking the class probabilities into account, and we express it in absolute percentage. Then, we consider the bass and chords weights: if they are both greater than, say, 20 % and lower than 80 %, then we can consider that the chunk belongs to the "Bossa nova" class. Such a rule could be also implemented in a classifier, so that the process is entirely auto-matic. An example of such a hybrid mode is displayed in Fig. 5.

Fig. 5. Identification of bass and chord parts in a bossa nova guitar audio signal

Although the frame classifier does not provide an accurate weight for each class within a chunk, the ability to detect when the musician is performing this hybrid playing mode brings new possibilities for building interactive applications. The pattern displayed on Fig. 5 is correctly detected, however it represents only a particular case of the bossa nova playing mode, in which bass and chords do not overlap. In the (fre-quent) case when they overlap, the classifier performance drops sharply.

6.3 Absolute Aggregation *vs.* Time Series

In this paper, we use the simple winner-take-all strategy to aggregate the 50 ms frames over the entire analysis window. This method does not take into account the time-series nature of a musical audio signal. For instance, guitar players sometimes use low-pitched notes in their melodic improvisation, and conversely, play walking bass with high-pitched notes. With our window-based scheme, the classifier uses the YIN pitch as a strong hint to distinguish the melody from the bass. As a consequence, the user might be surprised by some results for those notes with intermediary pitches (*e.g.*, in the range C3–E3) also, since there is no high-level musical analysis of the currently played phrase. The evolution and continuity between the different features values extracted within an audio chunk could be evaluated over time, leading to a smarter way to process these frames. We assume that a classifier that exploits such knowledge would be more accurate and could efficiently identify more sophisticated playing modes such as arpeggios, muted notes strumming, and, in general, playing modes based on longer temporal patterns.

7 Conclusion

We have presented a simple and fast method to classify in real time guitar audio signals into three basic playing modes: chords, melody, and bass. Our method is timbre-independent and proves accurate with four different types of guitar.

The good performance of our classifier paves the way for interactive musical systems allowing users to improvise with virtual copies of themselves to form, e.g., a guitar trio. Future designs of the algorithm, in particular taking into account the continuity between frame analyses, will be able to distinguish more complex playing modes, such as the bossa nova bass/chord mixing, thereby enabling the application to other musical genres.

Automatic playing mode classification brings a lot of potential for designing smarter augmented instruments. Interestingly, developing subtler and subtler playing mode classifiers, from polyphony-based detection as we presented here to the identification of player-specific patterns (Montgomery's octaves, Benson's licks or Van Halen's fast harmonic arpeggios), infringes on the emerging domain of style modeling.

Acknowledgments. This research is conducted within the Flow Machines project which received funding from the European Research Council under the European Union's Seventh Framework Programme (FP/2007-2013)/ERC Grant Agreement n. 291156.

References

1. Abesser, J., Lukashevich, H.M., Schuller, G.: Feature-based extraction of plucking and expression styles of the electric bass guitar. In: Proceedings of International Conference on Acoustics, Speech and Signal Processing, Dallas, pp. 2290–2293 (2010)
2. Abesser, J.: Automatic string detection for bass guitar and electric guitar. In: Proceedings of the 9th International Symposium on Computer Music Modelling and Retrieval, London, pp. 567–582 (2012)

3. Barbancho, I., Tardon, L.J., Sammartino, S., Barbancho, A.M.: Inharmonicity-based method for the automatic generation of guitar tablature. IEEE Trans. Audio Speech Lang. Process. **20**(6), 1857–1868 (2012)
4. De Cheveigné, A., Kawahara, H.: YIN, a fundamental frequency estimator for speech and music. J. Acoust. Soc. Am. **111**(4), 1917–1931 (2002)
5. Dixon, S.: Onset detection revisited. In: Proceedings of the 9th International Conference on Digital Audio Effects, Montreal, pp. 113–137 (2006)
6. Fohl, W., Turkalj, I., Meisel, A.: A Feature relevance study for guitar tone classification. In: Proceedings of the 13th International Study for Music Information Retrieval Conference, Porto (2012)
7. Guyon, I., Elisseef, A.: An Introduction to variable and feature selection. J. Mach. Learn. Res. **3**, 1157–1182 (2003). (http://www.jmlr.org)
8. Hartquist, J.: Real-time musical analysis of polyphonic guitar audio. Ph.D. thesis, California Polytechnic State University (2012)
9. Holmes, G., Donkin, A., Witten, I.H.: Weka: a machine learning workbench. In: IEEE Proceedings of the Second Australian and New Zealand Conference on Intelligent Information Systems, pp. 357–361 (1994)
10. Klapuri, A., Davy, M.: Signal Processing Methods for Music Transcription. Springer, New York (2006)
11. Lachambre, H., André-Obrecht, R., Pinquier J.: Monophony vs polyphony: a new method based on Weibull bivariate models. In: Proceedings of the 7th International Workshop on Content-Based Multimedia Indexing, Chania, pp. 68–72 (2009)
12. Lähdeoja, O., Reboursière, L., Drugman, T., Dupont, S., Picard-Limpens, C., Riche, N.: Détection des Techniques de Jeu de la Guitare. In: Actes des Journées d'Informatique Musicale, Mons, pp. 47–53 (2012)
13. Özaslan, T.H., Guaus, E., Palacios, E., Arcos, J.L.: Attack based articulation analysis of nylon string guitar. In: Proceedings of the 7th International Symposium on Computer Music Modeling and Retrieval, Malaga, pp. 285–297 (2010)
14. Pachet, F., Roy, P., Moreira, J., d'Inverno, M.: Reflexive loopers for solo musical improvisation. In: Proceedings of International Conference on Human Factors in Computing Systems (CHI), Paris, pp. 2205–2208 (2013). (Best paper honorable mention award)
15. Reboursière, L, Lähdeoja, O., Drugman, T., Dupont, S., Picard-Limpens, C., Riche, N.: Left and right-hand guitar playing techniques detection. In: Proceedings of New Interfaces for Musical Expression, Ann Arbor, pp. 30–34 (2012)
16. Ryynänen, M.P., Klapuri, A.P.: Automatic transcription of melody, bass line, and chords in polyphonic music. Comput. Music J. **32**(3), 72–86 (2008). (MIT Press)
17. Sinyor, E., Mckay, C., Mcennis, D., Fujinaga, I.: Beatbox classification using ACE. In: Proceedings of the 6th International Conference on Music Information Retrieval, London, pp. 672–675 (2005)
18. Stein, M., Abesser, J., Dittmar, C., Schuller, G.: Automatic detection of audio effects in guitar and bass recordings. In: Proceedings of the 128th Audio Engineering Society Convention, London (2010)
19. Stowell, D., Plumbley, M.D.: Delayed Decision-making in real-time beatbox percussion classification. J. New Music Res. **39**(3), 203–213 (2010)
20. Tindale, A., Kapur, A., Tzanetakis, G., Fujinaga, I.: Retrieval of percussion gestures using timbre classification techniques. In: Proceedings of the 5th International Conference on Music Information Retrieval, Barcelona, pp. 541–544 (2004)

Extracting Commands from Gestures: Gesture Spotting and Recognition for Real-Time Music Performance

Jiuqiang Tang and Roger B. Dannenberg[✉]

Carnegie Mellon University, Pittsburgh, USA
jiuqiant@andrew.cmu.edu, rbd@cs.cmu.edu

Abstract. Our work allows an interactive music system to spot and recognize "command" gestures from musicians in real time. The system gives the musician gestural control over sound and the flexibility to make distinct changes during the performance by interpreting gestures as discrete commands. We combine a gesture threshold model with a Dynamic Time Warping (DTW) algorithm for gesture spotting and classification. The following problems are addressed: i) how to recognize discrete commands embedded within continuous gestures, and ii) an automatic threshold and feature selection method based on F-measure to find good system parameters according to training data.

Keywords: Gesture spotting and recognition · Automatic threshold and feature selection · Dynamic time warping · Threshold model · F-measure evaluation

1 Introduction

In the field of computer music, real-time musical interaction has been a novel and attractive focus of research. It is related to all aspects of interactive processes including the capture and multimodal analysis of gestures and sounds created by artists, management of interaction, and techniques for real-time synthesis and sound processing. Moreover, with the development of gesture sensing technology, the measurement of gestures is becoming more and more accurate and can be utilized by interactive music systems.

In general, musicians' gestures can be interpreted as either discrete commands or as continuous control over a set of parameters. For instance, a temporal gesture, which consists of a cohesive sequence of movements, could represent a command to start a sound, enter a new state, or make a selection among several discrete choices. Alternatively, continuous control gestures may communicate sound parameters such as gain, pitch, velocity, and panning. Continuous parameter sensing is relatively easy since most physiological parameters captured by sensors are represented as a continuous stream. Converting this stream to a continuous parameter is often a simple matter of applying a mapping function to each sensor value to compute a control value. On the other hand, it can be very difficult to spot and recognize temporal gesture patterns within a continuous signal stream. Common solutions for command interfaces include special sensors such as buttons on a keyboard or multiple spatial positions as command

© Springer International Publishing Switzerland 2014
M. Aramaki et al. (Eds.): CMMR 2013, LNCS 8905, pp. 72–85, 2014.
DOI: 10.1007/978-3-319-12976-1_5

triggers. However, locating multiple physical keys or learning to reproduce absolute positions in live performance can be risky if activating command triggers is critical to the success of the performance. Some "natural" gestures, such as nodding the head or pointing, offer an alternative way to communicate commands.

Achieving a high recognition rate for continuous gestures is more challenging than recognizing static poses or positions because a sequence of sensor values must be considered. In this paper, we explore the recognition of discrete command gestures within a stream of continuous sensor data. The approach is based on the well-known dynamic time warping (DTW) sequence matching algorithm. While DTW provides a powerful mechanism for comparing two temporal sequences, it does not tell us what features will work best, how to pre-process the data to avoid outliers, how to spot a finite gesture in an infinite stream of input, or how to set thresholds to optimize recognition and classification performance. The goal of our study is to design and evaluate a gesture spotting and recognition strategy especially for music performance. We select features by searching over feature combinations, obtain optimal thresholds for each gesture pattern, and automatically generate a gesture recognizer.

2   Related Work

Recent research focuses on machine learning approaches for gesture-to-sound mapping in interactive music performance [4, 8–10]. Fiebrink's Wekinator [8] explores how end users can incorporate machine learning into real-time interactive systems, but the API/ Toolbox she provides uses a feature vector as input and creates a class as output. Users have to select features and models manually. Francoise built two models based on Hierarchical Hidden Markov Models to segment complex music gestures [9] in real time. He applied two strategies, a forward algorithm and Fixed-Lag smoothing, to recognize violin-bowing techniques during a real performance. His research mainly focused on how different strategies affect segmentation accuracy and recognition latency but did not clearly point toward a good combination over parameters that can increase detection accuracy.

In the field of gesture recognition, major approaches for analyzing spatial and temporal gesture patterns include Dynamic Time Warping [1, 3, 5, 11, 17], Neural Networks [7, 12, 18], Hidden Markov Models [14, 16] and Conditional Random Fields [6]. Many existing gesture spotting and recognition systems apply a threshold model for discriminating valid gesture patterns from non-gesture patterns [13, 14]. Lee and Kim developed an HMM-based adaptive threshold model approach [14]. They took advantage of the internal segmentation property of the gesture HMMs to build an artificial HMM that acts as the threshold model. The threshold model calculates the likelihood of a threshold of an input pattern and provides a confirmation mechanism for the provisionally matched gesture patterns. However, this method runs off-line and is not a suitable threshold model for real-time musical gesture recognition and identification. It still demonstrates to us that the calculated likelihood can be used as an adaptive threshold for selecting the proper gesture model. Krishnan et al. proposed an adaptive threshold model [13]. In their model, several weakest classifiers, which can satisfy a majority of samples of all the training classes, are used to test whether the input is too general. In our work, since the training process is based on a small limited-sample gesture vocabulary, the Adaboost method may not have enough features to train and get good performance. Additionally, in order to deal with multiple deformations in training gesture data, Miguel A Bautista et al. proposed a probability-based DTW for gestures on RGB-D data [3], in which the pattern model is discerned from several samples of the same gesture pattern. They used different sequences to build a Gaussian-based probabilistic model of the gesture pattern. Although our recognition system is not based on a probabilistic model, it still suggests that for a gesture recognition system, the detection threshold it generates for each gesture should both be able to tolerate deformation in training/testing gesture data (high recall score) and classify different gesture patterns clearly (high precision score). Similar to our work, Gillian et al. applied DTW to musical gesture recognition [11] and achieved over 80 % recognition accuracy spotting command gestures in a continuous data stream. Our work extends this approach with automated feature selection and threshold optimization.

3   System Overview

Our music gesture recognition system uses training data to learn gestures. In our terminology, a *feature* is a sensor reading or a processed sensor reading, a *feature vector*, or simply *vector*, is a set of simultaneous *features*, which typically include x, y, and z joint position coordinates. A gesture *sample* is a sequence of these *vectors*. A *template* is a *sample* that is representative of a particular command gesture. In operation, input is a continuous sequence of feature vectors. Overlapping windows of input are compared to templates using DTW, and output commands are issued when gestures are detected. We describe how input is compared to templates in Sect. 4.

Initially, the musician defines a gesture vocabulary, such as nodding their head, waving their hands, or making a circle motion. After defining a gesture vocabulary, the user records both gesture templates and test samples by using a motion capture sensor such as Microsoft Kinect or an on-body acceleration sensor.

Figure 1 illustrates the general architecture. Here we see the training process on the left (described in Sect. 5), where training samples are compared to templates using DTW using different parameters and features to obtain the best settings. The system in operation is shown on the right where the results of comparing continuous gesture input to templates are used to recognize gestures. Specifically, in the recognition process, the thresholds and feature combinations generated by the training process are applied. When a new feature vector is produced by the capture system, the features are pre-processed according to the feature preprocessing setting. In real-time testing, if the minimum distance between a gesture pattern and a test sequence is less than or equal to the threshold value, the gesture is said to be recognized. The timestamp where the minimum distance occurred will be treated as the end point of this gesture. Accordingly, by applying backtracking, the start point of the gesture can be estimated. Using this information, an output message is generated to report the type of gesture, the start time, and the end time. This message may then trigger some music events according to the detected gesture pattern.

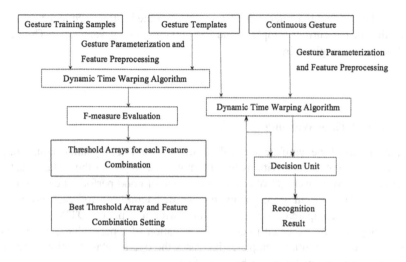

Fig. 1. General architecture of training and recognition processes.

4 Gesture Comparison with Dynamic Time Warping

4.1 Data Preprocessing

Since the data sequences captured by sensors are often loosely controlled, in order to eliminate out-of-range or missing data (e.g. the position of hand is not a number, or NaN), reduce unnecessary or redundant features (e.g. the position of knees is not useful for hand gesture recognition) and smooth each feature dimension, feature preprocessing is an essential step before applying gesture recognition. In our implementation, feature preprocessing is involving the following steps:

Sample Inspection. When the system receives a multidimensional feature vector, it will inspect each feature dimension separately. For each feature dimension, if the ratio of out-of-range or missing data is higher than 10 %, the feature dimension cannot be used in any training or recognition process.

Missing Data Prediction. Feature vectors with high out-of-range or missing data ratio are banned from use for training and recognition, but those feature vectors with low out-of-range or missing data ratio can still be utilized. We estimate missing data as the mean value among the nearest four valid data values.

Data Smoothing. For both the training and recognition process, data smoothing is applied before applying the matching algorithm. Since the data values in each feature dimension have redundancy (we assume that gestures are slow-moving compared to the sensor sample rate, or in signal processing terms, gestures are mainly low in frequency and thus oversampled), we can smooth the data points by the general information of each feature dimension to eliminate possibly inaccuracy measurement and reduce the impact of severe outliers. For real-time feature processing, the data we can utilize are only the past data points. The system implements the common smoothing method known as the exponential filter, which forms a smoothed output sequence as a linear combination of the current sample s_i and the previous output value s'_{i-1}. The derived smooth sequence is given by

$$s'_{i-1} = \alpha s_i + (1 - \alpha)s'_{i-1} \tag{1}$$

4.2 Dynamic Time Warping

Since the lengths of the template and real gesture are variable, Dynamic Time Warping (DTW) is one of the best algorithms for defining and computing the distance between these sequences. Moreover, DTW has the advantage of good performance with limited training data. The system stores many prerecorded templates for each gesture and each template is compared to the input data with a separate DTW computation. Multiple templates are expected to cover the variation of a particular gesture pattern. However, the use of multiple templates increases the overall classification time of the system, and some templates could be redundant.

The original DTW algorithm measures the distance or dissimilarity between two time series T and I based on distance function $dist(i, j)$ that measures the mismatch between any two vectors T_i and I_j, and penalties for inserting and deleting sequence elements. The default distance function is simply based on Euclidean distance, which is

$$dist(i,j) = \left(\sum_{d \, \in \, feature \; dimension} (T_{id} - I_{jd})^2 \right)^{\frac{1}{2}} \tag{2}$$

A cost matrix of size $m \times n$ is filled with values that represent distances between the first i vectors of T and j vectors of I. After computing a full cost matrix, the DTW algorithm can do backtracking from the last cell of the cost matrix, $C\,[m][n]$, to find a least distance path from the end to the beginning. The value of any cell $C(i, j)$ in the cost matrix can be calculated by following the simple rule:

$$C(i,j) = dist(i,j) + \min \begin{cases} C(i-1,j) + insert \; cost \\ C(i-1,j-1) \\ C(i,j-1) + deletion \; cost \end{cases} \tag{3}$$

Unfortunately, in our case we want continuous input I to match template T even if only the end of I is a good match. The standard DTW can be modified to remove penalties for skipping an initial prefix of the input; however, we find it useful to compute spatial coordinates relative to the gesture starting point to achieve position-independent gesture features. Therefore, we use a sliding window method that considers many gesture starting points within the continuous input I.

4.3 Dynamic Time Warping Implementation for Gesture Comparison

In order to use dynamic time warping for measuring the similarity between gesture sequences, at least two valid processed data sequences should be prepared and passed to the DTW method. Those data sequences should use corresponding features. In our implementation, each gesture recorded by Kinect or on-body sensor is saved as a file with a two-dimensional array of numbers. Moreover, DTW should also be informed of the costs of insertion and deletion for initializing the edge costs.

4.4   Dynamic Time Warping with Sliding Window

For each gesture template, the system allocates a queue Q with a capacity of n representing instances of DTW matchers. A new matcher is created every t input samples (the hop size in Fig. 2). Each new matcher replaces the oldest matcher in Q. Each matcher also retains the spatial coordinates of the first input; typically these are subtracted from successive samples to make them position independent before computing a new column of $C(i, j)$.

The system recognizes a gesture when the DTW-based distance to a template falls below the gesture threshold. The timestamp where the minimum distance occurred will be treated as the end point of this gesture. In addition, the start point of the gesture can be estimated by applying backtracking. Using this information, an output message is generated to report the type of gesture, the start time, and the end time. This message may then trigger some music events according to the detected gesture pattern. If more than one gesture type is matched at the same time, we use a KNN- based resolution algorithm to pick only one.

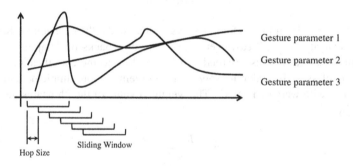

Fig. 2. The system runs a new DTW instance for each template in each window.

Generally speaking, the system applies the following decision method for each sample point until a command is recognized.

Step 1:   Read a new input feature vector

Step 2:   If it is time to begin a new window, create a new DTW instance, which keeps the current input vector as its start point. Destroy the oldest DTW instance in the queue

Step 3:   For each DTW instance, subtract its own starting point from the input vector and do data preprocessing

Step 4:   Compute the best alignment cost between template and preprocessed data vector

Step 5:   If the lowest cost is lower than that of the threshold model, set the gesture as a "candidate." If no threshold is exceeded, then no command is recognized

Step 6:   If only one candidate exists, output it as the recognition result

Step 7:   If the system provides more than one candidates, run the K-Nearest-Neighbor algorithm to find the best result

4.5   Solving Conflicts by K-Nearest-Neighbor

Although one hopes that only one gesture will be recognized at a given moment, it is possible that the best (lowest) alignment scores fall below the predetermined thresholds for two or more different gestures. In those cases, the system should choose one over several "candidate" gestures as the final result. The selection mechanism we implement uses the K-Nearest-Neighbor algorithm. The K-Nearest-Neighbor algorithm is a type of instance-based learning algorithm, which classifies objects based on the K closest training examples in the feature space. Since for each input vector, the system runs q DTW comparisons to align the input vector against q templates, it can get a set of best alignment scores S between each template and the input vector, $S = \{s_1, s_2, s_3, s_4, \ldots, s_q\}$. Considering the impact of the different threshold values, the algorithm normalizes the distance between each template and the real input vector by its threshold.

$$d_i = \frac{s_i}{threshold_i} \tag{4}$$

After ranking d_i from low to high, the system can make the decision by K-Nearest-Neighbor "majority voting." However, one of the drawbacks of "majority voting" is that an instance might be misclassified if it is too close to the classification boundary between two classes. In order to solve this problem, in our implementation, each neighbor votes with weighted values. The weighted value of the jth nearest neighbor is calculated by

$$v_j = \frac{K + 1 - j}{\sum_{j=1}^{K} j} \tag{5}$$

5   Training

5.1   Parameters

We use the users' personal gesture patterns and train the threshold model by trying each reasonable feature combination to find the best one. In our implementation, training on examples is used to select among the following parameters and features:

Input Feature. Sensors capture the motion of the users as a vector of N features consisting of values such as joint angles, spatial coordinates, and acceleration. Rather than search every combination (all 2^N), the system searches only a set of user-predefined feature combinations.

Preprocessing Function and Parameters. The system can also apply preprocessing functions to smooth or transform data. In our implementation we normally use an exponential smoothing method, testing four or five different smoothing values, α.

Insertion and Deletion Costs. For the DTW Algorithm, insertion and deletion costs can have a large effect on performance. To limit the search, insertion and deletion costs are chosen from 4 possible values: 0.0, 0.1, 0.3 and 0.5.

5.2 F-Measure Evaluation

In statistics, the F-measure is a measure of a test's accuracy. The F-measure considers both precision p and recall r of the test to compute its F-measure score f. Moreover, the score f can be interpreted as a weighted average of the precision p and recall r. The best score the F-measure can achieve is 1 and the worst score is 0.

Specifically,

$$p = \frac{correct\ result(true\ positive)}{correct\ result + unexpected\ result(false\ positive)} \tag{6}$$

$$r = \frac{correct\ result(truepositive)}{correct\ result + missing\ result(false\ negitive)} \tag{7}$$

$$f = \frac{2 \times precision \times recall}{precision + recall} \tag{8}$$

To evaluate the performance of the gesture threshold, the F-measure is a reasonable and effective measurement method. For each gesture, the threshold with the highest F-measure score will be considered as the most reliable threshold to be applied.

5.3 Threshold Selection

In the training process, for each gesture, we store n templates, and a gesture is considered recognized when one of its n templates matches the input with a distance less than a per-gesture threshold. For each gesture, we search for a single threshold that maximizes the F-measure. (Although one could use a separate threshold for each template, we decided to use only one threshold because the templates should all be similar.)

With multiple templates per gesture and the possibility of gestures matching multiple gestures (resolved with the K-Nearest-Neighbor algorithm), computing exact F-measures for a set of thresholds would involve a complete simulation of gesture recognition for each training sample. To save computation time and allow for greater exploration of parameters, we use a simplified version of gesture recognition to determine thresholds and to estimate the F-measure *independently for each gesture*. For positive samples of a gesture, we consider the sample to be recognized if the distance to *every* template is below threshold. For negative samples of a gesture, we consider the sample to be (wrongly) recognized if the distance to *any* template is below threshold. This tends to favor higher thresholds for positive samples, avoiding overfitting where the samples tend to match particular templates.

With these rules for determining true and false positives and negatives, it is sufficient to run the relatively expensive DTW algorithm just once to compute the alignment cost between each template and each training sample. The result is *Distance* $[i, j]$, where i denotes a template, and j denotes a training sample. Since the procedure is the same for each gesture, there are n templates and r training samples, so i ranges from $0 \ldots n - 1$ and j ranges from $0 \ldots r - 1$ in *Distance*$[i, j]$.

Next, we determine the minimum threshold for which sample j will be classified as positive. If sample j is labeled with the gesture, then the threshold is the maximum distance to any template:

$$T_j = \max_i(Distance[i, j]) \tag{9}$$

On the other hand, if sample j is labeled with another gesture, the threshold is considered to be the minimum to any template:

$$T_j = \min_i(Distance[i, j]) \tag{10}$$

Given T_j, we can quickly compute the F-measure for a given threshold T because if $T_j < T$, then sample j is classified as positive and otherwise negative. We consider each T_j as a possible threshold and pick the one that maximizes the F-measure. The algorithm first computes array T as shown in Fig. 3. Next, we search T for the threshold that maximizes the F-measure as shown in Fig. 4.

Alternatively, F-measure search also can be optimized by going through the thresholds of $T[j]$ in order, allowing for incremental updates to counts of true positives, false positives, and false negatives.

This algorithm, including the computation of *Distance*$[i, j]$, is repeated for each gesture class. We take the sum of the (best) F-measures from each gesture class to form an overall measure of the performance of the gesture recognizer.

Our training system performs a grid search on every reasonable combination of Input Feature, Preprocessing Function and Parameters, Insertion and Deletion Costs, and Thresholds to obtain the best result as evaluated by summing the F-measures obtained for all gestures. Moreover, users can customize and weight the feature combinations and adjust F-measure criteria to meet their needs. The F_2-measure, for example, can be used to favor recall over precision, leading to fewer false negatives.

```
Given: D[i,j] = distance from template i to sample j,
       L[j] = training sample labels, size r
       g = the label of the current gesture
initialize T[], an array of size r of thresholds
for each training sample j:
    if L[j] = g:
        T[j] = max(D[*,j])
    else
        T[j] = min(D[*,j])
```

Fig. 3. Calculation of Threshold array *T*.

```
best_f = 0
best_t = 0
for each element t    at index j   in T:
    for each element u    at index k in T  :
        if   u < threshold :
            if  L[k]  = g:
                true_pos + = 1
            else :
                false_pos += 1
        else  if L[k] = g:
            false_neg += 1
    precision =
        true_pos / (true_pos + false_neg)
    recall =
        true pos / (true_pos + false_neg)
    f  = (2 X precision   X recall ) / ( precision   +
recall )
    if f > best_f:
        best_f = f
        best_t = t
Result: best_t is the threshold for gesture g
```

Fig. 4. Calculation of the best threshold, the one that maximizes the F-measure, for a given gesture *g*.

6   Experiments and Results

To evaluate continuous gesture recognition, a human tester is asked to perform eight simple hand gestures (see Fig. 5) in front of a Microsoft Kinect sensor. Each of these "command" gestures is repeated five times to create templates. The tester is also asked to perform ten training gestures for each pattern. In order to reject the false detection of user's spontaneous motions, the system also requires the user perform several spontaneous motion samples, such as waving arms and shaking the body. Those non-gesture training samples are labeled with 0. Each sample in the template set and training set has the same approximate duration, which is about 2 s or 60 samples. The system estimates the best feature combination and threshold values based on the DTW comparisons between the template and training sets.

To evaluate the system, a tester performed 25 samples lasting 10–20 s. Each sample contains 1–3 gestures in the vocabulary and those gestures are hand labeled after recording. Figure 6 shows the two-dimensional hand trajectory of one of the test samples, which contains gesture 8 and gesture 1 in the vocabulary. The evaluation is

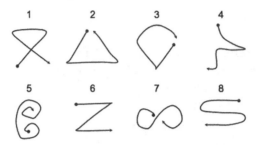

Fig. 5. Gesture vocabulary for testing. The start point of each gesture is labeled as a dot and the end of the gesture is labeled as an arrow.

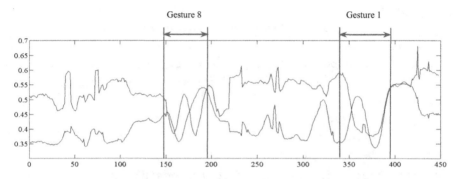

Fig. 6. Two-dimensional trajectory of one test sample, which contains gesture 8 and gesture 1.

based on recognition accuracy. A gesture is correctly recognized if the system finds the correct gesture within 6 samples (0.2 s) of the end point of the "true" label. Figure 7 shows how the alignment scores for Gestures 1 and 8 fall below the respective recognition thresholds (dotted lines) when the gestures are made.

Table 1. Continuous gesture recognition accuracy.

Feature vector	Relative position	Insertion cost	Deletion cost	F-score value	Recognition accuracy (%)
x-,y-axis left hand	False	0.0	0.0	6.37	72
x-,y-axis left hand	False	0.1	0.3	6.26	70
x-,y-axis left hand	False	0.0	0.0	6.44	75
x-,y-axis left hand	False	0.1	0.3	7.63	82
x-,y-axis elbow & left hand	False	0.1	0.3	6.10	67
x-,y-axis elbow & left hand	False	0.1	0.4	7.21	80
x-,y-axis elbow & left hand	True	0.1	0.4	6.67	75
x-,y-axis left hand	True	0.0	0.1	7.83	89

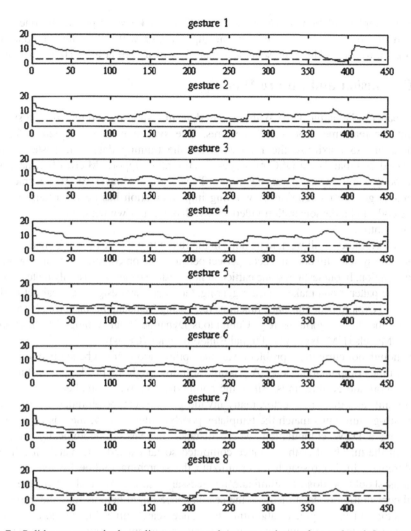

Fig. 7. Solid curves are the best alignment score between each template and each input vector. The dotted lines illustrate the thresholds of each gesture template.

When testing 55 gestures in 25 continuous sequences, we find there is a big difference in the recognition accuracy with different feature combination (See Table 1). Generally, the feature combination with the higher F-measure score achieves higher recognition accuracy. The highest recognition accuracy is 89 %, where the F-measure score is 7.83/8.0. (8 F-measures are summed, so the maximum score is 8.)

Execution time depends on several variables. Assume the system has m gestures and n templates of length of l, we create a DTW comparison every t vectors, and the computation for one DTW matrix cell is c. The total computation is $m \times n \times \frac{l}{t} \times c$.

In our implementation, $m = 8$, $n = 5$, $l = 60$ (2 s), $t = 4$, $c = 2.6$ μs, and for one DTW cell and the total cost for comparing one input vector with all gesture templates is 1.56 ms on average. This represents less than 5 % of a core at a 30 Hz input rate.

7 Conclusion and Future Work

In this paper, a Dynamic Time Warping based gesture spotting and recognition system is built for real-time "command" gestures. The system evaluates different feature combinations to maximize the F-measure for the training data. The system sends recognized commands via OSC messages. It currently supports Microsoft Kinect and an on-body wireless sensor as the input. The system achieves 89 % accuracy on continuous gesture recognition. A working implementation has been written in Java. Source code and a demonstration video are available: http://www.cs.cmu.edu/~music/mat/thesis.html.

However, there is still work to be done in the future to improve the performance of the system. The system still does not get a perfect performance on continuous gesture spotting and recognition. In our testing, some particular non-gesture patterns can easily match one of the gesture patterns and make a false triggering. Good gesture design is critical but further work could explore better distance functions (e.g. using Mahalanobis distance [2, 15]) and sequence matching algorithms (e.g. Continuous Dynamic Programming (CDP), Hidden Markov Models (HMMs) or Conditional Random Fields (CRFs)).

Although not currently a problem, various optimizations could be applied to reduce the real-time computational load. A possible solution might be breaking a gesture into several short sub-gesture units. Since the comparison is over a smaller space of sub-gesture units and the input vector, many invalid gestures can be eliminated early if the prefix sub-gesture units match the templates poorly. Alternatively, there is no point to continuing a DTW computation, where distance increases monotonically with the length of the match, after the distance computed so far exceeds the match threshold.

Moreover, further research on optimizing the searching routine for feature combinations should be done to eliminate unnecessary search. An analysis on the individual contribution of each factor in the search space might help us rank the impact of each factor and use a greedy algorithm to reduce search time. Furthermore, we will conduct user studies to evaluate our recognition system in practical contexts and develop systems with more gesture types providing a larger command set.

References

1. Akl, A., Valaee, S.: Accelerometer-based gesture recognition via dynamic-time warping, affinity propagation, and compressive sensing. In: ICASSP, pp. 2270–2273, (2010)
2. Alon, J., Athitsos, V., Yuan, Q., Sclaroff, S.: A unified framework for gesture recognition and spatiotemporal gesture segmentation. IEEE Trans. Pattern Anal. Mach. Intell. **31**, 1685–1699 (2008)
3. Bautista, M.A., Hernández, A., Ponce, V., Perez-Sala, X., Baró, X., Pujol, O., Angulo, C., Escalera, S.: Probability-based dynamic time warping for gesture recognition on RGB-D

data. In: Jiang, X., Bellon, O.R.P., Goldgof, D., Oishi, T. (eds.) WDIA 2012. LNCS, vol. 7854, pp. 126–135. Springer, Heidelberg (2013)

4. Bevilacqua, F., Schnell, N.: Wireless sensor interface and gesture-follower for music pedagogy. In: Proceedings of the 7th International Conference on New Interfaces for Musical Expression, pp. 124–129, (2007)

5. Corradini, A.: Dynamic time warping for off-line recognition of a small gesture vocabulary. In: Proceedings of the IEEE ICCV Workshop on Recognition, Analysis, and Tracking of Faces and Gestures in Real-Time Systems (RATFG-RTS'01). IEEE Computer Society. Washington, DC, USA (2001)

6. Elmezain, M., Al-Hamadi, A., Michaelis, B.: Robust methods for hand gesture spotting and recognition using hidden markov models and conditional random fields. In: IEEE International Symposium on Signal Processing and Information Technology (ISSPIT) (2010)

7. Fels, S., Hinton, G.: Glove-talk: a neural network interface between a data-glove and a speech synthesizer. IEEE Trans. Neural Netw. 4(1), 2–8 (1993)

8. Fiebrink, R.: Real-time human interaction with supervised learning algorithms for music composition and performance. Ph.D. dissertation, Faculty of Princeton University (2011)

9. Francoise, J.: Real time segmentation and recognition of gestures using hierarchical markov models. Master's thesis, Université Pierre et Marie Curie, Ircam (2011)

10. Gillian, N., Knapp, R.: A machine learning tool-box for musician computer interaction. In: Proceedings of the 2011 Conference on New Interfaces for Musical Expression (2011)

11. Gillian N., Knapp R.B., O'Modhrain, S.: Recognition of multivariate temporal musical gestures using N-dimensional dynamic time warping. In: Proceedings of the 11th International Conference on New Interfaces for Musical Expression, pp. 337–342 (2011)

12. Kjeldsen, R., Kender, J.: Visual hand gesture recognition for window system control. In: Proceedings of Int'l Workshop Automatic Face- and Gesture-Recognition, pp. 184–188, Zurich, Switzerland (1995)

13. Krishnan, N.C., Lade, P., Panchanathan, S.: Activity gesture spotting using a threshold model based on adaptive boosting. In: IEEE International Conference on Multimedia and Expo (ICME), vol. 1, pp. 155–160 (2010)

14. Lee, H., Kim, J.: An HMM-based threshold model approach for gesture recognition. IEEE Trans. Pattern Anal. Mach. Intel. 21(10), 961–973 (1999)

15. Liu, J., Wang, Z., Zhong, L., Wickramasuriya, J., Vasudevan, V.: uwave: Accelerometer-based personalized gesture recognition and its applications. In: IEEE International Conference on Pervasive Computing and Communications, pp. 1–9 (2009)

16. Murph, K.P., Paskin, M.A.: Linear Time Inference in Hierarchical HMMs. In: Dietterich, T., Becker, S., Gharahmani, Z. (eds.) Advances in Neural Information Processing Systems, vol. 2. MIT Press, Cambridge (2001)

17. Takahashi, K., Seki, S., Oka, R.: spotting recognition of human gestures from motion images (in Japanese). Technical report IE92 134. Institute of Electronics, Information and Communication Engineers, Japan, pp. 9–16 (1992)

18. Xu, D.: A neural approach for hand gesture recognition in virtual reality driving training system of SPG. In: International Conference on Pattern Recognition, vol. 3, pp. 519–522 (2006)

Music and Emotions: Representation, Recognition, and Audience/Performers Studies

Making Explicit the Formalism Underlying Evaluation in Music Information Retrieval Research: A Look at the MIREX Automatic Mood Classification Task

Bob L. Sturm[✉]

Audio Analysis Lab, AD:MT, Aalborg University Copenhagen,
A.C. Meyers Vænge 15, 2450 Copenhagen SV, Denmark
bst@create.aau.dk

Abstract. We make explicit the formalism underlying evaluation in music information retrieval research. We define a "system," what it means to "analyze" one, and make clear the aims, parts, design, execution, interpretation, assumptions and limitations of its "evaluation." We apply this formalism to discuss the MIREX automatic mood classification task.

Keywords: Evaluation · Systems analysis · Music information retrieval

1 Introduction

While a considerable amount of work contributes to making standard, systematic and rigorous the evaluation of systems for music information retrieval (MIR), e.g., [13,15,16,18,25,33,42], and some work contributes to the critical discussion of evaluation in MIR, e.g., [2,11,12,20,35,36,39,41,41–46,49,51–53], very little has been done to *formalize* evaluation in MIR research, i.e., *disambiguate evaluation to make explicit its aims, parts, design, implementation, analysis, interpretation, and all attendant assumptions and limitations.* An explicit formalization of evaluation helps one identify, motivate, and sufficiently define questions to be scientific, helps one design, implement and analyze experiments relevant to address these scientific questions, and helps one reach meaningful and valid conclusions for those scientific questions with fully specified limitations. Since the standard, systematic and rigorous evaluation practices currently and historically used in MIR research have by and large been adopted from disciplines like machine learning and information retrieval [16,39,42,46,50,53], the formalism of evaluation in MIR research remains for the most part implicit. These evaluation

This work was supported in part by Independent Postdoc Grant 11-105218 from Det Frie Forskningsråd. Part of this work was undertaken during a visit to the Centre for Digital Music at Queen Mary University of London, supported by EPSRC grant EP/G007144/1 (Plumbley).

© Springer International Publishing Switzerland 2014
M. Aramaki et al. (Eds.): CMMR 2013, LNCS 8905, pp. 89–104, 2014.
DOI: 10.1007/978-3-319-12976-1_6

approaches are thus assumed to be capable of producing valid conclusions for what appear to be scientific questions. In this work, we question the veracity of this assumption by making explicit the formalism underlying evaluation in MIR research. Through the lens it provides, we look at a specific task of the MIR Evaluation eXchange (MIREX) [13,15,18,33], and determine the kinds of conclusions one can draw from its results.

To be sure, the massive and concerted efforts of MIREX has enabled and promoted standard, systematic and rigorous approaches to evaluating MIR systems that were by and large missing before. Inspired by the Text Retrieval Conference (TREC) [16], Downie argued in 2003 [17] for the need to standardize evaluation practices in MIR, and thus coordinated three workshops on the topic [16], and developed MIREX [33]. Like TREC, MIREX aims to standardize *benchmarks* in MIR: realistic information needs and problem formulations (e.g., appropriately describing the mood of recorded music), test data collections (e.g., MIREX music mood dataset [25]), and performance measurement (e.g., accuracy of labels to "ground truth"). Every year since 2005, MIREX has systematically performed rigorous tests of new MIR systems proposed for such tasks as beat tracking, chord and onset detection, melody extraction, and genre and emotion recognition. That MIREX has had an impact is indisputable: the trials, techniques, data, and/or software of MIREX been cited in over 500 journal articles, conference papers, master's theses and PhD dissertations [13]; and much MIR research has followed suit in systematically and rigorously performing similar approaches to evaluation. The formalism of evaluation in MIR research, however, still remains implicit; and as long as it remains so, one cannot know if the standard, systematic and rigorous evaluation approaches that MIREX and MIR research employ can produce valid conclusions about MIR systems, or machine music listening in general.

There have been some challenges to the reliability or usefulness of particular approaches to evaluation in MIR research. Pampalk et al. [35] uncovered in 2005 a source of bias in the evaluation of music similarity algorithms: they found that laboratory evaluations of such algorithms produced significantly better outcomes when train and test datasets contain observations from the same artist or album, than when such tracks are isolated to only one of the datasets. This led to the recommendation of using an "artist filter" in evaluation to avoid such bias, and therefore to better estimate real-world performance. Flexer [20] has addressed the lack of but necessity for formal statistical testing in MIR evaluations in order for results to say anything meaningful; and Urbano et al. [51] question the meaningfulness of "statistical significance" with regards to the actual use of an MIR system. McKay and Fujinaga [32] argued in 2006 that the problem and evaluation of solutions for music genre recognition must be rethought, from building the datasets used for training and testing, to defining use cases. Whether the problem of music genre recognition is well-posed or not has been debated [3,5,11,32,34,46,55], but nearly 500 publications attest — implicitly or explicitly — to the importance of the problem [42]. Craft et al. [11,12] have pinpointed problems with music datasets having naturally vague labels, and propose a slightly different approach to evaluation taking ambiguity into account. That most datasets used in MIR evaluation are very small has motivated creating and using datasets of hundreds of thousands of songs in evaluation [9,40].

Very recently, four of eight articles in a special issue entitled, "MIRrors: The past of Music Information Research reflects on its future" (Journal of Intelligent Information Systems, vol. 41, no. 3, edited by P. Herrera-Boyer and F. Gouyon), critically reflect on aspects of current evaluation practices in MIR research [2,39, 44,53]. Aucouturier and Bigand [2] point out that the extent to which research and evaluation in MIR research is goal-oriented situate it outside the practice of science. Schedl et al. [39] highlight the near absence of the consideration of users in typical evaluations of MIR system. Urbano et al. [53] observe that current MIR evaluation practices play little role in the development of MIR systems: problems and success criteria are often artificial with no real use contexts; evaluation procedures are often weak, nonuniform, irreproducible and incomparable; and little to no effort is made to learn why and/or why not a system worked, and how to then improve it. In our article [44], we argue how the approach most used to evaluate music genre recognition systems is not useful for judging whether any system is itself addressing any musical problem, let alone which system is better than another.

In addition to these works, three curious results have appeared. First, Marques et al. [30,31] show that a very common approach to feature extraction in music genre recognition produces systems that have high accuracies, but the information carried by these features does not appear to be discriminative or representative of the very characteristic the systems are supposedly comparing or identifying. How can a classification system using features that do not encapsulate class information still be able to identify and discriminate between the classes of observations? Second, even though they are evaluated to have high accuracies, several state of the art MIR systems (genre recognition, emotion recognition, and autotagging) appear not to be considering the music they are supposedly describing [23,29,43–45,47,48]. If a classification system appears to not be considering the very content that is assumed to delimit and distinguish the classes of observations, then what has the system actually learned? Lastly, researchers have found that the performances of MIR systems, e.g., for artist or genre identification from audio signals [19], reach a limit below human performance — a "glass ceiling" [1,4,6,35] — that seems nearly impossible to surpass. This has been attributed to the limited amount of music information that can be extracted from audio samples [10,55], and used to motivate the development of new systems [26,27,41]. However, considering the two results above, might the "glass ceiling" merely be the signature of MIR systems reproducing the "ground truth" of standard datasets by using irrelevant factors confounded to some imperfect degree with the "ground truth" of a dataset, and evaluation approaches that are insensitive to such "cheating" [46,47]?

To resolve these questions, and advance the design, development, and evaluation of music machine listening systems, there is a need to make explicit the formalism underpinning the entire pursuit: What is the problem? What is a system?

What does it mean to evaluate a system? What is the aim of an evaluation? What are its parts? What is its design? How is it implemented? How can the results be interpreted and presented? What assumptions are made? What are the limitations of the conclusions drawn? Our work here attempts to illuminate the formalism of evaluation in MIR research. We first review the concept of a system, and what it means to analyze and evaluate one. We then review the formal design and analysis of experiments, and discuss relevance and scientific validity. Finally, we use this formalism to look at the evaluation performed in the MIREX automatic mood classification task (MIREX-AMC).

2   Formalization of System Evaluation

In this section, we define a system, and describe its analysis and evaluation. We then review formalized experimental design and analysis. We finally discuss relevance and scientific validity.

2.1   Systems and System Analysis

A *system* is a connected set of interacting and interdependent components that together address a use case [37]. Of the many systems in which MIR research is interested, there are four essential kinds of components: *operator(s)* (agent(s) that employ the system); *instructions* (specifications for the operator(s), like an application programming interface); *algorithms* (each a set of describable and ordered operations to transduce an input into an output); and *environment* (connections between components, external databases, the space within which the system operates, its boundaries). A system can fail to address a use case from any combination of errors on the parts of its components.

It is important to note here that our definition of a system is not a specification of several algorithms: *a system is a material thing of which one can make measurements, e.g., classification accuracy, latency, and confusions.* For instance, "the use of feature X with model Y for predicting Z" specify aspects of components of a system, but it is not a material system ready to run by some operator according to some instructions. One cannot measure, for instance, the mean squared error of "the use of feature X with model Y for predicting Z." If one hopes to show that the specification "the use of feature X with model Y for predicting Z" results in systems that produce "better" outcomes than systems resulting from the specification "the use of feature W with model Y for predicting Z", then this involves building many systems with both specifications, evaluating these systems in a way that adequately covers the problem domain and controls for all independent variables, a specification of "better," and finally the induction from evaluations of all those systems to say something about features "X" and "W".

To make the above more concrete, consider the following system: the Alpha-Numeric System for Classification of Recordings (ANSCR) [38] implemented in the music library at an imaginary university. A use case of this system is the cataloging of collected music recordings in the university music library. Its operators are the library staff, and its instructions specify the input (a piece of recorded material) and output (a labeled and physically placed piece of recorded material, an entry in the catalogue, and possibly a justification of the output — why it has been placed where it has been placed). One of its algorithms specifies how to categorize recorded music with respect to the task of organizing music content. Another of its algorithms specifies how to create and apply a label to the material. Yet another algorithm specifies how to add a new entry to the library catalogue to facilitate retrieval, avoid duplication, and so on. The environment of the system includes the physical library, its contents, the catalogue, the interactions between library staff and other components, and so on. A different system exists with the use case of facilitating for the students and staff of the university access to its collected and catalogued music recordings. A variety of aspects of these real systems can be measured. If ANSCR is replaced with a different classification method, if there is a change in library staff or equipment, if the instructions are changed, then new systems result.

An *analysis* of a system addresses questions and hypotheses related to its past, present and future, and its use cases. About its past, one can study the system history: why and how it came to be, the decisions made, past applications, its use case, its successes and failures, etc. About its present, one can study its implementation and applications, evaluate its success with respect to a use case, compare it to other systems, etc. About its future, one can predict its success, study ways to create improved systems with respect to a use case, perform a cost-benefit analysis, etc. These may involve breaking the system into its components, evaluating the components, and so on.

An essential part of a system analysis is an *evaluation*: a "fact-finding campaign" intended to address a number of relevant questions and/or hypotheses related to a use case of a system. In the case of the implementation of ANSCR at this university music library, (which has as its use case the cataloging of collected music recordings), an evaluation of it can attempt to answer polar questions, such as: "Can the system catalogue music recordings?" or, "Can the system catalogue minidisc music recordings?" or, "Can the system catalogue music recordings with no Internet connection?" An evaluation can attempt to answer evaluative questions, such as: "How well does the system catalogue music recordings?" or, "How does the system catalogue recordings having many artists?" or, "How many library staff members does the system require?" or, "What is the minimum amount of training that an operator of the system requires?" or, "How many music recordings can the system catalogue?" An evaluation can attempt to answer predictive questions, such as: "How can the system fail?" or, "If Dr. X donates his record collection, how well can the system handle these new materials?" or, "If an entirely new kind of music appears, how can the system handle the new recordings?" or, "If the database fails, what in the system can still work?" An evaluation can attempt to answer constructive questions, such as: "If the database fails, how can the system be adapted to minimize the risk of failure?" or, "How can the system instructions be changed to reduce training time?" An evaluation can attempt to answer comparative questions, such as: "How does a system using ANSCR2 perform differently from the one using ANSCR?" or, "Does ANSCR2 reduce operator error compared to ANSCR?" Finally, an evaluation can attempt to answer a *hypothesis* — a testable explanation of an observation — such as, "The particular results were (in)correct because the staff members bypassed ANSCR" or, "The system failed because of its instructions."

2.2 Experimental Design and Analysis

Evaluating a system is to scientifically address questions and hypotheses with respect to a use case by the design, implementation and analysis of relevant and valid experiments. An *experiment* consists of assigning and applying treatments to units, and measuring responses to determine the real effects of those treatments.[1] A *treatment* is the thing being evaluated. *Units* are the materials of the experiment. An *experimental unit* is a group of materials to which a treatment is applied, and an *observational unit* (or *plot*) is a group of materials from which one measures a response. An *experimental design* specifies how treatments are assigned to plots. A *response* is the "real" effect of a treatment, and its determination is the primary goal of an experiment. A *measurement* is a quantitative description of that response, relevant to the question or hypothesis being tested. The *analysis* of measurements involves the application of statistics to facilitate valid conclusions, implemented carefully to control all sources of variation and bias, in view of the hypothesis. An experiment is *valid* for a question or hypothesis when it can logically answer that question or hypothesis (whether or not the result is really "true").

Formally, the set of all N plots in an experiment is notated Ω, and the set of all t treatments is notated $\mathcal{T}$. The experimental design, $T : \Omega \to \mathcal{T}$, is a function that maps one plot to one treatment. For plot $\omega \in \Omega$, a measurement made of its response to a treatment is denoted y_ω. Denote as $\tau_{T(\omega)}$ the response of the treatment applied to ω. Thus, the measurement of plot ω treated with $T(\omega)$ thus produces y_ω, which is related in some way to the response $\tau_{T(\omega)}$. From the measurements then, one wishes to estimate the responses contributed by the treatments, and thereby quantify and compare the treatments.

To estimate responses, one must *model* measurements. A typical model is linear with measurements as realizations of random variables. For a plot ω, let its measurement be modeled by the random variable Y_ω arising from the non-random response of the treatment $\tau_{T(\omega)}$, and a random variable Z_ω encompassing measurement error, i.e., effects contributed by the plot independent of the treatment, and other unrelated factors. The measurement y_ω, a realization of Y_ω, thus includes things unrelated to the treatment, z_ω, a realization of Z_ω. With the *linear* model, one decomposes the measurement as $y_\omega = \tau_{T(\omega)} + z_\omega$, and models it by $Y_\omega = \tau_{T(\omega)} + Z_\omega$.

---

[1] We use the terminology and notation of Bailey [7].

Given t treatments and N measurements, an experiment is modeled by

$$\mathbf{Y} = \boldsymbol{\tau} + \mathbf{Z} = [\mathbf{u}_1 \, \mathbf{u}_2 \, \cdots \, \mathbf{u}_t]_{N \times t} \begin{bmatrix} \tau_1 \\ \tau_2 \\ \vdots \\ \tau_t \end{bmatrix} + \mathbf{Z} = \mathbf{X}\boldsymbol{\beta} + \mathbf{Z} \qquad (1)$$

where $\mathbf{Y}$ is a vector of N measurements, $\mathbf{Z}$ is a length-N random vector, and $\boldsymbol{\tau}$ is a vector of the N responses to the t treatments $\mathcal{T}$. The matrix $\mathbf{X} = [\mathbf{u}_1 \, \mathbf{u}_2 \, \cdots \, \mathbf{u}_t]$ is the *plan*, or experimental design: column i specifies which plots are treated with treatment i. Finally, the vector $\boldsymbol{\beta}$ contains the responses of the t treatments.

If the true means of $\mathbf{Y}$ and $\mathbf{Z}$ are known, the responses can be found exactly by solving $\mathbf{X}\boldsymbol{\beta} = E[\mathbf{Y}] - E[\mathbf{Z}]$. This knowledge is typically not possessed (an experiment would not be necessary then), and so one must build models of $\mathbf{Y}$ and $\mathbf{Z}$. From these, the responses can be estimated, notated $\hat{\boldsymbol{\beta}}$, *and* the relationship between them can be found, e.g., the bias and variance of the estimator, a bound on $|\boldsymbol{\beta} - \hat{\boldsymbol{\beta}}|^2$, positive correlation, and so on. Only then can one test hypotheses and answer questions subject to the strict assumptions of the selected models.

The *simple textbook model* [7] makes the assumption $\mathbf{Z} \sim \mathcal{N}(\mathbf{0}, \mathbf{I}_N \sigma^2)$, i.e., that $\mathbf{Z}$ is multivariate Gaussian with mean $E[\mathbf{Z}] = \mathbf{0}_N$ (a length-N vector of zeros), and $Cov[\mathbf{Z}] = \mathbf{I}_N \sigma^2$ for $\sigma^2 > 0$, where $\mathbf{I}_N$ is an identity matrix of size N. The choice of this model makes the assumption that the measurements of the responses are affected only by independent and identically distributed zero-mean white noise of power σ^2. In this case, $\mathbf{X}\boldsymbol{\beta} = E[\mathbf{Y}]$, and one knows the measurements will vary due to the noise as $Cov[\mathbf{Y}] = \mathbf{I}_N \sigma^2$. As an example, consider we measure the test scores of all students in a class. The simple textbook model assumes the test score for an individual student only comes from his or her knowledge of the material, and an error independent of the test, e.g., that the student skipped lunch. Considering the test scores of all students together under this model, we hope to estimate their knowledge of the material.

The simple textbook model may not fit the measurements when Ω is very heterogeneous, and/or when its units are selected randomly from a population. In such cases, "group effects" can bias the measurements, which then make estimates of $\boldsymbol{\beta}$ using the simple textbook model consistently poor. The *fixed-effects model* [7] decomposes $\mathbf{Z} = \boldsymbol{\alpha} + \mathbf{W}$ where the vector $\boldsymbol{\alpha}$ describes the contribution of each plot to each measurement invariant of the treatment, and $\mathbf{W}$ is a random vector, where $E[\mathbf{W}] = \mathbf{0}_N$ and $Cov[\mathbf{W}] = \mathbf{I}_N \sigma^2$. In this case, $\mathbf{X}\boldsymbol{\beta} = E[\mathbf{Y}] + \boldsymbol{\alpha}$, and $Cov[\mathbf{Y}] = \mathbf{I}_N \sigma^2$. As an example, consider we measure the test scores of the students in a class. We can decompose the test score for an individual student into a contribution of his knowledge of the material, a contribution of his skill in taking tests, and an error independent of the test, e.g., that the student skipped lunch. Considering the test scores of all students together under this model, we hope to estimate their knowledge of the material independent of their test taking abilities.

The *random-effects model* [7] decomposes $\mathbf{Z} = \mathbf{U} + \mathbf{W}$, where both $\mathbf{U}$ and $\mathbf{W}$ are random vectors. As in the fixed-effects model, $\mathbf{U}$ describes the contribution of each plot to each measurement invariant of the treatment, but it takes into account the uncertainty in the random sampling of the experimental units from the population. In this case, one assumes $E[\mathbf{W}] = E[\mathbf{U}] = \mathbf{0}_N$ and $Cov[\mathbf{W}] = \mathbf{I}_N\sigma^2$, and so $\mathbf{X}\beta = E[\mathbf{Y}]$, but $Cov[\mathbf{Y}] = Cov[\mathbf{U}] + Cov[\mathbf{W}] = Cov[\mathbf{U}] + \mathbf{I}_N\sigma^2$. As an example, consider we measure the test scores of a randomly selected subset of the students in a class. The test score for each student can be decomposed into a contribution of his knowledge of the material, the contribution of the his ability to take tests, and an independent error. To get an indication of how well *all* students in the class are doing with regarding to knowing the material, we must account for the fact that we have measured a random sample of the class. Hence, the contribution of the test taking ability of students will now be randomly distributed. There are also *mixed-effects models*, incorporating both random- and fixed-effects [54]. Since there are two sources of variance in these cases, the error of the response estimates can vary to a higher degree.

With a measurement model, and estimates of the responses, hypothesis testing becomes possible [7]. This involves specifying a null hypothesis and comparing its probability, to a pre-specified limit of statistical significance α, given all assumptions of the model. For example, a null hypothesis can be that the responses of all treatments are equivalent, i.e., $\tau_1 = \tau_2 = \ldots = \tau_t$. One then computes the probability p of observing the estimates of the responses given the null hypothesis and model assumptions are true. If $p < \alpha$, then the null hypothesis is rejected, i.e., it is unlikely with respect to α given the measurement model and observations that there are no differences between the responses of the t treatments.

2.3   Relevance and Scientific Validity

Even when estimates of responses have small error in some model, and null hypotheses are rejected, that does not mean an experiment has answered *the right question*. When the aims of the researcher are incompatible with the design, implementation and analysis of an experiment, an "error of the third kind" has occurred [24,28]: "giving the right answer to the wrong question." Furthermore, there is no assurance that, though something may be accurately measurable, it is thus relevant to the question of interest.[2] Experiments must thus be designed after the hypothesis is formulated, and the scientific and statistical questions are "deconstructed" [24].

The relationships between an experiment to what is intended center upon the concept of validity. One kind of validity is that a meaningful or scientific conclusion can come from the experiment. If the variances in the estimates of responses are too large for any meaningful conclusion about treatments, then the experiment has no *conclusion validity*, or is "scientifically vacuous" [14]. Another kind of validity is that the estimated responses come entirely from the treatments. When they come in part from unrelated but confounded factors not taken into account

---

[2] R. Hamming, "You get what you measure", lecture at Naval Post- graduate School, June 1995. http://www.youtube.com/watch?v=LNhcaVi3zPA.

in the measurement model, then a causal inference cannot be made between the treatments and the responses in an experiment, and it has no *internal validity*. Such problems arise from, e.g., a biased selection of units, the experimental design (mapping of treatments to units), the choice of measurements, who makes the measurements and how, and so on. A third kind of validity is the generalization of experimental results to the population, of which the experimental units are a subset. If the units are not a random sample of the population, or if an experiment has no conclusion and internal validity, then the experiment has no *external validity*. A good discussion of validity in relation to evaluation in MIR research is given by Urbano et al. [53].

3   The MIREX Automatic Mood Classification Task

The automatic mood classification task of MIREX (MIREX-AMC) has been organized the same way since 2007 [25,33], and aims each year to evaluate submitted systems in classifying audio recordings of music with single mood labels selected from five. The "best performance" in this task over the years has been argued to show progress on the problem of music mood recognition is slowing [26]. We now discuss MIREX-AMC in terms of the explicit formalism above, and whether an argument of "slowing progress" can be made from it.

3.1   Systems and System Analysis

A participant of MIREX-AMC has submitted implementations of two algorithms: a feature extraction algorithm, and a classification algorithm. The inputs and outputs of these algorithms are specified by the instructions of MIREX-AMC.[3] A MIREX-AMC organizer — i.e., the operator — then integrates these algorithms with the environment: a specific computer and its software, the private dataset used in the task, etc. Since MIREX-AMC evaluates each submission using 3-fold stratified cross-validation of the private dataset, one submission thus produces three systems, each one built with different training data.

MIREX-AMC evaluates each system by comparing its output labels to the "ground truth" labels in a test dataset. The measurements made include several figures of merit: mean accuracies per class (across all three systems), mean accuracies per fold (for each system), overall mean accuracy (across all systems and classes), and confusions. Since it only tests and compares systems in their reproduction of "ground truth" labels of a test dataset, no matter *how* that production happens, and does not address use cases of the systems it analyzes, the system analysis of MIREX-AMC is necessarily shallow. Its analysis is not concerned with, e.g., how a system makes its decisions, whether it is doing so in an "acceptable manner" with respect to some use case, whether any system is better than another with respect to some use case, how improved systems can be developed with respect to some use case, and so on.

---

[3] http://www.music-ir.org/mirex/wiki/2013:Audio_Classification_(Train/Test)_Tasks.

3.2   Experimental Design and Analysis

MIREX-AMC evaluates a submission by an operator applying the three resulting systems (treatments) to three folds (experimental units) of the test dataset. The experimental design of MIREX-AMC maps one system to the one fold not included in its environment. If a system was mapped to a different fold, then it would be tested using data on which it was trained. The operator measures for each of the five labels in a fold the proportion of matching labels produced by a system. Denote the five class labels by a, b, c, d, e. Hence, an observational unit is the set of excerpts in a fold from the same class, i.e., all excerpts with label a. Denote the measurements of system i applied to fold i, $\widehat{\mathbf{Y}}_i = [\hat{y}_{i,a}, \hat{y}_{i,b}, \dots, \hat{y}_{i,e}]^T$, where $\hat{y}_{i,a}$ is the number of excerpts in fold i that system i labels a correctly, divided by the number of excerpts in that fold with the "ground truth" label a.

MIREX-AMC reports several figures of merit for a submission: the *sequence of fold-specific mean classification accuracies* (we denote by $\mathbf{1}_n$ a length-n vector of ones divided by n)

$$\widehat{\mathcal{y}} := \left(\mathbf{1}_5^T \widehat{\mathbf{Y}}_1, \mathbf{1}_5^T \widehat{\mathbf{Y}}_2, \mathbf{1}_5^T \widehat{\mathbf{Y}}_3 \right) \tag{2}$$

the *class-specific mean classification accuracies*

$$\widehat{\mathbf{S}} := (\widehat{\mathbf{Y}}_1 + \widehat{\mathbf{Y}}_2 + \widehat{\mathbf{Y}}_3)/3 \tag{3}$$

and the *mean classification accuracy*

$$\hat{y} := \mathbf{1}_5^T \widehat{\mathbf{S}}. \tag{4}$$

MIREX-AMC 2007 reports only mean classification accuracy and confusion tables, but the results are further analyzed in [25]. In all years since, MIREX-AMC reports fold-specific mean classification accuracies, class-specific mean classification accuracies, mean classification accuracy, and confusion tables.

MIREX-AMC performs statistical tests to determine if there are significant differences between fold-specific and class-specific accuracies for all systems. Since 2008, MIREX-AMC tests two null hypotheses. First, for any of the three folds, the classification accuracies are the same for all L submissions, i.e.,

$$\mathcal{H}_0^{(i)} : \widehat{\mathcal{Y}}_1(i) = \widehat{\mathcal{Y}}_2(i) = \dots = \widehat{\mathcal{Y}}_L(i) \tag{5}$$

where $\widehat{\mathcal{Y}}_l(i)$ is the ith element of $\widehat{\mathcal{Y}}_l$, the sequence of fold-specific mean classification accuracies of submission l. Second, for any of the five classes, k, the classification accuracies are the same for all L machine learning algorithms, i.e.,

$$\mathcal{H}_0^{(k)} : \mathbf{e}_k^T \widehat{\mathbf{S}}_1 = \mathbf{e}_k^T \widehat{\mathbf{S}}_2 = \dots = \mathbf{e}_k^T \widehat{\mathbf{S}}_L \tag{6}$$

where $\mathbf{e}_k$ is the kth standard vector. To test these hypotheses, MIREX-AMC applies the *Method of Ranks* [21]. This approach builds a two-way table with the L treatments as columns and three (fold) or five (class) observational units as rows. Each measurement in a row is assigned a rank, with the largest value assigned L, the next largest $L-1$, and the smallest assigned 1.[4] If the classification accuracies are the same for all treatments, then the distribution of the ranks in the two-way table will be random. Assuming the measurements are mutually independent, the chi-squared test can then be used to test the null hypotheses. If either null hypothesis is rejected, then the fold-specific or class-specific mean classification accuracies show a dependence on the submissions.

Through the figures of merit it reports, and the statistical tests it performs, MIREX-AMC implicitly assumes the simple textbook model of its measurements. Furthermore, it assumes the same model applies to all systems it evaluates. To see this, consider the linear model explaining the measurements of MIREX-AMC:

$$\begin{bmatrix} \mathbf{Y}_1 \\ \mathbf{Y}_2 \\ \mathbf{Y}_3 \end{bmatrix} = \begin{bmatrix} \boldsymbol{\tau}_1 \\ \boldsymbol{\tau}_2 \\ \boldsymbol{\tau}_3 \end{bmatrix} + \begin{bmatrix} \mathbf{Z}_1 \\ \mathbf{Z}_2 \\ \mathbf{Z}_3 \end{bmatrix} = \boldsymbol{\beta} + \begin{bmatrix} \mathbf{Z}_1 \\ \mathbf{Z}_2 \\ \mathbf{Z}_3 \end{bmatrix} \tag{7}$$

where $\boldsymbol{\tau}_i = [\tau_{i,a}, \tau_{i,b}, \ldots, \tau_{i,e}]^T$ are the determinate responses of system i, and $\mathbf{Z}_i$ are contributions to the measurements that are not due to system i. The sequence of fold-specific mean classification accuracies is thus modeled

$$\mathcal{Y} := \left(\mathbf{1}_5^T (\boldsymbol{\tau}_1 + \mathbf{Z}_1), \mathbf{1}_5^T (\boldsymbol{\tau}_2 + \mathbf{Z}_2), \mathbf{1}_5^T (\boldsymbol{\tau}_3 + \mathbf{Z}_3) \right). \tag{8}$$

The expectation and variance of the ith member of this set are given by

$$E[\mathcal{Y}(i)] = \mathbf{1}_5^T (\boldsymbol{\tau}_i + E[\mathbf{Z}_i]) \tag{9}$$

$$Var[\mathcal{Y}(i)] = \mathbf{1}_5^T Var[\mathbf{Z}_i] \mathbf{1}_5. \tag{10}$$

The class-specific mean classification accuracies are thus modeled

$$\mathbf{S} = \frac{1}{3} \sum_{i=1}^{3} \boldsymbol{\tau}_i + \frac{1}{3} \sum_{i=1}^{3} \mathbf{Z}_i. \tag{11}$$

and the expectation and covariance of this are

$$E[\mathbf{S}] = \frac{1}{3} \sum_{i=1}^{3} \boldsymbol{\tau}_i + \frac{1}{3} \sum_{i=1}^{3} E[\mathbf{Z}_i] \tag{12}$$

$$Cov[\mathbf{S}] = \frac{1}{9} Cov \left[\sum_{i=1}^{3} \mathbf{Z}_i \right]. \tag{13}$$

Finally, the mean classification accuracy is thus modeled

$$y = \frac{1}{3} \sum_{i=1}^{3} \mathbf{1}_5^T \boldsymbol{\tau}_i + \frac{1}{3} \sum_{i=1}^{3} \mathbf{1}_5^T \mathbf{Z}_i. \tag{14}$$

---

[4] From the MATLAB implementation `friedman`.

and its expectation and variance are

$$E[y] = \frac{1}{3} \sum_{i=1}^{3} \mathbf{1}_5^T \boldsymbol{\tau}_i + \frac{1}{3} \sum_{i=1}^{3} E[\mathbf{1}_5^T \mathbf{Z}_i] \tag{15}$$

$$Var[y] = \frac{1}{9} Var \left[\sum_{i=1}^{3} \mathbf{1}_5^T \mathbf{Z}_i \right]. \tag{16}$$

The responses $\boldsymbol{\beta}$ can be estimated from $\widehat{\mathbf{S}}$ if $E[\mathbf{Z}_i]$ is known for all i. Typically, these are not known and must be modeled. Finally, the error of the estimate of $\boldsymbol{\beta}$ depends upon $Cov[\mathbf{S}]$, which itself depends on the covariance of each $E[\mathbf{Z}_i]$.

It is clear that since MIREX-AMC tests (5) and (6), it implicitly assumes for all i, $E[\mathbf{Z}_i] = \mathbf{0}_5$ (where $\mathbf{0}_5$ is a length-5 vector of zeros), and $Cov[\mathbf{Z}_i] = \sigma^2 \mathbf{I}_5$ for some σ^2. Otherwise, the measured fold-specific mean classification accuracies do not reflect the responses of the systems, and the measured class-specific mean classification accuracies do not reflect their "true" values for systems built from a submission. Furthermore, MIREX-AMC does not specify any bounds on the errors of the estimates, which come from the covariance of all $\mathbf{Z}_i$. Hence, only subject to the strict assumptions and limitations imposed by this measurement model — which is certainly mathematically convenient, but perhaps not appropriate for modeling the measurements — can the experiments of MIREX-AMC produce scientific knowledge [14].

3.3 Relevance and Scientific Validity

MIREX-AMC is principally concerned with the number of "ground truth" labels reproduced by systems built from submissions, but not how the systems select the labels. Whether or not it is acceptable to reproduce "ground truth" labels *by any means* depends on a use case; and thus the relevance of the measurements and comparisons made in MIREX-AMC depend on a use case. If the use case is "classifying music by moods" [25], and the preposition *by* denotes using criteria relevant to mood, for example, mode, tempo, topics of the lyrics, and vocal delivery, and not irrelevant factors that are confounded with the mood labels of the dataset, like low-level spectral information, then it is not relevant to measure the number of "ground truth" labels reproduced by a system, unless one makes the very strong assumption that label selection can only be either random or by relevant criteria in that dataset, or, equivalently, that the responses of the systems in the measurement model can be estimated with sufficiently small error bounds. In other words, classification accuracy is not enough for this use case [44–47].

With respect to the aim "classifying music by moods" then, MIREX-AMC has no conclusion validity (it does not unambiguously address whether a system is classifying music by mood), it has no internal validity (possible confounded factors are not controlled), and thus has no external validity. Since the experiments of MIREX-AMC cannot be related to the problem of music mood recognition — they do not say whether any system produced from any submission is working by using characteristics relevant to the problem of recognizing mood in recorded music, or working instead by confounds — the conclusion that progress on the problem of music mood recognition is slowing [26] does not logically follow. It may very well be the case that progress has never been made [46].

4   Conclusion

We have attempted to illuminate the formalism underlying evaluation in MIR research in order to make explicit its aims, parts, design, implementation, analysis, interpretation, and all attendant assumption and limitations. This includes defining what a "system" is and what it means to analyze one. This brings to the foreground the fact that MIR evaluation encompasses the design, implementation and analysis of experiments, and that crucial to the meaningfulness of an evaluation with regards to the use case of a system is the relevance of the measurements made in those experiments, and the kinds of validity brought about and restricted by the measurement model.

As a specific case, we discussed MIREX-AMC in terms of this formalism. This shows how its system analysis is quite shallow: of interest is only the number of "ground truth" labels reproduced by systems created from a submission, and not how the systems work, whether they work by using criteria relevant to mood, whether they are even considering the music embodied in digital signals, whether they work by confounds in the private dataset so far undetected by MIREX-AMC organizers, how improved systems can be built, and so on. In terms of formalized experimental design and analysis, we uncover the measurement model and its accompanying assumptions that have so far remained implicit in MIREX-AMC evaluations, as well as the critical lack of estimation error analysis. As Dougherty and Dalton write [14]: "any [work] that applies an error estimation rule without providing a performance characterization relevant to the data at hand is scientifically vacuous." We have shown that the measurement model implicit in MIREX-AMC from its hypothesis tests requires very strict assumptions about the nature of the measurements, i.e., the simple textbook model. There is no accompanying error estimation rule. Without evidence that such a measurement model holds for the experiment in MIREX-AMC, or that the error bounds are sufficiently small, no reasonable conclusions come from its seven years of results as regards to the extent to which the problem of automatic music mood recognition has been addressed, or which submissions are better than others for automatic music mood recognition.

It has been said that there are two obstacles to evaluating systems for music mood recognition [22], and indeed for any MIR system: a standardized dataset, and the generation of "ground truth". As we see from the explicit formalism of evaluation above, there are several other more fundamentally significant obstacles: squaring the aims of a system with the analysis, the explicit specification of the measurement model and all assumptions, the explicit specification of the errors in estimating the responses, and the guarantee of conclusion validity, internal validity, and external validity [44–47, 49, 50, 53]. Much, much more work has yet to be done to build the sophisticated approaches necessary to design, implement, and validly evaluate systems that have as a goal the extraction of human-relevant information from music signals, be it emotion, genre, or other descriptors encompassed by autotagging [8]. Just using more data with the same approach to evaluation is not a solution; but solutions can come from using in more creative ways the data that already exists [23, 29–31, 47, 48].

It has been suggested to have a moratorium on many organized MIR evaluation tasks like MIREX-AMC until questions of surrounding evaluation can be answered [2]. In some ways, such campaigns can provide good opportunity for publicity and community outreach, and they have certainly made clear the necessity for better approaches to evaluation in MIR research than before MIREX commenced; but in other ways they can divert attention to tasks that are actually meaningless with respect to solving any important problems of machine music listening, and they unfortunately promote the idea that a standardized, systematic and rigorous approach to evaluation is a *scientific* approach to evaluation. Validity in experiments forms a cornerstone in the foundation of progress in any science. There is thus little doubt that current evaluation practices in MIR research must change if scientific knowledge is the aim; and when the formalism of evaluation is explicit, then it is no longer difficult to judge which alternatives are or are not acceptable and why.

Acknowledgments. Many thanks to Mathieu Barthet for inviting this paper, and to Nick Collins for the fun discussions.

References

1. Aucouturier, J.J.: Sounds like teen spirit: computational insights into the grounding of everyday musical terms. In: Minett, J., Wang, W. (eds.) Language, Evolution and the Brain. Frontiers in Linguistic Series. Academia Sinica Press, Taipei (2009)
2. Aucouturier, J.J., Bigand, E.: Seven problems that keep MIR from attracting the interest of cognition and neuroscience. J. Intell. Info. Syst. **41**(3), 483–497 (2013)
3. Aucouturier, J.J., Pachet, F.: Representing music genre: a state of the art. J. New Music Res. **32**(1), 83–93 (2003)
4. Aucouturier, J.J., Pachet, F.: Improving timbre similarity: how high is the sky? J. Neg. Results Speech Audio Sci. **1**(1), 1–13 (2004)
5. Aucouturier, J.J., Pampalk, E.: Introduction - from genres to tags: a little epistemology of music information retrieval research. J. New Music Res. **37**(2), 87–92 (2008)
6. Aucouturier, J.J., Pachet, F., Roy, P., Beurivé, A.: Signal + context = better classification. In: ISMIR, pp. 425–430 (2007)
7. Bailey, R.A.: Design of Comparative Experiments. Cambridge University Press, Cambridge (2008)
8. Bertin-Mahieux, T., Eck, D., Mandel, M.: Automatic tagging of audio: the state-of-the-art. In: Wang, W. (ed.) Machine Audition: Principles, Algorithms and Systems. IGI Publishing, New York (2010)
9. Bertin-Mahieux, T., Ellis, D.P., Whitman, B., Lamere, P.: The million song dataset. In: Proceedings of ISMIR (2011). http://labrosa.ee.columbia.edu/millionsong/
10. Celma, O., Herrera, P., Serra, X.: Bridging the music semantic gap. In: Proceedings of International Conference Semantics and Digital Media Technology (2006)

11. Craft, A.: The role of culture in the music genre classification task: Human behaviour and its effect on methodology and evaluation. Technical report, Queen Mary University of London, Nov 2007

12. Craft, A., Wiggins, G.A., Crawford, T.: How many beans make five? The consensus problem in music-genre classification and a new evaluation method for single-genre categorisation systems. In: Proceedings of ISMIR, pp. 73–76 (2007)

13. Cunningham, S.J., Bainbridge, D., Downie, J.S.: The impact of MIREX on scholarly research. In: Proceedings of ISMIR, pp. 259–264 (2012)

14. Dougherty, E.R., Dalton, L.A.: Scientific knowledge is possible with small-sample classification. EURASIP J. Bioinform. Syst. Biol. **2013**, 10 (2013)

15. Downie, J., Ehmann, A., Bay, M., Jones, M.: The music information retrieval evaluation exchange: some observations and insights. In: Ras, Z., Wieczorkowska, A. (eds.) Advances in Music Information Retrieval, pp. 93–115. Springer, Heidelberg (2010)

16. Downie, J.S. (ed.): The MIR/MDL Evaluation Project White Paper Collection (2003). http://www.music-ir.org/evaluation/wp.html

17. Downie, J.S.: Toward the scientific evaluation of music information retrieval systems. In: Proceedings of ISMIR, Oct 2003

18. Downie, J.S.: The scientific evaluation of music information retrieval systems: foundations and future. Comput. Music J. **28**(2), 12–23 (2004)

19. Downie, J.S.: The music information retrieval evaluation exchange (2005–2007): A window into music information retrieval research. Acoust. Sci. Tech. **29**(4), 247–255 (2008)

20. Flexer, A.: Statistical evaluation of music information retrieval experiments. J. New Music Res. **35**(2), 113–120 (2006)

21. Friedman, M.: The use of ranks to avoid the assumption of normality in the analysis of variance. J. Am. Statist. Assoc. **32**, 675–701 (1937)

22. Fu, Z., Lu, G., Ting, K.M., Zhang, D.: A survey of audio-based music classification and annotation. IEEE Trans. Multimedia **13**(2), 303–319 (2011)

23. Gouyon, F., Sturm, B.L., Oliveira, J.L., Hespanhol, N., Langlois, T.: On evaluation validity in music autotagging (2014). http://arxiv.org/abs/1410.0001

24. Hand, D.J.: Deconstructing statistical questions. J. Royal Statist. Soc. A (Statist. Soc.) **157**(3), 317–356 (1994)

25. Hu, X., Downie, J.S., Laurier, C., Bay, M., Ehmann, A.F.: The 2007 MIREX audio mood classification task: lessons learned. In: Proceedings of ISMIR (2008)

26. Humphrey, E.J., Bello, J.P., LeCun, Y.: Feature learning and deep architectures: new directions for music informatics. J. Intell. Info. Syst. **41**(3), 461–481 (2013)

27. Karydis, I., Radovanovic, M., Nanopoulos, A., Ivanovic, M.: Looking through the "glass ceiling": a conceptual framework for the problems of spectral similarity. In: ISMIR (2010)

28. Kimball, A.W.: Errors of the third kind in statistical consulting. J. Am. Stat. Assoc. **52**(278), 133–142 (1957)

29. Marques, G., Domingues, M., Langlois, T., Gouyon, F.: Three current issues in music autotagging. In: Proceedings of ISMIR, pp. 795–800 (2011)

30. Marques, G., Langlois, T., Gouyon, F., Lopes, M., Sordo, M.: Short-term feature space and music genre classification. J. New Music Res. **40**(2), 127–137 (2011)

31. Marques, G., Lopes, M., Sordo, M., Langlois, T., Gouyon, F.: Additional evidence that common low-level features of individual audio frames are not representative of music genres. In: Proceedings of SMC, Barcelona, Spain, July 2010

32. McKay, C., Fujinaga, I.: Music genre classification: Is it worth pursuing and how can it be improved? In: Proceedings of ISMIR, pp. 101–106, Oct 2006

33. MIREX (2012). http://www.music-ir.org/mirex
34. Pachet, F., Cazaly, D.: A taxonomy of musical genres. In: Proceedings of Content-based Multimedia Information Access Conference, Paris, France, Apr 2000
35. Pampalk, E., Flexer, A., Widmer, G.: Improvements of audio-based music similarity and genre classification. In: Proceedings of ISMIR, pp. 628–233 (2005)
36. Peeters, G., Fort, K.: Towards a (better) definition of the description of annotated mir corpora. In: ISMIR, pp. 25–30 (2012)
37. Rowe, W.: Why system science and cybernetics? IEEE Trans. Syst. Cybernet. **1**, 2–3 (1965)
38. Saheb-Ettaba, C., McFarland, R.B.: The Alpha-numeric System for Classification of Recordings. Bro-Dart Publishing Company, Williamsport (1969)
39. Schedl, M., Flexer, A., Urbano, J.: The neglected user in music information retrieval research. J. Intell. Info. Syst. **41**(3), 523–539 (2013)
40. Schindler, A., Mayer, R., Rauber, A.: Facilitating comprehensive benchmarking experiments on the million song dataset. In: Proceedings of ISMIR, Oct 2012
41. Serra, X., Magas, M., Benetos, E., Chudy, M., Dixon, S., Flexer, A., Gómez, E., Gouyon, F., Herrera, P., Jordà, S., Paytuvi, O., Peeters, G., Schlüter, J., Vinet, H., Widmer, G.: Roadmap for Music Information ReSearch. Creative Commons (2013)
42. Sturm, B.L.: A survey of evaluation in music genre recognition. In: Proceedings of Adaptive Multimedia Retrieval, Oct 2012
43. Sturm, B.L.: Two systems for automatic music genre recognition: what are they really recognizing? In: Proceedings of ACM MIRUM Workshop, pp. 69–74, Nov 2012
44. Sturm, B.L.: Classification accuracy is not enough: on the evaluation of music genre recognition systems. J. Intell. Info. Syst. **41**(3), 371–406 (2013)
45. Sturm, B.L.: Evaluating music emotion recognition: Lessons from music genre recognition? In: Proceedings of ICME (2013)
46. Sturm, B.L.: The state of the art ten years after a state of the art: future research in music information retrieval. J. New Music Res. **43**(2), 147–172 (2014)
47. Sturm, B.L.: A simple method to determine if a music information retrieval system is a "horse". IEEE Trans. Multimedia (in press, 2014)
48. Sturm, B.L., Kereliuk, C., Pikrakis, A.: A closer look at deep learning neural networks with low-level spectral periodicity features. In: Proceedings of International Workshop on Cognitive Information Processing (2014)
49. Urbano, J.: Information retrieval meta-evaluation: challenges and opportunities in the music domain. In: Proceedings of ISMIR, pp. 609–614 (2011)
50. Urbano, J.: Evaluation in Audio Music Similarity. Ph.D. thesis, University Carlos III of Madrid (2013)
51. Urbano, J., McFee, B., Downie, J.S., Schedl, M.: How significant is statistically significant? the case of audio music similarity and retrieval. In: Proceedings of ISMIR, pp. 181–186 (2012)
52. Urbano, J., Mónica, M., Morato, J.: Audio music similarity and retrieval: evaluation power and stability. In: Proceedings of ISMIR, pp. 597–602 (2011)
53. Urbano, J., Schedl, M., Serra, X.: Evaluation in music information retrieval. J. Intell. Info. Syst. **41**(3), 345–369 (2013)
54. Venables, W.N., Ripley, B.D.: Modern Applied Statistics with S. Statistics and Computing, 4th edn. Springer, New York (2002)
55. Wiggins, G.A.: Semantic gap?? Schemantic schmap!! Methodological considerations in the scientific study of music. In: Proceedings of IEEE International Symposium Mulitmedia, pp. 477–482, Dec 2009

On the Perception of Affect in the Singing Voice: A Study of Acoustic Cues

Pauline Mouawad[1]([⊠]), Myriam Desainte-Catherine[1],
Anne Gégout-Petit[2], and Catherine Semal[3]

[1] University of Bordeaux and CNRS: LaBRI, Bordeaux, France
{pauline.mouawad,
myriam.desainte-catherine}@u-bordeaux.fr
[2] Institute Elie Cartan de Lorraine UMR CNRS, University of Lorraine,
7502 Nancy, France
anne.gegout-petit@univ-lorraine.fr
[3] University of Bordeaux and CNRS: INCIA, Bordeaux, France
catherine.semal@ipb.fr

Abstract. This study addresses the perception of affect in vocal and glottal recordings of a singing voice. An experiment was made to rate the samples on four broad affect terms describing the two-dimensional model of emotion. A cross-tabulation between the singing expressions and affect scores revealed their relationship with affect dimensions. Prosodic as well as spectral acoustic cues were extracted and statistical analysis performed on 22 features revealed a set of cues whose means are statistically significant with respect to valence and arousal, namely SPR, F5, B1, B4, mean pitch, mean intensity, brightness, jitter, shimmer, mean autocorrelation, mean HNR, mean LTAS, RMS, SPL, LPH, and LTAS slope. Principal component analysis was made for vocal and glottal features: 2 components explained 78.1 % and 73.5 % of the original variance of prosodic cues, and 2 components explained 86.3 % and 86.7 % of the original variance of prosodic and spectral cues.

Keywords: Vocal · Glottal · Spectral · Prosodic · Singing expressions · Affect dimensions

1 Introduction

Voice "is a primary instrument for emotional expression" [18]. In speech, there is a "universality in the recognition of vocal affects" [4] and "perception studies show that humans can identify affective states… with high accuracy" [17]; in singing, "emotional expression is an essential aspect" [22].

Although substantial research has addressed affect perception in speech, it is still in its early stages for the singing voice. Previous speech experiments have used "different phrases for different emotions" which made it "hard to distinguish a possible effect of the type of phrase from the effect of emotion" [6]. Other studies on the singing voice asked professional singers to perform songs according to a set of discrete emotions achieving results varying in accuracy and different emotions not identified equally well [6, 18]. Sundberg et al. [22] had a professional singer interpret "different phrases in an

© Springer International Publishing Switzerland 2014
M. Aramaki et al. (Eds.): CMMR 2013, LNCS 8905, pp. 105–121, 2014.
DOI: 10.1007/978-3-319-12976-1_7

emotional and a neutral way" thus emphasizing the difference between neutral and emotional singing rather than the inherent properties of the singing voice in the perception of emotion. In these studies, the stimuli consisted of phrases uttered or sung, hence the "possible interaction effect of phrase and emotion wasn't eliminated [6]". Furthermore, the explicit expression of a targeted emotion mediates the singer's emotional state to the listeners which influences their affect judgments. Therefore no judgment could be made as to the inherent faculty of the singing voice in conveying emotions independently of the singer's affect expression.

This study has two aims: first, to learn to what extent listeners perceive broad affect dimensions in a singing voice that doesn't portray a specific emotion using stimuli of singing voices without lyrics or music. And second if affect is perceived, to reveal the intrinsic role of the acoustical correlates of the singing voice in the perception of affect. To our knowledge, these questions have not been studied before.

2   Method

2.1   Stimuli

The stimuli was taken from the Singing Voice Database[1] and consisted of scale recordings of vocal as well as glottal sounds of a sung vowel 'ah' interpreted by professional singers (1 male and 1 female). The musical notes range from A2 to E4 and A3 to A5 for male and female voice respectively. The recordings are mono files in WAVE PCM format, at 16 bits and 44 kHz. The sound files were trimmed using MIRToolbox [8] to remove the silence at the beginning, and were segmented using R statistical software [15] so that only the first note of the scale is retained. The final dataset consisted of 44 sound samples, 22 vocal and 22 glottal of 1 s duration each in the following singing expressions (see footnote 1): bounce, hallow, light, soft, sweet, flat, mature, sharp, clear, husky and no expression. The female sound files don't include the flat singing expression. The type of the stimuli is relevant as the singers didn't perform specific emotions and there was no accompanying music or lyrics to influence the listener's affect perceptions, hence their judgments were expected to relate to the voice alone.

2.2   Procedure

Participants were asked to rate the perceived affect dimension of each voice sample on a 5-point Likert scale using the two-dimensional model of affect [16] represented by four broad affect terms: pleasant-unpleasant for valence, and awake-tired for arousal [20]. Considering that with today's internet bandwidth and sound technologies it has become possible to conduct psychoacoustic tests over the internet [3], the experiment was distributed through email with instructions explaining its objectives. Each participant could play the sound file more than once, and could at any time save their answers and come back to complete it later.

---

[1] http://crel.calit2.net/projects/databases/svdb.

Each participant could play the sound file more than once, and could at any time save the answer and come back to complete it later. Each sample occurred 3 times in the dataset and the order of the files was randomized. Duration of the experiment was 30 minutes. There were in total 15 participants, 9 males and 6 females, (age M = 26.1, SD = 9.6) of whom 1 is a professional singer and 4 have had some kind of formal singing training. 7 reported enjoying singing, 14 approved that music expresses emotions and that the singer's voice is important to their personal enjoyment of a song. All participants confirmed that the singer's voice is important in the expression of emotions in singing.

2.3 Acoustic Features

Both spectral and prosodic features contain emotional information and are therefore suitable for voice emotion recognition tasks [4, 7]. So a total of 22 acoustic features were selected according to their perceptual validity as established in the relevant literature (see Table 1) and were extracted from the original sound files using Praat software [1]. Pitch information was retrieved using a cross-correlation method for voice research optimization, with pitch floor and ceiling set to 75 Hz and 300 Hz respectively for male voice and to 100 Hz and 500 Hz respectively for female voice. The spectrum was obtained from the waveform using Fast Fourier Transform method with a dynamic range of 70 dB, a window length of 5 ms and a view range from 0 to 5000 Hz for male and from 0 to 5500 Hz for female voice.

Table 1. List of acoustic features and relevant literatures

Features	Literature
Singing formants: F2 to F4	Sundberg et al. [22], Ishi and Campbell [5], Millhouse and Clermont [11]
Singing power ratio (SPR)	Grichkovtsova et al. [4], Sundberg et al. [22], Omori et al. [12], Watts et al. [24], Lundy et al. [10]
Mean intensity, mean pitch	Jansens et al. [6], Patel et al. [13]
Jitter, shimmer, harmonicity: mean HNR, mean autocorrelation	Lundy et al. [10], Scherer K. [18]
Brightness	Ishi and Campbell [5]
LTAS	Scherer et al. [19], Sundberg et al. [23]
General voice acoustic attributes	http://www.sltinfo.com/acoustic-measures-norms

The singing power ratio (SPR) [10] is a measure that quantifies the singer's formant [11, 22] as well as the singing voice quality [12]. To this end the two highest spectrum peaks between 2 and 4 kHz and between 0 and 2 kHz were identified and SPR was obtained by computing the 'amplitude difference in dB between the highest spectral peak within the 2–4 kHz range and that within the 0–2 kHz range' [11].

Since the 'perceptual singer's formant' is 'contributed by the underlying acoustic formants F2, F3 and F4' [11], the means of F2, F3 and F4 were measured individually for each sound file, in addition to F1 and F5. The bandwidths B1 to B5 of the formants were also extracted, but B5 was subsequently discarded due to unknown values for some files. B4 was discarded for the glottal files only. The mean intensity of the sound was measured using energy averaging method. Root-mean-square was retrieved for the entire duration of the sample. Measures of jitter, shimmer mean autocorrelation and mean harmonics-to-noise ratio (HNR) were extracted from the voice report. Brightness was extracted using MIRToolbox [8]. Spectral features were extracted from the pitch-corrected long-term average spectrum (LTAS) with an analysis bandwidth of 100 Hz, a maximum frequency of 5000 Hz for male and 5500 Hz for female voice and pitch floor and ceiling values adjusted for male and female voice samples. The LTAS features are namely: sound pressure level (SPL), mean, local peak height (LPH), slope and spectral tilt or linear regression slope (LRS). The method detailing LTAS computation is detailed in [2].

3   Findings

3.1   Affect Ratings

Considering that the number of responses for each of the 5 categories on the Likert scale was slight therefore making it difficult to meet the assumptions of statistical validity for the ANOVA, the responses were grouped under 'pleasant', 'unpleasant', 'neutral' for valence, and 'awake', 'tired', 'neutral' for arousal. For example, responses for 'awake' and 'extremely awake' were grouped under 'awake'. The mean of the ratings for the 3 occurrences of each file was computed, and then the file was classified according to the emotion that brought the highest total number of votes. On the valence dimension, 16 were rated as pleasant (13 vocal, 3 glottal), 22 were rated as unpleasant (7 vocal, 15 glottal) and 6 were rated as neutral (2 vocal, 4 glottal). On the arousal dimension, 22 were rated as awake (17 vocal, 5 glottal), 17 were rated as tired (3 vocal, 14 glottal) and 5 were rated as neutral (2 vocal, 3 glottal).

3.2   Analysis

The entire analysis was carried out in the R statistical software environment [15].

Singing Expressions. To our knowledge, the relationship of various singing expressions to affect dimensions is not established in the literature. A cross-tabulation was done for the affect judgments and the singing expressions to determine the counts of the combination of each factor level.

On the valence dimension, all vocals in light, soft and sweet expressions as well as 67 % of those with no specific expression were perceived as pleasant; mature and sharp vocals were perceived as unpleasant. All glottals in bounce, husky, mature, sharp and no expression were perceived as unpleasant, and soft glottals were perceived as pleasant. On the arousal dimension, all vocals in bounce, clear, mature, sharp and no expression were perceived as awake, and those in soft and sweet expressions were perceived as tired (low energy). All glottals in clear, hallow, soft and sweet as well as 67 % of those having no specific singing expression were perceived as tired.

Acoustic Cues. A one-way ANOVA was performed for each acoustic measure with valence and arousal as factors with three levels each. The analysis results were verified using Tukey's multiple comparisons of means and were Bonferroni corrected.

On the valence dimension, acoustic cues whose means were statistically different for the pleasant-unpleasant factors are SPR, mean intensity, jitter, shimmer, mean autocorrelation, mean HNR, mean LTAS, RMS, SPL and LPH for vocal files (see Table 2), and brightness, mean intensity, shimmer, mean autocorrelation, B1 and F5 for glottal files, with brightness being significant for the pleasant-neutral factors as well (see Table 3). Contrasting vocal and glottal mean values, the shimmer's mean value in vocal sounds is lower for the pleasant dimension and higher for the unpleasant dimension. This is consistent with the thresholds of pathology[2] whereby a shimmer value > 3.810 % is considered to be a sign of potential pathology, which may explain why listeners judged files with a mean shimmer value of 5.120 % to be unpleasant. The same comment can be made for the jitter means of the vocal files, being <= 1.040 % (threshold (see Footnote 2)) for pleasant files and > 1.040 % for unpleasant files, as well as for mean HNR mean values being < 20 (see Footnote 2) for unpleasant files, potentially indicating a noticeable hoarseness. The mean intensity mean values are higher in glottal files for both pleasant and unpleasant dimensions.

On the arousal dimension, acoustic cues whose means were statistically different for the awake and tired factors are SPR, mean intensity, mean LTAS, RMS, LTAS slope for vocal files (see Table 4), in addition to B1, B4 for awake-neutral and tired-neutral, and LPH for awake-neutral (see Tables 5 and 6). For glottal files the cues are mean intensity, jitter, shimmer, mean HNR, mean pitch, F5, mean LTAS, RMS and

Table 2. p values, mean and standard deviation of vocal cues for pleasant-unpleasant

Acoustic features	p	Pleasant		Unpleasant	
		M	SD	M	SD
SPR	0.0020	28.580	7.470	15.900	5.990
Mean intensity	0.0006	53.940	5.020	62.670	1.830
Jitter	0.0300	0.650	0.330	1.160	0.470
Shimmer	0.0300	3.590	0.850	5.120	1.710
Mean autocorrelation	0.0040	0.980	0.006	0.950	0.031
Mean HNR	0.0010	21.440	2.130	16.200	3.300
Mean LTAS	0.0800[a] 0.0007	16.860	4.950	25.340	3.742
RMS	0.0600[a] 0.0001	0.109	0.006	0.026	0.008
SPL	0.0900[a] 0.0007	54.100	4.800	62.450	3.660
LPH	0.0910	0.380	5.610	6.460	6.250

[a] pleasant-neutral

---

[2] http://www.sltinfo.com/acoustic-measures-norms/.

Table 3. p values, mean and standard deviation of glottal cues for pleasant-unpleasant

		Pleasant		Unpleasant	
Acoustic features	p	M	SD	M	SD
Brightness	0.0300[a]	0.163	0.100	0.069	0.010
	0.0030				
Mean intensity	0.0200	59.420	7.170	65.890	2.600
Shimmer	0.0110	7.580	3.860	3.750	1.520
Mean autocorrelation	0.0420	0.970	0.020	0.980	0.007
B1	0.0220	187	83.060	533.400	421.780
F5	0.1300[a]	4727	206.610	4518	142.540
	0.0740				

[a] pleasant-neutral

Table 4. p values, mean and standard deviation of vocal cues for awake-tired

		Awake		Tired	
Acoustic features	p	M	SD	M	SD
SPR	0.0020	19.130	6.680	32.430	7.270
Mean intensity	0.0020	60.310	3.890	52.500	5.390
Mean LTAS	0.0640[a]	22.900	4.070	15.930	5.120
	0.0160				
RMS	0.0818[a]	0.021	0.008	0.009	0.005
	0.0093				
LTAS slope	0.0065	−7.340	4.600	−14.390	2.380

[a] awake-neutral

Table 5. p values, mean and standard deviation of vocal cues for awake-neutral

		Awake		Neutral	
Acoustic features	p	M	SD	M	SD
B1	0.0370	285.200	185.780	931.930	1109.203
B4	0.0001	293.600	162.660	1074	490.670
LPH	0.1500	4.640	5.560	−4.408	8.750

SPL, with mean HNR and F5 being also significant for the neutral-awake and tired-neutral factors respectively (see Table 7). Contrasting the mean values of both types of files, mean intensity, RMS and mean LTAS have higher values in glottal files for both affect dimensions.

In summary, the features whose means are statistically different for both affective dimensions are SPR, mean intensity, mean LTAS, RMS and LPH for vocal sounds, and mean intensity and shimmer for glottal sounds; and those that are significant for both vocal and glottal files are mean intensity, shimmer, and mean autocorrelation for valence, and mean intensity and shimmer for arousal.

Table 6. p values, mean and standard deviation of vocal cues for tired-neutral

		Tired		Neutral	
Acoustic features	p	M	SD	M	SD
B1	0.0530	275.100		931.300	1109.200
B4	0.0002	325.600		1074	490.670

Table 7. p values, mean and standard deviation of glottal cues for awake-tired

		Awake		Tired	
Acoustic features	p	M	SD	M	SD
Mean intensity	0.0200	68.840	2.330	63.510	3.910
Jitter	0.0070	0.560	0.130	1.280	0.420
Shimmer	0.0200	2.310	0.700	5.250	2.260
Mean HNR	0.0060	29.320	3.010	23.570	3.320
	0.0300[a]				
Mean pitch	0.0140	218.700	3.930	138.100	51.540
F5	0.1200[a]	4571.000	184.260	4690.000	233.600
Mean LTAS	0.0950	29.420	1.880	25.050	5.710
RMS	0.0800[b]	0.039	0.008	0.025	0.012
	0.1900				
SPL	0.1830[b]	66.560	1.920	62.240	5.530
	0.0950				

[a] awake-neutral
[b] tired-neutral

Dimension Reduction. A principal component analysis (PCA) was made on the acoustic correlates with two aims in mind: first, to identify the main components that best describe the stimuli and second, to project the sounds on a factorial plane that illustrates graphically their distribution on the valence-arousal dimensions alongside the acoustic correlates. A series of tests were carried on various combinations of acoustic correlates. First, the entire set of 24 features was analyzed and the first two components accounted for a mere 47.5 % and 21.5 % respectively of the total variance of vocal cues, and 40.63 % and 20.62 % respectively of that of glottal cues. Furthermore, the vocal and glottal files were quite dispersed on both affective dimensions (see Figs. 1, 2, 3 and 4).

Second, a test was made for the most relevant prosodic features (Table 1) namely, SPR, F2, F3, F4, mean pitch, brightness, shimmer, mean intensity, jitter, mean autocorrelation and mean HNR. Two components are retained that explain 78.1 % of the total variance of vocal cues and 73.5 % of that of the glottal ones.

Concerning the vocal cues result, the first component explains 57.7 % of the original variance and accounts mainly for variations in SPR, F4, mean pitch, opposed to jitter and mean intensity; the second component explains a further 20.4 % of the original variance and account mainly for variations in brightness. Figures 5 and 6 show that the vocal files projected onto the PC1-PC2 planes appear to cluster reasonably according to valence and arousal, although a bit weaker for arousal.

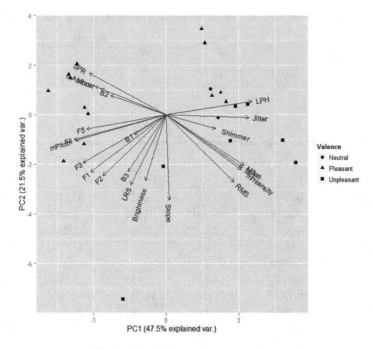

Fig. 1. Vocal files and cues on valence

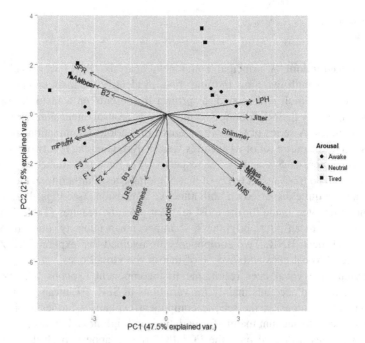

Fig. 2. Vocal files and cues on arousal

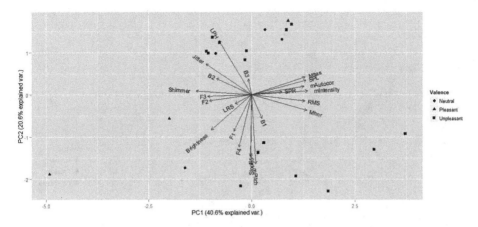

Fig. 3. Glottal files and cues on valence

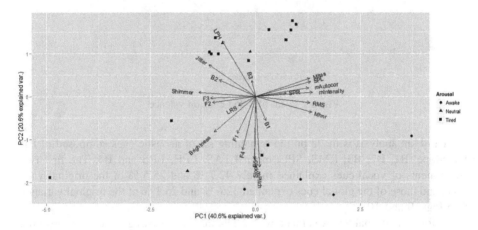

Fig. 4. Glottal files and cues on arousal

For example, pleasant sounds are those having higher values of SPR, F4 and mean pitch and lower values for jitter and mean intensity and/or lower values for brightness. Unpleasant sounds are those having higher values for jitter and mean intensity and lower values for SPR, F4 and mean pitch, and/or higher values for brightness. Sounds perceived as awake are those having higher values for jitter and mean intensity and rather lower values for brightness, and sounds perceived as tired are those having higher values for SPR, mean pitch and F4 and/or lower values for brightness.

For the glottal cues, the first component explains 53.4 % of the original variance and accounts for variations in shimmer, F2, F3, opposed to mean intensity, mean autocorrelation and mean HNR; the second component explains a further 20.1 % of the original variance and accounts for variations in mean pitch and F4 (see Figs. 7 and 8).

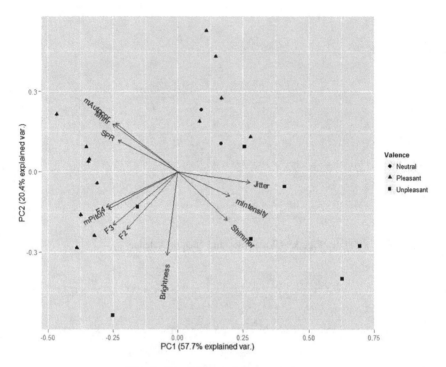

Fig. 5. Vocal files and cues on valence

Third, an analysis is made on the remaining set of acoustic cues composed of F1, F5, Slope, B1, B2, B3, RMS, SPL, mean LTAS, LPH, LRS and B4. The first two components of vocal cues explained merely 42.7 % and 25.5 % of the original variance, and those of the glottal cues explained 32.6 % and 25.1 % of the original variance (see Figs. 9 and 10).

A fourth and final test was made with a feature set consisting of selected prosodic and spectral features. The idea is to identify the largest possible set of features that is best accounted for by the components and that separates the sound files fairly well on the affective dimensions. The first two components of vocal features explain 86.3 % of the original variance and those of the glottal features explain 86.7 % of the original variance (see Figs. 11 and 12). A summary of the PCA tests and their first two components are in Tables 2 and 3.

For vocal cues, the first component explains 61.1 % of the original variance and accounts mainly for variations in SPR, F4, F5, and mean Pitch opposed to LPH and mean LTAS; the second component explains a further 25.2 % of the original variance and accounts for variations in LRS and Slope. Figure 11 shows that the vocal files projected onto the PC1-PC2 planes cluster fairly well on valence, with a better clustering noted for the pleasant-unpleasant factors than in the previous result. For example, unpleasant files are those having high values for LPH, mean LTAS, SPL and slope and low values for F4, F5 and mean pitch. Pleasant files are those having high values for F4, F5, mean pitch and SPR, and low values for mean LTAS, SPL, LPH and

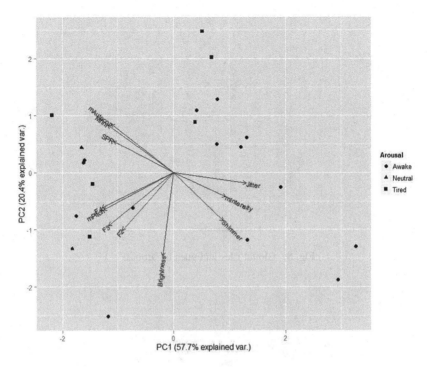

Fig. 6. Vocals files and cues on arousal

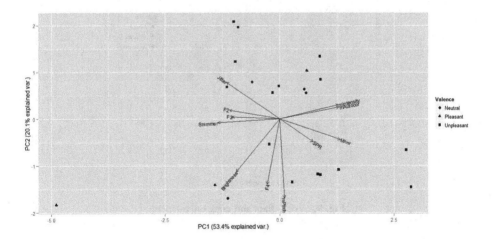

Fig. 7. Glottal files and cues on valence

mean intensity. Figure 12 shows an improved clustering of the vocal files on the awake-tired factors over the previous test result; sounds perceived as tired are those having high values for SPR and LPH and low values for RMS, slope, mean intensity and SPL. For glottal cues, the first component explains 62.9 % of the original variance

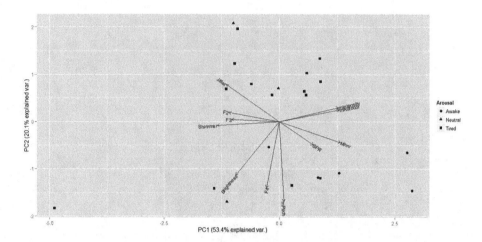

Fig. 8. Glottal files and cues on arousal

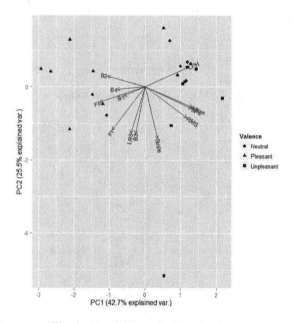

Fig. 9. Vocal files and cues on valence

and accounts for variations in mean LTAS, SPL, mean autocorrelation, mean intensity, RMS and mean HNR opposed to Shimmer and Jitter; the second component explains a further 23.8 % of the original variance and accounts for variations in Slope, mean pitch opposed to LPH. Figures 13 and 14 show that the glottal files projected on the PC1-PC2 plane cluster better for the pleasant-unpleasant factors than in the previous test result and rather quite better for the awake-tired factors. For example, unpleasant

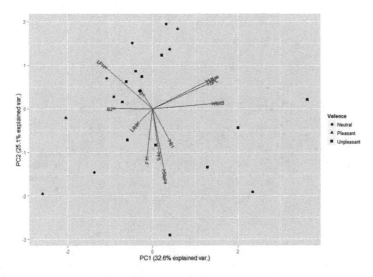

Fig. 10. Glottal files and cues on valence

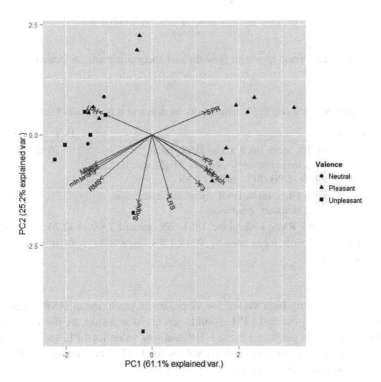

Fig. 11. Vocal files with prosodic and spectral features on valence

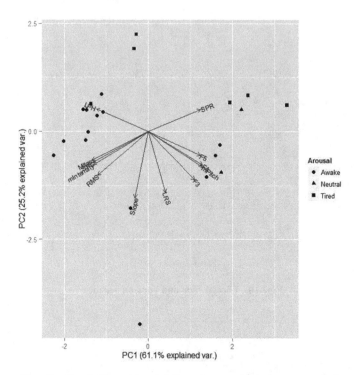

Fig. 12. Vocal files with prosodic and spectral features on arousal

Table 8. First two PCA components on different sets of vocal features

Set of vocal features	PC1	PC2
SPR, F1, F2, F3, F4, F5, mean pitch, mean HNR, mean autocorrelation, jitter, mean intensity, shimmer, brightness, B1, B2, B3, RMS, LRS, Slope, LPH, SPL, mean LTAS	47.50 %	21.50 %
SPR, F2, F3, F4, mean pitch, mean HNR, mean autocorrelation, jitter, mean intensity, shimmer, brightness	57.70 %	20.40 %
F1, F5, B1, B2, B3, B4, RMS, LRS, slope, LPH, SPL, mean LTAS	42.70 %	25.50 %
SPR, F3, F4, F5, mean pitch, mean intensity, RMS, LRS, slope, SPL, LPH, mean LTAS	61.10 %	25.20 %

sounds are those having high values for slope, mean pitch, mean HNR, mean LTAS and/or low values for jitter and LPH. Sounds perceived as awake are those having high values for slope, mean pitch and mean HNR and low value for LPH and jitter. Sounds perceived as tired are those having high values for LPH, Jitter, mean LTAS and low values for slope and mean pitch (Figs. 13 and 14).

Table 9. First two PCA components on different sets of glottal features

Set of glottal features	PC1	PC2
SPR, F1, F2, F3, F4, F5, mean pitch, mean HNR, mean autocorrelation, jitter, mean intensity, shimmer, brightness, B1, B2, B3, RMS, LRS, slope, LPH, SPL, mean LTAS	40.60 %	20.60 %
SPR, F2, F3, F4, mean pitch, mean HNR, mean autocorrelation, jitter, mean intensity, shimmer, brightness	53.40 %	20.10 %
F1, F5, B1, B2, B3, RMS, LRS, Slope, LPH, SPL, mean LTAS	32.60 %	25.10 %
Shimmer, jitter, mean pitch, mean autocorrelation, mean intensity, mean HNR, RMS, mean LTAS, slope, LPH, SPL	62.90 %	23.80 %

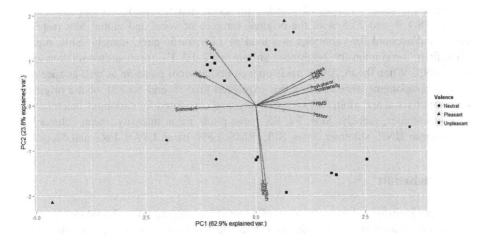

Fig. 13. Glottal files with prosodic and spectral features on valence

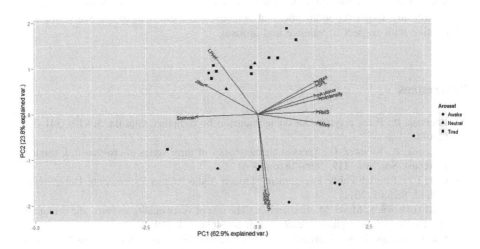

Fig. 14. Glottal files with prosodic and spectral features on arousal

4 Discussion

The statistical tests made on the acoustic features and the affective dimensions revealed a set of features that are statistically significant with respect to broad affect dimensions. Although it is not obvious to recommend an optimal feature set for studies investigating the perception of affect dimensions in the singing voice, some recommendations can be made concerning the pertinent features to extract depending on whether vocal or glottal files are studied. A feature set that is appropriate for the discrimination of both affect dimensions consists of SPR, mean intensity, mean LTAS, RMS, LPH in vocal recordings, and mean intensity and shimmer for glottal sounds. A feature set consisting of cues that are significant for both file types includes mean intensity, shimmer, and mean autocorrelation for valence, and mean intensity and shimmer for arousal.

The PCA made on a set of selected prosodic cues revealed 2 components that explain 78.1 % and 73.5 % of the original variance of vocal and glottal files respectively, and account for variations in a total of 11 acoustic cues, namely: SPR, mean pitch, jitter, mean intensity, brightness, shimmer, F2, F3, F4, mean autocorrelation and mean HNR. When the PCA was made on a combination of prosodic as well as spectral cues, 2 components were retained that explained 86.3 % and 86.7 % of the original variance of vocal and glottal files respectively, and accounted for variations in a total of 15 acoustic cues, namely: SPR, F4, F5, mean pitch, mean intensity, mean autocorrelation, mean HNR, shimmer, jitter, SPL, RMS, LPH, mean LTAS, LRS and Slope.

5 Conclusion

This paper investigated the perception of affect in the singing voice, based on vocal as well as glottal recordings. Prosodic as well as spectral features were extracted from the sound files. Statistical analysis revealed a set of acoustic cues that significantly discriminate the perception of broad affect dimensions in the singing voice. In conclusion, this paper has shown that affect dimensions can be perceived in a singing voice not expressing any target emotion, and that acoustic cues intrinsic to the voice are discriminative with respect to valence and arousal.

References

1. Boersma, P.: Praat, a system for doing phonetics by computer. Glot Int. 5(9/10), 341–345 (2001)
2. Boersma, P., Kovacic, G.: Spectral characteristics of three styles of croatian folk singing. J. Acoust. Soc. Am. 119, 1805–1816 (2006)
3. Cox, T.J.: Tutorial: Public Engagement Through Audio Internet Experiments. University of Salford, Salford (2011)
4. Grichkovtsova, I., Morel, M., Lacheret, A.: The role of voice quality and prosodic contour in affective speech perception. Speech Commun. 54(3), 414–429 (2012)
5. Ishi, C., Campbell, N.: Analysis of Acoustic-prosodic Features of Spontaneous Expressive Speech. Revista de Estudos da Linguagem 12(2), 38–49 (2012)

6. Jansens, S., Bloothooft, G., De Krom, G.: Perception and acoustics of emotions in singing. In: Proceedings of the 5th Eurospeech, vol. 4, pp. 2155–2158 (1997)
7. Joshi, A., Kaur, R.: A Study of speech emotion recognition methods. Int. J. Comput. Sci. Mob. Comput. (IJCSMC) 2(4), 28–31 (2013)
8. Lartillot, O., Toiviainen, P.: A Matlab toolbox for musical feature extraction from audio. In: Proceedings of the 10th International Conference on Digital Audio Effects (DAFx-07) (2007)
9. Lin E., Jayakody D., Looi V.: The singing power ratio and timbre-related acoustic analysis of singing vowels and musical instruments. In: Voice Foundation's 38th Annual Symposium: Care of the Professional Voice (2009)
10. Lundy, D.S., Roy, S., Casiano, R., Xue, J., Evans, J.: Acoustic analysis of the singing and speaking voice in singing students. J. Voice 14(4), 490–493 (2000)
11. Millhouse, T., Clermont, F.: Perceptual characterisation of the singer's formant region: a preliminary study. In: Proceedings of the Eleventh Australian International Conference on Speech Science and Technology, pp. 253–258 (2006)
12. Omori, K., Kacker, A., Carroll, L.M., Riley, W.D., Blaugrund, S.M.: Singing power ratio: quantitative evaluation of singing voice quality. J. Voice 10(3), 228–235 (1996)
13. Patel, S., Scherer, K.R., Björkner, E., Sundberg, J.: Mapping emotions into acoustic space: the role of voice production. Biol. Psychol. 87(1), 93–98 (2011)
14. Pittam, J., Gallois, C., Callan, V.: The long-term spectrum and perceived emotion. Speech Commun. 9(3), 177–187 (1990)
15. R development Core Team. R: A Language and Environment for Statistical Computing. R Foundation for Statistical Computing (2008)
16. Russel, J.: A circumplex model of affect. J. Pers. Soc. Psychol. 39(6), 1161–1178 (1980)
17. Scherer, K.R., Banse, R., Wallbott, H.G.: Emotion inferences from vocal expression correlate across languages and cultures. J. Cross Cult. Psychol. 32(1), 6–92 (2001)
18. Scherer, K.R.: Expression of emotion in voice and music. J. Voice 9(3), 235–248 (1995)
19. Scherer, K.R., Sundberg, J., Tamarit, L., Salomão, G.: Comparing the acoustic expression of emotion in the speaking and the singing voice. Comput. Speech Lang. 29(1), 218–235 (2013)
20. Schimmack, U., Grob, A.: Dimensional models of core affect: a quantitative comparison by means of structural equation modeling. Eur. J. Pers. 14, 325–345 (2000)
21. Sloboda, J.A., Juslin, P.: Psychological perspectives on music and emotion. In: Juslin, P.N., Sloboda, J.A. (eds.) Music and Emotion: Theory and Research, pp. 71–104. Oxford University Press, New York (2001)
22. Sundberg, J., Iwarsson, J., Hagegard, H.: A singer's expression of emotions in sung performance. Vocal Fold Physiology: Voice Quality Control, pp. 217–231 (1995)
23. Sundberg, J., Patel, S., Bjorkner, E., Scherer, K.R.: Interdependencies among voice source parameters in emotional speech. IEEE Trans. Affect. Comput. 2(3), 162–174 (2011)
24. Watts, C., Barnes-Burroughs, K., Estis, J. Blanton, D.: The singing power ratio as an objective measure of singing voice quality in untrained talented and nontalented singers. J. Voice, 20(1), 82–88 (2006)

Novel Methods in Facilitating Audience and Performer Interaction Using the Mood Conductor Framework

György Fazekas[✉], Mathieu Barthet, and Mark B. Sandler

School of Electronic Engineering and Computer Science,
Center for Digital Music, Queen Mary University of London, London, UK
{g.fazekas,m.barthet,m.sandler}@qmul.ac.uk

Abstract. While listeners' emotional response to music is the subject of numerous studies, less attention is paid to the dynamic emotion variations due to the interaction between artists and audiences in live improvised music performances. By opening a direct communication channel from audience members to performers, the Mood Conductor system provides an experimental framework to study this phenomenon. Mood Conductor facilitates interactive performances and thus also has an inherent entertainment value. The framework allows audience members to send emotional directions using their mobile devices in order to "conduct" improvised performances. Emotion coordinates indicted by the audience in the arousal-valence space are aggregated and clustered to create a video projection. This is used by the musicians as guidance, and provides visual feedback to the audience. Three different systems were developed and tested within our framework so far. These systems were trialled in several public performances with different ensembles. Qualitative and quantitative evaluations demonstrated that musicians and audiences were highly engaged with the system, and raised new insights enabling future improvements of the framework.

Keywords: Audience-performer interaction · Music · Performance · Emotion · Mood · Arousal · Valence · Improvisation · Live concert · Mobile technology · Smartphone app · Real time · Visualisation · Human computer interaction

1 Introduction

A large body of recent research in the area of music and emotions focusses on listeners' response to music, which may be studied in terms of expressed or *perceived* emotions, and in terms of induced or *felt* emotions. Thorough reviews of these works from the perspective of Psychological research as well as Music Informatics are presented in [4, 24] respectively. However, the role of emotions during expressive performances has been studied less frequently. Recent work [26] showed that performers experience both *music-related* and *practice-related* emotions.

© Springer International Publishing Switzerland 2014
M. Aramaki et al. (Eds.): CMMR 2013, LNCS 8905, pp. 122–147, 2014.
DOI: 10.1007/978-3-319-12976-1_8

For some artist or musician, performing involves feeling music-related emotions in order to "get into the mood" of the piece being played, whereas for others, performing is more a matter of deliberate conscious awareness and planned expressiveness, i.e. "knowing" music-related emotions, rather than "feeling" them [26].

Our present work deals with another aspect of music and emotion which is also scarcely studied: the communication of emotions between listeners (the audience) and performers. We describe a novel framework called Mood Conductor (MC) to create interactive music performances. The framework allows members of the audience to indicate the emotional content they find most desirable in the context of improvised music. The term "conductor" is used hereby metaphorically to refer to the act of conducting, which is the art of directing a musical performance by way of visible gestures. Through the use of the Mood Conductor App[1], audience members are able to communicate emotional intentions using their mobile devices: smart phones, tablets or laptops. Performers are made aware of the audiences' intentions by visual feedback operating in real-time. The framework is adapted to musical improvisation situations, which may be defined as a creative activity of immediate musical composition as well as spontaneous response to other musicians [11]. In our framework, the emotional intentions communicated from spectators to performers represent exogenous directions which constrain the musical improvisation in an interactive way.

The three main components of the Mood Conductor framework are a *(i)* web-based application optimised for mobile devices, *(ii)* a server side engine for aggregating and clustering data from the audience, and *(iii)* a visualisation client providing feedback for the musicians and the audience. The gradual development of the framework including the tuning of the systems' parameters was based on several interactive music performances over the course of almost two years. Concerts were held at Wilton's Music Hall in London, UK, during the 'New Resonances Festival' held in conjunction with CMMR 2012, at the Cathedral of Strasbourg in France, at Queen Mary University of London (QMUL), UK, at the Barbican Arts Centre in London, UK, and at an artistic event during the International Conference on Affective Computing and Intelligent Interaction (ACII 2013) in Geneva, Switzerland [9]. Different music ensembles were involved, including the vocal quartet 'VoXP', composed of four professional singers who graduated in Jazz and Classical Music from the Conservatoire National de Strasbourg, as well as a jazz/rock trio and quintet. The different systems were evaluated using online surveys as well as a controlled comparative study conduced in the lab environment at the Media and Arts Technology Laboratory of QMUL. The results of thorough formal evaluation of the first two systems are summarised in the present paper while more details can be found in [17,18].

The need for the Mood Conductor framework grew out of real-world problems the VoXP quartet was facing when trying to create interactive improvised performances. We invite the reader to watch a YouTube video[2] showing the system in use with the VoXP singer quartet[3].

---

[1] http://bit.ly/moodxp2.
[2] http://www.youtube.com/watch?v=o9Fd7nV2IWs.
[3] https://www.facebook.com/VoXPerformance.

The remainder of the paper is organised as follows. Section 2 highlights important related works and details the rationale behind selecting the underlying model of emotions for the interactive and visualisation interface of our systems. An overview of the architecture of the Mood Conductor framework is detailed in Sect. 3. Section 4 details the specific differences between the different MC systems, the different music performances, as well as the evaluations and the development iterations of the framework. Finally, in Sect. 5 we summarise our findings, outline our conclusions and the future perspectives for Mood Conductor.

2   Related Works and Model Selection

The most striking examples of constrained or directed improvisation occur in the theatre [14] when an improvisational troupe invites the audience to supply a theme and some constraints and then develops a rendition of the theme that also meets the constraints. This principle was adapted to the human computer interaction (HCI) domain by Hayes-Roth et al. who developed an interactive story application for children using intelligent agents [12]. In the rest of this section we detail on related works in music applications and affective sciences and introduce the mood model underlying our framework.

2.1   Interactive Systems in Musical Applications

In the musical domain, directed improvisation commonly occurs in jazz and other musical performances [8]. The literature on live music improvisation systems involving audience-performer interaction is however very scarce and to the best of our knowledge, Mood Conductor is the first system of its kind. The system fosters a new chain of communication between audience and performers which differs from the classic composer-performer-listener model adapted to Western written music [15]. A distributed interaction framework that supports audience and player interaction during interactive media performances was proposed in [23]. Reference [3] describes a "cheering meter" application offering a visualisation of audience reactions which was shown to increase the sense of participation in the audience during rap music performances. The system developed by [13] draws on facial emotion recognition technology to create art installations reacting to or mimicking audience changes in emotional expressions.

2.2   Arousal-Valence as a Model for Interaction and Visualisation

The Mood Conductor interface and visualisation components rely on the two-dimensional arousal-valence (AV) model proposed by Thayer [25] and Russell [19] to characterise core or basic emotions (such as "happy", "calm", "sad", "anger", etc.). The experiments described in [21] demonstrated that the AV model provides reliable means for collecting continuous emotional responses to music. In our framework, the AV space is used in a reciprocal way, to collect "emotional intentions" in real-time.

We choose the AV model as basis for both the Mood Conductor client and visualisation interfaces, because it overcomes some of the problems commonly associated with categorical emotion models, such as the discretisation of the problem into a set of landmarks. This would prevent emotions which differ from the landmarks to be considered. Additionally, the AV model was empirically shown to be a good representation of internal human emotion states [25], that is also relevant in the music domain, where emotion classes can be defined in terms of arousal or energy (how exciting/calming musical pieces are) and valence or stress (how positive/negative musical pieces are) [4].

Albeit higher dimensional models were also developed, such as [1], the interaction based on these models would almost certainly be less intuitive and the interface would be more cumbersome. It would also present a higher cognitive load distracting the audience members from the performance. We do not however rely solely on the AV model. The client interface also shows a mood tag closest to the selected position, allowing easier interpretation of the space, without restricting audience members to select a distinct emotion category, creating an interface that successfully fuses dimensional and categorical emotion models.

The graphical user interface of the Mood Conductor client shares similarities with that of 'MoodSwings' [16], a collaborative game that was developed for collecting music mood labels. However, in MC, the user interface displays mood tags, rather than emotion faces [22], to help users finding the relationships between locations in the space and their associated emotions, thus bridging the gap between the dimensional and categorical approaches [4].

3 Overview of the Mood Conductor Framework

The Mood Conductor framework consists of a shared system architecture and some common organising principles that facilitate a novel form of interaction between performers and the audience. Different systems have been built and evaluated so far within this framework. This section describes the common system components and principles, while the implementation details of the respective system variants are given in Sect. 4.

3.1 Common System Architecture

The Mood Conductor framework consists of three technical components that form a client-server architecture. The first component is a smartphone friendly Web-based client program. This client allows for any member of the audience with an internet and Web browser-enabled smartphone (or other mobile device) to indicate emotions during a music performance, thus to collaboratively "conduct" the performance.

The second component is a server-side application that provides two conceptually separate application programming interfaces (API) implemented within the same process. The smartphone client API allows for collecting data from the audience, and also exposes a JavaScript program that is run by the mobile client's web browser. The visual client API allows for retrieving aggregated and clustered user input from the server, as well as configuring some of the server-side parameters. Concerning client-server communication, Mood Conductor follows a representational state transfer (REST) style design [10]. More details about the server side implementation and the clustering process are provided in the respective descriptions of each Mood Conductor system variant.

The final component of Mood Conductor is a visualisation client that may be run on a conventional PC or laptop with video output. This client allows for projecting or otherwise visualising cumulative user input. The video output is displayed to the performers who may use this as guidance during improvisation. The visualisation is also projected on a (typically large) screen behind the performers for visual feedback to the audience. Figure 1 shows the components of the framework. In the rest of this section, we describe how these components work and interact.

3.2 Mobile Client Application

Mood Conductor opens a real-time communication channel in the context of improvised music performances. The mobile client allows the audience to indicate a target mood or emotion they would consider desirable, interesting, appropriate or otherwise aesthetically pleasing, and they would like to be expressed by the performers. This is achieved using a Web-based application suitable for smartphones that provides an easy to use interface to indicate emotion on the two-dimensional arousal-valence (AV) space [19,25], ranging from roughly positive to negative on the x axis, and calm to energetic on the y axis. The emotion tags closest to the selected point on the AV plane, such as "joyful" or "relaxed", are also shown on screen.

The client is a Web-based application written in JavaScript and HTML5 that runs in any modern Web browser. It is automatically downloaded when a designated URL[4] is dereferenced. This design allows Mood Conductor to be used in a platform independent manner on any mobile phone that is capable of accessing the internet and running a conventional Web browser. The client displays an interactive screen showing the arousal-valence space (see Fig. 3a) and allows the selection of an emotion coordinate. The client recognises the coordinates of prominent mood words using different databases of mood word to AV coordinate mappings. These databases are described in Sect. 4. The selected mood coordinates are communicated to the server by a designated API call using an XML HTTP request.

3.3 Mood Conductor Server

Individual user inputs are clustered by a server-side application that is also accessed by a visualisation client which produces a projection of the cumulative responses. The Mood Conductor server is a Python program written using

---

4 http://bit.ly/moodxp2.

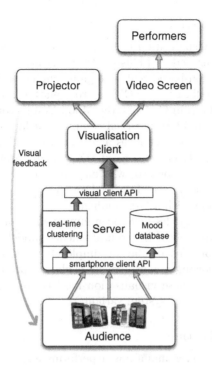

Fig. 1. Overview of the Mood Conductor framework. The audience interacts with the system using a Web-based smartphone application that allows to select emotion cues. Visual feedback is received via a projection of clustered responses situated behind the performers.

CherryPy[5], a self-contained Web application server library. The server provides two simple APIs for communication with the audience (mobile) and visualisation clients. Most importantly, the server accepts data from the audience and registers the coordinates of the selected emotion, as well as the corresponding time. Note that for simplicity potential network delays are ignored in the current implementation. The server aggregates the user input using a real-time constrained clustering process described in Sect. 4.1. The purpose of the clustering is to reduce the complexity of user inputs, and aid visualisation that facilitates the interpretation of audience interaction by the performers. Essentially, the server provides an API function to be accessed by the visualisation client to retrieve data from the server. This provides information such as the cluster centres, the number of input samples or observations assigned to each cluster, and the time when each cluster was spawned.

---

[5] http://www.cherrypy.org/.

3.4   Visualisation Client

The Mood Conductor visualisation client dynamically creates a graphical representation of the aggregated and clustered user input. The program is written using PyGame[6], a Python-based real-time game engine, which in turn is based on the Simple DirectMedia Layer (SDL), a cross-platform, free and open source multimedia library written in C. Thus, the Mood Conductor visualisation client can be executed on any modern personal computer or laptop. The visualisation client accesses the server and retrieves aggregated data from the audience via its REST-based API. In later versions of the system (from MC System 2), it also serves as a client for an operator who may modify the server side clustering parameters during a performance. The need for this capability became apparent when trialling the system with a large audience.

Different visualisation modes have been implemented, all relying on projecting aggregated user input into the arousal-valence model of emotions [19,25]. These modes range from the display of simple clustered data represented by coloured spheres, to showing a continuously evolving emotion trajectory in the AV space. The details of these visualisation models are presented in Sect. 4 in the context of each respective system variant.

3.5   User Data Collection

The Mood Conductor server maintains a performance log in which we collect information about the audience indicated emotions registered by the server. This process logs the IP address of each device for each received input, together with the coordinates of the indicated position on the AV plane, and the time of registration for each data point. The data collection is implemented simply by using the logging facilities of the web application server.

Table 1 summarises the data collected in four Mood Conductor performances in different venues and with significantly different audience sizes. Albeit the system logs IP addresses, individual user tracking is not yet implemented as we preferred an anonymous model for the interaction with the mobile client requiring no registration or login. However, we plan for assigning individual random identifier for connecting clients in the future, to make better use of individual emotion trajectories. As can be seen from the data, IP addresses alone cannot server this purpose, since mobile operators may assign IP addresses in a way that does not resolve individual clients, and also clients may be connected to a central WiFi network of the venue. This was the case during the last concert held in conjunction with the ACII2013 conference, hence the low number of registered IP addresses despite almost all conference participants were present during the conference and interacted with the application.

3.6   Performance Simulation

The Mood Conductor framework has the capability to simulate interaction based on data collected from previous performances as described in Sect. 3.5, or based

---

[6] www.pygame.org.

Table 1. Summary of data collected during the most well attended Mood Conductor performances.

Concert and venue	Approx. audience size	Unique IPs	Duration (min.)	Number of emotion cues	Mean response rate per sec
Cathedral of Strasbourg (Concert #2)	150	456	15	5392	6.22
Harold Pinter Drama Studio (Concert #3)	45	68	29	5429	3.72
Hack the Barbican (Concert #5)	70	49	60	5931	2.32
ACII Artistic Event (Concert #7)	200	11	45	11723	6.08

simply on random data. This data allows us to replay a performance, i.e. recreate the visualisation by providing the clustering and visualisation process with input data identical to what was sent by the audience during a concert performance. The purpose of simulation is twofold. On one hand, it enables fine tuning the visualisation parameters in the absence of a real audience. On the other hand, it serves the means of practicing the interpretation of the kind of visuals generated by the system during rehearsals. Albeit the initial concept of Mood Conductor was developed in collaboration with the VoXP quartet, several performances were held with a diverse range of artists who have not experienced the system before. The simulation capability proved very valuable in preparation for these performances. The simulator itself is implemented as a separate application that parses server logs and sends timestamped messages to the Mood Conductor server. Therefore it can also be used to test the capabilities of the network available at different performance venues.

4   Evaluations and Iterations of the Framework

The Mood Conductor framework follows a common system architecture and some basic principles with regards to the interaction and visualisation models. Several variants with different features have been built and evaluated so far. These variants can be grouped into three systems based on their user clients and visualisation modes, representing three landmarks in the development of the framework. Figure 2 illustrates the development process, the distinctive features of these systems, and their relation to concert performances and evaluations conducted in conjunction with these performances. In this section, we provide the technical details of each system, describe the respective performances where each system was used and trialled, detail on the evaluation methods and observations during these performances, and outline the results and conclusions which enabled further developments of the framework.

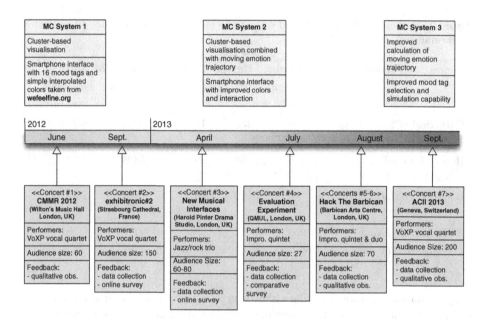

Fig. 2. Development timeline of the Mood Conductor Framework.

4.1 MC System 1

The initial version of Mood Conductor (MC System 1) was developed for the 'New Resonances Festival' held during the CMMR 2012 conference. This version featured the simplest mobile client interface and cluster-based visualisation as described in the following sections. System 1 was used during the first three Mood Conductor performances. Figure 3 shows its interface and a photo taken during concert #3 with the visualisation projected in the background.

Mobile Client Interface. The interface of the first system (see Fig. 3a) allows the user to indicate emotion on the two-dimensional arousal-valence (AV) space, which was shown to be a good representation of internal human emotion states [25] also relevant in the music domain. While this provides an effective way to gather the intent of each individual user in a continuous space, we do not consider the space to be readily interpretable by any member of the audience. We therefore combine the continuous representation with a discrete emotion model provided by a small number of mood tags displayed in the AV space. To find a mapping between mood words and AV coordinates, system one uses the Affective norm for English words (ANEW) database [5] developed to provide a set of normative emotional ratings for a large number of words in English. To avoid confusion resulting from the potential proximity of several words on the AV plane, especially when a small screen is considered, the system uses only some selected words from ANEW such as "serious", "relaxed", "calm", "fun" or "sad", that were deemed dominant in the authors opinion.

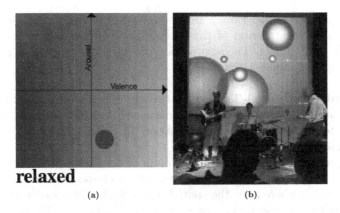

Fig. 3. (3a) Graphical user interface (GUI) of the Mood Conductor application for audience's suggestions. (3b) Visualisation of the audience's emotional directions with coloured spherical blobs. The higher the number of users indicating an emotion cue, the larger the blobs.

To prevent any single user from overwhelming the system by repeatedly selecting the same or different emotions, the client employs a blocking strategy that does not allow transmitting a different emotion within a predefined time limit. This time limit is experimentally defined, and currently set to 1000 ms. Albeit, this mitigates problems resulting form quickly repeated clicks, it still enables users to emphasise a certain area in the emotion space, potentially competing with other users.

Visualisation. The visualisation created by MC System 1 is also based on the arousal-valence model. Clustered user inputs are projected on the AV plane. Each cluster is represented by a spherical coloured blob drawn over dark background, whose size is proportional to the number of input samples associated with the cluster. The colours are selected using a gradient colour map that associate areas of the AV space with conventionally accepted colours[7] (e.g. anger with red) of prominent moods. While this selection is fairly subjective, it serves an aesthetic purpose in our application. Each blob is then drawn using a colour gradient generated between the selected emotion colour and the background. This produces a 3D effect which may create the impression that the clusters are represented by "planets" or "stars" in the "universe of emotions"[8]. The size of each sphere may be changed dynamically as new user inputs are assigned to clusters using a slow animation. To better reflect the continuously changing nature of emotion expressed by improvised music, the visualisation of each cluster is time limited. Unless new input is registered for a given cluster, its corresponding blob is faded towards the background colour at a constant rate by decreasing

---

[7] Colour codes for some prominent emotion were taken from the following resource: http://www.wefeelfine.org/data/files/feelings.txt.

[8] See photos at: http://bit.ly/moodcphotos.

its opacity (alpha channel value). In the current implementation, each blob is faded away in a fixed period of time (several seconds) after the last input is registered for that cluster. The next section provides more specific details about the clustering and visualisation method.

Time-Constrained Real-Time Clustering. The main algorithm driving the visualisation system uses a time-constrained real-time process, conceptually related to nearest neighbour classification [7], mean-shift clustering [6], and ensemble tracking [2].

User input is organised using a maximum of N clusters that correspond to blobs B_i ($i = 1, 2, ..., N$) visualised on screen. Each cluster is associated with the 3-tuple $(\boldsymbol{x}_i, c_i, t_i)$, where $\boldsymbol{x}_i$ is the spatial centre of the cluster on the AV plane, c_i is the number of observations or user inputs associated with cluster i, and t_i represents the time of the cluster object construction. Each input sample S received via the smartphone API is associated with the tuple $(\boldsymbol{x}_s, t_s)$, where $\boldsymbol{x}_s$ is the spatial coordinate of the user-indicated emotion on the AV plane, and t_s is the time when the input is registered. Let K_s be a spatial kernel such that

$$K_s(x) = \begin{cases} 1 & \text{if} \;\; ||x|| \leq \lambda_s \\ 0 & \text{if} \;\; ||x|| > \lambda_s, \end{cases} \tag{1}$$

and T_s a temporal kernel such that

$$T_s(t) = \begin{cases} 1 & \text{if} \;\; t \leq \tau_s \\ 0 & \text{if} \;\; t > \tau_s, \end{cases} \tag{2}$$

where λ_s and τ_s are server-side parameters representing spatial and temporal tolerances. For every user input S received via the smartphone API, a new cluster is constructed if nb_S in Eq. (3) evaluates to zero, that is, if we can not find an existing cluster within the spatial and temporal constraints designated by λ_s and τ_s to which the new input might be assigned to.

$$nb_S = \sum_{i=1}^{N} K_s(x_s - x_i) T_s(t_s - t_i) \tag{3}$$

In case $nb_s \geq 1$, the input is associated to the cluster denoted B' that minimises $d(x_s, x_i)$ for all B_i, where d is the Euclidean distance. In essence, this makes the process adhere to a nearest neighbour classification rule which minimises the probability of classification error [7]. The parameters of $B'(\boldsymbol{x}', c', t')$ are updated according to the following: $c' \leftarrow c+1$ while $t' \leftarrow t_s$; however, x', the spacial centre of the cluster remains unchanged in the current implementation. In an alternative implementation to be tested in the future, we may update x' to shift towards the cluster centre defined by the new sample mean of registered audience inputs, similarly to a k-means or mean-shift clustering approach [6]. However, this may create abrupt changes in the appearance of already displayed clusters. It remains future work to assess the usefulness of this alternative technique from our application's point of view.

In the current implementation, we set N, the number of clusters displayed at any one time, to an experimentally defined fixed value (see next section). Clusters and associated colour blobs are removed if this value is exceeded. The mechanism is implemented using a fixed length first-in, first-out (FIFO) queue. Moreover, regardless of their position in the queue, colour blobs are removed by the visualisation client when their age exceeds the predefined time threshold τ_c. This parameter is linked to the server side parameter τ_s, albeit they may be adjusted separately.

Performances with MC System 1. Three interactive music performances were organised using MC system 1 (see Fig. 2). The first two were held in collaboration with vocal VoXP, while the third performance was held in collaboration with a jazz/rock trio (drums, bass, guitar). These performances provided means for fine-tuning some of the parameters of the system during rehearsals, as well as for evaluating the system using feedback from the audience as well as the musicians.

Concert #1 was held during the CMMR 2012 "New Resonances Festival: Music, Machines and Emotions"[9] with an audience of about 60 people. The three primary parameters defined for the visualisation and clustering algorithm are N the total number of clusters or blobs allowed, λ_s the spatial proximity tolerance that governs how inputs are assigned to existing clusters, and τ_s the temporal constraint on clustering. During rehearsals these values were set to $N = 15$, $\lambda_s = 0.08$ (in normalised Euclidean space) and $\tau_s = 17s$.

Concert #2 was held as part of the Electroacoustic Music festival "exhibitronic#2". More than 150 members of the audience used the system[10]. During this concert, we used the same parameters as described above. While this worked well overall, we found that the visualisation became cluttered or chaotic during parts of the performance, especially in the first couples of minutes. This suggested that the clustering parameters need to be tuned differently for larger audiences, and also that there is a learning curve while the audience tries to familiarise with the application, and discover the meaning of locations and associated mood words on the AV plane. Musicians may also need time to learn how to adapt to more diverse responses of a large audience. Mutual adaptation however gradually allowed the performance to converge towards common directions and to become more uniform.

The third performance was held in the Harold Pinter Drama Studio as part of the 'New Musical Interfaces' concert, with a drums, bass and guitar trio, playing improvised music influenced by jazz and rock. During concert #3, the audience was asked to start and stop the performance using the Mood Conductor application to emphasise the idea of "conducting" the ensemble. To this end, the musicians started the performance as the audience started to interact, and stopped a piece as the audience stopped the interaction. This idea however was only partly successful as the audience preferred to interact continuously, therefore the

---

[9] http://cmmr2012.eecs.qmul.ac.uk/music-programme.
[10] Photos can be found online at http://bit.ly/moodcphotos.

performance consisted of a single improvised piece. Based on our experience from the Strasbourg performance, two modifications to the system were introduced before this concert, in order to better accommodate for a larger audience. We configured the visualisation parameters slightly differently ($N = 18$, $\lambda_s = 0.15$ and $\tau_s = 12s$), which provided smoother visual feedback with a larger audience. This is probably due to the fact that similar moods were clustered together as a result of the increased λ_s parameter, and higher number of colour blobs were allowed at any one time, resulting in fewer deletions as blobs are dropping out of a fixed length queue, i.e., more blobs were allowed to fade out gradually. Finally, to accommodate potentially swifter responses, the τ_s parameter was decreased.

Collected Data Analytics. We collected data from the audience during the performances in the Cathedral of Strasbourg (concert #2) and the Harold Pinter Drama Studio (concert #3, see summary in Table 1).

During concert #2, the system received between three to 17 indicated emotion responses each second with 6.22 responses per second on average. With respect to the AV plane [19,25], the highest number of responses occurred along the diagonal corresponding to "tiredness" vs. "energy" in Thayer's model, with a high number of responses in the negative-low ("melancholy", "dark", "atmospheric") and positive-high ("humour", "silly", "fun") quadrants. A richer cluster of responses was observed in the middle of the plane and at the positive end of the valence axis corresponding to mood words such as "happy", "pleased", or "glad".

During the third concert, between one to 15 indicated emotion responses were received each second with an average of 3.72. Since the performance was almost twice as long, but the size of the audience was smaller (about 40–50 % of that in concert #2), these data seem to indicate a very similar level of engagement during these two concerts. A similar pattern of audience responses can be observed with regards to the AV plane with one notable difference. A more emphasised cluster of mood indications can be observed in the quadrant corresponding to negative valence and high arousal ("aggressive", "energetic", "brutal"), which seems to suggest a different genre bias in case of the rock/jazz influenced performance.

Qualitative Observations. Informal observation on the evolution of these performance suggests that the behaviour of the audience members includes *exploratory*, genuinely *musical*, as well as possibly *game-like* interaction. Exploratory interaction commonly happens during the first phase of a performance, and may be explained by two factors: *(i)* the need for exploring the emotion space (e.g. the assignment of mood words to positions on the AV plane), and *(ii)* observing the initial response of the performers to the clustered and visualised audience input. This phase is occasionally followed by a period of time where audience members focus on different quadrants of the AV plane, or different contrasting emotions. This behaviour was observed for short time durations of up to 20–30 s. It may be interpreted as game-like, i.e., audience members converge, but try to steer the performance towards different contending directions.

As performances evolve and the audiences' understanding of the system deepens, a slower and more balanced interplay between performers and listeners develops. During this phase, the majority of audience members appear to focus on a prominent emotion area, typically indicating related emotions that are close to each other on the AV plane. The audience either moves slowly from a given emotion to other musically relevant emotion, or start to follow a new emotion selected by a minority in the audience. The observed convergence of listeners often leads to a slowly evolving trajectory spanning the AV plane, and allows the performers to express each emotion area more deeply, as well as to explore how musical improvisation techniques may be used to convey particular emotions. These informal observations allow us to form a number of hypotheses about the commonly occurring interaction types with Mood Conductor and the overall effectiveness of the system. Testing these hypotheses using the collected data (see Sect. 3.5) constitutes future work.

Evaluation. We conducted a user survey [17] to assess the various components of MC System 1 (web application, data visualisation technique), collect feedback on the experience and level of engagement during live performances, and collect suggestions for improvement. Two sets of self-completion questionnaires were designed for audience members and performers using the surveymonkey.com platform. Participants from Concerts #2 and #3 (see Fig. 2) were invited to take part in the online survey by email. In total, 35 participants comprising 29 audience members and 6 performers (3 singers, 1 guitarist, 1 bass player, 1 drummer) took part in the experiment. The answers from audience and performer participants are summarised in Fig. 4a and b.

As can be seen in Fig. 4a, about two thirds of the audience participants found the web application easy to use. This result highlighted the relevance and intuitiveness of the arousal/valence (AV) space as a means to convey emotional cues (note that audience members were given explanations on the AV space and how to use the app prior to the performances). Although a large proportion of participants found the mood tags and AV space colour mapping helpful, the fact that it didn't reach a consensus showed scope for improvement in the design of the user interface. The strongest flaw of the system was shown to be the cluster-based visualisation as more participants found it unclear and confusing rather than the opposite. Relatedly, most audience participants were not sure as to whether the emotional cues conveyed using the app had been followed by the performers well. The feedback from performers on the visualisation (see Fig. 4b) corroborates that of audience participants, as two third of the performers found the visualisation unclear and none of them found the emotional cues easy to follow. Although MC System 1 was considered somewhat distracting by performers when creating musical improvisation, all of them expressed a strong interest in performing again with the system and its future iterations.

The audience participants highlighted several issues with the web application. A better adaptation of the user interface to the dimensions of mobile devices' screen and a more attractive design was sought for. Some participants mentioned that there were some latency after selection on the screen. It is worth noting

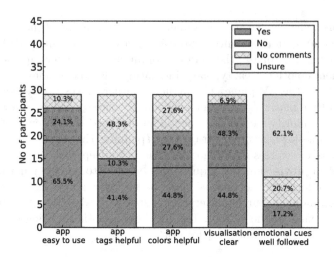

(a) Evaluation of the MC System 1 by audience participants.

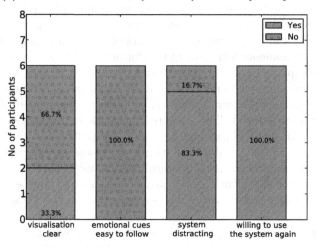

(b) Evaluation of the the MC System 1 by performers.

Fig. 4. Evaluation of the MC System 1 by audience participants.

that a delay was introduced intentionally to throttle the bandwidth, and also to prevent a single user from overwhelming the system. Some participants didn't know whether they had to tap a point continuously or only once on their touch screen for the data to be sent and wished to be able to see the mood tags before selecting an emotion point in the space. Refining the discretisation of the AV space to cover more mood categories was another suggested improvement. Some participants suggested to add an "introduction" or "clear instructions" in the application to guide users.

Table 2. Issues in the MC System 1 and proposed solutions.

MC System 1 web application issues	Proposed solutions in MC System 2
The interface does not consistently fit mobile devices' screen sizes	Platform-dependent adjustment of the UI size
More attractive user interface	Partial solutions: refinement of the color transitions in the AV space canvas
	Mood tags displayed in the AV space rather than at the bottom
No clear instructions on how to communicate with performers	Adding of help instructions in the web app
Data are sometimes sent unintentionally	Adding of a button to choose when to send the data
Occurrences of delay between selection and visualisation	Adding of warnings when emotional cues are sent too rapidly
MC System 1 visualisation issues	Proposed solutions in MC System 2
The clustered bubbles shown on screen are confusing	New visualisation
Audience and performers have difficulties to interpret the data	New visualisation
Changes of emotional intentions are too fast to follow for performers	Adding constraints on moving average trajectory

Some suggestions made by both audience participants and performers indicated that the visualisation would become clearer if it was possible to follow a single emotional cue, for instance the average of the audience's votes. Some participants indicated that, as in the app, mood tags should be displayed to help uncovering the emotions related to the clusters. The suggestions of the performers reached a consensus on several points: (i) when split votes occurred in the audience, it was very hard to figure out which emotional direction to follow, (ii) even in the case of a single emotional direction, time was required to be able to satisfactorily interpret the associated emotion, (iii) the changes of emotional directions were too fast to follow. Table 2 summarises the issues arising from the evaluation of MC System 1 and the proposed solutions implemented in MC System 2.

4.2   MC System 2

Mood Conductor System 2 was used during an evaluation experiment held at the Media and Arts Technology (MAT) Laboratory of QMUL. The system features an improved mobile device interface and a new visualisation model that uses a time-varying emotion trajectory projected in the AV space. The purpose of this was to evaluate the changes proposed in the previous section in a controlled laboratory environment. Figure 5 illustrates the new mobile client interface and the changes to the visualisation model. The following sections describe the implementation details between system 1 and system 2.

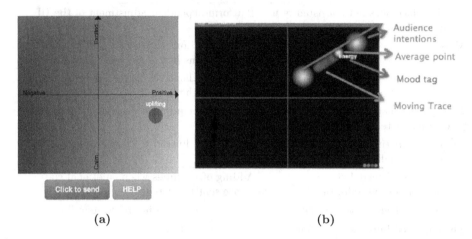

(a)   (b)

Fig. 5. (5a) Updated (GUI) of the Mood Conductor application for audience's suggestions. (5b) Visualisation of the audience's emotional directions including a moving blob and trace indicating an emotion trajectory.

Mobile Client Interface. The client interface of this system (see Fig. 5a) features a space with finer colour gradient on the canvas, and most importantly, a different interaction model that requires the user to press an additional button to send information to the server, rather than sending information at every touch of the screen (assuming a touchscreen device). Additionally, mood words are displayed next to a selected area in the AV space, and a help feature was added providing some information about the usage of the client interface.

The rationale behind changing the interaction model arose from two requirements. First, it became apparent during the evaluation of the previous system that audience members often need more time to discover the relationships between mood words and locations on the AV plane. This was supported both by survey data and qualitative observations as well as the tendency of the collected data following a uniform distribution during the first few minutes of the performance while audience members were experimenting with the interface. Second, although System 1 throttled the communication from client to server, it was still possible to overwhelm MC by continuously clicking on a single location, encouraging occasional game-like interaction between audience members. Having to press a button to send a new emotion direction is assumed to encourage more gradual changes in intent during interaction.

Visualisation in System 2. In MC System 1, clusters of emotional intentions are represented as blobs or spheres in the AV space whose size depends on the number of people who have selected an emotional intention in the corresponding area. Using this visualisation model, musicians typically relied on the dominant emotional intention to improvise. However, as pointed out by performers and audience members, it was not always easy to determine which blobs corresponds to the emotional intention of the majority, since blobs located in different parts of the AV space happened to have similar sizes, especially in the case of large audiences [18]. To overcome this issue, and thus ease the cognitive load on musicians interpreting the visualisation, a continuously moving sphere was added to the visualisation that intends to represent the average emotional direction indicated by the audience. This visualisation follows the normalised weighted average of all active clusters represented by the blob $M(x)$, where x is the spatial coordinate of the moving sphere. A gradually fading trace of $M(x)$ was also added to the visualisation. The coordinates of M are updated upon each change in the cluster configuration according to Eq. (4):

$$x = \frac{\sum_{i=1}^{N} B_i(x)B_i(c)}{\sum_{i=1}^{N} B_i(c)}, \tag{4}$$

where $B_i(x)$ is the spatial centre of cluster B_i, and $B_i(c)$ is the number of users inputs associated with that cluster.

4.3   Comparative Evaluation of MC Systems 1 and 2

We conducted an experiment to compare MC Systems 1 and 2 in the context of a live performance and to determine which of the two systems was judged best by the audience and performers [18]. An improvisation ensemble gathering 5 performers (harp and singer, flutist and singer, guitarist, drummer, keyboard player) was created for the purpose of the experiment which was held in the Performance space of the Media, Arts and Technology program at QMUL. A rehearsal was organised with the performers to let them become familiar with the two systems before the experiment. Two projector screens were used for visual feedback, one located behind the performers for the audience, and the other one located behind the audience, for performers.

27 audience participants were recruited amongst students and staff at QMUL (10 males and 17 females, aged between 21 and 43 years old). Each audience participant and performer was paid for the experiment. The audience participants were divided into two groups (a group of 13 and a group of 14). To account for possible order effects in judgements about the systems, the order of use of the two systems was alternated for the two groups. Each group was first introduced to the MC framework and was given explanations about the arousal/valence space. For each system, two short performances were given during which the audience participants had to use the MC app to convey emotional cues to the performers from their mobile devices or laptops. Right after the end of the interactive performances, the audience participants had to complete an online questionnaire[11] on

---

[11] Audience participants' questionnaires: session 1: http://bit.ly/mcs1q1 and http://bit.ly/mcs1q2 ; session 2: http://bit.ly/mcs2q1 and http://bit.ly/mcs2q2.

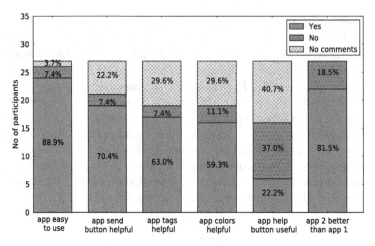

(a) Evaluation of the MC System 2 app by audience participants.

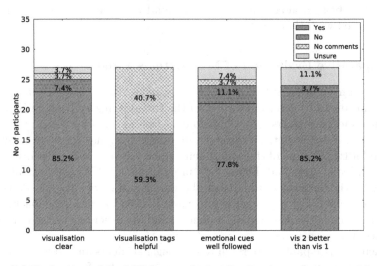

(b) Evaluation of the MC System 2 visualisation by audience participants.

Fig. 6. Evaluation of the MC System 2 app by audience participants.

computers from the MAT laboratory. The performers also completed an online questionnaire[12] after their performances.

Figure 6 presents a summary of the audience participants' assessment of the web application and visualisation technique used in MC System 2. 82 % of the participants preferred the app in MC System 2 which validated the benefit of the modifications made after the first evaluation listed in Table 2 (e.g. send button, refinement of color transitions, display of mood tags in AV space). However,

---

[12] Performers' questionnaire: http://bit.ly/mcperformer

only 22 % of the participants found the help button useful which showed that the instructions have to be presented in a better manner. The improvements in the visualisation of MC System 2 (moving average) were also clearly demonstrated by the survey as 85 % of the audience participants found it better than that of the initial system (cluster). While only 17 % of the audience participants had found that the emotional cues were well followed by the performers in the previous evaluation of MC System 1 (see Fig. 4a), most participants (79 %) found that the performers well followed their emotional cues with MC System 2 (see Fig. 6b). The visualisation improvements provided by MC System 2 were also acknowledged by performers who found (80 %) the second visualisation system was better than the previous one and all found that the emotional cues were easy to follow (see Fig. 7), albeit by qualitative judgement, the moving trace was not responsive enough and often stuck in the middle of the space.

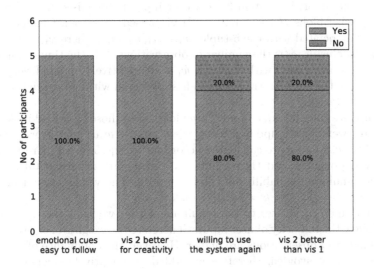

Fig. 7. Evaluation of the MC System 2 visualisation by performers.

4.4 MC System 3

The final system in our current framework builds upon the improvements of MC System 2 with additional modifications in the visualisation model. The main difference lies in the way the desired emotion trajectory is computed. Both mobile client interfaces remain usable in this system, but in the last performances (concerts #5-7) the user interface of System 2 was used. However, instead of using tags from the ANEW database, we used a music specific tag database obtained by mapping production music tags to locations in the AV space as described in [20].

Visualisation in System 3. To overcome some of the limitations in the way System 2 estimates the emotion trajectory suggested by the audience, we implemented a number of refinements in updating the location of the moving blob and associated trace. Intuitively, we would like new user input that is associated with larger clusters to be weighted higher than other user input, to avoid the emotion directions to be simply 'averaged out' over time. At the same time, to help the musicians' interpretation and artistic rendering of the trajectory, we would like relatively smooth transitions from one area of the emotion space to another, which still depends on choices made by the majority of the audience. However, previous experiments showed that audience members' emotional cues occasionally cluster in dissimilar emotion areas. Albeit we would like the system to be unbiased, artists following the emotion trajectory should be able to explore different areas of the space. To realise these divergent requirements, System 3 adopts the following model in estimating the emotion trajectory.

Adaptive Emotion Trajectory Estimation. Similarly to previous variants of Mood Conductor, in System 3 each user input is organised into N clusters associated with blobs B_i $(i = 1, 2, ..., N)$ visualised on screen. Clusters in this system are associated with the 5-tuple $(x_i, c_i, t_i, w_i, m_i)$, where x_i is the spatial centre of the cluster, c_i is the number of observations, t_i is the timestamp of the last user input associated with cluster i, w_i is an adaptively updated weight, and m_i is the time the emotion trajectory is first observed within a spacial tolerance λ_p of the cluster.

The update rules for x_i, c_i, and t_i are identical to those described in Sect. 4.1. The cluster weights are updated using $w' \leftarrow (w_c c + w_a a)^k p$ at every new user input, where c, a and p are calculated according to Eqs. 5, 6, and 7 respectively, while the exponent k and the weights w_c and w_a are experimentally defined using the simulation capability of the framework. The values are currently set to $w_c = 16$, $w_a = 0.5$ and $k = 7$.

The parameter c relates to the requirement that we want the trajectory to clearly follow the majority of user inputs. Therefore the weights of clusters with a higher number of observations are higher. However, the dominance of any single cluster should be avoided, therefore we added an adaptively calculated upper limit on the number of user inputs considered. This parameter is calculated as follows:

$$c = \begin{cases} B_i(c) & \text{if } B_i(c) < \lambda_c \\ \lambda_c & \text{otherwise,} \end{cases} \tag{5}$$

where λ_c represents the maximum number of user inputs considered. This value is updated once per second and depends on the current input rate, i.e., the number of audience directions sent to the server per second, reflecting the size and activity of the audience. The typical values of λ_c fluctuate between 15–30 with audience sizes of concerts #5-7 (see Table 1).

The parameter a allows clusters with newer audience responses to be weighted higher than clusters with older input. It is calculated according to Eq. 6:

$$a = \begin{cases} \tau_f - (t - B_i(t)) & \text{if } t - B_i(t) < \tau_f \\ 0 & \text{otherwise,} \end{cases} \tag{6}$$

where t is the current time and $B_i(t)$ is the time the last input was assigned to cluster B_i. Therefore $t - B_i(t)$ represents the relative age of the cluster. The time constant τ_f is experimentally defined and is set to 10s.

The parameter p depends on the time elapsed since the trajectory was first observed within a spacial tolerance ($\lambda_p = 0.13$ in the normalised Euclidean space) of cluster B_i. This parameter relates to the requirement that we would like to facilitate smooth transitions from one area to another on the AV plane, while avoiding a single emotion area to dominate the performance. The value of p is calculated as follows:

$$p = \begin{cases} \frac{1}{10(B_i(m)-\tau_p+1)} & \text{if} \quad B_i(m) \geq \tau_p \\ 1 & \text{otherwise,} \end{cases} \tag{7}$$

where $B_i(m)$ is the time the emotion trajectory is first observed within a spacial tolerance of the cluster, and τ_p is a time constant currently set to 35s. The value of $B_i(m)$ is zero until $M(x)$ is observed within the tolerance of B_i, that is, $d_{Eucl}(B_i(x), M(x)) > \lambda_p$. The effect of this rule is that the weight of cluster B_i is gradually diminished if the area has been active and the moving blob $M(x)$ has been close to the cluster for more than the time designated by τ_p. The actual visualisation of the trajectory then follows the normalised weighted average of all active clusters, similarly to Eq. 4, but with the adaptive cluster weighting $B_i(w)$ used in place of $B_i(c)$ which depends only on input counts.

Performances Observations. MC System 3 was used in two performances (Concerts #5 & 6) held at the end of the Mood Conductor residency during the Hack The Barbican festival (Barbican Arts Centre, London, August 2013)[13]. Concert #5 was given by an ensemble of five musicians including a singer/flutist, a singer/harpist, a keyboard player, a guitarist and a cahon/percussion player while Concert #6 was given in a duo configuration (vocals/flute and guitar). The video provided at the link below[14] shows some excerpts of Concert #5 corresponding to interactions in the four main quadrants of the arousal/valence space (funny, calm, depressive, scary). The concert was well-received with approximately 70 audience members including 49 active participants (see Table 1). Qualitative comparisons of video recordings from Concert #3 and #5 shows that the emotional cues from the audience spanned a wide range of emotions across the arousal/valence space in Concert #5 whilst cues in the "sad" and "angry" quadrants were predominant in Concert #3. We hypothesise that this finding comes from two factors, first the improved visualisation system (moving average) encourages the audience to build emotional trajectories in the AV space (in case of completely split votes, the average would be stuck in the middle resulting in neutral/boring performances, so audience members may choose their cues creating movements in the space), second, the emotional cues selected by the audience are influenced by the instrumentation due to a feedback loop with the music being played (the jazz/rock trio configuration of Concert #3 was

---

[13] http://lanyrd.com/scmwgx and http://lanyrd.com/scmxby.
[14] http://bit.ly/mcbarbican.

favourable to playing sad and angry music, therefore audience members tended to be biased toward these emotions, whereas the wide diversity of instruments in Concert #5 and the presence of a harp producing particularly soft timbres invited audience members to try the various quadrants of the AV space).

The Mood Conductor project was selected as the artistic event of the 5th International Conference on Affective Computing (ACII 2013). This concert was the one with the largest number of participants so far with an audience of about 200 people. The concert was performed by the Strasbourg-based vocal quartet VoXP. A video recording of the performance can be found at the link provided below[15]. As for Concert #5, a wide range of emotions spanning the AV space were performed by the vocal quartet over the course of the performance. Qualitative observations of the video recording show that the large amount of incoming data induce frequent changes of directions of the average cluster. Although this encourages musical diversity, this may hinder the performers to establish clear emotions which requires a sufficiently large time window. Finding additional mechanisms preventing too rapid shifts of the moving average in the case of "big" incoming data will be the focus of further research.

5   Conclusions and Future Work

We described Mood Conductor, a novel framework for audience-directed interactive performances that is well suited for facilitating improvisation in music, using a new form of audience feedback. The framework opens a new communication channel between the audience and musicians that proved to be valuable in seven public improvised music performances.

Several variants of the system were built and evaluated in substantially different venues with different audience sizes. We found that although some parameters of Mood Conductor are sensitive to the number of participants using its Web-based mobile application, the communication works even with suboptimal parameter settings after some adaptation by both the audience and the performers, supported by the analyses of a survey we obtained both from performers and audience members. Several solutions to the parameter optimisation problem might exist. An easily implemented extension allows the use of the new configuration API provided by the server, in order to manually tune the parameters during a performance. Further criteria might be introduced in the algorithm described in Sect. 4.1 to allow automatic adaptation to the rate and distribution of the incoming data. Lastly, data recorded during concerts may be replayed during rehearsals for further evaluation by the artists. This can be used to create a parameter database that allows for estimating the correct settings for each type of performance and for different audience sizes.

From a research perspective, one of the main merits and novelty of the Mood Conductor system is that it allows for examining the interaction between artists and audience using technology. The recorded data can be used in music emotion studies, and analysed in the context of recorded audio. More work is required

---

[15] http://bit.ly/mc_acii2013_video.

however to evaluate further aspects of the system. It may be possible to further improve the visualisation by employing different clustering strategies and additional visualisation models to the cluster and trajectory based models tested so far. For instance, mean-shift clustering [6] may represent the user input more accurately, on the expense of potentially more complex visualisations. The AV space may be replaced by other dimensional representations of emotions, and the blobs may be replaced by several continuous trajectories.

In the first parts of Concerts #5-7, the performers played several improvisations based on predetermined emotion trajectories (e.g. from calm to neutral to angry). Audience members were asked to use the MC app in a reverse manner, i.e. to rate the emotions perceived in the musical improvisations played by the performers, rather than to send emotional cues. Future research will look at finding the correlations between the emotional intentions of the performers and the listeners' data collected with the MC app.

An intriguing research question is presented by the need to define a reliable and objective measure of coherency that reflects the overall quality of communication between musicians and the audience. To this end, we may develop two alternative client interfaces that allow to split the audience into two groups: one conducting the performance as initially devised in our system, the other indicating perceived emotion. A possible way to define a coherency measure is then to select suitable correlation statistics to be calculated between the data sets collected from the two groups, appropriately corrected for a possible time lag.

Acknowledgments. The authors acknowledge the kind contribution of the vocal quartet VoXP who performed during some of the events detailed in this paper, and Matthias Gregori from SoundCloud Ltd. who implemented the client interface of MC System 1. This work was partly funded by the EPSRC Grant EP/K009559/1, the TSB funded "Making Musical Mood Metadata" project (TS/J002283/1), the EPSRC and AHRC Centre for Doctoral Training in Media and Arts Technology (EP/L01632X/1), and the EPRRC funded "Fusing Semantic and Audio Technologies for Intelligent Music Production and Consumption" (FAST-IMPACt) project (EP/L019981/1).

References

1. Asmus, E.P.: Nine affective dimensions. Technical report, University of Miami (1986)
2. Avidan, S.: Ensemble tracking. In: IEEE Computer Society Conference on Computer Vision and Pattern Recognition (CVPR'05), San Diego, California, USA (2005)
3. Barkhuus, L., Jørgensen, T.: Engaging the crowd: studies of audience-performer interaction. In: CHI '08 Extended Abstracts on Human Factors in Computing Systems, CHI EA '08, pp. 2925–2930. New York (2008)
4. Barthet, M., Fazekas, G., Sandler, M.: Music emotion recognition: from content- to context-based models. In: Aramaki, M., Barthet, M., Kronland-Martinet, R., Ystad, S. (eds.) CMMR 2012. LNCS, vol. 7900, pp. 228–252. Springer, Heidelberg (2013)

5. Bradley, M., Lang, P.J.: Affective norms for english words: instruction manual and affective ratings. Technical Report C-2, University of Florida (2010)
6. Cheng, Y.: Mean shift, mode seeking, and clustering. IEEE Trans. Pattern Anal. Mach. Intell. **17**(8), 790–799 (1995)
7. Cover, T.M., Hart, P.E.: Nearest neighbor pattern classification. IEEE Trans. Inf. Theor. **13**(1), 21–27 (1967)
8. Dean, R.: Creative Improvisation: Jazz, Contemporary Music and Beyond. Open University Press, Philadelphia (1989)
9. Fazekas, G., Barthet, M., Sandler, M.: Mood conductor: emotion-driven interactive music performance. In: International Conference on Affective Computing and Intelligent Interaction (ACII'13), Geneva, Switzerland, 2–5 September 2013 (2013)
10. Fielding, R.T., Taylor, R.N.: Principled design of the modern Web architecture. ACM Trans. Internet Technol. **2**(2), 115–150 (2002)
11. Gorow, R.: Hearing and Writing Music: Professional Training for Today's Musician, 2nd edn. September Publishing, Gardena (2002)
12. Hayes-Roth, B., Sincoff, E., Brownston, L., Huard, R., Lent, B.: Directed improvisation. Technical report, Stanford University (1994)
13. Iacobini, M., Gonsalves, T., Berthouze, N., Frith, C.: Creating emotional communication with interactive artwork. In: 3rd International Conference on Affective Computing and Intelligent Interaction and Workshops, pp. 1–6 (2009)
14. Johnstone, K.: Improvisation and the Theatre. Methuen Drama, London (2007)
15. Kendall, R.A., Carterette, E.C.: The communication of musical expression. Music Percept. **8**(2), 129–164 (1990)
16. Kim, Y., Schmidt, E.M., Emelle, L.: Moodswings: a collaborative game for music mood label collection. In: Proceeding of the International Society for Music Information Retrieval (ISMIR) Conference (2008)
17. Lou, T., Barthet, M., Fazekas, G., Sandler, M.: Evaluation of the Mood Conductor interactive system based on audience and performers' perspectives. In: Proceedings of the 10th International Symposium on Computer Music Multidisciplinary Research (CMMR), pp. 594–609 (2013)
18. Lou, T., Barthet, M., Fazekas, G., Sandler, M.: Evaluation and improvement of the mood conductor interactive system. In: 53rd AES Internationa Conference on Semantic Audio, London, UK, 26–29 January 2014 (2014)
19. Russell, J.A.: A circumplex model of affect. J. Pers. Soc. Psychol. **39**(6), 1161–1178 (1980)
20. Saari, P., Barthet, M., Fazekas, G., Eerola, T., Sandler, M.: Semantic models of musical mood: comparison between crowd-sourced and curated editorial tags. In: Proceedings of IEEE International Conference on Multimedia & Expo (ICME2013) International Workshop on Affective Analysis in Multimedia (AAM), San Jose, CA, USA, 15–19 July 2013 (2013)
21. Schubert, E.: Measuring emotion continuously: validity and reliability of the two-dimensional emotion-space. Aust. J. Psychol. **51**(3), 154–165 (1999)
22. Schubert, E., Ferguson, S., Farrar, N., Taylor, D., McPherson, G.E.: Continuous response to music using discrete emotion faces. In: Barthet, M., Dixon, S. (eds.) Proceedings of the 9th International Symposium on Computer Music Modeling and Retrieval (CMMR'12), pp. 3–19 (2012)
23. Sgouros, N.M.: Supporting audience and player interaction during interactive media performances. In: 2000 IEEE International Conference on Multimedia and Expo, 2000, ICME 2000, vol. 3, pp. 1367–1370 (2000)

24. Sloboda, J.A., Juslin, P.N.: Psychological perspectives on music and emotion. In: Juslin, P.N., Sloboda, J.A. (eds.) Music and Emotion Theory and Research. Series in Affective Science, pp. 71–104. Oxford University Press, Oxford (2001)
25. Thayer, R.E.: The Biopsychology of Mood and Arousal. Oxford University Press, New York (1989)
26. Van Zijl, A.G.W., Sloboda, J.: Performers' experienced emotions in the construction of expressive musical performance: an exploratory investigation. Psychol. Music **39**(2), 196–219 (2010)

The Art of Sonification

Making Data Sing: Embodied Approaches to Sonification

Adam Parkinson[✉] and Atau Tanaka

EAVI, Goldsmiths, University of London, London SE14 6NW, UK
{a.parkinson,a.tanaka}@gold.ac.uk

Abstract. We report on our experiences of two recent sonification pieces we have been involved in; composing for Peter Sinclair's *RoadMusic* project, and creating a multi-speaker installation with sound artist Kaffe Matthews which sonifies the movement of sharks around the Galapagos islands.

We describe these pieces in terms of translation of data into different modalities, and extending the affective capacity of the listener, allowing the data to be experienced viscerally and in an embodied manner, as opposed to intellectually or symbolically. We will discuss how this intersects with theoretical discourses drawn from cognitive science and philosophy.

Keywords: Sonification · Embodiment · Affect · Enaction

1 Introduction

Sonification is, at its most basic, the conversion of something from a non-sound medium into sound. Sonification occurs along a continuum from representation to abstraction. At the representative end of the spectrum we find auditory icons and sonification intended to represent and illustrate processes or data, often in order to educate or inform the listener [9]. The sound is a vessel for meaning, and might be used to illustrate some patterns that are less perceptible through other modalities. One example of this is Alberto di Campo's SonEnvir [3]. Another form of sonification seeks not to represent the data, but to abstract it and subsume it to compositional processes. The data might be used to introduce variety into textures, or to structure compositional ideas: a certain ratio, for instance, extracted from data might be used to structure certain musical relationships throughout a piece. Sonification becomes something of a compositional technique, a way for a composer to introduce elements or patterns that they might not otherwise manually score or sequence, not unlike algorithmic composition. Xenakis, in his piece *Pithoprakta*, used Brownian motion to score glissandi [2].

We propose an approach to sonification that foregrounds an embodied approach to musical experience: sonification can combine elements both of representation and abstraction to "Make Data Sing". The composer/programmer uses the sonification to extend the affective capacities of the listener and allow

© Springer International Publishing Switzerland 2014
M. Aramaki et al. (Eds.): CMMR 2013, LNCS 8905, pp. 151–160, 2014.
DOI: 10.1007/978-3-319-12976-1_9

an embodied experience of the data and the phenomenon behind the data. This chapter is organised as follows. We first describe the related work in sonification. We then describe our own experiences with sonification pieces. Finally, we present our approach within a certain theoretical context, drawing on concepts of embodiment, affect and enaction.

2 Related Work

Composer Larry Polanksy describes the two forms of sonification we introduced above, referring to "scientific" (or representative) sonification and what he terms "manifestation" or "artistic" sonification. To illustrate this, he suggests that a composer practising "manifestation" might use the Gaussian distribution not to hear the Gaussian distribution, rather she might use the Gaussian distribution to allow us to hear new music [12]. Salter et al. discuss these diverse approaches to sonification within the context of their own interactive work which combines different strategies for mapping (drawn from the field of digital instrument design) and sonification, highlighting the unexplored potential in "manifestation" for "computer controlled sound for artistic purposes" [14].

Hunt et al.'s *Sonification Handbook* gives an extensive overview of current sonification practices and research areas, focusing primarily on representative sonification, and the related practice of auditory displays [9]. Through taking advantage of the temporal nature of sound, sonification can represent data when visualization might be ineffective. Alberto di Campo's aforementioned SonEnvir, which facilitates such sonification and allows non-musicians to present data in a way that can be used to better analyse and understand that data, is discussed further in [3]. Ben Tal and Berger's work uses sonification in these two different ways. Some of this explores sonification and pattern detection, whilst they also describe deliberately avoiding representation, using data instead to help bring an "organic" feel into their work, and generate rich and varied sonic textures [2].

Somewhat bridging this dichotomy and moving towards our own position, Barrass and Vickers propose a design - oriented approach to sonification which frames it as a practice where data can be understood and even enjoyed [1]. In an article on sonification for the Oxford Handbook of Sound Studies, Jonathan Sterne notes, "Whilst it is true that in most cases the making audible of information is largely utilitarian, in many others the lines between scientific and artistic production are burnt" [16]. Sterne describes Andrea Polli's approach as blurring these through using acoustic instruments and clear compositional choices alongside more straightforward sonification of data in order to facilitate "the artistic creation of new languages of data interpretation" which articulate something about the phenomenon behind the data [13].

Sonification practices can problematise where we locate creative agency. A related practice which produces similar problems is algorithmic and generative composition. Nick Collins gives an overview of generative and algorithmic music, and engages with debates about the ontological status of these software and the creative and compositional strategies that might emerge from them [5].

Doornbusch discusses Xenakis's use of Brownian motion in scoring glissandi, and makes the important point that this use of sonification is considered composition. Whilst the data might be creating the music, there are still a great deal of compositional decisions taking place which shape how this data will sound.

The authors' experience with sonification extends beyond the specific works described. Tanaka has also worked on sonifying photographic images for a series of works described in [17]. Parkinson has worked with Kaffe Matthews on *Where are the Wild Ones?*, an opera which uses melodic material generated by the movements of wild salmon in the River Tyne. These projects begin to broach the conceptual and compositional issues approached here and through the pieces described.

We will discuss how sonification practices intersect with embodiment, which draws upon ideas of embodied cognition and the embodied mind, through the "extended mind" of Clark and Chalmers [4] and the "embodied enactivism" [18]. Central to these theses are ideas that cognitive processes, and the ways in which we understand and attribute meaning in the world grow out of our interactions with our environments. The mind cannot be thought of as being separate to our bodies, and our understanding of the world is routed in our bodily interactions with it. We also draw upon notions of affect, a concept which refers to interactions between bodies and the potential for bodies to change or be changed by such interactions [8]. Our interactions with the world might be seen as being constituted by affects, and sonification can thus extend our affective capacity by allowing us to hear or feel data that would otherwise remain visual. We relate this to Gilles Deleuze's extension of Spinozan affect, and some Deleuzian notions of the role of art and music in making perceptible certain imperceptible forces [6, 7].

3 Two Sonification Pieces

The first project we discuss involved working with Peter Sinclair's *RoadMusic* system which sonifies the movements of a car in real time for the driver and passengers.

RoadMusic uses. Pure Data software running on a single-board computer attached to the windshield of a car, much in the manner of a sat nav. Accelerometers and a webcam provide the computer with real time data generated during a drive (Fig. 1). The computer's audio output is connected to the car sound system, effectively replacing the car stereo with an interactive music system.

From the accelerometers, one has information about acceleration, deceleration, changes in the road surface, and bends in the road. The webcam gives information about colour balance (which can be used to detect when one enters a built up area, or if it is night or day), and blob tracking is used to detect oncoming objects (for instance, cars in the opposite lane of a motorway). There is also another level of data, as the system logs the frequency of events: from this, one can detect the "bendiness" of the drive or the "bumpiness" of a road, for instance [15].

Fig. 1. The RoadMusic FitPC, fitted with webcam and sensors. Image ©Peter Sinclair

Composers can use the modular nature of Sinclair's software to write their own Pure Data patch to sonify data from the host *RoadMusic* data processing patch. Sinclair commissioned a number of composers - the present authors included - to compose pieces for the system, and presented them at the 2013 Reevox Festival, Marseilles and the 2013 Seconde Nature Festival in Aix-en-Provence. A version of the software which runs as an Android app is soon to be released. The authors have reported on the scientific aspects "Composing for Car" [11].

In the second project, Parkinson worked with sound artist Kaffe Matthews on the installation *You Might Come Out of the Water Every Time Singing*. This piece sonifies data from shark movements in the Galapagos Islands, which was provided by researchers tagging and studying the sharks. The piece was based upon the artist's experience of a residency in Galapagos which involved working with scientists studying the sharks and diving with sharks herself. The piece has been exhibited as part of the Galapagos group show at the Bluecoat Gallery (Liverpool), the Haymarket Gallery (Edinburgh) and the Gulbenkian Museum (Lisbon).

The piece uses an ambisonic speaker setup, with sound spatialised in three dimensions through 8 speakers arranged in a cube, in a space measuring approximately 6 by 6 metres, along with two subwoofers. In the centre of the space is a wooden platform, covered in bamboo mats, and attached to the underside of this are transducers, which vibrate the platform according to the bass frequencies, adding to an embodied, immersive experience. Upon entering the dimly lit room, with the walls shrouded in felt curtains, people are encouraged to remove their shoes and lie upon the platform (Fig. 2).

The piece runs on an Apple Mac Mini, connected to a multichannel soundcard. On the computer, data describing the movements of six sharks in the

Galapagos Islands is cycled through by software written in Max MSP. This data consists of the longitude, latitude and depth of each shark at irregular intervals spanning a two-to-three day period. We also have the temperature of the water at every point of measurement. This gives us five values for each shark: latitude, longitude, depth, speed (derived from these) and temperature. Each shark is represented by a software oscillator, and the data is used to control both the spatial position and timbre of the oscillator associated with each shark. Some effects, such as filtering and reverb, can also be controlled by the data. The system allows Matthews to choose the speed at which the data is cycled through. For instance, a day in the life of a shark could take a day to cycle through, or all the data could be compressed into a few minutes.

The software also plays back samples: in this case, hydrophone recordings made by Matthews. Each sample has a 'spatlog' file associated with it which describes the way in which it is spatialised through time. She controls the way in which the shark data is routed to different parameters of the oscillator through a matrix, and makes a series of snapshots or presets which capture the routing and scaling. A master sequencer describes the relationships between different routing combinations and samples which is cycled through over the course of about 60 min. The same data often ends up having very different sonic effects, depending on the speed, routing and the number of sharks playing. Matthews has so far created three different master sequences, which are effectively compositions for the installation. The software, then, allows for the data to be sonified, but also for the artist/composer to fine tune and shape this data as an expressive material, through tweaking and tuning each preset, and creating the overall structure.

4   Making Data Sing

Through sonification these systems allowed us to "Make Data Sing", allowing for an embodied experience of the data and in some cases the experiential phenomena behind that data. In order to achieve this, data needs to be made expressive. The data is given voice through sonification and is not confined to a simple representational role. Mediated by the composer and expressed through the software and hardware of the installation or piece, it serves as a vessel for experience. This approach, falling neatly into neither wholly "artistic" nor "scientific" approaches to sonification, suggests a new role for musicians working with data, and for collaborations between artists and scientists.

In *RoadMusic*, through the work of the composer/programmer the people traveling in the car experience things such as the "bumpiness" of the road in a different level of abstraction. Their affective capacities are extended as they experience the bendiness of a road in terms of the way in which, say, the granulation of a sample evolves. The experience of *RoadMusic* is intensely embodied, as moments of synchronicity occur between the movements of the car and events in the music, and one is aware of an intimate connection between the two. The synchronicity can also be subverted or manipulated by the composer, bringing in dimensions of memory and sensorial transposition. The sensor data does not provide anything that the passenger or driver does not already experience: their body and eyes provide the same information as the webcam and accelerometers. However, *RoadMusic* turns this into an embodied, audio-visual and multi-modal experience, allowing the passenger to be affected by this data in a different way.

In this way, it is not a specific experience of driving that the composer is trying to extend to the audience, rather it is a way of extending the affective capacities of the passengers, allowing features of the drive - both specific events such as a bend, and higher level features such as the overall "bendiness" of the journey - to be experienced in new ways through different modalities.

Fig. 2. People experiencing the installation "You Might Come Out of the Water Every Time Singing" at the Bluecoat Gallery, with Kaffe Matthews. Image ©Kaffe Matthews

With the case of Kaffe Matthews's piece, the installation is intended to transmit a certain impressionistic experience from the data. The artist's direct experience of diving with hammerhead sharks served as a basis for the aesthetics, and informing how the data was used. One reviewer of the piece, writing in New Scientist, describes,

I lie perfectly still, listening to the sound of a hammerhead shark circling overhead. I hear another approaching, and another, until they are all around, arcing through the depths of the ocean. A deep rumbling begins then: the sound of a diving boat right above me. The platform I am lying on starts to vibrate and all the eerie sounds of the ocean crescendo around me [10].

From the raw data, which is essentially no more than the latitude, longitude and depth coordinates over time, a sensual, embodied experience (Matthews's own experience of swimming with sharks) is offered to the listener. The installation serves to extend the listener affective capacity, not just so they have a better understanding of the movement patterns and trajectories of hammerhead sharks, but so that they have an embodied experience of the data.

The composer has control over the sonification and is able to finely tune and adjust enough of the parts, so that although the data is represented, it also becomes a musical material which is shaped by the composer in order to articulate an experience. The data will have characteristics, and the composer has to treat this as something to sculpt with, through constraining certain parameters, exploring mappings and scalings, as well as filtering, processing and tuning of the sounds within the software. The data then becomes an expressive material for the composer to work with.

The addition of underwater field recordings further allows the composer to articulate an embodied experience of the phenomenon behind the data. The evocative power of hydrophone recordings allows the composer to articulate a sense of space. Similarly, adding reverb to the sounds controlled by the data can situate the audience within a certain, albeit artificial, space. We move away from a pure transcoding of data into sound and into a composed environment or what Sterne terms an "affective representation" [16].

5   Discussion: Extending Cognition

"Making the Data Sing" extends the sensory capacities of the listener by rendering sensible imperceptible forces, or translating them into different modalities. The writings of philosopher Gilles Deleuze, and his collaborator Felix Guattari, provide tools of talking about the materiality of art and music and the role of the human body in experiencing such things. In his writings on Spinoza and in *Mille Plateaux* with Guattari, Deleuze writes of "affect". This has since been taken up by scholars such as Brian Massumi, and some speak of an "affective turn" in theory: that is, theory that attempts to talk about works of art not in terms of abstraction and representation, but in terms of the bodies that make them and experience them. Deleuze writes of a body's capacity for being affected', that is, what it is capable of experiencing and what connections with other bodies it makes. Deleuze draws on the example of the tick, with its limited affective capacity delineated by strict thermal, light and olfactory sensitivity. The tick has a worldview (or *Umwelt*, as he adopts the terminology of Jakob von Uexkull) limited by the narrow bandwidth of senses which are sufficient for its survival [6]. Sonification becomes a way of extending a body's affective capacity and by consequences bandwidth. Shark movements becomes something experienced through the body on a rumbling platform, not studied on a graph or understood symbolically. We can feel data. This might not increase our understanding of it, and it is quite likely that should we want to study shark movements then the raw data and its representation in maps and graphs would be far more useful. Sonification instead opens up a cross-modal channel of experience. The body's capacity to be affected is extended, experiencing the rhythm of a shark's day in terms of an oscillating tone felt vibrating through the body, or the bumpiness of a road not through an uncomfortable journey but through the jitteriness of a melody or the timbre of a synthesised tone.

The affective experience can be tied to notions of extended and embodied cognition described by Clark and Chalmers [4] and Varela, Thompson and Rosch [18]. Whilst not proposing identical ideas, these authors all represent a school of thought that notes the mind is distributed into the environment, and doesn't stop at our corporeal membrane. We are involved in couplings - what Deleuze and Guattari would call assemblages - that extend and change our cognitive and affective capacities [6]. The projects we described are embodied insofar as we experience the data directly through our bodies as part of our environment, rather than symbolically from a detached semantic vantage point. There is a cognitive and thoroughly embodied process of sensemaking that is bound up in this embodied experience of our environment. We can only speculate what the outcomes of this are in the works discussed. Future work could include studies looking at the long term effects of driving whilst listening to the RoadMusic system, with our composition and others from the body of work commissioned by Sinclair, and we cannot expect them all to have the same effects. Whilst the type of sonification described here might allow for the people experiencing the piece to identify patterns or trends, as representative sonification traditionally facilitates, this is not the primary goal of the process. Nor is the data merely something which allows the composer to make music they would not make before. To "Make Data Sing" is neither purely "artistic" nor "scientific" sonification, and we start to see new, speculative ways in which we can imagine composers and artists to work with data. This is described well by Andrea Polli, who's sonification work augments the "pure" scientific sonification of data with live musicians or field recordings, and is intended to articulate an emotional or experiential dimension appropriate to the data. She suggests that such an approach can be useful in increasing understanding of the physical phenomenon that creates the data in the first place, writing,

As individuals and groups are faced with the interpretation of more and more large data sets, a language or series of languages for communicating this mass of data needs to evolve. Through an effective sonification, data interpreted as sound can communicate emotional content or feeling, and I believe an emotional connection with data could serve as a memory aid and increase the human understanding of the forces at work behind the data [13].

This is very much what we have termed "Making the Data Sing". Matthews's piece was routed in her personal experience swimming with sharks and leads audience members to comment on how they felt they had experienced - to some degree, at least - a similar thing through the piece. The audience do not come away with an internal representation of shark movements, traces upon a map, but a memory of a vicarious experience of being amongst sharks, even though they might just be sonic representations. Returning to Deleuze, we can see that sonification seemingly takes up one of his imperatives for painting and music, perhaps in a more direct or literal way than he intended; "The task of painting is defined as the attempt to render visible forces that are not themselves visible. Likewise, music attempts to render sonorous forces that are not themselves sonorous" [7]. Sonification as we have used it renders sonorous the non-sonorous road surface or the hunting pattern of a shark. It is the digitisation of sound and information that makes possible this very literal rendering sensible that we find in sonification, what Sterne describes as the "plasticity of data in digital schemes". Within the *RoadMusic* composition/programming environment, which we used in a numerical table can store a series of values that could represent either an audio waveform or any list of data: sound and information become interchangeable and transmutable, and there is a porous boundary between abstract data and sonic materiality as audio players can play back a list of data as a sound file, and a sound file is reconstituted as a list of data.

"Making the Data Sing" is ultimately a speculative proposition. Approaching sonification this way, artists and musicians might work with scientists and data to produce work which can extend the senses of the human body into new places. At the same time, things inaccessible to the senses can be experienced and experiences can move into different senses. Through this approach, we propose that we might find new ways of thinking about the physical processes and phenomena behind data.

References

1. Barrass, S., Vickers, P.: Sonification design and aesthetics. In: Hermann, T., Hunt, A., Neuhoff, J. (eds.) The Sonification Handbook. Logos Publishing House, Berlin (2011)
2. Ben-Tal, O., Berger, J.: Creative aspects of sonification. Leonardo Music J. **37**(3), 229–233 (2004)
3. Campo, A., Frauenberger, C., Holdrich, R.: Designing a generalized sonification environment. In: Proceedings of the International Conference on Auditory Display, Sydney (2004)
4. Clark, A., Chalmers, D.: The extended mind. Analysis **58**(1), 7–19 (1998)
5. Collins, N.: The analysis of generative music programs. Organised Sound **13**(3), 237–248 (2008)
6. Deleuze, G., Guattari, F.: A Thousand Plateaus: Capitalism and Schizophrenia. Continuum, London (2003)
7. Deleuze, G.: Francis Bacon: The Logic of Sensation. University of Minnesota Press, Minneapolis (2004)
8. Gregg, M., Seigworth, G. (eds.): The Affect Theory Reader. Duke University Press, Durham (2010)
9. Hermann, T., Hunt, A., Neuhoff, J. (eds.): The Sonification Handbook. Logos Publishing House, Berlin (2011)
10. de Lange, C. Bird-man and ultrasound sharks tell of Galapagos damage. In: New Scientist. http://www.newscientist.com/blogs/culturelab/2012/05/galapagos-ultrasound.html
11. Parkinson, A., Tanaka, A.: Composing for cars. In: Proceedings of the Sound Music Computing Conference, Stockholm (2013)
12. Polansky, L: Manifestation and Sonification (unpublished, 2002). http://eamusic.dartmouth.edu/larry/sonifi. Accessed 2 Oct 2013
13. Polli, A.: Atmospherics/Weather Works: A Multi-Channel Storm Sonification Project. In: Proceedings of the International Conference on Auditory Display, Sydney (2004)

14. Salter, C., Baalman, M., Moody-Grigsby, D.: Between mapping, sonification and composition: responsive audio environments in live performance. In: Computer Music Modeling and Retrieval, Copenhagen (2007)
15. Sinclair, P., Tanaka, A., Hubnet, Y.: RoadMusic: music for your ride from your ride. In: Adjunct Proceedings Automotive UI, Salzburg (2011)
16. Sterne, J., Akiyama, M.: The recording that never wanted to be heard and other stories of sonification. In: The Oxford Handbook of Sound Studies. Oxford University Press, Oxford (2011)
17. Tanaka, A.: The sound of photographic image. Ai Soc. **27**(2), 315–318 (2012)
18. Varela, F., Thompson, E., Rosch, E.: The Embodied Mind: Cognitive Science and Human Experience. MIT Press, Cambridge (1993)

Seismic Sound Lab:
Sights, Sounds and Perception
of the Earth as an Acoustic Space

Benjamin Holtzman[1]([✉]), Jason Candler[2], Matthew Turk[3,4], and Daniel Peter[5]

[1] Lamont Doherty Earth Observatory,
Columbia University, New York, USA
benh@ldeo.columbia.edu, http://www.seismicsoundlab.org
[2] Tisch School of the Arts, New York University, New York, USA
jason@guarsh.com
[3] Department of Astronomy and Astrophysics, Columbia University, New York, USA
matthewturk@gmail.com
[4] National Center for Supercomputing Applications,
University of Illinois at Urbana-Champaign, Champaign, USA
[5] Institute of Geophysics,
ETH (Swiss Federal Institute of Technology) Zurich, Zürich, Switzerland
peterda@ethz.ch

Abstract. We construct a representation of earthquakes and global seismic waves through sound and animated images. The seismic wave field is the ensemble of elastic waves that propagate through the planet after an earthquake, emanating from the rupture on the fault. The sounds are made by time compression (i.e. speeding up) of seismic data with minimal additional processing. The animated images are renderings of numerical simulations of seismic wave propagation in the globe. Synchronized sounds and images reveal complex patterns and illustrate numerous aspects of the seismic wave field. These movies represent phenomena occurring far from the time and length scales normally accessible to us, creating a profound experience for the observer. The multi-sensory perception of these complex phenomena may also bring new insights to researchers.

Keywords: Audification · Sonification · Seismology · Wave field visualization

1 Aims

An earthquake is a minute event in the vast and slow movements of plate tectonics; it is the smallest increment of plate motion that we can experience with our unenhanced senses. Over geologic time, earthquakes are tiny, discrete events that constitute smooth, slow motion of plates. An earthquake is a rapid (seconds to minutes) release of elastic potential energy that accumulates in the two plates separated by a fault. When the fault ruptures, some fraction of that energy

© Springer International Publishing Switzerland 2014
M. Aramaki et al. (Eds.): CMMR 2013, LNCS 8905, pp. 161–174, 2014.
DOI: 10.1007/978-3-319-12976-1_10

excites elastic waves, referred to as the seismic source. The seismic wave field is the ensemble of elastic waves that propagate through the planet after an earthquake. Only near the source can we directly feel these waves, but the wave fields from sources with magnitudes above about 4.5 can be measured globally by seismometers. The resulting seismograms are the raw data used to study both the internal structure of the planet and the nature (magnitude and orientation) of the fault rupture. The aim of this project is to develop methods for making this global wave field perceptible, as illustrated in Fig. 1.

Here, we construct a sensory experience of the global seismic wave field by making a vast shift in its time and length scales. The most basic element is to create sounds from seismograms. We shift the frequencies into an audible range by time compression of the data (as illustrated in Fig. 2 and discussed in the Appendix), referred to as "audification" or "sonification" [18]. Sounds from several seismic data sets simultaneously recorded at different locations on the globe play through speakers in the same relative positions as the seismometers to produce spatialized sound. We then produce 4D renderings of the seismic wave field from global simulations and synchronize the sound with the movies, which are played in audio-visual environments in which the listener is situated "inside" the Earth. The sounds are unmistakably natural in their richness and complexity; they are artificial in that they are generated by a simple transformation in time. We are not trying to simulate the experience of being in an earthquake; rather, as observers seek meaning in the sounds and images, they grapple with the magnitude of this shift. In a subliminal way, these sounds can bring people to realize how fragile and transient is our existence, as well as a fundamental curiosity about the planet.

Humans perceive a great deal of physical meaning through sound– for example, the motion of approaching objects, the mood of a voice, the physical character of material breaking (distinguishing snapping wood from shattering glass), the nature of motion on a frictional interface (roughness of the surface and the speed of sliding). Also, perception of motion through sound often triggers our mind to look for visual cues. This perception of motion is very sensitive to frequency [5]. While our hearing has better temporal resolution, our eyes are very sensitive to spatial gradients in color from which we decipher spatial information, texture, etc. Due to these differences, "multi-sensory integration" is much more powerful than sound or image alone in eliciting in the observer a range of responses, from the instinctual to the rational.

After some historical background of signification of seismic data in Sect. 2, we describe how we produce sounds and images, in Sects. 3 and 4 respectively. In Sect. 5, we discuss how we synchronize sounds and images to illustrate one fundamental aspect of the physics of the seismic wave field in the Earth. In Sect. 6, we elaborate on the pedagogical questions, approaches and potential. Multi-sensory perception of wave fields in the Earth provokes a wide range of questions in the observer; those questions depend on their experience. The signals in seismic waves measured at any seismometer depend on the nature of the earthquake source, the distance from the source and the structure of the Earth; questions provoked in the listener reflect any or all of these aspects.

2   Background and Development of the Project

The earliest example (to our knowledge) of earthquake sonification is a record from 1953, called "Out of this World" (Road Recordings, Cook Laboratories), recorded by Prof. Hugo Benioff of Caltech, brought to our attention by Douglas Kahn [7]. He ran seismic data from 2″ magnetic tape directly to vinyl print, accelerating the tape playback so that the true frequencies of the seismic signal would be shifted into our range of hearing. A concise description of the frequency shifting process in an analog system is found in the liner notes: "*It is as though we were to place the needle of a phonograph cartridge in contact with the bedrock of the earth in Pasadena... and we "listen" to the movement of the Earth beneath a stable mass, or pendulum, which is the seismometer... But even during nearby earthquakes, the rate of motion is so slow in terms of cycles per second that the taped signals cannot be heard as sound... It is somewhat as though we played a 33-1/3 rpm record at 12,000 rpm,*" Sheridan Speeth at Bell Labs used this technique to distinguish between seismic signals from bomb tests and earthquakes, in the early days of nuclear test monitoring [7,15]. Based on his experiments with sonification of active-source seismic data (explosions, not earthquakes as the source of elastic waves) in the 1970's, David Simpson wrote "*Broadband recordings of earthquakes...provide a rich variety of waveforms and spectral content: from the short duration, high frequency and impulsive 'pops'; to the extended and highly dispersed rumbles of distant teleseisms; to the rhythmic beat of volcanic tremor; to the continuous rattling of non-volcanic tremor; and the highly regular tones of Earth's free oscillations*" [14]. A small number of people have continued to develop these efforts with scientific and artistic aims. Those we are aware of include, in some roughly chronological order, David Simpson [14], Florian Dombois [3], John Bullitt [2][1], Andy Michael, Xigang Peng, Debi Kilb [12]. Our impression is that many of these people (including us) had the initial raw idea to time-compress seismograms that felt completely original and obvious, then later discovered that others had preceded them with the same excitement.

We began in 2005 with a low budget system of 8 self-powered speakers and an audio interface, interested in using the spatialized sound to understand the nature of earthquakes, wave propagation through the planet as an acoustic space. In subsequent years, our large step forward was to couple the sounds with animations of the seismic wave field from both real data and simulations. Seeing the wave field while hearing the sounds enables an immediate comprehension of the meaning of the sounds that is a huge leap from the sound alone, as discussed above. Our first effort to couple the sound and image was to add sound to the animation of smoothed seismic data across Japan from the 2007 Chuetsu-oki (Niigata) earthquake (Magnitude 6.8)[2], using the method of [4]. This kind of wave field visualization is only possible for very dense arrays of seismometers, where the station spacing determines the minimum wavelength that can be

---

[1] http://www.jtbullitt.com/earthsound.

[2] http://www.eri.u-tokyo.ac.jp/furumura/lp/lp.html.

seen and the areal coverage of the area determines the maximum wavelength. With the advent of the USArray program and its transportable array (TA), such images have become possible for long period waves across the continental US. These "ground motion visualizations" (GMVs) were developed by Charles Ammon and Robert Woodward at IRIS (Integrated Research Institutions for Seismology[3]). The TA contains more than 400 broadband seismometers with an aperture of more than 1000 km, with station spacing of 70 km, such that there is a sampling of the wavelengths across the seismic spectrum that can be seen in the data. We currently synchronize multi-channel sound to these GMVs, but that project will be described in future work.

Subsequently, we synchronized sounds to visualizations of simulations of the global seismic wave field, which is the focus of this paper, as illustrated in Fig. 1. The simulations are generated using SPECFEM [8–10], a numerical (spectral element) model that calculates the elastic wave field in the whole Earth resulting from an earthquake. Candler and Holtzman began a collaboration with Turk, in the context of a grant from the National Science Foundation (see Acknowledgements) to develop this material for the Hayden Planetarium at the American Museum of Natural History in New York City, with its 24-channel sound system and a hemispheric dome.

3   Sound Production

Here, we first describe the methodology for making a sound using data from a single seismometer and then for an array of seismometers for spatialized sound. At present, most of the following processing is done in MATLAB, unless otherwise noted.

3.1   For a Single Seismometer

For a chosen event, the data is downloaded from IRIS (using the package "Standing Order for Data" (SOD)[4] or "obspy"[5]), with de-trending performed in SAC (Seismic Analysis Code). The signal in SAC format is read into MATLAB (Fig. 2a). We choose initial values of f_e (a reference frequency in the seismic signal, where the subscript e refers to "earth", from some part of the spectrum that we want to shift to the center of the sonic band) and f_s (the frequency in the sonic range to which we would like to shift f_e, as illustrated in Fig. 2b and c), listen and repeat, until achieving the desired sound and time-compression. We also specify what time derivative we would like to listen to (displacement, velocity or acceleration). The sounds are sharper and some volume compression occurs with each successive time derivative. We then design a filter (low-pass, high-pass or band-pass Butterworth), using MATLAB functions, as illustrated in Fig. 2d. We then sweeten and apply additional cleaning/filtering/compression

---

[3] www.iris.edu.

[4] http://www.seis.sc.edu/sod/.

[5] http://www.obspy.org.

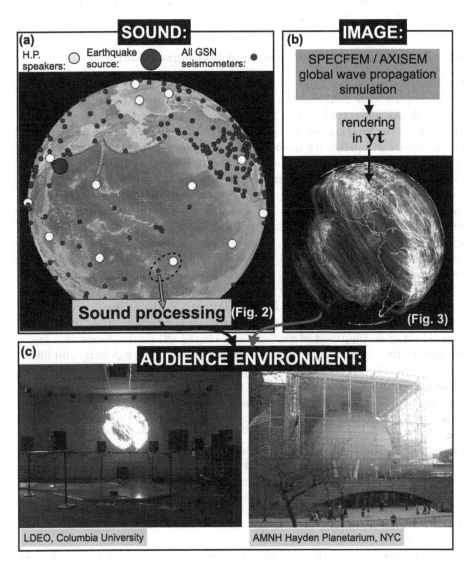

Fig. 1. (a) Sound processing: for a given earthquake, we obtain a list of active seismic stations on the globe (black dots), decide on the speaker geometry (white dots) and the relation of it to the earthquake source (large black dot), and then find the nearest stations to the speaker locations (dashed oval), download the data for those stations from IRIS, and then run them through our sound generating/processing programs. **(b)** Image generation: for that given event, we run a simulation either in SPECFEM3D or AXISEM, render the graphics in yt and then synchronize with the sounds. **(c)** We have a small multi-channel (16) sound system with a projector at LDEO, but have developed this material for the Hayden Planetarium.

utilizing iZotope RX and Reaper audio software. Alternative methods are under development using python and SoX[6].

3.2 For Multiple Seismometers and Spatialized Sound

For a single earthquake, we generate sounds from multiple seismometers to convey the entire wave field and the motion of seismic waves through and around the Earth. As illustrated in Fig. 1a, for a chosen speaker geometry, we build a 3D image of the locations of the speakers on a sphere in MATLAB (white dots). For a given earthquake, we download a list of seismometers that were active at that time (for whatever spatial scale we are interested in, but in this case, global), from http://global.shakemovie.princeton.edu/ (black dots). We then orient the Earth (or the earthquake source and the array of seismometers) relative to the speaker locations and find the nearest seismometers to each speaker. We run the multi-channel sounds and synchronize with the animation in Reaper, which is also capable of varying time-compression of audio and video interactively. Reaper actions can be scripted using python and driven externally using Open Sound Control, forming the platform for installations and exhibits.

Our current speaker geometries include a flexible array of 24 speakers in the Seismic Sound Lab[7] at the Lamont Doherty Earth Observatory (LDEO) and the 24-speaker dome system in the Hayden Planetarium. At LDEO, the 24 channel array is comprised of an 8-channel ring of self-powered monitors and a 16 channel array of mid-range satellite speakers powered by car-audio amplifiers, with a subwoofer and a infra-speaker platform on the floor. The audience can sit inside the ring (on the infraspeaker) or outside the ring, illustrated in Fig. 1c. The infra-speaker floor adds a great deal of dynamic range to the experience, as listeners often are not aware that their perception of the sound has changed from the sonic to the sub-sonic as the seismic waves disperse and decrease in frequency. At the Hayden Planetarium, the 24-channel speaker array resides behind the hemispheric screen, as shown in Fig. 1c (12 at the horizon, 8 at the tropic, 3 at the apex and one subwoofer track).

4   Image Production

In the last decade, a major advance in theoretical seismology has come from the development of the spectral element method (SEM) for simulating the wave fields that emanate from an earthquake. SEM combines the geometric flexibility of the finite element method with the temporal and spatial resolution of the spectral methods [8–10]. At the global scale, the SPECFEM3D code, implementing SEM, can model wave fields with a broad range of frequencies, for realistic crustal structure (e.g. CRUST2.0), limited only by the computational resources available. The movies and synthetic seismograms can be downloaded several hours

---

[6] http://sox.sourceforge.net.
[7] www.seismicsoundlab.org.

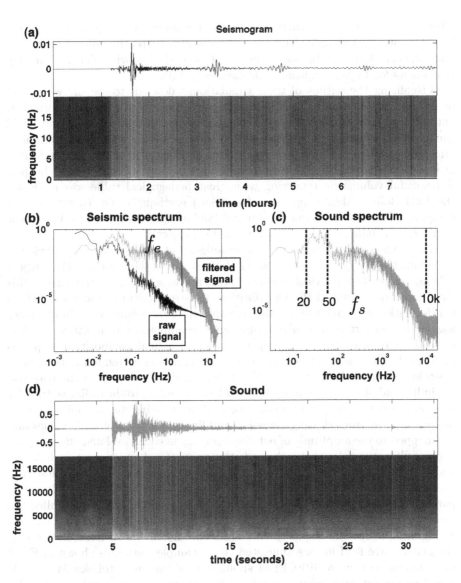

Fig. 2. Our standard plots for sound generation and analysis. This data is from the 2011 Tohoku, Japan, M9 earthquake. (**a**) Seismic waveform and its spectrogram. (**b**) Fourier transform of the signal (black) and filtered signal (grey), in this case a high pass filter. The red line marks the reference frequency (f_e) used for calculating the time-compression factor (Appendix 1). (**c**) FFT of the sound signal (f_e has been shifted to f_s). The black dashed lines mark the ranges of our sound systems (20–50 for bass and 50-10k Hz for mid-upper ranges). (**d**) Sound waveform and its spectrogram. Note the difference between the original seismogram and the sound signal due to the high pass filter; the large pulses, which are the surface waves, are absent in the sound, and much more high frequency detail is apparent in the "coda". Without the high-pass filter, the surface waves dominate the sound.

after any event for which there is a centroid moment tensor produced (CMT, M > 5.5, http://www.globalcmt.org). We are also currently using AXISEM, a quasi-3D code based on the same numerical methods, but with higher symmetry that allows for higher frequency calculations [1, 11][8].

Visualizing the output of these simulations allows us to see the wave field in motion. A "membrane" rendering the wave field at the Earth's surface is automatically constructed as part of the Shakemovie[9] output [16]. The wave field can also be rendered on a 2D cross section through the Earth, on, for example, a great circle section[10]. Combined cross section and spherical membrane renderings give a good sense of the 3D wave field and are computationally much cheaper. A beautiful volumetric rendering with great pedagogical value was made for the 1994 Bolivia M8.2 deep focus (∼630 km) earthquake [6]. To render such complex volumetric forms in a meaningful (and inexpensive) way is an important visualization challenge and major aim of this project.

The `python` environment "yt" [17] is designed to process, analyze and visualize volumetric data in astrophysical simulations, but in the context of this project is being adapted to spherical geometries relevant to seismology. To visualize this data, techniques used in the visualization of astrophysical phenomena such as star formation and galaxy evolution were applied to the seismic wave fronts. Data was loaded into `yt` in a regular format and decomposed into multiple patches, each of which was visualized in parallel before a final composition step was performed. The visualization was created using a volume rendering technique, wherein an image plane traversed the volume and at each step in the traversal the individual pixels of the image were evolved according to the radiative transfer equation, accumulating from absorption and attenuating due to emission. Colormaps are constructed using Gaussian and linear functions of RGB values and are mapped to the amplitude of net displacement in each voxel and time step. In a given filter, the color shows the radiative value (local emission at each point) and the curvature of the top of the filter shows the alpha value, that describes the transparency (alpha = 1 is completely opaque, alpha = 0 is completely transparent). The combination of the color map and the alpha function is called the "transfer function", as illustrated in Fig. 3. This approach results in a smooth highlighting of specific displacement values throughout the volume, illustrating the global wave field for one time step. The example snapshots shown in Fig. 3 were generated from a SPECFEM simulation of the 2011 Tohoku Magnitude 9 earthquake (at www.seismicsoundlab.org), discussed further below. Graphics are rendered for flat screen and 180-degree fisheye projections.

5   Synchronization of Sound and Image

Our ongoing challenge is to synchronize the natural sounds and synthetic images into a meaningful cinematic object, in order to convey physical aspects of the

---

[8] http://www.seg.ethz.ch/software/axisem.

[9] http://global.shakemovie.princeton.edu.

[10] http://seis.earth.ox.ac.uk/axisem/.

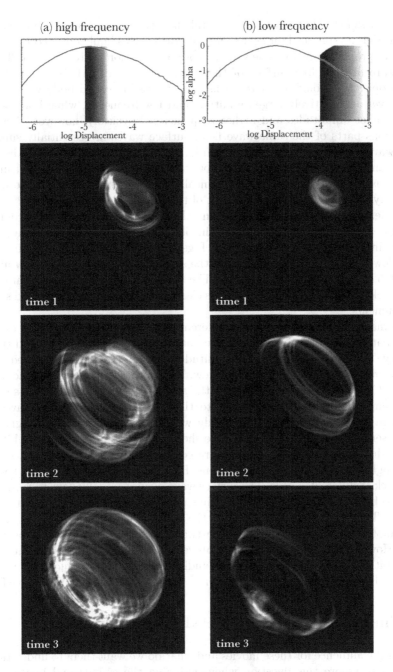

Fig. 3. Three time steps of yt-rendered animations, **(a)** Small displacement transfer function (top) corresponds predominantly to body waves (high frequency). **(b)** Large displacement transfer function (top) corresponds predominantly to the surface waves (low frequency). This simulation is of the first 4 hours after the 2011 Tohoku, Japan, Mag. 9.1 earthquake.

seismic wave field. The most fundamental character of the Earth as an acoustic space is that its spherical (or near spherical) form with a liquid outer core controls the wave propagation [13]. The waves whose propagation is always controlled by or "aware of" the free surface of the sphere are called surface waves. Those that propagate through the interior as wave fronts are called body waves. Surface waves are relatively large amplitude and low frequency, while body waves have smaller amplitudes and higher frequencies. Physically, however, they are continuous parts of the same wave field; surface waves are essentially sums of body waves. However, because they can be identified in seismograms as discrete phases and are thus separable, seismologists analyze them using different methods. Thus, we want to visually and sonically distinguish between surface waves and body waves, to explore this aspect of the physics.

To demonstrate this difference, using the data and the simulation from the Tohoku earthquake, our initial efforts involve filtering both the images and the sounds in parallel, as summarized in Figs. 3 and 4. To make the sounds, we run a low pass and high pass filter on the seismic data, above and below about $1.0 - 0.5$ Hz, as illustrated in Fig. 4a. The surface waves clearly propagate as a wave packet, and the coherent motion is clear when listening in spatialized sound environments.

To make the images, we apply different transfer functions centered on different bands of displacement amplitude, mapping amplitude to color and transparency. The larger displacement amplitudes correspond to the lower frequency surface waves, as shown in Fig. 3, top row. The surface wave transfer function is modified from one designed to render the appearance of a plasma. The smaller displacement amplitudes correspond to the higher frequency body waves, as shown in Fig. 3, bottom row. The body wave transfer function is designed to render semi-transparent, semi-reflective sheets moving through space (a bit like a jellyfish). The wave fields, when separated like this, look very different. Correspondingly, the sounds are very different. Furthermore, the movies with sounds play back at different speeds. The surface wave movies actually have to be shifted more to be in the audible range and thus play back faster than the body wave movies. The synchronization is tight; the sounds correspond to events in the wave motion, and the meaning of the two aspects of the wave field becomes clear. However, much potential for improvement remains in the development of quantitative relationships between the audio and image filters, such that we can explore the behavior of narrower frequency (band-pass) aspects of the wave field.

6   Emerging Scientific and Pedagogical Questions

Who is the audience for these movies and what do we want them to understand? We largely ignore this question when designing the sounds and images, but give it full importance when designing presentations and exhibits. We design the material to be as rich in visual and auditory information as possible. In the spirit of Frank Oppenheimer and the Exploratorium, our belief is that the material should contain as much of the richness of the process itself as possible;

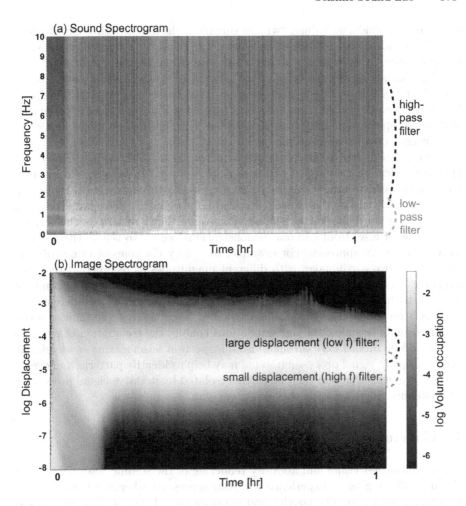

Fig. 4. (a) Sound spectrogram with approximate filter bands indicated. (b) Image spectrogram showing displacement on the y-axis and the volume occupied by pixels with that displacement value, represented by the greyscale spectrum. These filtering and rendering methods are works in progress.

that richness is what attracts peoples innate curiosity and will be understood in different terms at every stage of experience. Filtering of information to isolate certain patterns (for example, as a function of frequency) should be done late in the production, ideally by the observer as part of the process of understanding through experimentation.

There is large diversity in people's sonic and visual perception, as well as ranges of experience in perceiving and interpreting physical behavior. The movies may provoke very similar questions, but the language used to articulate those questions will be very different for a 5-year old than for a professional seismologist. In past presentations, people have used interesting physical analogies to describe the sounds, including: "whales singing in the distance through the deep ocean", "hands clapping once in an empty warehouse", "a loose piece of sheet metal flapping in the wind", "a tree bough cracking in a cold winter night", "a bowling ball hitting the dirt with a thud", "a trailer truck bouncing over a bump in the highway as you cling to the underside of its chassis". These analogies speak to the detailed information we associate with sound on the acoustic properties of different spaces and the physical processes that produce sound, and also to the diversity of sounds in seismic data.

As discussed above, the phenomena in the sounds can be separated into (1) the physical characteristics of the rupture process, (2) the mechanical properties of the rock volumes that the waves are passing through and (3) the geometry or acoustic space– the internal structure of the Earth. The spatialization is important for conveying relative location of events, depth relative to the surface, and motion of wave fronts. In our demonstrations, we try to isolate these effects by a comparative approach. For example, to convey the concept of magnitude, we listen to two earthquakes with different magnitudes as recorded at one seismometer. To convey the concept of the Earth as an acoustic space and compare different paths through it, we listen to one earthquake recorded at different seismometers on the globe. For Seismologists, our intent is that the multi-sensory presentation of seismic data and simulations enables the recognition of patterns that would be missed only through visual inspection seismograms as waveforms and subsequent signal processing; sound may help us identify patterns and events in the waveforms that can then be further isolated by iterative signal processing and listening. Work towards this aim is ongoing.

7 Conclusions

The synchronized visual and auditory rendering of the seismic wave field in the Earth is allowing us to experience with our senses an otherwise imperceptible natural phenomenon. The novelty and information-richness of these movies has enormous educational value, but also is beginning to provide new questions and insights for researchers. We have much work to do in the technical aspects of the visualization and sonification and their union, that will improve the perceptibility of patterns in the data.

Acknowledgments. We have the good fortune of working with Pritwiraj Moulik, Anna Foster, Jin Ge, Yang Zha, Pei-ying Lin and Matthew Vaughan at LDEO and Lapo Boschi at Univ. Paris VI. They have taught us a great deal of Seismology and contributed generously to many aspects of the project. In addition to co-author Daniel Peter, Vala Hjorleifsdottir, Brian Savage, Tarje Nissen-Meyer and Jeroen Tromp have all contributed to bringing SPECFEM and AXISEM into this project. Art Lerner-Lam gave us the initial financial support and scientific encouragement when we began this project for the LDEO Open House in 2006. David Simpson, Douglas Repetto, Nolan Lem, George Lewis and Dan Ellis have provided encouragement and assistance on computer music/sound aspects. Denton Ebel, Carter Emmart and Rosamond Kinzler have made possible bringing this project to the Hayden Planetarium. This work is directly supported by NSF grant EAR-1147763, "Collaborative Research: Immersive Audio−Visualization of Seismic Wave Fields in the Earth (Earthscope Education & Outreach)" to B. Holtzman and NSF grants ACI-1339624 and ACI-1048505 to M. Turk.

Appendix: Scaling Frequency and Duration

In the process of shifting the frequency of a seismic signal, the number of samples (or data points) in the waveform signal (n) does not change. All that changes is the time interval assigned between each sample, dt, where the sampling frequency, $f_{Sam} = 1/dt$. Broadband seismometers generally have sampling rates of 1, 20 or 40 Hz. For sound recording a typical sampling frequency is 44.1 kHz. In the context of frequency shifting, consider an arbitrary reference frequency f_{Ref} such that $f_{Ref}/f_{Sam} < 1$, because f_{Ref} must exist in the signal. When considering frequency shifting in which the number of samples does not change, this ratio must be equal before and after frequency shifting.

In the problem at hand, we refer to the original sampling rate of the seismic data as f^e_{Sam} (for "earth"), with reference frequency f^e_{Ref}, and the shifting sampling rate and reference frequency as f^s_{Sam} and f^s_{Ref}, (for "sound") respectively, such that

$$\frac{f^e_{Ref}}{f^e_{Sam}} = \frac{f^s_{Ref}}{f^s_{Sam}} \tag{1}$$

As illustrated in Fig. 2, we look at the Fourier transform (FFT) of the original signal, choose a reference frequency based on what part of the signal spectrum that we want to hear (e.g. 1 Hz for body waves), and then choose a reference frequency to shift that value to (e.g. 220 Hz, towards the low end of our hearing). We then re-arrange Eq. 1 to determine the new sampling rate:

$$f^s_{Sam} = \frac{f^s_{Ref}}{f^e_{Ref}} f^e_{Sam} \tag{2}$$

which is entered as an argument into the "wavwrite" function in MATLAB.

Similarly, duration is $t = n.dt$ where n is the total number of samples, and dt is the time step in seconds between each data point or sample. Since n is constant for the original data and the sound ($n_e = n_s$), we can write $\frac{t_e}{dt_e} = \frac{t_s}{dt_s}$. This is usefully re-arranged to

$$t_s = \frac{f^e_{Sam}}{f^s_{Sam}} t_e, \tag{3}$$

which is useful for synchronizing the sounds with animations.

References

1. Nissen-Meyer, T., van Driel, M., Stähler, S.C., Hosseini, K., Hempel, S., Auer, L., Fournier, A.: AxiSEM: broadband 3-D seismic wavefields in axisymmetric media. Solid Earth Discuss. 6(1), 265–319 (2014). doi:10.5194/sed-6-265-2014. http://www.solid-earth-discuss.net/6/265/2014/
2. Baker, B.: The internal 'orchestra' of the Earth. The Boston Globe, January 2008
3. Dombois, F.: Auditory seismology: on free oscillations, focal mechanisms, explosions and synthetic seismograms. In: Proceedings of the 8th International Conference on Auditory Display (2002)
4. Furumura, T.: Visualization of 3D wave propagation from the 2000 Tottori-ken Seibu, Japan, earthquake: observation and numerical simulation. Bull. Seismol. Soc. Am. 93(2), 870–881 (2003)
5. Hartmann, W.M.: How we localize sound. Phys. Today 52(11), 24–29 (1999)
6. Johnson, A., Leigh, J., Morin, P., van Keken, P.: Geowall: stereoscopic visualization for geoscience research and education. IEEE Comput. Graph. 26, 10–14 (2006)
7. Kahn, D.: Earth Sound Earth Signal. University of California Press, Berkeley (2013)
8. Komatitsch, D., Ritsema, J., Tromp, J.: The spectral-element method, beowulf computing, and global seismology. Science 298(5599), 1737–1742 (2002)
9. Komatitsch, D., Tromp, J.: Introduction to the spectral element method for three-dimensional seismic wave propagation. Geophys. J. Int. 139(3), 806–822 (1999)
10. Komatitsch, D., Tromp, J.: Spectral-element simulations of global seismic wave propagation - I. Validation. Geophys. J. Int. 149(2), 390–412 (2002)
11. Nissen-Meyer, T., Fournier, A., Dahlen, F.A.: A 2-D spectral-element method for computing spherical-earth seismograms-I. Moment-tensor source. Geophys. J. Int. 168, 3 (2007)
12. Peng, Z., Aiken, C., Kilb, D., Shelly, D.R., Enescu, B.: Listening to the 2011 magnitude 9.0 Tohoku-Oki, Japan, earthquake. Seismol. Res. Lett. 83(2), 287–293 (2012)
13. Shearer, P.: Introduction to Seismology, 2nd edn. Cambridge University Press, Cambridge (2009)
14. Simpson, D., Peng, Z., Kilb, D.: Sonification of earthquake data: from wiggles to pops, booms and rumbles. AGU Fall Meeting 2009, January 2009
15. Speeth, S.D.: Seismometer sounds. J. Acoust. Soc. Am. 33(7), 909–916 (1961)
16. Tromp, J., Komatitsch, D., Hjörleifsdóttir, V., Liu, Q., Zhu, H., Peter, D., Bozdag, E., McRitchie, D., Friberg, P., Trabant, C., Hutko, A.: Near real-time simulations of global CMT earthquakes. Geophys. J. Int. 183(1), 381–389 (2010)
17. Turk, M.J., Smith, B.D., Oishi, J.S., Skory, S., Skillman, S.W., Abel, T., Norman, M.L.: yt: a multi-code analysis toolkit for astrophysical simulation data. Astrophys. J. Suppl. 192, 9 (2011)
18. Walker, B., Nees, M.: Theory of Sonification. Principles of Sonification: An Introduction to Auditory Display and Sonification Chap. 2, pp. 1–32 (2006)

Music with Unconventional Computing: A System for Physarum Polycephalum Sound Synthesis

Edward Braund$^{(\boxtimes)}$ and Eduardo Miranda

Interdisciplinary Centre for Computer Music Research (ICCMR),
Plymouth University, Plymouth, UK
edward.braund@students.plymouth.ac.uk,
eduardo.miranda@plymouth.ac.uk

Abstract. The field of computer music is evolving in tandem with advances in computer science. Our research is interested in how the developing field of unconventional computation may provide new pathways for music and music technologies. In this paper we present the development of a system for harnessing the biological computing substrate *Physarum Polycephalum* for sonification. *Physarum Polycephalum* is a large single cell with a myriad of diploid nuclei, which moves like a giant amoeba in its pursuit for food. The organism is amorphous, and although without a brain or any serving centre of control, can respond to the environmental conditions that surround it.

Keywords: Music with unconventional computing · *Physarum polycephalum* · Sonification · Bionic engineering · Unconventional computing

1 Introduction

Since its invention, the computer has become increasingly ubiquitous in everyday life. In music it offers a seemingly limitless paradigm for composition and consumption. Historically, one of the first known computer music implementations was during the 1950s. Here, the musical curiosity of a computer scientist enticed him to programme the CSIR Mk1 machine to play a selection of popular melodies [9]. Shortly after his experiments, composers and scientists began exploring the computer's ability to be a tool in the composition of music. One of the first pieces to contain computer generated material was the *Illiac Suite for String Quartet* [10], which was written by a mathematician and composer in the late 1950s. Since these early computer music experimentations, advances in computer science and music/sound have demonstrated a close correlation. Consequently, computational advancements have impacted instrumentation and compositional practices resulting in novel genres of music as well as new methods of distribution [15,16]. There are genres of music today which consist mainly of computer generated sounds. It is therefore expected that future developments in

© Springer International Publishing Switzerland 2014
M. Aramaki et al. (Eds.): CMMR 2013, LNCS 8905, pp. 175–189, 2014.
DOI: 10.1007/978-3-319-12976-1_11

computer science will continue to have a strong influence on the field of music and related technologies.

We are interested in exploring ways in which the advancing field of unconventional computation may offer new pathways for computer music. Unconventional computing is a branch of computer science that addresses computing paradigms other than the conventional Von Neumann architecture and Turing machine, which have dominated computing since the 1930s. These non-standard models look to the information processing abilities of biological, chemical and physical systems, and how they may be exploited as either a genuine or utopian computational model. In this paper we report on the initial results of our work into harnessing the biological organism *Physarum polycephalum*, henceforth known as *P.polycephalum*, for use in the field of computer music. Specifically, we present the development of a system for recording the behaviour of *P.polycephalum* for sonification. At this early stage of our research, we are focusing on how the technique of sonification can be used to begin understanding the behaviour of this emerging computing substrate. We anticipate that this will provide us with an indication of which direction to take our research going forward.

This paper is structured as follows. First, some background information on the project is explained, offering knowledge on unconventional computing, some details on other projects in the area and an introduction to *P.polycephalum*. Next, the development of our system for collecting behavioural information from *P.polycephalum* is presented, followed by its testing. Then, the implementation of a simple sonification experiment is explained. Finally, the paper ends with final remarks.

2   Project Background

To cite this research let us first look to the development of today's conventional computer, which lays its ancestral roots with the Turing Machine pioneered in the 1930s [21]. This abstract computational model was developed by formalising the behaviour of 'real world' computers: large groups of people who carried out calculations following a strict procedure [8]. Shortly after this invention, Von Neumann developed a stored-program computing architecture [7], which widened the scope of the computing machine. These inventions saw the deterioration of 'real world' computers and, through the course of 80 years, have become the father of today's conventional computer. Over this period the premise of computation has remained relatively unchanged, with Turing's idea of a computing machine leading to the ideology of a universal computer that could solve most mathematical or logic based problems. This left non-standard computing models mainly residing in the theoretical domain until recently where momentum has been building due to a growing need for faster and more efficient technology.

Unconventional computing models currently being developed harness abstractions from a wide selection of phenomena. These range from reaction-diffusion [4] to emerging quantum computers [11]. Such computing devices, amongst several others, are exciting scientists who speculate that if this area of computer science is developed at the same frequency as the Turing Machine then *"Seventy years from now, the technology will be unrecognisable from today's ideas"* [19].

In regards to music, we consider there to be two approaches to harnessing unconventional computing. We refer to these as the algorithmic and sonic approaches. The algorithmic approach relates to how unconventional techniques are harnessed within other disciplines. For instance, an algorithmic implementation could produce the arrangement of musical sections or create an environment for working and interacting with music. The sonic approach on the other hand is uniquely attributed to unconventional computation in computer music. Here the computational behaviour of the harnessed phenomena is exploited to produce sound in a sonification model. Its behaviour can then be controlled to alter the model's parameters, allowing variations in sonic material to be produced. This approach lends itself to the development of new instrumentation.

The technique of sonification can be described as the art of using non-speech audio to convey information, and has a truly interdisciplinary background with it being employed for purposes ranging from recreational to scientific. Sonification is an elementary starting point for harnessing unconventional computation in computer music. This is because it allows for knowledge of natural systems to be realised and relationships to be drawn between behaviours and music/sound. The outcome of which could indicate possible computer music applications that the phenomena may be suited to.

Although research into unconventional computing in music is in its infancy, there are a number of projects beginning to emerge. To the extent of our knowledge, these mainly adopt a sonic approach. One early example explored using chemical computing by way of a Cellular Automata model to control a granular synthesiser [14]. Another example investigated synthesising sounds with a hybrid wetware-silicon device using in vitro neuronal networks [13].

Regarding our research, there are many unconventional computing prototypes currently being developed that could hold potential for computer music. However, many of these require expensive laboratory equipment along with specialist knowledge to allow computational prototypes to be developed. At this stage of our research we needed a more accessible medium to begin conducting our experiments. Uniquely, the biological substance *P.polycephalum* requires comparatively less resources than most other unconventional computing substrates: the organism is cheap, openly obtainable, considered safe to use and has a robustness that allows for ease of application. Moreover, *P.polycephalum* has been building presence in unconventional computation studies with evolving notions of it being a *"universal computer"* [1]. For these reasons, we have selected *P.polycephalum* as the computing substrate for our research.

3   P. Polycephalum

P.polycephalum is an acellular slime mould belonging to the order *Physarales*, subclass *Myxogastromycetidae*, class *Myxomycete*. In the field, this organism exhibits a dynamic life cycle of thirteen phases, which sees it develop from spore

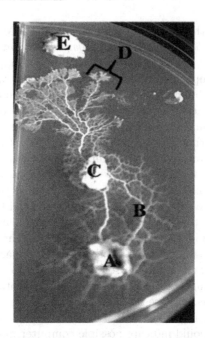

Fig. 1. A photograph of plasmodium of *P.polycephalum* showing: (A) inoculation of plasmodium into the environment, (B) protoplasmic network connecting areas of colonisation, (C) colonised food sources, and (D) extending pseudopods forming a search front along a gradient to food marked by (E).

germination to its main vegetative plasmodium state. It is *P.polycephalum's* plasmodium state that yields interest for unconventional computation.

As plasmodium, *P.polycephalum* exists as a large single cell (visible to the unaided eye) with a myriad of diploid nuclei, which divide in natural synchrony through mitosis every ten or so hours. The organism displays negative phototaxis and subsequently resides in dark, cool and damp environments. Its appearance is a yellow mass of protoplasm that moves like a giant amoeba in its pursuit for food. Plasmodium propagates towards chemo-attractants and away from chemo-repellents, which have formed a gradient on a substrate. Propagation is achieved by extending pseudopods, which disperse forming a search front while building a route-efficient network of protoplasmic veins connecting foraging efforts and areas of colonisation (Fig. 1). Upon discovery of food, the plasmodium surrounds it with pseudopods and feeds through the process of phagocytosis, ingesting nutrients that are spread across the organism via cytoplasmic streaming. Conversely, if matter is discovered which does not entice the appetite of the plasmodium, the area is avoided. Over time, given the correct environmental conditions, the organism can grow to become a considerable size and propagate at speeds of up to 5 cm/h. The visual result of a fully-grown culture is a planar graph with nodes represented by areas of colonization and edges by protoplasmic veins, as shown in Fig. 2.

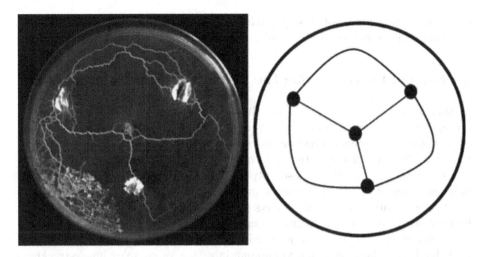

Fig. 2. The visual result of a culture of plasmodium in relation to a planar graph. Shown are several areas of colonisation (nodes) connected via a network of protoplasmic veins (edges).

The intracellular topology of plasmodium has been described as a network of biochemical oscillators [18]: waves of contraction or relaxation which collide inducing cytoplasmic streaming. This intracellular activity produces fluctuating levels of electrical potential, typically in the range of $\pm 50\,$mV, displaying oscillations at periods of approximately 50–200 s with an amplitude of 5–10 mV [12]. If recorded in isolated zones of colonisation over the duration of it being active, patterns emerge that correlate to spatial activity and environmental conditions. Adamatzky and Jones have examined such patterns and have reported that they can be used to denote the plasmodium's behaviour and physiological state [6].

P.polycephalum has been the subject of advancing research in recent years due to the sophisticated behaviour it demonstrates while foraging: the organism reacts to environmental stimuli with parallelism; allowing it to find efficient routes to food, build an optimised network of protoplasmic veins, and avoid unfavourable environmental factors. In computer science, researchers have explored using the organism as a parallel computing device capable of solving a wide selection of problems. The genesis of computing with *P.polycephalum* was a maze solving experiment [17], which developed methods of manipulating its chemotaxis to produce a route-efficient protoplasmic vein network from the entrance to the exit. Since this early experiment, use of the organism has advanced to more complex applications such as robot control [20]. In this project scientists developed a six-legged robot whose movement was controlled remotely by *P.polycephalum*. The robot was fitted with light sensors that relayed intensity information to a computer. This information was then used to project white light onto select areas of the *P.polycephalum* culture. The resulting phototaxis was recorded and used to naturally manoeuvre the robot away from light.

Other laboratory proofs of *P.polycephalum's* computational ability include route planning [2,5], colour sensing [3] and numerous others [1].

4   System for Recording the Behaviour of *P.Polycephalum*

In this section, our system for recording the behaviour of *P.polycephalum* is presented. To ensure we produced a system fit for purpose, two criteria focused the development process. The first was to select methods of recording behaviour that were discrete, ensuring they had no effect on *P.polycephalum*. The second was to construct a system whose output could be adaptable to accommodate different types of future experimentation.

As the organism takes several days to exhibit substantial growth, the possibility of harnessing it in real-time is limited. As a result, *P.polycephalum* computational devices are commonly recorded using time-lapse imagery. This allows for behaviour to be interpreted via human interface, or complex image-tracking algorithms, both of which are not efficient or guaranteed to be accurate. For sonification, we needed to develop more tangible methods of gathering detailed information of its behaviour. To achieve this, we looked to the research discussed previously regarding *P.polycephalum's* electrical activities [6]. This method of recording behaviour provides a high level of detail regarding the organism's evolving physiological states, in a form that is very usable. Recording behaviour this way requires electrodes to be positioned at points of colonisation and isolated from one another using a non-conductive material. As a single entity, this, unfortunately, would not allow the organism's propagation trajectories between electrode zones to be recorded. To combat this, we proposed the use of both time-lapse imagery and electrical potentials to record behaviour, as it provides information on stationary colonisation, as well as propagation trajectories.

4.1   The System

To enable us to capture *P.polycephalum's* behaviour, two forms of hardware are required: a camera with a flash and an ADC interface with a high resolution. The camera we selected was a USB high definition microscope with a manual focus. This device has eight white light LEDs that can be used as a flash to illuminate the foraging environment appropriately: it is important that the environment is only illuminated momentarily for image capture to avoid affecting *P.polycephalum's* phototaxis. To record the electrical activity, a 20-bit ADC high-resolution interface manufactured by Pico Technology UK was selected. This device can facilitate up to eight single-ended electrodes. When using this interface to record *P.polycephalum*, electrode arrays are arranged with one reference and a number of measurement electrodes.

To facilitate the collection and collation of information from these hardware devices, we designed a piece of bespoke software suitable for our research. We programmed this in Max, by Cycling 74, as it offers a comprehensive tool kit for data acquisition, as well as continuing operations from the collation stage.

We developed our software to offer two collation frameworks for sampling electrical activity: Electrical Potential Collation (EPC) and Custom Collation (CC). EPC operates one systematic collation protocol for all inputs, at definable intervals. The CC framework consists of two selectable collation protocols: Electrical Potential Difference collation (EPD) and Conditional Collation Gate (CCG). EPD calculates the potential difference between a selected reference input and a selection of other active inputs. This protocol collates at definable intervals and includes a reference line at the beginning of each collation to denote its contents: a line of text that states the name of the reference source and each selected input. Such a collation is particularly useful as it compares the level of activity across an environment. CCG differs from the previous two protocols as it does not conform to set intervals. The protocol collates readings from each input at the exact time one of them reaches a definable increment/decrement threshold from their previous stored reading. This acts as a method of compressing incoming data to retain only changes at a threshold that is deemed necessary. To allow for data to be viewed visually, the contents of each collation is plotted in a live graph.

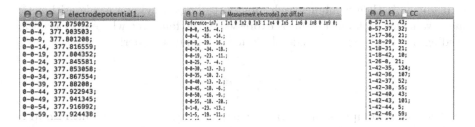

Fig. 3. Collation files created by each of the system's collation protocols. From left to right: EPC, EPD and CCG.

The software's image collation framework operates either at independent intervals or in synchrony with EPC. In addition to this, another collation protocol can be enabled that collates in tandem with CCG, allowing for points of heightened activity to be visually recorded. All collated image files are stored in a predefined directory and can be compiled to produce either a 15 fps or 30 fps video file.

All the collected data is organised using a global time-elapsed indexing system, which consists of three selectable formats: hours-minutes-seconds, seconds, and reading number. Furthermore, real world time and date information is embedded into each collated image, allowing for changes in behaviours due to daylight or other time-based factors to be recorded. Figure 4 shows the software's user interface, with annotations denoting the function of each panel.

In addition to these operations, the software also offers two methods of post-collation data compression. These are related to electrical activity readings and are included as they will further expand the system's usability. The first compression algorithm groups the collation into blocks containing a defined quantity

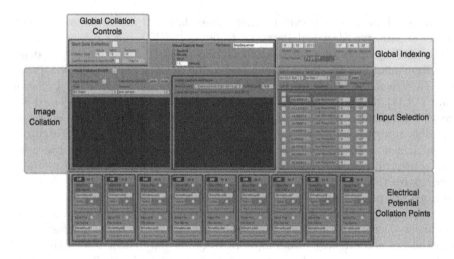

Fig. 4. Collation system's user interface with annotations.

of readings. It then combines each input's readings, leaving a single arithmetic mean value for each block. This is expressed in the following where e = electrical reading, r = readings in a single block and a = input number:

$$\frac{1}{r}\sum_{i=1}^{r} e_i^a \tag{1}$$

The second compression algorithm views the data not as individual electrode readings but as sets of entries at each collation interval. It then compresses the data set as follows: n entry is only retained if m number of measurements from k amount of readings presents a change over b threshold from the previous entry stored (first entries are always retained). This is expressed in the following where if $x(C) = 1$ the entry is withheld, otherwise it is lost:

$$\sum_{i=1}^{k} x(|a_i^n - a_i^{n-1}| \geq b) \geq m \tag{2}$$

4.2   System Testing

To ensure the operational success of our system, we initially tested the hardware and software in a basic scenario. Here, two electrodes coated in non-nutrient agar were arranged in a linear fashion, with the left elected as reference and inoculated with *P.polycephalum* and the right furnished with an attractant. The system was then initialised to enable all collation systems relating to the single measurement electrode. Figure 5 depicts the hardware setup and electrode arrangement.

This testing experiment was left to run over the course of three days, and was only halted when no change in electrical potential had been exhibited for a period

Fig. 5. Photographs of the experimental step up used to test the our system.

of time. The resulting collation was then scrutinised to ensure it accurately represented behaviour, and that the appropriate correlation existed between recorded activities in time-lapse imagery and electrical potential. Furthermore, the collations were compared to research put forward by Adamatzky and Jones [6] on the connotation of the electrical behaviour of *P.polycephalum*. This reinforced that the collected data was accurate and in line with accepted research within this area. Figure 6 shows this comparison and confirms the system's operations and output were a success.

5   Experimental Sonification

We are currently experimenting with a number of applications that harness behaviour recorded by the system presented in this paper. One of these is briefly explained in this section: the *P.polycephalum* step sequencer. This application is one of our more novel approaches to sonifying behaviour, taking the form of a compositional tool that allows a user to define certain parameters of the sonification model.

Step sequencers are devices that loop through a defined number of steps at predetermined time intervals. Normally, each step can exist in either an active or inactive state, which regulates whether a sound event is triggered when the sequencer reaches its respective position in the loop. The idea of a *P.polycephalum* step sequencer was conceived when reviewing sets of time-lapse images with correlating electrical activities. We noticed how the substance oscillates protoplasm around a network of veins to colonised regions, and how this relates to the architecture of a musical step sequencer. Resulting from this

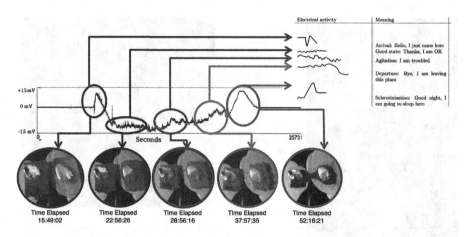

Fig. 6. Correlations between activity recorded in electrical readings and images. Shown is a connotation table courtesy of Adamatzky and Jones [6], which denotes the meaning of electrical patterns.

thought, we conceptualised a sequencer where *P.polycephalum* controlled step activation through propagation trajectories/colonisation, and sound event triggering with fluctuating levels of electrical activity.

To implement this experiment, we first developed a growth environment that could represent a step sequencer. Here, we arranged six electrodes in a circular fashion with a reference electrode placed in the centre (Fig. 7). Each electrode was coated in a non-nutrient agar with an attractant positioned on top to entice propagation and facilitate colonisation. *P.polycephalum* was then inoculated onto the reference electrode and left to forage in a dark enclosure. We programmed our system to take readings from each electrode at two-second intervals, and to capture images every two-minutes. Presented in Fig. 9 are graphs produced by our system representing each measurement electrode's activity.

This collation process took five days to complete and generated an excessive 330,000 electrical readings for each measurement electrode. Harnessing this quantity of data would have resulted in an extremely long and undynamic output. To circumvent this, we applied both of our software's compression algorithms. First, sets of ten readings were averaged. Then, we only retained readings if they presented a change over a defined threshold. This process reduced the quantity of entries to circa 5500, while maintaining behavioural patterns and the voltage gradients between them.

The step sequencer itself was programmed in Max with a small amount of data handling operations being outsourced to Java. This application's architecture mimics the growth environment used to record behaviour in and operates as follows. Six steps, arranged in a circular fashion, are paired with their respective electrode collation. These collations are recalled at a user-defined speed and are altered to become absolute values. A global metronome then ticks through each step at a user-defined BPM in a 360 loop taking a reading from each data stream.

Fig. 7. Images of the step sequencer growth environment.

Fig. 8. *P.polycephalum* fully grown within the step sequencer growth environment.

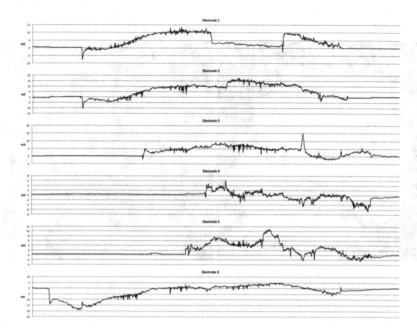

Fig. 9. A summary of electrical activity recorded on each of the six steps over the course of one week.

Steps only become active within the sequence once populated by *P.polycephalum*. Until this time, no reading is taken. Step activation is achieved by the application initially applying a high level smoothing expression to each data stream whose output activates the step when it reaches a threshold above zero. Readings taken by the sequencer are used to trigger a set of nine MIDI notes that are programmed in by the user. All steps are allocated a set of four notes from the nine available, which are then each assigned to a voltage trigger range. When a note is triggered, its velocity is produced through scaling the step's current electrical potential value to the MIDI data range. In order to determine the duration of a note, the current average potential of all other steps (active and non-active) is calculated, and then compared to the triggered step's voltage to produce a potential difference value. The higher this value, the more significant the note duration will be within the sequence, with a maximum duration being four beats. The sequencer is limited to only allow six notes to sound at a time; if a note is triggered but is unavailable due to being made active by another step, a note with the closest value in the step's priority list will sound. All of the sequencer's parameters can be altered in real-time.

As with any musical device, the user interface is an integral part of its function. Within this sequencer, the interface is built around the time-lapse imagery, inducing a connection between the user, the recorded behaviour, and the resulting sonic output. Here the time-lapse imagery is played back in perfect synchrony to the electrical collations and is positioned in the centre of the user interface

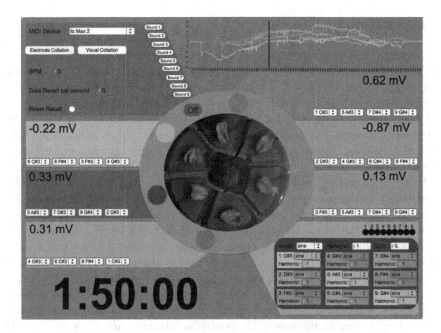

Fig. 10. The *P.Polycephalum* step sequencer user interface.

with each step's parameter controls arranged next to their corresponding electrode (Fig. 10).

This sequencer outputs a progressive arrangement of notes, which correspond morphologically to the recorded foraging behaviour. As a sonification of behaviour, the produced output does convey auditory representation of voltage levels quite accurately. This is because each note's velocity is produced directly by the respective step's voltage - a parameter that directly relates to energy. Moreover, by producing each note's duration with a potential difference value, it is possible to compare activity on each step through listening. From a musical perspective, having note velocity controlled this way is slightly undynamic due to voltage levels also controlling which notes are triggered: each note is played with a similar velocity every time. Going forward, this parameter may need to be controlled by another behavioural aspect that provides an additional dimension to the sonification.

Although currently this device's implementation is simplistic, a range of different results can be achieved through utilising the available parameters. However, the quantity of original material produced through the extended use of this device maybe limited due to the application using only a single set of recorded behaviour. Future versions of the sequencer could be developed to embody a model of *P.polycephalum*, allowing for different behaviour to be produced and harnessed in real-time.

6 Final Remarks

This paper presented the development of a system for recording the behaviour of *P.polycephalum*. The purpose of such a system is to enable a set of sonification experiments to be completed, marking the start of our investigation into how the area of unconventional computing may be used in computer music.

At this time it is difficult to evaluate the success of our system due to its limited employment. The testing scenario did however give a preliminary indication that it was operationally sound. Also, our early experimentation does suggest a degree of usability. This was demonstrated by the step sequencer, which was implemented using data collected by our system without any major compatibility issues occurring. Moreover, its output gave a basic auditory perception of both *P.polycephalum's* developing morphology and electrical activities, indicating that our system recorded behaviour with levels of accuracy. To speculate on issues and limitations that could arise; the electrical potential collation frameworks may cause some problems. This is in regards to the quantity of data accumulated from recording behaviour. Such large quantities of information may be overly excessive to employ, and any compression applied could damage the integrity of recorded behaviour. If any problems such as this occur, we will improve our system as necessary. Moreover, as advances are made in the field of unconventional computing with *P.polycephalum*, we will review our system to ensure we are best positioned to take advantage of these.

In regards to our continued work in this area, we are extensively conducting experiments that harness the behaviour of *P.polycephalum* in several different ways. As these experiments develop, success levels will indicate areas of computer music that may benefit from the unconventional computing paradigm. We are also currently researching methods of controlling *P.polycephalum's* behaviour in order to develop degrees of predictable control during its use. This is an active area of research both in the field of biology and unconventional computing. Advances made in this area will improve *P.polycephalum's* compatibility with employment in computer music by allowing for behaviour to be manipulated with musical/creative intent.

In summary, our research is still very much in its infancy, but so is unconventional computing with *P.polycephalum*. To begin understanding how this branch of computer science may be used in music, we need to immerse its application across the field. This process will widen our appreciation and lead to innovative advances as the computing paradigm lends itself to certain applications.

Undoubtedly, further research and development into unconventional models of computation will be innovatively fruitful for the field of computer music.

References

1. Adamatzky, A.: Physarum Machines: Computers from Slime Mould, vol. 74. World Scientific, Singapore (2010)
2. Adamatzky, A.: Physarum machines for space missions. Acta Futura **6**, 53–67 (2013)

3. Adamatzky, A.: Towards slime mould colour sensor: recognition of colours by Physarum polycephalum. Org. Electron. **14**(12), 3355–3361 (2013)
4. Adamatzky, A., Costello, B.D.L., Asai, T.: Reaction-Diffusion Computers. Elsevier, New York (2005)
5. Adamatzky, A., Jones, J.: Road planning with slime mould: if Physarum built motorways it would route M6/M74 through Newcastle. Int. J. Bifurcat. Chaos **20**(10), 3065–3084 (2010)
6. Adamatzky, A., Jones, J.: On electrical correlates of Physarum polycephalum spatial activity: can we see Physarum machine in the dark? Biophys. Rev. Lett. **6**(01n02), 29–57 (2011)
7. Aspray, W.: John von Neumann and the Origins of Modern Computing, vol. 191. Mit Press, Cambridge (1990)
8. Copeland, B.J.: The modern history of computing (2008)
9. Doornbusch, P.: Computer sound synthesis in 1951: the music of CSIRAC. Comput. Music J. **28**(1), 10–25 (2004)
10. Hiller, L.A., Isaacson, L.M.: Experimental Music; Composition with an Electronic Computer. McGraw-Hill, New York (1959)
11. Ladd, T.D., Jelezko, F., Laflamme, R., Nakamura, Y., Monroe, C., OBrien, J.L.: Quantum computers. Nature **464**(7285), 45–53 (2010)
12. Meyer, R., Stockem, W.: Studies on microplasmodia of physarum polycephalum V: electrical activity of different types of microplasmodia and macroplasmodia. Cell Biol. Int. R. **3**(4), 321–330 (1979)
13. Miranda, E.R., Bull, L., Gueguen, F., Uroukov, I.S.: Computer music meets unconventional computing: towards sound synthesis with In vitro neuronal networks. Comput. Music J. **33**(1), 9–18 (2009)
14. Miranda, E.R.: Granular synthesis of sounds by means of a cellular automaton. Leonardo **28**(4), 297–300 (1995)
15. Miranda, E.R.: Composing Music with Computers, vol. 1. Taylor & Francis, London (2001)
16. Miranda, E.R., Wanderley, M.M.: New Digital Musical Instruments: Control and Interaction Beyond the Keyboard, vol. 21. AR Editions Inc., Middleton (2006)
17. Nakagaki, T., Yamada, H., Tóth, A.: Intelligence: maze-solving by an amoeboid organism. Nature **407**(6803), 470 (2000)
18. Nakagaki, T., Yamada, H., Ueda, T.: Modulation of cellular rhythm and photoavoidance by oscillatory irradiation in the Physarum plasmodium. Biophys. Chem. **82**(1), 23–28 (1999)
19. Stepney, S.: Programming unconventional computers: dynamics, development, self-reference. Entropy **14**(10), 1939–1952 (2012)
20. Tsuda, S., Zauner, K.P., Gunji, Y.P.: Robot control with biological cells. Biosystems **87**(2), 215–223 (2007)
21. Turing, A.M.: On computable numbers, with an application to the entscheidungsproblem. Proc. Lond. Math. Soc. **42**(2), 230–265 (1936)

When Auditory Cues Shape Human Sensorimotor Performance

Intensity Shaping in Sustained Notes Encodes Metrical Cues for Synchronization in Ensemble Performance

Bogdan Vera[(⊠)] and Elaine Chew

Centre for Digital Music, Queen Mary University of London, London, UK
{b.vera,elaine.chew}@qmul.ac.uk

Abstract. We investigate the use of musical prosody as a coordination strategy in ensemble performance, focussing on the metrically ambiguous case of long sustained notes, where little rhythmic information can be obtained from the sparse note onsets. Using cluster analysis of the amplitude power curves of long notes in recordings of a violin-cello duo, we examine the use of varying intensity to communicate timing information over the duration of these sustained notes. The elbow method provides the optimal number of clusters, and we present the common intensity shapes employed by the violinist and by the cellist. Analysis of peaks in the intensity curves uncovers correspondences between peak positions and natural subdivisions of musical time: performers tend to use consistent curve shapes that peak at metrical subdivisions within notes, namely, at around the 0.25 and 0.75 points of the note event. We hypothesize that the 0.75 point intensity peak functions as an upbeat indicator and the 0.25 point peak serves to propel the note forward. We surmise that knowledge of the placements of these intensity peaks may be useful as auditory cues for marking musical time in held notes, and discuss how this knowledge might be exploited in anticipatory accompaniment systems and audio-score alignment.

Keywords: Ensemble interaction · Auditory musical cues · Prosodic gestures · Time series clustering

1 Introduction

Synchronization is a key aspect of ensemble performance. Previous research [3,5,8,14] has shown that musicians use various types of gestural cues to assist in ensemble synchronisation. Performance cues can be visual, as in instrument or body motion [6], or auditory, as in breathing [13].

Such overt synchronization cues are necessary only on relatively rare occasions over the course of performance of a piece. In rhythmic passages, and in parts of the music that are more densely populated with notes, the music itself carries sufficient cues on timing for synchronization, and simple entrainment to these implicit cues can allow musicians to stay together. In parts of the music

© Springer International Publishing Switzerland 2014
M. Aramaki et al. (Eds.): CMMR 2013, LNCS 8905, pp. 193–203, 2014.
DOI: 10.1007/978-3-319-12976-1_12

where timing can be hard to predict, such as during periods of long pauses or having sustained notes with little rhythmic information, the importance of extra-musical cues increases. This study is concerned with musical situations under which gestural cues are necessary for coordination beyond simple entrainment when musicians play together.

In a recently published study [12], we described an experiment in which a violin and cello duo was asked to play two specially composed pieces under three conditions of line of sight: normal line of sight (face-to-face performance), no line of sight (separation by an opaque screen), and partial line of sight condition (musicians were presented only the others' silhouettes created by casting shadows on the screen as shown in Fig. 1). The opaque screen removed visual contact completely, while the silhouettes allowed observation of two-dimensional motion only without facial expression.

Fig. 1. Partial line of sight (silhouettes) scenario in ensemble interaction experiment described in [12].

The first of the two composed pieces consisted of long sustained notes separated by equally long pauses. The second piece comprised of long notes with no pauses. Our results showed a significant effect on musician synchronisation when line of sight was removed for the first piece, but no significant effect in the second piece; we also found no effect when the musicians could see each others' shadows, suggesting that detection of motion through silhouettes (akin to peripheral vision) provided sufficient timing cues to contribute to more effective synchronisation.

These results complement those of Keller and Appel [4], who performed a similar experiment with pianists playing with and without line of sight, and found that visual contact was not necessary for congruence between sound synchrony and interpersonal body sway, which guaranteed basic ensemble coordination.

Together the results of these studies suggest that visual communication is not vitally important outside of critical sections where synchronisation becomes difficult with only timing cues implicit in the music.

In this paper we present the continuation of our study. We hypothesize that when notes are sustained on instruments that allow for continuous sound control, such as the violin or cello, some information about timing may be encoded within this expression, allowing musicians to synchronize in the absence of visual contact.

Here, we show that during the long notes in the second composed piece (comprising of long notes with no pauses), the intensity of the notes was shaped by the musicians in such a way as to provide information on the passage of musical time. Another musician paying attention to these auditory cues could then use them to understand their partner's perception of musical time and anticipate note onsets/offsets based on the shaping of the musical note. We also demonstrate that some types of expression curves tend to be reused for the same passage in a piece, over several performances, and present a clustering analysis of the expression curves employed by the duo. Finally, we discuss the possibility of using this expression data to improve synchronization in musician-computer interaction and automatic accompaniment.

2 Experimental Set-Up

The violinist and cellist in our study were recorded with attached instrument pick-ups, to isolate the sound sources as much as possible. The musicians were recorded playing the piece 10 times in total. While the pieces were performed under various conditions of line of sight as part of the related experiment, we do not study the effects of line of sight obstruction here. No clear difference was found between the expression used in different line-of-sight scenarios, suggesting that this type of expressive intensity shaping is inherent in string performance.

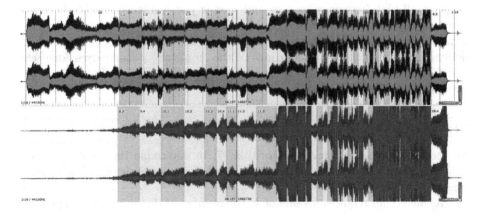

Fig. 2. Onset annotations.

The onset of each note was annotated manually in Sonic Visualiser [1], as shown in Fig. 2. Manual annotation was required due to difficulties in obtaining reliable note onset annotations automatically from bowed instruments.

3   Analysis

Using the recordings and the onset annotations created, an analysis of the intensity expression was conducted, focusing on the longest notes in the piece, all of which are two bars long. This amounts to 90 notes in total for the cello part and 60 for the violin part. Some of these notes were played in counterpoint, as shown in the score excerpt in Fig. 3. The tied semi-breve notes were annotated as single continuous note events for the purpose of the analysis.

Fig. 3. The first part of the piece, where the chosen long notes occur.

The audio for each recording was processed with a gaussian smoothing filter, removing all high frequency content and leaving just a smooth amplitude envelope representing large scale changes in intensity. The segments were all length normalized to the 0.0–1.0 interval by resampling them as a series of 200 samples, yielding scale-invariant representations of the amplitude power curves for each note. The curves were also normalized to peak at 1.0 amplitude. Figure 4 shows the collection of all extracted curves.

3.1   Cluster Analysis

We use the k-means clustering algorithm [7] to determine the most common curve shapes in the dataset, and to estimate the number of distinct basic curve types.

The algorithm requires a value of k, the number of distinct curve shapes, to be first chosen. k must be chosen in such a way as to account for the perceptibly

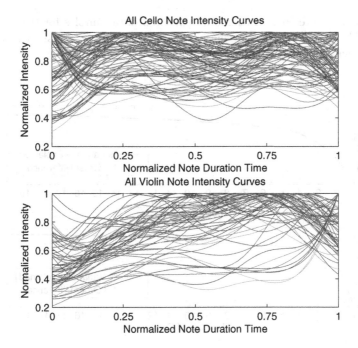

Fig. 4. All intensity curves.

distinct curve shapes without generating clusters with similar centroids. Clustering is often subjective, and it can be difficult to choose an optimal value for the number of clusters. Higher numbers of clusters can produce clusters representing what the algorithm designates as different shapes, which may effectively be scaled or shifted versions of the same curve.

One heuristic for choosing an optimal k value in k-means clustering is the elbow method [9]. Suppose the within-cluster sum of squares quantifies the degree to which the cluster centroids fit the data. As k increases, so does the fit. However, a large k would over-fit the data and produce less generalizable results. In the elbow method, the objective is to find the k at the elbow of the graph of the within-cluster sum of squares over k. Additionally, one may consider the percentage of variance explained by increasing k, and find a similar elbow point.

This elbow analysis, averaged over 10 clustering runs for k values up to 20, shown in Fig. 5, indicates that $k = 4$ is optimal for the cello curves. This analysis is consistent with observations of the centroids, as higher values of k resulted in highly similar cluster centroid shapes.

The violin elbow graph decreases rapidly, however there are two possible elbows in the curve, the first at $k = 2$ and the second at $k = 4$. Around 30 % of variance remains unexplained even with $k = 4$; this is likely because the curves are of overall similar shape, or are simply scaled or shifted versions of one another, which provides an additional challenge to constructing a classifier for the curves.

The curves were treated as 200-dimensional data samples for the clustering process. The resulting centroid shapes for each performer are shown in Fig. 6, within the violin curves clustered with both $k = 2$ and $k = 4$.

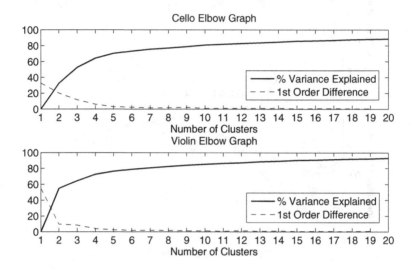

Fig. 5. K-means clustering elbow heuristic.

Tables 1 and 2 show the cluster assignments of (i.e. nearest centroids for) each note's curve (with $k = 4$ for cello and violin), for every take, for both instruments. The numbers correspond to the centroids as labeled in Fig. 6. Interestingly, we observe that for some of the notes, the cellist used the same type of curve. For example, notes 4 and 8 were played with the same type of curve each time. For note 9 the same type of curve accounted for 9 out of 10 takes, and for note 2 and 6 one curve was used in 8 out of the 10 takes. The violinist showed less tendency to use the same expression, however note 2 had the same type of intensity curve each time and, for note 5, one curve was used for 8 out of 10 takes.

3.2 Peak Position Analysis

By inspection, we observe that the curves tend to have either one or two peaks, coinciding roughly with the 0.25 and 0.75 points, which mark the minim, i.e. half note, time intervals away from the note boundaries. We posit that these emphasis points constitute an auditory cue that can communicate the passage of time during a long note. A simple feature was chosen for analysis: peak position. Figure 7 illustrates two such peaks, extracted with an existing peak finder algorithm [16].

The peaks were extracted automatically, generating a list of all significant peaks from all the cello's tied whole notes. Histograms of the peak position data for each instrument are shown in Fig. 8. For both performers we see a strong

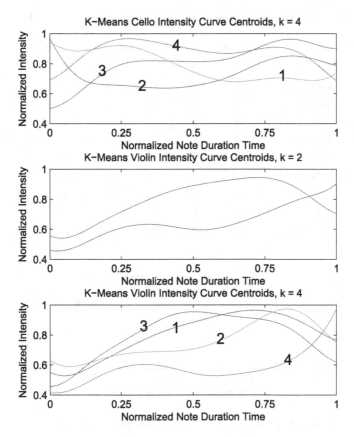

Fig. 6. Cluster centroids from k-means clustering of cello and violin intensity curves. Centroids for cello and violin with $k = 4$ are numbered for later reference.

Table 1. Cluster assignments for each cello note in every take.

	Note 1	Note 2	Note 3	Note 4	Note 5	Note 6	Note 7	Note 8	Note 9
Take 1	3	1	4	1	3	2	1	1	4
Take 2	1	2	1	1	1	2	3	1	2
Take 3	1	2	2	1	1	4	4	1	4
Take 4	4	2	4	1	4	2	4	1	4
Take 5	1	2	4	1	3	2	3	1	4
Take 6	1	4	3	1	3	4	3	1	4
Take 7	1	2	4	1	3	2	1	1	4
Take 8	4	2	4	1	3	2	4	1	4
Take 9	1	2	4	1	1	2	4	1	4
Take 10	1	2	4	1	3	2	4	1	4

Table 2. Cluster assignments for each violin note in every take.

	Note 1	Note 2	Note 3	Note 4	Note 5	Note 6
Take 1	3	2	3	2	3	2
Take 2	4	2	4	1	3	2
Take 3	3	2	2	1	4	1
Take 4	3	2	3	4	3	1
Take 5	2	2	1	4	3	4
Take 6	4	2	3	4	3	1
Take 7	3	2	1	2	1	2
Take 8	3	2	3	1	3	1
Take 9	4	2	1	2	3	2
Take 10	4	2	3	2	3	2

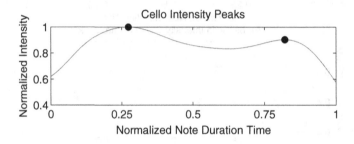

Fig. 7. Example peaks in one cello intensity curve.

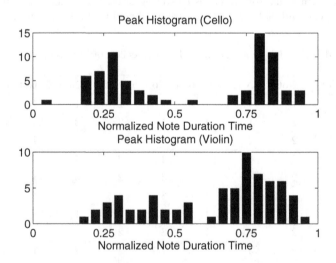

Fig. 8. Histogram of all cello and violin intensity peak positions.

tendency to peak close to three quarters of the way through the note event. The cellist's peak positions were more focused, and had a lower standard deviation, than the violinist's. In addition, the cellist showed a strong tendency to peak one quarter of the way through the note event. As these points correspond to natural subdivisions of musical time, expressive emphases that correspond to these time points can serve as useful auditory cues marking the passage of time through the notes. The peak near 0.75 acts as an upbeat to the next onset, and the peak near 0.25 functions as a virtual impetus for the continuation of the note.

4 Discussion

The results of our study show a clear correspondence between expressive emphasis and musical timing. Our results mirror those of other researchers such as Yang et al. [15], who also found similar beat-synchronized expression in other parameters such as vibrato depth in violin and erhu performances, suggesting that the effect may be generalized. It is possible that increased vibrato intensity correlates positively with loudness, and may even cause the perception of increased loudness. It is difficult to determine this from our results as our method for retrieving amplitude envelopes hides the vibrato.

Aside from being an auditory cue for ensemble musicians during long notes, should metrical encoding in expression prove to be common and reasonably consistent over a set of note types or a section of a piece, an algorithm may be built to analyze the signal to make predictions about parameters such as note length. One potential application would be in automatic accompaniment, where the accompanying system must synchronize effectively with performers who vary their tempo or prolong notes expressively. While previously developed algorithms for audio-to-score alignment and automatic accompaniment have focused primarily on note onset information (see [2]), our study suggests that with continuously sounding instruments such as the violin or cello, there may be useful metrical information encoded in the shaping of the notes themselves that could be exploited.

Recent research at IRCAM [10] has shown that it is possible to improve audio-to-score alignment by considering the musicians' gestural movements as part of the alignment. It would be possible to further augment this technology by using auditory features such as the ones we have described to aid in alignment. We envision two possible approaches similar to those used commonly in aligning common audio signals. First, an algorithm such as On-line Dynamic Time Warping [2] can align ongoing expressive shaping to templates learned from rehearsals. The second approach can use a statistical model, which describes probability distributions for the time occurrence of expressive peaks. The metrical information encoded in the expressive shaping of notes can then be used to estimate likely locations for beats, and the alignment can be improved.

5   Further Work

As this experiment was performed with a modest dataset, analysis of recordings from multiple ensembles would shed further light on this type of musical communication. It would be interesting to discover the degree to which musicians share similar types of expressive shaping cues, or if particular ensembles develop their own cueing strategies.

Other expressive parameters such as pitch (and vibrato, for example) might be of interest, and could be analyzed in similar ways. Furthermore, understanding this expressive shaping could lead to possibilities of classifying or recognizing expression shapes, with applications to music information retrieval. As previously described, one application is the estimation of performance parameters, such as tempo and phrasing, by analyzing ongoing notes.

One aspect we have not investigated in this study is the effect of changing tempo on the placement of intensity shape peaks. In our study the musicians were asked to keep the tempo as steady as possible, however in many forms of music, the tempo can evolve as a series of continuous tempo arcs (see [11]), and performers may spontaneously choose to exercise rubato or extend notes as agogic accents.

Acknowledgments. The authors thank Kathleen Agres and Laurel Pardue for their participation in the line of sight ensemble interaction experiments. This research was funded in part by the Engineering and Physical Sciences Research Council (EPSRC).

References

1. Cannam, C., Landone, C., Sandler, M.: Sonic visualiser: An open source application for viewing, analysing, and annotating music audio files. In: Proceedings of the ACM Multimedia 2010 International Conference (2010)
2. Dixon, S.: Live tracking of musical performances using on-line time warping. In: Proceedings of the 8th International Conference on Digital Audio Effects (DAFx05) (2005)
3. Godoy, R.I., Leman, M.: Musical Gestures Sound, Movement and Meaning. Routledge, New York (2010)
4. Keller, P.E., Appel, M.: Individual differences, auditory imagery, and the coordination of body movements and sounds in musical ensembles. Music Percept. Interdisc. J. **28**, 27–46 (2010)
5. Levine, M., Schober, M.: Visual and auditory cues in jazz musicians. In: International Symposium on Performance Science (2011)
6. Lim, A.: Robot musical accompaniment: Real time synchronisation using visual cue recognition. In: Proceedings of (IROS) IEEE/RSJ International Conference on Intelligent RObots and Systems (2010)
7. MacQueen, J.: Some methods for classification and analysis of multivariate observations. In: Proceedings of 5th Berkeley Symposium on Mathematical Statistics and Probability (1967)
8. McCaleb, M.: Communication or interaction? applied environmental knowledge in ensemble performance. In: Proceedings of the CMPCP Performance Studies Network International Conference (2011)

9. Ng, A.: Clustering with the k-means algorithm. http://calypso.inesc-id.pt/docs/KM1.pdf
10. Ritter, M., Hamel, K., Pritchard, B.: Integrated multimodal score-following environment. In: Proceedings of the International Computer Music Conference (2013)
11. Stowell, D., Chew, E.: Bayesian map estimation of piecewise arcs in tempo time-series. In: Proceedings of the International Symposium on Computer Music Modeling and Retrieval (2012)
12. Vera, B., Chew, E., Healey, P.G.T.: A study of ensemble synchronisation under restricted line of sight. In: Proceedings of the 14th International Society for Music Information Retrieval Conference (2013)
13. Vines, B.W., Wanderley, M.M., Krumhansl, C.L., Nuzzo, R.L., Levitin, D.J.: Performance gestures of musicians: what structural and emotional information do they convey? In: Camurri, A., Volpe, G. (eds.) GW 2003. LNCS (LNAI), vol. 2915, pp. 468–478. Springer, Heidelberg (2004)
14. Williamon, A.: Coordinating duo piano performance. In: Proceedings of the Sixth International Conference on Music Perception and Cognition (2000)
15. Yang, L., Rajab, K., Chew, E.: Vibrato performance style: A case study comparing erhu and violin. In: Proceedings of the International Conference on Computer Music Modeling and Retrieval (2013)
16. Yoder, N.: Peakfinder. www.mathworks.co.uk/matlabcentral/fileexchange/25500-peakfinder

Moving with Beats and Loops: The Structure of Auditory Events and Sensorimotor Timing

Matthew W.M. Rodger[✉] and Cathy M. Craig

School of Psychology, Queen's University Belfast, Belfast, UK
{m.rodger, cathy.craig}@qub.ac.uk

Abstract. Traditionally, audio-motor timing processes have been understood as motor output from an internal clock, the speed of which is set by heard sound pulses. In contrast, this paper proposes a more ecologically-grounded approach, arguing that audio-motor processes are better characterized as performed actions on the perceived structure of auditory events. This position is explored in the context of auditory sensorimotor synchronization and continuation timing. Empirical research shows that the structure of sounds as auditory events can lead to marked differences in movement timing performance. The nature of these effects is discussed in the context of perceived action-relevance of auditory event structure. It is proposed that different forms of sound invite or support different patterns of sensorimotor timing. Hence, the temporal information in looped auditory signals is more than just the interval durations between onsets: *all metronomes are not created equal*. The potential implications for auditory guides in motor performance enhancement are also described.

Keywords: Sound structure · Perceptual events · Movement timing · Sensorimotor synchronization

1 Introduction

As humans, we are uniquely able to time our movements to patterns of sounds with a high degree of accuracy, as exemplified by dancers, marching bands, and ensemble musicians. In order to understand this complex ability better, it is necessary to ask how our sensorimotor systems pick up information about time through auditory sensation, and use this information to control ongoing movements. It is the position of the present paper that this question is best approached by considering sounds as perceptual events, the different structures of which support or invite different forms of movement timing. This approach is here explained, with examples given of empirical studies that investigate the relationships between auditory event structure and timing of actions.

Historically, the predominant paradigm for studying the timing of movements to sounds (and other sensory timing cues) has been to ask experimental participants to tap in time with a metronomic stimulus, and/or continue tapping in time after the stimulus presentation has ceased [31]. There is a seemingly reductionist appeal of this approach: a discrete, intermittent sound constitutes a pure, uncluttered temporal interval as a stimulus; while a finger tap is a small enough response to minimize the disruption to timing from a noisy, dumb motor system. Hence, extraneous variables in the

© Springer International Publishing Switzerland 2014
M. Aramaki et al. (Eds.): CMMR 2013, LNCS 8905, pp. 204–217, 2014.
DOI: 10.1007/978-3-319-12976-1_13

sensorimotor timing process can be minimized or removed, giving a 'true' picture of the underlying mechanisms involved. Factors in the input stimulus that are often varied in this research paradigm include interval duration between metronome tones, slight offsets from isochrony of consecutive tones, or presentation of timing cues to different sensory modalities [29, 30, 48]. In turn, mathematical models of timing errors in motor output are generated to explain the supposed underlying processes in participants' synchronization performance. A common assumption seems to be that there is a clock-like process somewhere in the mind [45, 47], i.e. a regular intermittent pulse-like signal that transmits timing information to wherever it is needed in the brain. It is further assumed that by stripping back the movement timing task to its simplest form, the characteristics of this mental clock can be discerned by peering through the tea-leaves of messy perceptual and motor systems.

Although somewhat unfairly caricatured, the above description portrays a prevalent theoretical stance towards researching movement timing in relation to sounds. In contrast, we believe that this approach fails to capture important characteristics of how people move with sounds in the real-world. For example, movements of larger scales than finger-tapping can successfully be performed in time with auditory events, e.g. a percussionist striking a timpani drum can require movement of her full arm. Furthermore, sounds in the world rarely occur as metronomic pure tone islands in a sea of silence, but rather in a continuous unfolding stream, the structure of which varies in pitch, intensity, timbre and other auditory properties. With this in mind, it is important to think of sound-based timing cues not as extension-less points on an artificial timeline, but as events; an event being something that "occupies a restricted portion of four-dimensional space-time" [10]. Thus, to fully understand the capacity to move in time with sounds, it is necessary to consider a broader range of perceptual and motion factors in one's experimental investigations. At a more theoretically fundamental level, the established picture of sensorimotor synchronization as *sensory input* → *mental clock processing* → *motor output* belies the embodied, dynamic nature with which we interact with our perceptual environments [6, 12, 18].

These concerns may be remedied by adopting a more ecological stance to the questions of how we are able to time our actions to sounds. The ecological approach in psychology considers agents (people/organisms) as active perceivers of their surrounding environments [16]. Moreover, environments give a structure to the energy (e.g. light, air vibrations) that excite sensory organs (e.g. retina, cochlea), such that patterns of sensation are specific to the geometric properties of objects, surfaces and events that cause them [42]. On the whole, these world-specifying patterns are not clear from a static perspective, but reveal themselves through ongoing movement, such as how the visual field moves as we move our eyes. This means that there is sensory information available for active perceivers that directly informs about events in the world [38]. In the case of sounds, patterns of vibration in the air are specific to the events (scrapes, collisions, drops...) that give rise to them [14]. Furthermore, auditory events are not isolated atoms of sensation in time, but rather they unfold temporally, and the form of this unfolding is essential for perceiving the nature of sound-causing physical interactions [4]. Finally, the ecological approach in psychology puts a firm emphasis on action, asserting that the job of perception is to help us move successfully through the world [16]. In this picture, the brain is not an indifferent processor of detached sense data, but rather it is a tuning fork for action, selecting appropriate responses to the changing environmental scene [5]. Hence, perceptual information is constrained and defined by how it invites or dictates particular actions [49].

Considering this theoretical framework – one that is more ecological/embodied in perspective – the important questions for our current purposes should be: how do the structures of auditory events support or invite time-sensitive actions, and conversely, how do people control timed movements for different event-specifying sounds? By adopting this approach, it is still possible to scientifically investigate the manner in which auditory factors can give rise to different movement timing behaviors in a controlled, rigorous manner. For example, most of the research presented here involves a paradigm in which participants are asked to make a number of repetitive upper limb movements at a rate that matches the tempo specified by different looping sounds. An important step in this process is considering the structure of sound in a perceptual event, that is, how do auditory parameters (e.g. pitch, intensity) change over time, and how might differences in these structure (e.g. onset attack, slope) be meaningfully related to action. By generating synthetic sounds that possess clear differences in auditory structure, and looking at subsequent differences in performance when participants have to perform simple actions in time with such sounds, one can carefully study the relationship between auditory events and sensorimotor timing. The proposed advantage of framing such an investigation in this way is that it allows experimental conclusions to be drawn that will more likely provide insight into how sounds guide actions in real-world scenarios.

2   Extrinsic and Intrinsic Information for Action

If we are to consider the timing of action as guided by the available information specifying temporal intervals, it is important to consider the nature of this information and where it comes from. A useful framework for addressing this question can be found in the outline of David Lee's *General Tau Theory* [20–22]. According to this theory, the control of any action (big or small) can be thought of as the closure of a *motion gap* between the limb's current state and its goal state. For example, catching a ball involves closing the motion gap between one's hand and the ball's trajectory. Successful actions involve closing this motion gap within a suitable *temporal gap*, i.e., getting to the right place at the right time. For example, playing a drum in time involves closing the motion gap between the end of the stick/beater and the surface of the drum within the temporal gap that closes between consecutive beats. More complex movements may involve the closure of multiple motion gaps concurrently, e.g. marching in time with others involves closing the motion gap between foot and ground at the same instant that those around you do the same. The sensorimotor control of this process, therefore, involves coupling the closure of motion gaps to appropriate dynamic information that will lead to the successful spatial-temporal execution of an action.

An important question at this stage is *where* within the agent-environment system the information is found with which to guide the closure of a given motion gap. According to the theory, a distinction can be made between *extrinsic* or *intrinsic* information for movement guidance. Extrinsic information entails a relevant, event-specifying *sensory gap* to which the unfolding motion gap may be coupled. For example, in the case of catching a ball, the sensory gap exists visually between the ball and the hand. By coupling these together, such that both gaps close to zero at the same time, a successful interceptive action will be achieved. Hence, extrinsic guidance of movement implies that the information is available in the dynamics of events in our environment. When there is not information available in the environment to guide closure of the relevant motion gap, as in the case of self-paced actions, intrinsic information must be generated within the nervous system. For example, a golfer making a putt has no external timing information to guide her swing, and so must use an unfolding internally-generated *neural gap* to control her action [7]. Thus, although intrinsic and extrinsic guidance of action involve different processes, both can be characterized as the coupling of movement to information about a closing spatial-temporal gap [20].

General Tau Theory goes further to say that the nature of the informational variable used for both extrinsic and intrinsic guidance of action is the time-to-closure of a gap (motion, sensory, neural) at its current rate of closure. This variable, *tau*, can be directly sensed as the ratio between the current magnitude of a gap and its current rate of closure. In the case of extrinsic guidance, the tau of the motion gap can be coupled to the tau of a sensory gap, such as the visual angle on the retina relative to its rate of change [20]. In the case of intrinsic guidance, a motion tau is coupled to the neural power gap, relative to its rate of change [21]. Without going into too much detail, it can be noted that there is a great deal of support for this variable in the control of actions in which there is external dynamic sensory information, such as, long-jumpers taking run-ups [23] or drivers controlling the timing of braking [19], as well as for actions that require internal guidance, such as, infants sucking [8], singers initiating vocal pitch glides [37], and musicians' expressive performance gestures [35].[1] The important point for the present purposes is that General Tau Theory carves sensorimotor control of action into two distinct forms (extrinsic and intrinsic), depending on the availability of perceptual information for online guidance of movement, while also offering a candidate informational 'currency' that may be used in both cases.

2.1   Discrete and Continuous Sounds

Following the preceding discussion, it is possible to unpack the distinction between intrinsic and extrinsic information for guiding action in the context of synchronizing movement with sound. As mentioned in the introduction, a common sound type for assessing sensorimotor synchronization is a metronome, the general form of which is a short tone, followed by a period of silence, repeated at a set inter-onset interval. Although the presence of intermittent tones may be considered an extrinsic source of timing information, there is no information about the unfolding temporal gap between tone onsets with which to couple individual movements (e.g. taps). Thus, according to present theory, each metronome tone is a discrete event, and the information for timing

---

[1] For a more comprehensive list of empirical studies relating to General Tau Theory, please visit http://www.pmarc.ed.ac.uk (Last accessed: 24/06/2013).

movements between individual tones must be neurally generated [9]. An alternative way to present cues for time intervals is to have a sound that changes along some auditory parameter (e.g. pitch or intensity) continuously throughout the duration of each interval, looping back to the initial parameter at the end of the duration. Figure 1a illustrates the distinction between these two interval-specifying sound types. For each discrete interval, because there is no sensory information between tones, an intrinsic neural guide must fill in the temporal gap onto which the motion gap is coupled [9]. For each continuous interval, there is sensory information present in the changing auditory parameter about the unfolding temporal gap. Hence, according to the present theory, these different sound structures would likely recruit different movement timing processes.

By plotting auditory parameters as a function of time, one can characterize the structure of each sound as differently shaped perceptual events, and in turn, consider the structure of different movements that may be invited by a particular sound structure.[2] As shown in Fig. 1b, discrete sounds may be better suited to discrete movements (quick changes in displacement followed by recuperation or waiting), whereas continuous sounds may more likely invite smoother continual change in displacement over time. It is worth noting that tapping can be thought of as a discrete movement with a sharp change in displacement to the target surface followed by recuperation and pausing between subsequent actions. Hence, asking participants to tap to sound may bias the form of the observed movement trajectory. In cases where the form of movement to be made by a participant is less strictly specified by the task, as is the case in moving between lateral targets, different movement strategies can be found [2].

Rodger and Craig [34] reported a study which investigated the idea that different sound structures (discrete vs. continuous) can differentially affect timing and movement trajectory in a sensorimotor synchronization task. Participants (n = 23) had to repeatedly move their index finger reciprocally between two separate targets in synchrony with either discrete tones or looped continuous pitch ramp sounds. Different interval durations (temporal gaps) were used (1 s, 2.5 s, 4 s) and movement distances between targets (motion gaps) were also varied (20 cm and 70 cm). Results showed differences in sensorimotor synchronization between sounds types: timing errors were greater for continuous sounds (arriving in target too early), but variability of timing errors was lower in this condition, when compared with discrete sounds. Moreover, movements between targets were more harmonic in form (the relationship between velocity and displacement was closer to sinusoidal) for continuous sounds than discrete. Thus, the difference in structure of sound led to marked differences in sensorimotor synchronization performance and shape of movement. These effects were most pronounced for longer interval durations, suggesting that auditory-driven differences in intrinsic vs. extrinsic movement timing processes have a greater effect when temporal gaps are larger. It can be noted that these findings from Rodger and Craig [34] are supported by results from an experiment by Varlet et al. [43], which found similar changes in movement timing and trajectory when synchronizing wrist rotation movements with discrete (metronomic) and continuous (pitch oscillating) sounds.

---

[2] More complex sound events may be thought of as multiple dimensions of auditory parameters changing over time relative to each other.

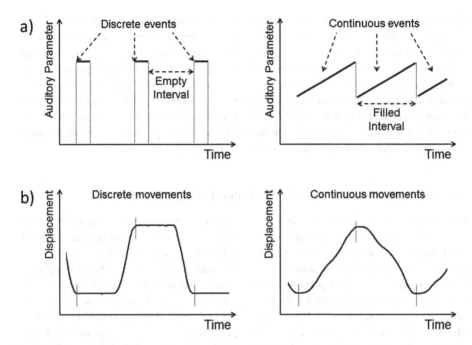

Fig. 1. Representation of sound and movement structures across time. A): Discrete and continuous sound events represented as changes in auditory parameters against time. Discrete sound events (e.g. metronome) are represented as instantaneous changes to a set auditory parameter (tone, intensity, etc.) followed quickly by instantaneous change to zero, separated in time by empty (silent intervals). Continuous sound events (e.g. pitch ramp loops) are represented as constant change in the value of an auditory parameter during each interval, in this case with an instantaneous change to the initial value at interval boundaries. B): Movement represented as displacement of a point on a limb over time. In these examples, movement is of an index finger between two lateral targets. Data is taken from a participant synchronizing with discrete and continuous sound events shown in A with 2.5 s intervals. Discrete movements involve waiting in target zones for the majority of the interval with quick movements between targets to intercept subsequent beats, while continuous movements involve gradual change in displacement throughout each of the interval durations. Dashed vertical lines indicate synchronization points with sounds.

In terms of relating the movement timing behavior to the sounds as auditory events, the differences in the shape of movement between targets may be understood as differences in the type of action invited by different auditory structures, as depicted in Fig. 1. However, it is still necessary to explain differences in timing caused by sound structure, that is, synchronization error and variability. This may be addressed by considering the information specifying perceptual event boundaries. Phillips et al. [28] provide evidence that sound intensity onsets mark the edges of new perceptual events. Discrete sounds have clear intensity (and technically, pitch) onsets at the start of each interval, marking a clear boundary for the perceptual event. For the continuous pitch ramps, the intensity is constant, while the instantaneous pitch drop at the end of each interval may form a more ambiguous event boundary than that created by discrete tones.

This could explain why synchronization errors were smaller for discrete sounds.[3] The reduced variability in synchronization errors for continuous sounds may have to do with the more oscillatory nature of the ongoing perceptual events. That is, the overarching temporal form of the ongoing sound is consistently maintained in movement timing, without individual actions necessarily lining up neatly with individual event boundaries. In other terminology, there is a consistent but non-zero phase relationship between the movement and sound in this condition. The important point is that by considering the time-related structure of these different auditory events, it is possible to offer an account of observed effects on the temporal aspects of corresponding actions.

2.2   Perceptually-Driven Changes in Motor Timing Behavior

The present approach to understanding movement timing and the structure of sound events can also speak to a distinction often made in the motor control literature: that of event-based and emergent timing [11, 24]. Tasks in which participants have to, for example, draw circles continuously in time with a metronome – as compared to tapping – result in markedly different patterns of timing error and movement trajectory [13, 39]. Typically, temporal errors are greater and less self-correcting for emergent timing (e.g. circle drawing) than for event-based timing (e.g. tapping). There is some debate as to whether this reflects different motor timing processes, or is the manifestation of two extremes of the same pulse-based motor control system [11, 33]. What is often not considered is the manner in which the action matches the available perceptual information specifying time, i.e. the metronome. If the timing information was presented as continual sound, would this lead to improvements in synchronization in emergent-timing tasks, relative to discrete sounds for timing? This question draws attention to the limitations of solely focusing on motor outputs to understand movement timing in response to sound cues.

More generally, the current position would encourage that one asks what is the information available to control movement, and how does this information invite a particular form of action over another. By characterizing sensorimotor synchronization problems in this way, resulting answers should be more commensurate with the way behavior is guided in real-world, non-laboratory situations.

3   Structure of Auditory Events and Re-Enacted Duration

In addition to cases where movement is synchronized with sound, there may also be scenarios in which sound is used to set-up a movement timing pattern for subsequent action.

---

[3] Another possible explanation is that the increasing tone and intensity ramps were perceived as looming sounds (objects approaching the listener), which have been shown to bias action responses to be earlier [26]. The explanation given for this effect is that looming sounds are likely to specify a prospective collision, and so we are more likely to respond early to avoid this. Although this account signifies the relevance of the ecological meaning of sounds in influencing actions, the fact that the pitch ramps were looped would likely mean that any looming effect would likely be attenuated by repetition.

As an anecdotal example, imagine a footballer singing a familiar song to herself as a way to get the timing right in the run-up for a penalty kick. In such a case, the temporal structure of the sound resonates in the timing of the following action. Scientifically, the effects of timing cues on subsequent motor actions is often studied in the context of a continuation paradigm in which participants are presented with a metronomic stimulus and then asked to maintain the stimulus tempo after the sound has stopped [31]. As with the previous discussion, a relevant question for the present position is how the structure of a given sound within a time-setting interval may affect the subsequent continuation motor timing. That is, how does the sound resonate in the action after it has sounded? There is evidence that the structural content of an interval does influence perceived and enacted timing, and the current account offers a potential explanation for why this may be so.

It has been established that the content of two different sound events can affect their perceived durations, even if the physical durations are identical. Looming sounds are perceived as longer than receding sounds [17]; while emotionally negative sounds last longer perceptually than neutral ones [27]. A particularly well-studied instance of this general phenomenon is the observation that filled intervals have greater perceived duration than empty ones [3, 41, 46]. For example, a continuous tone in an interval marked by silent gaps will be perceived as longer than a silent interval marked by short tones [46]. Also, discrete tone intervals are perceived as longer depending on the number of sub-interval tones they contain [3]. Thus, perceptual time is not a faithful recreation in the mind of the 'physical passing' (the regular passage of a clock-measured fourth dimension), but rather it is modulated by the sensory information contained within an event. A putative explanation of this phenomenon is that the magnitude of energy/work specified by a sound event dilates the perception of that events duration. Hence, intervals that contain sustained energy, changing parameters, or sub-events will be perceived as lasting longer than more empty/static intervals, as these factors imply work of some kind on the part of the sound generator. This phenomenon carries into motor timing behavior. Repp and Bruttomesso [32] observed that pianists would slow the overall tempo of their playing when required to play more notes in a musical interval (beat). As will be seen below, the structure of an auditory event in terms of parameter change and event density also affects subsequent reproduction of timed actions.

3.1 Smooth (Single-Event) and Ridged (Multiple-Event) Continuous Sounds

The notion that the magnitude of physical energy specified by the structure an auditory event can dilate its experienced and re-enacted duration was investigated in a previously unpublished study conducted by the present authors. The task was similar to that described in Rodger and Craig [34]: participants (n = 38, female = 23; M_{age} = 21.2 years) had to move their index finger between lateral targets to synchronise with different interval durations (1 s, 2 s, and 3 s) specified by different sounds types (detailed below). However, in this study, a continuation paradigm was used in which participants heard the sounds for a set number of repetitions before having to produce timed movements at the tempo of the just-heard timing cues. Two of the sounds used

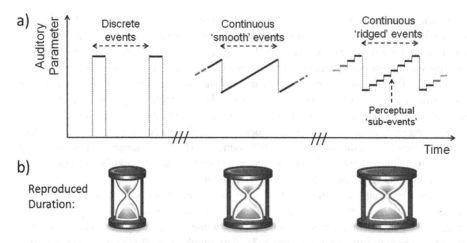

Fig. 2. Effects of auditory event structure on continuation movement timing. A): Sounds used in this study were *discrete* tones, continuously increasing pitch ramps (*continuous-smooth*), and concatenations of individual tones, which increased consecutively in pitch over the same distance as for the pitch ramps (*continuous-ridged*). B): Results from this study showed that participants altered the duration of their movements in a continuation task depending on the structure of the auditory event, with longest movement durations in the continuous-ridged condition, and shortest in the discrete condition.

were identical to those used in [34]: discrete tones and pitch ramps. A third sound type was also introduced: a series of end-to-end discrete tones rising in pitch chromatically over the duration of the interval before looping back to the initial pitch after each interval boundary. Each of these sounds is depicted as changes in auditory parameters in Fig. 2a. Pitch ramps and tone scales are designated continuous-smooth and continuous-ridged sounds, respectively. The structural difference between continuous-smooth sounds and continuous-ridged sounds is that the ridged sound's steps in pitch form perceptual sub-events within the larger looping interval-length event.

The results from the continuation phase of this experiment are depicted symbolically in Fig. 2b, and graphically in Fig. 3. Overall, there was a significant effect of sound type on participants' reproduced interval durations ($F_{(2,74)} = 41.96, p < .001$, $\mu^2_p = .53$). In keeping with previous research [3, 41, 46], filled intervals were reenacted as longer in duration than empty discrete intervals. In addition, filled interval events that contained multiple sub-events (continuous-ridged sounds) were re-enacted as longer in duration than intervals that were filled with a single whole event (continuous-smooth sounds). This order of effect between sound types occurred in all duration and movement distance task conditions. The findings of this study, therefore, provide support for the proposition that the structure of auditory events (discrete/continuous; smooth/ridged) can affect the re-enaction of time in subsequent movements. Thus, the perceived temporal structure of sound echoes in movement timing, even after the sound is no longer perceptually present.

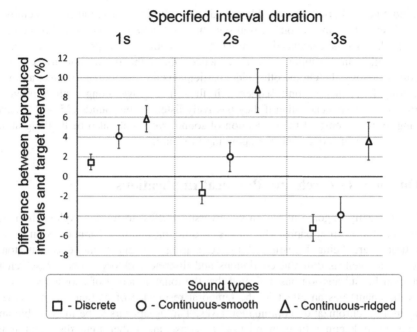

Fig. 3. Mean percentage differences between participants' reproduced interval durations in a continuation task relative to the interval durations specified by the different sound types (positive percentages indicate that reproduced intervals were longer than as specified by the previously heard sounds). Error bars denote standard error of the mean.

3.2   Timing in Perceptual Events Mediated by Action Salience

It should be asked at this point why the structural content of an auditory event should modulate the perceived/enacted duration of the sound. As indicated above, one explanation is that the perceived magnitude of work/energy in an event is positively related to its perceived duration [44]. The current account would take this idea further by suggesting that the reason for this has to do with the perceived action-salience of a sound: sounds that invite or suggest a greater magnitude of action effort on the part of the listener are likely to be perceived as occupying a greater expanse of time.

This proposition comes back to the ecological approach to perception and action, which states that our experience is mediated by the opportunities for action that our senses pick up. Gibson [15] said that "time is the ghost of events", intimating that the experience of time and duration are not detached from our active perception of the world, but are rather properties of the events we purposefully sift through for potential actions. In the previously described experiment, the difference in reproduced duration between the continuous-smooth and continuous-ridged sounds was that the sub-events within the ridged sounds supported the possibilities for sub-actions within the larger movements. Hence, these sounds invited a greater complexity of movement within intervals than the smooth sounds, even if this complexity was not acted upon. This idea is still very speculative, but is being further investigated by the first author.

A more general point that should be made about timing and sound is the reciprocal nature of perception and action. Gibson said that we 'move to perceive and perceive to move' [16]. This is evidenced in research into audio-motor processes. Perceived melodic motion in a simple musical sequence affects the timing and trajectory of subsequent actions [1]. On the other side, participants are better able to detect a timing offset irregularity in a sound sequence if they first move along with a previous isochronous tone sequence than if they passively listen to the sounds [25, 40]. Hence, in trying to make sense of the perception of sound, we should also be thinking about the possible role of movement in responding to sound.

4   Ongoing Research and Practical Implications

Work is currently ongoing at Queen's University Belfast to further explore the ideas laid out in this position paper. The effects of different auditory parameters on movement timing are being investigated by comparing consonant and dissonant tonal structures, as well as different continuous and discrete auditory events. Research in preparation for submission has indicated that the tonal structure of chords (consonant versus dissonant) has an effect on the temporal resonance of participants movement timing in a synchronization-continuation tasks. Timing appears to be more stable and accurate when keeping time in relation to consonant rather than dissonant tonal intervals, which may relate to the ecological preference in humans and certain animals towards consonant sounds, such as human vocalizations. Further work is currently being conducted to understand the relationships between auditory structures of sound and sensorimotor timekeeping.

In addition to these sensorimotor timing investigations, the ability of people to perform spatio-temporally constrained goal-direct actions through perceived auditory events is being studied through a number of experiments. These research projects aim to further elucidate the relationships between the structure of sounds and the structure of timed movements. Furthermore, as acknowledged in the introduction, the synthesized sounds described in this paper are not necessarily typical of those found in real-world interactions, which are much more complex in structure [4]. Research needs to be conducted to assess the extent to which the claims made here obtain when auditory events are more like those found in everyday experience.

There is also a more practical motivation for tackling these theoretical issues. A strong driving force for the current authors' engagement with these theoretical questions is the potential for using sound guides to enhance movement performance, in both motor rehabilitation and skill acquisition contexts. For example, footstep sound events have been shown to successfully convey spatio-temporal walking information to healthy participants [50], and the possibly beneficial effects of this have now been observed in a study of patients with Parkinson's disease [51]. In the latter study, patients with Parkinson's disease were found to increase their step length while listening to recordings of long strides on gravel. Interestingly, the advantage of these sounds was also observed when patients were played these sounds and then asked to walk without them, showing that the resonance of auditory events in the minds of the patients can continue to influence motor action even when such sounds have ceased.

A new step has also been to synthetically sonify in real-time the swing phase of Parkinson's disease patients' steps, so that they can now hear the silent portion of their gait while walking [36]. This new development has shown promising benefits to patients, most likely through the augmented action-relevant feedback that these sounds provide through moving. In summary, by understanding better the ways that sounds can specify information for action, we may be able to design more optimal sensory guides that optimally scaffold motor performance for individuals with movement deficits.

5 Conclusions

The theoretical position outlined in this paper is that auditory sensorimotor processes are best understood by considering the structure of auditory events and the form of movement and motor timing supported by this structure. Hence, sounds in this context can be thought of as perceptual events that invite or align with particular forms of action. This can be seen in the effects of discrete and continuous sounds as distinct auditory structures on sensorimotor synchronization performance. Additionally, sound structure can influence re-enacted interval duration in a sensorimotor continuation task. Although there is much work still to be done, a case is forming for the argument that sound structure and movement timing are intimately linked when people act on sounds and that audio-motor processes are best examined by asking what is the available information for action in the structure of an auditory event. In practice, this work may have implications in the design of auditory guides as a potential strategy for movement rehabilitation.

Acknowledgments. The work presented here was partly supported by a Starting Independent Researcher's Project funded by the European Research Council (TEMPUS-G 210007 StIG) awarded to Cathy M. Craig.

References

1. Ammirante, P., Thompson, W.: Continuation tapping to triggered melodies: motor resonance effects of melodic motion. Exp. Brain Res. **216**, 51–60 (2012)
2. Bieńkiewicz, M.M.N., Rodger, M.W.M., Craig, C.M.: Timekeeping strategies operate independently from spatial and accuracy demands in beat-interception movements. Exp. Brain Res. **222**, 241–253 (2012)
3. Buffardi, L.: Factors affecting the filled-duration illusion in the auditory, tactual, and visual modalities. Percept. Psychophys. **10**, 292–294 (1971)
4. Carello, C., Wagman, J., Turvey, M.: Acoustic specification of object properties. In: Anderson, J.D., Anderson, B.F. (eds.) Moving Image Theory: Ecological considerations, pp. 79–104. Southern Illinois University Press, Carbondale (2005)
5. Cisek, P., Kalaska, J.F.: Neural mechanisms for interacting with a world full of action choices. Annu. Rev. Neurosci. **33**, 269–298 (2010)
6. Clark, A.: Being there: putting brain, body, and world together again. MIT Press, Cambridge (1997)

7. Craig, C.M., Delay, D., Grealy, M.A., Lee, D.N.: Guiding the swing in golf putting. Nature **405**, 295–296 (2000)

8. Craig, C.M., Lee, D.N.: Neonatal control of sucking pressures: evidence for an intrinsic (tau)-guide. Exp. Brain Res. **124**, 371–382 (1999)

9. Craig, C.M., Pepping, G.J., Grealy, M.A.: Intercepting beats in pre-designated target zones. Exp. Brain Res. **165**, 490–504 (2005)

10. Cutting, J.: Six tenets for event perception. Cognition **10**, 71–78 (1981)

11. Delignières, D., Torre, K.: Event-based and emergent timing: dichotomy or continuum? A reply to repp and steinman. J. Motor. Behav **43**, 311–318 (2010)

12. Dewey, J.: The reflex arc concept in psychology. Psychol. Rev. **3**, 357–370 (1896)

13. Elliott, M.T., Welchman, A.E., Wing, A.M.: Being discrete helps keep to the beat. Exp. Brain. Res. **192**, 731–737 (2009)

14. Gaver, W.: What in the world do we hear?: an ecological approach to auditory event perception. Ecol. Psychol. **5**, 1–29 (1993)

15. Gibson, J.J.: Events Are perceived but time is not. In: Fraser, J.T., Lawrence, N. (eds.) The Study of Time, vol. 2, pp. 295–301. Springer, New York (1975)

16. Gibson, J.J.: The Ecological Approach to Visual Perception. Houghton Mifflin, Boston (1979)

17. Grassi, M., Pavan, A.: The subjective duration of audiovisual looming and receding stimuli. Atten. Percept. Psychophys. **74**, 1321–1333 (2012)

18. Hurley, S.L.: Consciousness in Action. Harvard University Press, Cambridge (1998)

19. Lee, D.N.: A theory of visual control of braking based on information about time to collision. Perception **5**, 437–459 (1976)

20. Lee, D.N.: Guiding movement by coupling taus. Ecol. Psychol. **10**, 221–250 (1998)

21. Lee, D.N.: General Tau theory: evolution to date. Special issue: landmarks in perception. Perception **38**, 837–858 (2009)

22. Lee, D.N., Georgopoulos, A.P., Clark, M.J., Craig, C.M., Port, N.L.: Guiding contact by coupling the taus of gaps. Exp. Brain Res. **139**, 151–159 (2001)

23. Lee, D.N., Lishman, J.R., Thomson, J.A.: Regulation of gait in long jumping. J. Exp. Psychol. Hum. Percept. Perform. **8**, 448–459 (1982)

24. Lemoine, L., Delignières, D.: Detrended windowed (lag one) autocorrelation: a new method for distinguishing between event-based and emergent timing. Q. J. Exp. Psychol. **62**, 585–604 (2009)

25. Manning, F., Schutz, M.: "Moving to the beat" improves timing perception. Psychon. Bull. Rev. **20**, 1133–1139 (2013)

26. Neuhoff, J.G.: An adaptive bias in the perception of looming auditory motion. Ecol. Psychol. **13**, 87–110 (2001)

27. Noulhaine, M., Mella, N., Samson, S., Ragot, R., Pouthas, V.: How emotional auditory stimuli moderate time perception. Emotiion **7**, 697–704 (2007)

28. Phillips, D.P., Hall, S.E., Boehnke, S.E.: Central auditory onset responses, and temporal asymmetries in auditory perception. Hear. Res. **167**, 192–205 (2002)

29. Repp, B.H.: Phase correction, phase resetting, and phase shifts after subliminal timing perturbations in sensorimotor synchronization. J. Exp. Psychol. Hum. Percept. Perform. **27**, 600–621 (2001)

30. Repp, B.H.: Rate limits in sensorimotor synchronization with auditory and visual sequences: the synchronization threshold and the benefits and costs of interval subdivision. J. Mot. Behav. **35**, 355–370 (2003)

31. Repp, B.H.: Sensorimotor synchronization: a review of the tapping literature. Psychon. Bull. Rev. **12**, 969–992 (2005)

32. Repp, B., Bruttomesso, M.: A filled duration illusion in music: effects of metrical subdivision on the perception and production of beat tempo. Adv. Cogn. Psychol. **5**, 114–134 (2009)
33. Repp, B., Steinman, S.: Simultaneous event-based and emergent timing: synchronization, continuation, and phase correction. J. Motor. Behavior. **42**, 111–126 (2010)
34. Rodger, M.W.M., Craig, C.M.: Timing movements to interval durations specified by discrete or continuous sounds. Exp. Brain Res. **214**, 393–402 (2011)
35. Rodger, M.W.M., O'Modhrain, S., Craig, C.M.: Temporal guidance of musicians' performance movement is an acquired skill. Exp. Brain Res. **226**, 221–230 (2013)
36. Rodger, M.W.M., Young, W.R., Craig, C.M.: Synthesis of walking sounds for alleviating gait disturbances in parkinson's disease. IEEE Trans. Neural. Syst. Rehabil. Eng. **22**, 543–548 (2014)
37. Schogler, B., Pepping, G.-J., Lee, D.N.: TauG-guidance of transients in expressive musical performance. Exp. Brain Res. **189**, 361–372 (2008)
38. Shaw, R.E., Flascher, O.M., Mace, W.M.: Dimensions of event perception. In: Prinz, W., Bridgeman, B. (eds.) Handbook of Perception and Action, vol. 1, pp. 345–395. Academic Press Ltd, London (1996)
39. Studenka, B.E., Zelaznik, H.N.: Circle drawing does not exhibit auditory-motor synchronization. J. Motor. Behav. **43**, 185–191 (2011)
40. Su, Y.-H., Poppel, E.: Body movement enhances the extraction of temporal structures in auditory sequences. Psychol. Res. **76**, 373–382 (2012)
41. Thomas, E., Brown, I.: Time perception and the filled-duration illusion. Percept. Psychophys. **16**, 449–458 (1974)
42. Turvey, M.T., Shaw, R.E., Reed, E.S., Mace, W.M.: Ecological laws of perceiving and acting: in reply to fodor and pylyshyn. Cognition **9**, 237–304 (1981)
43. Varlet, M., Marin, L., Issartel, J., Schmidt, R.C., Bardy, B.G.: Continuity of visual and auditory rhythms influences sensorimotor coordination. PLoS ONE **7**, e44082 (2012)
44. Walsh, V.: A theory of magnitude: common cortical metrics of time, space and quantity. Trends Cogn. Sci. **7**, 483–488 (2003)
45. Wearden, J.H.: Do humans possess an internal clock with scalar timing properties? Learn. Motiv. **22**, 59–83 (1991)
46. Wearden, J.H., Norton, R., Martin, S., Montford-Bebb, O.: Internal clock processes and the filled-duration illusion. J. Exp. Psychol. Hum. Percept. Perform. **33**, 716–729 (2007)
47. Wing, A., Kristofferson, A.: Response delays and the timing of discrete motor responses. Percept. Psychophysic. **14**, 5–12 (1973)
48. Wing, A.M., Doumas, M., Welchman, A.E.: Combining multisensory temporal information for movement synchronisation. Exp. Brain Res. **200**, 277–282 (2010)
49. Withagen, R., de Poel, H.J., Araujo, D., Pepping, G.J.: Affordances can invite behavior: reconsidering the relationship between affordances and agency. New Ideas Psychol. **30**, 250–258 (2012)
50. Young, W., Rodger, M., Craig, C.M.: Perceiving and reenacting spatiotemporal characteristics of walking sounds. J. Exp. Psychol. Hum. Percept. Perform. **39**, 464–476 (2013)
51. Young, W.R., Rodger, M.W.M., Craig, C.M.: Auditory observation of stepping actions can cue both spatial and temporal components of gait in parkinson's disease patients. Neuropsychologia **57**, 140–153 (2014)

Learning Movement Kinematics
with a Targeted Sound

Eric O. Boyer[1,2]([✉]), Quentin Pyanet[1], Sylvain Hanneton[2],
and Frédéric Bevilacqua[1]

[1] IRCAM STMS-CNRS-UPMC, 1 place Igor Stravinsky, 75004 Paris, France
{eric.boyer,frederic.bevilacqua}@ircam.fr,
quentin.pyanet@gmail.com
[2] Laboratoire de Psychologie de la Perception UMR CNRS 8242,
UFR STAPS - Université Paris Descartes, 45 rue des Saints Pères,
75006 Paris, France
sylvain.hanneton@parisdescartes.fr

Abstract. This study introduces an experiment designed to analyze
the sensorimotor adaptation to a motion-based sound synthesis system.
We investigated a *sound-oriented* learning task, namely to reproduce a
targeted sound. The motion of a small handheld object was used to control a sound synthesizer. The object angular velocity was measured by a
gyroscope and transmitted in real time wirelessly to the sound system.
The targeted sound was reached when the motion matched a given reference angular velocity profile with a given accuracy. An incorrect velocity
profile produced either a noisier sound or a sound with a louder high harmonic, depending on the sign of the velocity error. The results showed
that the participants were generally able to learn to reproduce sounds
very close to the targeted sound. A corresponding motor adaptation was
also found to occur, at various degrees, in most of the participants when
the profile is altered.

Keywords: Gesture · Sound · Sensorimotor · Learning · Adaptation ·
Interactive systems · Auditory feedback · Sound-oriented task

1 Introduction

There is growing interest in using tangible interfaces and motion sensing technology to interact gesturally with digital sound processes. In particular, a research
community has been established over the last ten years around the development of gestural digital musical instruments (DMIs). The NIME conference
(New Interfaces for Musical Expression) [3] has centralized several important
research results. While the evaluation methodology of such interfaces is recognized as important, it has generally been considered from a user experience point
of view, most often ignoring fundamental aspects of sensorimotor learning. Nevertheless, we believe that sensorimotor learning should be fully addressed for the
development and evaluation of digital musical interfaces.

© Springer International Publishing Switzerland 2014
M. Aramaki et al. (Eds.): CMMR 2013, LNCS 8905, pp. 218–233, 2014.
DOI: 10.1007/978-3-319-12976-1_14

This research topic is close to applications using *movement sonification,* where digital sound processes are designed to react to movements, hence providing additional information about the movement/performance. Typically, the auditory feedback is thought to supplement other sensory modalities (such as proprioception and vision) and to facilitate sensorimotor learning. Such an approach has been proposed for example for the facilitation of skills acquisition in sports [28] or in physical rehabilitation [20]. Although there is a growing number of publications studying the mechanisms whereby auditory feedback can improve motor control and learning, there is still a lack of formalism and consensus on the use of such auditory feedback.

We have started to study sensorimotor learning in DMIs and interactive sound systems for movement training/rehabilitation, within a single research project[1]. We take advantage of the fact that these applications can share identical technology (motion sensing and processing) and also share similar questions about the action-perception loop involved in motion-sound interaction.

While the different applications might imply similar sensorimotor learning processes, they can still be categorized based on the different tasks they imply. In the case of DMIs, the task can be expressed as *sound-oriented.* The users adjust their movements in order to achieve a specific goal expressed in terms of sonic/musical characteristics. In the case of motion training (i.e. sport or rehabilitation), the task can be expressed as *motion-oriented.* The users get auditory feedback to adjust their movements and to achieve a specific goal in terms of motion characteristics. In Fig. 1 we schematically describe the information flow of movement sonification in the cases of *motion-oriented* and *sound-oriented* tasks. The figure emphasizes that both concepts share the same architecture.

In this paper, we focus only on the first case: the *sound-oriented* task. In this case, the user's attention is drawn on the sound produced by the action and the auditory-motor loop is regulated by the perceived sound properties. We present an experiment where we evaluate the movement adaptation of subjects who are asked to control a specific sound quality.

The paper is structured as follows. First, we present a short overview of related works. Second, we describe the experimental setup, methodology and motion analysis. Third, we present the results, and fourth, we discuss our findings and their implications for further experiments.

2   Related Works

We first describe here the few studies that explicitly reported on a *sound-oriented* task. We then report on other *motion-oriented* tasks that showed the interest of using auditory feedback.

---

[1] Legos project, http://legos.ircam.fr.

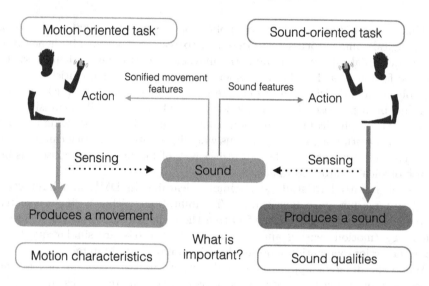

Fig. 1. Concept of Motion-oriented vs Sound-oriented task.

2.1 Sound-Oriented Task

A small number of studies have examined the concept of *sound-oriented* task. Early works were performed focusing on the evaluation of gesture-sound mappings. Hunt et al. in [14] presented such an evaluation by asking subjects to reproduce a target sound using different mapping strategies. Only simple interfaces such as a mouse and sliders were used. It resulted that, while complex gesture-sound mappings were more difficult to master, they appeared to be more engaging for the subjects. This implies that the type of implicit learning involved in this case was perceived as beneficial.

Gelineck et al. [9] also studied input interfaces and compared knobs and sliders for a task consisting in reproducing reference sound samples. Subjects were musicians and were asked to reproduce four sounds with temporal timbral variations (synthesized with a physical model of flute and friction). A qualitative evaluation was performed showing that no significant difference was found between the use of knobs and the use of sliders. Note that these studies did not explicitly address sensorimotor learning or adaptation in their questionnaire-based evaluation.

Pointing towards auditory targets can also be considered as a sound-oriented task. Recently, we investigated the effect of sound feedback on blindfolded pointing movements towards auditory targets spatialized with HRTF binaural technique [4]. We found that the auditory target should last enough to be heard during the task. The potential advantage to additionally sonifying the hand was not apparent in such a case. Forma et al. [8] showed that blindfolded participants are also able to point towards targets in a auditory virtual environment using sound as sensory substitution. Interestingly participants succeeded in the task whether the virtual listener was congruent with their ears or placed on one of their hands.

The concept of a *sound-oriented* task can be linked to recent studies on the relationship between body motion occurring during various sound/music stimuli [5,10,11,17,18]. In particular, Godøy et al. [10] investigated motion trace that subjects performed on a 2-dimensional surface in response to a sound stimuli. Other studies were reported on hand gestures performed while listening to either abstract synthesized sounds [18], or stimuli derived from environmental sounds [5]. As expected these studies showed that the motion related to sound stimuli depends on several different sound aspects and varies greatly between subjects. Nevertheless, such studies offer novel perspectives in showing experimentally that some sounds can favor specific motions.

2.2   Auditory Feedback in Motion-Oriented Task

The other types of related studies concern investigations of *motion-oriented* tasks to establish whether auditory feedback can be beneficial for learning and performance. Rath and Schleicher [19] studied a virtual balancing task under different feedback conditions, including auditory feedback to guide movements. They found that the auditory feedback was beneficial in terms of rapidity, the best results being found when sonifiying the ball velocity. They also found small differences between ecological and abstract sounds. More recently, Rosati et al. [22] showed that a tracking task can be improved using an auditory feedback (in addition to a visual feedback) related to the task achievement or, to a lesser extent, giving information about the error.

Vogt et al. [27] proposed a movement sonification system to improve perception of body movements. Sonification and "positive"sounds were beneficial for task understanding and increased the subject motivation. Effenberg [6] focused on an ecological approach, insisting there is a close relationship in kinesiology between movement kinetics and sound. He showed that supplementary auditory information improves the perception and reproduction of sport movements compared to vision alone. These results appeared independent from the qualitative assessment of the sounds qualities by the subjects. Takeuchi [25] previously pointed out that sound is a very useful information channel in sports. Avanzini et al. [2] insist on the role played by auditory information in multimodal interactions. Wolf et al. [28] and Effenberg et al. [7] showed that subjects can benefit from multimodal motor representation in a rowing-type task.

Wolf et al. also report that auditory feedback can reduce spatial error and improve synchronization when the feedback is related to the internal representation of the task rather than short-time features of the movement. Karageorghis and Terry [15] suggested as well that sound feedback can improve mood, hence performance, in sports and leisure activities.

Sport and musical control are not the only domains where auditory interaction can improve motor learning. Thoret et al. [26] studied the sonification of drawings to investigate whether subjects could recognize a drawn shape from recorded and synthesized friction sounds. They noticed that people were able to identify gesture trajectories with the friction sound they produced and the model-generated sounds which used movement velocity as input.

A recent review by Sigrist et al. [23] presents experimental studies of sonification techniques. The authors formalize the different type of auditory feedback in the framework of motor learning theories. They insist on the fact that, despite important applications, several questions on auditory feedback for motor learning remain insufficiently explored.

Recent studies show that an additional feedback can improve physical rehabilitation processes and there is growing interest in using additional auditory feedback to guide movements of impaired or stroke patients [1,20,21,24]. For instance Huang et al. [13] designed a multimodal biofeedback with musical tracks in a reaching task with stroke patients and found that visual and auditory feedback together helped patients producing smoother and more accurate movements.

3   Materials and Methods

3.1   Experimental Setup

The *sound-oriented* task is based on the manipulation of a specific motion interface that allows for the continuous control of sound synthesis. Subjects are seated in front of a table on which two spots are drawn, named 1 and 2, marking the spatial starting and ending areas of the movement they will have to make. Subjects carry in their hand the motion interface, consisting of a small object containing 3D accelerometers and a 3-axis gyroscope. Figure 2 depicts schematically the setup. Data are transmitted wirelessly to a receiver through the IEEE protocol 182.15.4 (2.4 GHz Band), that transmits them to the computer using Open Sound Control (through the UDP protocol). A software programmed using the Max environment (Cycling '74) includes real-time data processing, sound synthesis and data logging (data, sound and video recordings of each subject). The subjects listen to the sound using headphones.

The angular velocity around the Z axis of the interface is used as input. The sound is synthesized from the difference between the performed velocity profile

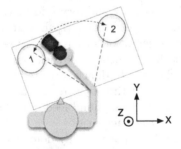

Fig. 2. Experimental setup. The subjects move the tangible interface from 1 to 2 in order to continuously control the sound and aim the targeted sound.

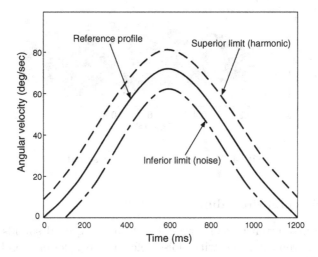

Fig. 3. Reference profile and the associated thresholds enabling the change in the sound qualities (noise or loud higher harmonic).

and a defined velocity profile, the *reference profile*, that varies between different conditions. This profile is a bell shape curve (derived from a Gaussian profile), corresponding roughly to the velocity profile typically found while moving the hand between two points [16], with a maximum peak velocity around 70 deg.s^{-1}.

The velocity signal is mapped to a sound synthesizer using Modalys[2] in Max. A resonator, a string model, is used to filter three types of input sound signal: one square sound signal at a fundamental frequency equal to 260 Hz (corresponding to C4), matching the second harmonic of the string, one square sound signal at a fundamental frequency equal to 910 Hz, matching approximately the 7th harmonic and pink noise (constant power per octave). The difference between the performed profile and the reference profile modulates the intensity of the higher harmonic or the noise inputs: positive values boost the higher harmonic, negative values boost the noise sound. This choice is motivated by the analogy with the velocity/pressure adjustments in bowing a string in a violin: low velocity might produce a noisy sound (with sufficiently high pressure), while increasing the velocity produces higher frequencies.

The sound level of the added effect is effective only when the difference reaches a given threshold, of constant value over the whole profile of velocity, as illustrated in Fig. 3. Once the threshold is reached, the intensity of the effect depends linearly on the difference between the performed and reference velocity values. Our interest was to investigate how the subjects can learn a specific movement without guessing it directly from the sound morphology of the reference sound. As shown in Fig. 4, the intensity morphology of the target sound does not match the reference profile.

---

[2] Modalys (Ircam), http://www.forumnet.ircam.fr/product/modalys. The object used is "MONO-STRING", see documentation for details.

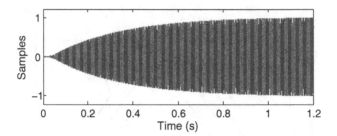

Fig. 4. Waveform of the target sound.

3.2 Experimental Procedure

The subjects first listen to the target sound and to typical sounds associated to incorrect movements: one with noise referring to a lower angular velocity movement and one with an extra harmonic note referring to a higher angular velocity. All the sounds are 1.2 s long. The subjects can listen to the sounds as many times as they wish until they feel comfortable distinguishing the different sound characteristics. Figure 5 shows the spectrogram of the three example sounds, which are chosen to be easily discriminated by the subjects according to their frequency content.

Subjects are then instructed to move the object with their dominant hand between areas 1 and 2 to produce the target sound. Their motion should last as long as the sound (1.2 s). The subjects do not have control anymore on the sound produced beyond 1.2 s.

During the first phase, we call *Exploration*, subjects perform 60 movements (30 rightward and 30 leftward) with the normal symmetrical profile called E as a

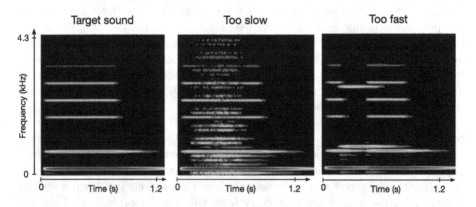

Fig. 5. Sonograms of the three example sounds; left: target sound produced if the movement matches exactly the target velocity profile *i.e.* the plain line in Fig. 3; middle: sound containing noise produced by a slow movement; right: sound with the higher harmonic produced by a too fast movement.

reference for feedback generation. Between each movement, they must wait until a *beep* is emitted, which occurs randomly between 2.5 and 3.5 s. This random start is set to avoid the creation of a rhythmic pattern in chaining the movements.

In the second phase, *Adaptation*, subjects are blindfolded and asked to perform three blocks of 50 movements. For each block, the reference velocity profile was changed following the sequence A - B - A, without informing the subjects. As illustrated in Fig. 6, the profiles A and B were obtained from profile E by shifting the temporal position of the maximum velocity. Figure 6 also shows the changes in the initial slope, which is approximated between start point and maximum of the profile. Profile A thus exhibits a higher acceleration and a slower deceleration. Profile B exhibits the opposite variation: a lower acceleration and higher deceleration.

The subjects are asked to fill in a questionnaire at the end of the experiment. It contains questions about their musical abilities, whether they are used to manipulate digital interfaces, asks whether they noticed modifications in the system in both phases, and invites them to rate the difficulty and the degree of control they experienced.

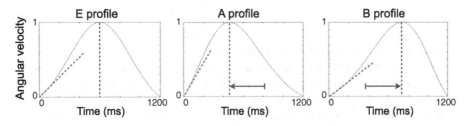

Fig. 6. Reference profiles of angular velocity used in the different phases of the experiment, showing initial slopes and peak shifts; amplitudes are normalized.

3.3 Subjects

Fourteen subjects volunteered for the experiment. All were healthy and reported normal hearing. They were 23.6 ± 1.9 years old and three of them were left-handed (21 %). All were familiar with digital interfaces such as computers, and were familiar with music from recreational to professional levels (1 to 20 years of instrumental practice). All subjects gave written informed consent for the experiment.

3.4 Data Analysis

The analysis is based on the comparison between the angular velocity time profile performed by the subjects v_i and the reference profile u_i, where i is the ith time sample (50 Hz sampling frequency). The recorded profiles are low-pass filtered with a 10 Hz cutoff Savitsky-Golay filter. As described below, different measures are estimated to capture specific features of the performed profiles. In a second step, the time evolutions of these measures were examined to find trends over the series of the subjects' trials, using t-tests and ANOVAs.

3.5   Angular Velocity Profile Parameters

The different measures described below were considered:

First, the mean error can be evaluated for each trial by taking the standard deviation of the difference between performed angular velocity v_i and the reference profile u_i:

$$mean\ error = \frac{1}{(N-1)}\sqrt{\sum_{i=1}^{N}[v_i - u_i]^2} \tag{1}$$

N being the total number of samples.

Second, the mean or first order moment of the profile was computed. It allows us to characterize where the largest velocity values are reached.

$$first\ moment = \Delta t\frac{\sum_{i=1}^{N} v_i i}{\sum_{i=1}^{N} v_i} \tag{2}$$

Δt being the time interval between two samples.

Third, we computed an approximation of the initial slope of the velocity profile. The changes in dynamics to A and B profiles come from the modification of the last two parameters, it is thus natural to compute these measures to evaluate subjects adaptation to the changes in the mapping. Table 1 gathers the parameter modifications in profiles E, A and B.

Table 1. 1st order moment and initial slope of the different reference angular velocity profile phases.

Profil	1st Moment [ms]	Initial slope [deg]
E	600	34.6
A	536	41.0
B	684	28.4

4   Results

We first investigated the evolution of the performance by comparing average error values at the beginning (8 first movements) and at the end (8 last movements) of each block (E, A, B, A). A general statistical analysis (ANOVA) was performed with three factors: the 4-level 'block' factor, the 2-level 'beginning/end' factor and the 8-level 'trial' factor. The analysis revealed a significant effect of the 'beginning/end' factor alone ($F_{(1,13)} = 26.3$, $p < 0.005$) which was not the case for the 'trial' factor. The interaction of 'beginning/end' and 'block' factors interestingly presented a significant effect on the performance ($F_{(3,39)} = 9.2$, $p < 0.005$), but the post-hoc tests indicated significant error reduction only within the first block (the Exploration phase). This shows that there is significant learning occurring in the Exploration phase which we further examined using individual t-tests.

4.1   Exploration Phase

During the Exploration phase, each subject starts with a spontaneous motion from area 1 to 2. By listening to the auditory feedback, they are able to adapt their movement to reach, more or less, the reference profile. A typical example is shown in Fig. 7, where the first and last profiles are plotted along with the reference profile. In this case, the ending profile is clearly closer to the reference profile than the initial one.

The mean error values of the velocity profile are shown in Fig. 8 for each subject. Error bars indicate the standard deviation across the profiles for a given subject. A large variability between the subjects can be observed on the initial movements (dark grey bars). This was expected since no specific instruction was given to the subjects about the dynamics of the movement they had to perform. These differences can thus be directly linked to the variability of the spontaneous movements performed by the subjects. After more than 45 trials, the variability between the subjects is largely reduced (by 50 %), which indicates

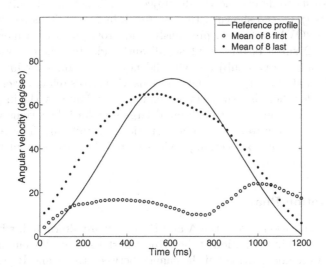

Fig. 7. Example of angular velocity profiles during the exploration phase (subject #7). The comparison between the first and last profiles clearly shows that the subject modified his movement towards the reference profile.

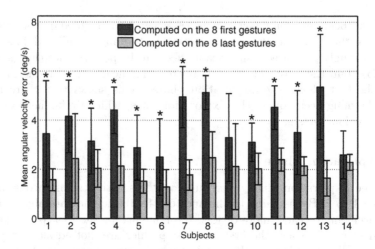

Fig. 8. Mean error results on angular velocity profile for each subject during the Exploration phase E; error bars indicate standard deviation; the asterisks indicate significant error reduction at the end of the Exploration phase ($p \leq 0.05$).

they were able to use the sound feedback to constraining their motion towards the reference profile.

Importantly, Fig. 8 also shows that for all subjects the mean error is lower in the last trials than in the first trials, which is also a strong indication of the positive effect of the auditory feedback. To characterize this quantitatively, we performed t-tests to determine which subjects exhibited statistically significant improvements ($p < 0.05$ shown with an asterisk in Fig. 8). This result confirms the general ANOVA performed previously, and provides us with more detailed information: 12 subjects out of 14 significantly adapted their motion during phase E. Among the two subjects who did not show significant improvement, subject #14 spontaneously performed motions with errors relatively close to that of last profiles for the other subjects, which might explain why the improvement was less significant. Subject #9 exhibited large standard deviations which also explains why the improvement is not statistically significant. The Adaptation phase discussed in the next section provides more information about the performance of these subjects.

4.2   Adaptation Phase

During the Adaptation phase, the A and B profiles are alternated, which allows for a more detailed investigation of the subject performances. We emphasize that the subjects were not informed of the change between the A and B profiles. The main difference between these profiles can be characterized by the variations of the first moment, or by the initial slopes (see Table 1). The first moment is actually close to the relative time to peak velocity (rTPV). Nevertheless, we found the computation of rTPV less robust, due to irregularities sometimes

Table 2. Significance of the parameter variations during the Adaptation phase, between the 14 last trials of each block ($p \leq 0.05$)

Subject	1	2	3	4	5	6	7	8	9	10	11	12	13	14
1st moment A → B	★	★		★		★	★		★	★	★		★	★
1st moment B → A	★	★	★			★	★				★		★	
Initial slope A → B		★		★		★	★			★	★	★	★	★
Initial slope B → A		★	★	★		★	★			★	★	★	★	

occurring in the velocity profiles. Therefore, we focused on the first moment and the initial slopes and performed statistical tests to examine whether significant adaptation can be observed within the transitions A to B and B to A. The results are reported in Table 2.

The individual t-test results show that we can separate the subjects into three groups. First, 5 subjects show significant adaptation for all blocks (#2, #6, #7, #11, #13). Two subjects show no significant adaptation (#5, #8). The other 7 subjects show some adaptations depending on the considered parameters. This can be explained by the fact that subjects adopt different strategies. For example, subject #1 adapted his profile globally as shown by the significant variation of the 1st moment. On the contrary, subject #12 principally adapted the beginning of the profile, as evidenced by the significant variation of the initial slope.

We performed a general statistical analysis (ANOVA) over the three blocks of the Adaptation phase for the 1st moment and initial slope parameters, respectively left and right on Fig. 9. The analysis revealed a significant effect of the phase factor for both parameters: $F_{(2,26)} = 6.7$, $p < 0.005$ and $F_{(2,26)} = 11.5$, $p < 0.005$ respectively. Post-hoc tests indicated a significant change between transitions A-B and B-A for the 1st moment and only for A-B transition for the initial slope. Therefore, these results show that subjects adapted their movement between the ends of each block, and this adaptation appeared more significant

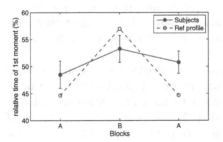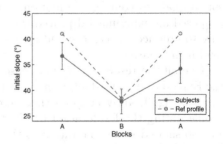

Fig. 9. Evolution of the relative time to 1st moment (left) for the 14 last trials averaged for all subjects (plain lines) showing an underestimation of this parameter, and initial slope (right) showing the overshoot. Error bars indicate 95 % confidence interval.

on 1st moment. Interestingly, subjects tend to underestimate the adaptation of the 1st moment position, indicating it might be difficult to modify that much this dynamic property of the movement. They also overshoot the initial slope towards small values, indicating they generally initiated their movement too slowly.

4.3   Qualitative Comments of the Subjects

The questionnaire filled by each subject offers additional information about the experiment. Concerning the Exploration phase, 8 subjects (out of 14) were positive that no change occurred in the system and 6 were unsure. Concerning the Adaptation phase, 8 subjects noticed that some changes occurred in the system, 5 were certain that no changes occurred, and 1 subject was convinced that the changes he perceived were solely due to his motion.

The subjects rated the difficulty of the task as 3.1 ± 0.9 and 3.1 ± 0.8 for the Exploration and Adaptation phases respectively (from 1-easy to 5-difficult). Subjects were also asked to evaluate the level of control they experienced over the system (from 1-no control at all, to 5-complete control). The results are close to the median : 2.3 ± 0.7 for the exploration phase and 2.8 ± 0.7 for the adaptation phase. Finally, they were asked questions concerning the system design. Subjects reported neither particular physical nor auditory fatigue (1.4 ± 0.6 and 1.2 ± 0.4 respectively, rated from 1 to 5). The perceived quality of the sounds produced was rated as 2.9 ± 0.9 over 5.

The performances of the subjects were not correlated with their sensation of control or success. Despite the fact that they all declared to be familiar with digital interfaces and practicing music (at a recreational level for most of them) we obtained quite heterogeneous results in terms of adaptation. It appears as though musical abilities or non-professional training is not a particular natural tendency to obtain better results in this particular adaptation task.

5   Discussion and Conclusion

We investigated the concept of *sound-oriented* task and questioned whether sound qualities could guide motion, and, in particular, its velocity profile. We proposed an experimental procedure to quantify how subjects adapt their gesture to produce a specific sound by avoiding either the presence of noise or of a loud higher harmonic.

Overall the results show that sensorimotor adaptations were found in both the Exploration and Adaptation experimental phases. In particular, 12 out of 14 subjects significantly adapted their movement to match the reference velocity profile during the Exploration phase. During the Adaptation phase, 12 out of 14 also showed some adaptation to the reference profiles, even if they were not informed of the sudden changes.

Nevertheless, important differences were noticed between subjects, which require further investigation. Several explanations can be put forward. First, participants, even musicians, appeared not to be used to manipulate sound with such a digital interface. The qualitative assessments of the subjects confirmed that the task was relatively difficult, which also indicates that the sensorimotor adaptation should be designed as more gradual. It is also noted that some subjects who obtained positive results did not notice the reference profiles variations. These observations are in favor of the presence of a strong implicit learning.

The type of extrinsic auditory feedback we developed in our experiment cannot be simply described using the well-known categories knowledge of result *KR* and knowledge of performance *KP* [12]. Knowledge of result provides user with information on the success of the task, as a score for instance. Knowledge of performance provides user with information on the performance itself, such as information about kinematics or joint angles. In our case, the auditory feedback is used to adjust the angular velocity profile (faster or slower). In particular, it leads to corrections occurring in two steps, first during the motion to adapt it, and second, after the motion when planning for the next trial. The first role of the auditory feedback here is thus to provide information during the motion, which could be considered as KP. Nevertheless, the subjects also make use of the general auditory feedback during one trial in order to plan the next trial. The quantity of noise or harmonic they heard during a movement informs them on the success of their trial. Such a feedback could be considered to be similar to KR. This might explain why we did not observe a smooth improvement rate during the trials, but rather improvements based on trials and errors corrections.

From a sensorimotor loop perspective, the auditory feedback we propose is continuous. Moreover, the auditory feedback is designed as the task itself (as opposed to a motion-oriented task). This experiment served us as a first step to design more complete investigations of sensorimotor adaptation driven by *sound-oriented* tasks. In particular, it shows the limit of using standard feedback categories for continuous auditory feedback. Additional formal investigation and experimental works is thus necessary to establish a new framework to describe interactive auditory feedback and the regulation of the auditory-motor loop using these systems.

In conclusion, our results establish that learning movement kinematics is possible in a auditory task and allow us to support the notion of *sound-oriented* task for the study of sensorimotor learning. They open up towards new experiments which we are being pursued.

Acknowledgements. We acknowledge support by ANR French National Research Agency, under the ANR-Blanc program 2011 (Legos project ANR- 11-BS02-012) and additional support from Cap Digital. We thank all the participants of Legos project for very fruitful discussions.

References

1. Avanzini, F., De Götzen, A., Spagnol, S., Rodà, A.: Integrating auditory feedback in motor rehabilitation systems. In: Proceedings of International Conference on Multimodal Interfaces for Skills Transfer (SKILLS09) (2009)

2. Avanzini, F., Rochesso, D., Serafin, S.: Friction sounds for sensory substitution. In: Proceedings of ICAD 04, pp. 1–8 (2004)
3. Bevilacqua, F., Fels, S., Jensenius, A.R., Lyons, M.J., Schnell, N., Tanaka, A.: Signime: music, technology, and human-computer interaction. In: CHI '13 Extended Abstracts on Human Factors in Computing Systems, CHI EA '13, pp. 2529–2532. ACM, New York (2013)
4. Boyer, E.O., Babayan, B.M., Bevilacqua, F., Noisternig, M., Warusfel, O., Roby-Brami, A., Hanneton, S., Viaud-Delmon, I.: From ear to hand: the role of the auditory-motor loop in pointing to an auditory source. Frontiers Comput. Neurosci. **7**, 26 (2013)
5. Caramiaux, B., Susini, P., Bianco, T., Bevilacqua, F., Houix, O., Schnell, N., Misdariis, N.: Gestural embodiment of environmental sounds: an experimental study. In: Proceedings of the International Conference on New Interfaces for Musical Expression, Oslo, Norway, pp. 144–148 (2011)
6. Effenberg, A.: Using sonification to enhance perception and reproduction accuracy of human movement patterns. In: Internation Workshop on Interactive Sonification 2004, pp. 1–5 (2004)
7. Effenberg, A., Fehse, U., Weber, A.: Movement sonification: audiovisual benefits on motor learning. In: BIO Web of Conferences, The International Conference SKILLS 2011, vol. 00022, pp. 1–5 (2011)
8. Forma, V., Hoellinger, T., Auvray, M., Roby-Brami, A., Hanneton, S.: Ears on the hand: reaching 3D audio targets. BIO Web of Conferences, vol. 00026, pp. 1–4 (2011)
9. Gelineck, S., Serafin, S.: A quantitative evaluation of the difference between knobs and sliders. In: Proceedings of the International Conference on New Interfaces for Musical Expression (2011)
10. Godøy, R.I., Haga, E., Jensenius, A.R.: Exploring music-related gestures by sound-tracing: A preliminary study. In: Proceedings of the COST287-ConGAS 2nd International Symposium on Gesture Interfaces for Multimedia Systems (GIMS2006) (2006)
11. Godøy, R.I., Haga, E., Jensenius, A.R.: Playing "air instruments": mimicry of sound-producing gestures by novices and experts. In: Gibet, S., Courty, N., Kamp, J.-F. (eds.) GW 2005. LNCS (LNAI), vol. 3881, pp. 256–267. Springer, Heidelberg (2006)
12. Hartveld, A., Hegarty, J.: Augmented feedback and physiotherapy practice. Physiotherapy **82**(8), 480–490 (1996)
13. Huang, H., Ingallas, T., Olson, L., Ganley, K., Rikakis, T., He, J.: Interactive multimodal biofeedback for task-oriented neural rehabilitation. In: Annual International Conference of the IEEE Engineering in Medicine and Biology Society, pp. 3–6 (2005)
14. Hunt, A., Kirk, R.: Mapping strategies for musical performance. In: Wanderley, M.M., Battier, M. (eds.) Trends in Gestural Control of Music, pp. 231–258. Ircam - Centre Pompidou (2000)
15. Karageorghis, C.I., Terry, P.C.: The psychophysical effects of music in sport and exercise: a review. J. Sport Behav. **20**(1), 54 (1997)
16. Mitrovic, D., Klanke, S., Osu, R., Kawato, M., Vijayakumar, S.: A computational model of limb impedance control based on principles of internal model uncertainty. PLoS One **5**, e13601 (2010)
17. Nymoen, K., Glette, K., Skogstad, S., Torresen, J., Jensenius, A.: Searching for cross-individual relationships between sound and movement features using an svm

classifier. In: Proceedings of the International Conference on New Interfaces for Musical Expression (2010)

18. Nymoen, K., Caramiaux, B., Kozak, M., Torresen, J.: Analyzing sound tracings: a multimodal approach to music information retrieval. In: Proceedings of the 1st International ACM Workshop on Music Information Retrieval with User-Centered and Multimodal Strategies, MIRUM '11, pp. 39–44. ACM, New York (2011)

19. Rath, M., Schleicher, R.: On the relevance of auditory feedback for quality of control in a balancing task. Acta Acust. United Acust. **94**, 12–20 (2008)

20. Robertson, J.V.G., Hoellinger, T., Lindberg, P., Bensmail, D., Hanneton, S., Roby-Brami, A.: Effect of auditory feedback differs according to side of hemiparesis: a comparative pilot study. J. Neuroengineering Rehabil. **6**, 45 (2009)

21. Rosati, G., Oscari, F., Reinkensmeyer, D., Secoli, R., Avanzini, F., Spagnol, S., Masiero, S.: Improving robotics for neurorehabilitation: enhancing engagement, performance, and learning with auditory feedback. In: 2011 IEEE International Conference on Rehabilitation Robotics (ICORR), pp. 1–6 (2011)

22. Rosati, G., Oscari, F., Spagnol, S., Avanzini, F., Masiero, S.: Effect of task-related continuous auditory feedback during learning of tracking motion exercises. J. Neuroengineering Rehabil. **9**(1), 79 (2012)

23. Sigrist, R., Rauter, G., Riener, R., Wolf, P.: Augmented visual, auditory, haptic, and multimodal feedback in motor learning: a review. Psychon. Bull. Rev. **20**(1), 21–53 (2013)

24. Subramanian, S.K., Massie, C.L., Malcolm, M.P., Levin, M.F.: Does provision of extrinsic feedback result in improved motor learning in the upper limb poststroke? A systematic review of the evidence. Neurorehabilitation Neural Repair **24**(2), 113–124 (2010)

25. Takeuchi, T.: Auditory information in playing tennis. Percept. Mot. Skills **76**(3 Pt 2), 1323–8 (1993)

26. Thoret, E., Aramaki, M., Kronland-Martinet, R., Velay, J.L., Ystad, S.: Sonifying drawings: characterization of perceptual attributes of sounds produced by human gestures. In: Proceedings of the Acoustics 2012 Nantes Conference, pp. 23–27, April 2012

27. Vogt, K., Pirro, D., Kobenz, I., Höldrich, R., Eckel, G.: Physiosonic - Movement sonification as auditory feedback. In: ICAD 2009, pp. 1–7 (2009)

28. Wolf, P., Sigrist, R., Rauter, G., Riener, R.: Error sonification of a complex motor task. In: BIO Web of Conferences, vol. 1, p. 00098, Dec 2011

Audio-Motor Synchronization: The Effect of Mapping Between Kinematics and Acoustic Cues on Geometric Motor Features

Etienne Thoret[1]([✉]), Mitsuko Aramaki[1], Christophe Bourdin[2],
Lionel Bringoux[2], Richard Kronland-Martinet[1], and Sølvi Ystad[1]

[1] LMA, CNRS, UPR 7051, Aix-Marseille Université, Ecole Centrale Marseille,
Marseille Cedex 20, France
{thoret,aramaki,kronland,ystad}@lma.cnrs-mrs.fr
[2] Aix-Marseille Université, CNRS, ISM, UMR 7287,
13288 Marseille Cedex 09, France
{christophe.bourdin,lionel.bringoux}@univ-amu.fr

Abstract. This paper presents an experiment dealing with the sensorimotor relation between auditory perception and graphical movements. Subjects were asked to synchronize their gestures with synthetic friction sounds. Some geometrical and dynamical parameters of the motor productions are analyzed according to the different mappings. This experiment provides a formal framework for a wider study which aims to evaluate the relation between audition, vision and gestures.

Keywords: Auditory perception · Sensorimotor loop · Friction sounds · Gestures

1 Introduction

When we are interacting with the material world, we often think that only the visual modality is engaged to guide our actions, like for instance when we are walking, reaching a glass or drawing on a paper. The use of other modalities, like the proprioceptive system or the audition is more subtle and not as well conscious as vision which seems to occupy most of our attention. Nevertheless, several studies have shown our ability to recognize a geometric shape only by touching it [18], or to recognize events only from the sounds they produce [10,11]. For instance, we are able to recognize and re-enact characteristic walking patterns from listening to the produced footsteps [28]. Other studies have focused on the sounds produced by continuous interactions and showed that we can discriminate rubbing, scratching and rolling sounds from the sounds they produced [6,7]. Another study focused on the sounds produced by interactions such as squeaking, squeaking or squealing and highlighted specific patterns responsible of their auditory recognition [20]. From rubbing sounds, we are also able to identify biological movements in the case of graphical gestures from sound.

© Springer International Publishing Switzerland 2014
M. Aramaki et al. (Eds.): CMMR 2013, LNCS 8905, pp. 234–245, 2014.
DOI: 10.1007/978-3-319-12976-1_15

More precisely, these studies revealed that we are able to identify a gesture, and to a certain extent the shape, drawn by a human only from the friction sound generated by the pen mine rubbing the paper [19,21].

The interaction between vision or proprioception and movements has already been studied. In different seminal studies, Viviani and colleagues have largely investigated such relations. For vision, they showed that we are more accurate when we follow a spotlight target which respects the dynamics of biological movements, also called the 1/3 power law. This law links the velocity of a movement to the curvature of its trajectory [14,24,25]. The blindfolded manual reproduction of a kinesthetic stimulus has also been studied in another experiment [27] that likewise revealed that subjects based the reproduction of the kinesthetic stimulus on the velocity of the target.

From the auditory point of view, the manual production associated to the timbre variations of an acoustical stimulus has not been studied in the same way. Some studies investigated the relation between a sound and a gesture in specific situations. In particular, the case of musical gesture has been widely studied [12,15,16]. Such relations were for instance investigated in an experiment where subjects were asked to imitate a musical excerpt in three dimensions with their hands [5]. This study revealed that the subjects synchronized gesture parameters – mainly the velocity and the acceleration – on specific sound descriptors, mainly the pitch and the loudness. In another study, Caramiaux et al. [4] asked subjects to imitate environmental sounds with their hands, in order to distinguish different behaviors according to the *causality* of the imitated sound event.

In this article, a work in progress about the direct relationship between the auditory system and the graphical motor competency is presented. Our aim is to investigate how audition can guide a graphical gesture in a synchronization task. Moreover, we aimed at investigating the relation between sound and graphical movements with calibrated auditory stimuli which clearly evoked motions. In the case of vision, it is easy to create a calibrated stimulus which evokes a movement and to control its velocity using for instance a moving spot light. In the case of auditory stimuli, the problem is less simple. As mentioned before, the friction sound produced by a mine pen rubbing a paper clearly evokes a movement and has already been used to investigate the gesture evoked by such friction sounds [19]. Here, we used the same kind of sound to create calibrated auditory stimuli as acoustical targets evoking a specific movement. Rather than using recorded frictions sounds of someone drawing, we will use synthesized ones. Synthesis indeed enables to precisely control the friction sound produced by an object rubbing a surface by isolating one aspect, for instance the kinematic, linked to the movements that produced the sound.

This paper therefore presents an experiment where subjects were asked to synchronize their gestures on different synthesized friction sounds. They were asked to draw ellipses or circles according to the sound, and to translate the evocations of the sounds in their graphical productions. In particular, we investigated the influence of different mapping strategies between the gesture velocity and the sound parameters on the motor production task. The paper is organized in two parts, the synthesis process is firstly presented, in a second time the experiment and the results are presented and discussed.

2   Synthesis of Friction Sounds

In this study, timbre variations of friction sounds will be used as the acoustical target evoking movements. Such sounds naturally evoke movements according to their timbre variations without any spatialization processes. To synthesize such variations, we used a phenomenological model that has been proposed by Gaver [10] and improved by Van den Doel et al. [23]. This model supposed that the sound produced by the friction between a plectrum and a rough surface results from a series of impacts on a resonator. The quicker the plectrum rubs the surface, the higher the number of impacts, and therefore the higher the pitch of the sound. From a signal point of view, the surface can be modeled by a noise[1]. And finally, the friction sound produced by the motion of the plectrum on the surface can be synthesized by low pass filtering the noise with a cutoff frequency proportional to the velocity of the plectrum (see [7] for a recent implementation). The modeling of the resonator is done by filtering the low pass filtered noise with a resonant filter bank tuned to the modal characteristics of the rubbed object [1,2].

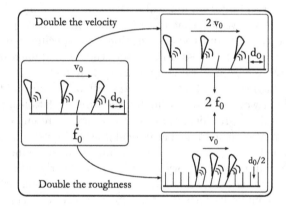

Fig. 1. A simple example of the phenomenological model of friction sounds. The three cases presented illustrate the ambiguity between velocity and roughness in the produced friction sound.

Mapping Strategy. The synthesis process necessitates the determination of a mapping between gesture (velocity) and sound (cutoff frequency of the lowpass filter) parameters. The cutoff frequency of the low pass filter is linked to the velocity of the plectrum by a proportionality coefficient α: $f_c(t) = \alpha v_T(t)$. This coefficient is linked to the surface roughness, and the proposed mapping encompasses two physical effects: the roughness of the surface and the relative velocity of the pen that interacts with the paper. The relationship between these parameters can be illustrated by the following example. We consider a simple surface,

---

[1] The more classical model of roughness for a surface is the fractal one, whose spectrum is defined by $S(\omega) = \frac{1}{\omega^\beta}$. When β is null, the noise is white, when β equals 1 the noise is pink. The higher the β the smoother the modeled surface is [23].

with regularly spaced asperities separated from a distance d_0, as presented in Fig. 1. If the surface is rubbed at a velocity v_0, the pitch of the produced sound will be proportional to v_0 and inversely proportional to d_0. If the surface is now rubbed at a velocity that by two times greater, the pitch of the friction sound produced will be also doubled. In the same way, if the distance d_0 is divided by two, the pitch will be doubled. Finally, when we listen to such a friction sound, there is an ambiguity about the conveyed information. When increasing α, do we imagine that the surface become rougher, or do we imagine that the rubbing is twice as faster?

3 Experiment

The goal of the experiment was to evaluate the characteristics of the evocation induced by a friction sound using a synchronization task between a graphical gesture and a friction sound in visual open loop (i.e. the subjects were blindfolded during the task). It was effectuated in different acoustical conditions corresponding to different mappings between the velocity and the cutoff frequency to evaluate their influence on the produced graphical movements.

3.1 Methods

Subjects and Apparatus. 12 participants took part in the experiment: two women and nine men. The average age was 24.17 years (SD = 2.55). All the participants were right handed. None of the subjects were familiar with the topic of the study before the test. The subjects were blindfolded in front of a desk. The sounds were played through Sennheiser HD-650 headphones. The graphical gestures were collected through a Wacom Intuos 5 graphic tablet at a time rate of 133 Hz and with a spatial precision of 5.10^{-3} mm.

Geometric Shapes. Two geometric shapes were used. An ellipse of eccentricity 0.9 and semi-major axis of 9.05 cm, and a circle with a radius of 6.36 cm (i.e. an ellipse with null eccentricity and a semi major axis of 3.18 cm). The perimeters equal to 43.86 cm for the ellipse and 40 cm for the circle.

Velocity Profiles. The dynamic along the shapes were defined according to the Lissajous motion:

$$\begin{cases} x(t) = a \cos\left(\frac{2\pi}{T}t\right) \\ y(t) = b \sin\left(\frac{2\pi}{T}t\right) \end{cases} \tag{1}$$

where a and b are respectively the semi-major and semi-minor axis of the ellipse (equal in the case of a circle). The chosen period T was 1.8 s, and 19 periods were generated. Thus, the durations of the stimuli were equal to 34.2 s. Such a configuration of an ellipse (a fortiori a circle) implies that the motion follows the 1/3 power law (i.e. a biological motion). In the case of the ellipse selected for the experiment, the tangential velocity varies between 13.88 cm.s^{-1} and 31.66 cm.s^{-1}. In the case of the circle, the tangential velocity is constant over the entire trajectory and equals 22.7 cm.s^{-1}.

Acoustical Stimuli. Synthesized friction sounds were generated with the phenomenological model previously presented, and from the velocity profiles defined in the previous paragraph. The role of the mapping coefficient α is here evaluated, we arbitrarily chose 6 different values: 5, 10, 20, 50, 100 and 300 Hz.s.m^{-1}. These values provide friction sounds with very different timbres and influences mainly brightness of the friction sound. The higher the α the brighter the sound. The Table 1 presents the minimal and maximal values of the cutoff frequency induced by these different values of α. Finally, 12 stimuli were generated: 2 (shapes) × 6 (mappings).

Table 1. Minimal and maximal values of the low pass filter cutoff frequency in Hertz. In the case of the circle, the cutoff frequency is constant for all the stimuli as the velocity is constant.

		Ellipse	Circle
α	f_{min}	f_{max}	f
5	69	159	111
10	138	318	223
20	276	635	445
50	690	1588	1135
100	1380	3176	2227
300	4140	9528	6681

Task and Procedure. The task consisted in drawing a shape – a circle or an ellipse – while being guided by the friction sound played through the headphones. The subjects were asked to synchronize their movement on the sound variations in the counterclockwise direction during the 34.2 s of the friction sound. To investigate the direct relationship between the auditory modality and the evoked gesture, subjects were blindfolded throughout the duration of the experiment (also called in open loop) and encouraged to translate the evocation of the timbre variations in their production. It was explicitly asked to lift the elbow to make sure that the joint used during the movement involved both the shoulder and the elbow, and not the handle as during a handwriting task. The test was preceded by a training phase during which subjects would train on an example of such a circle and an ellipse. It was explicitly stated to the subjects that these two shapes were present. Subjects could also adjust the height of the seat before the beginning of the experiment. Finally, each subject performed 36 trials: 2 (shapes) × 6 (mappings) × 3 (repetitions), which were randomized for all the subjects. The subjects were not aware about the size nor the orientation of the shapes. An experiment lasted about 45 min and the subjects were encouraged to make a break when they felt the need.

Data Analysis. Recorded data correspond to the coordinates of the stylus position on the tablet over time. Data analysis focuses on the geometric and kinematic characteristics of the motor performance. A data preprocessing is performed prior to the study of these two characteristics in order to overcome from the digital artifacts that appears when calculating the first and second derivatives of the data. The methods for calculating the different descriptors have been established in various articles of Viviani and colleagues [17, 26, 27].

Pre-processing. A smoothing of the data is performed by using Savitzky-Golay filters. Moreover, since subjects were blindfolded during the task, their graphic productions are not spatially accurate during the entire movement, and a low frequency deviation appears. In order to avoid the deflection of the center of gravity over time, a high-pass filtering is performed at 0.5 Hz on the recorded coordinates.

The recordings lasted 34.2 s for each trial. Since it took some time for the subjects to produce a regular and synchronous movement with the sound (in the case of ellipses), the first six periods were excluded from the analysis, which corresponds to the first 10.8 s. Finally, the following 12 periods were selected, which corresponds to 21.6 s.

Geometric and Kinematic Characteristics:

- *The eccentricity.* Eccentricity of an ellipse is defined with the following formula: $e = \sqrt{\frac{a^2 - b^2}{a^2}}$, where a and b are respectively the semi major and minor axis of the ellipse. To determine the average eccentricity of the drawn shape, we used a method proposed by Viviani [26]. We considered each recording as a group of pointlike unitary masses and we computed the inertial tensor. It is well known in classical mechanics that the inertial tensor of a two-dimensional structure can be modeled by an ellipse whose characteristics are linked to the eigenvalues of the inertial tensor. The precise method will not be described here, but we refer to the Viviani studies and to the Goldstein book for more details [13].
- *The tilt.* Tilt of an ellipse corresponds to its inclination relative to a horizontal axis. It is well known that when we draw an ellipse, the preferred coordination pattern corresponds to a an ellipse inclined of 45 degrees [9]. It can easily be calculated by using a similar method than for the eccentricity in diagonalizing the inertial tensor, the tilt corresponds to the angle between the eigenvectors with the horizontal axis.
- *The perimeter.* This is calculated from the recorded trace on the twelve analyzed periods.
- *The mean velocity.* This is computed from the 10 recorded cycles of movement.

3.2   Results

All the results are summarized in the Table 2. For each descriptor and each geometrical shape, a repeated measures ANOVA is performed to evaluate whether the mapping has affected the geometric and kinematic characteristics of the performances. Each significant effect is widely analysed with a Newman-Keuls post-hoc test to highlight interactions between the different mapping conditions.

Table 2. Marginals means and standard errors for the three geometrical descriptors.

	α	$\bar{e}$	$\overline{Perimeter}$ (cm)	$\overline{Tilt}$ (degrees)	$\bar{v}$ (cm/s)
Circle	5	.72 ±.044	7.4±1.11	55.4 ±7.23	4.26 ±0.991
	10	.63 ±.030	7.0±.92	47.9 ±5.78	4.06 ±0.817
	20	.63 ±.047	7.4±1.03	50.7 ±8.46	4.36 ±1.013
	50	.63 ±.042	6.9±1.03	38.7 ±6.69	4.34 ±1.178
	100	.59 ±.029	7.6±1.10	47.6 ±6.28	4.5 ±1.067
	300	.55 ±.032	5.3±1.23	48.9 ±7.08	3.42 ±1.324
Ellipse	5	.93 ±.016	15.7±1.82	37.9 ±6.20	8.74 ±1.981
	10	.93 ±.011	15.8±1.37	32.9 ±5.20	8.63 ±1.487
	20	.94 ±.009	15.9±1.57	39.4 ±6.27	8.84 ±1.693
	50	.94 ±.013	16.1±1.62	32.7 ±7.28	9.00 ±1.773
	100	.95 ±.010	15.9±1.45	24.9 ±5.17	8.87 ±1.592
	300	.94 ±.013	16.4±1.89	35.2 ±7.77	9.19 ±2.102

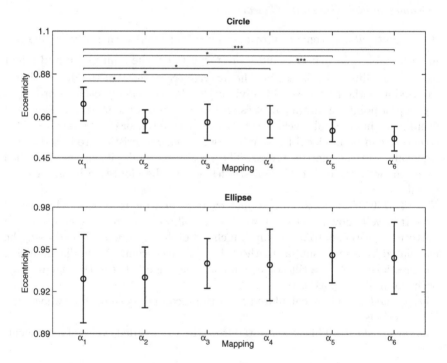

Fig. 2. Eccentricities: Marginal means and 95 % confidence intervals

– *Eccentricity.* The eccentricity was significantly affected by the mapping for
  circles but not for the ellipses, $F(5,55) = 5.907, p < .001$ and $F(5,55) =
  2.295, p = .0576$ respectively. In the case of circles, post-hoc tests revealed
  that the mapping $\alpha = 5$ provided significantly flatter circles than the five

others conditions ($p < .05$ for all comparisons). Moreover, $\alpha = 20$ provided significantly flatter circles than $\alpha = 300$, see Fig. 2.

- *Tilt.* The orientation wasn't significantly modified both for circles and ellipses, $F(5,55) = .854, p = .52$ and $F(5,55) = 1.695, p = .151$ respectively, see Fig. 3. It is noticeable that the orientation of the shape was higher for circles than for ellipses.
- *Perimeter.* As for the tilt, no significant effect of the mapping was observed both for the circles and the ellipses, $F(5,55) = 1.642, p = .16$ and $F(5,55) = .569, p = .72$, see Fig. 4. These results reveal that whatever the mapping, the size of the drawn shape wasn't affected, it's really interesting because it supports the hypothesis that in this task of synchronization, the mapping is not perceived as a change of velocity but as a change of the surface roughness, higher the mapping, higher perceived roughness is.
- *Mean Velocity.* No significant effect of the mapping was observed both for the circles and the ellipses, $F(5,55) = 1.604, p = .17$ and $F(5,55) = .581, p = .71$, see Fig. 5. These results confirm the previous ones, for each shape, a change in the mapping is not perceived as a change in the velocity but as a change of roughness.

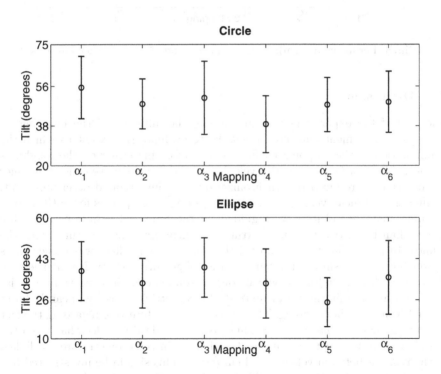

Fig. 3. Tilts (in degrees): Marginal means and 95 % confidence intervals

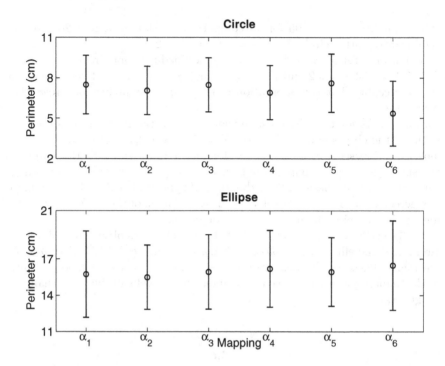

Fig. 4. Perimeters (in cm): Marginal means and 95 % confidence intervals

3.3 Discussion

The goal of the experiment was to evaluate the influence of the mapping on the evoked movement and more precisely, to evaluate the extent to which the manipulation of the mapping coefficient α – informing either on the roughness of the rubbed surface or on the velocity of the evoked movement – modifies the movement produced by synchronization. The investigated descriptors, tilt, perimeter, and mean velocity, did not differ between mappings for both shapes, meaning that the subjects were guided by the temporal variations of timbre rather than the intrinsic sound texture to synchronize their gestures with the sounds. In particular, results showed that the mapping effect was perceived as a modification of a surface roughness rather of gesture velocity. Nevertheless, in the case of drawn circles, for which friction sounds contained no timbre varia-tions and had a uniform sound texture, the eccentricity was significantly lower for high values of the mapping. This observation is interesting regarding the fact that mean velocities have not been affected, this indeed revealed that when the sound evoke any velocity variations, the changes in the geometry are not linked to the relation between velocity and curvature. This should be investigated fur-ther to better explain this, a possible hypothesis is that as the velocities are very low (about 4 cm/s for each mapping) it is more difficult to produce a regular movement than when the velocity is higher. This could be investigated by asking

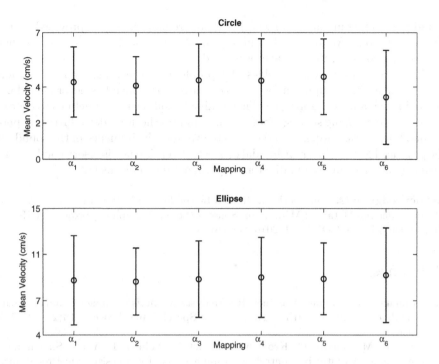

Fig. 5. Mean Velocities (cm/s): Marginal means and 95 % confidence intervals

subjects to draw circles more or less slowly without sounds to evaluate whether it should modify the geometrical regularity. Finally, these results revealed that in a synchronization task, the temporal variations of timbre contained in the ellipses dominated over the absolute information given by the sound texture. Another interesting point to highlight is the average eccentricity value of .93 observed for the drawn ellipses. This result confirms classical results about preferred coordination patterns observed in different studies that have highlighted that ellipses of .91 eccentricities were the easiest to draw [3,8]. It shows that the mapping and the synchronization task do not influence such motor attractors.

4   Conclusion and Perspectives

This experiment enables to conclude that the mapping – expressed by the proportionality coefficient α – between the sound parameter and the velocity of a rubbing plectrum modifies the produced synchronized movements only if there are no slower timbre variations as in the case of the ellipses. It enables to conclude that, from a perceptual point of view, the α coefficient is more related to the roughness of the rubbed surface than to the velocity of the gesture. Further analysis should be conducted to completely assess the results presented here. In addition, the analysis of asynchrony between the gestures and the acoustical sound parameters might reveal whether there are mappings that provided better synchronizations. An analysis by subject should also enable to evaluate whether intrinsic personal strategies have been used.

This preliminary study tackles the problem of the sensorimotor relation between an auditory input and a produced movement which has never been done before in such a formal approach. The obtained results will also help us to choose the adequate mapping strategy for friction sound synthesis model in further experiments. Such a framework should enable to evaluate the influence of the sound on the produced gesture in a multimodal context. Potential multisensory conflicts are currently being evaluated in different experimental conditions [22].

Acknowledgments. This work was funded by the French National Research Agency (ANR) under the MetaSon: Métaphores Sonores (Sound Metaphors) project (ANR-10-CORD-0003) in the CONTINT 2010 framework.

References

1. Aramaki, M., Kronland-Martinet, R.: Analysis-synthesis of impact sounds by real-time dynamic filtering. IEEE Trans. Audio Speech Lang. Process. **14**(2), 695–705 (2006)
2. Aramaki, M., Gondre, C., Kronland-Martinet, R., Voinier, T., Ystad, S.: Thinking the sounds: An intuitive control of an impact sound synthesizer. In: Proceedings of ICAD 09–15th International Conference on Auditory Display (2009)
3. Athenes, S., Sallagoïty, I., Zanone, P.G., Albaret, J.M.: Evaluating the coordination dynamics of handwriting. Hum. Mov. sci. **23**(5), 621–641 (2004)
4. Caramiaux, B., Susini, P., Bianco, T., Bevilacqua, F., Houix, O., Schnell, N., Misdariis, N.: Gestural embodiment of environmental sounds: An experimental study. In: Jensenius, A.R., et al. (eds) Proceedings of the International Conference on New Interfaces for Musical Expression, (NIME 2011) (2011)
5. Caramiaux, B., Bevilacqua, F., Schnell, N.: Towards a gesture-sound cross-modal analysis. In: Kopp, S., Wachsmuth, I. (eds.) GW 2009. LNCS, vol. 5934, pp. 158–170. Springer, Heidelberg (2010)
6. Conan, S., Derrien, O., Aramaki, M., Ystad, S., Kronland-Martinet, R.: A synthesis model with intuitive control capabilities for rolling sounds. IEEE/ACM Trans. Speech Audio Lang. Process. **22**(8), 1260–1273 (2014)
7. Conan, S., Thoret, E., Aramaki, M., Derrien, O., Gondre, C., Kronland-Martinet, R., Ystad, S.: An intuitive synthesizer of continuous interaction sounds: rubbing, scratching and rolling. Comput. Music J. **38**(4) (2014) (In press)
8. Danna, J., Athènes, S., Zanone, P.G.: Coordination dynamics of elliptic shape drawing: Effects of orientation and eccentricity. Hum. Mov. Sci. **30**(4), 698–710 (2011)
9. Dounskaia, N., Van Gemmert, A.W.A., Stelmach, G.E.: Interjoint coordination during handwriting-like movements. Experimental Brain Research **135**(1), 127–140 (2000)
10. Gaver, W.W.: What in the world do we hear? An ecological approach to auditory event perception. Ecol. Psychol. **5**(1), 1–29 (1993)
11. Gaver, W.W.: How do we hear in the world? Explorations in ecological acoustics. J. Ecol. Psychol. **5**(4), 285–313 (1993)

12. Godøy, R.I., Leman, M.: Musical Gestures: Sound, Movement, and Meaning. Taylor & Francis, New York (2010)
13. Goldstein, H.: Classical Mechanics. Addison-Wesley, New York (1962)
14. Lacquaniti, F., Terzuolo, C.A., Viviani, P.: The law relating kinematic and figural aspects of drawing movements. Acta Psychologica **54**, 115–130 (1983)
15. Leman, M.: Embodied Music Cognition and Mediation Technology. MIT Press, Cambridge (2007)
16. Rasamimanana, N.: Geste instrumental du violoniste en situation de jeu: analyse et modélisation. Ph.D Thesis - Université Pierre et Marie Curie - Paris VI (2008)
17. Stucchi, N., Viviani, P.: Cerebral dominance and asynchrony between bimanual two-dimensional movements. J. Exp. Psychol. Hum. Percept. Perform. **19**(6), 1200–1220 (1993)
18. Theurel, A., Frileux, S., Hatwell, Y., Gentaz, E.: The haptic recognition of geometrical shapes in congenitally blind and blindfolded adolescents: is there a haptic prototype effect? PloS one **7**(6), e40251 (2012)
19. Thoret, E., Aramaki, M., Kronland-Martinet, R., Velay, J.-L., Ystad, S.: Reenacting sensorimotor features of drawing movements from friction sounds. In: Aramaki, M., Barthet, M., Kronland-Martinet, R., Ystad, S. (eds.) CMMR 2012. LNCS, vol. 7900, pp. 130–153. Springer, Heidelberg (2013)
20. Thoret, E., Aramaki M., Gondre C., Kronland-Martinet, R., Ystad, S.: Controlling a non linear friction model for evocative sound synthesis applications. In: Proceedings of the 16th International Conference on Digital Audio Effects (DAFx), Maynooth, Ireland, Sept 2013 (2013)
21. Thoret, E., Aramaki, M., Kronland-Martinet, R., Velay, J.L., Ystad, S.: From sound to shape: Auditory perception of drawing movements. J. Exp. Psychol. Hum. Percept. Perform. **40**, 983–994 (2014)
22. Thoret, E., Aramaki, M., Bringoux, L., Kronland-Martinet, R., Ystad, S.: When acoustic stimuli turn visual circles into ellipses: sounds evoking accelerations modify visuo-motor coupling, Poster at the 15th International Multisensory Research Forum (IMRF), Amsterdam 11–14 June 2014
23. Van Den Doel, K., Kry, P.G., Pai, D.K.: FoleyAutomatic: Physically-based sound effects for interactive simulation and animation. In: Proceedings of the 28th Annual Conference on Computer Graphics and Interactive Techniques, pp. 537–544. ACM (2001)
24. Viviani, P., Terzuolo, C.: Trajectory determines movement dynamics. Neuroscience **7**(2), 431–437 (1982)
25. Viviani, P., Campadelli, P., Mounoud, P.: Visuo-manual pursuit tracking of human two-dimensional movements. J. Exp. Psychol. Hum. Percept. Perform. **13**(1), 62–78 (1987)
26. Viviani, P., Schneider, R.: A developmental study of the relationship between geometry and kinematics in drawing movements. J. Exp. Psychol. Hum. Percept. Perform. **17**, 198–218 (1991)
27. Viviani, P., Baud-Bovy, G., Redolfi, M.: Perceiving and tracking kinesthetic stimuli: Further evidence of motor-perceptual interactions. J. Exp. Psychol. Hum. Percept. Perform. **23**(4), 1232–1252 (1997)
28. Young, W., Rodger, M., Craig, C.: Perceiving and re-enacting spatio-temporal characteristics of walking sounds. J. Exp. Psychol. Hum. Percept. Perform. **39**(2), 464–476 (2013)

Movement Sonification for the Diagnosis and the Rehabilitation of Graphomotor Disorders

Jérémy Danna[1,2(✉)], Vietminh Paz-Villagrán[1], Annabelle Capel[3],
Céline Pétroz[3], Charles Gondre[4], Serge Pinto[2], Etienne Thoret[4],
Mitsuko Aramaki[4], Sølvi Ystad[4], Richard Kronland-Martinet[4],
and Jean-Luc Velay[1]

[1] LNC, CNRS, UMR 7291, Aix Marseille Université, FR 3C FR 3512,
13331 Marseille cedex 3, France
{jeremy.danna,vietminh.paz,
jean-luc.velay}@univ-amu.fr
[2] LPL, CNRS, UMR 7309, Aix Marseille Université,
13100 Aix-en-Provence, France
serge.pinto@univ-amu.fr
[3] Département D'Orthophonie, Faculté de Médecine, Aix Marseille Université,
Marseille, France
annabelle.celine@gmail.com
[4] LMA, CNRS, UPR 7051, Aix Marseille Université, Centrale Marseille,
13402 Marseille Cedex 20, France
{gondre,thoret,aramaki,ystad,
kronland}@lma.cnrs-mrs.fr

Abstract. The dynamic features of sounds make them particularly appropriate for assessing the spatiotemporal characteristics of movements. Furthermore, sounds can inform about the correctness of an ongoing movement without directly interfering with the visual and proprioceptive feedback. Finally, because of their playful characteristics, sounds are potentially effective for motivating writers in particular need of any writing assistance. By associating relevant sounds to the specific variables of handwriting movement, the present chapter aimed at reporting how supplementary auditory information allows an examiner (teacher or therapist) to assess the movement quality from his/her hearing. Furthermore, a writer could also improve his/her movement from this real-time auditory feedback. Sonification of some movement characteristics would be a relevant tool for the diagnosis and the rehabilitation of some developmental disabilities (e.g. dysgraphia) or acquired disorders (e.g. Parkinson's disease).

Keywords: Motor control · Kinematics · Auditory feedback · Dysgraphia · Parkinson's disease

1 Introduction

Audition takes on a share of diagnosis from a long time. The stethoscope is a proof. The first reason of using audition is that it is particularly suitable for reaching temporal

© Springer International Publishing Switzerland 2014
M. Aramaki et al. (Eds.): CMMR 2013, LNCS 8905, pp. 246–255, 2014.
DOI: 10.1007/978-3-319-12976-1_16

occurrences. Secondly, auditory information can be used as a time reference to get visual information. Finally, it is well established that multisensory (audio-visual) integration improves perception [11]. Altogether, these reasons make sound also relevant for motor rehabilitation. The additional benefit of audition in rehabilitation is that pleasant or funny sounds can improve the motivation of the subject, thanks to their affective valence.

In this book chapter, we focus on a particular activity: handwriting. Handwriting is one of the motor skills for which human expertise is the largest and most shared. Consequently, the study of handwriting disorders has an important societal issue, both in terms of education, to help children with specific handwriting difficulties, and in the clinical field, to reveal more general disorders.

1.1 Principle of Handwriting Movement Sonification

The strategy of sonification consists in using an intuitive mapping between sound and handwriting movement. Indeed, the impact of an auditory feedback depends considerably on the natural and correct interpretation of the applied mapping functions and metaphors.

It is thus possible to evoke motion by sounds, provided that we have already had the experience of hearing these sound-producing events. The Theory of Event Coding considers that all the sensory modalities involved in the perception of an action (visual if we see it, auditory if we hear it, and/or proprioceptive if we do it) would be integrated during experience together with the motor commands in order to provide a unified percept [13]. Then, this multimodal representation would be reactivated in unimodal conditions. This is why for instance, the auditory perception of a rhythm can activate motor regions of the brain [5], or executing silent finger movements on a piano keyboard can produce "audible tones inside the head" [2]. Consequently, the sonification of silent movements can be exploited to create a more stable and accurate cognitive representation of these movements. As a result, the multisensory integration of a sonified movement seems to improve both its perception and reenactment [25, 27].

In this context, the idea is to associate intuitive sounds to "hidden" variables of the handwriting movement, which are not (or not easily) visible, to make them naturally perceptible for an external examiner or for the writer him/herself. Handwriting sonification would then be useful for the diagnosis of handwriting difficulties as well as rehabilitation.

1.2 Sonifying Handwriting for the Diagnosis of Handwriting Difficulties

Specific handwriting difficulties, or dysgraphia, are considered here as a learning disorder of the mechanical writing skills, unrelated to any other learning abilities as reading or spelling [23]. It is not quite easy to distinguish a child who has a poor handwriting and a child with an actual dysgraphia. Dysgraphia is diagnosed by the therapist, thanks to dedicated and standardized tests (e.g. in European countries: the Concise Evaluation Scale for Children's Handwriting – the BHK test) [12]. Usually, the diagnosis consists in evaluating the legibility of the written trace and the slowness of handwriting production, determined by the number of letters written in a given time (5 min). Consequently, the children handwriting analysis is mainly based on the subjective appreciation of the therapist. Therefore, sonifying handwriting would help the therapist to take into account new information about the ongoing movement, which are not accessible when looking at the written trace.

How sonifying handwriting movement? Several strategies of sonification are possible [22]. In the present case, the first step was to determine the variables that inform at best about the handwriting quality. The second step was to identify the most relevant sounds to be associated with these variables in order to optimize handwriting perception. To validate these two steps, we conducted a first experiment based on the auditory perception of sonified handwriting [9]. Adult participants had to listen to and score the sonified handwriting of various writers. These writers were children with dysgraphia, children without dysgraphia and adults without dysgraphia. Handwriting samples of these 3 groups of writers were previously recorded on a graphic tablet and transformed into sound files. The rationale was that, if the sonification was correct, the listeners would be able to recognize dysgraphic handwriting only "by ear", without seeing it. The results of this experiment revealed that listeners scored poor handwriting significantly less than skilled handwriting, thus validating the variable/sound associations.

This experiment validated the sonification of selected variables (including the movement velocity and fluency) for characterizing dysgraphia. We propose that the pen-and-paper test used for the diagnosis of dysgraphia (e.g. the BHK test [12]) be realized on graphic tablet in order to assess both the handwriting product and process.

1.3 Sonifying Handwriting for the Rehabilitation of Handwriting Difficulties

After validating the sonification for the diagnosis of handwriting difficulties, the second step was to apply the same sonification as a real-time feedback for the rehabilitation of dysgraphic handwriting. Although the use of an additional auditory feedback in handwriting rehabilitation is not a novelty [19], the development of numeric technologies provides now the writer with the possibility of real-time computer-assisted feedback.

So far, auditory feedback has been explored as a means of compensating disabilities in different sensorimotor deficits. For example, Baur and colleagues associated an auditory feedback with the grip force for the treatment of writer's cramp [3]. As a sound was presented, its frequency changed with the variation in force applied to the pen by the fingers. Results revealed a significant reduction of vertical pressure exerted on the tablet by the tip of the writing stylus and an improvement in performance. Plimmer and colleagues proposed a multimodal system based on auditory and haptic feedback for signature learning in blind children [18]. An auditory feedback varied as a function of the x and y position of the stylus, and a haptic guidance pulled the user's hand around a predefined trajectory. The authors concluded that the multisensory feedback was efficient in helping the blind children to learn how to sign.

Recently, we tested the effect of movement sonification as real-time auditory feedback on handwriting learning in adults [8]. The task consisted in learning new characters with the non-dominant hand. Half of the characters were learned with the auditory feedback and the other half were learned without supplementary feedback. Beneficial effects of the auditory feedback were revealed on handwriting movements, which were faster and more fluent. This study demonstrated the efficacy of this method of sonification in proficient adults. The aim of the present study was to go a step further and to test it in a real rehabilitation protocol with children with dysgraphia. We hypothesized that if the handwriting variables and the sounds were appropriately selected, children with dysgraphia would be able to hear what is not correct in their handwriting movements and hence to improve them.

2 Experiment

2.1 Method

Seven children with dysgraphia (all boys, mean age 8.1 years) diagnosed by means of the BHK test [4, 12], and following a handwriting rehabilitation program, participated in the experiment. Prior to the experiment, parents signed an informed consent form. The experiment was conducted in agreement with the Aix Marseille University guidelines. Data were collected by the authors in the therapist's office.

The rehabilitation program was designed as a training session per week, during 4 weeks. The experiment was comprised of a classic "pre-test/training/post-test" longitudinal protocol (see Fig. 1).

The pre- and post-tests were run at the beginning and end of each training session. They consisted in tracing six alternating downward and upward loops ($\partial\partial\partial$), and in writing the French sentence '*la nuit, la lune est belle*' ('in the night, the moon is beautiful') in cursive letters. The training consisted in producing various strokes, elliptic and circular shapes, and loops with the real-time auditory feedback. The mean duration of the training with sounds was twenty minutes. As a whole, each session lasted thirty minutes.

Based on our previous study [9], three variables were selected for real-time sonification: the instantaneous pressure exerted by the pen on the paper, the instantaneous tangential velocity and the supernumerary velocity peaks, which inform specifically on movement fluency. Tangential velocity and pressure were supplied by the graphic tablet (Wacom, Intuos3 A4, sampling frequency 200 Hz). The supernumerary velocity peaks were determined from a specific variable, the Signal-to-Noise velocity peak difference (SNvpd) [10]. SNvpd is computed by subtracting the number of velocity peaks when velocity is filtered with a cutoff frequency of 5 Hz from the number of velocity peaks when velocity is filtered with a cutoff frequency of 10 Hz.

The instantaneous tangential velocity was sonified by a rubbing [1, 26] or a squeaking sound [24] on a metallic plate, when it was lower than 1.5 cm.s^{-1}. Concerning rubbing sound synthesis, the model simulates the physical sound source resulting from successive impacts of a pencil on the asperities of a given surface. The surface roughness was modeled by a white noise reflecting the height of the surface

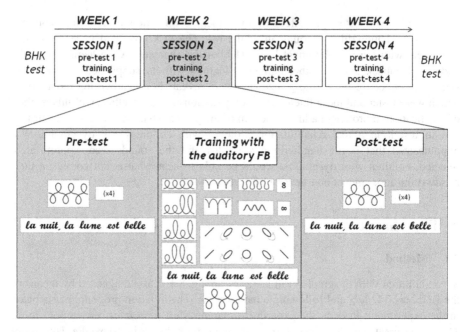

Fig. 1. Description of the longitudinal experiment, with the presentation of the tasks realized during the pre-test, the training, and the post-test in a typical session (in grey).

asperities. This noise was low pass filtered with a cut off frequency mapped to the tangential velocity of the writer. Concerning squeaking sound synthesis, the model simulates the sound source of an object strongly rubbing a metallic plate with a harmonic spectrum whose fundamental frequency is linked to the velocity of the movement. Supernumerary velocity peaks were sonified using an impact sound. Finally, the instantaneous pen vertical pressure was associated to the sound volume. While the pen was in contact with the tablet, the sound volume varied slightly with pen pressure. During pen lifts, no sound was emitted.

Within- and between-session evolutions were evaluated by comparing the pre- and post-test performances for each session (short-term effect) and by comparing the pre-tests of sessions 2, 3 and 4 to the pre-test of session 1 (long-term effect). Performances in loop production were determined on the basis of two kinematic variables, 1- Movement Time (MT), and 2- the SNvpd. The sentence writing performances were determined on the basis of the same kinematic variables. In addition, sentence legibility was estimated by six items extracted from the BHK test (items 3, 5, 6, 9, 11 and 13). Note that one of the children did not succeed in sentence writing: sentence writing analyses were carried out for six children only. Repeated measures ANOVAs (followed by Fisher's LSD post hoc test with Bonferroni's correction) were performed for each of the dependent variables.

Finally, a second BHK test was administrated to all children two months after the fourth training session. The speed and legibility scores obtained in the first and second BHK tests were compared by means of a non-parametric test (Wilcoxon test).

2.2   Results

Loops. Analysis of MT in the pre- and post-tests of the four sessions revealed a long-term effect ($F(3,18) = 6.37$, $p < .01$), a short-term effect ($F(1, 6) = 22.71$, $p < .01$), and a significant interaction ($F(3, 18) = 3.25$, $p < .05$). Post hoc analysis showed that MT significantly decreased between the first pre-test and the pre-test of the three other sessions ($p < .0001$, Fig. 2).

Analysis of SNvpd revealed a long-term effect ($F(3, 18) = 8.55$, $p < .001$), a short-term effect ($F(1, 6) = 20.67$, $p < .01$), and an interaction ($F(3, 18) = 4.31$, $p < .05$). Post hoc tests confirmed that movement fluency improved between the first pre-test and the pre-test of the three other sessions ($p < .0001$, Fig. 2).

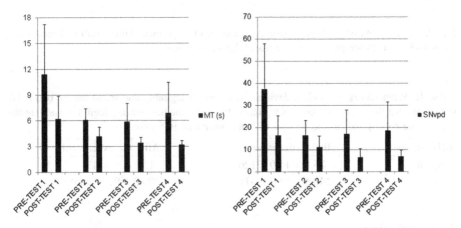

Fig. 2. Loops production. Mean (standard deviation) of Movement Time (MT) and movement fluency (SNvpd) in the pre- and post-tests of the four sessions.

Sentence. Comparison of pre- and post-tests of the four sessions revealed a significant within-session decrease in MT ($F(1, 5) = 9.24$, $p < .05$). Post hoc test showed that the MT decrease was significant only between the first pre-test and the pre-tests of the third and fourth sessions ($p < .05$ and $p < .01$, respectively).

Movement fluency showed a within-session improvement (short term effect, $F(1, 5) = 7.65$, $p < .05$). In addition, post hoc tests revealed that movement fluency improved between the first pre-test and the pre-tests of the three other sessions (long term effect, $p < .01$, $p < .001$, and $p < .0001$, respectively, see Fig. 3).

Finally, analysis of sentence legibility did not show any significant between- and/or within-session variation (p > 0.26).

BHK. Comparisons of the two BHK tests confirmed that both handwriting legibility and speed were greater after the four weeks of rehabilitation than before (see Table 1, $p < .05$).

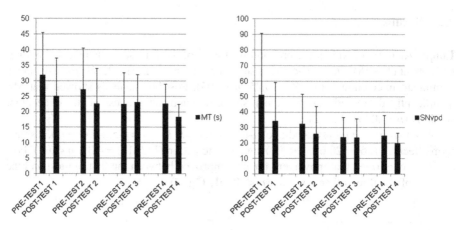

Fig. 3. Sentence writing. Mean (standard deviation) of Movement Time (MT) and movement fluency (SNvpd) in the pre- and post-tests of the four sessions.

Table 1. Mean scores, ± standard deviation (median) of legibility and speed for the two BHK tests. Note that the lower the score of legibility, the better the handwriting legibility and that the speed score corresponds to the number of letters produced in 5 min.

BHK scores	Before the experiment	After the experiment
Legibility	25.5 ± 11.0 (21.5)	15.2 ± 4.4 (13)
Speed	140.5 ± 58.3 (147)	203.0 ± 91.4 (205)

3 Conclusion

3.1 Main Results

The improvement of performance both within and across sessions confirmed the beneficial effect of the sonification procedure: children with dysgraphia were able to improve their handwriting movements after four sessions of twenty minutes of rehabilitation with sonification. Sentence writing results showed that real-time auditory feedback helped children with dysgraphia to write faster and more fluently without reducing writing legibility. These results are promising even if legibility did not increase across the four weeks of rehabilitation. Probably, children were focusing on their handwriting fluency and trying to write with less effort without paying much attention to their legibility. However, we can suppose that, with a longer period of rehabilitation with sonified handwriting, legibility may improve also. Indeed, a comparison of the two BHK tests, one before and one after the experiment, confirmed that handwriting legibility increased for all children. However, due to the long delay between the two tests (three months), it is hard to disentangle handwriting improvements related to the development of children from those related to the specific effect of the rehabilitation.

Obviously, we cannot ensure that there was a specific effect of adding sounds due to the lack of a control group who would have performed the same protocol without auditory feedback. For practical and ethical reasons, it was not possible but this specific effect was evaluated in adults [8] and the results confirmed the efficiency of the auditory modality for providing online supplementary feedback about handwriting movements.

An important issue that needs to be addressed is the emotional and aesthetic aspects of auditory feedback. The sounds have to be pleasant for the children, otherwise their impact could be negative. With this in mind, we envisage using an adaptation of the Questionnaire for User Interface Satisfaction [6] for children. The goal, here, would be to individualize the sounds used as a feedback to optimize the motivation of children with dysgraphia, who are very often reluctant to write. The option of applying more musical sounds is also possible and currently evaluated.

Finally, we need to pay particular attention to ensure that learners do not become dependent upon the supplementary feedback, a phenomenon known as the 'guidance hypothesis of information feedback' [20]. Although these authors demonstrated that, in a motor learning task, learners are less dependent on auditory than visual augmented feedback, it is important to avoid such a dependence since our aim is to facilitate the improvement of dysgraphic handwriting without the permanent assistance of auditory feedback.

In conclusion, auditory feedback may be applied as an interesting means of providing information on kinematic characteristics of handwriting movements. Sounds may be used to assist proprioceptive and visual feedback which is naturally used by the writer, thereby making "hidden" dynamic and kinematic variables perceptible.

3.2   Perspectives: Sonifying Handwriting for the Early Diagnosis of Movement Disorders in Adults

If handwriting sonification helps for the diagnosis of specific handwriting difficulties, it might also be a useful tool for the diagnosis of other movement disorders that affect handwriting. For this purpose, handwriting sonification of patients with Parkinson's disease (PD) is currently investigated.

Today, the diagnosis of Parkinson's disease (PD) is mainly based on the clinical-motor assessment of the TRAP syndrome (Tremor at rest, Rigidity, Akinesia and Postural instability), using the Unified Parkinson's Disease Rating Scale [14]. Handwriting is not included in the diagnosis of PD. Yet, it is often one of the first signs alerting the patient and leading him/her to consult. In the description of the disease made by James Parkinson in 1817, the alteration of writing precedes that of walking [16]. McLennan and colleagues reported a case of PD patient who had changes in his handwriting two years before other clinical symptoms appeared [15].

Theoretically, the main behavioral manifestations of PD can be assessed in handwriting movement analysis. Freezing of upper limb can be investigated by analyzing pen stops [17], tremor by the lack of handwriting fluency [10], bradykinesia and akinesia by the pen velocity, and rigidity by the pen pressure [21]. Therefore, sonifying handwriting movement might be used both for the early diagnosis of the disease, and for evaluating the effects of treatments on the symptom. However, because handwriting in PD patients differs from handwriting in children with dysgraphia, the first step is to identify the handwriting variables which are the most affected in PD.

We are currently running an experiment in which sixteen patients with idiopathic PD are required to perform several handwriting tasks on a graphic tablet with ('on') and without ('off') pharmacological treatment (basically, L-dopa medication). Results on spiral drawing revealed that the movement fluency and velocity, the number and the cumulative duration of movement stops, as well as the axial pen pressure exerted on the tablet were significantly different with and without L-dopa [7]. These preliminary results confirm that handwriting movements are affected in PD patients. The question is now to try to know whether the handwriting perturbations can be detected before the other main symptoms. To answer this question, we are investigating handwriting characteristics in *de novo* PD patients, who have just diagnosed with PD and not yet on treatments.

In conclusion, transforming relevant handwriting variables into sounds may allow the neurologists to consider supplementary objective criteria and thus, to help them to evaluate PD patients. Sounds may be used as a supplementary tool to access information about kinematics of handwriting movements. In this sense, handwriting sonification can be compared to a new stethoscope which allows identifying by ear the first behavioral manifestation of Parkinson's disease.

Acknowledgements. This work, carried out within the Labex BLRI (ANR-11-LABX-0036), has benefited from support from the French government, managed by the French National Agency for Research (ANR), under the project title Investments of the Future A*MIDEX (ANR-11-IDEX-0001-02) and by the ANR project METASON (CONTINT 2010: ANR-10-CORD-0003).

References

1. Aramaki, M., Besson, M., Kronland-Martinet, R., Ystad, S.: Controlling the perceived material in an impact sound synthesizer. IEEE Trans. Audio Speech Lang. Process. **19**(2), 301–314 (2011)
2. Bangert, M., Häusler, U., Altenmüller, E.: On Practice: how the brain connects piano keys and piano sounds. Ann. N.Y. Acad. Sci. **930**, 425–428 (2001)
3. Baur, B., Fürholzer, W., Marquart, C., Hermsdörfer, J.: Auditory grip force feedback in the treatment of writer's cramp. J. Hand Ther. **22**, 163–171 (2009)
4. Charles, M., Soppelsa, R., Albaret, J.M.: BHK - Échelle d'Evaluation Rapide de l'Ecriture chez l'Enfant. Editions et Applications Psychologiques, Paris (2003)
5. Chen, J.L., Penhume, V.B., Zatorre, R.J.: Listening to musical rhythms recruits motor regions of the brain. Cereb. Cortex **18**(12), 2844–2854 (2008)
6. Chin, J., Diehl, V., Norman, K.: Development of an instrument measuring user satisfaction of the human-computer interface. In: Proceedings of ACM CHI '88, ACM Press, New York (1988)
7. Danna, J., Eusebio, A., Azulay, J.P., Witjas, T., Pinto, S., Velay, J.L.: Computerized analysis of spiral drawing in Parkinson's disease. Mov. Disord. **29**(Suppl. 1), 313 (2014)
8. Danna, J., Fontaine, M., Paz-Villagrán, V., Gondre, C., Thoret, E., Aramaki, M., Kronland-Martinet, R., Ystad, S., Velay, J.L.: The effect of real-time auditory feedback on learning new characters. Hum. Mov. Sci. (in revision)

9. Danna, J., Paz-Villagrán, V., Gondre, C., Aramaki, M., Kronland-Martinet, R., Ystad, S., Velay, J.L.: Handwriting sonification for the diagnosis of dysgraphia. In: Nakagawa, M., Liwicki, M., Zhu, B. (eds.) Recent Progress in Graphonomics: Learn from the Past – Proceedings of the 16th Conference of the International Graphonomics Society, pp. 123–126. Tokyo University of Agriculture and Technology Press, Tokyo, Japan (2013)

10. Danna, J., Paz-Villagrán, V., Velay, J.L.: Signal-to-noise velocity peak difference: a new method for evaluating the handwriting movement fluency in children with dysgraphia. Res. Dev. Disabil. **34**, 4384–4675 (2013)

11. Effenberg, A.O.: Movement sonification: effects on perception and action. IEEE Multim. **12**, 53–59 (2005)

12. Hamstra-Bletz, L., DeBie, J., den Brinker, B.: Concise Evaluation Scale for Children's Handwriting. Swets & Zeitlinger, Lisse (1987)

13. Hommel, B.: Event files: feature binding in and across perception and action. Trends Cogn. Sci. **8**(11), 494–500 (2004)

14. Jankovic, J.: Parkinson's disease: clinical features and diagnosis. J. Neurol. Neurosur. Psychiatry **79**, 368–376 (2008)

15. McLennan, J.E., Nakano, K., Tyler, H.R., Schwab, R.S.: Micrographia in Parkinson's disease. J. Neurol. Sci. **15**(2), 141–152 (1972)

16. Parkinson, J.: An Essay on the Shaking Palsy. Whittingham and Rowland for Sherwood, Neely & Jones, London (1817)

17. Paz-Villagrán, V., Danna, J., Velay, J.L.: Lifts and stops in proficient and dysgraphic handwriting. Hum. Mov. Sci. **33**, 381–394 (2014)

18. Plimmer, B., Reid, P., Blagojevic, R., Crossan, A., Brewster, S.: Signing on the tactile line: a multimodal system for teaching handwriting to blind children. ACM T. Comput.-Hum. Interact. 18(3), Article 17, 1–29 (2011)

19. Reavley, W.: The Use of biofeedback in the treatment of writer's cramp. J. Behav. Ther. Exp. Psychiatry **6**, 335–338 (1975)

20. Ronsse, R., Puttemans, V., Coxon, J.P., Goble, D.J., Wagemans, J., Wenderoth, N., Swinnen, S.P.: Motor learning with augmented feedback: modality dependent behavioral and neural consequences. Cereb. Cortex **21**, 1283–1294 (2011)

21. Rosenblum, S., Samuel, M., Zlotnik, S., Erikh, I., Schlesinger, I.: Handwriting as an objective tool for Parkinson's disease diagnosis. J. Neurol. **260**(9), 2357–2361 (2013)

22. Sigrist, R., Rauter, G., Riener, R., Wolf, P.: Augmented visual, auditory, haptic, and multimodal feedback in motor learning: a review. Psychon. Bull. Rev. **20**(1), 21–53 (2013)

23. Søvik, N., Arntzen, O.: A Comparative study of the writing/spelling performances of "normal", dyslexic and dysgraphic children. Eur. J. Spec. Needs Educ. **1**(2), 85–101 (1986)

24. Thoret, E., Aramaki, M., Gondre, C., Kronland-Martinet, R., Ystad, S.: Controlling a non linear friction model for evocative sound synthesis applications. In: Proceedings of 16th International Conference on Digital Audio Effects (DAFx), Maynooth, Ireland, pp. 1–7 (2013)

25. Thoret, E., Aramaki, M., Kronland-Martinet, R., Velay, J.L., Ystad, S.: From sound to shape: auditory perception of drawing movements. J. Exp. Psychol. Hum. Percept. Perform. **40**, 983–994 (2014)

26. Van den Doel, K., Kry, P.G., Pai, D.K.: Foleyautomatic: physically-based sound effects for interactive simulation and animation. In: Proceedings of SIGGRAPH '01, pp. 537–544. ACM Press, New York (2001)

27. Young, W., Rodger, M., Craig, C.M.: Perceiving and reenacting spatiotemporal characteristics of walking sounds. J. Exp. Psychol. Hum. **39**(2), 464–476 (2013)

Music and Sound Data Mining

MidiFind: Similarity Search and Popularity Mining in Large MIDI Databases

Guangyu Xia$^{(\boxtimes)}$, Tongbo Huang, Yifei Ma, Roger Dannenberg, and Christos Faloutsos

School of Computer Science, Carnegie Mellon University,
Pittsburgh, PA, USA
{gxia,tongboh,yifeim,rbd,christos}@andrew.cmu.edu

Abstract. While there are perhaps millions of MIDI files available over the Internet, it is difficult to find performances of a particular piece because well labeled metadata and indexes are unavailable. We address the particular problem of finding performances of compositions for piano, which is different from often-studied problems of Query-by-Humming and Music Fingerprinting. Our *MidiFind* system is designed to search a million MIDI files with high precision and recall. By using a hybrid search strategy, it runs more than 1000 times faster than naive competitors, and by using a combination of bag-of-words and enhanced Levenshtein distance methods for similarity, our system achieves a precision of 99.5 % and recall of 89.8 %.

Keywords: Music search · Similarity search · Large scale string matching · Data mining · Popularity mining · MIDI

1 Introduction

As music computing becomes more advanced, we have the opportunity to incorporate more data from human performances and to apply machine learning and music analysis to make computer music systems more musical and more expressive. Most existing human performances databases, e.g., the CrestMuse dataset [1] and the ones used in Widmer's works [23,24], are collected manually and take years to build. Moreover, they are either small in scale or not openly available for research. Potentially, an excellent source of music performance information is MIDI files on the Internet. There are at least one million MIDI files online and there are reasons to expect the number to increase. The online MIDI files are often free and they are also very easily distributed since their size is about 1000 times smaller than audio files.

However, these files are disorganized and difficult to search by metadata due to careless or casual labeling. Our goal is to automatically retrieve and organize these files so that comparative studies of different performances of the same pieces can be carried out on a large scale. Hence, we need a method to search on the order of one million MIDI files quickly, in a way that robustly deals

© Springer International Publishing Switzerland 2014
M. Aramaki et al. (Eds.): CMMR 2013, LNCS 8905, pp. 259–276, 2014.
DOI: 10.1007/978-3-319-12976-1_17

with performance variation, and without using metadata, which would be too unreliable. Specifically, we aim to solve the following problem:

- Given: A query MIDI file
- Find: *similar pieces*, i.e., different performance versions (including pure quantized versions) of the same composition, and also *popular pieces*, i.e., the compositions that have most performance versions.

The main challenges to solve these problems are the search quality and scalability. I.e., the system should be both accurate and fast enough to deal with a database with a million MIDI files.

The logical structure of our solution is shown in Fig. 1. The first step is to guarantee good search quality by carefully designing different similarity measurements for different representations. We present novel features for MIDI data based on a bag-of-words idea and melodic segments, and introduce a new variation of Levenshtein distance that is especially suitable for music melody. The second step is to dramatically speed up the search process. We present different hybrid indexing strategies that combine different representations and similarity measurements. The final step is to find the ideal thresholds for different similarity measurements.

To evaluate the system, we use a small and labeled MIDI dataset with 325 files. We also use a large unlabeled dataset that is downloaded and combined from several smaller datasets which are all free from the Internet. The large database contains 12,484 MIDI files with around 2,000 similar pieces.

Our *MidiFind* system is now deployed and hosted on http://www.cmumidifind. com:9000/. The main contributions of the system are:

- It is *effective*: it achieve **99.5 % precision** and **89.8 % recall**, compared to pure Levinshtein distance measurement, which achieves 95.6 % precision and 56.3 % recall.
- It is *scalable*, with sub-linear complexity for queries, and outperforms naive linear scanning competitors by more than **1000 times**.

The following section describes related work. Section 3 describes feature extraction and search quality. Section 4 discusses various strategies to achieve scalability. Section 5 describes the construction of the *MidiFind* system. We present experimental results in Sect. 6, and present some findings from our *MidiFind* system in Sect. 7.

2 Related Work

Music Information Retrieval has emerged as an active research area in the past decade. Much work has been done on music search. Both Music Fingerprinting systems [7,10] and Query-by-Humming systems [5,8,11,15,16,21,22,25] are related to our work.

For Music Fingerprinting systems, users record a short period of audio to query the system and the results are expected to be an *exact* match, i.e., the

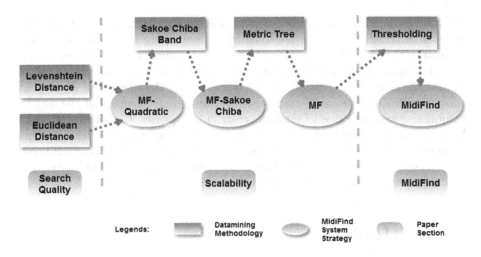

Fig. 1. The logical structure of Sects. 3, 4, 5 of the paper.

query audio must be a copy of a fragment of the reference audio. These systems are generally very robust to audio noise but a query of the same song with a slightly different performance will almost always lead to a failure. On the contrary, our *MidiFind* system deals with *similar* match, i.e., given a query, we aim to find different performance versions. Audio noise is out of our consideration since our query inputs are pure MIDI files.

Query-by-Humming systems share a similar architecture with *MidiFind* system. Most of them store MIDI files as references and they also implement approximate matching since human performances are not exact. The differences lie in the query part and the goal of the system. The queries of Query-by-Humming systems are usually very short audio snippets, while the queries for our *MidiFind* system are much longer MIDI files. Therefore, we can take advantage of the discrete nature of MIDI data and the full information contained in the full-length MIDI query, but at the same time have to deal with larger variations and a potentially longer matching process for longer sequences. The goals of Query-by-Humming systems are usually Nearest-Neighbor search, while our *MidiFind* system deals with range query, which aims to find out all different performance versions of the same composition.

Early Query-by-Humming systems [8,16,22] used melodic contour (defined as a sequence of up, down, and same pitch intervals) and string matching to match similar melodies. Later on, melodic contour was proved unable to distinguish melodies in large datasets [21] and researchers started to resort to dynamic time warping on melody notes [5,11,15,25]. One method studied is a brute-force fashion of dynamic time warping [15] which is certainly slow due to the $O(mn)$ complexity (m is the length of query and n is the total length of references) but serves as a baseline for future research. Different methods have been tested to speed up the searching process. Two of them [5,25] are closely related to our work in that they both use a 2-step pipeline approach to first shrink the target of candidates and then use dynamic time warping to test the surviving candidates. However, the first method relies only on dynamic time warping and has a limitation on the length of music. It cannot handle long queries and also requires segmentation labels on the reference music. The method of [5] has an innovative idea to combine N-grams with dynamic time warping but the search performance was poor due to random errors in the queries. Compared to them, the query of our *MidiFind* system is longer with few errors, at least at the beginning and ending. This enables us to use bag-of-words and novel clipped melody features to dramatically shrink the target of candidates and speed up the string comparison process, respectively.

3   Search Quality

We begin by parsing MIDI files into music note strings. After that, we design two different representations for each piece of music: the bag-of-words and clipped melody representation. For the bag-of-words representation, we adopt Euclidean distance; while for the clipped melody representation, we use enhanced Levenshtein distance.

3.1   Euclidean Distance for Bag-of-Words Representation

Inspired by the bag-of-words idea, we create a bag-of-words feature for music. Every piece of music is treated as a sequence of words, where each note is considered as a word by ignoring its length and octave. We consider each word as one of the 12 pitch classes within an octave (in other words, we use the MIDI key number modulo 12. We can also use modulo 24 and so forth) and consider the word count as the total number of times that each pitch occurs within the piece of music. (We actually first tried to incorporate the timing information in the feature vector but the performance was much worse.) Finally, the word count is normalized by the total number of pitch occurrences, resulting in a probability mass table. In the case of 12 pitch classes, this is equivalent to pitch class histograms often used in key finding [12].

The similarity of two pieces of music is measured by the Euclidean distance, as shown in Definition 1, between the corresponding bag-of-words feature vectors. This method works well, or at least is capable of filtering out most of the different pieces, since different pieces of music usually have different distributions over the pitch classes.

Definition 1. *The Euclidean distance (ED) between S and T, where $|S| = |T|$, is defined as:*

$$ED(S,T) = \sqrt{\Sigma_{i=1}^{n}(S_i - T_i)^2}$$

3.2   Enhanced Levenshtein Distance and Melody Representation

Besides the bag-of-words representation, we extract the melody from each piece of music as in most Query-by-Humming systems [8,16,22]. As suggested by G.Widmer [24], we can simply use the highest pitch at any given time as an estimate of the melody for each piece of music. The detailed extraction algorithm is described in Algorithm 1. We then use Levenshtein distance measurement with different enhancements on the extracted melodies.

Algorithm 1. Melody Extraction Algorithm

Data: Note Strings
Result: Melody Strings
sortedNotes = sort(all notes, prioritize higher pitches);
melodyNotes = empty list;
while *sortedNotes is not empty* **do**
> note = the note with highest pitch in sortedNotes;
> remove note from sortedNotes;
> **if** *the period of note is not entirely covered by notes in melodyNotes* **then**
>> split note into one or more notes of the same pitch named splitNotes, where each note corresponds to time period that has not been covered;
>> insert every note in splitNotes into melodyNotes;
>
> **end**

end
return melodyNotes;

Standard Levenshtein Distance. Levenshtein distance (a kind of Dynamic Time Warping) has been shown empirically to be the best distance measure for string editing [6], and this is the reason that it is also named string editing distance as shown in Definition 2. To calculate Levenshtein distance of two melody strings S and T of length m and n, we construct an m-by-n *Levenshtein matrix* where the (i^{th}, j^{th}) element of the matrix is the Levinshtein distance between the prefix of S of length i and the prefix of T of length j. However, it suffers high computational complexity, $O(mn)$, which we will discuss in Sect. 4. For our melody string distance, we set insertion, deletion, and substitution costs to be 1. (We actually tried to incorporate the note durations in the melody representation and weight the costs by the durations, but the performance turned out to be much worse.)

Definition 2. *The Levenshtein (string editing) Distance [2] between two sequences is the minimal number of substitutions, insertions, and deletions needed to transform from one to the other. Formally, the Levenshtein distance between the prefixes of length i and j of sequences S and T, respectively, is:*

$$lev_{S,T}(i,j) = \begin{cases} \max(i,j), & \textit{if } min(i,j) = 0 \\ \min \begin{cases} lev_{S,T}(i-1,j)+1 \\ lev_{S,T}(i,j-1)+1 \\ lev_{S,T}(i-1,j-1) \\ +(S_i \neq T_j) \end{cases} & \text{otherwise} \end{cases}$$

Enhancement 1: Lev-400. As previously discussed, standard Levenshtein distance is a good metric for measuring difference between strings. However, it does have one drawback in that the distance is strongly correlated to the string length. Unfortunately, melody string lengths vary significantly within our database. Figure 2 shows the histogram of melody string lengths.

Observation 1. *The distribution over the length of melody strings follows a power law.*

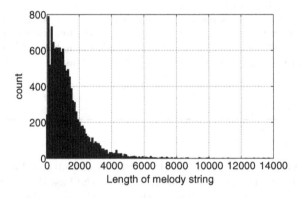

Fig. 2. Melody string length histogram on largest dataset. Mean: 1303. Standard Deviation: 1240. This follows a power-law pattern.

Such a large variance on the length will cause problems in matching. For instance, two melody strings S_1 and T_1 both have length 500, and the other two melody strings S_2 and T_2 both have length 1000. If we get a Levenshtein distance of 100 from both pairs, the first pair is trivially more different from each other compared to the second pair. This inspires us to find a way to turn melody strings into equal length and we find a nice property that chopping and concatenating the first 200 and last 200 notes of long melody strings actually increases Levenshtein distance accuracy in a large-scale dataset, as in Observation 2. For melody strings shorter than 400 notes, we do not modify them but scale up the distances. The reason that this manipulation works is that (1) a unified length leads to a unified threshold for Levenshtein distance, (2) similar melodies tend to share more common notes at the beginning and the ending of the music piece, while performers tend to introduce larger variation in the body part. We call this enhanced Levenshtein distance *Lev-400.*

Observation 2. *Chopping and concatenating the first 200 and last 200 notes of long melody strings increases Levenshtein distance accuracy in a large-scale dataset.*

Enhancement 2: Lev-400SC. Lev-400 gives us melody strings with $l \leq 400$, where l is length of any string. A by-product of the Levenshtein distance computation is the sequence of notes that is shared by both strings, which can also be considered the *alignment* of the strings. By checking how strings align, we find another property of similar MIDI files: The optimal melody alignment path stays close to the diagonal in the Levenshtein matrix for similar MIDI files, as described in Observation 3. The reason for this observation is that we expect the entire pieces to match without any major insertions or deletions on the notes, so that the best alignment for similar strings should fall along the diagonal in the Levenshtein matrix. This property suggests using the Sakoe-Chiba Band, which constrains the string alignment path by limiting how far it may divert from the diagonal [18]. An illustration of the Sakoe-Chiba Band is shown in Fig. 3. We propose using a Sakoe-Chiba Band and finding a reasonable band width to balance the trade off between speed and accuracy. The speed factor will be discussed in Sect. 4. We call this enhanced distance metric *Lev-400SC*.

Observation 3. *The melody string alignment path corresponding to the smallest Levenshtein distance stays close to the diagonal for similar MIDI files in large-scale datasets.*

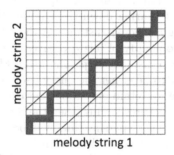

Fig. 3. The illustration of Sakoe-Chiba Band (between thin diagonal black lines) that acts as a global constraint on the Levenshtein alignment path of a Levenshtein matrix.

4   Search Scalability

The similarity measurements mentioned in Sect. 3 lay the groundwork for accurate matching between MIDI files. However, since there are at least one million MIDI files on the Internet, to search through all those files and find similar ones for any query can be very time consuming. That is why we design a set of hybrid methods (MF-Q, MF-SC, MF) that combine advantages from both similarity measurements and provide a way to search through the database that is both fast and accurate.

4.1   MF-Q: Combine Euclidean and Lev-400 Distance

We have discussed in Sect. 3 that using Euclidean distance on the bag-of-words representation can differentiate MIDI files that are dramatically different. However, we also need to consider the fact that some MIDI files might share the same notes but have entirely different orderings. Bag-of-words will not differentiate such MIDI files since mapping them to a low dimension (multiples of 12 depending on number of octaves involved), we lose a big chunk of information. The parsing step for the Euclidean distance will convert note sequences to low dimensional vectors. The complexity is linear to the size of MIDI files, and it only needs to be performed once. However, after finishing the parsing step, the calculation of Euclidean distance between two files is very fast: proportional to d, where d is the dimension of the word space.

Levenshtein distance is generally considered to be highly accurate but time consuming. All calculations are performed on melody strings extracted from the note strings, as introduced in Sect. 3.2. For two melody strings S and T with length m and n, the runtime is proportional to $m \cdot n$. By clipping and concatenating melody strings to 400 notes, we effectively set an upper bound on the runtime of Lev-400: $\min\{m, 400\} \cdot \min\{n, 400\} < 400 \cdot 400$. As shown in Fig. 2, the average length of melody strings is 1303; therefore, the clipped melody representation will lead to a speed-up of about 10.

Building on the two representations and similarity measurements, we design a hybrid method that runs bag-of-word first and then further filters the result by using Levenshtein distance. This is named *MF-Q* (short for MidiFind-Quadratic). The idea is that we want to shrink down the number of possible similar MIDI candidates by thresholding Euclidean distance. Although the candidate set from this step contains high probability of false-positives, they will be identified and removed by the Levenshtein distance step. The MIDI files returned in the final result has high probability to be either the query itself or some variation of that same music piece. Assume we retain only a percentage of p out of total melody strings through bag-of-words thresholding, then the total runtime needed to find similar pieces (excluding one-time parsing time) will be proportional to $(d + (400 \cdot 400)p)N$, where d is the bag-of-words dimension and N is the total number of MIDI files. We finally achieve a p as small as 0.025 which leads to a further speed-up of about 40. Therefore, the *MF-Q* speeds up the system about 400 times. We will discuss how to choose the p in Sect. 5 and give detailed experimental results in Sect. 6.

4.2   MF-SC: Sub-Quadratic Levenshtein Distance
with Sakoe-Chiba Band

MF-Q combines two distance metrics, but the Lev-400 step is still time-consuming. As mentioned in the Lev-400SC distance metric, we can limit the string editing path in the Levenshtein matrix. Consider our MIDI dataset and take melody string S and T with length m and n as an example, we limit the bandwidth to be

$$b = \max\{0.1 \cdot \min\{m, n, 400\}, 20\}$$

which is at least 20 notes and increases with the actual length. After using Sakoe-Chiba Band, the complexity of string comparison is sub-quadratic: $min\{m, n, 400\} \cdot b$. We call this method *MF-SC* (short for MidiFind-Sakoe-Chiba). MF-SC can achieve an accuracy performance that is close to MF-Q with a speed-up of about 10. We show the experimental results in Sect. 6.

4.3   MF: Search Using Metric Tree

MF-SC speeds up the Levenshtein distance step. We propose a further speed-up for the Euclidean distances by adopting the Metric Tree (M-tree), and call this method *MF*. An M-tree is constructed with a distance metric and relies on the triangle inequality for efficient range and k-NN queries. It is very effective when there is a clear threshold to differentiate close nodes and distant nodes [4]. However, it is not very effective when overlaps are big among similar and distant nodes and there is no clear strategy to avoid them. The M-tree has a hierarchical structure just like other common tree structures (R-tree, B-tree), and it tries to balance its nodes according to the given metric. Each node has a maximum and minimum capacity c. When exceeding the maximum capacity, the node will be split into two nodes according to a given splitting policy. For MF, we tried using two splitting policies: maximum lower bound on distance and minimum sum of radii, as in Definitions 3 and 4, we also set the maximum and minimum capacity of nodes to be 8 and 4.

Definition 3. *Let N be the current node and S be the set of N and its children, then the maximum lower bound on distance is achieved by promoting S_i and S_j to be new center nodes, in which $S_j \equiv N$, and S_i s.t. $d(S_i, N) = \max_j\{d(S_j, N)\}$.*

Definition 4. *Let N be the current node and S be the set of N and its children, then the minimum sum of radii is achieved by promoting S_i and S_j to be new center nodes, and assign all nodes in S to S_i or S_j, which gives the smallest sum of radii.*

The trade-off is that Minimum Sum of Radii needs to calculate every possible distance pair in S, but is a better split spatially and ensures minimum overlap. It is faster while performing range queries but the performance decays as the threshold increases. The actual data entries in M-trees are all stored in leaf nodes while non-leaf nodes are duplicates of the leaf nodes. Optimally, M-trees can achieve $O(log_c|D|)$, where c is the maximum capacity of nodes and D is the dataset. However, the M-tree performance degrades rapidly when there are overlaps between nodes. By testing different thresholds, we finally achieve a speed-up of a factor of 2 to compute the Euclidean distances. More detailed experimental results will be given in Sect. 6.

5   MidiFind: A Music Query System

In this section, we describe how to build the *MidiFind* system by taking both searching quality in Sect. 3 and searching scalability in Sect. 4 into consideration. We start by finding ideal thresholds for different similarity measurements, and then formally present the pipeline searching strategy which achieves both effectiveness and efficiency in similarity search.

5.1 Find Similarity Measurement Thresholds

The goal of threshold setting is to maximize the benefits from both similarity measurements. We first compute the precisions, recalls, and F-measures as functions of different thresholds. Then, we choose the Lev-400SC distance threshold (ϵ_{Lev}) that leads to the largest F-measure, and choose the Euclidean distance threshold (ϵ_{ED}) that leads to a large recall and a reasonable time cost.

It is important to notice the different roles between ϵ_{ED} and ϵ_{Lev}. The role of ϵ_{ED} is to not only dramatically shrink the number of target candidates, but also retain a high recall. In other words, the candidates returned by using ϵ_{ED} should balance the number of false negatives and retained candidates. The role of ϵ_{Lev} is to identify similar MIDI performances accurately. Therefore, we choose ϵ_{Lev} that leads to the highest F-measure. Our final *MidiFind* system uses $\epsilon_{ED} = 0.1$ and $\epsilon_{Lev} = 306$.

5.2 MidiFind System Pipeline

Here we formally present the pipeline strategy to find similar MIDI pieces based on a user-submitted MIDI file query Q to the *MidiFind* system, as shown in Algorithm 2.

Algorithm 2. MidiFind System Algorithm

Data: The query melody string Q, and reference melody strings
$\quad\quad \mathcal{R} = \{R_1, R_2, \cdots, R_{|R|}\}$
Result: The set of similar melody string $\mathcal{M}$
Step1: Within $\mathcal{R}$, do range query on Euclidean distance (M-tree) based on bag-of-words representation and get a set of candidates $\mathcal{S}_{B\imath\mathcal{W}}$, where the distance between each element of $\mathcal{S}_{B\imath\mathcal{W}}$ and Q is less than ϵ_{ED};
Step2: Within $\mathcal{S}_{B\imath\mathcal{W}}$, do range query on melody Lev-400SC distance (Sequential Scan) and get $\mathcal{M}$, where the distance between each element of $\mathcal{M}$ and Q is less than ϵ_{Lev} ;
return $\mathcal{M}$;

---

6   Experiments

6.1 Quality Experiments

In these experiments, we examine how well our proposed similarity measurements can find pairs of MIDI performances of the same music composition on real datasets. In essence, we claim a discovery of a pair if their distance is smaller than a given threshold. Since truly different performances of a same music composition should indeed be very similar at some threshold, our algorithms can discover these pairs with high precision and recall.

The MIDI files in these experiments come from the Music Performance Expression Database, which belongs to the CrestMuse Project [1]. There are 325 different MIDI files consisting of 79 unique compositions and 2,289 pairs of MIDI files sharing the same composition. Our goal is to discover all these 2,289 pairs.

We compared four discovery methods based on the following three feature sets and their corresponding similarity measurements:

- ED (Sect. 3.1): Each MIDI file is represented by a 12-dimensional vector where every element is the proportion of melody notes that is played on this key at any octave. The ED similarity of two MIDI files corresponds to the Euclidean distance of their two 12-dim vectors.
- Standard-Lev (Sect. 3.2): Each MIDI file is represented by a string of melody pitches without any truncation. The Standard-Lev similarity of two MIDI files corresponds to the Standard Levenshtein distance.
- Lev-400SC (Sect. 3.2): Each MIDI file is represented by a string of melody pitches. The string is then truncated to have the first 200 and the last 200 notes only. The Lev-400SC similarity of two MIDI files corresponds to the Levenshtein distance with Sakoe-Chiba band of their two length 400 strings. In the case that a melody string has length smaller than 400, the distance is scaled up.

The four discovery methods we compare are:

- ED-thresholding: Claiming two MIDI files to be different performances of the same music composition if their ED distance is below some threshold.
- Lev-400SC-thresholding: Claiming two MIDI files to be different performances of the same music composition if their Lev-400SC distance is below some threshold.
- Standard-Lev-thresholding: Claiming two MIDI files to be different performances of the same music composition if their standard Levenshtein distance is below some threshold.
- MF-thresholding: Claiming two MIDI files to be different performances of the same music composition if both their ED distance and their Lev-400SC distance are below some thresholds.

We first consider the precisions, recalls, and F-measures of all methods with different threshold parameters. The true set of MIDI file pairs is hand labeled. As can be seen in Fig. 4 (a)–(d), better precision appears when the thresholds ϵ are set smaller, because this eliminates many false positives. On the other hand, better recall appears when ϵ is set larger. We can clearly see that the accuracy of Lev-400SC thresholding dramatically outperforms Standard-Lev thresholding. The fact that both precision and recall become high at some $\hat{\epsilon}$, (the choices and their qualities are in Table 1), and remain high in its neighborhood indicates that there is a big overlap between the true similar set and the similar set we found. This fact also give us some flexibility to tune the parameters.

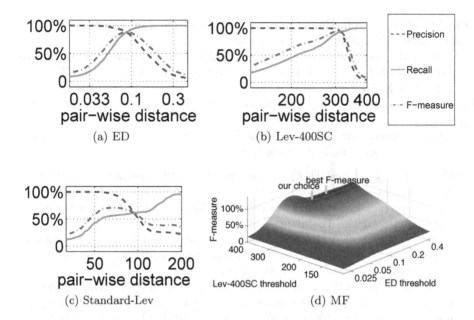

Fig. 4. (a)–(c): Precision, recall, and F-measure of the four methods against various distance threshold parameters. (d): F-measure of the MF method against different threshold parameters.

Finally, the best parameter set that optimizes the F-measure for the MF-thresholding method is $(0.18, 306)$ with F-measure 96.6% whereas our choice of $(0.1, 306)$ which balances quality and scalability achieves an F-measure of 94.4% (Fig. 4(d)).

Table 1. Best thresholds and their qualities

Method	Threshold	Precision	Recall	F-measure
ED	0.087	88.6%	88.3%	88.4%
Lev-400SC	302	98.5%	94.3%	96.4%
Standard-Lev	66	95.6%	56.3%	70.8%
MF (our choice)	(0.1, 306)	99.5%	89.8%	94.4%
MF (optimal)	(0.18, 306)	98.6%	94.7%	96.6%

6.2 Scalability Experiments

The scalability experiments are conducted by using the large dataset which contains 12484 MIDI files that come from several small datasets. The experiments all run on a 3.06 GHz, 2-core (Intel Core i3) machine with 4 GB Memory, so that users of *MidiFind* system could achieve similar performance by using personal computers.

We begin the scalability experiments by testing how much speed we can gain by using a hybrid searching strategy. Intuitively, more candidates will be filtered out if a smaller threshold for Euclidean distance (ϵ_{ED} in Algorithm 2) is adopted for bag-of-words features, and vice versa. Figure 5 shows the relationship between the Euclidean threshold and the fraction of remaining candidates. It is clearly shown that we can filter out about 97.5 % if we adopted a threshold $\epsilon_{ED} = 0.1$.

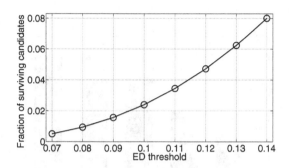

Fig. 5. The relationship between ϵ_{ED} and the fraction of remained candidates.

We then test how much speed we can gain by using different M-tree algorithms mentioned in Sect. 4.3. Figure 6 shows the relationship between the Euclidean threshold ϵ_{ED} and the fraction of candidates whose Euclidean distances need to be checked. It can be seen that the maximum lower bound approach works better, and with $\epsilon_{ED} = 0.1$, we can skip 55 % of the candidates when we compute the Euclidean distance.

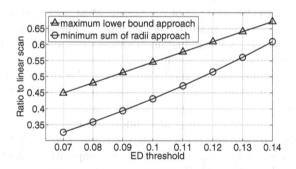

Fig. 6. Search time comparison between M-tree split policies. The y-axis is the fraction of Euclidean distance calculations compared to linear scan. Minimum sum of radii has fewer calculations than maximum lower bound on distance, but it takes longer to build the M-tree. The advantage on search time decreases as threshold increases.

Finally, we compare the speed of all mentioned searching strategies based on how many MIDI files can be searched within one second. As shown in Fig. 7, the fastest method is MF which takes less than 0.1 s even if the dataset size is more than 10, 000. The MF-SC is slightly slower than MF since MF only speeds up the procedure of computing Euclidean distances, which is less costly than computing Levenshtein distances. MF-Q is about 10 times slower than MF, while the linear scanning on Lev-400 distances is about 400 times slower. Compared with the naive linear scan competitor (standard-Lev), our MF method is more than 1000 times faster.

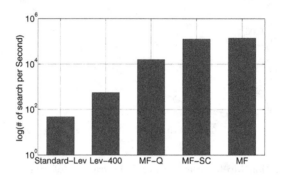

Fig. 7. A comparison of the speed of all searching strategies.

7   Discovery: What Are the Most Popular Pieces

We used Gephi software [3] with OpenOrd algorithm [14] to visualize all similar pairs of MIDI files discovered by our MF method. The results are shown in Fig. 8. Here, MIDI files are nodes and the edges between nodes indicate similar pairs.

Figure 8(a) shows the overview of the layout. Most nodes are singletons, that is they are not claimed to share the same music composition with any other node, whereas some nodes form clusters. The sizes of the clusters largely follow power law distribution (shown later in Fig. 9).

Figure 8(b) examines the detailed structure of the clusters. The nodes are colored according to which datasets they come from. Clearly, a larger size of cluster indicates a more popular piece. Besides that, several observations can be made. First, the connected clusters are almost always densely connected (and thus only clouds can be seen). This shows the consistancy that two nodes connected by one node, i.e. sharing the same music composition with the bypassing node, should also be connected. However, such consistency is not common with arbitrary graphs.

Second, although it is very possible, given such a large dataset, that one noisy node being close to only a few nodes in two bigger clusters join these two clusters and make them indistinguishable, it does not appear often here. This is thanks to the dual-filtering effects our MF method. Notice that any two MIDI

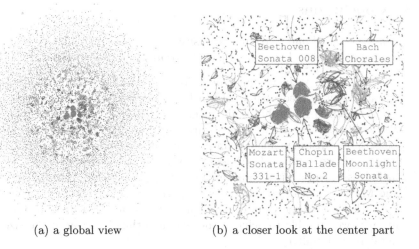

(a) a global view   (b) a closer look at the center part

Fig. 8. A visualization of similar pairs among 12,484 MIDI files.

files sharing the same music score have to be similar under both metrics. Thus, our proposed MF harnesses multiple aspects of the nature of music.

Finally, the cluster sizes follow a power law distribution, that is larger-sized clusters appear exponentially fewer than smaller-sized clusters. We plot the cluster-size-vs-rank distribution in Fig. 9. In this figure, we sort all the clusters in an descending order according to their sizes. The most popular music compositions are also listed there.

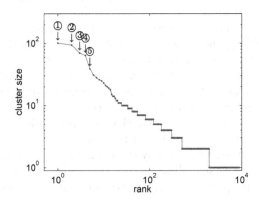

Fig. 9. Power law of number of copies of music pieces. Most popular music pieces are: ① Mozart Sonata 331-1, ② Bach Chorales, ③ Beethoven Sonata 008 Pathétique, ④ Chopin Ballade No.2, and ⑤ Beethoven Moonlight Sonata.

8   Conclusions

We present *MidiFind*, a MIDI query system for effective and fast searching of MIDI file databases. The system has the properties we mentioned earlier:

- *Effectiveness*: it achieves high precision and recall by using novel similarity measurements based on bag-of-words and melody segments, which outperforms standard Levenshtein distance.
- *Scalability*: our *MidiFind* system is dramatically faster than the naive standard Levenshtein distance linear scanning, which is $O(mnN)$, where m and n are lengths of two compared strings and N is the size of the database. By using melody segments representation, bag-of-words filtering, Sakoe-Chiba Band, and M-tree, we achieve speed-ups of 10, 40, 10, and 1.05, respectively, which finally leads to a speed-up of more than 1000 times. Since the methods scale linearly, we are able to achieve one search within 10 s even if the size of the database is 1 million.

9   Future Work

Potentially, we can improve the *MidiFind* system by substituting existing rule-based methods by more machine-learning based approaches. Here, we discuss the possibilities in terms of both effectiveness and scalability.

Effectiveness: We see a small gap of recall between the optimal threshold choice and our choice in Table 1. The optimal parameters are not chosen since it will lead to a very low precision for Euclidean distance, which will create a very large overhead for the next string matching step. It is possible to learn a representation from data which could achieve higher precision than the current bag-of-words representation.

One possibility is to design more "words" based on musical knowledge, and then use Principle Component Analysis (PCA) [20] to reduce the dimensionality. The advantage of PCA is that it automatically "groups" the related information, so that the final representation contains richer information and pays less attention to uninformative details. Another possibility is to use Kernel PCA [19] to directly learn a representation from the strings of various lengths. By using a string kernel [13,17], we can also take the structure of the string into account rather than just counting the number of the words.

We also see that though the melody string matching process is very accurate, it may rely on the fact that highest pitches are representative enough for piano pieces. For non-piano pieces, we may need more advanced melody extraction algorithms.

Scalability: We see a speed-up factor of 2 to compute the Euclidean distance by using M-tree indexing. It might be possible to increase the speed-up factor by using locality-sensitive hashing (LSH) [9]. Someone may argue that this step is not very critical since that the overhead of Euclidean distance computation is just about 10 % of the one of whole computation. However, it is possible that the fraction of Euclidean distance computation will increase as the data size increases to 1 million, in which case the Euclidean distance computation step will become more significant.

We could adopt a k-bit (e.g., 32-bit or 64-bit based on the CPU architecture) LSH function which could basically perform a query in a constant time. There is certainly a trade-off between accuracy and speed. As for precision, the LSH can at least return a rough set of candidates very quickly. After performing LSH, we can check the true Euclidean distance between the set of candidates and the query by linear scanning. In other words, LSH will serve as another filter, so that we end up using a pipeline approach to sequentially filter the candidates by using LSH, Euclidean distance, and finally the actual string matching. As for recall, our pipeline approach will unavoidably create some false negatives, though it has been shown that the false negative probability can be driven very low by tuning the parameters. However, considering our goal of searching 1 million files, a small trade-off on recall, we would argue, will not be a big issue.

References

1. Crestmuse. http://www.crestmuse.jp/pedb/
2. Levenshtein distance. http://en.wikipedia.org/wiki/Levenshtein_distance
3. Bastian, M., Heymann, S., Jacomy, M.: Gephi: an open source software for exploring and manipulating networks. In: International AAAI Conference on Weblogs and Social Media (2009)
4. Ciaccia, P., Patella, M., Zezula, P.: M-tree: an effcient access method for similarity search in metric spaces. In: Proceedings of the 23rd Athens International Conference on VLDB, pp. 426–425 (1997)
5. Dannenberg, R.B., Birmingham, W.P., Pardo, B., Hu, N., Meek, C., Tzanetakis, G.: A comparative evaluation of search techniques for query-by-humming using the musart testbed. J. Am. Soc. Inf. Sci. Technol. 58(5), 687–701 (2007)
6. Ding, H., Trajcevski, G., Scheuermann, P., Wang, X., Keogh, E.: Querying and mining of time series data: experimental comparison of representations and distance measures. Proc. VLDB Endow. 1(2), 1542–1552 (2008)
7. Ellis, D., Whitman, B., Jehan, T., Lamere, P.: The echo nest musical fingerprint (ENMFP). In: International Symposium on Music Information Retrieval (2010)
8. Ghias, A., Logan, J., Chamberlin, D., Smith, B.C.: Query by humming: musical information retrieval in an audio database. In: ACM Multimedia, pp. 231–236 (1995)
9. Gionis, A., Indyk, P., Motwani, R.: Similarity search in high dimensions via hashing. In: Proceedings of the 25th International Conference on Very Large Data Bases, VLDB '99, pp. 518–529. Morgan Kaufmann Publishers Inc., San Francisco (1999)
10. Haitsma, J., Kalker, T.: A highly robust audio fingerprinting system. In: International Symposium on Music Information Retrieval (2002)
11. Jang, R., Lee, H.: Hierarchical filtering method for content-based music retrieval via acoustic input. In: Proceedings of the ACM Multimedia, pp. 401–410. ACM Press (2001)
12. Krumhansl, C.L.: Cognitive Foundations of Musical Pitch. Oxford University Press, New York (2001)

13. Lodhi, H., Saunders, C., Shawe-Taylor, J., Cristianini, N., Watkins, C.: Text classification using string kernels. J. Mach. Learn. Res. **2**, 419–444 (2002)
14. Martin, S., Brown, W.M., Klavans, R., Boyack, K.W.: Openord: an open-source toolbox for large graph layout. In: IS&T/SPIE Electronic Imaging, pp. 786806–786806. International Society for Optics and Photonics (2011)
15. Mazzoni, D., Dannenberg, R.B.: Melody matching directly from audio. In: International Symposium on Music Information Retrieval, pp. 17–18 (2001)
16. Mcnab, R.J., Smith, L.A., Bainbridge, D., Witten, I.H.: The new zealand digital library MELody inDEX. D-Lib Mag. **3**(5), 4–15 (1997)
17. Paass, G., Leopold, E., Larson, M., Kindermann, J., Eickeler, S.: SVM classification using sequences of phonemes and syllables. In: Elomaa, T., Mannila, H., Toivonen, H. (eds.) PKDD 2002. LNCS (LNAI), vol. 2431, p. 373. Springer, Heidelberg (2002)
18. Papapetrou, P., Athitsos, V., Potamias, M., Kollios, G., Gunopulos, D.: Embedding-based subsequence matching in time-series databases. ACM Trans. Database Syst. (TODS) **36**(3), 17 (2011)
19. Scholkopf, B., Smola, A., Müller, K.R.: Kernel principal component analysis. In: Schölkopf, B., Burges, C.J.C., Smola, A.J. (eds.) Advances in Kernel Methods - Support Vector Learning, pp. 327–352. MIT Press, Cambridge (1999)
20. Shlens, J.: A tutorial on principal component analysis. In: Systems Neurobiology Laboratory, Salk Institute for Biological Studies (2005)
21. Uitdenbogerd, A., Zobel, J.: Manipulation of music for melody matching. In: ACM Multimedia, pp. 235–240 (1998)
22. Uitdenbogerd, A., Zobel, J.: Melodic matching techniques for large music databases. In: Proceedings of the Seventh ACM International Conference on Multimedia (Part 1), Multimedia '99, pp. 57–66. ACM, New York (1999)
23. Widmer, G., Flossmann, S., Grachten, M.: YQX plays Chopin. AI Mag. **30**(3), 35–48 (2009)
24. Widmer, G., Tobudic, A.: Playing Mozart by analogy: learning multi-level timing and dynamics strategies. J. New Music Res. **32**(3), 259–268 (2003)
25. Zhu, Y., Shasha, D.: Warping indexes with envelope transforms for query by humming. In: Proceedings of the 2003 ACM SIGMOD International Conference on Management of Data, SIGMOD '03, pp. 181–192. ACM, New York (2003)

Finding Repeated Patterns in Music: State of Knowledge, Challenges, Perspectives

Berit Janssen[1,2](✉), W. Bas de Haas[3], Anja Volk[3],
and Peter van Kranenburg[1]

[1] Meertens Institute, Amsterdam, The Netherlands
{berit.janssen,peter.van.kranenburg}@meertens.knaw.nl
[2] Institute for Language, Logic and Computation, Amsterdam University,
Amsterdam, The Netherlands
[3] Department of Information and Computing Sciences,
Utrecht University, Utrecht, The Netherlands
{w.b.dehaas,a.volk}@uu.nl

Abstract. This paper discusses the current state of knowledge on musical pattern finding. Various studies propose computational methods to find repeated musical patterns. Our detailed review of these studies reveals important challenges in musical pattern finding research: different methods have not yet been directly compared, and the influence of music representation and filtering on the results has not been assessed. Moreover, we need a thorough understanding of musical patterns as perceived by human listeners. A sound evaluation methodology is still lacking. Consequently, we suggest perspectives for musical pattern finding: future research can provide a comparison of different methods, and an assessment of different music representations and filtering criteria. A combination of quantitative and qualitative methods can overcome the lacking evaluation methodology. Musical patterns identified by human listeners form a reference, but also an object of study, as computational methods can help us understand the criteria underlying human notions of musical repetition.

Keywords: Musical pattern finding · Musical pattern discovery · Musical pattern matching · Music analysis · Music cognition · Music information retrieval

1 Introduction

Repetitions are a fundamental structuring principle in many musical styles. They guide the listener in their experience of a musical piece through creating listening experiences, and facilitate the recall process [25, p. 228 ff.]. As such, the study of repetition is an important research topic in many fields of music research, and computational methods enable researchers to study musical repetitions quantitatively in large music collections. Musical pattern finding is important in several areas of music research. In Music Information Retrieval, repetitions have been

© Springer International Publishing Switzerland 2014
M. Aramaki et al. (Eds.): CMMR 2013, LNCS 8905, pp. 277–297, 2014.
DOI: 10.1007/978-3-319-12976-1_18

used as indicators of musical segmentation [21], or to find themes or choruses in large databases [49]. In Music Analysis, analytical approaches based on repetition, for instance Réti's motivic analysis [52], have been formalized and evaluated by developing a computer model [5]. In Folk Music Research, computational discovery of shared patterns between folk song variants offers the potential to detect moments of stability, i.e. melodic elements that change relatively little through the process of oral transmission [58]. Hypotheses on memory, recall and transmission of melodies can be tested on large databases using musical pattern finding [26].

As we show in this article, there are many different kinds of repetition that different researchers investigate: large repeated structures, such as themes, chorusses, or stanzas; smaller repeated units, such as motifs; but also building blocks of improvized music, such as formulae or licks. For these different purposes, and for different genres, the authors of the discussed studies have formalized repetition in different ways. What may be considered as a variation or as musically unrelated depends on a great number of factors, factors which yet need to be understood [57].

A computational method to find musical repetitions can contribute to an understanding of principles of repetition and variation. Using computational methods, researchers can model and test knowledge on the cognitive principles underlying musical repetition. Cognitive and computational models can cross-pollinate each other in such an overarching research question, as argued, for instance, by Honing [22,23]. In this paper, we explore computational methods for finding repeated musical patterns, which we will refer to as musical pattern finding.

Currently, the knowledge of musical pattern finding is dispersed across different fields of music research. Miscellaneous studies present various approaches to the problem, but there is no systematic comparison of the proposed methods yet. Moreover, the influence of music representation, and filtering of algorithmic results on the success of musical pattern finding is currently unknown. This lack of comparative assessment is further complicated by the lack of a sound methodology for the evaluation of musical pattern finding.

This paper provides a comprehensive overview, review and discussion of the field of musical pattern finding. We present the essence of assorted studies, and we proceed to clarify the relationships between different methods, proposing a taxonomy of musical pattern finding approaches, and discussing various studies according to the criteria of music representation, filtering, reference data, and evaluation. Furthermore, we identify current challenges of musical pattern finding and conclude with steps to overcome these challenges.

2   State of Knowledge on Musical Pattern Finding

We conducted a comprehensive literature survey on musical pattern finding. In this section, we provide an overview of the various studies. First, we discuss the methods that the surveyed studies used, introducing a taxonomy within which the different approaches can be placed. We continue by considering different forms of music representation, different methods of filtering algorithmic results, and close with an overview of reference data and evaluation methods used in the studies.

In this survey, our focus lies on studies using symbolic music representations. Several studies work with audio representations [9,44], but we will not discuss the problems related to transforming audio representations for musical pattern finding. For this, and other methods for the audio domain, we refer the reader to the overview by Klapuri [28].

We present our overview of studies on musical pattern finding in Table 1. The tables' columns refer to the study, naming the first author and year (please refer to the references for the full list of authors). The second column mentions the goals of the authors in exploring musical pattern finding. We list the musical pieces that each study used. Further categories, which we will discuss in more detail below, are the method the studies employed, the music representation that was used, what kind of filtering of the algorithmic results was performed, the reference of musical patterns against which the results were compared, represented by first author and year, and finally, which evaluation methods were applied. Empty cells denote that the category in question is not applicable to a particular study.

2.1 Methods

As can be gleaned from the various goals of the studies presented in Table 1, the interest for musical pattern finding is diverse, spanning different music research disciplines and musical genres. This might be the reason why various authors present their algorithms without stating how their method relates to most of the other research on musical pattern finding.

To assess the relationship of different methods, we propose a taxonomy in which the various methods can be placed in perspective, which is represented in Fig. 1. Below, we will explain the distinctions within the taxonomy.

Pattern Discovery or Pattern Matching. Musical pattern discovery, on the one hand, aims at the identification of motifs, themes, and other musical structures in a piece of music, or between related pieces of music (intra-, and inter-opus discovery). Typically, algorithms applied for pattern discovery do not presuppose prior knowledge of possible candidates.

Musical pattern matching, on the other hand, strives to recognize pre-defined patterns in a musical piece, or a corpus of music [53]. Applications of pattern matching include the identification of fugue subjects and counter-subjects in Bach fugues [19] or variations of themes, as in some works by Mozart [18], among others.

In terms of the applied techniques, there is an overlap of pattern matching with classification problems in music retrieval, which aim at the identification of similar musical pieces in a large database (e.g. [24,33]). However, in this paper,

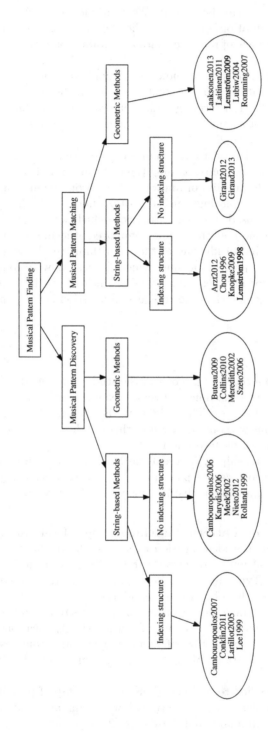

Fig. 1. A schematic representation of a taxonomy for musical pattern finding methods. For each category, relevant studies are listed.

Table 1. Overview of research on musical pattern finding in music

Study	Goals	Musical pieces	Method	Music representation	Filtering	Reference data	Evaluation
Arzt2012 [1]	Fast identification of piece and score position from a performance	Selected pieces by Mozart and Chopin	Generation of fingerprints by sampling pitches at fixed time intervals, which are matched as hash keys	pitch, inter onset intervals		Performance data of musical pieces	Precision of results in terms of piece and score position
Buteau2009 [6]	Computer-aided motivic analysis	Schumann's *Träumerei*	topological model: motifs as shapes in n-dimensional space	pitch and onset	shape clustering	Repp1992 [51]	Qualitative comparison with music theorist Repp's segmentation of Schumann's *Träumerei*
Cambouropoulos2006 [7]	Segmentation based on musical repetitions	Sonatina No. 2 in C Major by Anton Diabelli (soprano voice)	set partitioning method[16]	pitch intervals; step-leap	frequency of occurrence, pattern length	Koniari2001 [32]	Quantitative comparison with human segmentations of a sonatina by Anton Diabelli
Cambouropoulos2007 [8]	Finding motifs in musical pieces		Searching maximal pairs in suffix trees	pitch interval, step-leap representation of pitch			
Chou1996 [9]	Content-based retrieval of music from large data bases		Suffix trees	representation of chords			
Collins2010 [12]	Finding translational patterns in musical pieces to support music analysis	two sonatas by Scarlatti, two Bach preludes (polyphonic)	Structure Induction Algorithms (extension of Meredith2002)	pitch interval, onset	*compactness trawling*: prefer patterns with adjacent data-points	Collins2010 [12]	Quantitative comparison with motif annotations in two sonatas by Scarlatti and two Bach preludes; using Precision and Recall
Conklin2011 [15]	Classifying Cretan folk songs based on characteristic patterns	106 monophonic Cretan folksongs	sequential pattern mining; finding maximally general distinctive patterns (MGDP) in a search tree	pitch intervals	frequency of occurrence		Qualitative analysis of patterns as parts of Cretan folk music genres

(Continued)

Table 1. (*Continued*)

Study	Goals	Musical pieces	Method	Music representation	Filtering	Reference data	Evaluation
Giraud2012 [19]	Finding fugue subjects	24 fugues from Bach's Wohltemperiertes Clavier	Alignment of a fugue subject with the remaining fugue	(interval, onset, length), (pitch, onset, length)	Threshold of similarity	Bruhn1993 [3]	Qualitative; precision and recall
Giraud2013 [18]	Finding variations of a theme	Two works by W.A. Mozart: K. 331 and K. 265	Alignment of theme and variation using fragmentation	pitch, onset, length	length, at least one pitch equal, equivalent position	Musical form	Precision, recall
Karydis2006 [27]	Finding themes in large music databases	Assorted MIDI files (unspecified)	Finding maximum-length repeating patterns with set partitioning method	pitch			Computation speed
Knopke2009 [30]	Analysis of Palestrina's contrapuntal structure	masses by Palestrina (separated into voices and phrases)	4 suffix arrays for each phrase (indicated by rests), for original, inversion, retrograde, retrograde inversion	pitch and duration intervals, mapped to UTF-8 tokens			Qualitative analysis of selected patterns, especially longest patterns and most frequent patterns
Laaksonen2013 [34]	Finding time-scaled and time-warped permutations of fugue subjects	unspecified music databases	Dynamic time warping	onset times, pitches			Performance speed
Laitinen2011 [35]	Finding more efficient algorithms for exact and approximate matches, time-scaled and time-warped	Music data from Musitopia database (unspecified)	Dynamic time warping	pitch against time			Performance speed

Table 1. (*Continued*)

Study	Goals	Musical pieces	Method	Music representation	Filtering	Reference data	Evaluation
Lartillot2005 [36]	Assisting music analysis with computational discovery of motifs	monophonic melodies from different genres	construction of a pattern tree, which can have cyclic structures	pitch intervals, duration	maximally specific patterns, filtered during the tree construction		Qualitative analysis of selected patterns
Lee1999 [37]	Content-based retrieval of music from large data bases	100 songs in MIDI format (unspecified)	Different suffix tree algorithms	pitch interval, quantized duration (combined and separate)			Computation speed
Lemström1998 [38]	Translation-invariant retrieval from music databases	154 pieces of music from different genres	Suffix tree	pitch/duration tuples for different abstraction levels			occurrences of search keys, and quantity of melodies containing search keys
Lemström2009 [39]	Content-based music retrieval of motifs and themes	Polyphonic music (not specified)	defining vectors connecting lexicographically ordered points within patterns, detecting them in a large database	pitch against time	comparison of 7 different filters for exact and approximate matching		Precision and recall of patterns artificially inserted into the database
Lubiw2004 [42]	Finding matches of musical patterns translated in pitch and time	Bach invention, Bach fugue, Mozart sonata	Alignment with weights following Mongeau and Sankoff [46]	onset, offset, pitch			Qualitative analysis of patterns
Meek2001 [44]	Discovering themes in Western art music	60 polyphonic pieces from different epochs of Western art music	Stream segregation; matching keys representing pitch intervals in a base 26 numerical system	pitch intervals	frequency of occurrence; hill-climbing optimisation of different pattern features	Barlow1948 [2]	Quantitative comparison of selected examples against *Dictionary of musical themes* (Barlow): the evaluation procedure is not described

(*Continued*)

Table 1. (*Continued*)

Study	Goals	Musical pieces	Method	Music representation	Filtering	Reference data	Evaluation
Meredith2002 [45]	Assisting music analysts and composers by finding repeated patterns in music	52 polyphonic pieces, mostly from Bach's *Wohltemperiertes Clavier*	Structure Induction Algorithms: tones represented as points in n-dimensional space	pitch intervals, onset	Suggestions, not reported		Demonstration of one discovered pattern
Nieto2012 [47]	Finding motifs in musical works	Monophonic melodies from 6 musical pieces (Bach, Mozart, Beethoven, Haydn)	string-based pattern discovery; Gestalt rules applied for candidate motifs	pitch intervals, duration	clustering candidate motifs		Score based on amount of overlap between annotated motifs in the pieces and those discovered by algorithm
Rolland1999 [53]	Automatizing pattern discovery in jazz improvisation	10 Charlie Parker solos	Knuth-Morris-Pratt approximate matching with star center algorithm, alignment for similarity	duration, intervals, metric levels, contour	Frequency of occurrence	Owens1974 [48]	Qualitative comparison of selected patterns with Owens' catalogue of Charlie Parker's patterns
Romming2007 [54]	Finding matches of musical patterns in polyphonic music, shifted in pitch and time and meter-invariant	"Fuggi, fuggi, da questo cielo" with variations; Bach's Goldberg Variation No.14	Comparison of alignment based on Hausdorff metric and geometric hashing	pitch, duration, onset			Qualitative analysis
Szeto2006 [56]	Discovering structures in post-tonal music	Arnold Schoenberg's Klavierstücke, op. 11 no.1	Graph with notes as vertices, edges linking simultaenous and sequential events	pitch class, onset	Clustering of graph vertices	Wittlich1974 [59]	Quantitative comparison with musicological analysis (Wittlich1974): counting number of matches and approximate matches

we focus on the problem of identifying a musical subsequence in a larger piece of music.

In Fig. 1, musical pattern discovery algorithms are presented on the left; musical pattern matching approaches can be found on the right side of the diagram.

String-Based or Geometric Methods. A piece of music can be represented by a series - or string - of tokens. For instance, the notes of a melody could be represented by a string of pitches (A; G; A; D), as MIDI note numbers (57; 55; 57; 50), or as tokens representing both pitch and duration of the note ((A, 1.5), (G, 0.5),(A, 1.0), (G, 1.0)). These multiple possibilities will be further discussed in the section on music representation below.

One approach to musical pattern finding is to search for identical subsequences of tokens in a string representation of a melody or multiple melodies. This approach has been derived from techniques developed within Computational Biology to compare gene sequences. Gusfield [20] provides a thorough overview of these techniques.

In geometric methods, a melody is considered as a shape in an n-dimensional space. Repeated patterns are then identified as (near-)identical shapes. Geometric methods are especially interesting for polyphonic music, as they can deal more efficiently with note events occurring at the same time [45, p. 328]. Meredith's *Structure Induction Algorithms* (SIA) [45] order the pitch/onset points lexicographically, and search for vectors of pitch and time relationships which repeat elsewhere in a musical piece. This concept, used by Meredith and Collins [12, 45] for pattern discovery, has been applied by Lemström et al. [39] for pattern matching.

The musical pattern discovery approaches by Buteau and Vipperman [6] and Szeto and Wong [56] rely on a similar conceptualisation of music as n-dimensional shapes. In the latter study, the geometric relationships are represented as nodes and edges in graphs [56]. Laaksonen [34], Laitinen and Lemström [35], Lubiw and Tanur [42] and Romming and Selfridge-Field [54] represent musical pieces as point sets of onset times and pitch, which can be shifted in the time or pitch domain, which is handled through substitution weights in an alignment algorithm.

Use of Indexing Structures. Within the string-based methods we can define two categories: namely, whether or not indexing structures are used. Such indexing structures typically are a graph of tree-like structure, in which the repetitions contained in a string are represented, and can therefore be efficiently found. We will first present those studies that do not use indexing structures for the music pattern discovery, then those which do use them.

The simplest string-based approach to finding repeated patterns in a melody M consists of sliding all possible patterns P past M, and recording all found matches. This approach is taken by Nieto and Farbod [47]. There are some extensions of this simple approach, which skip some comparison steps between

P and M without missing any relevant patterns. One of these extensions, the algorithm by Knuth, Morris and Pratt [31], has been applied by Rolland [53] for musical pattern discovery.

Yet another approach is Crochemore's set partitioning method [16], which recursively splits the melody M into sets of repeating tokens. Cambouropoulos [7] used this method to find maximally repeating patterns (i.e. repeated patterns which cannot be extended left or right and still be identical) in musical pieces. Karydis et al. [27] refine the set-partitioning approach to find only the longest patterns for each musical piece, with the intuition that these correspond most closely to musical themes.

Meek and Birmingham's [44] algorithm transforms all possible patterns up to a maximal pattern length to keys in a radix 26 system (representing 12 intervals up or down, unison, and a 0 for the end of the string). After a series of transformations, which consolidate shorter into longer patterns, identical patterns are encoded by the same numerical keys.

There are number of studies which do use indexing structures [8,9,15,30, 36,37]. Knopke and Jürgensen [30] use suffix arrays representing phrases of Palestrina masses. Conklin and Anagnostopoulou [15] use a sequence tree to represent search spaces of patterns in Cretan folk songs, which is pruned based on the patterns' frequency of occurrence. Lemström and Laine compare suffix tries to the more compressed form of suffix trees on a varied music corpus [38]. Lartillot [36] employs a pattern tree to model musical pieces; what is special about this indexing structure is that it allows for cyclic structures within the graph, which can capture repetitions of short patterns, forming building blocks within larger repeated structures.

Exact or Approximate Matching. Next to searching for exact matches, approximate matching is also of great interest to musical pattern finding. Rhythmic, melodic and many other conceivable variations are likely to occur, such as the insertion of ornamentations during a repetition, the speeding up or slowing down of a musical sequence, deviations in pitch, or transpositions.

Several ways to define approximate matching for musical pattern finding have been proposed. Approximate matching algorithms typically distinguish between approximate matches and irrelevant patterns based on a threshold on a given similarity measure. This can be the number of allowed mismatches, referred to as *k-mismatch*, the Hausdorff-distance, which refers to the Euclidian distance between sets of points [54], or the length of the longest common subsequence [40]. If musical pieces are represented as sequences of numbers (e.g. pitch values), it is also possible to define a threshold on the difference between values of two compared sequences – δ-matching – or on the sum of all differences between the values in two compared strings – γ-matching – as suggested by Clifford and Iliopoulos [10]. However, to our knowledge, δ-matching and γ-matching have not been used for musical pattern finding to this date.

Furthermore, the threshold can also be defined as a maximum amount of edit operations in an alignment algorithm (also known as edit distance or Levenshtein distance) [41]. This way, also strings of different length, or strings containing gaps in relation to each other, can be considered as approximate matches. Giraud et al. [19] use edit distance as a similarity measure for Bach fugues. For the comparison of Mozart themes and variations, Giraud and Cambouropoulos [18] extend the alignment metric with another operation, fragmentation. Fragmentation was introduced by Mongeau and Sankoff [46] so that musical embellishments cause smaller edit distances between patterns than with the classical definition of edit distance.

In a generalisation for patterns repeated on different time scales, alignment algorithms have also been developed further so as to consider patterns shifted by time constants or ratios. This approach, generally referred to as dynamic time warping, has been applied, among others, by Laitinen and Lemström [35] to a database of music from different genres, and by Laaksonen [34] in order to find augmentations and diminuations of fugue subjects.

To our knowledge, only Rolland [53] applied approximate matching to musical pattern discovery, using the Levenshtein distance to compare a pattern with a match candidate. Implicitly, however, approximate matching can also be achieved through more abstract music representations, as Cambouropoulos et al. [8] point out. We will discuss this in more detail below.

2.2 Music Representation

There are different musical dimensions to be considered for comparisons of musical patterns: rhythm, pitch, but also dynamics, timbre, and many more. Moreover, there are different conceivable abstraction levels at which to represent these dimensions: in terms of absolute values; in terms of categories or classes; in terms of contours indicating only the direction of change; among others. This is closely related to Conklin's [13] notion of musical viewpoints.

A glance at the music representation column reveals that the majority of the studies on musical pattern finding use pitch or pitch intervals as the music representation, in some of the studies this is combined with rhythmic representations such as note onset or duration.

Chou et al. [9] extract a more abstract representation from the musical surface: they represent polyphonic musical pieces as chords, which are automatically extracted from simultaneous pitches, even though the paper does not report the results of such an approach. Similarly, Arzt et al. [1] match patterns with a symbolic fingerprint that is derived from pitch values sampled at specific time intervals.

Three studies [8,37,53] suggest multiple music representations. Rolland [53] allows the users of his *FlExPat* software to switch between different music representations, but he does not report how this influences the results of his musical pattern discovery algorithm. Cambouropoulos et al. [8] suggest to compare a pitch interval representation with a more abstract step-leap representation, but results of these two representations are not discussed by the authors. Lee and Chen [37] state that pitch and duration can be either represented in independent suffix trees, or in a combined suffix tree which contains tuples of pitch and duration values. They do not find either approach satisfying, so they suggest two new indexing structures, *Twin Suffix Trees*, and *Grid-Twin Suffix Trees*, as possible alternatives. They do not report any results produced by these different representations.

2.3 Filtering

A frequently described problem in musical pattern discovery is the great amount of algorithmically discovered patterns as compared to the patterns that would be considered relevant by a human analyst. For the task of computer-aided motivic analysis, Marsden recently observed that "... the mathematical and computational approaches find many more motives and many more relationships between fragments than traditional motivic analysis." [43].

Therefore, most of the presented studies employ a filtering step, which is supposed to separate the wheat from the chaff. One approach is to consider only relatively long patterns. Cambouropoulos [7] filters according to pattern lengths. Likewise, Collins' *compactness trawling* to refine the result of Structure Induction Algorithms [12] is based on such a filtering, in which patterns of adjacent notes are preferred over patterns with many intervening notes.

Another frequently employed filtering method is based on the assumption that patterns which occur more often might also be considered as more important by human analysts, and is applied in several studies [7,53].

Conklin and Anagnostopoulou [15] are also interested in a pattern's frequency of occurrence, but weigh it against its frequency in a collection of contrasting music pieces, the *anticorpus*. This process is designed to favour patterns that are characteristic for the analyzed piece. Conversely, also patterns which are characteristically not represented in specific pieces or genres can be interesting for music researchers [14].

Nieto and Farbod filter according to Gestalt rules during the search process, which means that pattern candidates containing relatively long notes or rests, or relatively large intervals will be rejected [47].

Lartillot's detection of maximally specific patterns [36] filters for patterns which occur in different musical domains: a pattern which repeats the rhythm as well as the pitch of another pattern is considered as more specific than one that repeats in one of these domains alone.

It is also possible to employ several filtering parameters, and adjust their relative weights using an optimisation algorithm. Meek and Birmingham [44] take this approach. They let the algorithm select those filtering parameters which give the best agreement between the discovered patterns and Barlow and Morgenstern's *Dictionary of Musical Themes* [2].

Lemström et al. [39] apply seven different filtering methods to their pattern matching results: these filters are based on the relationships between the points in the query patterns (*intra-pattern vectors*). The least frequent intra-pattern vectors are considered the best candidates for meaningful matches.

2.4   Reference Data

Some of the presented studies use annotated musical patterns to evaluate the results of their musical pattern discovery algorithm, which we will denote as reference data. Such reference data ranges from overviews of frequently used licks in jazz improvisation [48] to themes in Western art music [2]. This reference data is typically assembled by domain specialists, annotating what they consider the most relevant patterns of the analyzed music collection.

Such reference data can serve as a ground truth to evaluate musical pattern discovery: if there is a good agreement between an algorithm and a reference, the algorithm emulates human judgements on relevant patterns, and might therefore be more useful for tasks such as assisting music analysis for this genre.

2.5   Evaluation

Many studies discussed here evaluate qualitatively: the discovered patterns are scrutinized. Typically, selected examples are presented to the reader in this case. If there is no reference against which the results can be compared, the researchers' and readers' judgements form the post hoc reference.

For available reference data, several researchers evaluate the discovered patterns quantitatively by counting the number of agreements between algorithm and reference data [12, 18, 19, 44, 47, 56].

Sometimes, the reference data takes the form of a segmentation. In this case, the starting and end positions of algorithmically discovered patterns can be compared with segmentation boundaries [6, 7].

In a number of the studies [34, 35, 37], the researchers aimed for fast solutions, which make the algorithms more interesting for practical use. Therefore, computation speed is used as an evaluation metric in these cases. This does not give an indication of the usefulness of the automatically found patterns, however.

Several quantitative evaluation measures have been suggested for musical pattern finding, but there seems to be no common methodology among the reported studies. This is one of the points to which we will turn in the next sections, in which we will discuss the current challenges in the field of musical pattern discovery.

3   Challenges of Musical Pattern Finding

We have now observed that in various studies, different approaches to musical pattern discovery have been proposed. There are some common challenges which can be derived from these observations, which will be discussed below, following the same order as the previous section.

3.1   Methods

The approaches to musical pattern finding presented above all aim to find specific kinds of patterns, in specific genres and for specific applications. This is a good starting point, as a restriction to one part of the research field enables researchers to formulate more concrete questions, and to interpret results more easily.

However, it is crucial to know how different methods compare to each other, and to answer questions such as the following: how many relevant and irrelevant patterns does each algorithm find in relation to given reference data? Are there specific advantages of a string-based over a geometric approach for a given pattern finding task, or vice versa? In short: which musical pattern finding method performs best as compared against a given set of reference data?

3.2 Music Representation

As of yet, there is no systematic analysis of the influence of the music representation on musical pattern finding. The presented studies use various representations, but they do not directly evaluate the influence of the music representation on the musical pattern discovery results.

This is another challenge of musical pattern finding: do more abstract representations lead to more irrelevant discovered patterns? Or is some abstraction desired for the description of some musical parameters? Which musical dimensions are important for a given musical genre? Which music representation approximates best the judgements on repeating patterns of a human listener, as manifested in reference data?

3.3 Filtering

We have also seen manifold filtering criteria applied in various studies. Again, the influence of different filtering parameters on the quality of musical pattern finding has not yet been systematically investigated.

Are the most frequent patterns the ones human listeners would judge to be the most relevant? Or is it, conversely, just the unique patterns which capture our attention? Which filtering criteria match those of a human annotator of a given reference annotation most closely?

Insights on the influence of filtering are not only needed to improve musical pattern finding methods; filtering criteria of a computational method can also serve as a model of the criteria human listeners apply when they isolate themes, motifs, or other salient musical patterns in musical pieces.

3.4 Reference Data

As the preceding paragraphs show, there is a great need for references of human judgements on repeated patterns in music.

The literature overview pointed out a number of resources which can be used as reference data for musical pattern finding. As this reference data is very diverse, and highly subjective, matching the results of a computational method closely to one set of reference data does not necessarily imply that the whole problem of musical pattern finding has been solved.

This is another challenge of musical pattern finding: will an algorithm that performs well on finding licks in jazz improvisation also perform well for finding themes in Western art music? What exactly *is* the data contained in a reference annotation?

3.5 Evaluation

Further advances in repeated melodic pattern finding research hinges on a good evaluation of different methods. Many of the above studies report some successful results, yet how do we know these results are not only the grains the proverbial blind hen happens to find?

One very essential approach is of course a qualitative evaluation, in which discovered patterns are compared to those in reference data. However, for large corpora this is unfeasible, and it is hard to report the relative success of a method using qualitative evaluation, unless the lengthy analysis would be reported.

We showed above that some studies use quantitative measures, derived from the number of agreements between algorithmically found patterns and patterns in reference data. Yet the definition of an agreement is problematic: do we only consider patterns which match those in a reference exactly, or should there also be a (penalized) score for partial matches?

Collins et al. suggest to allow a certain number of differences between algorithmically discovered or matched, and reference patterns [12]. A window around the start and end position of a pattern, allowing patterns to be counted as matches which are slightly shorter or longer than the reference patterns, might be another worthwhile approach. Recently, Collins [11] suggested a cardinality score as a similarity measure, which expresses the amount of the overlap between patterns. From this, several potentially interesting measures can be derived (see [11] for details).

So far, it is not clear whether some of these evaluation measures might be too tolerant, including too many patterns as agreements between algorithm and reference, or too strict, and register almost no patterns as matches between algorithm and reference. In both extremes, the performances of different methods, music representations and filtering techniques would probably be hard to assess.

Finding an effective, unified methodology of evaluation represents another challenge to the field of musical pattern finding.

4 Perspectives of Musical Pattern Finding

From the above mentioned challenges, we conclude important perspectives for future research on musical pattern finding. These perspectives relate to the influence different methods, different music representations and different filtering techniques have on the results of musical pattern discovery, what we can learn from annotated patterns in reference data, and which evaluation measures should be used.

4.1 Comparison of Methods

In order to assess different methods for repeated melodic pattern finding, it is indispensable to compare them in a more direct way, even if they have been designed to find specific kinds of patterns, or to find patterns in a specific genre. We suggested in our overview a taxonomy of different approaches to pattern finding, which helps to put the many different methods in perspective.

Ideally, next to the qualitative comparison of results, also a quantitative comparison should take place, which necessitates that methods be tested on the same corpus, and compared against the same reference data. The recently introduced MIREX track on musical pattern discovery [11] is an important step into this direction. Similar incentives to compare approaches in musical pattern matching would be highly desirable.

4.2 Comparison of Music Representations

We have noted the importance of understanding the influence of music representation on musical pattern finding. Future research can amend this gap of knowledge by systematically comparing results from different representations to reference data. This way, we can learn more about the musical dimensions, abstraction levels and concepts of similarity that human analysts rely on for finding musical patterns.

Results from experimental studies (e.g. [17,29,55]) on music perception and recall should also be taken into account for choosing music representations. They provide theories which can be employed and tested by musical pattern finding. The comparison of musical pattern finding using different music representations with human annotations and with perceptual theories will generate insights which can feed back into research on similarity and variation in music theory and music cognition.

4.3 Comparison of Filtering Techniques

The systematic investigation of filtering techniques is also marked out as a fruitful direction of future research. By applying different filtering criteria and comparing the resulting patterns to reference data, we can better understand what conditions a pattern needs to fulfill in order to be considered relevant by human analysts.

Moreover, insights from research on long-term musical salience [4] can lead to models of how human listeners filter musical patterns according to salience or relevance. Musical pattern finding can benefit from and contribute to this research area in music cognition.

4.4 Reference Data

We have shown that there is a need for reference data of musical patterns annotated by human listeners. At the same time, the available reference data is a challenge in itself, as different references are based on subjective judgements of human analysts who annotated different kinds of patterns, working in different genres.

Researchers in musical pattern finding can treat their algorithms as models of human analysis, and through relative successes and failures of these models, we can understand better which criteria underlie human judgements on repeated musical patterns.

Therefore, another perspective of this research area is the study of reference data itself by comparison to computational results. Such a study will promote knowledge on the concept of musical repetition, as applied by different human listeners in different genres. Such knowledge is important for various disciplines of music research interested in the nature of musical repetitions.

4.5   Towards an Evaluation Methodology

We infer that the best way to quantitatively evaluate musical pattern finding algorithms consists of a combination of the several proposed measures. In combination, these different evaluation measures should give a reasonable impression of the respective successes of different approaches.

Many of the presented studies have performed a qualitative analysis of selected patterns. This should remain an indispensable evaluation step: for musical pattern discovery, patterns which quantitatively correspond to reference data exceptionally well, but also those which correspond exceptionally badly should be investigated qualitatively. In musical pattern matching, those patterns should be investigated which are found by the algorithm, but have not been annotated by human listeners, and those which have been annotated, but were overseen by the algorithm. Only with such an accompanying qualitative analysis can the behaviour of a pattern finding algorithm be truly understood.

Quantitative and qualitative methods can also be combined in a learning process, by which quantitative measures are fitted to qualitative judgements. This method has been applied to improve the automatic generation of musical patterns by Pearce and Wiggins [50]. A use of qualitative judgements in combination with different quantitative measures will not only contribute to the improvement of musical pattern finding, but will also greatly benefit related research in other fields, e.g. music cognition, musicology and music theory, as notions of what constitutes a repetition are quantified.

5   Conclusion

Our literature overview has shown that between the many approaches to musical pattern finding, there are important challenges left unaddressed. There is a need to investigate how methods developed for a specific goal generalize to other tasks within musical pattern finding, and how different methods perform on the same reference data. Moreover, the influence of different music representations and filtering on the results of musical pattern finding algorithms is not yet unravelled, which demands further research. The different idiosyncrasies of reference annotations, and their semantics are poorly understood. Finally, no standardized evaluation measure for musical pattern finding has yet been established, which we suggest to overcome by combining various quantitative measures with a qualitative evaluation.

As stated in the introduction, much is to be gained for diverse music research disciplines from musical pattern finding. Some successes have already been achieved, which makes further research in this field an intriguing effort to pursue. This thorough investigation of the state of the art in musical pattern finding, its challenges and perspectives, should help to mark out the field in which further fruitful research can take place.

Acknowledgments. We thank Henkjan Honing and the reviewers for their useful comments, which greatly helped to improve this paper. Berit Janssen and Peter van Kranenburg are supported by the Computational Humanities Programme of the Royal Netherlands Academy of Arts and Sciences, under the auspices of the Tunes&Tales project. For further information, see http://ehumanities.nl. Anja Volk and W. Bas de Haas are supported by the Netherlands Organisation for Scientific Research through an NWO-VIDI grant to Anja Volk (276-35-001).

References

1. Arzt, A., Sebastian, B., Widmer, G.: Fast identification of piece and score position via symbolic fingerprinting. In: International Symposium for Music Information Retrieval (2012)
2. Barlow, H., Morgenstern, S.: A Dictionary of Musical Themes. Crown Publishers, New York (1948)
3. Bruhn, S.: J. S. Bach's Well-Tempered Clavier: In-depth Analysis and Interpretation. Mainer, Hong Kong (1993). http://www-personal.umich.edu/siglind/text.htm
4. Burgoyne, J.A., Bountouridis, D., Van Balen, J., Honing, H.: Hooked: a game for discovering what makes music catchy. In: Proceedings of the 14th International Society for Music Information Retrieval Conference (2013)
5. Buteau, C., Mazzola, G.: Motivic analysis according to Rudolph Réti: formalization by a topological model. J. Math. Music Math. Comput. Approaches Music Theory Anal. Compos. Perform. **2**(3), 117–134 (2008)
6. Buteau, C., Vipperman, J.: Melodic clustering within motivic spaces : visualization in OpenMusic and application to Schumann's Träumerei. In: Klouche, T., Noll, T. (eds.) Mathematics and Computation in Music, pp. 59–66. Springer, Berlin (2009)
7. Cambouropoulos, E.: Musical parallelism and melodic segmentation: a computational approach. Music Percept. **23**(3), 249–268 (2006)
8. Cambouropoulos, E., Crochemore, M., Iliopoulos, C.S., Mohamed, M., Sagot, M.F.: All maximal-pairs in step-leap representation of melodic sequence. Inf. Sci. **177**(9), 1954–1962 (2007). http://linkinghub.elsevier.com/retrieve/pii/S0020025506003525
9. Chou, T.C., Chen, A.L.P., Liu, C.C.: Music databases: indexing techniques and implementation. In: Multimedia Database Management Systems, pp. 46–53 (1996)
10. Clifford, R., Iliopoulos, C.: Approximate string matching for music analysis. Soft Comput. **8**, 597–603 (2004)

11. Collins, T.: Discovery of repeated themes and sections, Sect. 4. http://www. music-ir.org/mirex/wiki/2013:Discovery_of_Repeated_Themes_%26_Sections. Accessed 4 May 2013

12. Collins, T., Thurlow, J., Laney, R., Willis, A., Garthwaite, P.H.: A comparative evaluation of algorithms for discovering translational patterns in Baroque keyboard works conference item. In: International Symposium for Music Information Retrieval (2010)

13. Conklin, D.: Multiple viewpoint systems for music prediction. J. New Music Res. **24**(1), 51–73 (1995)

14. Conklin, D.: Antipattern discovery in folk tunes. J. New Music Res. **42**(2), 161–169 (2013). http://www.tandfonline.com/doi/abs/10.1080/09298215.2013.809125

15. Conklin, D., Anagnostopoulou, C.: Comparative pattern analysis of cretan folk songs. J. New Music Res. **40**(2), 119–125 (2011). http://www.tandfonline.com/doi/abs/10.1080/09298215.2011.573562

16. Crochemore, M.: An optimal algorithm for computing the repetitions in a word. Inf. Process. Lett. **12**(5), 244–250 (1981)

17. Dowling, W.J.: Scale and contour: two components of a theory of memory for melodies. Psychol. Rev. **85**(4), 341–354 (1978)

18. Giraud, M., Cambouropoulos, E.: Fragmentations with pitch, rhythm and parallelism constraints for variation matching. In: Proceedings of the 10th International Symposium on Computer Music Multidisciplinary Research, pp. 241–252 (2013)

19. Giraud, M., Groult, R., Levé, F.: Subject and counter-subject detection for analysis of the Well-Tempered Clavier fugues. In: International Symposium on Computer Music Modelling and Retrieval (CMMR), vol. 2012 (2012)

20. Gusfield, D.: Algorithms on Strings, Trees and Sequences: Computer Science and Computational Biology. Cambridge University Press, Cambridge (1997)

21. de Haas, W.B., Volk, A., Wiering, F.: Structural segmentation of music based on repeated harmonies. In: Proceedings of IEEE International Symposium on Multimedia (ISM2013), pp. 255–258 (2013)

22. Honing, H.: Computational modeling of music cognition: a case study on model selection. Music Percept. **23**(5), 365–376 (2006)

23. Honing, H.: Lure(d) into listening : the potential of cognition-based music information retrieval. Empir. Musicology Rev. **5**(4), 146–151 (2010)

24. Huang, T., Xia, G., Ma, Y., Dannenberg, R., Faloutsos, C.: MidiFind: fast and effective similarity searching in large MIDI databases. In: Proceedings of the 10th International Symposium on Computer Music Multidisciplinary Research, pp. 209–224 (2013)

25. Huron, D.: Sweet Anticipation: Music and the Psychology of Expectation. MIT Press, Cambridge (2007)

26. Janssen, B., Honing, H., van Kranenburg, P., Grijp, L.: Stability of melodic patterns in oral transmission. In: Proceedings of the Society for Music Perception and Cognition (2013)

27. Karydis, I., Nanopoulos, A., Manolopoulos, Y.: Finding maximum-length repeating patterns in music databases. Multimed. Tools Appl. **32**, 49–71 (2007). http://link.springer.com/10.1007/s11042-006-0068-5

28. Klapuri, A.: Pattern induction and matching in music signals. In: Exploring Music Contents, 7th International Symposium, CMMR 2010, Málaga, Spain, pp. 188–204 (2010)

29. Klusen, E., Moog, H., Piel, W.: Experimente zur mündlichen Tradition von Melodien. In: Jahrbuch für Volksliedforschung, pp. 11–23 (1978)

30. Knopke, I., Jürgensen, F.: A system for identifying common melodic phrases in the masses of Palestrina. J. New Music Res. **38**(2), 171–181 (2009). http://www.tandfonline.com/doi/abs/10.1080/09298210903288329
31. Knuth, D.E., Morris, J.H., Pratt, V.R.: Fast pattern matching in strings. SIAM J. Comput. **6**(2), 323–350 (1977)
32. Koniari, D., Predazzer, S., Mélen, M.: Categorization and schematization processes used in music perception by 10- to 11-year-old children. Music Percept. Interdisc. J. **18**(3), 297–324 (2001)
33. Kranenburg, P.V.: A computational approach to content-based retrieval of Folk song melodies. Ph.D. thesis, University of Utrecht (2010)
34. Laaksonen, A.: Efficient and simple algorithms for time-scaled and time-warped music search. In: Proceedings of the 10th International Symposium on Computer Music Multidisciplinary Research, pp. 621–630, No. 118653 (2013)
35. Laitinen, M., Lemström, K.: Dynamic programming in transposition and time-warp invariant polyphonic content-based music retrieval. In: 12th International Society for Music Information Retrieval Conference (ISMIR 2011), pp. 369–374. Ismir (2011)
36. Lartillot, O.: Multi-dimensional motivic pattern extraction founded on adaptive redundancy filtering. Journal of New Music Research **34**(4), 375–393 (2005). http://www.tandfonline.com/doi/abs/10.1080/09298210600578246
37. Lee, W., Chen, A.L.P.: Efficient multi-feature index structures for music data retrieval. In: Electronic Imaging, pp. 177–188. International Society for Optics and Photonics (1999)
38. Lemström, K., Laine, P.: Music information retrieval using musical parameters. In: International Computer Music Conference, vol. 26, pp. 341–348 (1998)
39. Lemström, K., Mikkilä, N., Mäkinen, V.: Filtering methods for content-based retrieval on indexed symbolic music databases. Inf. Retr. **13**(1), 1–21 (2009). http://link.springer.com/10.1007/s10791-009-9097-9
40. Lemström, K., Ukkonen, E.: Including interval encoding into edit distance based music comparison and retrieval. In: Proceedings of the AISB'2000 Symposium on Creative and Cultural Aspects and Applications of AI and Cognitive Science, Birmingham (2000)
41. Levenshtein, V.I.: Binary codecs capable of correcting deletions, insertions and reversals. Sov. Phys. - Dokl. **10**(8), 707–710 (1966)
42. Lubiw, A., Tanur, L.: Pattern matching in polyphonic music as a weighted geometric translation problem. In: International Society for Music Information Retrieval Conference (ISMIR 2004), pp. 369–374 (2004)
43. Marsden, A.: Counselling a better relationship between mathematics and musicology. J. Math. Music Math. Comput. Approaches Music Theory Anal. Compos. Perform. **6**(2), 145–153 (2012)
44. Meek, C., Birmingham, W.P.: Thematic extractor. In: International Symposium for Music Information Retrieval, pp. 119–128 (2001)
45. Meredith, D., Lemström, K., Wiggins, G.A.: Algorithms for discovering repeated patterns in multidimensional representations of polyphonic music. J. New Music Res. **31**(4), 321–345 (2002)
46. Mongeau, M., Sankoff, D.: Comparison of musical sequences. Comput. Humanit. **24**, 161–175 (1990)
47. Nieto, O., Farbood, M.M.: Perceptual evaluation of automatically extracted musical motives. In: Proceedings of the 12th International Conference on Music Perception and Cognition, pp. 723–727 (2012)

48. Owens, T.: Charlie Parker: techniques of improvisation. Ph.D. thesis (1974)
49. Paulus, J., Müller, M., Klapuri, A.: State of the art report: audio-based music structure analysis. In: Proceedings of ISMIR, pp. 625–636 (2010)
50. Pearce, M.T., Wiggins, G.A.: Evaluating cognitive models of musical composition. In: Proceedings of the 4th International Joint Workshop on Computational Creativity, London, pp. 73–80 (2007)
51. Repp, B.H.: Diversity and commonality in music performance: an analysis of timing microstructure in schumann's träumerei. J. Acoust. Soc. Am. **92**, 227–260 (1992)
52. Réti, R.: The Thematic Process in Music. Macmillan, New York (1951)
53. Rolland, P.Y.: Discovering patterns in musical sequences. J. New Music Res. **28**(4), 334–351 (1999)
54. Romming, C.A., Selfridge-Field, E.: Algorithms for polyphonic music retrieval: the hausdorff metric and geometric hashing. In: International Society for Music Information Retrieval Conference (ISMIR 2007), pp. 457–462 (2007)
55. Sloboda, J., Parker, D.: Immediate recall of melodies. In: Howell, P., Cross, I., West, R. (eds.) Musical structure and cognition, pp. 143–167. Academic Press, London (1985)
56. Szeto, W.M., Wong, M.H.: A graph-theoretical approach for pattern matching in post-tonal music analysis. J. New Music Res. **35**(4), 307–321 (2006). http://www.tandfonline.com/doi/abs/10.1080/09298210701535749
57. Volk, A., de Haas, W.B., van Kranenburg, P.: Towards modelling variation in music as foundation for similarity. In: Proceedings of ICMPC, pp. 1085–1094 (2012)
58. Volk, A., van Kranenburg, P.: Melodic similarity among folk songs: an annotation study on similarity-based categorization in music. Musicae Sci. **16**(3), 317–339 (2012). http://msx.sagepub.com/lookup/doi/10.1177/1029864912448329
59. Wittlich, G.: Interval set structure in schoenberg's op. 11, no. 1. Perspect. New Music **13**, 41–55 (1974)

Fragmentations with Pitch, Rhythm and Parallelism Constraints for Variation Matching

Mathieu Giraud[1]([✉]), Ken Déguernel[1], and Emilios Cambouropoulos[2]

[1] Laboratoire d'Informatique Fondamentale de Lille (LIFL), UMR CNRS 8022,
Université Lille 1, Villeneuve d'Ascq, France
{mathieu,ken}@algomus.fr
[2] Department of Music Studies, Aristotle University of Thessaloniki,
Thessaloniki, Greece
emilios@mus.auth.gr

Abstract. Composers commonly employ ornamentation and elaboration techniques to generate varied versions of an initial core melodic idea. Dynamic programming techniques, based on edit operations, are used to find similarities between melodic strings. However, replacements, insertions and deletions may give non-musically pertinent similarities, especially if rhythmic or metrical structure is not considered. We propose, herein, to compute the similarity between a reduced query and a melody employing *only fragmentation* operations. Such fragmentations transform one note from the reduced query into a possible large set of notes, taking into account pitch and rhythm constraints, as well as elementary parallelism information. We test the proposed algorithm on four "theme and variations" piano pieces by W. A. Mozart and L. van Beethoven and show that the proposed constrained fragmentation operations are capable of detecting simple variations with high sensitivity and specificity.

Keywords: Melodic similarity · Reduced melody · Variations · Fragmentation · Musical parallelism

1 Introduction

Ornamentation, embellishment, elaboration, filling in are common strategies employed by composers in order to generate new musical material that is recognized as being similar to an initial or reduced underlying musical pattern. This way musical unity and homogeneity is retained, whilst at the same time, variation and change occur. This interplay between repetition, variation and change makes music "meaningful" and interesting. Listeners are capable of discerning common elements between varied musical material primarily through *reduction*, i.e. identifying "essential" common characteristics. Systematic music theories

© Springer International Publishing Switzerland 2014
M. Aramaki et al. (Eds.): CMMR 2013, LNCS 8905, pp. 298–312, 2014.
DOI: 10.1007/978-3-319-12976-1_19

(e.g. Lerdahl and Jackendoff [19]) explore such processes, as do high-level descriptions [10, 22] or semi-Schenkerian computational models [20]. We try here to identify *ornamentations of a given reduced melodic pattern*. The proposed pattern matching algorithm employs not only pitch information but also additional rhythmic properties and elementary parallelism features.

Pattern matching methods are commonly employed to capture musical variations, especially melodic variations, and may be based on dynamic programming techniques. Similarity between melodies can be computed by the Mongeau-Sankoff algorithm [23] and its extensions, or by other methods for approximate string matching computing edit-distances, that is allowing a given number of restricted edit operations [7, 9, 13, 14]. The similarities can be computed on absolute pitches or on pitch intervals in order to account for transposition invariance [4, 11, 16, 25]. Note that some music similarity matching representations do not use edit-distance techniques [1, 8, 17, 21]. Geometric encodings also provide transposition invariance [18, 26, 27].

In edit-distance techniques, the allowed edit operations are usually matches, replacements, insertions, deletions, consolidations and fragmentations. However, edit operations such as replacements, insertions and deletions of notes are adequate for various domains (e.g. bioinformatics [12]) but present some problems when applied to melodic strings. In the general case, insertions or deletions of notes in a melodic string seriously affect metrical structure, and the same is true for substitutions with a note of different duration. Fragmentations and consolidations may be a further way to handle some aspects of musical pattern transformation [6, 23]. In [2], Barton et al. proposed to focus only on consolidation and fragmentation operations on pitch intervals: the sum of several consecutive intervals in one melodic sequence should equal an interval in another sequence. Their algorithm identifies correctly variations, including transposed ones, of a given reduced pattern, but incorrectly matches a large number of false positives, the consolidation and the fragmentation being applied only on the pitch domain.

In this paper it is asserted that identifying simple variations (that contain ornamentations) of a given reduced melodic pattern is best addressed using fragmentation operations, taking into account both *pitch* and *rhythm* information, along with other higher level musical properties such as *parallelism*. Apart from leaving aside replacement, insertion and deletion operations (only fragmentation is employed), this paper gives emphasis to rhythmic properties of melodic strings and other higher level structural features (e.g. similar ornamentations are introduced for similar underlying patterns) showing that such information increases both sensitivity and specificity of melodic variation detection.

The current study is not meant to provide a general method for identifying variations of a given melodic pattern, but rather an exploration of some factors that play a role in some "prototypical" cases of musical variation. The chosen set of variations (W. A. Mozart K. 265, K. 331, K. 455 and Beethoven WoO 64) are commonly used in composition as prototypical examples illustrating a number of basic variation techniques (ornamentation, rhythmic variation, modal change); these apparently simple sets of variations are already quite challenging for computational modeling as the number of notes varies significantly between different versions (some variations may have 8 times or more notes than the underlying thematic pattern). Variations, however, appear in many guises and musical similarity is very difficult to pin down and define systematically in a general way [3]; further research that takes into account a much larger variation dataset will be necessary. In the last section, limitations of the current proposal are discussed and future developments suggested.

The paper is organized as follows. Section 2 presents some definitions, Sects. 3 and 4 describe the algorithm and its results on three sets of variations by Mozart and one set of variations by Beethoven, totaling 728 bars in 4 themes and 31 variations. The best results are obtained while combining pitch, length and parallelism constraints, with sensitivity between 70 % and 85 % and precision between 60 % and 100 %. Section 5 discusses some perspectives of this work.

2   Definitions

A *note* x is described by a triplet (p, o, ℓ), where p is the pitch, o the onset, and ℓ the length. The pitches can describe diatonic (based on note names) or semitone information. We consider ordered *sequence of notes* $x_1 \ldots x_m$, that is $x_1 = (p_1, o_1, \ell_1), \ldots, x_m = (p_m, o_m, \ell_m)$, where $0 \le o_1 \le o_2 \le \ldots \le o_m$ (see Fig. 1). All the sequences used in this paper are *monophonic*: there are never two notes sounding at the same onset, that is, for every i with $1 \le i < m$, $o_i + \ell_i \le o_{i+1}$. We do not handle overlapping notes.

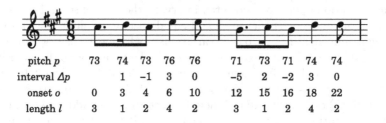

pitch p		73	74	73	76	76		71	73	71	74	74
interval Δp			1	−1	3	0		−5	2	−2	3	0
onset o		0	3	4	6	10		12	15	16	18	22
length l		3	1	2	4	2		3	1	2	4	2

Fig. 1. A monophonic sequence of notes, represented by (p, o, ℓ) or $(^\Delta p, o, \ell)$ triplets. In this example, onsets and lengths are counted in sixteenths, and pitches and intervals are represented in semitones through the MIDI standard.

Approximate matching through edit operations. Let $S(a, b)$ the score of the best *local* alignment between two monophonic sequences $x_{a'} \ldots x_a$ and $y_{b'} \ldots y_b$. This score can be computed by dynamic programming [23]:

$$S(a, b) = \max \begin{cases} S(a - 1, b - 1) + \delta(x_a, y_b) & \text{(match, replacement)} \\ S(a - 1, b) + \delta(x_a, \varnothing) & \text{(insertion)} \\ S(a, b - 1) + \delta(\varnothing, y_b) & \text{(deletion)} \\ S(a - k, b - 1) + \delta(\{x_{a-k+1} \ldots x_a\}, y_b) & \text{(consolidation)} \\ S(a - 1, b - k) + \delta(x_a, \{y_{b-k+1} \ldots y_b\}) & \text{(fragmentation)} \\ 0 & \text{(local alignment)} \end{cases}$$

Fig. 2. The two first measures of the theme and variations of the Andante, K. 331, by Mozart, preceded by a reduction R of the theme. In the theme, the circled D of the first measure is a *neighbor tone*, as the $C^\#$ of the second measure. This neighbor tone D can also be found in the variation VI, as an appoggiatura. The D that is present in the first measure of the other variations is better analyzed as a *passing tone* between $C^\#$ and E (a similar role of passing tone can be also argued in a medium-scale interpretation of the theme). Finally, there are no such Ds in variation I. A "note for note" alignment between the theme and variation III, IV and V that would align all these Ds but include some deletions and insertions does not lead here to a satisfactory analysis. Less errors are done when considering fragmentations between the reduced pattern and the variations.

δ is the score function for each type of mutation. If the last line (0) is removed, this equation computes the score for the best *global alignment* between $x_1 \ldots x_a$ and $y_1 \ldots y_b$. Moreover, initializing to 0 the values $S(0, b)$, the same equation computes the score for the best *semi-global* alignment, that is the score of all candidate occurrences of the sequence $x_1 \ldots x_a$ (seen as a pattern) inside the sequence $y_1 \ldots y_b$.

The complexity of computing $S(m, n)$ is $O(mnk)$, where k is the number of allowed consolidations and fragmentations.

3   A Fragmentation Operation for Variation Matching

Allowing many fragmentations may produce many spurious matches: often fragmentations are thus restricted to only 2, 3 or 4 notes, of same length and pitch. However, fragmentation with more notes and with different pitches does occur in real cases, especially when a pattern is ornamented. Moreover, if we consider a reduced pattern, then almost any variation of the pattern can be seen as a fragmentation of this reduction. For example, the variations of the *Andante grazioso* of Mozart K. 331 (Fig. 2) can be seen as a fragmentation of a reduced pattern in 2 to 6 notes, using chord tones but also ornamental tones.

More specifically, we take fragmentation to mean that a relatively long note is fragmented into shorter notes of the same overall duration (*length* constraint), and that the pitch of at least one of the shorter notes matches with the initial long note (*pitch* constraint). Finally, if the given reduced theme (query) comprises repeating pitch and/or rhythm patterns, we assume that the same ornamentation transformations will be applied on the repeating pitch/rhythm patterns (this *parallelism* constraint is enforced in a post-processing stage).

We thus propose here to consider a semi-global pattern matching between a reduced pattern $x_1 \ldots x_a$ and a monophonic sequence $y_1 \ldots y_b$ with only fragmentations:

$$S(a,b) = \max_k \; S(a-1, b-k) + \delta(x_a, \{y_{b-k+1}\ldots y_b\})$$

The only operation considered here is the fragmentation of a note x_a into k notes $\{y_{b-k+1}\ldots y_b\}$. We require that the score function $\delta(x_a, \{y_{b-k+1}\ldots y_b\})$ checks the following constraints:

– *length* constraint – the total length of the notes $\{y_{b-k+1}\ldots y_b\}$, with their associated rests, is exactly the length of x_a;
– *pitch* constraint – at least one of the pitches $y_{b-k+1}\ldots y_b$ must be equal to the pitch of x_a, regardless of the octave. To match minor variations, we simply use a "diatonic equivalence", considering as equal pitches differing from only one chromatic semitone (or, when the pitch spelling is not known, allowing ± 1 semitone between the sequences, as in the δ-approximation [5,24]).

We are not interested here into fine-tuning error costs: $\delta(x_a, \{y_{b-k+1}\ldots y_b\})$ equals 0 when the constraints are met, and $-\infty$ otherwise. Note that with these simplified costs, a consequence of the length constraint is that, at each position, there is at most one fragmentation for each note x_a – so dynamic programming can be implemented in only $O(mn)$ time.

Finally, we also propose a post-filtering that applies very well to the variations technique. Usually, inside a variation, the same transformation pattern is applied on several segments of the theme, giving a unity of texture. In Fig. 2, variation I could be described by "sixteenths with rest, using chromatic neighbor tones", possibly with the help of some high-level music formalism [10,19,22]. We propose here a simple filter that will be very computationally efficient. The unity of texture often implies that the underlying base pitch is heard at similar places (+ marks on the Fig. 2). We thus applied a refinement of the *pitch* constraint:

– *pitch position parallelism* filtering – when applying the pitch constraint on a pattern divided into segments, at least one matched pitch must be found at the same relative position in at least two segments.

For example, on Fig. 2, all + marks, except the ones in parentheses in variation V, occur at the same relative position in both measures.

4   Results

4.1   The Corpus

In order to evaluate the proposed algorithm, we apply it on the following sets of "theme and variations" (see Table 1). We started from either .krn Humdrum [15] or .mid files, keeping only the melody (without acciaccaturas):

- the first movement *Andante grazioso* of the Piano Sonata 11 in A major (K. 331) by W. A. Mozart,
- the variations on *Ah vous dirai-je maman* (K. 265) by W. A. Mozart,
- the variations on *Wilhelm von Nassan* (K. 25) by W. A. Mozart,
- and the *Six Easy Variations on a Swiss Song* (WoO 64) by Ludwig van Beethoven.

Table 1. Sets of variations used in this study. For Mozart K. 331, we started from the .krn Humdrum files available for academic purposes at kern.humdrum.org, and kept only the melody. For the other pieces, the melody has been extracted manually and encoded in .mid or .krn symbolic notation.

Mozart	K. 331	A major	6/8	Theme + 6 variations	144 bars
Mozart	K. 265	C major	2/4	Theme + 12 variations	363 bars
Mozart	K. 25	D major	4/4	Theme + 7 variations	144 bars
Beethoven	WoO 64	F major	4/4	Theme + 6 variations	77 bars

Table 2. Reduced themes used as query for the fragmentation matching, and number of ground truth occurrences of these themes in the considered sets of variations. The "parallelism" column display the number of segments used to check the parallelism constraint. Note that the length of the patterns is manually adapted for variations with another meter than the theme (variation 12 of K. 265, in 3/4, and variation 10 of K. 455, in 6/8).

		Reduced theme	Length	Occurrences	Parallelism
Mozart	K. 331	$C^{\#}EBD$	2 bars	7×3	$\times 2$
Mozart	K. 265	$CGAGFEDC$	2 bars	13×2	$\times 4$
Mozart	K. 25	$DEF^{\#}EGF^{\#}$	4 bars	8×2	$\times 2, \times 2$
Beethoven	WoO 64	$CFACGFCCEFDC$	6 bars	7×1	$\times 2$

In a study on the recognition of variations using Schenkerian reduction [20], the author uses 10 sets of variations by Mozart; only the first four bars of each theme (10 themes) and variations (77 variations) are used for testing the proposed system.

In the current study, the corpus has a total of 4 themes and 31 variations. This number may seem low, but the set of variations is used here searching for a reduction of the theme *in the whole melodic surface* of the piece (728 bars on the four pieces). Moreover, the search is not restrained to full bars – there could be an occurrence starting from any note. However, in the majority of cases, the length constraint will enforce the metrical structure of the pattern in the occurrences.

For each variation set, a reduced version of the theme (or part of the theme) is given as the query (Table 2). The algorithm then identifies matches of this theme in the piece. The following paragraphs details the results on the four sets. Some alignments corresponding to the best constraints can be downloaded from www.algomus.fr/variations.

4.2 *Andante grazioso*, Piano Sonata 11 (K. 331)

The query is the reduced theme melody R (top of Fig. 2), consisting of the four notes $C^{\#} E B D$. We choose this pattern, having three occurrences in each variation, instead of the full eight-notes pattern $C^{\#} E B D A B C^{\#} B$ which has only one complete occurrence in each variation.

Table 3. Number of occurrences of the reduced pattern $C^{\#} E B D$ found in the theme and variations of the *Andante grazioso* of the Piano Sonata 11 by Mozart (K. 331). Several fragmentation operations are tested. The columns "sens" and "prec" represents the sensitivity (recall) and precision of the proposed algorithm compared to the ground truth (3 occurrences in the theme and each variation). In all the cases, these 3 occurrences are found by the method (true positives), except for the variation III, in minor, when not using diatonic pitch matching. The "no constraint" line is directly related to the number of notes of the variation – there are matches everywhere.

	theme	variations						sens	prec
		I	II	III	IV	V	VI		
number of notes	88	156	201	201	121	351	304		
no constraint (all frag. 1...20)	85	153	198	198	118	348	301	100%	<2%
pitch	79	108	186	129	112	327	260	100%	<2%
length	36	45	37	40	55	37	81	100%	6%
length + pitch	3	3	8	0	3	14	13	83%	41%
length + pitch + parallelism	3	3	6	0	3	3	4	83%	82%
length + pitch (diatonic)	3	3	8	5	4	14	14	100%	46%
length + pitch (diatonic) + parallelism	3	3	6	3	3	3	4	100%	84%
ground truth	3	3	3	3	3	3	3		

Results are summarized on Table 3. In the theme and each variation, 3 occurrences have to be found. As our fragmentations can handle very large sets of notes, the 3 truth occurrences are always found, except for the variation III, in minor, when using pitch matching without diatonic equivalence.

The algorithm has thus an almost perfect sensitivity (recall), and should be evaluated for his precision. Allowing any fragmentation (even starting only on beats) leads to many spurious results. Adding only the pitch constraint does not help so much. Adding only the length constraint gives matching every sequence of two measures against the pattern.

As soon as both pitch and length constraints are enforced, the algorithm gives good results, with very few false positives: In the majority of the variations, only the 3 true occurrences are found. The best results are here when using afterwards the "pitch parallelism" constraint (on two halves of the pattern), filtering out some spurious matches (see Fig. 3). This method has an overall 84 % precision.

m13@288 → m15@336 | Score = 4
Check pitch parallelism: [×2 ?] ++ Parallelism [×2] found.

m14@312 → m16@360 | Score = 4
Check pitch parallelism: [×2 ?] – – [×3 ?] – – [×4 ?] – – no common pitch position → discarding

Fig. 3. Two overlapping matches found on the minor variation of K. 331, at measures 13 and 14, including each one 4 fragmentations into 6 notes (F6), with length and pitch ±1 constraints. The * marks indicate the pitches that are identical to the query (with the approximation $C = C^\#$). (Top.) The real match is confirmed by the parallelism of pitch positions (sixteenths number 1, 5, 7 and 10 inside each measure) (Bottom.) This spurious match is discarded, as the position of the matching pitches are different in the two measures.

False (or inexact) positives can still happen in some situations (Fig. 4), but they are very few: only 4 in this piece. Moreover, some false positives are overlapping with true matches, and could be discarded with a more precise scoring system.

4.3 Variations on *Ah vous dirai-je maman* (K. 265)

For *Twelve Variations on "Ah vous dirai-je, Maman"* (K. 265), we selected a query as the eight notes $C\,G\,A\,G\,F\,E\,D\,C$, this full theme appearing twice in each variation, totaling 26 occurrences. The parallelism constraint here applies

Fig. 4. A false positive in variation III of K. 331, that has also common pitch positions. This false positive occurs (with overlapping) one measure later than a true occurrence, at measure 5, that is correctly detected.

Table 4. Number of occurrences (occ) of the reduced pattern $C\,G\,A\,G\,F\,E\,D\,C$ found in *Twelve Variations on "Ah vous dirai-je, Maman"* by W. A. Mozart (K. 265, 1387 notes in our encoding). The ground truth has 2 occurrences in the theme and each variation, totaling 26 occurrences. The column "(tp)" shows the number of true positives found by each method, and the columns "sens" and "prec" give the associated sensibility and precision. As we encoded the files in MIDI, without pitch spelling information, we used here a ± 1 semitone pitch approximation to match the minor variation (but it also brings some spurious occurrences).

	occ	(tp)	sens	prec
Length + pitch	39	(20)	77 %	51 %
Length + pitch + parallelism	29	(20)	77 %	69 %
Length + pitch ($\pm$ 1)	71	(22)	85 %	31 %
Length + pitch ($\pm$ 1) + parallelism	36	(22)	85 %	61 %
Ground truth		(26)		

Table 5. Number of occurrences of the reduced pattern found in *Wilhelm von Nassan* (K. 25) by W. A. Mozart. The ground truth has 2 occurrences in the theme and each variation, totaling 16 occurrences.

	occ	(tp)	sens	prec
Length + pitch ($\pm$ 1)	35	(12)	75 %	34 %
Length + pitch ($\pm$ 1) + parallelism	20	(12)	75 %	60 %
Ground truth		(16)		

on the four segments of one measure, requiring that at least two measures share common pitch positions.

Results are summarized on Table 4. With pitch, length and parallelism constraints, the algorithm outputs 20 true positive occurrences (sensitivity of 77 %) with regular pitch matching, and 22 true positive occurrences (sensitivity of 85 %) with ± 1 pitch matching.

Note that the sensitivity is not as perfect as in K. 331: For example, on some variations, the length constraint can not be enforced (see Fig. 5, bottom).

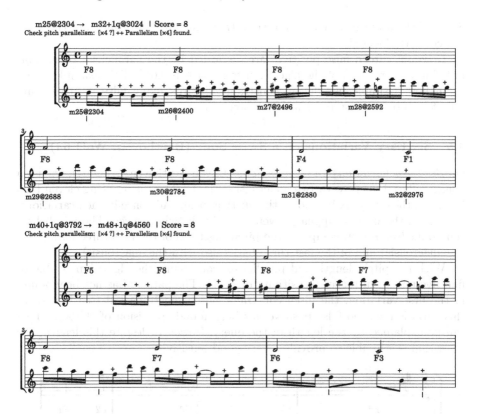

Fig. 5. Two matches found in the first variation of K. 265. (Top.) Good match and alignment. (Bottom.) Although the end of this match is a true positive, the alignment is wrong: the true occurrence should be shifted a quarter before, but the ties on the melody prevent a good alignment respecting the length constraint across the fragmentations.

Again, there are very few false positives, especially when the parallelism constraint is required.

4.4 Variations on *Wilhelm von Nassan* (K. 25)

On the variations on *Wilhelm von Nassan* (K. 25), the query appears twice in each variations, totaling sixteen occurrences (Fig. 6). Since the reduced query is not symmetrical (two whole notes, then four half notes), we choose here to apply the parallelism constraint in two separated parts, first checking the first two bars together, and then the third and fourth bars.

With the pitch, length and parallelism constraint, the algorithm is able to find twelve true occurrences (sensitivity of 75 %). The results are summed up in Table 5. Even with the parallelism constraint, eight false positives are found.

Some of them are in fact true positives that are shifted in time, and therefore not correctly located.

However, fifteen false positives are discarded by the parallelism constraint, bringing the precision of the algorithm from 34 % to 60 %. This example shows again how a simple parallelism constraint discards many false positives, and therefore provides results with better precision.

4.5 Six Easy Variations on a Swiss Song (Beethoven, WoO 64)

On *Six Easy Variations on a Swiss Song* (L. van Beethoven, WoO 64), we use a longer reduced query with two anacrousis (Fig. 7). The theme being eleven bars long, and the query six bars long, the query only once in each variations. Therefore, the pattern appears seven times in the whole piece. The parallelism constraint (see Fig. 9) compares the pitch positions of the first three bars (with the anacrousis) and of the last three bars (also with the anacrousis).

With the pitch, length and parallelism constraint, the algorithm is able to find five true occurrences (sensitivity of 71 %). The pattern has not been found in the first variation, the pitch constraint not being respected (see Fig. 8). In this variation set, no false positive has been found (precision of 100 %), which can be explained by the length of the query. However, despite this length, the algorithm is still able to provide a very good sensitivity.

Fig. 6. Query used for the Variations on *Wilhelm von Nassan* (K. 25) aligned to the theme.

Fig. 7. Reduced theme of Beethoven's Six Easy Variations on a Swiss Song used as a query in the algorithm.

5 Discussion

In this paper, we have shown that a unique edit operation – a fragmentation – gives very good results in matching a reduced query against a theme and a set of variations. The key point in our approach is to focus on musically relevant fragmentations, allowing very large fragmentations, but restricting them with rhythm and pitch information along with some parallelism.

Such an approach with fragmentations works because we start from a reduced query. Moreover, a very simplified matching procedure and error cost have been used in this study. This simple model has produced good results in four sets of variations that contain instances of extensive ornamentation. However, the model may be improved in many ways. For instance, fine-tuning scores for the δ function could improve the results, allowing imperfect fragmentations and some other classical operations. The "parallelism" constraint that was tested here is also very simple (one common pitch position on several segments of a pattern), and the number and the position of segments were manually selected for each piece. This parallelism constraint could be extended to become more generic, but its current simplicity makes it very suitable for efficient computation. Finally, theses ideas could also be adapted to interval matching, to be transposition invariant.

5.1   Analysis of Elaborated Sets of Variations

An important limit of this present study is that the four chosen sets of variations are easy or intermediate piano pieces, and that their composition technique almost always respects the global layout of the theme. At the opposite end of the spectrum, one could look for example to the 15 "Eroica" Variations (op. 35) or the 33 "Diabelli" Variations (op. 120) by Beethoven. Such pieces exhibit much complex transformations of the musical material. The proposed algorithm could extract *some* of these variations, but will be limited by the following facts:

– In many cases, there is not a single melody that can be extracted from the polyphonic texture, or the melody can alternate between several voices (see Fig. 10);
– However, even in the cases where a melody can be extracted, further ornamentation and transformation sometimes do not respect the *length* constraint.

Fig. 8. First bars of the first variation of WoO 64. The A in the first bar does not respect the pitch constraint (F in the query), and therefore this occurrence is not found.

Fig. 9. A positive match found in the fifth variation of WoO 64. The parallelism constraint is enforced for at least one position in both segments.

Fig. 10. Example of a more complex transformation on the "Eroica" variations by Beethoven (op. 35).In this set of variations, two melodies are transformed: the theme and the bass line. In the variation no. XIV, these melodies are tangled: During the first eight bars, the transformed bass line is played at the soprano, and the transformed is played at the bass. Then, the roles are exchanged.

We used in this study only fragmentations, and not the usual insertion/ deletion/substitution operations from [23], but, as stated in the introduction, these operations break the metrical structure as soon as they affect durations of individual notes. For us, a good generic solution based on the fragmentation operation could include some relaxation of the *length* constraints – thus allowing insertion of notes or group of notes – but at the same time shall include a *reinforcement of high-level constraints*, such as the parallelism operation.

5.2 Towards a Unique *Transformation* Operation

Going a step further, we argue that relevant similarities between two melodies – and maybe even between polyphonic pieces – should be computed with *a unique high-level transformation operation* of a group of several notes $\{x_1, x_2...x_\ell\}$ into another group of notes $\{y_1, y_2...y_k\}$. The traditional edit operations of match/replacement/insertion/deletion, along with fragmentation and consolidation, can be seen as particular cases of this transformation operation, one set of notes being reduced to a singleton or to the empty set. In such a framework, computing $\delta(\{x_1, x_2...x_\ell\}, \{y_1, y_2...y_k\})$ may require several steps, possibly including dynamic programming with the more classical operations. Seeing transformation as the basic operation could yield musical similarities that span a larger range than usual operations.

References

1. Ahlbäck, S.: Melodic similarity as a determinant of melody structure. Musicae Scientiae Discussion Forum **4A**, 235–280 (2007)
2. Barton, C., Cambouropoulos, E., Iliopoulos, C.S., Lipták, Z.: Melodic string matching via interval consolidation and fragmentation. In: Artificial Intelligence and Innovations Conference (AIAI 2012), pp. 460–469 (2012)
3. Cambouropoulos, E.: How similar is similar? Musicae Scientiae Discussion Forum **4A**, 7–24 (2009)
4. Cambouropoulos, E., Crawford, T., Iliopoulos, C.S.: Pattern processing in melodic sequences: challenges, caveats and prospects. In: Artifical Intelligence and Simulation of Behaviour (AISB 99), pp. 42–47 (1999)
5. Cambouropoulos, E., Crochemore, M., Iliopoulos, C.S., Mouchard, L., Pinzon, Y.J.: Algorithms for computing approximate repetitions in musical sequences. Int. J. Comput. Math., 129–144 (1999)
6. Clausen, M.: Modified Mongeau-Sankoff algorithm. http://www-mmdb.iai.uni-bonn.de/forschungprojekte/midilib/english/saddemo.html
7. Clifford, R., Iliopoulos, C.S.: Approximate string matching for music analysis. Soft. Comput. **8**(9), 597–603 (2004)
8. Conklin, D., Anagnostopoulou, C.: Segmental pattern discovery in music. INFORMS J. Comput. **18**(3), 285–293 (2006)
9. Crawford, T., Iliopoulos, C.S., Raman, R.: String matching techniques for musical similarity and melodic recognition. Comput. Musicology **11**, 71–100 (1998)
10. Deutsch, D., Feroe, J.: The internal representation of pitch sequences in tonal music. Psychol. Rev. **88**(6), 503–522 (1981)
11. Giraud, M., Groult, R., Levé, F.: Subject and counter-subject detection for analysis of the Well-Tempered Clavier fugues. In: Computer Music Modeling and Retrieval (CMMR 2012) (2012)
12. Gusfield, D.: Algorithms on Strings, Trees, and Sequences. Cambridge University Press, New York (1997)
13. Hanna, P., Ferraro, P., Robine, M.: On optimizing the editing algorithms for evaluating similarity between monophonic musical sequences. J. New Music Res. **36**, 267–279 (2007). http://hal.archives-ouvertes.fr/hal-00285560
14. Hewlett, W.B., Selfridge-Field, E. (eds.): Melodic Similarity: Concepts, Procedures, and Applications. MIT Press, Cambridge (1998)
15. Huron, D.: Music information processing using the Humdrum toolkit: concepts, examples, and lessons. Comput. Music J. **26**(2), 11–26 (2002)
16. Kageyama, T., Mochizuki, K., Takashima, Y.: Melody retrieval with humming. In: International Computer Music Conference, pp. 349–351 (1993)
17. Lartillot, O.: Motivic pattern extraction in symbolic domain. In: Intelligent Music Information Systems: Tools and Methodologies, pp. 236–260 (2007)
18. Lemström, K., Ukkonen, E.: Including interval encoding into edit distance based music comparison and retrieval. In: Symposium on Creative and Cultural Aspects and Applications of AI and Cognitive Science (AISB 2000), pp. 53–60 (2000)
19. Lerdhal, F., Jackendoff, R.: A Generative Theory of Tonal Music. MIT Press, Cambridge (1983, 1996)
20. Marsden, A.: Recognition of variations using automatic Schenkerian reduction. In: International Society for Music Information Retrieval Conference (ISMIR 2010), pp. 501–506 (2010)

21. Marsden, A.: Interrogating melodic similarity: a definitive phenomenon or the product of interpretation? J. New Music Res. **41**(4), 323–335 (2012)
22. Meredith, D.: A geometric language for representing structure in polyphonic music. In: International Society for Music Information Retrieval Conference (ISMIR 2012) (2012)
23. Mongeau, M., Sankoff, D.: Comparison of musical sequences. Comput. Humanit. **24**, 161–175 (1990)
24. Mäkinena, V., Navarro, G., Ukkonen, E.: Algorithms for transposition invariant string matching (extended abstract). In: Alt, H., Habib, M. (eds.) STACS 2003. LNCS, vol. 2607, pp. 191–202. Springer, Heidelberg (2003)
25. Müllensiefen, D., Frieler, K.: Modelling experts' notion of melodic similarity. Musicae Scientiae Discussion Forum **4A**, 183–210 (2007)
26. Typke, R.: Music retrieval based on melodic similarity. Ph.D. thesis, Univ. Utrecht (2007)
27. Ukkonen, E., Lemström, K., Mäkinen, V.: Geometric algorithms for transposition invariant content based music retrieval. In: International Conference on Music Information Retrieval (ISMIR 2003), pp. 193–199 (2003)

Predicting Agreement and Disagreement in the Perception of Tempo

Geoffroy Peeters[(⊠)] and Ugo Marchand

STMS - IRCAM - CNRS - UPMC - 1, pl. Igor Stravinky, 75004 Paris, France
{geoffroy.peeters,ugo.marchand}@ircam.fr
http://www.ircam.fr

Abstract. In the absence of a music score, tempo can only be defined by its perception by users. Thus recent studies have focused on the estimation of perceptual tempo defined by listening experiments. So far, algorithms have only been proposed to estimate the tempo when people agree on it. In this paper, we study the case when people disagree on the perception of tempo and propose an algorithm to predict this disagreement. For this, we hypothesize that the perception of tempo is correlated to a set of variations of various viewpoints on the audio content: energy, harmony, spectral-balance variations and short-term-similarity-rate. We suppose that when those variations are coherent, a shared perception of tempo is favoured and when they are not, people may perceive different tempi.We then propose several statistical models to predict the agreement or disagreement in the perception of tempo from these audio features. Finally, we evaluate the models using a test-set resulting from the perceptual experiment performed at Last-FM in 2011.

Keywords: Tempo estimation · Perceptual tempo · Tempo agreement · Tempo disagreement

1 Introduction

Tempo is one of the most predominant perceptual element of music. For this reason, and given its use in numerous applications (search by tempo, beat-synchronous processing, beat-synchronous analysis, musicology ...) there has been and there are still many studies related to the estimation of tempo from an audio signal (see [9] for a good overview).

While tempo is a predominant element, Moelants and McKinney [14] highlighted the fact that people can perceive different tempi for a single track. For this reason, recent studies have started focusing on the problem of estimating the "perceptual tempo" and perceptual tempo classes (such as "slow", "moderate" or "fast"). This is usually done for the subset of audio tracks for which people agree on the tempo. In this paper we study the case where people disagree.

© Springer International Publishing Switzerland 2014
M. Aramaki et al. (Eds.): CMMR 2013, LNCS 8905, pp. 313–329, 2014.
DOI: 10.1007/978-3-319-12976-1_20

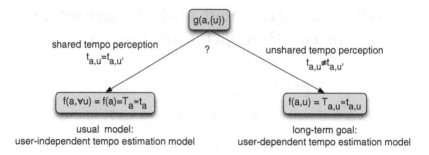

Fig. 1. $g(a, u)$ is a function that predicts tempo agreement and disagreement. Based on this prediction a user-independent or a user-dependent tempo estimation model is used.

1.1 Formalisation

We denote by a an audio track and by t_a its tempo. The task of tempo estimation can be expressed as finding the function f such that $f(a) = T_a \simeq t_a$. Considering that different users, denoted by u, can perceive different tempi for the same audio track, the ideal model can be expressed as $f(a, u) = T_{a,u} \simeq t_{a,u}$.

Previous research on the estimation of perceptual tempo (see Sect. 1.2) consider mainly audio tracks a for which the perception of the tempo is shared among users. This can be expressed as $t_{a,u} = t_{a,u'}$. The prediction model is therefore independent of the user u and can be written $f(a, \forall u) = f(a) = T_a$.

Our long-term goal is to create a user-dependent tempo prediction model $f(a, u) = T_{a,u} \simeq t_{a,u}$. As a first step toward this model, we study in this paper the prediction of the audio tracks a for which the perception is shared ($t_{a,u} = t_{a,u'}$) and for which it is not ($t_{a,u} \neq t_{a,u'}$). For this, we look for a function $g(a, \{u\})$ which can predict this shared perception for a given audio track a and a given set of user $\{u\}$ (see Fig. 1). We consider that this disagreement of tempo perception is due to

1. the preferences of the specific users (which may be due to the users themselves or to the listening conditions such as the listening environment),
2. the specific characteristics of the audio track; it may contain ambiguities in its rhythm or in its hierarchical organization.

In this work we only focus on the second point. We therefore estimate a function $g(a)$ which indicates if an ambiguity exists and which can therefore be used to predict whether users will share the perception of tempo (agreement) or not (disagreement).

1.2 Related Works

Studies on Tempo Agreement/Disagreement Estimation. One of the first studies related to the perception of tempo and the sharing of its perception is the one by Moelants and McKinney [14]. This study presents and discusses the results of three experiments where subjects were asked to tap to the beat of musical excerpts. Experiments 1 and 2 lead to a unimodal perceived tempo distribution with a resonant tempo centered on 128 bpm and 140 bpm respectively[1]. They therefore assume that a preferential tempo exists around 120 bpm and that "... pieces with a clear beat around 120 bpm are very likely to be perceived in this tempo by a large majority of the listeners.". An important assumption presented in this work is that "the relation between the predominant perceived tempi and the resonant tempo of the model could be used to predict the ambiguity of tempo across listeners (and vice versa)... if a musical excerpt contains a metrical level whose tempo lies near the resonant tempo, the perceived tempo across listeners (i.e., perceived tempo distribution) is likely to be dominated by the tempo of that metrical level and be relatively unambiguous". In our work, this assumption will be used for the development of our first prediction model. In [14], the authors have chosen a resonant tempo interval within [110–170] bpm. During our own experiment (see Sect. 3), we found that these values are specific to the test-set used. In [14], Moelants proposes a model to predict, from acoustic analyses, the musical excerpts that would deviate from the proposed resonance model.

Surprisingly no other studies have dealt with the problem of tempo agreement/disagreement except the recent one of Zapata et al. [22] which uses mutual agreement of a committee of beat trackers to establish a threshold for perceptually acceptable beat tracking.

In the opposite, studies in the case of tempo agreement ($t_{a,u} = t_{a,u'}$) are numerous. In this case, the model simplifies to $f(a, \forall u) = T$ and aims at estimating "perceptual tempo", "perceptual tempo" classes or octave error correction.

Studies on "Perceptual Tempo" Estimation. Seyerlehner [20] proposes an instance-based machine learning approach (KNN) to infer perceived tempo. For this, the rhythm content of each audio item is represented using either a Fluctuation Patterns or an Auto-correlation function. Two audio items are then compared using Pearson correlation coefficient between their representations. For an unknown item, the K most similar items are found and the most frequent tempo among the K is assigned to the unknown item.

Chua [3] distinguishes perceptual tempo from score tempo (annotated on the score) and foot-tapping tempo (which is centered around 80–100 bpm). He proposes an Improved Perceptual Tempo Estimator to determine automatically the perceptual tempo This IPTE determines the perceptual tempo (with frequency sub-band analysis, amplitude envelope autocorrelation then peak-picking) on 10 seconds-length segment, along with a likelyhood measure. The perceptual tempo is the tempo of the segment with the highest likelihood. On a test-set

---

[1] Experiment 3 is performed on musical excerpts specifically chosen for their extremely slow or fast tempo and leads to a bi-modal distribution with peaks around 50 and 200 bpm. Because of the specificities of these musical excerpts, we do not consider the results of it here.

of 50 manually annotated musical excerpts, he evaluates his IPTE. The model failed for only 2 items.

Studies on "Perceptual Tempo" Classes Estimation. Hockman [10] considers only two classes: "fast" and "slow" tempo classes. Using Last.fm A.P.I., artists and tracks which have been assigned "fast" and "slow" tags are selected. The corresponding audio signals are then obtained using YouTube A.P.I. This leads to a test-set of 397 items. 80 different audio features related to the onset detection function, pitch, loudness and timbre are then extracted using jAudio. Among the various classifiers tested (KNN, SVM, C4.5, AdaBoost ...), AdaBoost achieved the best performance.

Gkiokas [8] studies both the problems of continuous tempo estimation and tempo class estimation. The content of an audio signal is represented by a sophisticated set of audio features. For this 8 energy bands are passed to a set of resonators. The output is summed-up by a set of filter-bank and DCT is applied. Binary one-vs-one Support Vector Machine (SVM) classifier and SVM regression are then used to predict the tempo classes and continuous tempo. For the later, peak picking is used to refine the tempo estimation.

Studies on Octave Error Correction. Chen [2] proposes a method to automatically correct octave errors. The assumption used is that the perception of tempo is correlated to the "mood" ("aggressive" and "frantic" mood usually relates to "fast" tempo while "romantic" and "sentimental" mood relates to "slow" tempi). A system is first used to estimate automatically the mood of a given track. Four tempo categories are considered: "very slow", "somewhat slow", "somewhat fast" and "very fast". A SVM is then used to train four models corresponding to the tempi using the 101-moods feature vector as observation. Given the estimation of the tempo category, a set of rules is proposed to correct the estimation of tempo provided by an algorithm.

Xiao [21] proposes a system to correct the octave errors of the tempo estimation provided by a dedicated algorithm. The idea is that the timbre of a track is correlated to its tempo. To represent the timbre of an audio track, he uses the MFCCs. An 8-component GMM is then used to model the joint MFCC and annotated tempo t_a distribution. For an unknown track, a first tempo estimation T_a is made and its MFCCs extracted. The likelihoods corresponding to the union of the MFCCs and either T_a, $T_a/3$, $T_a/2$ ... is evaluated given the trained GMM. The largest likelihood gives the tempo of the track.

Studies that Uses Real Annotated Perceptual Tempo. As opposed to previous studies, only the following works use with real annotated perceptual tempo data.

McKinney [13] proposes to model the perceptual tempi assigned by the various users to a track by a histogram (instead of the single value used in previous studies). This histogram is derived from user tappings along 24 10-sec music excerpts. He then studies the automatic estimation of these histograms using

3 methods : resonator filter-bank, autocorrelation and IOI Histogram. All three methods perform reasonably well on 24 tracks of 8 different genres. The methods usually find the first and the second largest peaks correctly, while having a lot of unwanted peaks.

Peeters et al. [18] studies the estimation of perceptual tempo using real anno-tated perceptual tempo data derived from the Last-FM 2011 experiment [12]. From these data, he only selects the subset of tracks for which tempo percep-tion is shared among users ($t_{a,u} = t_{a,u'}$). He then proposes four feature sets to describe the audio content and proposes the use of GMM-Regression [4] to model the relationship between the audio features and the perceptual tempo.

1.3 Paper Organization

The goal of this paper is to study the prediction of the agreement or disagreement among users on tempo perception using only the audio content. We try to predict this agreement/disagreement using the function $g(a)$ (see Sect. 1.1 and Fig. 1).

For this, we first represent the content of an audio file by a set of cues that we assume to be related to the perception of tempo: variation of energy, short-term-similarity, spectral balance variation and harmonic variation. We successfully validated these four functions in [18] for the estimation of perceptual tempo (in the case $t_{a,u} = t_{a,u'}$). We briefly summarize these functions in Sect. 2.1.

In Sect. 2.2, we then propose various prediction models $g(a)$ to model the relationship between the audio content and the agreement or disagreement on tempo perception. The corresponding systems are summed up in Fig. 2.

In Sect. 3, we evaluate the performance of the various prediction models in a usual classification task into tempo Agreement and tempo Disagreement using the Last-FM 2011 test-set.

Finally, in Sect. 4, we conclude on the results and present our future works.

2 Prediction Model $g(a)$ for the Prediction of Tempo Agreement and Disagreement

2.1 Audio Features

We briefly summarize here the four audio feature sets used to represent the audio content. We refer the reader to [18] for more details.

Energy Variation $d_{ener}(\lambda)$. The aim of this function is to highlight the pres-ence of onsets in the signal by using the variation of the energy content inside several frequency bands. This function is usually denoted by "spectral flux" [11]. In [16] we proposed to compute it using the reassigned spectrogram [5]. The later allows obtaining a better separation between adjacent frequency bands and a better temporal localization. In the following we consider as observation, the autocorrelation of this function denoted by $d_{ener}(\lambda)$ where λ denotes "lags" in second.

Short-Term Event Repetition $d_{sim}(\lambda)$**.** We make the assumption that the perception of tempo is related to the rate of the short-term repetitions of events (such as the repetition of events with same pitch or same timbre). In order to highlight these repetitions, we compute a Self-Similarity-Matrix [6] (SSM) and measure the rate of repetitions in it. In order to represent the various type of repetitions (pitch or timbre repetitions) we use the method we proposed in [17]. We then convert the SSM into a Lag-matrix [1] and sum its contributions over time to obtain the rate of repetitions for each lag. We denote this function by $d_{sim}(\lambda)$.

Spectral Balance Variation $d_{specbal}(\lambda)$**.** For music with drums, the balance between the energy content at high-frequency and at low-frequency at a given time depends on the presence of the instruments: low > high if a kick is present, high > low when a snare is present. For a typical pop song in a 4/4 m, we then observe over time a variation of this balance at half the tempo rate. This variation can therefore be used to infer the tempo. In [19] we propose to compute a spectral-balance function by computing the ratio between the energy content at high-frequency to the low-frequency one. We then compare the values of the balance function over a one bar duration to the typical template of a kick/snare/kick/snare profile. We consider as observation the autocorrelation of this function, which we denote by $d_{specbal}(\lambda)$.

Harmonic Variation $d_{harmo}(\lambda)$**.** Popular music is often based on a succession of harmonically homogeneous segments named "chords". The rate of this succession is proportional to the tempo (often one or two chords per bar). Rather than estimating the chord succession, we estimate the rate at which segments of stable harmonic content vary. In [18] we proposed to represent this using Chroma variations over time. The variation is computed by convolving a Chroma Self-Similarity-Matrix with a novelty kernel [7] whose length represents the assumption of chord duration. The diagonal of the resulting convolved matrix is then considered as the harmonic variation. We consider as observation the autocorrelation of this function, which we denote by $d_{harmo}(\lambda)$.

Dimension Reduction. The four feature sets are denoted by $d_i(\lambda)$ with $i \in \{ener, sim, specbal, harmo\}$ and where λ denotes the lags (expressed in seconds). In order to reduce the dimensionality, we apply a filter-bank over the lag-axis λ of each feature set. For this, we created 20 filters logarithmically spaced between 32 and 208bpm with a triangular shape. Each feature vector $d_i(\lambda)$ is then multiplied by this filter-bank leading to a 20-dim vector, denoted by $d_i(b)$ where $b \in [1, 20]$ denotes the number of the filter. To further reduce the dimensionality and decorrelate the various dimensions, we also tested the application of the Principal Component Analysis (PCA). We only keep the principal axes which explain more than 10 % of the overall variance.

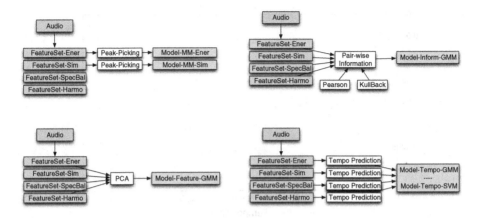

Fig. 2. Flowchart of the computation of the four prediction models

2.2 Prediction Models

We propose here four prediction models to represent the relation-ship between the audio feature sets (Sect. 2.1) and the agreement and disagreement on tempo perception. The four prediction models are summed up in Fig. 2.

A. Model MM (Ener and Sim). As mentioned in Sect. 1.2, our first model is based on the assumption of Moelants and McKinney [14] that "if a musical excerpt contains a metrical level whose tempo lies near the resonant tempo, the perceived tempo across listeners is likely to be dominated by the tempo of that metrical level and be relatively unambiguous". In [14], a resonant tempo interval is defined as [110–170] bpm. Our first prediction model hence looks if a major peak of a periodicity function exists within this interval. For this, we use as observations the audio feature functions in the frequency domain: $d_i(\omega)$ (i.e. using the DFT instead of the auto-correlation) and without dimensionality reduction. We then look if one of the two main peaks of each periodicity function $d_i(\omega)$ lies within the interval [110–170] bpm. If this is the case, we predict an agreement on tempo perception; if not, we predict a disagreement.

By experiment, we found that only the two audio features $d_{ener}(\omega)$ and $d_{sim}(\omega)$ lead to good results. We make two different models: MM (ener) or MM (sim).

Illustration: We illustrate this in Fig. 3 where we represent the function $d_{ener}(\omega)$, the detected peaks, the two major peaks, the [110–170] bpm interval (green vertical lines) and the preferential 120 bpm tempo (red dotted vertical line). Since no major peaks exist within the resonant interval, this track will be assigned to the disagreement class.

B. Model Feature-GMM. Our second model is our baseline model. In this, we estimate directly the agreement and disagreement classes using the audio features $d_i(b)$. In order to reduce the dimensionality we apply PCA to the four

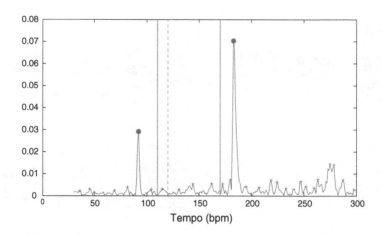

Fig. 3. Illustration of the Model MM (ener) based on Moelants and McKinney preferential tempo assumption [14].

feature sets[2]. Using the reduced features, we then train a Gaussian Mixture Model (GMM) for the class agreement ($\mathcal{A}$) and another for the class disagreement ($\mathcal{D}$). By experimentation we found that the following configuration leads to the best results: 4-mixtures for each class with full-covariance matrices. The classification of an unknown track is then done by maximum-a posteriori estimation.

C. Model Inform-GMM (Pearson and KL). The feature sets $d_i(b)$ represent the periodicities of the audio signal using various viewpoints i. We assume that if two vectors $\underline{d}_i$ and $\underline{d}_{i'}$ bring the same information on the periodicity of the audio signal, they will also do on the perception of tempo, hence favoring a shared (Agreement) tempo perception.

In our third model, we therefore predict $\mathcal{A}$ and $\mathcal{D}$ by measuring the information shared by the four feature sets. For each track, we create a 6-dim vector made of the information shared between each pair of feature vectors $\underline{d}_i$: $\underline{C} = [c(\underline{d}_1, \underline{d}_2), c(\underline{d}_1, \underline{d}_3), c(\underline{d}_1, \underline{d}_4), c(\underline{d}_2, \underline{d}_3) \ldots]$. In order to measure the shared information, we will test for c the use of the Pearson correlation and the use of the symmetrized Kullback-Leibler divergence (KL) between $\underline{d}_i$ and $\underline{d}_{i'}$.

The resulting 6-dim vectors $\underline{C}$ are used to train a GMM (same configuration as before) for the class agreement ($\mathcal{A}$) and disagreement ($\mathcal{D}$). The classification of an unknown track is then done by maximum-a posteriori estimation.

Illustration: In Fig. 4, we illustrate the correlation between the four feature sets for a track belonging to the agreement class (left) and to the disagreement class

---

[2] As explained in Sect. 2.1, we only keep the principal axes which explain more than 10 % of the overall variance. This leads to a final vector of 34-dimensions instead of 4*20 = 80 dimensions.

(a) Agreement   (b) Disagreement

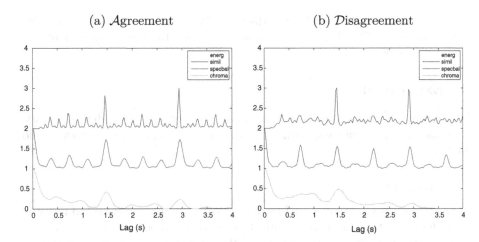

Fig. 4. [Left part] from top-to-bottom ener, sim, specbal and harmo functions for a track belonging to the agreement class; [right part] same for the disagreement class.

(right)[3]. As can be seen on the left (Agreement), the positions of the peaks of the ener, sim and specbal functions are correlated to each other's. We assume that this correlation will favour a shared perception of tempo. On the right part (Disagreement), the positions of the peaks are less correlated. In particular the sim function has a one-fourth periodicity compared to the ener function, the specbal a half periodicity. We assume that this will handicap a shared perception of tempo.

D. Model Tempo-GMM and Model-Tempo-SVM. Our last prediction model is also based on measuring the agreement between the various viewpoints i. But instead of predicting this agreement directly from the audio features (as above), we measure the agreement between the tempo estimation obtained using the audio features independently.

For this, we first create a tempo estimation algorithm for each feature sets: $T_i = f(d_i(\lambda))$. Each of these tempo estimation is made using our previous GMM-Regression methods as described in [18]. Each track a is then represented by a 4-dim feature vector where each dimension represent the prediction of tempo using a specific feature set: $[T_{ener}, T_{sim}, T_{specbal}, T_{harmo}]$. The resulting 4-dim vectors are used to train the final statistical model. For this, we compare two approaches:

– training a GMM (same configuration as before) for the class agreement ($\mathcal{A}$) and disagreement ($\mathcal{D}$); then use maximum-a posteriori estimation,

---

[3] It should be noted that for easiness of understanding we represent in Fig. 4 the features $d_i(\lambda)$ while the $\underline{C}$ is computed on $d_i(b)$.

- training a binary Support Vector Machine (SVM) (we used a RBF kernel with $\gamma = 0.001$ and $C = 1.59$) to discriminate between the classes agreement ($\mathcal{A}$) and disagreement ($\mathcal{D}$).

3 Experiment

We evaluate here the four models presented in Sect. 2.2 to predict automatically the agreement or disagreement on tempo perception using only the audio content.

3.1 Test-Set

In the experiment performed at Last-FM in 2011 [12], users were asked to listen to audio extracts, qualify them into 3 perceptual tempo classes and quantify their tempo (in bpm). We denote by $t_{a,u}$ the quantified tempo provided by user u for track a. Although not explicit in the paper [12], we consider here that the audio extracts have constant tempo over time and that the annotations have been made accordingly. The raw results of this experiment are kindly provided by Last-FM. The global test-set of the experiment is made up of 4006 items but not all items were annotated by all annotators. Considering the fact that these annotations have been obtained using a crowd-sourcing approach, and therefore that some of these annotations may be unreliable, we only consider the subset of items a for which at least 10 different annotations u are available. This leads to a subset of 249 items.

For copyright reason, the Last-FM test-set is distributed without the audio tracks. For each item, we used the 7-Digital API in order to access a 30 s audio extract from which audio features has been extracted. This has been done querying the API using the provided artist, album and title names. We have listened to all audio extracts to confirm the assumption that their tempi are constant over time.

Assigning a track to the Agreement or Disagreement class: We assign each audio track a to one of the two classes agreement ($\mathcal{A}$) or disagreement ($\mathcal{D}$) based on the spread of the tempo annotations $t_{a,u}$ for this track. This spread is computed using the Inter-Quartile-Range (IQR)[4] of the annotations expressed in log-scale[5]: $\text{IQR}_a (\log_2(t_{a,u}))$. The assignment of a track a to one the two classes is based on the comparison of IQR_a to a threshold τ. If $\text{IQR}_a < \tau$, agreement is assigned to track a, if $\text{IQR}_a \geq \tau$, disagreement is assigned. By experimentation we found $\tau = 0.2$ to be a reliable value. This process leads to a balanced distribution of the test-set over classes: $\#(\mathcal{A}) = 134$, $\#(\mathcal{D}) = 115$.

Illustration: In Fig. 5 we represent the histogram of the tempi $t_{a,u}$ annotated for each track a and the corresponding IQR_a derived from those.

---

[4] The IQR is a measure of statistical dispersion, being equal to the difference between the upper and lower quartiles. It is considered more robust to the presence of outliers than the standard deviation.

[5] The log-scale is used to take into account the logarithmic character of tempo. In log-scale, the intervals [80–85] bpm and [160–170] bpm are equivalent.

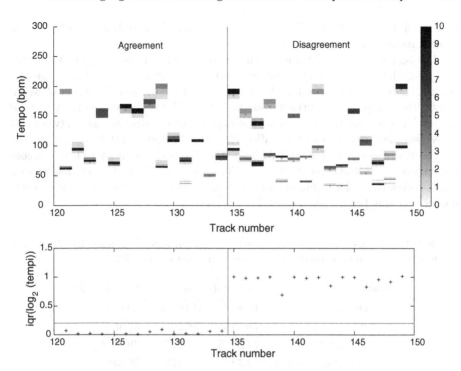

Fig. 5. [Top part] For each track a we represent the various annotated tempi $t_{a,u}$ in the form of a histogram. [Bottom part] For each track a, we represent the computed IQR_a. We superimposed to it the threshold τ that allows deciding on the assignment of the track to the agreement (left tracks) or disagreement (right part).

3.2   Experimental Protocol

Each experiment has been done using a five-fold cross-validation, i.e. models are trained using 4 folds and evaluated using the remaining one. Each fold is tested in turn. Results are presented as mean value over the five-folds. When GMM is used, in order to reduce the sensitivity on the initialization of the GMM-EM algorithm, we tested 1000 random initializations.

In the following, we present the results of the two-classes categorization problem ($\mathcal{A}$ and $\mathcal{D}$) in terms of class-Recall[6] (i.e. the Recall of each class) and in terms of mean-Recall, i.e. mean of the class-Recalls[7].

3.3   Results

The results are presented in Table 1. For comparison, a random classifier for a two-class problem would lead to a Recall of 50 %. As can be seen, only the

---

[6] $\text{Recall} = \frac{\text{True Positive}}{\text{True Positive} + \text{False Negative}}$.

[7] As opposed to Precision, the Recall is not sensitive on class distribution hence the mean-over-class-Recall is preferred over the F-Measure.

models MM (Sim), Inform-GMM (KL), Tempo-GMM and Tempo-SVM lead to results above a random classifier.

The best results are obtained with the Tempo-GMM and Tempo-SVM models (predicting the agreement/disagreement using four individual tempo predictions). Their performances largely exceed the other models. In terms of Mean Recall, the Tempo-SVM outperforms the Tempo-GMM classifier (74.9 % instead of 70.1 %). However this is done at the expense of the distribution between the agreement and disagreement Recalls: while the Tempo-GMM has close Recalls for the two classes (73.7 % and 66.5 %), the Tempo-SVM model clearly recognizes more easily the class $\mathcal{A}$ (87.3 %) than the class $\mathcal{D}$ (44.3 %, i.e. less than a random classifier). This unbalancing of Recall makes us prefer the Tempo-GMM model over the Tempo-SVM model.

Table 1. Results of classification into agreement and disagreement using five-fold cross-validation for the various prediction models presented in Sect. 2.2.

Model	Recall($\mathcal{A}$)	Recall($\mathcal{D}$)	Mean Recall
MM (Ener)	62.69 %	42.61 %	52.65 %
MM (Sim)	56.71 %	58.26 %	57.49 %
Feature-GMM	55.21 %	45.22 %	50.22 %
Inform-GMM (Pearson)	51.51 %	49.57 %	50.54 %
Inform-GMM (KL)	61.17 %	50.43 %	55.80 %
Tempo-GMM	**73.73 %**	**66.52 %**	**70.10 %**
Tempo-SVM	**87.35 %**	**44.35 %**	**74.85 %**

3.4   Discussions on the Model Tempo-GMM

The Tempo-GMM model relies on the agreement between the four individual tempo estimations $T_{ener}, T_{sim}, T_{specbal}, T_{harmo}$. In Fig. 6 we represent the relationship between these four estimated tempi for data belonging to the classes agreement (red plus sign) and disagreement (blue crosses)[8]. As can be seen, the estimated tempi for the class agreement are more correlated (closer to the main diagonal) than the ones for the class disagreement (distribution mainly outside the main diagonal). This validates our assumption that the sharing of the perception of tempo may be related to the agreement between the various acoustical cues.

We now investigate the usefulness of each of the four tempi estimation T_{ener}, $T_{sim}, T_{specbal}, T_{harmo}$ for our agreement/disagreement estimation. As a reminder, T_i is the tempo estimation obtained with $d_i(\lambda)$ using GMM-Regression:

---

[8] It should be noted that we didn't plot the relationship between T_{harmo} and the other estimated tempi because the effect we wanted to show was less clear. We will investigate why in the next paragraph.

(a) $t_1 = T_{ener}/t_2 = T_{sim}$

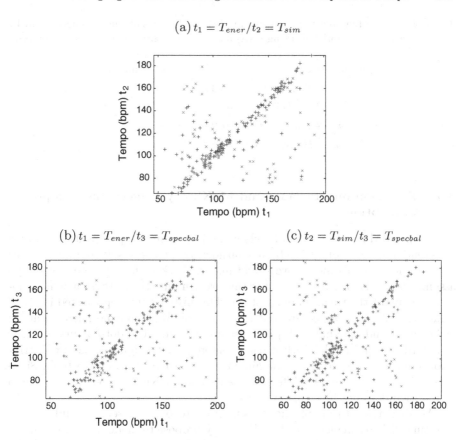

Fig. 6. Each panel represents the relationship between the estimated tempo for (a) $t_1 = T_{ener}/t_2 = T_{sim}$, (b) $t_1 = T_{ener}/t_3 = T_{specbal}$, (c) $t_2 = T_{sim}/t_3 = T_{specbal}$. Red plus signs represent data belonging to the agreement class, blue crosses to the disagreement class.

$T_i = f(d_i(\lambda))$. The question is twofold: are the values we expect to have for T_i the correct ones? Is T_i useful? In order to test the first, we only consider the subset of tracks for which people agree on the tempo (the 134 items belonging to the class $\mathcal{A}$). In this case, $T_i = f(d_i(\lambda))$ should be equal to the shared perceptual tempo t. Table 2 indicates the tempo accuracy at 4 % obtained with each $d_i(\lambda)$. The best results are obtained with the Energy variation f(78.3 %), followed by the Short-term event repetition (55.0 %) and the Spectral balance variation (47.0 %). The Harmonic variation is strongly inaccurate (only 20.5 %). A similar observation has been made by [18]. Because its estimation is strongly inaccurate, it is likely that T_{harmo} is actually not useful for the prediction of tempo agreement/ disagreement. Actually, using only $T_{ener}, T_{sim}, T_{specbal}$ as input to our Tempo-GMM model allows increasing the classification into agreement ($\mathcal{A}$) and disagreement ($\mathcal{D}$) by 1 % (71.2 % without using T_{harmo} compared to 70.1 % when using it).

Table 2. Correct tempo estimation (in %) of the 134 tracks of the class agreement by a GMM-Regression algorithm, using $d_i(\lambda)$ as input ($i \in [ener, sim, specbal, harmo]$).

Audio feature	Correct tempo estimation
$T_{ener} = f(d_{ener}(\lambda))$	78.3 %
$T_{sim} = f(d_{sim}(\lambda))$	55.0 %
$T_{specbal} = f(d_{specbal}(\lambda))$	47.0 %
$T_{harmo} = f(d_{harmo}(\lambda))$	20.5 %

3.5 Discussion on Moelants and McKinney Preferential Tempo Assumption

The model MM is derived from Moelants and McKinney experiment assuming a preferential tempo around 120 bpm. Considering the bad results obtained in our experiment with this model, we would like to check if their preferential tempo assumption holds for our test-set. For this, we compute the histogram of all annotated tempi for the tracks of our test-set. This histogram is represented in Fig. 7 (blue vertical bars). We compare it to the one obtained in experiments 1 and 2 of Moelants and McKinney [14] (represented by the green dotted curve). Their distribution is uni-modal with a peak centered on 120 bpm while our distribution is bi-modal with two predominant peaks around 87 and 175 bpm. Since these distributions largely differ, Moelants and McKinney preferential tempo assumption does not hold for our test-set.

We then tried to adapt their assumption to our test-set. We did this by adapting their resonance model. In [15], they propose to model the tempo annotations distribution by a resonance curve: $R(f) = \frac{1}{\sqrt{(f_0^2 - f^2)^2 + \beta f^2}} - \frac{1}{\sqrt{f_0^4 - f^4}}$, where f is the frequency, f_0 the resonant frequency and β a damping constant. The resonant model that best fits our distribution has a frequency of 80 bpm (instead of 120 bpm in [14]). It is represented in Fig. 7 by the red curve.

We then re-did our experiment changing the preferential tempo interval in our prediction model to [60–100] bpm (instead of [110–170] bpm in [14]). Unfortunatelly it didn't change our results in a positive way: mean-Recall(MM-Ener) = 50.39 %, mean-Recall(MM-Sim) = 42.49 %.

Note that, the difference of resonant frequency may be due to the different test-sets, experimental protocols and users[9]. Note also that the bad results we

---

[9] Firstly the test-set for our experiment and the one of [14] largely differ in their genre distribution. In [14], the tracks are equally distributed between classical, country, dance, hip-hop, jazz, latin, reggae, rock/pop and soul. In our test-set, most of the tracks are pop/rock tracks (50 %), soul and country (about 10 % each). The other genres represent less than 5 % each. The experimental protocols also largely differ. Our test-set comes from a web experiment, done without any strict control on the users, whereas McKinney and Moelants had a rigorous protocol (lab experiment, chosen people). Users have then very different profiles. In McKinney and Moelants experiment, the 33 subjects had an average of 7 years of musical education. In our case, we reckon that almost nobody had a musical training.

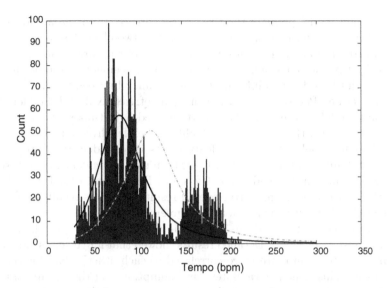

Fig. 7. Histogram of tempi annotation for the tracks of the Last-FM test-set. We super-imposed to it the resonant model as proposed by Moelants and McKinney [14] with a frequency of 80 bpm (red line) and with a frequency of 120 bpm (green dotted line). The 80 bpm model has been fitted from our test-set. The 120 bpm model corresponds to the McKinney and Moelants experiment.

obtained with Moelants and McKinney model may also be due to our audio features that are not suitable for this kind of modeling. These acoustical cues are more adapted to a tempo-estimation task since they have a lot of peaks (at the fundamental tempo and at its integer multiples). It makes the tempo estimation more robust but hampers the selection of the two pre-dominant peaks.

4   Conclusion

In this paper, we studied the prediction of agreement and disagreement on tempo perception using only the audio content. For this we proposed four audio feature sets representing the variation of energy, harmony, spectral-balance and the short-term-similarity-rate. We considered the prediction of agreement and disagreement as a two classes problem. We then proposed four statistical models to represent the relationship between the audio features and the two classes.

The first model is based on Moelants and McKinney [14] assumption that agreement is partly due to the presence of a main periodicity peak close to the user preferential tempo of 120 bpm. With our test-set (derived from the Last-FM 2011 test-set) we didn't find such a preferential tempo but rather two preferential tempi around 87 and 175 bpm. The prediction model we created using [14] assumption reached a just-above-random mean-Recall of 57 % (using the sim function).

The second model predicts the two classes directly from the audio features using GMMs. It performed the same as a random two-class classifier.

The third and fourth model use the *agreement* of the various acoustical cues provided by the audio features to predict tempo agreement or tempo disagreement. The third model uses information redundancy between the audio feature sets (using either Pearson correlation or symmetrized Kullback-Leibler divergence) and models those using GMM. It reached a just-above-random mean-Recall of 55 % (with the symmetrized Kullback-Leibler divergence).

The fourth model uses the four feature sets independently to predict four independent tempi. GMMs (then SVM) are then used to model those four tempi. The corresponding model leads to a 70 % mean-Recall (and 74 % for the SVM). Although SVM classifier has better overall results, the class-result are far from being equally-distributed (87 % for the agreement class against 44 % for the disagreement one). This made us prefer the GMM classifier (which has well-distributed results by class). Detailed results showed that for the class agreement, the four estimated tempi are more correlated to each other's than for the class disagreement. This somehow validates our assumption that the sharing of tempo perception (agreement) is facilitated by the coherence of the acoustical cues. In a post-analysis, we found out that our harmonic variation feature, because of its inaccuracy, was not beneficial for predicting tempo agreement and disagreement. Further works will therefore concentrate on improving this feature. Future works will also concentrate on studying the whole model, i.e. introducing the user variable u in the tempo estimation $f(a, u) = T_{a,u}$. However, this will require accessing data annotated by the same users u for the same tracks a.

Acknowledgments. This work was partly supported by the Quaero Program funded by Oseo French State agency for innovation and by the French government Programme Investissements d'Avenir (PIA) through the Bee Music Project.

References

1. Bartsch, M.A., Wakefield, G.H.: To catch a chorus: Using chroma-based representations for audio thumbnailing. In: IEEE Workshop on the Applications of Signal Processing to Audio and Acoustics, pp. 15–18 (2001)
2. Chen, C.W., Cremer, M., Lee, K., DiMaria, P., Wu, H.H.: Improving perceived tempo estimation by statistical modeling of higher-level musical descriptors. In: 126th Audio Engineering Society Convention. Audio Engineering Society, Munich (2009)
3. Chua, B.Y., Lu, G.: Determination of perceptual tempo of music. In: Wiil, U.K. (ed.) CMMR 2004. LNCS, vol. 3310, pp. 61–70. Springer, Heidelberg (2005)
4. En-Najjary, T., Rosec, O., Chonavel, T.: A new method for pitch prediction from spectral envelope and its application in voice conversion. In: Proceedings of the INTERSPEECH (2003)
5. Flandrin, P.: Time-Frequency/Time-Scale Analysis, vol. 10. Academic Press, San Diego (1998)
6. Foote, J.: Visualizing music and audio using self-similarity. In: Proceedings of the Seventh ACM International Conference on Multimedia (Part 1). pp. 77–80 (1999)

7. Foote, J.: Automatic audio segmentation using a measure of audio novelty. In: Proceedings of IEEE International Conference on Multimedia and Exp (ICME), vol. 1, pp. 452–455 (2000)
8. Gkiokas, A., Katsouros, V., Carayannis, G.: Reducing tempo octave errors by periodicity vector coding and svm learning. In: Proceedings of the 13th International Society for Music Information Retrieval Conference (ISMIR), pp. 301–306 (2012)
9. Gouyon, F., Klapuri, A., Dixon, S., Alonso, M., Tzanetakis, G., Uhle, C., Cano, P.: An experimental comparison of audio tempo induction algorithms. IEEE Trans. Audio Speech Lang. Process. 14(5), 1832–1844 (2006)
10. Hockman, J., Fujinaga, I.: Fast vs slow: learning tempo octaves from user data. In: Proceedings of the 11th International Society for Music Information Retrieval Conference (ISMIR), pp. 231–236 (2010)
11. Laroche, J.: Efficient tempo and beat tracking in audio recordings. J. Audio Eng. Soc. 51(4), 226–233 (2003)
12. Levy, M.: Improving perceptual tempo estimation with crowd-sourced annotations. In: Proceedings of the 12th International Society for Music Information (ISMIR), pp. 317–322 (2011)
13. McKinney, M.F., Moelants, D.: Extracting the perceptual tempo from music. In: 5th International Conference on Music Information Retrieval (ISMIR) (2004)
14. Moelants, D., McKinney, M.: Tempo perception and musical content: what makes a piece fast, slow or temporally ambiguous. In: Proceedings of the 8th International Conference on Music Perception and Cognition, pp. 558–562 (2004)
15. van Noorden, L., Moelants, D.: Resonance in the perception of musical pulse. J. New Music Res. 28(1), 43–66 (1999)
16. Peeters, G.: Template-based estimation of time-varying tempo. EURASIP J. Adv. Sign. Process. 2007, 067215 (2007). doi:10.1155/2007/67215
17. Peeters, G.: Sequence representation of music structure using higher-order similarity matrix and maximum-likelihood approach. In: Proceedings of the International Conference on Music Information Retrieval (ISMIR), pp. 35–40 (2007)
18. Peeters, G., Flocon-Cholet, J.: Perceptual tempo estimation using gmm-regression. In: Proceedings of the Second International ACM Workshop on Music Information Retrieval with User-Centered and Multimodal Strategies, pp. 45–50 (2012)
19. Peeters, G., Papadopoulos, H.: Simultaneous beat and downbeat-tracking using a probabilistic framework: theory and large-scale evaluation. IEEE Trans. Audio Speech Lang. Process. 19(6), 1754–1769 (2011)
20. Seyerlehner, K., Widmer, G., Schnitzer, D.: From rhythm patterns to perceived tempo. In: Proceedings of the 8th International Conference on Music Information Retrieval (ISMIR), pp. 519–524 (2007)
21. Xiao, L., Tian, A., Li, W., Zhou, J.: Using statistic model to capture the association between timbre and perceived tempo. In: Proceedings of the 9th International Conference on Music Information Retrieval (ISMIR). pp. 659–662 (2008)
22. Zapata, J.R., Holzapfel, A., Davies, M.E., Oliveira, J.L., Gouyon, F.: Assigning a confidence threshold on automatic beat annotation in large datasets. In: 13th International Society for Music Information Retrieval Conference (ISMIR). pp. 157–162 (2012)

Interactive Sound Synthesis

Music: Ars Bene Movandi

Jean-Claude Risset[✉]

Laboratoire de Mécanique et d'Acoustique, CNRS, Marseille, France
jcrisset@lma.cnrs-mrs.fr

Introduction

I thank Richard Kronland-Martinet for inviting me to this exciting Symposium, which gathered participants from around the world in the Laboratoire de Mécanique et d'Acoustique of Marseille (LMA), where I have been working for more than thirty years.

I wish to give a few instances of the importance of motion in sound and music, and I shall evoke some early research. I concluded my presentation at the symposium with a demonstration of an interactive process of piano accompaniment: this process will be described at the end of this article, and references will be provided.

1 Motion and Sound

A "keynote speech" is supposed to suggest a tonality (in the figured sense). The pitch standard used in a musical performance (for instance **A** 440 Hz) is specified by the motion of a tuning fork. When I hit a tuning fork in front of an audience, the sound is too weak for the listeners to hear it, unless I touch a table with the vibration fork. The intermediate vibrations of the table act as an impedance adaptor between the fork and the air. Then the listeners can hear the **A** because the vibratory motion of the tuning fork is effectively radiated and propagated to their ears by the air.

Sound is very important for us because we live on Earth, a planet with an atmosphere, unlike the moon. Mechanical motions (such as hitting, blowing and scraping) produce perturbations in the atmospheric pressure, and these perturbations will propagate in the air over substantial distances, even in the presence of obstacles that would stop visual signals. Thus evolution has favored the appearance of the sense of hearing, a kind of remote touch, which is extraordinarily sensitive to vibratory motions - for instance one can hear 1000 Hz vibrations of a membrane even when their amplitude is less than the dimensions of a single atom. The sense of hearing gives warnings about motions occuring in the surrounding environment: this is invaluable for predators as well as for their potential preys.

Perception and action take place in a universe where interactions are mostly mechanical. True, most people hear music today through loudspeakers, and there is a lot of communication through telephones. However the evolution of living organisms has occured in a mechanical world, and our senses are well equipped to detect motions in the environment.

© Springer International Publishing Switzerland 2014
M. Aramaki et al. (Eds.): CMMR 2013, LNCS 8905, pp. 333–345, 2014.
DOI: 10.1007/978-3-319-12976-1_21

2   Where and What?

In particular hearing is able to infer the **where** and **what** of the auditory signals, that is, to locate the source of acoustic sounds, and to infer their causality, that is, the mechanical process which produced them.

Where? Hearing gives us information about the location of the sound source - it points to the direction of the source and it evaluates the distance of the source. Hearing can follow the motion of a sound source.

The understanding of the auditory cues for direction, distance and motion has enabled John Chowning (1971) to perform striking illusions of source motions. Using only four fixed loudspeakers, Chowning controls the cues for the apparent positions and motions of virtual sound sources. In particular Chowning suggests a given distance of the virtual source of sound by controlling the ratio of direct sound to reverberated sound: this ratio gets smaller when a source recedes in the distance. Chowning also simulates the Doppler effect to reinforce the feeling of motion and speed. This has lead to a milestone of kinetic music, Chowning's *Turenas* (1973).

At the Groupe de Musique Expérimentale de Marseille, Laurent Pottier has developed *Holophon*, an advanced software for computer music which permits to specify prescriptions for illusory motions - this research is pursued by Charles Bascou.

What? Hearing is well equipped to infer how heard sounds were produced: it hints at the mechanical cause of the sound - blowing, hitting, scraping ... This capacity has developed during the course of evolution, which has happened in a world where most sounds are generated by mechanical motions and vibrations.

However the hearing mechanism to detect the source is at a loss with a general source of sound such as the loudspeaker, designed to produce a variety of different sounds.

3   Sound Synthesis

Max Mathews had started computer sound synthesis in 1957: his modular synthesis programs (Music3, Music4, Music5) calculate the sound signal directly.

By carefully designing synthetic sounds, it is possible to mimic musical instruments and the human voice, as demonstrated by Dexter Morrill and myself for the trumpet, Max Mathews for the violin, John Chowning and Johan Sundberg for the singing voice.

John Chowning and myself have attempted in the 1960s and 1970s to synthesize novel musical timbres. Many of the synthetic timbres we stumbled upon lacked a strong sense of identity and of presence. We found that it was easier to impart a vivid identity when we generated sounds that could be interpreted by listeners as having been produced by a mechanical process - such as hitting, plucking, scraping, blowing, bowing. We also got some aggressively artificial sounds with doubtful musical utility.

So, even though our perception has developed so as to deal with a mechanical world, the digital production of sound and images can imitate - or escape - the constraints of mechanics. Yet if one wants to produce sounds with strong identities and significance, one must understand what cues our perception uses to provide information about our environment.

4 Physical Modelling

Physical modelling does not try to imitate the acoustic signals produced by the mechanical motions of objects: it produces sounds by directly simulating these motions, taking in account the laws of physics.

One of the earliest applications of physical modelling to sound was *Daisy, a bicycle built for two*, a song "sung" in 1963 by computer synthesis programs designed by John Kelly, Carol Lochbaum and Max Mathews at Bell Telephone Laboratories. While Mathews's synthetic piano-like accompaniment does not use a physical model, a special program articulates the lyrics thanks to a physical model of the vocal tract, which moves between target shapes corresponding to the vowels. The computer has an electrical accent, but the lyrics are quite comprehensible (*Daisy, Daisy, give me answer, do, I'm half crazy all for the love of you...*). Stanley Kubrick alluded to this in his film *2001: A Space Odyssey*.

Physical modelling of musical sounds was pioneered by Pierre Ruiz, Claude Cadoz and others. In the late 1960s, Ruiz synthesized violin-like tones by modelling the vibratory motion of bowed strings. In the late 1970s, Cadoz and his colleagues of ACROE in Grenoble wrote the equations for the fall and bounce of an abstract virtual mass, using Newton's law and elasticity data: their resolution by computer produced a vivid suggestion of a bouncing ball. In fact no actual ball was used: the computer only calculated the timings of the virtual bounces.

Physical modelling tends to produce sounds with strong identity and presence, for instance the impressive trumpet simulations by Christophe Vergez, and recently the clarinet-like synthesis performed in LMA by Kergomard, Guillemain and Voinier. Several composers resort to physical modelling: among them Luedger Bruemer, Giuseppe Gavazza, Mesias Maïguiaschka. When using physical modelling, one does not have to limit oneself to sounds related to the mechanical world: one could model imagined worlds where the laws of physics would be different.

5 Motion and Music

St Augustinus has written "*music is **ars bene movandi***" - the art of moving well, a graceful dance of sounds. This statement is more than a metaphor. According to Johan Sundberg and his colleagues in Stockholm, "our listening refers to experiences of movement": thus "an aesthetically pleasing performance is similar to a graceful motoric pattern". Researchers studying musical performance, especially Johan Sundberg and Neil McAngus Todd, have shown for instance that pleasing musical accelerandi or rallentendi are similar to the ways athletic runners (such Jesse Owens or Usain Bolt) speed up or slow down.

Changes in time akin to mechanical or bodily motions may be a strong key to naturalness and musical expressivity. Graceful motions have been generated through physical modelling by Chi Min Sieh, a dancer who has worked in ACROE with Annie Luciani on applying physical modelling to image animation. Indeed evolution has shaped our senses in a mechanical world.

Motion is important in many respects. Thermal motion of atoms, molecules and ions relates with temperature. A bicycle will only stand if it moves. A person reading a book or a musical score or looking at a picture performs very specific eye movements, which can now be tracked precisely (cf. the research of Eckhard Hess, François Molnar, Bernhard Hess, Walter Kropfl, John Krauskopf, Kenneth Gaarder, Bela Julesz). With Bela Julesz, Enrico Chiarucci has realized a revealing movie where each frame is made up of random dots. No figure emerges from any frame of this movie, however distinct patterns such as letters can be seen when the film is shown in motion: the eye and brain extract these patterns through correlating the successive images. The sections of a musical works are called *movements*. People long dreamed of achieving perpetual motion, but science states it is impossible - even though Victor Hugo argued that science itself is a perfect example if perpetual motion. *Perpetuum mobile* is a musical form, illustrated from Paganini to Ravel and Arvo Pärt.

Fig. 1. Fraser spiral

One often claims that "seeing is believing". At first glance, the curve shown of Fig. 1, known as a "Fraser spiral", indeed looks like a spiral. However, if one follows the curve, one is convinced that it actually consists of concentric circles. Passive looking is not enough: moving along is believing.

In the same vein, Roger Shepard and I have illustrated the circularity of pitch hy generating endless pitch ascents (A B C D E F G A...) and descents (do si la sol fa mi ré do). At LMA, Loïc Kessous has devised a process generating in real time a similar pitch circular motion by drawing a circle on a graphic pad. Here action and perception are combined - a key concept of *enaction*, a significant mode of cognition introduced by Francisco Varela and emphasized in the work of ACROE in Grenoble.

Musical performance is sensitive to the acoustic environment. Around 1990, Simon Bolzinger and myself have shown that pianists playing in small rooms unconsciously try to compensate increased room dryness by playing louder, even when they do not fully succeed: the resistance felt by the pianists in their fingers could made some of them believe that the keyboard had been made harder.

6   Audio and Sub-audio

Periodic vibrations at audio frequencies are heard as pitched sensations. Slow sub-audio frequencies are perceived as modulation envelopes, as trackable changes of amplitude, not as pitches.

For instance, a cluster of sine waves of constant amplitude with frequencies 125 Hz, 128, 131, 134, 137, 140 Hz will not sound like a stationary cluster, but like a percussive sound repeated 3 times per second. This is due to the phenomenon of beats: the beat frequency is 3 Hz, a sub-audio frequency. The multiplication of components 3 Hz apart increases the selectivity, just as in a Fabry-Perot inter-ferometer.

Thus one can slow down a recording of speech without changing pitches. In the late 1980s, Daniel Arfib wrote the software *Sound Mutations*, a precursor of IRCAM's *Audiosculpt*. It permits in particular to perform extreme slowing down (by factors higher than 100) without loosing speech intelligibility: this is done by slowing down only the voiced parts of speech, in order to avoid a distorsion of the consonant that would alter their recognition. For instance, slowing down syllables like pa, ta or ka would mess up the cue allowing to identify p, t or k (namely the duration of the occlusion between the consonant and the following vowel). Here the identification of the consonants depends upon the ballistics of the vocal tract articulators.

The perceived difference between audio and sub-audio can lead to paradoxes. I have produced a curious rhythmical beat: when played on a tape recorder, it seems to slow down a bit when one switches speed from 7 1/2 ips to 15 ips [10].

In the 1960s, John Chowning discovered a completely novel way to use frequency modulation for synthesizing complex audio spectra. The process can be linked to the vibrato used by Western violonists for expressivity: the violonists move their left hand back and forth to modulate the string frequency at a rate of approximately 5 to 7 Hz. Chowning synthesized frequency-modulated sine waves - modulated carriers, and he increased the modulation rate from sub-audio to audio rates, up to the frequency of the carrier and above. This turned out to be a powerful synthesis technique, which has considerable utility if it is used effectively. To achieve such a modulation in the mechanical world, a violonist would have to vibrate his left hand at frequencies such as 440 Hz or more.

In 1999, Chowning performed a crucial "analysis by synthesis" which solved the unison enigma: how can the ear sort out two tones in unison, corresponding to the same note - for instance A 440? Chowning added two tones in unison with spectra typical of sung vowels: if they are strictly periodic, they tend to fuse and to be heard as a single tone. Chowning then affected the two tones with two different "micromodulations" (for instance two vibratos at different rate): the ear could then easily discriminate the two tones. This is the sonic counterpart of the principle of "common fate" favoring fusion, enunciated by the German Gestalt psychologists of the early XXth century. Chowning produced powerful sonic and video demonstrations. The visual cue of common fate is easy to demonstrate using two transparent sheets. If one draws a dense could of random dots on one transparent, and on the other one a distinct figure (for example a human face) made up of a few dots, this figure disappears when the two transparents are superposed, but it will surge immediately if one of the sheets is set in motion in respect to the other. Vibratory coherence is a case of common fate: it induces fusion.

7   The Myth of the Resonating Body

I want to argue against a prevalent myth. Rameau's theory of harmony states that vibrating bodies produce a series of sub-vibrations, called harmonics, which occur at frequencies that are integer multiples of the fundamental frequency. According to Rameau's view, the intervals between harmonics play an essential role in harmony. Rameau thought that resonating bodies - *la résonance du corps sonore* - produced harmonic components: according to him, this was a natural foundation for his theory of harmony. However hitting most **resonant** bodies will not produce an harmonic motion: percussive sounds, such as bells, gongs and drums, even the piano, have *inharmonic* spectra, that is, the frequency components are **NOT** equally spaced in frequency. Only sustained quasi-periodic sounds - such as bowed violins, wind instruments or voiced sounds - have harmonic spectra.

With usual acoustic instruments, it is difficult to produce sustained sounds having inharmonic spectra: but it is quite easy with computer synthesis. Thus Chowning, in his work *Stria*, has used a scale related with the specific inharmonic structures of the sounds he synthesized, and he was able to preserve a notion of consonance with unusual scales and tones.

8 Musical Performance Controlled by Gestures

Let me go back to the vibration of the tuning fork. It only carries two informations: its pitch, informative about the frequency of vibration, and its loudness, related to the amplitude of the vibration. A strictly periodic sound does not convey a flow of information: sound is informative only insofar as it varies. If the sound is produced by an acoustic source, variations must be produced by modifications of this vibratory source. In the case of musical instruments, such modifications are usually produced by the motions of the musical performer, i.e. the gestures of the instrumentalist.

The art of musical instrument makers must take in account the physical laws of acoustics as well as the specifics of both auditory perception and human motricity in order to construct machines that will effectively convert the energy of the motions of the performer into audible acoustic energy.

The performer controls his or her instrument by gestures that are specific to that instrument. These are expert gestures: the instrumentalist has to be overtrained to be able to fulfill the demands of virtuosity of the score. John Sloboda has shown that even gifted musicians need thousands of hours of training to perform instruments at a professional level.

Human gestures act, but they also bring information about the body and the outside world. One can distinguish between two basic archetypes of instruments: the violin player controls his sound from beginning to end, while the percussionist, as soon as he or she has triggered a sound, can attend to the next one. In this respect, the voice and the wind instruments are similar to the violin, while piano, guitar, harp or harpsichord are similar to the percussion.

Digital instruments use the MIDI protocol (Musical Instrument Digital Interface). Performance nuance is easier to control through MIDI parameters for percussion-type instruments than for voice-type instruments, even though certain MIDI wind controllers sense variations of parameters throughout the note, such a as breath and lip pressure (Kergomard, Guillemain and Voinier used such a controller for the real-time performance of their clarinet simulations).

Claude Cadoz has proposed a typology of musical gestures. Marcelo Wanderley has performed revealing analyses of the gestures produced by performers, pioneering the study of the expressive role of looking at the gestures of musical performers.

A present challenge for research on performing with digital instruments is to capture gestures and to map them to significant musical parameters. The motion capture tutorial by James Yang has addressed this challenge in the course of the CMMR 2013 Symposium. The meeting NIME - New Instrument for Musical Expressions - is dedicated to this question. In the 2000s, a group directed by Daniel Arfib has worked at LMA on the problem of mapping - capturing gestures from pads, tablets, driving wheels, accelerometers, or from video image analysis ...

In the 1960s, Alvin Lucier, Richard Teitelbaum and Manfred Eaton demonstrated the possibility of controlling music through brain waves and the *biofeedback* - a difficult endeavour pursued by Atau Tanaka, David Rosenboom, Eduardo

Mirando and Joel Eaton. In CNMAT Berkeley, Adrian Freed is working on wearable instruments: clothes that sense the bodily motions and turn them into musical effects.

9   Expressivity and Deviations in Musical Performance

In music, one expects expressive performances: the instrumentalist must deviate in appropriate ways from a mathematically accurate rendering of the score. The computer has facilitated further understanding of musical performance, permitting to study it through analysis - detecting the deviations realized by performers and interpreting them - but also by using the paradigm of *analysis by synthesis* - evaluating by ear the effect of such or such deviation from an accurate rendering. Bengtsson and Gabrielson effectively used this paradigm. For instance they realized a simplified rendering of the beginning of *The Fledermaus (The Bat)* by of Johan Strauss: they could suggest the character of the waltz by simply introducing proper deviations in the timings of the notes.

The deviations occurring in performance are not erratic. In masterful performers, the deviations are consistent and systematic. Sunberg interprets them as a way to make the structuration of the music more intelligible to the listener. His group has determined some performance rules defining deviations that help inject expressivity in the rendering of a score (cf. [17]). Some of these rules depend upon the musical style (for instance the tonal syntax has its idiosyncrasies), but a few seem universal - for instance slightly speeding up when going up a scale and slowing down when going down.

In the early 1970s, Max Mathews and F. Richard Moore have designed *Groove*, a hybrid real-time system permitting to control electronic music in real time using non-conventional controllers such as music keyboards, switches and potentiometers, including a 3-D potentiometer enabling to control 3 parameters with one hand. Mathews has used *Groove* to perform revealing performance studies. In this system, the music is specified in terms of functions of time (for instance pitch and intensity as functions of time). These functions can be defined in different ways and they can be combined. Thus a pitch function defined by a step-wise function extracted from a musical score can be slightly altered by motions exerted on a potentiometer to produce a vibrato. One can build up a performance in successive passes, introducing refinements one at a time. Mathews asked several musicians to construct their own Groove performance of existing works (a movement of Ravel's quartet and Webern's *Bagatelles*): the results were vastly different, showing that the system allows for personal expression. This raised the interest of Pierre Boulez, who is keen on performing or conducting electronic music live rather than presenting it as a fixed medium.

10   Motion in Hearing and Other Senses

The living organism has to integrate the signals it receives from the various sensory modalities. The concept of motion could be a key paradigm for the understanding of various aspects of sound, in particular its relation with image.

In many situations, vision dominates audition (seeing is believing): but sound is more *dynamogenic*. Small children cannot refrain from dancing on music with a strong beat, whereas they will not dance on a periodic recurrence of images. Galileo had no chronometer: he resorted to musical monks beating time.

Speeding up is exciting, slowing down is depressing, even when the slow-down is circular and endless.

I have synthesized a paradoxical sound which slows down yet ends faster, which also goes down in pitch but ends higher, and also seems to rotate in space faster and faster: there is a sort on conflict between a strange slowing rhythm and an accelerating circular motion. This can be heard at the end of my work *Moments newtoniens*.

Simonne Marquès, a musician and music teacher working in Marseille, has for long let high school students move at leisure at the sound of the music she played instead of forcing them to stay seated. The kids enjoyed it, and it led them to appreciate the music and to develop their own *expression corporelle* (free bodily expression). We are on the border of dance here.

Dance is body motion associated with music. Dancers n+n Corsino have dealt with this association during the CMMR 2013 Symposium. In the ballet *Phosphones*, realized in the 1970s, an extreme synchronization between sound and lighting could be achieved with the help of the system *Groove*. The music was composed by the late Emmanuel Ghent, who was very concerned with rhythmic coordination. With the help of the kinetic sculptor James Seawright, Groove produced the control signals for both the music and the lighting. The dancers belong to the company of Mimi Garrard, who did the choreography.

11   Motion Universals

Are there motion universals? Researchers from MIM - Musique et Informatique de Marseille, a musical group created by Marcel Frémiot - has tried to find some basic temporal figures, genuine universals of motion, in the hope to apply the same analysis tools to both instrumental music and electroacoustic music - perhaps even to all arts of time. The elementary motion components selected were called *Semantic Temporal Units* (TSU - in French *Unités Sémantiques Temporelles*, UST - cf. [16]). Nineteen of them have been specified at the moment, such as Falling, Rotating, Stationary, Suspended ... The results of analysis are encouraging, but it seems too early to conclude whether these are really fundamental components of motion, or if there is some arbitrariness in the choice (cf. [5,16]).

12   Interactive Disklavier Performance

I ended my presentation at CMMR 2013 by demonstrating an interactive process of accompaniment in the acoustic domain, using a *Disklavier*, a mechanized acoustic piano built by Yamaha. I describe this process in more details below, and I indicate a couple of web sites presenting demonstrations. I have developed this in 1989 in M.I.T., when Barry Vercoe invited me in the Music and Cognition Group, Media Laboratory, M.I.T., and I pursue it at LMA.

In this interactive process, the key motions of the pianist trigger a response in terms of motions of mechanical keys rather than motions of a loudspeaker membrane: the live pianist is followed by a virtual partner playing on the same piano an accompaniment which depends on what the pianist plays and how he or she plays. So all sounds are in the acoustic domain, even though a computer mediates the interaction.

I called this process *Duet for one pianist*: in addition to the pianist's part, a second part is played on the same acoustic piano by a computer which follows the pianist's performance. The pianist has a "partner" - but an invisible, virtual one. The computer program "listens" to what the pianist plays, and instantly adds its own musical part on the same piano: this part is not a mere recording, it depends upon what the pianist plays and how he plays. Hence we have a genuine duet: the pianist's partner, although unreal and computerized, is sensitive and responsive.

This requires a special piano - a Yamaha Disklavier - equipped with MIDI input and output. On this piano, each key can be played from the keyboard, but it can also be activated by electrical signals: these signals trigger motors, which actually depress or release the keys and the pedals. Each key also sends out information as to when and how loud it is played. The information to and from the piano is in the MIDI format, used for synthesizers. A computer receives this information and sends back the appropriate signals to trigger the piano playing: the programming determines in what way the computer part depends upon what the pianist plays. This programming was made easy thanks to the real-time graphic software *Max* written by Miller Puckette at M.I.T. and at IRCAM. I acknowledge the highly dedicated and competent help of Scott Van Duyne for the writing of the Max patches.

I realized short pieces - *sketches* and *etudes* - in which I have tried to explore and demonstrate different processes of live interaction between the pianist and the computer. The pieces enumerated below exemplify some of these processes.

Echo. The computer echoes the pianist - not as a mere repetition: the echoes are transposed in pitch and in tempo, and they can occur with different delays with respect to the original utterance.

Double. The pianist plays alone, then he or she repeats with ornaments added by the computer. These ornaments were established in advance: they are called when the pianist plays certain notes, with tempo and nuances influenced by performance of the pianist.

Fractals. To each note played, the computer adds five notes spaced approximately - but not exactly - one octave apart. Thus the pitch patterns played by the pianist are distorted in strange ways: an octave jump is heard as a semitone descent.

Resonances. This piece takes advantage of the resonances on the same soundboard of notes played by either the pianist or his virtual partner. At the beginning, the computer plays long sustained chords. Then the pianist plays mute chords: the strings are set in resonance by the sequences played by the computer.

Narcisse. Here the relation is akin to a mirror reflection: the pitch intervals are inversed -a fifth is reflected into a fourth and vice-versa. The center of symmetry is a note of the keyboard, which varies throughout the piece. The reflection can also be retarded with different delays.

Metronomes. This begins by a short canon: the computer echoes the pianist on transposed pitches and at different tempos. It later plays simultaneously different sequences at different tempos. Then it repeats the same pitches, but again at different metronomic tempos, either preset (as in Ligeti's *Symphonic Poem for one hundred metronomes*) or set by the pianist.

Mercure. In this kind of scherzo, the pianist triggers arpeggioes at different speeds. The speed is set either by the tempo of certain patterns played by the pianist, or by the pitch played, or by the loudness. Fast arpeggioes move through pitch space somewhat like shapes in a kaleidoscope.

Such an interaction could be used beyond the field of contemporary music composition. The potential applications for pedagogy are numerous. There are obvious applications in aiding the practice of pieces for more than one pianist. Special performing environments could be prepared, for instance to try out compositional algorithms, or to stimulate improvisation: the field of jazz would lend itself to the piano-computer live interaction with its generally structured rhythmic and harmonic patterns.

In a broader context, one might even think of exploiting this interaction for fast and sophisticated controls, even completely out of the field of music. Through a specific response on the same piano (for instance consonant if all goes well, dissonant otherwise), the pianist-controller could have fast and elaborate feedback that could instruct him or her what to play next, that is, what to do next if in a non-musical context. Such man-machine interaction would be hard to beat in speed and complexity: a good pianist sight-reading a score performs great feats of ergonomy.

Parting Remarks

The CMMR 2014 symposium permitted a fruitful exchange of new research data on the combined study of *music and motion*: this is a rapidly expanding field with very promising perspectives.

Video Demonstrations

Chi Minh Sieh: Miroirs. Video_DVD ICA-ACROE 2005-2009, 2 (2009)

Dars, J.F., Papillaut, A.: Film on the research of J.C. Risset, beginning by a demonstration of the real-time interaction "Duet for one pianist" (French, partial English dubbing, 17 min) (1999). This film can be seen at: http://videotheque.cnrs.fr/video.php?urlaction=visualisation&method=QT&action=visu&id=394&type=grandPublic

Mathews, M.V., presenting Ghent & Garrard Phosphones (1971). In The early gurus of electronic music, Ohm, Ellipsis Arts, 2005 (DVD 3694)

Risset, J.C.: Démonstration vidéo (in French) de l'interaction temps réel "Duo pour un pianiste" sur Disklavier, MESH, Lille, Thé?tre du Nord, (circa 28 min) 3 february 2009, http://live3.univ-lille3.fr/video-campus/concert-diskclavier-jean-claude-risset-2.html

Risset, J.C.: Conference in English, including a video demonstration of the live interaction "Duet for one pianist" on Disklavier, CIRMMT, McGill University, Montreal, 17 march 2011 (1h26mn) http://www.cirmmt.mcgill.ca/activities/distinguished-lectures/Risset

References

1. Ambiant and Instrumental Creativity / Créativité Instrumentale et Créativité Ambiante. ACROE/Enactive Systems Books publisher (2011). http://aicreativity.eu
2. Bolzinger, S., Risset, J.C. A preliminary study on the influence of room acoustics on piano performance. Comptes Rendus du 2ème Congrès Français d'Acoustique, Arcachon (Editions du Journal de Physique 1992), pp. 93–96 (1992)
3. Chowning, J.M.: The simulation of moving sound sources. J. Audio Eng. Soc. **19**, 2–6 (1971)
4. Chowning, J.M.: Frequency modulation synthesis of the singing voice. In: Mathews, M.V., Pierce, J.R. (eds.) Current Directions in Computer Music Research. MIT Press, Cambridge (1989)
5. Frey, A., Hautbois, X., Yeh, Y.S.: An experimental validation of Temporal Semiotic Units and Parametrized Time Motifs. Musicae Scientiae **18**(1), 99–123 (2014)
6. Marquès, S.: Musique et mouvement à l'école. Edisud (1990)
7. Mathews, M.V., Boulez, P.: Conducting program. J. Acoust. Soc. Am. **57**, S22 (1975). http://dx.doi.org/10.1121/1.1995123
8. Mathews, M.V., Pierce, J.R. (eds.): Current Directions in Computer Music Research. MIT Press, Cambridge (1989)
9. Pottier, L.: Dynamical spatialization of sound. HOLOPHON: a graphic and algorithmic editor for Sigma1, Proceedings of the Digital Audio Effects Meeting (1998). Accessible on the GMEM web site: http://www.gmem.org/index.php?option=com_content&view=article&id=35&Itemid=45#sthash.24Rv6x9r.dpuf
10. Risset, J.C.: Pitch and rhythm paradoxes: comments on "Auditory paradox based on a fractal waveform". J. Acoust. Soc. Am. **80**, 961–962 (1986)
11. Risset, J.C.: Speech and music combined: an overview (with 40 sound examples on CD). In: Sundberg, J., Nord, L., Carlson, R. (eds.) Proceedings of the Wenner-Gren International Symposium "Music, Language; Speech and Brain", McMillan, pp. 369–379, 451–452 (1991)
12. Risset, J.C.: Le son numérique: une acoustique affranchie de la mécanique ? Comptes Rendus du 2ème Congrès français d'Acoustique, Arcachon, Editions du Journal de Physique, 3–11 (1992)
13. Risset, J.C.: Rhythmic paradoxes and illusions: a musical illustration. In: Proceedings of the International Computer Music Conference, Thessaloniki 1998, ICMA, pp. 7–10 (1998)
14. Risset, J.C., Mathews, M.V.: Analysis of instrument tones. Phys. Today **22**(2), 22–30 (1969)

15. Risset, J.C., Van Duyne, S.C.: Real-time performance interaction with a computer controlled acoustic piano (with sound examples on CD enclosed in the Journal). Comput. Music J. **20**(1), 62–75 (1996)
16. Rix, E., Formosa, M. (ed.): Vers une sémiotique générale du temps dans les arts. Actes du colloque "Les Unités Sémantiques Temporelles (UST), nouvel outil d'analyse musicale: théories et applications", Delatour (2008)
17. Sundberg, J.: The Science of Musical Sounds. Academic Press, San Diego (1991)
18. Torra-Mattenklott, C.: Illusionisme musical. Dissonance **64**, 4–11 (2000)
19. Wessel, D.L.: Timbre space as a musical control structure. Comput. Music J. 3(2), 45–52 (1979); Reprinted in Roads, C., Strawn, J., (eds.) Foundations of Computer Music. MIT Press, Cambridge (1985)
20. Zölzer, U.: Digital Audio Effects. Wiley, New York (2011)

A Virtual Reality Platform for Musical Creation: GENESIS-RT

James Leonard[1(✉)], Claude Cadoz[1,2], Nicolas Castagne[1],
Jean-Loup Florens[2], and Annie Luciani[1,2]

[1] ICA Laboratory, University of Grenoble Alpes, Grenoble, France
{james.leonard, Claude.Cadoz, Nicolas.Castagne,
Annie.Luciani}@imag.fr
[2] ACROE, University of Grenoble Alpes, 46 Avenue Félix Viallet,
38000 Grenoble, France
Jean-Loup.Florens@imag.fr

Abstract. We present GENESIS-RT, a Virtual Reality platform conceived for musical creation. It allows the user to (1) interactively create physically-based musical instruments and sounding objects, and (2) play them in real time in a multisensory fashion, by ways of haptics, 3D visualisation during playing, and sound. The design of this platform aims for full physical coupling, or *instrumental interaction*, between the musician and the simulated instrument. So doing, it differs from both traditional Digital Musical Instrument architectures and Virtual Reality system architectures. By presenting our environment, we discuss several scientific underlying questions: (1) possible ways to manage simultaneous audio-haptic-visual cooperation during real time multisensory simulations; (2) the Computer Aided Design functionalities for the creation of new physically-based musical instruments and sounding objects, and (3) the synchronous real time features, in terms of software and hardware architecture. Finally the article reviews a series of exemplary models and instrumental situations using the proposed platform.

Keywords: Physical modelling · Haptics · Force-feedback interfaces · Virtual reality · Musical creation · Multisensory interaction · Instrumental interaction · Digital musical instruments

1 Introduction

In this paper, we focus on how the domain of Computer Music can be enhanced by Virtual Reality concepts and developments. Indeed, Digital Musical Instruments (DMIs) are one of the major research axes of Computer Music, but are rarely conceived as or considered full-fledged VR systems. On other hand, Virtual Reality environments are multi-modal by nature, but sound is rarely the main focus and is often overlooked in these systems. Consequently, very few of them are conceived for musical creation. We propose a new modelling and simulation platform, which draws on concepts from both of the above and enables designing virtual musical instruments and playing them in real time with multisensory interaction.

© Springer International Publishing Switzerland 2014
M. Aramaki et al. (Eds.): CMMR 2013, LNCS 8905, pp. 346–371, 2014.
DOI: 10.1007/978-3-319-12976-1_22

The term *multisensory interaction* with a virtual object or scene generally bears various meanings, depending whether considered from a Computer Music perspective, a VR perspective, or a physical perspective. Our system aims for multisensory interaction in the physical sense, *i.e.* a dynamic physical coupling with a simulated physical object, by means of force feedback technologies and real-time synchronous computation of physically-based models. It displays a complete virtual scene construction environment based on mass-interaction physical modelling and a real time interactive simulation environment that generates haptic, auditory and visual feedback during the multisensory manipulation of the virtual scene. To our knowledge, this dynamical coupling-based, or *instrumental* approach to interaction with simulated objects or instruments remains a rare feature in both Computer Music and in general VR systems.

First, we will present the domains of virtual musical instruments and virtual reality, with a physical interaction perspective. We will then present the GENESIS-RT platform and its main features. Finally we will show various models of virtual musical instruments created with this platform, and discuss the results.

2 Virtual Musical Instruments and Virtual Reality

2.1 Virtual Musical Instruments

Sound Synthesis. Over the last 50 years, research has yielded numerous technologies and concepts for sound synthesis, which have in turn rapidly been integrated as compositional tools for musicians [24, 54, 55]. Many of the most well known synthesis methods are signal-based, in that they are based on direct manipulation of parameters related to the signal itself, such as amplitudes, frequencies, attack, decay, etc. [20, 46]. Software such as Max/MSP [47], PureData [53] or SuperCollider [48] all allow for numerous signal-based synthesis techniques. More recently, an alternative solution to this approach proposes to model the sound source rather than the sound itself, for instance using physically-based modelling techniques, such as digital waveguide physical models [59] or mass-interaction physical models [9]. This is particularly relevant in cases where it is very difficult, or impossible, to obtain a given sound by direct manipulation of the signal's parameters, whereas characterising the sound source's properties can be easier. Moreover, causal modelling of the sound source naturally allows obtaining a variety of resulting synthesised sounds, as the sound source responds differently to various types and dynamics of excitation (plucking, bowing, striking, hard, soft, etc.). In this respect, physical modelling can be considered a mentally economical approach for obtaining relevant and diverse synthesised sounds, which present *natural* perceptive qualities, as they are based on the modelling of physically plausible mechanical structures [18].

A number of physical modelling environments and tools have been issued in the last 25 years. We propose to split them into two main categories:

- Software dedicated to the synthesis of specific categories of instruments, such as BRASS (Arturia/IRCAM) [8, 63] or String Studio (Applied Acoustics Systems) [2] and more generally all the physics-based "audio synthesis plug-ins". Each of these tools generally focuses on a specific category of instruments, aiming to convincingly imitate a real world counterpart. They provide plug-and-play simple usage, but are limited to a certain category of sounds.

- Modular environments allowing building virtual instruments, such as Reaktor [49], CYMATIC [35], MODALYS [1, 25], TASSMAN [2] or GENESIS [16]. These systems generally aim to produce sounds presenting "natural" perceptive qualities, due to the physical nature of the sound source, but are not restricted to a specific category of instruments, or even imitating existing instruments.

Inside this second category, systems vary in terms of the level of modularity: Reaktor, TASSMAN and MODALYS essentially revolve around pre-built macro-elements, such as strings, membranes, plates, etc. whose parameters can be globally controlled and that can be assembled together by the user. In contrast, GENESIS offers an entirely modular formalism, in which instruments can be entirely created from the ground up by designing mass-interaction networks. It also allows modelling other non-vibrating sections of the instrument, such as bows, plectrums and hammers with the same principles and the same level of detail as the vibrating structure, allowing to fully craft complete virtual musical instruments.

Digital Musical Instruments. While technology initially imposed that sound synthesis be calculated off-line, the fast evolution of computing power has rapidly allowed nearly all techniques to operate in real time, with the expansion of the real time user-control of sound synthesis systems, as related by [60]. In this scenario, systems designed for the gestural control of digital sound synthesis are generally referred to as Digital Musical Instruments (DMIs) [64]. Such Digital Musical Instruments are usually decomposed into two distinct sections: the gestural control section, which captures and interprets various user actions or gestures (via sensors, cameras, etc.), and the sound synthesis section that computes one or several audio signals according to the gestural input parameters.

The mapping of gestural information to various audio synthesis parameters is a determining factor for the DMI, as it fundamentally affects the instrument's expressivity and playability [38]. As a consequence, the study and strive for optimal and general mapping strategies for DMIs has been a major research axis over the last 15 years [36, 37], and is still ongoing. Possibility of an arbitrary mapping from gesture to sound opens many possibilities for innovative sound control; however, re-creating a meaningful association between an input gesture and the variation of an acoustical property is still considered a difficult task, often requiring complex mapping strategies in order to obtain satisfying control of the instrument [39].

In DMIs, the modalities for the musician/instrument interaction are essentially gestural and auditory. Visual representations of the virtual instrument are most often control visualisations for the audio synthesis or completely detached visualisation processes. Thus, we cannot speak of complete visual-auditory interaction with a virtual object.

Physically-based virtual instruments can of course also be driven by arbitrary mapping processes, in the same way as other signal-based synthesis techniques. However, they also lend themselves to an alternative solution: maintaining the physical link between the user and the instrument, i.e. creating a unified physical structure composed of both the gestural section and the vibrating structure, and directly interacting with this physical structure. This approach eliminates the need to build mapping strategies, and has the advantage of enabling consistent and physically meaningful control over sound dimensions.

2.2   Haptics and Virtual Musical Instruments

To further reinforce the metaphor of tangible physical interaction with the virtual instrument itself, many recent developments aim to integrate tactile and/or haptic feedback into DMIs [30, 50, 57], giving a stronger meaning to the term virtual instrument: the user can now feel the instrument in addition to hearing it. Various works have demonstrated the relevance of such feedback in improving the musician's performance with a computer-based instrument [3, 51], showing that the additional feedback can make for increased expressiveness when playing [50].

Although the uses of haptics in Computer Music are very diverse, we propose to gather them into two main categories, being (1) the addition of haptic feedback to a traditional DMI architecture based on the control of digital sound synthesis processes and (2) using haptics in order to achieve physical coupling with a simulated musical instrument (or vibrating virtual object).

Haptic-augmented DMIs. In this first scenario, audio synthesis is generally driven by data provided by the haptic interaction between the user and a local mechanical model [3, 50, 57]. Mapping strategies are employed in order to provide the adequate control of audio properties in accordance to properties of the interaction with the local mechanical model. The general architecture of such systems is given in Fig. 1. It is generally based on several loops running at different rates: the audio synthesis engine runs at the highest rate, whereas the haptic interaction occurs at a lower rate, typically 1 kHz, and the physical dynamics of the local mechanical model can be computed at lower rates still, such as 60 or 100 Hz [41, 57], for instance using rigid body dynamics. These loops communicate with each other, often asynchronously.

Haptics for Instrumental Interaction. The use of force-feedback systems for re-creating a dynamic physical coupling between a musician and a virtual instrument

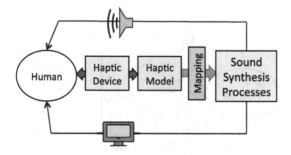

Fig. 1. Addition of haptic feedback to a mapping-based control of digital sound synthesis processes

refs to the *ergodicity* [7] of the instrumental situation, as introduced by Cadoz, or to the concept of *instrumental interaction* [12]. With acoustical instruments, the acoustic outcome of the physical interaction between the musician and his instrument is the result of a continuous and intimate exchange of energy between the two parties [13]. The energetic exchange, or *ergotic* function of instrumental interaction, conveys meaning and is a key factor for expressiveness in the sound of a musical instrument.

When considered in the context of digital systems, this analysis corresponds to a strong change in paradigm [17] compared to the traditional DMI mapping-based architecture, as it strives for an enactive situation [26], yielding natural physical interaction with the instrument. It requires for the complete simulation chain, depicted in Fig. 2, to allow for coherent exchange of energy between user and instrument, and what's more covering a frequency spectrum comparable to that of the rate of the simulated instrument's physical deformations. This implies the need for high performance haptic devices, an appropriate physically-based simulation formalism, and specific hard real time constraints for the simulation's computational scheme.

Mimicking the real world interaction with a virtual object lends itself particularly well to physically-based modelling methods as proposed in [27]. Mass-interaction physical modelling is well suited in this case, one of the main reasons being that the vibrating structure of the instrument and the elements related to the gestural interaction can be modelled within the same framework. Other techniques can be used, such as using the digital waveguide method to simulate the vibrating structure, which is then interfaced with the haptic device, for instance via a variable spring and damper [4, 58].

Recently, some works have started studying how and why achieving instrumental interaction with digital technology has power to dramatically improve instrumental playing. For instance, [44] show that the believability of a bowed string increases considerably when the haptic feedback is able to convey the acoustic vibrations of the string to the musician's hand. This result has been obtained by running the haptic parts at the simulation rate of the string, i.e. at the sampling acoustic rate of 44.1 kHz, and has been proved to help the musician in performing complex musical tasks, such as reversing the direction of the bow, while maintaining the vibration of the string.

Regardless of the above typology, the existence of tools able to support the design of virtual instruments is crucial, in particular as they are determining factors for ensuing musical uses. Noticeably, in the case of mapping-based DMIs, many hardware and software systems exist and interoperate, allowing the final user to design the DMI, using

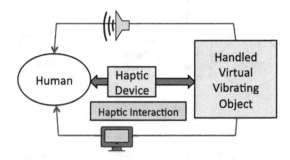

Fig. 2. Direct, closed-loop haptic interaction with a virtual vibrating object

various tools for the gestural input (possibly including haptics [56]), the sound synthesis [21, 53], as well as the mapping itself [45]. Conversely, only a smaller number of systems aim at designing physically-based virtual musical instruments and interacting with them [5, 35], and as of yet none have targeted full instrumental interaction.

2.3   Virtual Reality and Sound

One of the main pursued goals of Virtual Reality is to introduce interaction with a computer in a similar form to interaction with an object of the real world. This naturally addresses multiple senses: at least tactile /haptic, visual, and sometimes auditory. Indeed, VR systems were initially centred almost exclusively on visual environments, displaying complex scenes composed of objects that can be seen, manipulated, moved... These systems very rarely consider sound with the same level of importance as the visual or gestural aspects. Also, most VR platforms are dedicated to specific applications (simulation & training, surgery, rehabilitation, automotive, showrooms, etc.), and very few of them are used for music. Indeed, even though a few applications such as [6, 22] put emphasis on the sound produced when interacting with a virtual object, audio is often left out entirely, or integrated as a rather secondary feature, giving audio cues for example [42].

VR environments are often based on geometric approaches including complex computational processes such as collision detection between complex shapes in large 3D scenes, and sometimes physical modelling [32]. The addition of force feedback devices and haptic interaction into virtual reality systems usually leads to a trade off between the usual computation rate of the 3D objects (usually 25–100 Hz) and the haptic interaction (classically of 1 kHz or more) [34], leading to the dissociation of geometry and haptic related aspects through the concept of *haptic rendering* of the 3D scene through the haptic device. Such a trade – off is critical in terms of the balance between the reachable complexity of the 3D scenes and the quality of the haptic interaction in terms of inertia, peak force or acceleration [33], haptic algorithms being then executed within a dedicated thread called the haptic loop. This trade–off becomes even more complex when introducing sound synthesis. Indeed, except in cases where sounds are simply pre-recorded, then triggered, or more rarely parameterised, by an event occurring and detected in the VR 3D scene (a collision detection for instance), introducing sound synthesis in haptic-powered VR systems leads to novel questions at least in terms of the organisation of the models into several sections running at different frame rates: the sound synthesis sections (namely 44,1 kHz), require a frame rate greater than not only the 3D geometrical parts (25–100 Hz) but also the haptic parts (1 kHz at least).

Whatever the intended use, the believability of a VR scene is tied as much to the consistency between the multisensory outputs (sounds and images) as to the realism of the haptic interaction. In both cases, physical modelling gains significant importance in increasing the believability of the virtual world. This is why the VR environment proposed here is based on physical modelling as the common point for sound generation, haptics as well as for animated image generation.

2.4   System Architectures for VR and Computer Music

In the case of haptically augmented control of mapping-based audio synthesis, the general architecture resembles that of usual VR systems, in that the coupling between the haptic device – if any – and the next component, a local mechanical model, can be bi-directional, but the coupling between this section and the following components (for example, the vibrating processes) is usually unidirectional, oriented and from upstream to downstream.

Differently, full physical coupling with a virtual physical instrument leads to consider that all the physical instrumental components composing the whole action-sound chain, from gestures to sounds, are connected in a bi-directional way. For example, such a system would present a bidirectional physical coupling between the haptic device and the mechanical exciter manipulated by the user, but also a physical mechanical coupling between this exciter and rest of the instrument including the vibrating structure, allowing for the vibrating structure to physically react on the upstream physical elements.

This requirement leads to a second difference: in order to allow energetically coherent couplings from the haptic device to the virtual vibrating object, the simulation has to rely on synchronous real time computing [62], within the haptic local loop as usual but also all along the instrumental physical chain. This differs from the traditional DMI architecture, as in these systems the unidirectional couplings can be done asynchronously. However, the consequence of full physical coupling is that it necessitates reconsidering the hardware and software architecture of the system.

This fundamental difference impacts the frame rate cooperation inside the system: within a unidirectional and asynchronous framework, various sections can be computed at different rates depending on, amongst other things, which modality they are addressing (visual, haptic, audio). In the case of synchronous physical coupling, the separation into multiple frame rates is a more delicate process, requiring complex synchronous multi-rate architectures that maintain the energetic coherence of the physical coupling. Hence, in the work presented in this article, virtual objects are modelled as a whole, and simulated at the single highest needed frame rate – that is: the audio frame rate.

2.5   An Instrumental VR System for Musical Creation

In both Computer Music and Virtual Reality, and to our knowledge, no existing systems have merged an end-user design tool for interactive construction of virtual musical instruments and a high-quality haptics simulation system enabling full dynamic physical coupling with these instruments. The aim of our work is to integrate the principles of VR into the context of musical creation and virtual musical instruments, offering a platform for the interactive design of these instruments and means for multisensory dynamic physical coupling with them, associating haptics, sound and vision.

Concerning modelling, we propose a modular environment for constructing virtual instruments and scenes composed of many interacting instruments and sound objects based on mass-interaction physical modelling.

Concerning haptics, we implemented the situation in which the haptic interaction is supported by a high performance haptic device, and is closely linked to the physical modelling of the instrument, for instance by running at the same high frame rate as that of the sound rate simulation. Thus, the instrumentalist is intimately in contact (is physically *coupled*) with his/her instrument during playing. We mean here that the instrumentalist truly physically interacts with vibrating object, increasing the realism, the believability and the embodiment [31] of the virtual instrument during the playing, as demonstrated in [44].

Concerning vision, we believe that introducing visualisation in the design and the playing of virtual musical instruments will considerably improve the playability, the pleasure, the efficiency, and the creativeness in the musical playing. By visualisation, we mean not only seeing the geometry of the instrument, but a new functionality consisting in rendering visible some features of the vibrating behaviour of the instruments, in order to reinforce their presence and believability.

Concerning sounds, they are produced by means of physically-based simulation for all the parts of the instruments: vibrating and non-vibrating sections, as well as interactions between multiple instruments.

The auditory, haptic and 3D visual feedback of the manipulated physical objects occur in real time during simulation, and all stem from the physical behaviour of the unique simulated vibrating object, which is not the case with analysis-synthesis approaches such as [22]. Therefore, GENESIS-RT can be considered a full multisensory VR platform for musical creation, allowing for *Instrumental Virtual Reality*.

The following section will present the GENESIS-RT platform, first by introducing the formalism and tools used to construct virtual physical objects, then characterising the essential features of our simulation system. We will then discuss examples and models of virtual musical instruments.

3   The GENESIS-RT Virtual Reality Platform

GENESIS-RT is a virtual reality platform for musical creation, based on, for the first time, the integration of three basic components: (1) the CORDIS-ANIMA physical modelling and simulation formalism [11], (2) the GENESIS interactive modeller for musical creation [16, 19] and (3) the high fidelity ERGOS haptic technology [28]. The environment is composed of two communicating parts: a modelling section in which the user is able to design his/her own physically-based musical instrument or sounding object in an interactive way, and a second section in which he/she is able to play with his/her virtual instrument by way of real time haptic, audio and 3D visual multisensory interaction. We will now introduce each component of our system.

3.1   An Interactive Modeller to Design Physically-Based Musical Instruments

The CORDIS ANIMA Formalism. The modelling and simulation processes used in GENESIS-RT are based on the CORDIS-ANIMA formalism [11], a modular language and system that allows building physical objects by creating mass-interaction networks based on Newtonian physics and simulating them. Briefly, it formally defines a small number of basic physical modules that represent elementary physical behaviours. These modules can be assembled in order to build complex physical objects. There are two main modules types in CORDIS-ANIMA, depicted in Fig. 3:

- <MAT> (mass type modules): punctual material elements, possessing a spatial position and inertia.
- <LIA> (interaction type modules; LIA stands for the French work *liaison*: link): modules that define an interaction between two <MAT> modules.

Thanks to the formal modules schemes, a wide variety of <LIA> modules can be developed and inserted into the modelling system, from simple linear interactions such as springs and dampers, to more complex nonlinear ones such as dry friction as needed in modelling bow-string rosin interactions for violin or cello simulations.

The majority of CORDIS-ANIMA modules exist in various spatial dimensionalities. For instance, unidimensional modules, in which state variables are simple scalars, are well suited to create topological networks that represent vibratory deformations such as those found in the mechanics of musical instruments; moreover, they are the fastest to compute, hence suited for audio-rate real time simulations. In contrast, three-dimensional modules can be used to model 3D scenes, adding geometric properties, such as Euclidian distances, to the topological CORDIS model [43]. These 3D models are generally computed at a lower rate, often similar to the temporal dynamics of haptics/human gestures, as the vibratory behaviour is not the focus.

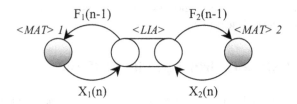

Fig. 3. Schematic representation of the CORDIS ANIMA formalism, composed of MAT (material points) and LIA (interaction) modules. X and F represent the dual position/force variables, and n represents the time step.

A specific implementation of CORDIS ANIMA has been integrated into a new simulation engine, which is specifically tailored for our presented platform. We will discuss this engine in Sect. 3.3.

GENESIS as a Virtual Reality Modeller. GENESIS [16, 19] is a physical modelling software for musical creation. Its modelling language is based on a subset of CORDIS-ANIMA module types. It disposes of advanced tools for creating physical structures and tuning their acoustic and mechanical properties and has matured into a complete, elaborate and user-friendly environment for musical creation by means of physical modelling. We have extended GENESIS into a VR haptic modeller for real time force-feedback interaction with simulated physical models.

GENESIS was initially designed to create complex physical models of vibrating physical structures for off-line simulation, aimed not only at sound synthesis but also at musical composition. It allows for the design of complex instruments and sounding objects [61], dynamically interacting together through physical interactions, composing complex instrumental structures as used in the physically-based orchestra shown in Fig. 4, composed of tens of thousands interacting physical elements [14].

For sounding objects, the simulation as well as the synthesis rate must be at the audio/acoustical scale, i.e. at 44,1 kHz, in respect to the vibrating qualities of the virtual objects. The audio output signals are directly built as being equal to the successive positions of chosen material <MAT> modules during the simulation.

GENESIS models are computed in a 1D space, meaning that all physical elementary modules are computed along a single vibration axis (*unidimensional* version of CORDIS-ANIMA). Acoustics of musical instruments show that, in many cases, the one-dimensional main deformation, such as for example the transversal deformation of a string or a plate, is the major contributor to the sound. This is why synthesis tools usually compute one or several scalars signals that are those finally sent to the loudspeakers. This choice allows for optimised computation, enabling the design of very large physical structures. Nevertheless, auditory phenomena linked to spatiality can be obtained in a 1D simulation space by using non-linear spring interactions, as related in [15], at a fraction of the cost of full 3D computation.

However, as it is based on multi-scalar non-meshed physical models, GENESIS has been extended with visualisation processes, which aim to reconstruct a 3D real time representation of the acoustical deformations of the instruments (cf. Sect. 3.5).

Extending GENESIS as a VR haptic modeller requires introducing the representation of haptic devices within the modelling functions. Here, we introduce a representation of the haptic device inside the model, following the same formalism, as a general <MAT> module. Thus, it can be connected to virtual objects in the same way as any other module, for instance with percussive buffer interactions, plucking or bowing interactions which can be designed by non-linear interaction modules, and so forth.

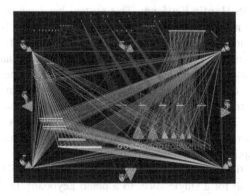

Fig. 4. Representation in GENESIS of a complex physically-based orchestra by C. Cadoz, for his musical piece "pico.. TERA" [14]

3.2   Real-Time Simulation Platform

The first haptic device aimed for dynamic coupling with simulated instruments was designed by Florens in 1978 [29]. This research has continued over the years [10] and evolved into the ERGOS high fidelity haptic technology [28] developed by ACROE and ERGOS Technologies, which is used in GENESIS-RT. The system is composed of the haptic device itself, called TGR (*transducteur gestuel rétroactif*), with its electronic rack, and a dedicated "haptic board" co-processor [23], connected to a host computer. The haptic board is implemented on a TORO DSP board from Innovative Integration, which allows real time synchronous floating-point operations, with ADC and DAC converters for the haptic device position input and force feedback output. The physical simulations run in real time on the haptic board within a single-sample, synchronous, high-speed computational loop. The complete simulation architecture for the GENESIS-RT platform is shown in Fig. 5.

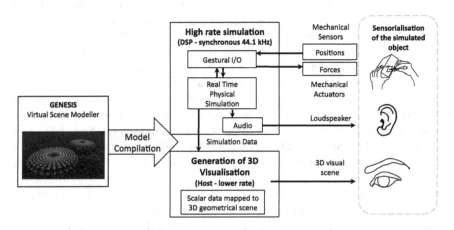

Fig. 5. The GENESIS-RT Virtual Reality platform

The 12 DoF ERGOS Haptic Platform. This system has been developed in relation with the context and needs of artistic creation, specifically in the field of instrumental arts such as music and animated image synthesis. Therefore, its primary aim is to restore the dynamic qualities of the interaction between the user and a traditional real physical object in a user/virtual instrument situation. Thus, a strong emphasis has been put on the platform's dynamic performances, suited for instrumental musical gestures, as opposed to most traditional VR haptic systems centred on shape and geometrical property rendering. This concerns, among others, the reactivity of the electro-mechanical transducer, and maximum peak force feedback (approx. 200 N).

Thanks to the haptic device's modular *sliced motor* technology [28], one of its main features is the potentially high number of degrees of freedom (DoF) offered by the system: from one DoF for a single slice, to a piano keyboard. In the following, each DoF will be called "a key". As opposed to most haptic systems, the ERGOS Haptic device offers several working spaces all derived from the same base design, meaning that it can be adapted for various types of manipulation of virtual objects, using morphological end-effectors ranging from separate one-dimensional keys (Fig. 7), to 3 or 6 DoF joysticks, 3DoF bow manipulators (Fig. 6).

From this technology, GENESIS-RT disposes of a 12 DoF ERGOS Haptic system that can be configured with various combinations of end-effectors. The range of possibilities of this setup is complementary to the various interactions that can be modelled between the musician and the virtual instruments: striking, bowing, plucking, pulling, damping... The user is free to choose from a panoply of end-effectors, which allow him/her to adapt the morphology of the modular haptic device to the specific needs for his/her virtual instrument, and to adapt to a wide variety of playing styles.

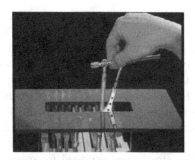

Fig. 6. ERGOS Haptic device equipped with a bow end-effector.

Fig. 7. 12-key ERGOS haptic device equipped with piano-key end effectors.

A Reactive DSP Simulation Architecture. We consider synchronous computing architecture to be a key feature for allowing true physical coupling with the simulated instrument, allowing for fully reactive dynamical coupling at audio-rates. Indeed, the TORO DSP board allows running completely synchronous physical simulations, including sound simulation and production at very high rates (ranging from 1 kHz up to 44.1 kHz) and with very low latency (less than 23 μs at 44.1 kHz), including communication with haptic devices at the same rate [23, 44]. This provides high fidelity in the rendering of very stiff contacts that are crucially important in percussive musical gestures and accurate frictions of bowed-string interactions.

Below, we show the typical sequencing of a simulation step:

- Haptic device key positions are fed to the ADC converters.
- A step of the physical simulation is calculated on the DSP chip.
- The calculated force feedback is sent to the DAC converters, with an exact single-sample time delay, which is fed to the electronic amplification system for the ERGOS haptic device's actuators.
- The DSP board also generates the audio-output of the simulation (with single sample latency).

Connection to the Host Environment. During the simulation, the haptic board communicates with a host system, which controls and monitors the simulation and deals with the real-time visualisation of the model, tasks that are not subject to the same latency constraints as the physical simulation haptic loop.

Various simulation data is streamed from the haptic board to the host system in real time: the deformations of all the masses in the model, composed of the exciters (striking devices, bows, etc.) and the vibrating structures (strings, plates, etc.) are sent. From this data, the host builds a visual scene for each frame, at a lower rate than the DSP's physical simulation, rendered according to a mapping from the multi-scalar deformation data to the geometrical space.

3.3   An Optimised Simulation Engine

Using the TORO board for the physical simulation of acoustical vibrating objects necessarily induces a trade-off between processing power and reactivity. The TMS320C6711 DSP chip presents less processing power than many general-purpose PC processors, however it does allow completely deterministic computation at rates such as 44.1 kHz. Therefore we developed a new CORDIS-ANIMA simulation engine, optimised for the DSP, which allows us to take full advantage of the chip's features.

An essential feature for the simulation engine is its modularity, or compatibility for automatic allocation from a physical model description. This is critical for a virtual reality scene modelling and simulation system, as a non-modular simulation engine would revert to a one-shot approach, with custom simulations designed for specific models. This was the case for the previous real time simulations created at ACROE-ICA, such as [44], which were designed with ad hoc, hand-optimised simulation programs.

A benchmarking and testing procedure has been conducted for various software architectures of DSP real time simulation engines. Throughout this procedure, we have been able to bring forward a number of important design choices for a new real time simulator. The main performance critical criteria for the new DSP simulation engine have been found to be:

- Reducing the number of function calls (up to 70 % gain by factorising the physical module functions).
- Vectorising the various data structures, including management of the DSP memory specificities (a further 70 % gain).
- Using static memory allocation.
- Optimising the C++ expressions of the CORDIS-ANIMA algorithms for the DSP (excluding all division operations in the critical real time code sections, minimising conditional sections, etc.).

The new simulation engine features optimised data structures, model reorganisation for vectorised calculation of the physical algorithms and optimisation of the physical algorithm calculations according to the DSP board's architecture, while retaining a modular approach that is compatible with the generic description of physical models.

Figure 8 shows performance comparison between GENESIS-RT's optimised modular simulation engine and the previous non-modular real time engine as well as the initial off-line modular GENESIS engine.

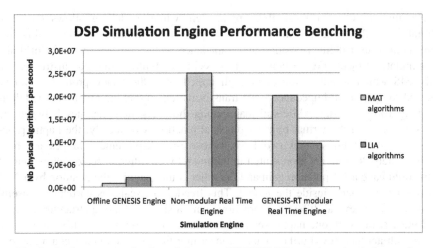

Fig. 8. Performance evaluation of the new GENESIS-RT real time simulation engine

The results of this work have lead to a new real time simulation engine with maximal efficiency of the physical algorithms, thus, increasing the complexity of the physical models that can be simulated at audio sample rates on the DSP.

Our current simulation architecture allows simulating models composed of approximately 130 to 150 modules, depending on the types of modules, number of haptic DoF… While these models are only a small subset of possible GENESIS models (which can grow to contain tens of thousands of interacting physical components), the allowed complexity is sufficient to create simple yet rich vibrating structures with up to 12 haptic interaction points (as our ERGOS Haptic device has 12 individual 1D keys). We will illustrate some typical virtual musical instruments in the examples section.

3.4   Real/Virtual Interconnection

The quantitative relations between the real and virtual world, especially through force-feedback devices, are rarely studied with Virtual Reality systems. However, in our case the virtual world is designed with specific physical properties that we want to hear, see and feel in the real world. Specifically for the haptic perception of the virtual object, the user/simulation chain must be entirely characterised and calibrated, so that a given mechanical property in the simulation (for example an inertia or viscosity) is projected into the real world through the haptic device with a completely controlled and mea-surable equivalency between the two.

The interconnection properties between the real world and the simulation are defined by three parameters linked to the user/simulation chain:

- The real/simulation position gain,
- The simulation/real force feedback gain,
- The sampling rate of the simulated world, which in our case is 44.1 kHz.

Having control over these three parameters while modelling allows complete calibration of the system with metrological precision. Furthermore, they allow the adjustment of user-defined position and impedance scales between the real world and the simulated object. For instance, it is possible to build a musical instrument in GENESIS which weighs a ton (very high impedance); the haptic properties can be adjusted to operate an impedance scale transformation so that the instrument is felt as weighing 100 g or 1 kg, while still maintaining the energetic coherency between the user's actions and the virtual object's physical reaction. Conversely, the haptic properties can be set up so that two keys, whose real displacement ranges are both approximately 20 mm, are represented in the model with different scale factors: one of them could have a 1:1 position gain and the other could magnify the position by a 20:1 or even 1000:1 factor inside the model. This freedom of scales is particularly useful when designing several different interactions with a single vibrating structure, such as plucking a string with one haptic key and simultaneously fretting the string at a given length with another key. Further details concerning the user/simulation chain and our developed software tools are presented in [40].

3.5   Reconstructing a 3D Visualisation of the Virtual Scene

As stated in the previous sections, GENESIS modelling is based on multi-scalar non-geometrical physical models. Consequently, the 3D geometry needed for the visualisation has to be reconstructed from the available multi-scalar data representing the acoustical deformations produced by the simulation. In other words, rather than having constructed a 3D vibrating object, which would have been inadequate for the relevancy of the resulting sounds and for our simulation needs, we simulate its dynamic acoustical behaviour and try to visualise this behaviour, not only from signal representations, but by visualising it in the 3D space, offering a better understanding of the vibrating properties of the object that will help the user's playing.

Designing a model in GENESIS consists in placing <MAT> modules on a blackboard and in designing their interactions. Thus, such a representation is a topological representation of the structure of the model, in which interactions represent dynamic coupling between 1D deformations supported by the 1D displacement of the masses. The geometrical mapping in GENESIS is represented in Fig. 9. It consists in: (1) assigning spatial coordinates (X and Y) to the location (Bh, Bv) on the blackboard, and (2) assigning the scalar representing the position of the masses on the single simulation axis (which we will call a in Fig. 9) at the Z coordinate of the geometrical 3D space.

During real time simulation, the X and Y positions in the 3D space are fixed, and the Z displacements (representing the physical deformations of the object) are communicated asynchronously from the DSP board for real time visualisation at the visualisation frame rate.

This mapping stage is part of the modelling activity in the sense that 3D representation must be coherent with the dynamics of the deformations. For instance, a string allows visualising the mechanical deformations associated to the wave propagation if the placement of the mass modules on the blackboard and the design of the geometrical mapping are consistent. Placing the modules randomly on the blackboard would be impossible to interpret visually, even if it generates the same exact behaviour.

Figure 9 shows how the data is mapped to build the visualisation, and Fig. 10 shows an example with a GENESIS model, on the modelling blackboard, then during simulation. The string topology of the mass-interaction network is matched with the representation on the blackboard. During simulation, if the mapping is correctly designed, this spatial structure will show the waves propagating back and forth along the string.

All these components constitute GENESIS-RT, an Instrumental Virtual Reality platform for musical creation. For the first time, GENESIS models can be played haptically in real time. Furthermore, these new developments provide our first generic modelling system for the interactive design of multisensory real time simulations based on the CORDIS-ANIMA formalism. In the following section, we present a number of models and examples designed and manipulated with GENESIS-RT.

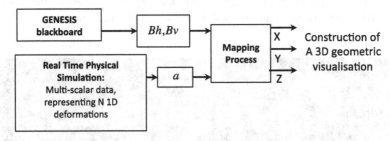

Fig. 9. 3D geometrical mapping process of a GENESIS model for the real time visualization

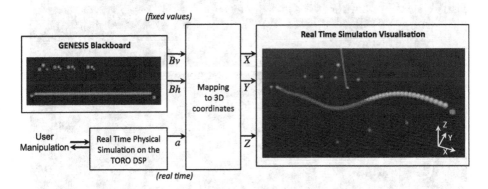

Fig. 10. Example of a GENESIS model and the final animation produced during simulation.

4 Models and Examples

The first objective of this work has been to create an extensive and user-friendly platform for designing and manipulating virtual musical instruments. In this respect, two major strengths of this system are the ease with which virtual scenes can be built and the qualities of the instrumental interaction when playing these instruments.

New models can be created and played with in a matter of minutes, with no need for expert knowledge neither in haptic technologies nor in real time programming. The only prerequisite is being comfortable with the GENESIS physical modelling paradigm, for which ACROE already disposes of pedagogical tools. Below we demonstrate some of the first models created with this platform. Needless to say, this modelling and creation phase is still under way, and many more virtual instruments and scenes are in the works.

4.1 A Piano-Inspired Model

This model, shown in Fig. 11, aims to explore the full potential of our 12-key force-feedback device. It is constituted of 12 separate "Haptic keys". These keys are linked to small "hammer" masses, which strike individual vibrating structures ("oscillators" on Fig. 11), tuned to various audio pitches. A physical "bridge" gathers all the vibrations from the vibrating structures and is used as the sound output source.

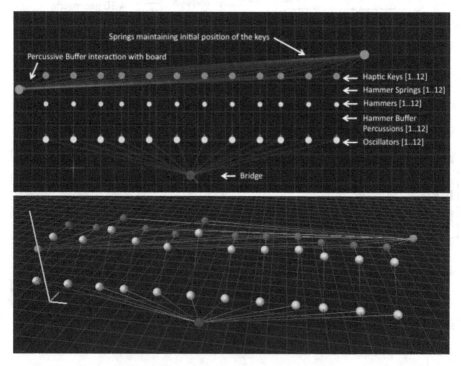

Fig. 11. The Piano model: the GENESIS model on the blackboard (above) and the 3D animation during real time simulation (below), with the haptic keys coloured in red (Colour figure online).

The model contains multiple elements for configuring the piano-key feel:

- The stiffness of the buffer interaction between the key and the board, as well as the distance between them, can be adjusted, making the mechanical feel harder/softer, and configuring the displacement range to press down the keys.
- The stiffness of the spring maintaining the key in its initial position changes the effort required to press the keys down, hence the feel of the instrument's rigidity.
- The entire hammer mechanism, and the position of the oscillators in regards to these hammers along the simulation axis, are also key factors in tuning the instrument's playability: one must allow for easy striking of the oscillators, but avoid double bounces, and other undesirable physical behaviours.

This model shows the many aspects that come into play when crafting a physically-based virtual musical instrument. The fine-tuning of the instrument's "feel" can be performed iteratively, by developing successive prototypes of the instrument, or can also be studied in the offline GENESIS context. The basic model presented here can be extended to incorporate more subtle components of the key mechanism and also more complex vibrating structures, although the DSP-based architecture limits attainable complexity today. Indeed, further work on the simulation hardware architecture is currently underway to allow implementing much more complex models for all 12 keys.

4.2   A Ring Structure

This model, shown in Fig. 12, generates inharmonic bell-like sounds with "Gamelan-like" acoustic properties. It is composed of a main ring structure divided into four heterogeneous sections, modelling a structure with uneven matter distribution. Each section is delimited by visco-elastic relations, which connect them to a heavy bridge oscillator. Four striking devices hit the different sections of this ring. Depending on the stiffness of the section delimiters, the user can control the ratio between the propagation of the vibrations in the full ring and the local propagation limited to the excited sub-section.

Fig. 12. Screenshot of the ring structure during simulation.

During playing, the instrument shows different sound responses depending on where, and how heavily it is hit. Furthermore, the striking devices can also be used as dampers, to block certain sub-sections of the ring, stopping certain vibrations and modifying the response of the structure. Figure 13 shows the lower spectrum of the audio output, for strikes on two different sections of the ring.

Although the vibrating structure contains the same modes in both cases, striking different sections excites them very differently. For instance, Fig. 13a) shows an apparent fundamental frequency of 395 Hz, and many higher modes, whereas Fig. 13b) shows a strike on a heavier section, which results in stronger /additional lower modes (including the 322 Hz fundamental frequency, which is almost completely absent in Fig. 13a), and weaker high modes.

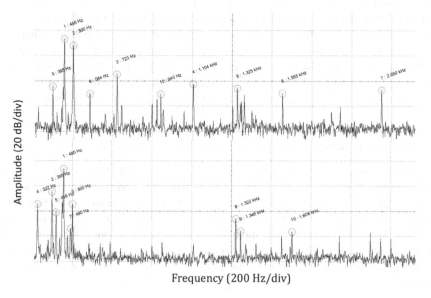

Fig. 13. Lower audio spectrum (300 Hz–2200 Hz) for the ring structure, struck in two different locations: (a) on a medium weighted section (top) and (b) on a heavy section (bottom).

4.3   A Bowed String Model

The model, resumed in Fig. 14, is composed of a string, attached to two fixed points. The string is excited by a 1D haptic key, via a velocity-driven non-linear interaction that presents a similar profile to the usual physicists' models of the real world stick-slip interaction of a bow with a string. As GENESIS functions in a one-dimensional space, the friction interaction is restricted to the displacement axis, thus there is no modification of the interaction properties according to a pressure parameter. Previous work by F. Poyer's allows addressing this while remaining in 1D [52] and is scheduled for integration into future models.

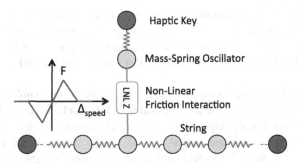

Fig. 14. Structure of the bowed string model, which uses a non-linear friction (LNL Z) interaction (force/velocity profile shown on the left).

Figure 15 shows a user manipulating this string model with GENESIS-RT. Figure 16 shows the behaviour of the string at the friction point during bowing. We can observe the Helmoltz motion of the string, caused by the stick-slip interaction.

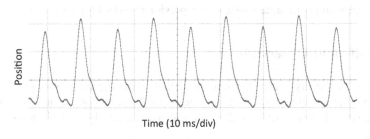

Fig. 15. Using the GENESIS-RT platform to play the bowed string model.

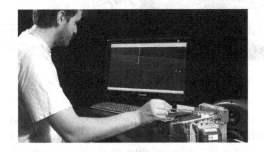

Fig. 16. Position of the string over time (observed at the bowing point). We can note the stick-slip Helmoltz motion.

4.4 The Paddleball

This model is very simple: a sheet or membrane made of MAS (mass) and REF (visco-elastic interaction) elements is connected to a haptic key though each of its extremities, the key acting as a "floating" fixed point for the membrane. Vibrations from the membrane are sent to the audio output. The other component of the model is a single MAS module, which we will call the ball. It is given gravity by applying a constant downward force value, and is connected to the membrane with a buffer-spring interaction. In its initial state, the ball rests against the membrane and nothing specific happens.

When manipulating the haptic key, hence the height of the whole membrane, the user can launch the ball up in the air. The ball then falls back down and bounces (with damping) on the membrane, until it rests completely against it. However, with well-timed impulses to the membrane section, the ball can be sent back into the air, and the bounces can be sustained, for as long as the user can keep his gestures synchronised with the ball's motion. In short, this model reproduces a 1D paddleball, as shown in Fig. 17-right.

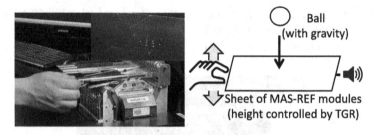

Fig. 17. The paddleball model.

The impacts of the ball on the membrane are felt, heard and seen by the user. Succeeding in maintaining the ball's bounces is not a trivial task, and proves very difficult when removing information relative to certain sensory channels (muting the audio, removing the force feedback, or removing the visualisation). This goes to show the importance of physically coherent sensory feedback from a virtual object for instrumental manipulation, as discussed in previous works [44].

5   Results and Observations

Real time multisensory manipulation of the virtual scenes depicted above proves highly satisfying, offering subtle and intimate control over the sound production by respecting the energetic coherence between the user and the virtual object. Four points can be mentioned:

First, the properties of the TGR haptic device and the architecture of the platform make for a high quality restitution of the mechanical properties of the virtual objects. Hard contacts can be rendered and the mechanical feel of an instrument can be modelled. This makes the system very versatile, as we can truly craft the virtual instruments for the desired feel and playability. Our piano-inspired model, for instance, although it does not entirely model the mechanical complexity of the real instrument, proposes a complete, precisely tuneable, and playable musical interface.

Furthermore, the 3D visualisation of the physical object's deformations during manipulation is an asset of our system that is not present in the natural instrumental situation. More than just seeing the instrument during playing, our system offers an extensive and tuneable visual representation of the simulated physical object, allowing for instance to magnify the visualisation of chosen physical deformations. Not only can the user manipulate a complete coherent multisensory simulated instrument, but he/she can also simultaneously benefit from a detailed visualisation of the vibratory behaviour of the instrument during playing (imagine playing a violin and being able to simultaneously visualise all the vibratory deformations of the strings and body!). From our qualitative studies, we can say that such a visual representation, allowed by our VR approach, adds to the understanding of the instrument's physical behaviour, and to the experience of playing the instrument.

Thirdly, our first qualitative observations gathered with a group of 20 participants (musicians and non-musicians) and through various demonstration sessions show promising preliminary results concerning the user-instrument relationship. Subjects very quickly and naturally take the instruments in hand and learn how to produce a wide variety of (sometimes surprising) sounds. Furthermore, we observed that users actively explore the possibilities in terms of gestures and sounds, of causes and consequences, and often like spending a surprising amount of time, e.g. tens of minutes, experimenting with one single simple instrument, exploring all of its instrumental possibilities. Though preliminary, these observations are highly satisfying. In the same way as [31], it seems that the virtual instruments present a positive assimilation curve, acquisition of knowledge and skill increase through the interaction. It seems that a true deepness has been achieved with this platform in regards to the quality of instrumental interaction. This leads us to say that the musician/instrument relation is somewhat similar to that of a traditional musical instrument, in the sense that the instrument is intuitively apprehended and embodied by the user, and provides a rich gesture-sound-vision relation.

Finally, as pointed out by the paddleball model, the scope of this platform is larger than virtual musical instruments alone. Any number of virtual scenes and scenarios can be imagined and created, presenting the user with a full, physical and energetically coherent audio-visual-haptic experience.

6 Conclusions

This paper has presented GENESIS-RT, a new virtual reality platform for musical creation composed of the GENESIS physical modelling environment, a high performance ERGOS haptic device, and a real time simulation environment for haptic interaction with virtual scenes.

From a musical perspective, the quality of the haptic device and the full physical modelling of the virtual objects enable full dynamic coupling between the musician and his instrument, resulting in expressive playing. From a larger perspective, this platform is a complete audio, visual and haptic virtual reality station, presenting an advanced scene modeller and a complete simulation environment, offering a unique tool for further exploring the influence of the coherence of visual, haptic and audio feedback for designing perceptually convincing virtual objects.

This work raises several new questions and perspectives.

First, generally speaking, it may open path to new research in regards to possible structure and design of "coupling-based" Digital Musical Instruments and "Instrumental" Virtual Reality systems, as defined in this article.

It also raises the question of the adequate hardware/software architecture design for real time physical simulations. Using a dedicated haptics-board or *Haptics Processing Unit,* as done in this work, such as the TORO board allows reaching the needed levels of time determinism which are not attainable on standard computers, but at the cost of lower computing power, restraining the size of implantable models. New architectures are currently being studied to address this limitation.

Thirdly, it encourages further reflexion on an optimal frame rate for the haptic and mechanical sections of the virtual instruments, allowing for the conceptual separation of a gesture, or "mechanical" space, and an aero-acoustical vibrating space, both remaining physically coupled. The introduction of multi-rate physical models could hence be a promising perspective, in which the purely mechanical sections of the instrument would be computed at a lower rate than the vibrating sections.

Fourth, we believe that existence of platforms such as GENESIS-RT, providing both user-friendly modelling means and possibility of multisensory physical coupling while playing virtual instruments, opens possibility of new research in the domain of cognitive sciences, for example on rather unstudied questions in regards to the true nature and key dimensions of human-instrument interaction, and in regards to the core phenomena which constitute such an interaction.

Finally, the developments achieved with GENESIS-RT make it possible to explore the new possibilities opened to musical creation by the instrumental concepts reified by the platform.

Acknowledgments. This research has been supported by: the French Ministry of Culture; the French Agence Nationale de la Recherche through the cooperative project DYNAMé - ANR-2009-CORD-007; the Grenoble Institute of Technology; and the Doctoral Studies College of Grenoble-Alpes University.

References

1. Adrien, J.M.: Etude de structures complexes vibrantes, application à la synthèse par modèles physiques. Ph.D. thesis, Université Paris VI, Paris (1988)
2. Applied Acoustics Systems. http://www.applied-acoustics.com (2014). Accessed Mar 2014
3. Berdahl, E., Niemeyer, G., Smith, J.O.: Using haptics to assist performers in making gestures to a musical instrument. In: Proceedings of NIME'09, pp. 177–182. USA (2009)
4. Berdahl, E., Niemeyer, G., Smith, J.O.: Using haptic devices to interface directly with digital waveguide-based musical instruments. In: Proceedings of the Ninth International Conference on New Interfaces for Musical Expression, pp. 183–186. Pittsburgh, PA (2009)
5. Berdahl, E., Smith, J.O.: An introduction to the Synth-A-Modeler compiler: Modular and open-source sound synthesis using physical models. In: Proceedings of the Linux Audio Conference (2012)

6. Berthaut, F., Hachet, M., Desainte-Catherine, M.: Piivert: percussion-based interaction for immersive virtual environments. In: IEEE Symposium on3D User Interfaces (3DUI) 2010, IEEE, pp. 15–18 (2010)
7. Boissy, J.: Cahier de termes nouveaux: 1992. Conseil international de la langue française (1992)
8. BRASS. http://www.arturia.com/evolution/en/products/brass/ (2014). Accessed Mar 2014
9. Cadoz, C., Luciani, A., Florens, J.L.: Responsive input devices and sound synthesis by stimulation of instrumental mechanisms: The CORDIS system. Comput. Music J. **8**(3), 60–73 (1984)
10. Cadoz, C., Lisowski, L., Florens, J.L.: A modular feedback keyboard design. Comput. Music J. **14**(2), 47–51 (1990)
11. Cadoz, C., Luciani, A., Florens, J.L.: CORDIS-ANIMA: a modeling and simulation system for sound and image synthesis: the general formalism. Comput. Music J. **17**(1), 19–29 (1993)
12. Cadoz, C.: Le geste, canal de communication homme/machine: la communication "instrumentale". Tech. Sci. Informatiques **13**, 31–61 (1994)
13. Cadoz, C., Wanderley, M.M.: Gesture – music. In: Battier, M., Wanderley, M. (eds.) Trends in Gestural Control of Music, pp. 71–93. Editions IRCAM, Paris (2000)
14. Cadoz, C.: The physical model as metaphor for musical creation: "pico..TERA", a piece entirely generated by physical model. In: Proceedings of the 2002 International Computer Music Conference (2002)
15. Castagné, N., Cadoz, C.: Physical modeling synthesis: balance between realism and computing speed. In: Proceedings of the Digital Audio Effects Conference (DAFx-00), Verona, Italy (2000)
16. Castagne, N., Cadoz, C.: GENESIS: a friendly musician-oriented environment for mass-interaction physical modelling. In: Proceedings of the International Computer Music Conference (ICMC'02), pp. 330–337. Sweden (2002)
17. Castagne, N., Cadoz, C., Florens, J. L., Luciani, A.: Haptics in computer music: a paradigm shift. In: Proceedings of EuroHaptics (2004)
18. Castagné, N. Cadoz, C.: A goals-based review of physical modeling. In: Proceedings of the International Computer Music Conference (ICMC'05), pp. 343–346 (2005)
19. Castagné, N., Cadoz, C., Allaoui, A., Tache, O.: G3: GENESIS software environment update. In: Proceedings of the International Computer Music Conference (ICMC), pp. 407–410 (2009)
20. Chowning, J.: The synthesis of complex audio spectra by means of frequency modulation. Comput. Music J. **1**(2), 46–54 (1977)
21. Cook, P.R., Scavone, G.: The synthesis toolkit (stk). In: Proceedings of the International Computer Music Conference, pp. 164–166 (1999)
22. Corbett, R., Van Den Doel, K., Lloyd, J.E., Heidrich, W.: Timbrefields: 3d interactive sound models for real-time audio. Presence: Teleoperators Virtual Environ. **16**(6), 643–654 (2007)
23. Couroussé, D.: Haptic board. In: Luciani, A., Cadoz, C. (eds.) Enaction and Enactive Interfaces: A Handbook of Terms, pp. 126–127. Enactive Systems Books, Grenoble (2007). ISBN 978-2-9530856-0-48
24. De Poli, G., Piccialli, A., Roads, C.: Representations of Musical Signals. MIT press, Cambridge (1991)
25. Eckel, G., Iovino, F., Caussé, R.: Sound synthesis by physical modelling with Modalys. In: Proceedings of the International Symposium of Music Acoustics (1995)
26. Essl, G., O'modhrain, S.: An enactive approach to the design of new tangible musical instruments. Organised sound **11**(3), 285–296 (2006)

27. Florens, J.L.: Real time Bowed String Synthesis with Force Feedback Gesture. In: Invited paper. 585, Mus. 06, vol. 88, Acta Acustica (2002)

28. Florens, J.L., Luciani, A., Castagne, N., Cadoz, C.: ERGOS: a multi-degrees of freedom and versatile force feedback panoply. In: Proceedings of Eurohpatics 2004, Germany, pp. 356–360 (2004)

29. Florens, J.L.: Coupleur Gestuel Rétroactif pour la Commande et le Contrôle de Sons Synthétisés en Temps-Réel. Ph.D. thesis, Institut National Polytechnique de Grenoble (1978)

30. Gillespie, B.: The virtual piano action: design and implementation. In: Proceedings of the International Computer Music Conference (ICMC'94), pp. 167–170 (1994)

31. Gillespie, B., O'Modhrain, S.: Embodied cognition as a motivating perspective for haptic interaction design: a position paper. In: Proceedings of World Haptics Conference (WHC), pp. 481–486 (2011)

32. Gutiérrez, T., De Boeck, J.: Haptic board. In: Luciani, A., Cadoz, C. (eds.) Enaction and Enactive Interfaces: A Handbook of Terms, pp. 130–132. Enactive Systems Books, Grenoble (2007). ISBN 978-2-9530856-0-48

33. Hayward, V., Ashley, O.: Performance measures for haptic interfaces. In: Giralt, G., Hirzinger, G. (eds.) Robotics Research: The 7th International Symposium, pp. 195–207. Springer, London (1996)

34. Hayward, V., Astley, O.R., Cruz-Hernandez, M., Grant, D., Robles-De-La-Torre, G.: Haptic interfaces and devices. Sens. Rev. 24(1), 16–29 (2004)

35. Howard, D.M., Rimell, S., Hunt, A.D., Kirk, P.R., Tyrrell, A.M.: Tactile feedback in the control of a physical modelling music synthesiser. In: Proceedings of the 7th International Conference on Music Perception and Cognition, pp. 224–227 (2002)

36. Hunt, A., Wanderley, M.M., Kirk, R.: Towards a model for instrumental mapping in expert musical interaction. In: Proceedings of the International Computer Music Conference (ICMC-00), pp. 209–212 (2000)

37. Hunt, A., Kirk, R.: Mapping strategies for musical performance. In: Battier, M., Wanderley, M. (eds.) Trends in Gestural Control of Music, pp. 71–93. Editions IRCAM, Paris (2000)

38. Hunt, A., Wanderley, M.M., Paradis, M.: The importance of parameter mapping in electronic instrument design. J. New Music Res. 32(4), 429–440 (2003)

39. Kvifte, T.: On the description of mapping structures. J. New Music Res. 37(4), 353–362 (2008)

40. Leonard, J., Castagné, N., Cadoz, C., Florens, J.L.: Interactive Physical Design and Haptic Playing of Virtual Musical Instruments. In: Proceedings of the International Computer Music Conference (ICMC'13), Perth, Australia (2013)

41. Liu, J., Ando, H.: Hearing how you touch: real-time synthesis of contact sounds for multisensory interaction. In: Conference on Human System Interactions, pp. 275–280 (2008)

42. Lokki, T., Grohn, M.: Navigation with auditory cues in a virtual environment. IEEE Multimedia 12(2), 80–86 (2005)

43. Luciani, A., Jimenez, S., Florens, J.L., Cadoz, C., Raoult, O.: Computational physics: a modeler simulator for animated physical objects. Proc. Eurographics 91, 425–436 (1991)

44. Luciani, A., Florens, J.L., Couroussé, D., Castet, J.: Ergotic sounds: a new way to improve playability, believability and presence of virtual musical instruments. J. New Musical Res. 38, 303–323 (2009)

45. Malloch, J., Sinclair, S., Wanderley, M.M.: Distributed tools for interactive design of heterogeneous signal networks. Multimedia Tools and Applications 2014, 1–25 (2014)

46. Mathews, M.V.: The digital computer as a music instrument. Science 142(11), 553–557 (1963)

47. Max/MSP. http://cycling74.com/products/max/ (2014). Accessed Mar 2014

48. McCartney, J.: Rethinking the computer music language: SuperCollider. Comput. Music J. **26**(4), 61–68 (2002)
49. Native Instruments Reaktor. www.native-instruments.com/en/products/komplete/synths-samplers/reaktor-5/ (2014). Accessed Mar 2014
50. Nichols, C.: The vBow: development of a virtual violin bow haptic human-computer interface. In: Proceedings of the 2002 Conference on New Interfaces For Musical Expression (NIME '02), pp. 1–4 (2002)
51. O'Modhrain, M.S., Chafe, C.: Incorporating haptic feedback into interfaces for music applications. In: 8th International Symposium on Robotics with Applications, ISORA, 2000, World Automation Congress WAC (2000)
52. Poyer, F., Cadoz, C.: Sound synthesis and musical composition by physical modelling of self-sustained oscillating structures. In: Proceedings of the Sound and Music Computing conference (SMC'07), pp. 14–21 (2007)
53. Puckette, M.: Pure data: another integrated computer music environment. In: Proceedings of the Second Intercollege Computer Music Concerts, pp. 37–41 (1996)
54. Roads, C. (ed.): The music machine: selected readings from Computer music journal. MIT press, Cambridge (1992)
55. Roads, C., Pope, S.T., Piccialli, A., De Poli, G. (eds.): Musical signal processing. Swets & Zeitlinger, Leiden (1997). (Reedited by Routledge 2013)
56. Sinclair, S., Wanderley, M.M.: Defining a control standard for easily integrating haptic virtual environments with existing audio/visual systems. In: Proceedings of the 7th International Conference on New Interfaces for Musical Expression, pp. 209–212 (2007)
57. Sinclair, S., Wanderley, M.M.: A run time programmable simulator to enable multi-modal interaction with rigid body systems. Interact. Comput. **21**, 54–63 (2009)
58. Sinclair, S., Scavone, G.: Audio-haptic interaction with the digital waveguide bowed string. In: Proceedings of the International Computer Music Conference (2009)
59. Smith, J.O.: Physical modeling using digital waveguides. Comput. Music J. **16**(4), 74–91 (1992)
60. Smith, J.O.: Virtual acoustic musical instruments: review and update. J. New Music Res. **33**(3), 283–304 (2004)
61. Tache, O., Cadoz, C.: Organizing mass-interaction physical models: the cordis-anima musical instrumentarium. In: Proceedings of the International Computer Music Conference, pp. 411–414 (2009)
62. Uhl, C., Florens, J.L., Luciani, A., Cadoz, C.: Hardware architecture of a real time simulator for the cordis-anima system: physical models, images, gestures and sounds. In: Proceedings of Computer Graphics International '95 - Leeds (UK), pp. 421–436 (1995)
63. Vergez, Christophe, Tisserand, Patrice: The BRASS project, from physical models to virtual musical instruments: playability issues. In: Kronland-Martinet, Richard, Voinier, Thierry, Ystad, Sølvi (eds.) CMMR 2005. LNCS, vol. 3902, pp. 24–33. Springer, Heidelberg (2006)
64. Wanderley, M.M., Depalle, P.: Gestural control of sound synthesis. Proc. IEEE **92**(4), 632–644 (2004)

Interactive Sound Texture Synthesis Through Semi-Automatic User Annotations

Diemo Schwarz[1]([⊠]) and Baptiste Caramiaux[2]

[1] IRCAM–CNRS–UPMC, Paris, France
schwarz@ircam.fr
[2] Goldsmiths College, University of London, London, UK
b.caramiaux@gold.ac.uk

Abstract. We present a way to make environmental recordings controllable again by the use of continuous annotations of the high-level semantic parameter one wishes to control, e.g. *wind strength* or *crowd excitation level*. A partial annotation can be propagated to cover the entire recording via cross-modal analysis between gesture and sound by canonical time warping (CTW). The annotations serve as a descriptor for lookup in corpus-based concatenative synthesis in order to invert the sound/annotation relationship. The workflow has been evaluated by a preliminary subject test and results on canonical correlation analysis (CCA) show high consistency between annotations and a small set of audio descriptors being well correlated with them. An experiment of the propagation of annotations shows the superior performance of CTW over CCA with as little as 20 s of annotated material.

Keywords: Sound textures · Audio descriptors · Corpus-based synthesis · Canonical correlation analysis · Canonical time warping

1 Introduction

Environmental sound textures or atmospheres, such as rain, wind, traffic, or crowds, are an important ingredient for cinema, multi-media creation, games and installations.

In order to overcome the staticality of fixed recordings, we propose a method to make these recordings controllable again via a high-level semantic parameter so that they can be adapted to a given film sequence, or generated procedurally for games and installations. We have the two following use cases in mind:

Use Case 1 — Film Post-Production: A film sound designer or producer works on editing the sound track for a windy outdoor scene. On the rushes used for the scene, the sound is not available or unusable for some reason, but other rushes capture the intended sound atmosphere of the scene well. The sound designer annotates 30 s of these audio tracks for "wind strength" and the system propagates that annotation automatically to the rest of the recording. The sound

© Springer International Publishing Switzerland 2014
M. Aramaki et al. (Eds.): CMMR 2013, LNCS 8905, pp. 372–392, 2014.
DOI: 10.1007/978-3-319-12976-1_23

designer is then able to directly and interactively create, by moving one slider, the evolution of the sound to match the wind in the edited scene, observable on trees and objects. This relieved him from having to find contiguous audio sequences with the right temporal evolution, and to cut and splice them together.

Use Case 2 — Computer Games: In a sports game, the stadium crowd has to react to actions made by the players. Instead of preparing several sound samples or loops, and specifying the allowed transitions and superpositions, the game sound designer annotates a small corpus of stadium sounds and has it controlled by the game engine with one single parameter. The sound designer then stores the corpus to be reused for the next version of the game.

The method we propose in this article makes use of a 1D continuous manual annotation of an environmental recording that describes the sound quality one wishes to control, e.g. *wind strength* or *crowd excitation level*, or even a totally subjective parameter. The time/annotation relationship is then inverted to retrieve segments of the original recording via target annotation values by means of corpus-based concatenative synthesis [14]. The idea is to automatically retrieve the relationship between the sound and the annotation allowing for a subjective understanding of "strength" or "excitation level" in sound. The basic workflow is summarised in Fig. 1.

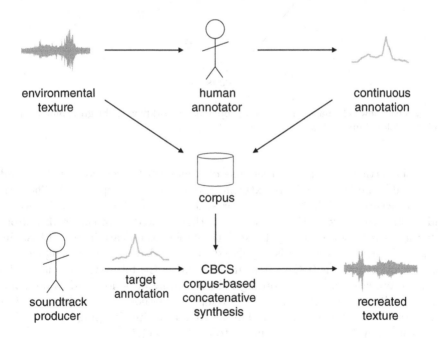

Fig. 1. Overview schema of the basic retexturing workflow.

In addition to this automatic analysis, we aim at providing a tool that allows the annotator to be able to annotate only a part of the sound and that propagates the annotation to the remaining recording. The term *semi-automatic* hence refers to the ability of the method to draw upon a user's incomplete annotation and to propagate it accurately to the whole sound. The workflow how the annotation propagation is enriching the corpus is shown in Fig. 2, the resynthesis staying the same as in Fig. 1.

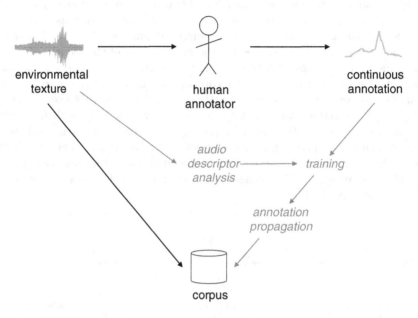

Fig. 2. Overview schema of annotation propagation workflow (light grey/blue parts in italics) (Color figure online).

In this article we report on the use of Canonical Correlation Analysis and Canonical Time Warping for retexturing and annotation propagation. The article is structured as follows. We will present our *ReTexture* method in Sect. 3 and a preliminary evaluation subject test, that allowed us to collect data from annotations from several users. These data enabled us to learn in Sect. 4 how the percept of e.g. *wind strength* is correlated to sound descriptors by using canonical correlation analysis (CCA). This might allow in the future to automatise the inversion process. For long recordings, the recording does not need to be annotated over its entire length, since we developed a method to propagate a partial annotation to the rest of the recording by canonical time warping (CTW), that is presented, evaluated, and compared to CCA in Sect. 5.

2   Previous and Related Work

The present research draws on previous work on corpus-based sound texture synthesis [16,17]. A state-of-the-art overview on sound texture synthesis in general can be found in [15].

Gestural responses to sound have been studied from different perspectives. In psychology of music, prior work investigated how people would represent controlled stimuli made of pure tones on a 2-dimensional surface [7]. In ecological psychology, other authors investigated the relationship between the gestural description of environmental sounds and the perception of their sound source [1], or in musicology, bridging theoretical concepts of sound study and body motion [10]. These methods draw upon embodied music condition theory [8] to provide insights on the relationships between physical motion properties and sound characteristics.

Based on this theoretical background, other prior work tried to use statistical techniques to automatically investigate the link between sound stimuli and gestural responses. The motivation behind the use of automatic techniques borrowed from data mining is to be able to find the function that links the sound to the gestures in order to invert it for gesture-based control of sound. Caramiaux et al. [4] make use of Canonical Correlation Analysis to automatically retrieve the implicit mapping between listened sound and synchronously performed arm movements. The set of sounds comprised various types such as musical excerpt, environmental sound, etc. Later, Nymoen et al. [9] used the same method to find the implicit mapping in terms of correlation between controlled sounds and movement of a stick in 3-dimensional space. Unfortunately, a major drawback of this technique, already mentioned in [2,4], is that the canonical analysis is based on correlation, meaning that both the sound and the gesture signals must be temporally aligned in order to be analyzed. An approach has been to use a different gesture–sound metric than the correlation, namely a probabilistic alignment based on hidden Markov models [3]. However these methods do not allow for feature selection but rather both the motion and the sound features must be chosen beforehand.

We base our work on the same methodology as above, but use a simpler and more focused task (annotate one specific sound quality) and input modality (a 1D slider), serving our concrete application in post-production.

Extensions of CCA have been proposed in order to overcome its inherent shortcomings. A kernel-based CCA is used to overcome the linear constraint between datasets [6] and has been recently proposed and used in an application of music recommendation based on body motion [11]. On the other hand, the synchronicity constraint has been shown to be relaxed by introducing a dynamical temporal alignment together with CCA. This model is called Canonical Time Warping and has been proposed by Zhou and De la Torre [18,19] for spatio-temporal alignment of human motion. The methods proceed in alternating between solving the time warping using DTW and computing the spatial projection using CCA, by the mean of a modified Expectation–Maximization (EM) method.

3 Interactive Sound Texture Synthesis Through Inversion of Annotations

We will now explain the *ReTexture* method of interactive sound texture synthesis through subjective user annotations (Sect. 3.1), followed by a subject experiment (Sect. 3.2) that allowed to evaluate the method, and to gather a database of annotations (Sect. 3.3).

3.1 The ReTexture Method

We collect a continuous one-dimensional annotation of a subjective quality of an environmental recording via a slider on a computer screen (see Fig. 3) or on an external MIDI controller. The slider is moved by a human annotator while listening to the recording.

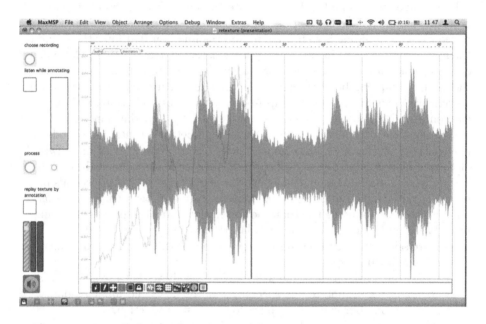

Fig. 3. Retexturing annotation interface.

The collected 1D break-point function is then used as a descriptor for corpus-based concatenative synthesis (CBCS), i.e. as an index to retrieve sound segments to be concatenated by annotation value. The index is implemented efficiently using a kD-tree.

For interactive recreation of a new texture, the user moves the same annotation slider that now controls the target value for concatenative resynthesis: Lookup is performed by choosing the 9 segments of length 800 ms around the annotated values closest to the given target value. One of the segments is chosen randomly (avoiding repetition), cosine windowed, and played with 400 ms overlap.

The prototype annotation application is implemented in MAX/MSP using the MUBU extensions for data management, visualisation, granular and corpus-based synthesis [13]. Examples of recreated evolutions of wind sounds can be heard online[1].

3.2 Subject Test

We performed a pre-test with 5 expert subjects with good knowledge of sound synthesis and gestural control to validate the annotation interface (Fig. 3), get first feedback on the workflow and control efficacy, and start collecting annotations. These provided us with the knowledge on what audio descriptors correlate best with the chosen sounds (Sect. 4) and ground truth data used for training of the propagation of annotations (Sect. 5).

The test corpus consisted of 4 sound files to be annotated: two wind recordings of 1:33 made by sound designer Roland Cahen, and two stadium crowd recordings of about 40 s length from a commercial sound library. These recordings and the annotation data are available online for reference.

The test procedure was as follows: After an explanation of the aim of the test, the qualities to annotate (wind strength and crowd excitation level, respectively) were made clear. Then, for each of the 4 sound files to be annotated, the subject could first explore the recording by starting playback at any time (by clicking on a point in the waveform), in order to familiarise herself with the different sound characters and extrema present. Then, the waveform was hidden in order not to bias annotation by visual cues on energy peaks, and recording of the annotation input via an on-screen slider started in parallel to playback of the whole sound file. At the end of this process, the raw annotation data was saved to a file, and the subject could then re-control the sound file using the annotation slider as control input, after which first impressions and free feedback were gathered.

After the whole corpus was annotated, the subject answered a questionnaire about the process with 6 questions, soliciting responses on a 5-point Likert scale (strongly disagree = 1, disagree = 2, neither agree nor disagree = 3, agree = 4, strongly agree = 5). The questions and mean ratings over the 5 subjects are given in Table 1.

3.3 Annotation Results

Figure 4 shows, for each of the 4 sound files, the annotation curves of the 5 subjects, individually normalised to zero mean and unit standard deviation.

---

[1] http://imtr.ircam.fr/imtr/Sound_Texture_Synthesis.

Table 1. Questionnaire and mean and standard deviation of response values.

Question	μ	σ
Q1: It was easy to annotate the sound quality during listening	4.0	0.71
Q2: It was often not clear which character of sound or type of events should be annotated with what value	1.8	0.45
Q3: It was easy to recognise the annotated sound qualities when replaying via the control slider	3.6	0.89
Q4: It was easy to recreate a desired evolution in the sound with the control slider	4.0	0.71
Q5: One can precisely control the desired sound character via the annotations	3.0	0.71
Q6: The created sound sequence is natural	4.4	0.55

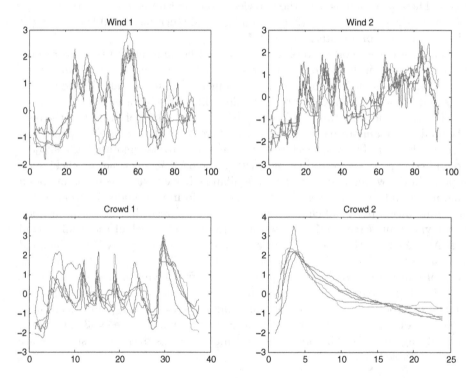

Fig. 4. All normalised subject annotations for each sound file over time [s].

We can see that there is a high concordance between subjects, except sometimes at the very beginning of some sounds, presumably due to a start-up effect (the slider was left in the previous position, and some subjects needed a fraction of a second to home in to the value they intended for the beginning of the sound).

4 Correlation Between Annotations and Descriptors

In this section, we will investigate if there is a correlation between the collected annotations and some audio descriptors. More precisely, we will extract the audio descriptors (or linear combinations of audio descriptors) that better correlate with the user-generated annotations.

4.1 Audio Descriptor Analysis

The 20 annotations collected in the preliminary subject test described in Sect. 3.2 were correlated with a large set of audio descriptors [12], covering temporal, spectral, perceptual, and harmonic signal qualities.

The descriptors were calculated with the IRCAMDESCRIPTOR library outputting 47 descriptors of up to 24D in up to 6 scaling variations in instantaneous and median-filtered versions, resulting in 437 numerical features. Figure 5 shows a subset of the descriptors for each of the 4 audio files.

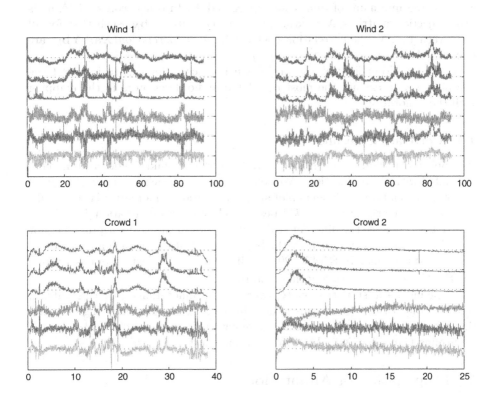

Fig. 5. Normalised descriptors for each sound file over time [s]. From top to bottom: *Loudness, Harmonic Energy, Noise Energy, Spectral Spread, Perceptual Spectral Slope, Spectral Centroid.*

4.2   Correlation Analysis

In order to get a first hint on what descriptors best represent the annotated quality of the sounds, canonical correlation analysis (CCA) was applied to the two data sets.

CCA is a common tool for investigating the linear relationships between two sets of variables in multidimensional reduction. In our case, the first (mono variate) set is the annotation (resampled and interpolated to the time base of the descriptors), and the second are the descriptors. Formally, if we let $\mathbf{X}$ and $\mathbf{Y}$ denote two datasets, CCA finds the coefficients of the linear combination of variables in $\mathbf{X}$ and the coefficients of the linear combination of variables from $\mathbf{Y}$ that are maximally correlated. The coefficients of both linear combinations are called *canonical weights* and operate as projection vectors. The projected variables are called *canonical components*. The correlation strength between canonical components is given by a correlation coefficient ρ. CCA operates similarly to Principal Component Analysis (PCA) in the sense that it reduces the dimension of both datasets by returning N canonical components for both datasets where N is equal to the minimum of dimensions in $\mathbf{X}$ and $\mathbf{Y}$. In other words, CCA finds two projection matrices $\mathbf{A} = [\mathbf{a}_1 \ldots \mathbf{a}_N]$ and $\mathbf{B} = [\mathbf{b}_1 \ldots \mathbf{b}_N]$ such that for all h between $1 \ldots N$, the correlation coefficients $\rho_h = correlation(\mathbf{X}\mathbf{a}_h, \mathbf{Y}\mathbf{b}_h)$ are maximised and ordered $(\rho_1 > \cdots > \rho_N)$.

Finally, a closer look at the projection matrices allows us to interpret the mapping, i.e. to extract the most correlated audio descriptors in the mapping with the annotation.

4.3   Correlation Results

We applied correlation analysis to our data in order to find the descriptors most correlated with the annotations. We collect the rank of each feature in the sorted vector of correlation coefficients ρ of all 20 annotations in a matrix $\mathbf{R}(437 \times 20)$, i.e. if $r_{ij} = k$, feature i has the kth best correlation with annotation j.

We then coalesce the different scaling variations of the 47 descriptors, i.e., for each descriptor, we conserve only the best ranked feature for each annotation in a coalesced rank matrix $\mathbf{R'}(47 \times 20)$, i.e. if $r'_{ij} = k$, *some* feature of descriptor i has the kth best correlation with annotation j.

Applying basic statistics on $\mathbf{R'}$ over the 20 annotations, given in Table 2, shows us that the 3 highest-ranked descriptors have a consistently high correlation with the annotations across the different audio files and different subjects, confirming Caramiaux's findings for environmental sounds [5].

5   Propagation of Annotations

When the environmental recording is long, as in use case 1, where rushes were used, annotating can be time consuming. To speed up the annotation process, we developed a method whereby a partial annotation can teach the system how to automatically annotate the rest of the recording.

Table 2. Best 8 ranked correlations between the 20 annotations and audio descriptors.

Descriptor	Mean rank	Stddev. of Rank	Min. Rank	Max. Rank
Loudness	1.95	1.47	1	5
Relative specific loudness	5.50	2.01	3	12
Harmonic energy	6.30	5.90	1	19
Noise energy	14.30	15.00	3	53
Harmonic tristimulus	23.45	22.27	3	71
Perceptual tristimulus	29.25	31.82	3	105
Perceptual spectral spread	33.10	24.15	13	113
Perceptual spectral slope	41.45	30.44	11	107

This propagation uses the partial annotation as training data to derive a mapping between annotation and audio descriptors, and applies the inverted mapping to the descriptors of the rest of the recording to reconstruct an annotation that can then be used to resynthesise the texture interactively as in Sect. 3. Of course, the part chosen by the human annotator should be representative of the whole recording.

5.1 Temporally Aligned Correlation Analysis

In our aim of propagating annotations, we have to take into account the fact that annotations and audio stimuli are not synchronised. This would consequently affect the correlation analysis and propagate errors over time (note that we will come back to this issue in the presentation of our experimentations). To deal with this issue, we propose here the use of an extension of CCA that includes a time warping in between both datasets. The technique is called *Canonical Time Warping* (CTW) [18,19].

Similarly to CCA, running canonical time warping returns projection matrices $\mathbf{V}_x, \mathbf{V}_x$. In addition CTW returns the alignment matrices $\mathbf{W}_y, \mathbf{W}_x$ from dynamic time warping, that are used for the reconstruction of the aligned CTW annotation from the descriptors: $\mathbf{R}_{CTW} = D\mathbf{V}_y\mathbf{V}_x^{-1}$.

5.2 Training of Annotation Propagation

We base the automatic propagation of the partial human annotation T, used to train the propagation method, and D, a normalised and median-smoothed subset of the audio descriptor data of the recording. The subset has been determined by the correlation analysis in Sect. 4 and contains 76 features from the 12 descriptors *Loudness, Harmonic Energy, Total Energy, Relative Specific Loudness, Noise Energy, MFCCs, Spectral Spread, Perceptual Spectral Spread, Spectral Slope, Perceptual Spectral Slope, Perceptual Spectral Centroid, Spectral Flatness*. D_t are the descriptors corresponding to the annotated segment.

We run CTW on the data and compute the reconstruction $\mathbf{R}_{CTW}$ as explained above. For the evaluation in Sect. 5.3, we also use CCA to reconstruct the annotation from descriptors: $\mathbf{R}_{CCA} = DBA^{-1}$, where $\mathbf{A}, \mathbf{B}$ are the projection matrices from CCA.

The reconstruction and evaluation is done per individual annotation of one sound by one user, since this is closest to the use case where one expert sound designer needs to work on one specific sound. Nevertheless, we'll examine in the following the statistical influence of various parameters of the reconstruction over all our 20 examples, to obtain recommendations of minimum training segment length and robustness.

5.3   Evaluation of Annotation Propagation

We will in this section evaluate the power of annotation propagation by cross-validation on the annotation data we collected, and compare it with CCA as baseline method.

We split each of the 20 annotations into a training segment T, apply CCA and CTW training on T and D_T, and reconstruct the annotations R_{CCA} and R_{CTW} from the audio descriptors D as described above.

This procedure is performed for 5 different lengths l_i of T of 5, 10, 20, 30 s and the whole length of the recording $l_5 = L$, and with 5 equally distributed starting positions s_i between 0 and $L - l_i$ for each length l_i, except for the whole length $l_5 = L$, where there is only $s_1 = 0$.

Two examples of original and reconstructed annotations are given in Figs. 6, 7, 8, 9, 10 and 11. Figures 6, 7 and 8 for recording *Wind 2* show the robustness of CCA and CTW when the segment length is $l_3 = 20$ s or more. They also show the "start-up effect" (see Sect. 3.3) of this particular annotator, that makes the reconstruction be less stable when trained at the beginning s_1. Figures 9, 10 and 11 show the more difficult example *Crowd 2*, where the prominent peak at the beginning makes the reconstruction over- or undershoot when trained outside of it, presumably because the annotated slope does not have the right relation between the peaky part and the decreasing part. That is a pathological case of not picking a representative segment to train the annotation. We can also see that CTW is clearly more robust to this difficulty than CCA.

For a quantitative evaluation, the reconstructed annotations are then compared to the whole annotation taken as ground truth using three comparison methods: the absolute global correlation c, the euclidean distance e, and the total DTW cost d.

First we aim at examining the influence of the factors segment length and start position on the reconstruction errors (given by c, e, d) from CCA and CTW. Figure 12 illustrates the influence of the training segment length and start position on these measures. We can see that the variability of the segment start diminishes or disappears from $l_3 = 20$ s onwards, and that CTW is always better or at least equal to CCA in terms of correlation.

To determine the effect of the two factors segment start position s_i and size l_i on the metrics between the reconstruction and the annotation under the

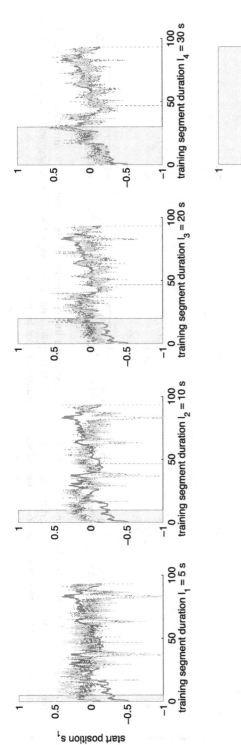

Fig. 6. CCA (dotted dark grey/red line) and CTW (dashed light grey/green line) reconstructions of one human annotation (solid middle grey/blue line) of the *Wind 2* example for different durations l_i and start positions s_1 of the training segment (visualised as grey rectangle). X-coordinates are in seconds, Y are normalised coordinates.

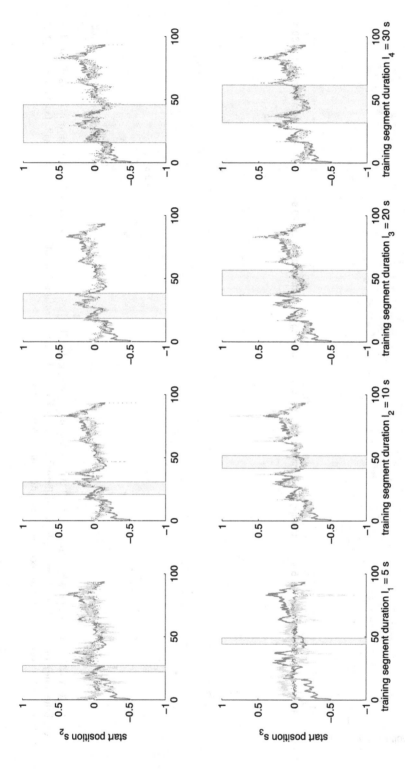

Fig. 7. CCA (dotted dark grey/red line) and CTW (dashed light grey/green line) reconstructions of one human annotation (solid middle grey/blue line) of the *Wind 2* example for different durations l_i and start positions s_2 and s_3 of the training segment (visualised as grey rectangle). X-coordinates are in seconds, Y are normalised coordinates (Color figure online).

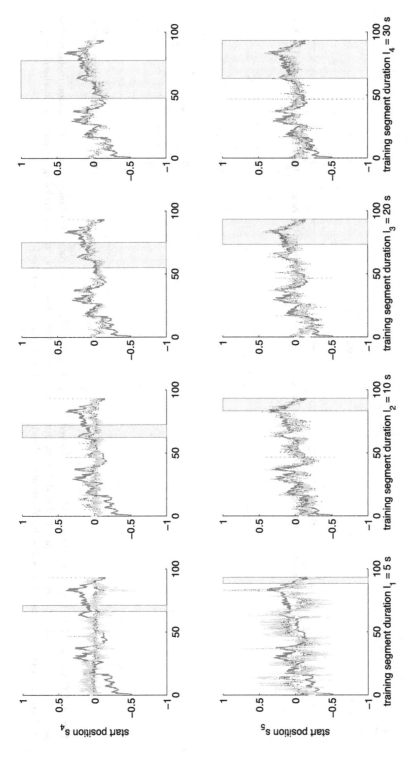

Fig. 8. CCA (dotted dark grey/red line) and CTW (dashed light grey/green line) reconstructions of one human annotation (solid middle grey/blue line) of the *Wind 2* example for different durations l_i and start positions s_4 and s_5 of the training segment (visualised as grey rectangle). X-coordinates are in seconds, Y are normalised coordinates (Color figure online).

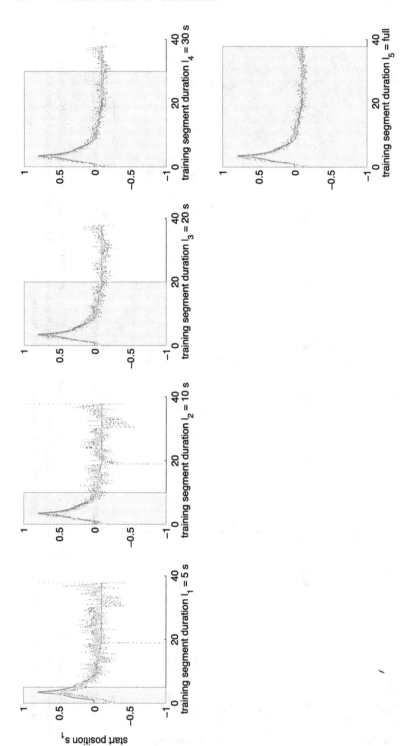

Fig. 9. CCA (dotted dark grey/red line) and CTW (dashed light grey/green line) reconstructions of one human annotation (solid middle grey/blue line) of the *Crowd 2* example for different durations l_i and start position s_1 of the training segment (visualised as grey rectangle). X-coordinates are in seconds, Y are normalised coordinates (Color figure online).

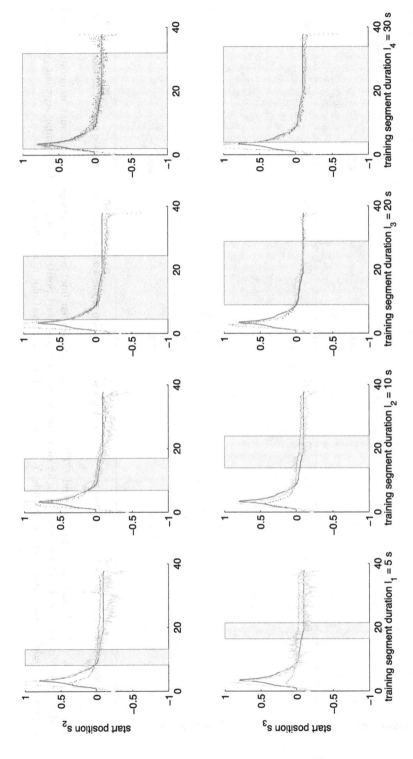

Fig. 10. CCA (dotted dark grey/red line) and CTW (dashed light grey/green line) reconstructions of one human annotation (solid middle grey/blue line) of the *Crowd 2* example for different durations l_i and start position s_2 and s_3 of the training segment (visualised as grey rectangle). X-coordinates are in seconds, Y are normalised coordinates (Color figure online).

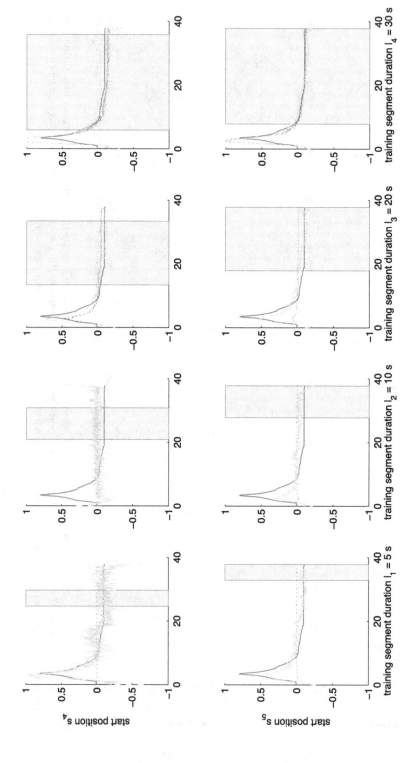

Fig. 11. CCA (dotted dark grey/red line) and CTW (dashed light grey/green line) reconstructions of one human annotation (solid middle grey/blue line) of the *Crowd 2* example for different durations l_i and start position s_4 and s_5 of the training segment (visualised as grey rectangle). X-coordinates are in seconds, Y are normalised coordinates (Color figure online).

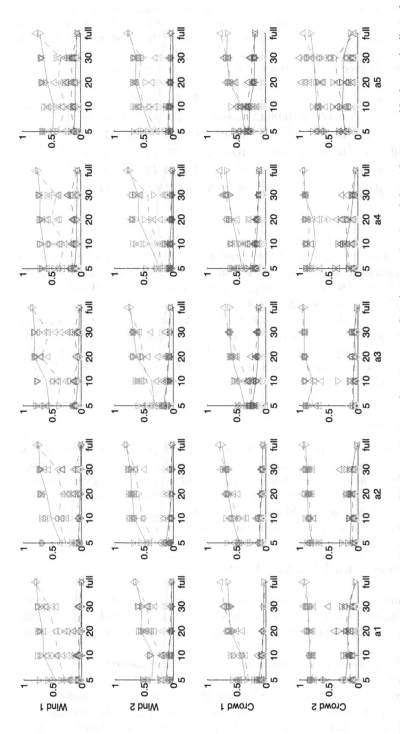

Fig. 12. Scatterplot and mean of absolute global correlation c (medium grey/blue), normalised euclidean distance e (dark grey/red), and normalised total DTW cost d (light grey/green) of CCA ($\triangle$, dashed line) and CTW ($\triangledown$, straight line) for training segment length l_i [s] (x-axis) and all segment start positions s_i (scatter) for all 20 annotations of the 4 sounds (rows) and by annotators a1...a5 (columns) (Color figure online).

Table 3. Mean metrics (global correlation c, euclidean distance e, total DTW cost d) of reconstruction over all data sets per training segment length l_i in seconds. Best values are in bold. The column h expresses the result of the t-test whether the null hypothesis (the means are equal) can be rejected with 5 % confidence ($\alpha = 0.05$). Note that the table only reports the h values (1 if $p < 0.05$, 0 otherwise).

l_i	c_{CCA}	c_{CTW}	h	e_{CCA}	e_{CTW}	h	d_{CCA}	d_{CTW}	h
5	0.45	**0.47**	0	**0.0042**	0.0044	0	484.96	**474.63**	0
10	0.46	**0.55**	1	0.0043	**0.0037**	0	**347.06**	397.17	0
20	0.59	**0.68**	1	0.0038	**0.0030**	1	**276.07**	319.76	0
30	0.65	**0.72**	1	0.0035	**0.0028**	1	**248.75**	289.53	0
all	0.84	**0.99**	1	0.0019	**0.0003**	1	232.63	**197.17**	0

two conditions CCA and CTW, we performed an ANOVA. The analysis shows that start position does not affect the correlation of the reconstruction with the ground truth annotation, but segment size influences significantly the correlation metric ($F(3, 792) = 97.5$, $p < 0.01$), and stabilises with the 20 s length (no significant difference between 20 and 30 s).

We further show the inequality between CCA and CTW for each segment size via Student's T-test. This test allows us to quantify if each mean metric differs significantly ($alpha = 0.05$) between the two conditions CCA or CTW. Its results are given in Table 3 and show that CTW is better except for the shortest segment.

5.4   Discussion

All these tests conclude that 20 s is a viable and surprisingly short length of annotation that allows to propagate the annotation to the rest of the recording. In addition, the starting position does not affect the reconstruction which means that it can be the beginning of the sound. This is in favour of our application context: a sound designer could annotate the 20 first seconds of a sound, and the method would propagate the annotation accurately.

6   Conclusion and Future Work

The evaluation and results reported here showed promising first results, encouraging us to believe that the method presented in this article could make a significant contribution to sound texture authoring for moving image or in interactive settings.

The results and feedback gathered in the subject test showed us a number of points to improve: First, one could observe a systematic and consistent lag in the annotation compared to the events in the sound (gusts of wind or climaxes in the crowd cheers), presumably due to the reaction time taken by the brain to go from perception to action, and also by a possible persistence of momentum (when to inverse the direction the annotation takes). In future work, this lag could be measured and corrected for in the lookup, thus improving control accuracy on resynthesis of textures.

In the resynthesis phase, several subjects were very apt in discovering what they considered "errors" in their annotation. This hints at giving the possibility to edit and refine the annotation interactively.

In future work, to streamline the exploration phase of the sound to be annotated, we could think of automatic selection of the n most diverse excerpts, to convey an idea of the extreme points for the annotation. This will be especially important for much longer recordings to be annotated.

The comparison of automatic propagation of the annotation by CCA versus CTW showed that CTW is more robust and needs less annotated training material than CCA. Already with surprisingly short 20 s human annotation can the rest of the recording be reliably automatically annotated.

Further questions concern the dimensionality of annotation. The one dimension of "strength" asked for was intuitively clear to every subject, but some tried to linearly include special features into the annotation (e.g. reserve a region of annotation values for the presence of horns in the crowd examples).

In a future version of the subject test, certain improvements should be applied: The questions of the subject test should all be the same scale (higher is better) or present randomised scales. Cross-subject listening tests on the resynthesised sound could remove a possible bias of the subject having produced the resynthesis.

Finally, a more systematic study of the most appropriate input device for annotation should be carried out. Candidates (with maximum dimensionality in parentheses) are the mouse on a slider or free movement (2D), digitizer tablets (2D and pressure) hardware faders (n × 1D), game controllers such as joystick or Wiimote (2D).

Acknowledgments. The work presented here is partially funded by the French *Agence Nationale de la Recherche* within the project *PHYSIS*, ANR-12-CORD-0006. The authors would like to thank Sarah, Alejandro, Jules, and Louis.

References

1. Caramiaux, B., Bevilacqua, F., Bianco, T., Schnell, N., Houix, O., Susini, P.: The role of sound source perception in gestural sound description. ACM Trans. on Applied Perception 11(1) (2014)
2. Caramiaux, B.: Studies on the gesture-sound relationship for musical performance. Ph.D. thesis, Université Pierre et Marie Curie (Paris 6), Paris (2012). http://articles.ircam.fr/textes/Caramiaux11f/
3. Caramiaux, B., Bevilacqua, F., Schnell, N.: Analysing gesture and sound similarities with a HMM-based divergence measure. In: Proceedings of the Sound and Music Computing Conference, SMC, vol. 11 (2010)
4. Caramiaux, B., Bevilacqua, F., Schnell, N.: Towards a gesture-sound cross-modal analysis. In: Kopp, S., Wachsmuth, I. (eds.) GW 2009. LNCS, vol. 5934, pp. 158–170. Springer, Heidelberg (2010). http://articles.ircam.fr/textes/Caramiaux09d/

5. Caramiaux, B., Susini, P., Bianco, T., Bevilacqua, F., Houix, O., Schnell, N., Misdariis, N.: Gestural embodiment of environmental sounds: an experimental study. In: New Interfaces for Musical Expression (NIME) (2011). http://articles. ircam.fr/textes/Caramiaux11a/
6. Hardoon, D.R., Szedmak, S., Shawe-Taylor, J.: Canonical correlation analysis: an overview with application to learning methods. Neural Comput. 16(12), 2639–2664 (2004)
7. Küssner, M.B., Leech-Wilkinson, D.: Investigating the influence of musical training on cross-modal correspondences and sensorimotor skills in a real-time drawing paradigm. Psychol. Music 42(3), 448–469 (2013)
8. Leman, M.: Embodied Music Cognition and Mediation Technology. MIT Press, Cambridge (2008)
9. Nymoen, K., Caramiaux, B., Kozak, M., Torresen, J.: Analyzing sound tracings–a multimodal approach to music information retrieval. In: ACM Multimedia, Workshop MIRUM (2011). http://articles.ircam.fr/textes/Nymoen11a/
10. Nymoen, K., Godøy, R.I., Jensenius, A.R., Torresen, J.: Analyzing correspondence between sound objects and body motion. ACM Trans. Appl. Percept. (TAP) 10(2), Articleno. 9 (2013)
11. Ohkushi, H., Ogawa, T., Haseyama, M.: Music recommendation according to human motion based on kernel CCA-based relationship. EURASIP J. Adv. Signal Process. 2011(1), 1–14 (2011)
12. Peeters, G.: A large set of audio features for sound description (similarity and classification) in the Cuidado project. Technical report version 1.0, IRCAM - Centre Pompidou, Paris, France, April 2004. http://www.ircam.fr/anasyn/peeters/ ARTICLES/Peeters_2003_cuidadoaudiofeatures.pdf
13. Schnell, N., Röbel, A., Schwarz, D., Peeters, G., Borghesi, R.: MuBu & friends - assembling tools for content based real-time interactive audio processing in Max/MSP. In: Proceedings of the International Computer Music Conference (ICMC), Montreal, Canada, Aug 2009
14. Schwarz, D.: Corpus-based concatenative synthesis. IEEE Signal Process. Mag. 24(2), 92–104 (2007). (Special Section: Signal Processing for Sound Synthesis)
15. Schwarz, D.: State of the art in sound texture synthesis. In: Proceedings of the COST-G6 Conference on Digital Audio Effects (DAFx), Paris, France, September 2011
16. Schwarz, D., Cahen, R., Hui, D., Jacquemin, C.: Sound level of detail in interactive audiographic 3D scenes. In: Proceedings of the International Computer Music Conference (ICMC), Huddersfield, UK (2011)
17. Schwarz, D., Schnell, N.: Descriptor-based sound texture sampling. In: Proceedings of the International Conference on Sound and Music Computing (SMC), Barcelona, Spain, pp. 510–515, July 2010
18. Zhou, F., De la Torre, F.: Canonical time warping for alignment of human behavior. In: Advances in Neural Information Processing Systems Conference (NIPS), December 2009
19. Zhou, F., De la Torre, F.: Generalized time warping for multi-modal alignment of human motion. In: IEEE Conference on Computer Vision and Pattern Recognition (CVPR) (2012)

Intonaspacio: A Digital Musical Instrument for Exploring Site-Specificities in Sound

Mailis G. Rodrigues[1,2](✉), Marcelo M. Wanderley[2], and Paulo F. Lopes[1]

[1] CITAR - School of Arts, UCP,
Rua Diogo Botelho, n. 1327, 4169-005 Porto, Portugal
mailisr@gmail.com, pflopes@porto.ucp.pt
[2] IDMIL - CIRMMT, McGill University,
527 Sherbrooke st. West, Montreal, QC H3A 1E3, Canada
marcelo.wanderley@mcgill.ca

Abstract. The integration of space as a parameter in the composition of an art work as been relegated to a secondary role. Site-specific art is a branch of the visual arts whose main goal is to fuse space in the art work, i.e., the piece belongs to the space where it is placed and its meaning is lost once it is removed. There's an idea of bi-directionality beneath the conception of the work, where space defines the perception of the piece and the piece interferes in the perception of space.

In music and especially in sound art, there are some examples of site-specific works, but they are sparse and mainly centered on the idea of installation. Site-specificity in sound is an open and not yet fully explored field. Our research purposes a new digital musical instrument (DMI) Intonaspacio, which allows the access to the sound of the room, and the integration of it in the music in real time. Intonaspacio provides the performer with tools to create site-specific sound, i.e., to integrate space as part of the creative work.

In this paper we present Intonaspacio, focusing attention on the design of the physical interface. Up until now we have designed two versions of Intonaspacio. From the first version to the second one, we have modified the material of the frame, which led us to reconsider some of our previous decisions on the choice of sensors and their placement. We also designed different mappings that present several approaches to the site-specific question.

Keywords: Musical interfaces · Gestural control of sound synthesis · Motion and gesture

1 Introduction

Bachelard [4] presented the relation between sound and place as being responsible for defining the boundaries of a place. Silence would represent an infinite space, while sound would limit and confine. Hence, sound would give us the means to transform space in an adjustable place - whose boundaries were contracted

© Springer International Publishing Switzerland 2014
M. Aramaki et al. (Eds.): CMMR 2013, LNCS 8905, pp. 393–415, 2014.
DOI: 10.1007/978-3-319-12976-1_24

or expanded depending on the existence or non existence of sound. Place would redesign itself, perceptually speaking, along with the sound present in the room.

One of the characteristics of sound is to inform us about space. Muecke [24] reinforces this idea by stating that "the reverberation of sound in space and the quality of reflected sound, both affected by geometry, proportion and material - in other words, by architecture - could considerably enrich the sense of volume and space". Low and high frequencies give different perceptual images of space and contribute to modulate the boundaries of a place.

Carpenter [9] insists in these same ideas, when he refers that the auditory space (the space defined by the range of sound perceptible to our ears), "It's a sphere without fixed boundaries, space made the thing itself, not space containing the thing. (...) dynamic, always in flux, creating it's own dimensions moment by moment. It has no fixed boundaries". Carpenter justifies this volatility of auditory space based on the ear's characteristic of having a wide range of attention. Similarly, Labelle [19] understands sound as a something that can grant us access to space - what we listen in a place is in reality a convolution between the original sound and the response of the room, "as the wave travels, it is charged by each interaction with the environment" (Barry Truax cited in [19]).

The questions raised by this relationship (sound - place) are not new. Several thinkers and artists have already raised questions that relate sound to space. Although we still observe that there is a lack of music pieces where space is more than a physical parameter (adapting the acoustics of a room for a specific task), but truly a creative parameter in sound and music composition.

2 Prior Work - Place and Sound Interactions

The 20th century has a some examples where this assimilation of space in sound and music creation is present. This is obtained in different directions. First, by opening the musical range of what is consider musical. Daily life sounds are increasingly introduced in music. We can no longer remain in the classic concept of music [19], nor rely on the same traditional palette of musical sounds [8,30–32]. Second, composers search more and more for unusual performance places, different from the usual concert hall. For example, Erik Satie [36] in 1917 proposes the *Musique d'Ameublement*. Also, John Cage composed for Muzak [34], a system for music ambiance in public spaces such as restaurants, elevators, hotel lobbies, etc., places where the goal is to discretely disseminate music through speakers installed in the space.

Finally, composers search for new architectures for the concert hall, more suitable for the music they compose. The Phillips Pavilion at the Expo 58 at Brussels, designed by Le Corbusier and Xenaquis for the public presentation of *Poèmes Electroniques* from Edgar Varèse, is a good example. Another one is the German pavilion at the Expo Osaka in 1970, the first spherical concert hall, where the intention was that the audience could have an immersive experience with the sound. Stockhausen explains the sensation he sought for the audience:

"To sit inside the sound, to be surrounded by the sound, to be able to follow and experience the movement of the sounds, their speeds and forms in which they move: all this actually creates a completely new situation for musical experience." (Stockhausen cited in [18]).

In this last example, Stockhausen is referring to the spatialisation of sound. There is usually a mingling between the concepts of spatialisation and site-specific sound. Our research however, does not deal directly with spatilisation questions. Site-specific sound is not translated by spatialisation, they are actually placed at opposite moments in the sound creation process. Sound spatialisation refers to the output of the sound, it is the design of the space as the way sound will travel in it, as Nunes [25] explains: "spatialisation is oriented perception". Several techniques exist nowadays to perform sound spatialisation (wavefield synthesis, ambisonics and so on) but the majority is applied at the end of the sound chain, with few exceptions [33].

Site-specific relate to the input of space in sound. The aim of site-specific art is to incorporate place and its characteristics within the sound art work. Thus, it cannot be added after the composition of the sound, since when sound is generated it already incorporates place characteristics.

Despite the fact that sound spatialisation and place-specific sound art are considerably different procedures on sound creation, they are not mutually exclusive. *Quodlibet*, a music piece composed by Emmanuel Nunes is a good example on how to combine both methods. This piece was composed exclusively to be performed at Coliseu dos Recreios at Lisbon, where he benefits from the acoustics of the room to perform a spatialisation of the sound. Nunes understands how each instrument propagates its sound in space and in which way the acoustics of the room will influence the timbre of the instruments. By placing the musicians around the concert hall, Nunes creates a relation between several elements - the distance the audience is from each instrument, the way each instrument diffuses in the room, and finally, the different reverberations each location in the Coliseu generates [25]. Nunes defines place as an ensemble of micro-specifities; acoustic characteristics that are particular to each location - propagation, amplitude, distance, direction, timber, filter, levels of recognition of the sound location and so on. These compose a filter or an envelope of "hauteurs et/ou de rythmes"[1], that defines what he calls the *Espace composable*.

Labelle [19] refers that sound must be inherently site-specific since it is always the result of a reflection within place and bears a portrait of it. Sound is "boundless on one hand and site-specific in another".

In Background Noise, Labelle presents an extensive review on site-specific sound art. From it we can deduce several ways to integrate space in sound, we will refer to some, as they somehow inspired us to design the mapping for Intonaspacio.

---

[1] "Pitch and/or rhythmns". Translated by the author.

2.1 Silence as an Open Door for Place

John Cage presents silence as the ensemble of non-intentional sounds, i.e., sounds that are not produced by a performer. Silence represents, according to Bachelard [4] the epitome of the connection between daily life and music, trough it we have access to the architecture of the place. Silence is the ensemble of found sounds, and 4'33" the silent composition of Cage [8,17], is actually an *assemblage d'objets trouvés*. The composition enables the listener to perceive place, by listening to the sounds that are associated to it, without any intervention by the performer. Cage refers that silence and sound share the same features, both have five characteristics: pitch, amplitude, timber, duration and morphology. Together they define a position of a sound of what Cage specifies as a "total sound-space" [8], a space composed of sounds with the boundaries fixed by the ear. To change one parameter in any sound is to alter its position in space.

2.2 Where Sound Meets Acoustic

Michel Ascher's work [3,19] searches to fuse the sounds that are present outside and inside the room within the art work. Ascher modifies the architecture of the room as to enable the sounds, the lights and the air flow from outside to enter the room, and once inside, place is modified in such a way that it amplifies or absorbs the exterior elements (using walls with dumping properties, or sound generators tuned to resonate with the room, playing with white and black walls to reflect or absorb light, and so on). By acting on the acoustics of the room, he fully integrates place in the work. As Labelle suggests, Ascher construct his installations with "the found environment as sound-producing source" [19]. Michel Ascher continues the approach of Cage, he also uses silence as the material of his installations, but at the same time he extends it, introducing the use of acoustic phenomena to direct the viewer to place itself.

2.3 Listening to Place

In 1969 Alvin Lucier presents his sound installation *I am sitting in a room* [19]. The work consists in Lucier's voice recorded while he reads a text where he explains the procedure of the work itself. The act of recording the same speech over and over again in space, will corrupt the initial recorded sound little by little, until we are no longer able to discern Lucier's voice. We rather ear a slow, low pitch melody where only the rhythm of the speech prevails. Lucier ground this work in an acoustic phenomena where the resonant frequencies of the room are excited by his voice. It is a process in time as well as in space. Feedback helps to notice the filtering effect of place, the physical action of space on sound.

Since his early works, Lucier has been interested in spatial issues, namely this blend between acoustics and music [11]. He creates these sounding spaces, where a precarious equilibrium is achieved between the several elements of the work (place, sound, viewer), and the smallest change cause "the space to sound" [11].

Lucier's work no longer uses silence (non-intentional generated sound) as a material for his music, like Cage or even Ascher, instead we produces sound hints that trigger a response from place. He crossed the frontier to acoustics, Labelle [19] calls these sounds, the inherent sounds of the room, the resonant frequencies that are dependent of the architectural structure of the room. Both the sound works are movable from one place to another, but the connection with place is not lost with the relocation. The work is the same but the sound result is different because one of the parameters in the creation has changed.

2.4   Place - A Musical Instrument

Sound art demonstrates that there is an unbreakable link between sound and place. Both influence each other. Still, we perceive in some works a more solid presence of place, where we understand its own sounds. A room has an inner spectrum that amplifies and absorbs certain frequencies. When amplified these are audible and can be used as musical content. Consequently, place can be understood as a musical instrument of its own, with a sound generator and a resonator system. Still, these qualities are hard to control and to integrate in the sound work without easily fall in uncontrollable feedback. Thus, we purpose the utilization of a digital musical instrument (DMI) as a mediator between performer and place, in order to give control to the former over place. A DMI that would extent the possibilities of place.

3   Intonaspacio

Intonaspacio, Fig. 1, is a DMI that enables the integration of space as a composition parameter. It allows the performer to record the ambient sound of the room, including the noises produced by the audience, the instruments from other performers and the resonance modes of the room, as well as it detects the most predominant frequencies in the room. Intonaspacio has a ball shape built with a set of arcs connected to each other in two points (top and bottom of the sphere). This frame is covered by fabric, that acts as a skin or a membrane of the instrument. At the center is a platform with a set of different sensors that allow the performer to modulate the sound and control some parameters of a sound synthesis algorithm. These provide more control over the generated sound and improve the level of expressiveness of the instrument.

Intonaspacio is not a self-contained instrument, it works coupled with a computer. Intonaspacio sends wireless the ensemble of signals generated by the sensors to the computer. Here the data is analyzed and each extracted featured is mapped to control a certain sound parameter.

3.1   Playing Music with a Ball

One of the main reasons this design is commonly used is because it is a known object, thus easy to interact with. People have previous knowledge on how to

Fig. 1. Intonaspacio

manipulate the object and what to expect from it. A ball has a playful function, is commonly used in games, thus it is easy getting people to interact with it.

There are a number of DMIs that use a ball shape [1,2,5–7,12,14,23,27, 35,39–41]. This shape is usually used to design collaborative musical instrument, where two or more performers can play the instrument at the same time. The idea of collaboration is visible in the type of gestures performed with this instruments - throwing the instrument between performers [40,41]; and also in the kind of activities it is used - to apply data sonification to collective sports like soccer or basketball ball [14,27].

When designing a DMI with a ball shape, it is important to look for a weightless and resistant material. A ball, always inspires gestures like throw, roll, dribble, among others. Several different materials are used to shape the instrument, the most common is plastic [2,5–7,23,39], some use sponge [40], and others use fabric [12,41], however not as a sensitive part of the instrument as in Intonaspacio. Another main concern on this design is the easiness of access to the sensors, and their stability. The sensors must be in a stable position in order to read correctly. Finally, it is important that the instrument can be wireless, especially if the interface is thought to be shared or played by more than one person at a time. Two main solutions are used: bluetooth [40] and radio frequency transmission [2,23,39].

Common to all these DMIs is the use of a 3-axis accelerometer to calculate orientation, tilt and shock (when the instrument is thrown away). A ball doesn't have necessarily a visual clue to distinguish top and bottom, front and back. This can become a tricky question, concerning orientation. In Intonaspacio, this identification is made by using visual clues, to play it correctly the performer must hold the instrument with the IR sensor facing him. Orientation usually controls continuous parameters of the sound.

Piezoelectric sensors are also widely used to calculate percussive gestures, and as sound triggers [7,41], sometimes this sensors are coupled with an FSR

(Force Sensitive Resistor) that measures the surface deformation [12,14]. Two of the DMIs we studied use haptic feedback [6,14] using devices that produce small vibrations that are sensed by the performer, through its skin.

Some examples use IR to calculate distance [23,39] but only one of them uses the distance between the body and the instrument as in Intonaspacio.

Intonaspacio has fairly different goals from these DMIs, and looks for a different combination of gestures. First, it is a musical instrument to be played by one performer only. The combination of sensors used in our design gives more complexity and expressivity to the instrument, because the interface has more sensitive areas and a larger number of freedom degrees. Also, none of the previous DMIs look for the integration of space as a creative parameter for composition. Finally, in Intonaspacio we have integrated the whole structure as part of the instrument, i.e., the whole instrument is sensitive to the performers gestures. We achieved that by placing the sensors in specific locations where we could get a larger sensing area.

3.2   Frame and Gestural Acquisition

To design the frame of Intonaspacio we looked for a material that was strong enough to get us a stable structure for the sensors, since some are fragile. We also had to devise a stable platform for the sensors. Stability is very important, especially for the inertial sensors, were readings can be severe affected. For that reason our concern was to have a central base that would support all the electronic apparatus. This base is mounted in the middle of the sphere. Finally, we had to provide easy access to the central board for circumstance where we would need to change batteries, remove sensors, cables, wires or correct connections. This is particularly important in a performance situation where one must be able to quickly solve any technical problem. Whence the use of fabric to cover the instrument that works as a removable skin with an opening who granted direct access to the main electronic area in Intonaspacio.

We have designed two versions of Intonaspacio. The major difference between the two versions is the material that we use for the frame. In the first version, we use strips of plastic, commonly used to design corsets and cage skirts; and for the second version we use Commercially Pure Titanium (Ticp). This gives us a greater stability while preserving the lightness of the instrument. In Figs. 2 and 3 you can compare both versions.

The sensors we use in Intonaspacio, were chosen according to a set of movements inferred by the shape itself. In Fig. 4, you can see some of this movements, namely orientation of the instrument in space, impact on the surface and distance from the instrument to the body of the performer.

Orientation. To calculate orientation of Intonaspacio we used the Mongoose 9 Dof, an IMU board developed by CkDevices [10]. An IMU is a device that combines several inertial sensors: accelerometers, magnetometers and gyroscopes. Combining them prevents drift errors that are common when just one sensor is used; and allow the measurement of orientation in the three euler angles - pitch,

Fig. 2. Intonaspacio: Version 1 (structure)

Fig. 3. Intonaspacio: Version 2 (structure)

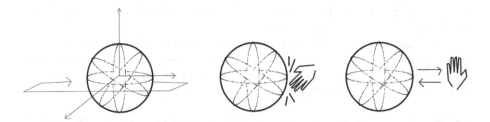

Fig. 4. Intonaspacio: sensed movements (from left to right - orientation, impact and distance).

yaw and roll. The Mongoose board has embedded a 3-axis accelerometer, a 3-axis gyroscope and a 3-axis magnetometer. The output values are already combined by the firmware included on the board. We have, however, access to the raw data of the sensors.

With this IMU we are able to know in real-time at what direction the performer is pointing the instrument. However, since Intonaspacio is ball, the directionality is not clear, because a sphere doesn't have a top/bottom, front/back defined. To compensate for this problem, in version 1, we added visual clues in the skin (fabric that covers the structure) of Intonaspacio that clearly indicates to the performer the directions in the instrument. In version 2, the fabric does not cover the whole instrument, leaving the front open and thus indicating the front of Intonaspacio.

Impact. Percussive gestures bring great possibilities in the design of a musical instrument. To sense impact, shock or vibration several methods can be used. One of them is using an accelerometer to calculate impact or vibration (high frequencies in the accelerometer signal). Another technique is the use of piezoelectric sensors. Intonaspacio has two different piezoelectric sensors, which differ in the shape and sensitivity. This way we intended to create several sensitive zones introducing more degrees of freedom in the manipulation of the instrument. Each sensor has a complementary limiting circuit proposed by Maloch [20] for the T-stick [21], to prevent it from output voltages above 5V. One of the piezoelectric sensors, that we will, refer to as Piezo 1 has a disc shape. The second piezoelectric sensor, Piezo 2, is a tiny film with a small mass at the end, this characteristic make it more responsive than Piezo 1 to small vibrations Figs. 5 and 6. Both sensors were placed in opposite arcs. They present some sensitiveness to actions on neighbor arcs, this characteristic increases the sensing area.

Fig. 5. Piezoelectric disc

Fig. 6. Piezoelectric film with mass

Distance. To calculate distance, in version 1 of Intonaspacio, we used two different sensors: an infrared sensor (IR) and a bend sensor. In the second version of the instrument, since the material of the structure does not present the same bendable characteristics as the one used in the first version, we did not used the bend sensor. Intonaspacio uses a Sharp GP2D120 mounted at the center of the sphere facing the performer. Our first option was to cover the entire surface of the instrument with fabric. However, the IR sensor presents some sensibility to changes in opacity. We performed some tests in order to understand the response of the sensor. Fabrics were chosen according to two main characteristics: the height - it had to have some height in order to be rigid enough as to keep the shape when the instrument was hit by the performer; and the opacity - it had to have some degree of translucence, in order to enable a wide range of measurements with the IR sensor.

We chose two cotton fabrics for the first version of Intonaspacio. One white, very translucent, and one yellow somewhat translucent. We observed how different were the response of the sensor for each situation - white fabric, yellow fabric, both combined. Tests showed that the response was quite similar between the two fabrics, but the combination of the two outputted substantially different values. The idea, then, was to create a combination of these two options creating two zones of different sensibility. Despite our measurement, this solution did not reveal to be very interesting. Thus in version 2, we opted by leaving the IR sensor without any obstacle, (Fig. 7). This decision led to new ways of grabbing the instrument.

Pressure. The motivation behind the decision of covering the frame of Intonaspacio with fabric was based on the possibility of having a tunable instrument. Fabric would be the skin or membrane of Intonaspacio. The performer could adjust the stiffness and consequently change the overall pitch of the sound of the

Fig. 7. Intonaspacio version 2. Detail.

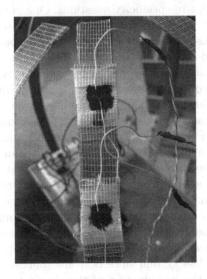

Fig. 8. Fabric sensor

instrument. We decided to implement a Force-sensitive Resistor (FSR) textile sensor in Intonaspacio, Fig. 8. The sensor was inspired by Wilson [26] recipe, made with homemade conductive ink, combining graphite and nail polish. The sensor presented a very good response. We wanted this sensor to be the size of a finger pulp, thus we designed smaller sensors and glued them to some of the arcs of the instrument. When installed, however, they revealed several weaknesses. In version 2 we still did not have found a good design solution to implement these.

Fig. 9. Binaural microphone

4   Getting Access to Space

Our research deals with site-specificity questions. One of our biggest challenges is how to actually have access to space in order to create site-specific sounds. Technically speaking the most direct path to introduce space in sound is using a microphone that records the sound ambiance of the room. We can then provide two ways of feeding space in sound, direct and indirect. A direct process is the one that consists in recording these sounds and reproducing them immediately afterwards. Whereas the indirect method implies an analysis of the captured sound, in order to extract a spectrum analysis of the room. Several techniques can be used like FFT (Fast Fourier Transform), convolution or spectral density.

For the first version of Intonaspacio, we designed an homemade binaural microphone, Fig. 9. The motivation for using a binaural technique related to the possibility of having a stereo image of the sound present in the room[2]. Intonaspacio would behave like an autonomous entity that listens to the space. We used two condenser microphone capsules with an omnidirectional pattern, spaced about 30 cm (the diameter of the sphere) and sewed in the cover of the instrument. This approach had some limitations, namely the impossibility of having a complete wireless system since both microphones need to be supplied with a 3 volts charge (the introduction of the circuit to feed the microphones would cause an undesired increasing on the weight of the instrument).

We opt for using a wireless microphone. This microphone is set up at the central platform of the instrument and is connected to a FM transmitter. It has an omnidirectional pattern and a fairly flat response in all the audible frequency range. The main goal was to have an even recording of the sound, with no particular amplification over a set of frequencies. This microphone also has some limitations, especially because it has to be tuned to a frequency that most of the time introduces noise in the sound. Each time the performer uses the instrument

---

[2] By present in the room we mean the sound ambiance of the room as well as the resonant frequencies of the room as defined by Labelle [19].

in a different room it is always necessary to calibrate the FM receiver. Another limitation is the noise introduced by the antenna that is in contact with all the metallic parts of the structure of Intonaspacio. Besides the performer needs to find a good position where the instrument captures the signal with a higher signal-to-noise ratio, which can be stressful for him. We are still performing tests as to find a better solution for the microphone.

4.1 Future Design

We have performed some changes to this design (version 2.2). We clustered together the electronics at the center of the sphere and divided the central platform into a two-stage platform, in order to better distribute the weight of the components. In the top platform we placed the sensors that requires regular access (changing battery, turning on and off, and so on).

We are currently preparing a third version of the hardware, in collaboration with the visual artist Mario Ângelo. This new version would be substantially different from the previous ones. The ball shape will be kept, but it will be structured as a modular shape, where every piece is printed in 3-D printer. Intonaspacio would have an internal sphere where all the electronic apparatus would be stored, and the sensors would be less accessible to the performer (it will have special cases to place each sensor and the wires will pass inside the hoops that connect the structure). This would allow for a greater protection of the sensors. In this version we will not use fabric to cover the instrument, mainly due to aesthetically reasons. In Fig. 10 you can see the 3-D model of version 3 of Intonaspacio.

Fig. 10. Intonaspacio version 3 (3-D model).

5 Mapping Strategies

Mapping is the element where gesture and sound parameters are combined in different relations. The associations between both parameters - control and sound generation, are arbitrary, and only dependent of the intention of the DMI's designer. Two types of mapping approaches are possible: generative mapping, and "explicit mapping techniques" [15].

Explicit mapping techniques are relations created by the designer of the instrument that relate control gestures to sound generation and modulation parameters. These can be of several types:

- One-to-one (A variable in ensemble 1 corresponds to a change in a variable in ensemble 2)
- One-to-many (A variable in ensemble 1 corresponds to a change in several variables in ensemble 2 - Divergent [28,29])
- Many-to-one (Several variables in ensemble 1 corresponds to a change in a variable in ensemble 2 - Convergent mapping [28,29])
- Many-to-many (Several variables in ensemble 1 corresponds to a change in several variables in ensemble 2)

There is a trend in the design of digital musical instruments to opt for simple mappings, where one-to-one strategies are used [15]. Designers tend to establish simple connections where the effect of the gesture is immediately perceived by the performer. However, this strategy presents several weaknesses, in a long term usage of the DMI. Lack of expressivity is the most evident.

In an acoustic musical instrument several parameters contribute to a change in the sound - convergent techniques are the most common. Hunt [15,16] exemplifies with the violin where the speed of the bow, the pressure, the string played and the position of the finger, all together contribute to control the intensity of the sound. Similarly, several authors [16,29,38] demonstrate that complex mappings are more expressive than simple mappings. Thus performers are more inclined to explore this DMIs and feel more engaged and interested in it [13,15]. Comprehensibly this situation leads to a longer learning time and to an increased frustration, specially in an initial stage of the exploration.

Another reason to design complex mappings is to opt for different relations than a direct proportion from the extracted feature of the gestural layer and the sound parameter in the synthesis algorithm. One can construct derivatives relations, where the rate of change in the input controls the output, or an integrational one, where the history of the input controls the output. Combining these three options (PID theory - proportiona-integral-derivative [13]) contributes to a more complex mapping with more available options.

Mappings can balance expressivity and complexity with a simpler approach which enables the performer to understand, without greater difficulty, the behavior of the instrument. Some DMIs, especially the ones that replicate an acoustic instrument (its shape rather than its playing technique), take advantage from the performer's previous knowledge on how to manipulate these instruments. Some others, as Intonaspacio, suggest a combination of gestures because the shape is familiar. Complex mappings also benefit from the use of high level language. Instead of controlling frequency and amplitude, for example, the mapping can enable the control of timbre [21], the DMI would result in a interface that could control and modulate timbral spaces [37]. Maloch [21] suggests the subdivision of mapping in several layers where the gestural acquisition would be separated from the sound synthesis parameters and in-between would exist a semantic layer where these abstractions would take place[3]. If we have generic features that are extracted from the instrument, and at the same time generic parameters in the synthesis algorithm, is simpler to create dynamic mappings. It also facilitates the use of different synthesis algorithms controlled by one DMI and vice-versa [22].

We had mainly two goals when designing the mapping to Intonaspacio: one, the integration of space in the sound process, and second, the creation of a musical expressive instrument. Following Maloch [21] suggestion, we created distinct layers on the mapping. One layer for the gestural interface and a second one for the sound synthesis algorithm. This separation was necessary to make a clear distinction between the extracted features from the performers gestures and the sound generation. In our perspective the gestural acquisition should be a closed section of the DMI, i.e., the mapping is not changeable, for consistency reasons. It is hard enough for a performer to learn a new instrument, he does not need to be faced with a different instrument every week. Also, and since in our work, we collaborated with some composers, that do not necessarily need to know the electronics and the programming that is behind the operation of Intonaspacio, it was mandatory to have a fixed set of parameters with which they could work with.

Most of the signals extracted from the sensors were noisy. Hence, the first step was to smooth the output signal, pulling out an average signal. Except for the IR, all signals outputted from the sensors were somehow "cooked" - they had to be transposed to values more suitable to work with[4]. We used Max/MSP to process the signals and to design the sound synthesis, and Libmaper [22] to create the mappings. Libmapper allows for dynamically change between different mappings, which made it easier to test with several options of mapping.

6   Interacting with Intonaspacio

The interaction process in Intonaspacio was somehow inspired by the same mechanisms that underlie the experience with an acoustic instrument - there must be a transmission of energy from the performer to the musical instrument and this energy must be, in some way, reflected in the generated sound. These relations in Intonaspacio were made by the analysis of the incoming signal (rate of variation, amplitude of the signal, integration and so on). We also attributed functions of

---

[3] By abstractions Maloch refers to the transformation of the extracted features in meaningful actions. For example if the signal of an accelerometer presents high frequencies and high amplitude, one can associate it to jerky movements. By creating these abstractions it is easier to others than the designer to create mappings with the DMI.

[4] In Max/MSP the amplitude of sound must be between 0. and 1., else it will be distorted, hence signals that control this variable must be confined to this range.

excitation and dumping to specific gestures - strike one of the piezoelectric sensors would initiate a sound with the same amplitude as the one reported by the sensor (the stronger the impact, the louder the sound). Obstruct the IR will dump the sound, and eventually stop it according to the time the performer rests with the instrument in the same position.

We designed two initial mappings with two different approaches of integrating space in the generated sound. Mapping 1 would allow the recording of sound ambiance samples, these could be reproduced generating a loop of sound that would excite the resonant frequencies of the room that work as a filter on some of the parameters of the sound file. In mapping 2, space acts indirectly, extracting some features of the incoming sound that are used to control several parameters of the sound synthesis algorithm. In Figs. 11 and 12 is presented a schema that shows both approaches.

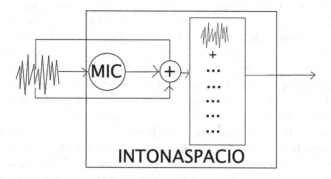

Fig. 11. Different approaches to space integration in sound (sample recording) - mapping 1

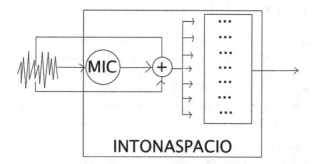

Fig. 12. Different approaches to space integration in sound (FFT analysis) - mapping 2

Piezoelectric Sensors. The output signal from the piezoelectric sensors informs when the sensor is struck and how intense. This information, as we explained before, is used in Piezo 1, to initiate the sound with an amplitude which is proportional to the amplitude of its output. Additionally, we also extracted the number of times both sensors were taped, and the velocity of each strike, i.e., how fast each sensor reached its maximum amplitude, these features can be combined with the amplitude to help us perceive the intensity of the strike.

Piezo 1 and piezo 2 are both used as triggers. We have also add a sequential triggering where the performer needs to strike sequentially both sensors. This feature was introduced by Clayton Mamedes as part of the mapping of Entoa, one of the musics composed for Intonaspacio.

Accelerometer. The accelerometer is used to detect impact on the surface - jab (jerky movements) and regular taping on the surface of the instrument. In order to detect jab, we add up the signal of the three-axes accelerometer (x, y and z) and analyze the amplitude of the signal. If it exceeds a certain threshold, then the system reports a jab gesture. This detection method is, however, not completely reliable. A better process would be to perform an analysis of the frequency of the signal of the accelerometer - hi-frequency would represent jab movements, and low-frequency tilt movements. These would prevent misrepresentations of jab gestures.

Infra Red. The output signal of the IR give us information about the distance to the body or hand of the performer. We then separate the signal into three zones that correspond to three distances: far, close and covered. After it, we integrate the values collected at each zone, and we were able to know how much time the instrument was kept in the same zone. This led us to map the IR signal to the overall amplitude of the sound. By changing the distance towards his/her body, the performer can alter the intensity of the sound played. If the performer keeps the instrument close enough to his body by a certain amount of time, he/she can also dump the sound and eventually stop it, when a fixed time threshold is reached.

Pitch, Roll and Yaw. Finally, the IMU unit allows us to extract the euler angles - pitch, roll and yaw. These are used to control different parameters in the sound, namely some sound effects such as reverberation, speed of reproduction or spatialisation variables. These, depend mostly on the chosen mapping. In mapping 2 some of the parameters are controled by the extracted frequencies of the sound input analysis.

7   Looking for an Instrumental Technique

We are currently trying to understand if we can extract a set of common gestures when playing Intonaspacio. This would allows us to establish the basis of an instrumental technique of Intonaspacio, as well as defining a gestural grammar for musical notation (Table 1).

We have performed an experiment at CIRMMT, at McGill University, to understand the experience users had with the interface and the relation of

Table 1. Features extracted from Intonaspacio

Sensor	Features
P1	trigger
	amplitude
P2	trigger
	amplitude
P1 + P2	sequential trigger
Accelerometer	jab
IMU	yaw
IMU	pitch
IMU	roll
Accelerometer	gesture amplitude (x axis)
IMU	change in yaw
IMU	change in pitch
IMU	change in roll
IR	time spent
IR	amplitude
accelerometer	variation rate
Mic	frequencies

Intonaspacio with place (how perceptible it is, how does it change the performance of each user, and so on). The test included three trials where the participants could play freely with Intonaspacio, around the room. Each trial had a correspondent mapping. The three mappings contained different ways of integrating place in sound. Mapping 1 would allow the user to record samples of the sound ambiance of the room and reproduced it in a loop. Mapping 2 performs an indirect integration of place in sound, the sound input is analyzed and the fifteen most present frequencies in the sound are extracted. The instrument performs a rough acoustic room analysis that changes over time and with the sounds that interact in space. Thus, if the performer generates other sounds, such as vocal sounds, tapping on surfaces, etc., these will affect the reading in the room analysis. This intrusion is highly desirable, we believe it can create interesting relations between the three actors of this interaction - performer, place and musical instrument. The extracted data was mapped to control some of the sound parameters in a Max/MSP patch (time of reverberation, modulation frequency). Finally, mapping 3 did not include any form of place integration, the goal was to understand if users would prefer integration of place in sound against no integration at all.

We recorded the data outputted from all the sensors at each trial, and recorded a video from each participant. The video will help us to analyze the gestures each participant uses the most. We are looking at similarities between mappings (the same participant would have a gestural consistency between each trial) and participants (the same gesture pattern would be repeated by more than one user).

Subjects also had to answer to a questionnaire, at the end of the test. The questionnaire was divided into two main subjects: interface and site-specificity of Intonaspacio. With regard to interface, questions centered around the usability of Intonaspacio - sensation of control, easiness of manipulation, repeatability of behavior and so on. The second part of the survey centered most on the perception and interest of integration of place in sound.

8 Composing a Repertoire

In addition to defining an instrumental technique for Intonaspacio, we are also trying to collaborate with composers and musicians with the purpose of assembling a repertoire for Intonaspacio. For the moment, we collaborated with two composers that wrote two pieces for Intonaspacio - Entoa by Clayton Mamedes and Intonéspacio by José Alberto Gomes. The approach in each piece is substantially different.

Entoa has a dynamic mapping, where different gestures relate to different sound parameters along the five movements of the music. Clayton Mamedes created several conditions for each movement on the music that are mutable along time. The same gesture can control different parameters at different moments of the piece. The action-sound relation, however is always very straightforward. The performer has to learn the exact gestures that trigger the sound the composer has described in the score. In spite of this aspect, the performer still has some freedom and he is responsible for same important choices in music, such as the duration of each movement (with same exceptions), and the weight of the sound effects (harmonizer, spatialisation control and so on).

Intonéspacio is divided in two movements, and at each one we have a crescendo in intensity. The time of each movement is controlled by the performer's manipulation of the instrument. The composer establish very interesting relations between continuous gestures and discrete actions, for example, changes in orientation will trigger specific changes in timbre. They will also trigger the reproduction of sound samples. Once more there are some gestures that are not common to both movements.

Intonaspacio has also been used in improvisation context, namely as part of the FVLC group, a laptop/new music instruments ensemble at CITAR, Porto. We have played with Intonaspacio in one of our Christmas presentations. The performers followed a graphic score, where time hints were given. Besides these, the performer was free to play any sound he/she wanted to, within that time cluster.

9 Conclusion

Intonaspacio is a DMI designed in order to integrate space in the generation and control of sound. It is an interface that creates site-specific sound. The musical instrument has a ball shape which requires to think about some questions related with stability, robustness and lightness of the structure. At the same time this shape inspires a set of gestures that comes from the experience of playing with balls. The previous knowledge on how to play with a ball, facilitates the first approach of a performer to the instrument. This situation also help us to predict a set of actions that the instrument has to sense, and what are the most suitable sensors to measure them. With this point of departure we designed a first version of the instrument, where the frame was made with very bendable plastic stripes. These enabled the instrument to be very pliable and thus easier to carry from one place to another. The frame however presented several problems and we had to change the material of the strips to Ticp - Commercially Pure Titanium. From version one to version two some of the sensors had to be different since the characteristics of the material were not the same. Ticp is a rigid material, thus tests with different bend sensors coupled at the structure showed that there was not significant changes when someone bent the structure.

The choice of the sensors was made based in the set of actions we wanted to capture - orientation of the instrument, impacts on its surface, distance from the instrument to the performer, deformation of the surface (in version 1) or pressure applied by the performer in the surface of Intonaspacio. Our DMI has implemented a set of 4 sensors - an IMU, two piezoelectric sensors and an IR sensor. For each we performed several tests to understand their general behavior and their dynamic ranges. Based on these tests we chose the best position to place the sensor and what kind of features we could extract from it.

We used a microphone to capture the sound present in the room (sound generated by the performer itself, sound generated by other players in the room, noise or the resonant frequencies generated by the room). We opted for a wireless mic that uses a FM transmitter to transmit the audio signal. Previously we had tested a pair of binaural microphones but this solution brought enormous constraints - these microphones need a supply of 3 V to work and this situation prevents Intonaspacio to be completely wireless. The wireless microphone is not, however, the best solution. It introduces noise in the signal and its frequency of emission has to be adjusted every time Intonaspacio is moved to another room.

We have designed two different mappings for Intonaspacio, where each one presents a different approach to integrate place on sound. The first mapping allowed the performer to record samples of the sound ambiance of the room, and then reproduce it in a loop that will excite the resonant frequencies of the room an introduce changes in the sound file. Mapping 2 presents an indirect approach, the input sound is analyzed and we extract the 15 frequencies with greatest magnitude in the spectrum. Hence, we can have a rough spectral analysis of the room. This information is then used to control some sound parameters in a sound synthesis algorithm.

At present, we aim to understand if it is possible to compile a gestural grammar for Intonaspacio that would be the basis for the creation of an instrumental technique. This grammar can, as well, become the foundation of a gestural notation adapted to instruments with the same characteristics as Intonaspacio.

We understand that a notation can facilitate the creation of a repertoire, the preservation and circulation of Intonaspacio among musicians and composers.

Intonaspacio has several musical applications, it can be played on an improvisational context as well as with a written score. At the moment we have already two music pieces written for Intonaspacio, Entoa and Intonéspacio, both apply different perspectives on the relations established between gesture and sound.

Acknowledgments. This research was funded by FCT (Foundation for Science and Technology, Portugal). The authors would like to thank Benjamin Bacon for his precious help, the composers Clayton Mamedes and José Alberto Gomes, and all those who in any way have participated in this project (Avrum, Carolina, Joe, André, André, João, Vasco, Mário).

References

1. Music 250a final projects 2001. http://ccrma.stanford.edu/~verplank/250a/2001.html
2. Aimi, R., Young, D.: A new beatbug: revision, simplifications and new directions. In: Proceedings of ICMC (2004)
3. Ascher, M.: Writtings 1973–1983 on works 1969–1979. The Press of the Nova Scotia College of Art and Design and The Museum of Contemporary Art Los Angeles, Hallifax, Nova Scotia
4. Bachelard, G.: A Poética do Espaço, 2 edn. Martins Fontes, São Paulo (2008)
5. Blaine, T.: The outer limits: a survey of unconventional musical input devices. Electronic Musician (2000)
6. Bowen, A.: Soundstone: a 3-d wireless music controller. In: Proceedings of NIME (2005)
7. Broson, C.: The orbison: designing a digital musical instrument for collaborative performance (2011), mUMT McGill
8. Cage, J.: Silence: Lectures and Writtings, 21st edn. Marion Boyars, London (2009)
9. Carpenter, E., McLuhan, M.: Explorations in Communication, An Anthology. Beacon Press, Boston (1960)
10. CkDevices: Mongoose 9 dof. http://store.ckdevices.com/products/Mongoose-9DoF-IMU-with-Barometric-Pressure-Sensor-.html
11. Davis, R.: '...and what they do as they're going...': sounding space in the work of alvin lucier. In: Organised Sound, vol. 8. Cambridge University Press, Cambridge (2003)
12. Gan, S.L.: Squeezables: tactile and expressive interfaces for children of all ages. Master's thesis. MIT (1998)
13. Goudeseune, C.: Interpolated mappings for musical instruments. Org. Sound 7(2), 85–96 (2002). http://dx.doi.org/10.1017/S1355771802002029
14. Hermann, T., Krausse, J., Ritter, H.: Real-time control fo sonification models with a haptic interface. In: Proceedings of International Conference on Auditory Display (2002)
15. Hunt, A., Wanderley, M.M.: Mapping performer parameters to synthesis engines. Org. Sound 7, 97–108 (2002). http://journals.cambridge.org/article_S1355771802002030

16. Hunt, A., Wanderley, M.M., Kirk, R.: Towards a model for instrumental mapping in expert musical interaction. In: Proceedings of International Computer Music Conference, Berlin, Germany (2000)
17. Joseph, B.W.: John cage and the architecture of silence. October **81**, 81 (1997)
18. Kurtz, M.: Stockhausen: A Biography. Faber and Faber, London (1991)
19. Labelle, B.: Background Noise - Perspectives on Sound Art. Continuum, New York (2006)
20. Malloch, J.: Building a sopranino t-stick. https://josephmalloch.wordpress.com/projects/mumt619/
21. Malloch, J.: A consort of gestural musical controllers: design, construction and performance. Master's thesis, McGill University (2008)
22. Malloch, J., Sinclair, S., Wanderley, M.M.: Libmapper (a library for connecting things). In: Proceedings of the International Conference on Human Factors in Computing Systems, Paris, France, pp. 3087–3090 (2013)
23. Milk, C.: Summer into dust documetary. www.chrismilk.vrb.com
24. Muecke, M., Zach, M.: Essays on the Intersection of Music and Architecture. Resonance (Ames, Iowa), Culicidae Architectural Press (2007). http://books.google.pt/books?id=ZhYg30P7QI0C
25. Nunes, E.: Espaces, chap. Temps et spatialité: En quête des lieux du temps. No. 5 in les cahiers de l'IRCAM: recherche et musique, IRCAM, Paris (1994)
26. Perner-Wilson, H., Buechley, L.: Making textile sensors from scratch. In: Proceedings of the Fourth International Conference on Tangible, Embedded, and Embodied Interaction (2010)
27. Rasamimanana, N., Fléty, E., Bevilacqua, F., Bloit, J., Schnell, N., Cera, A., Frechin, J.L., Petreviski, U.: The urban musical game: usong sport balls as musical interfaces. http://articles.ircam.fr/textes/Rasamimanana12a/index.pdf
28. Rovan, J.B., Wanderley, M.M., Dubnov, S., Depalle, P.: Instrumental gestural mapping strategies as expressivity determinants in computer music performance. In: Kansei - The Technology of Emotion Workshop, Genova, Italia, October 1997
29. Rudraraju, V.: A tool for configuring mappings for musical systems using wireless sensor networks. Master's thesis, McGill University (2011)
30. Russolo, L.: The Art of Noises. Pendragon Press, New York (1986)
31. Schaeffer, P.: Traité des objets musicaux: Essai interdisciplinaires. Éditions du Seuil, Paris (1966)
32. Schafer, R.M.: The soundscape: our sonic environment and the tuning of the world. Destiny Books; Distributed to the book trade in the United States by American International Distribution Corp., Rochester, Vt.; [United States] (1994)
33. Schumacher, M., Bresson, J.: Compositional control of periphonic sound spatialization. In: Proceedings of the 2nd International Symposium on Ambisonics and Spherical Acoustics, Paris, France (2010)
34. Vanel, H.: John cage's muzak-plus: the fu(rni)ture of music. Representations **102**(1), 94–128 (2008)
35. Verplan, B.: Music 250a final projects 2002. http://ccrma.stanford.edu/~verplank/250a/2002/2002.html
36. Vogel, O.: Erik satie and his three concepts of musique d'ameublement. In: Music and Sonic Art: Practice and Theories, vol. I. International Institute for Advanced Studies in System Research and Cybernetics, Canada (2010)
37. Wessel, D.: Timbre space as musical control structure. Comput. Music J. **3**, 42–52 (1979)

38. Winkler, T.: Making motion musical: gesture mapping strategies for interactive computer music. In: Proceedings of the 1995 International Computer Music Conference (1995)
39. Yamaguchi, T., Kobayashi, T., Ariga, A., Hashimoto, S.: Twinkleball: a wireless musical interface for embodied sound media. In: Proceedings of New Interfaces for Musical Expression (2010)
40. Yeo, W.: The bluetooth radio ball interface (brbi): a wireless interface for music/sound control and motion sonification. In: Proceedings of ICMC (2006)
41. Yeo, W.S., Yoon, J.W., Cho, H.Y.: The stringball: a ball interface with strings for collaborative performance. In: Proceedings of ICMC (2007)

Non-stationarity, Dynamics
and Mathematical Modeling

The Large Time-Frequency Analysis Toolbox 2.0

Zdeněk Průša[1]($\boxtimes$), Peter L. Søndergaard[2], Nicki Holighaus[1],
Christoph Wiesmeyr[3], and Peter Balazs[1]

[1] Acoustics Research Institute, Austrian Academy of Sciences,
Wohllebengasse 12–14, 1040 Vienna, Austria
{zdenek.prusa,nicki.holighaus,peter.balazs}@oeaw.ac.at
[2] Oticon A/S, Kongebakken 9, 2765 Smørum, Denmark
pesg@oticon.dk
[3] Numerical Harmonic Analysis Group, Faculty of Mathematics,
University of Vienna, Oskar-Morgenstern-Platz 1, 1090 Vienna, Austria
christoph.wiesmeyr@univie.ac.at

Abstract. The Large Time Frequency Analysis Toolbox (LTFAT) is
a modern Octave/Matlab toolbox for time-frequency analysis, synthesis, coefficient manipulation and visualization. It's purpose is to serve
as a tool for achieving new scientific developments as well as an educational tool. The present paper introduces main features of the second
major release of the toolbox which includes: generalizations of the Gabor
transform, the wavelets module, the frames framework and the real-time
block processing framework.

Keywords: Frames · Fourier transform · Gabor transform · Wavelet
transform · Real-time audio processing

1 Introduction

Time-Frequency analysis is a very important tool for signal processing and its
applications in audio, video and acoustics. It allows a representation showing
simultaneously (to some extent) the frequency and time content of a signal.
Typical representations are the Gabor [16] or wavelet [17] transforms. In recent
years more flexible transforms, in the form of adapted and adaptive representations were a very active topic of research, see e.g. [3]. For all those concepts
the mathematical theory of frames has proven to be highly significant, as frames
allow a very flexible approach, a wide range of possible analysis parameters and
properties, while still guaranteeing perfect reconstruction. For applications in
particular the implementation of related algorithms are important, an efficient,
and possibly real-time, realization being preferable. For a reproducible research
it is important to have a stable, well-documented toolbox.

Dealing with those concepts, LTFAT is an open-source Matlab/Octave toolbox freely available at http://ltfat.sourceforge.net/. The toolbox is well documented both in the code itself and in the form of a documentation web page.

© Springer International Publishing Switzerland 2014
M. Aramaki et al. (Eds.): CMMR 2013, LNCS 8905, pp. 419–442, 2014.
DOI: 10.1007/978-3-319-12976-1_25

The features of the first version of the toolbox were presented in [37] which was focused mainly on the *Discrete Gabor Transform – DGT* and window design. This paper focuses on the new additions, which are generalizations of the Gabor transform, both changing the lattice, as well as allowing varying windows; the wavelet modules, including wavelet filterbank trees and wavelet packet transforms; the frames framework, also dealing with multipliers and sparsity; and real-time block processing. The rest of the paper is organized as follows: Sect. 2 gives a brief overview of the frame theory in a finite setting and introduces the frames framework which allows users to effectively work with different transforms using a common interface. Sections 3 and 4 describe generalizations of Gabor systems to systems defined on non-separable and on non-regular time-frequency grids respectively. Section 5 deals with the discrete wavelet transform and derived algorithms. Section 7 provides examples for those sections. Section 6 contains description of several algorithms generalizing the Fourier transform. Section 8 describes the block-stream processing framework which enables real-time audio processing directly in Matlab/Octave. Section 9 discusses the design of the toolbox and states further plans.

1.1 Notation

To be consistent with [37], we use the same notation and assumptions. We regard all signals, windows and transforms as finite-dimensional and periodic. This assumption greatly simplifies the formulas and produces the fastest algorithms but at the same time introduces an unnatural behavior at signal boundaries. The signals are represented as vectors $x = \{x(0), x(1), \ldots, x(L-1)\} \in \mathbb{C}^L$ which are assumed to be column vectors with cyclic indexing such that $x(l + kL) = x(l)$ for $l, k \in \mathbb{Z}$. By $\overline{x}$ we denote a complex conjugation of each element in x. The scalar product on $\mathbb{C}^L$ is defined as $\langle x, y \rangle = \sum_{l=0}^{L-1} x(l)\overline{y}(l)$ and the induced norm as $\|x\| = \sqrt{\langle x, x \rangle}$. A linear operator $\mathcal{O} : \mathbb{C}^L \longrightarrow \mathbb{C}^M$ is represented by a $M \times L$ matrix vector multiplication $(\mathcal{O}x)(m) = \sum_{l=0}^{L-1} o(m,l)x(l)$ for $m \in \{0, \ldots, M-1\}$. All operators mentioned are linear. Finally, we denote $\widehat{x}(k) = \frac{1}{\sqrt{L}} \sum_{l=0}^{L-1} x(l)e^{-2\pi ikl/L}$ for $k \in \{0, \ldots, L-1\}$ as a (unitary) Discrete Fourier Transform (DFT) of x.

Here we give a brief summary of the DGT which maps a signal $f \in \mathbb{C}^L$ to a set of coefficients $c \in \mathbb{C}^{M \times N}$ using (circular) time shifts and modulations of a window $g \in \mathbb{C}^L$ such that

$$c(m, n) = \sum_{l=0}^{L-1} f(l)e^{-2\pi ilm/M}\overline{g}(l - an) \qquad (1)$$

assuming $L = Mb = Na$. Here M denotes the number of frequency channels and a denotes the time step or a hop size in samples. The input length restrictions can be handled either by truncating or by padding[1] of f. The coefficients capture

---

[1] The toolbox does a zero padding implicitly.

a time-frequency representation of the signal allowing one to study its time-frequency distribution. The choice of g, a and M determines the time-frequency localization of the signal. The windows g can be either full-length or be nonzero only on some smaller interval (FIR). In order to be able to reconstruct signals from their coefficients, $MN \geq L$ is required. This condition is necessary for the system

$$g_{m,n}(l) = \left\{ e^{2\pi ilm/M} g(l - an) \right\} \tag{2}$$

with $m \in \{0, \ldots, M-1\}$, $n \in \{0, \ldots, L/a - 1\}$ and $l \in \{0, \ldots, L-1\}$ to form a Gabor *frame* for $\mathbb{C}^L$, see also Sect. 2. In this case, the reconstruction can be done using the same parameters a, M but this time using a dual window $\widetilde{g}$ such that

$$f(l) = \sum_{n=0}^{N-1} \sum_{m=0}^{M-1} c(m,n) e^{2\pi iml/M} \widetilde{g}(l - an). \tag{3}$$

The fact that the (canonical) dual frame of a Gabor frame has the same structure is a central property of Gabor frames. An overview of the theory of Gabor frames can be found in [21].

Actual Matlab/Octave functions are referred to in a typewriter style (functionname).

2 The Frames Framework

A *frame* in $\mathbb{C}^L$ is a collection of vectors $\Psi = \{\psi_\lambda\}_{\lambda \in \{0,\ldots,\Lambda-1\}}$, $\psi_\lambda \in \mathbb{C}^L$ such that *frame bounds* $0 < A \leq B < \infty$ exist with

$$A\|f\|^2 \leq \sum_{\lambda=0}^{\Lambda-1} |\langle f, \psi_\lambda \rangle|^2 \leq B\|f\|^2,$$

for all $f \in \mathbb{C}^L$. A frame is redundant (oversampled) if $\Lambda > L$ and it is called *tight* if $A = B$. The basic operators associated with frames are the *analysis* and *synthesis operators* which take the form of matrix multiplications. The analysis operator acts as follows: $c = \mathbf{C}_\Psi f = \{\langle f, \psi_\lambda \rangle\}_{\lambda \in \{0,\ldots,\Lambda-1\}}$, where $c \in \mathbb{C}^\Lambda$ is a $\Lambda \times 1$ vector, $\mathbf{C}_\Psi \in \mathbb{C}^{\Lambda \times L}$ is a $\Lambda \times L$ matrix

$$\mathbf{C}_\Psi = \begin{pmatrix} - & \overline{\psi_0} & - \\ - & \overline{\psi_1} & - \\ & \vdots & \\ - & \overline{\psi_{\Lambda-1}} & - \end{pmatrix}$$

and $f \in \mathbb{C}^L$ is a $L \times 1$ vector. The synthesis operator act as $f = \mathbf{D}_\Psi c = \sum_{\lambda=0}^{\Lambda-1} c(\lambda)\psi_\lambda$, where $\mathbf{D}_\Psi \in \mathbb{C}^{L \times \Lambda}$ is a $L \times \Lambda$ matrix being the conjugate transpose of the analysis matrix such that $\mathbf{D}_\Psi = \mathbf{C}_\Psi^*$. Their concatenation $\mathbf{S}_\Psi = \mathbf{D}_\Psi \mathbf{C}_\Psi$ is referred to as the *frame operator* $\mathbf{S}_\Psi \in \mathbb{C}^{L \times L}$. Any frame admits a, possibly non-unique, dual frame, i.e. a frame Ψ^d such that the identity can be represented as $\mathbf{I} = \mathbf{D}_{\Psi^d}\mathbf{C}_{\Psi} = \mathbf{D}_{\Psi}\mathbf{C}_{\Psi^d}$. The most widely used dual is the so called *canonical dual* that can be obtained by applying the inverse frame operator $\mathbf{S}_{\Psi}^{-1}$ to the frame elements. When we prefer to have a tight system for both analysis and synthesis, we can instead use the *canonical tight frame* $\Psi^t = \{\psi_\lambda^t\}_{\lambda \in \{0,\ldots,\Lambda-1\}}$, defined by $\psi_\lambda^t = \mathbf{S}_{\Psi}^{-\frac{1}{2}}\psi_\lambda$ and satisfying $\mathbf{I} = \mathbf{D}_{\Psi^t}\mathbf{C}_{\Psi^t}$. See e.g. [2] for more detailed description of frames in the finite setting.

It is usually not computationally feasible to work with the matrices directly, when considering processing e.g. audio signals, as they normally consist of many thousand samples. Therefore, the frames framework provides an operator-like interface for working with frames without explicitly creating the matrices exploiting fast algorithms whenever they are possible.

2.1 Frames and Object Oriented Programming

The notion of a frame fits very well with the notion of a *class* in the object oriented programming paradigm. A class is a collection of methods and variables that together form a logical entity. A class can be *derived* from another class, in such a case that the derived class *inherits* properties of the original class, and it can extend them in some way. It can supply an implementation of abstract methods or override the existing ones. The derived class can still be referred to as the parent class and thus the same code can be used to work with different derived classes in a unified way. In the frame framework presented in this paper, the frame class serves as the abstract base class from which all other classes are derived. In the following text, we give an overview of the framework interface.

An object of type `frame` is instantiated by the user providing information about which type of frame is desired, and any additional parameters (like a window function, the number of channels etc.) necessary to construct the frame object. This is usually not enough information to construct a frame for $\mathbb{C}^L$ in the mathematical sense, as the dimensionality L of the space is not supplied. Instead, when the analysis operator of a frame object is presented with an input signal, it determines a value of L larger than or equal to the length of the input signal and only at this point is the mathematical frame fully defined. The construction was conceived this way to simplify work with different signal lengths without the need for a new frame for each signal length.

Therefore, each frame type must supply the `framelength` method, which returns the next larger length for which the frame can be instantiated. For instance, a dyadic wavelet frame with J levels only treats signal lengths which are multiples of 2^J. An input signal is simply zero-padded until it has admissible length, but never truncated. Some frames may only work for a fixed length L.

The `frameaccel` method will fix a frame to only work for one specific space $\mathbb{C}^L$. For some frame types, this involves precomputing the data structures to speed up the repeated application of the analysis and synthesis operators. This is highly useful for iterative algorithms, block processing or other types of processing where a predetermined signal length is used repeatedly.

Basic information about a frame can be obtained from the `framebounds` methods, returning the frame bounds, and the `framered` method returning the redundancy $\frac{A}{L}$ of the frame.

2.2   Analysis and Synthesis

The workhorses of the frame framework are the `frana` and `frsyn` methods, providing the analysis and synthesis operators $\mathbf{C}_\Psi$, $\mathbf{D}_\Psi$ of the frame Ψ respectively. These methods use a fast algorithm if available for the given frame. They are the preferred way of interacting with the frame when writing algorithms. However, if a direct access to the operators is needed, the `frsynmatrix` method returns a matrix representation of the synthesis operator.

The `framedual` and `frametight` methods represent the $\mathbf{S}_\Psi^{-1}$ and $\mathbf{S}_\Psi^{-\frac{1}{2}}$ operators respectively. Again, the matrices are not created and inverted explicitly if a fast algorithm exists. For some frame types, e.g. `filterbank` and `nsdgt`, the canonical dual frame is not necessarily again a frame with the same structure, and therefore it cannot be realized with a fast algorithm. Nonetheless, analysis and synthesis with the canonical dual frame can be realized iteratively. The `franaiter` method implements iterative computation of the canonical dual analysis coefficients using the frame operator's self-adjointness via the equation $\langle f, \mathbf{S}_\Psi^{-1}\psi_\lambda\rangle = \langle \mathbf{S}_\Psi^{-1}f, \psi_\lambda\rangle$. More precisely, a conjugate gradient method (`pcg`) is employed to apply the inverse frame operator $\mathbf{S}_\Psi^{-1}$ to the signal f iteratively, such that the analysis coefficients can be computed quickly by the `frana` method. Note that each conjugate gradient iteration applies both `frana` and `frsyn` once. The method `frsyniter` works in a similar fashion to provide the action of the inverse of the frame analysis operator. Furthermore, for some frame types the diagonal of the frame operator $\mathbf{S}$ calculated by `framediag` can be used as a preconditioner, providing significant speedup whenever the frame operator is diagonally dominant, see e.g. [6].

While both methods `franaiter` and `frsyniter` are available for all frames, they are recommended only if no means of efficient, direct computation of the canonical dual frame exists or its storage is not feasible. Their performance is highly dependent on the frame bounds and the efficiency of `frana` and `frsyn` for the frame type used.

2.3   Advanced Operations with Frames

A *frame multiplier* [4] is an operator constructed by multiplying frame coefficients with a symbol $s \in \mathbb{C}^A$ such that

$$\mathbf{M}_s f = \sum_{\lambda=0}^{A-1} s(\lambda) \langle f, \psi_\lambda^\mathrm{a}\rangle \, \psi_\lambda^\mathrm{s},$$

where ψ_λ^a and ψ_λ^s are simply the λth elements of the analysis and synthesis frames, respectively. The analysis and synthesis frames need not be of the same type, but they must have exactly the same redundancy. Under which conditions a frame multiplier is invertible, and when this again is a frame multiplier, are non-trivial questions [39,40]. In the LTFAT the inverse `iframemul` is generally computed iteratively by a conjugate gradient method `pcg`.

For a frame Ψ and an input signal $f \in \mathbb{C}^L$, the `franalasso` function returns coefficients $c \in \mathbb{C}^A$ which minimize the following objective function

$$\frac{1}{2}\|f - \mathbf{D}_\Psi c\|^2 + \gamma\|c\|_1, \tag{4}$$

where $\|c\|_1 = \sum_{\lambda=0}^{A-1}|c(\lambda)|$ and $\gamma \geq 0$ is a penalization coefficient which controls a tradeoff between the "sparsity" of c and the approximation error. The actual minimization is done using the Fast Iterative Soft Thresholding algorithm [8,13]. Another function `franagrouplasso` works similarly but the objective function employs a mixed norm [24] enforcing sparsity along the time or the frequency axis. Currently, this routine only works with frames which have a regular time-frequency distribution of atoms.

Sometimes, the phase of the frame coefficients is lost. For a generic frame more than 4 times redundant, the signal can be reconstructed from the magnitude of the coefficients only [1]. The `frsynabs` function attempts to reconstruct the signal using the iterative Griffin-Lim algorithm [20] or it's fast version [29].

Examples for the mentioned operations can be found in Sect. 7.

3   Discrete Gabor Transform on Non-separable Grids

The parameters a and M used in the classical DGT result in a regular, i.e. rectangular grid in the time-frequency plane. On the other hand, Gabor systems on general subgroup lattices $\Lambda \leq \mathbb{Z}_L \times \mathbb{Z}_L$ retain all theoretical properties of Gabor systems on rectangular grids, e.g. that the canonical dual of any *Gabor frame* is again a Gabor frame with respect to the same lattice.

A general lattice can be uniquely defined by using a third parameter $\lambda = \lambda_1/\lambda_2$ in addition to a and M. The *lattice type* λ is an irreducible fraction describing the displacement of neighboring (nonempty) columns in the lattice, relative to the frequency shift $\frac{L}{M}$, see Fig. 1 for an illustration. The corresponding Gabor system is

$$g_{m,n}(l) = \left\{e^{2\pi i(m+w(n))l/M}g(l-an)\right\}, \tag{5}$$

with m, n as before and $w(n) = \mathrm{mod}(n\lambda_1, \lambda_2)/\lambda_2$. More details on Gabor systems on general lattices and their implementation can be found in [44].

In the toolbox, both the classical and the non-separable DGT are available as `dgt`, `idgt` and dual Gabor windows can be computed with `gabdual`. For rectangular and quincunx grids only, `dgtreal` and `idgtreal` facilitate analysis and synthesis of purely real-valued signals, ignoring time-frequency coefficients on negative frequency channels.

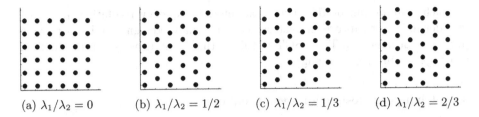

(a) $\lambda_1/\lambda_2 = 0$ (b) $\lambda_1/\lambda_2 = 1/2$ (c) $\lambda_1/\lambda_2 = 1/3$ (d) $\lambda_1/\lambda_2 = 2/3$

Fig. 1. The figure shows the placement of the Gabor atoms for four different lattice types in the time-frequency plane. The displayed Gabor system has parameters $a = 6$, $M = 6$ and $L = 36$. The lattice (a) is called *rectangular* or *separable* and the lattice (b) is known as the *quincunx* lattice.

4 Nonstationary Discrete Gabor Transform and Filterbanks

The nonstationary Gabor transform (NSGT) theory [5] generalizes the classical Gabor theory, where the window g, the time step a and the number of frequency channels M are fixed; to systems with evolving properties over either time or frequency. A central result of [5] is the definition of conditions on the window properties which result in *painless* nonstationary Gabor frames which admit an efficient computation of the canonical dual system with the same structure. In this setup, the frame operator is diagonal and its inversion is a simple operation. In the non-painless case, reconstruction is still possible, assuming the system is a frame, but computation of the dual system is not straightforward and it might not retain the original structure.

The painless conditions can be applied either in time or in frequency domain. To avoid confusion, both cases will be shown separately.

4.1 Changing Resolution over Time

Instead of a single window with the fixed time step a, assume a set of N windows $\{g_n\}_{n\in\{0,...,N-1\}}$, with g_n centered around the origin and considering M_n frequency channels. The resulting discrete nonstationary Gabor system is given by

$$g_{m,n}(l) = \left\{e^{2\pi i(l-a_n)m/M_n}g_n(l - a_n)\right\}, \tag{6}$$

for $n \in \{0, \ldots, N - 1\}, m \in \{0, \ldots, M_n - 1\}$ and $l \in \{0, \ldots, L - 1\}$. In contrast to (2) the complex exponentials shift along with the windows due to the $(l - a_n)$ term. This *phase locked* convention was chosen to simplify the impementation. The system is *painless* given the following conditions are satisfied:

1. Each of the windows g_n is compactly supported with support length being less or equal to M_n. This means that the windows have nonzero values only in some area around the time position.
2. The adjacent windows overlap so that $0 < A \le \sum_{n=0}^{N-1} |g_n(l - a_n)|^2 \le B < \infty$, for some positive A and B, for all $l \in \{0, \ldots, L - 1\}$.

Such systems can be designed to adapt the frequency resolution over time in order to better capture characteristics of an analyzed signal and still provide perfect reconstruction. The NSGT in this setting is implemented in the toolbox as nsdgt, its inverse as insdgt.

4.2   Changing Resolution over Frequency

Exploiting the duality in time and frequency domains, we assume M compactly supported windows $\{\widehat{g_m}\}_{m\in\{0,\ldots,M-1\}}$ in the frequency domain centered around frequency 0. Again, if the frequency support of each $\widehat{g_m}$ is less or equal to N_m and if the windows overlap sufficiently and cover the whole frequency spectrum, the collection

$$\widehat{g_{m,n}}(l) = \left\{ e^{-2\pi i l n/N_m} \widehat{g_m}(l-b_m) \right\}, \tag{7}$$

for $m \in \{0,\ldots,M-1\}$, $n \in \{0,\ldots,N_m-1\}$ and $l \in \{0,\ldots,L-1\}$ defines the DFT of painless nonstationary Gabor system atoms. An alternative interpretation of this result is that $\{\widehat{g_m}\}$ are band-limited frequency responses of filters in a perfect reconstruction filterbank and each of them is followed by a subsampling operation with a possibly non-integer factor $a_m = \frac{L}{N_m}$. In digital signal processing terms, the analysis filterbank does not introduce aliasing in subbands, and therefore no aliasing cancellation property of the synthesis filterbank is needed. This construction proved to be very useful, because it allows designing perfect reconstruction filterbanks with frequency bands adapted to a specific needs, e.g. the constant-Q Transform (CQT) in [5]. The filters in a CQT are placed along the frequency axis with a constant ratio of center frequency to bandwidth, or Q-factor. This transform is particularly interesting for an acoustic signal processing because it can be tuned to mimic the musical scale allowing to choose the octave resolution (number of filters per octave). An example of a CQT spectrogram is in Fig. 2 on the left.

Another application of the frequency adapted NSGT is the ERBlet transform [27] in which the filters are tuned to mimic the psychoacoustic ERB scale (erblett). An example of the ERBlet spectrogram is in Fig. 2 on the right.

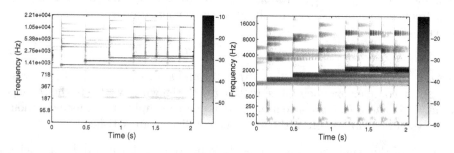

Fig. 2. Examples of the CQT spectrogram (left) and the ERBlet spectrogram (right) of an excerpt of the gspi test signal. The figures can be reproduced by running demo_filterbanks.

In the toolbox, the frequency adapted nonstationary Gabor systems are implemented in the context of the more general `filterbank` and `ifilterbank` routines.

4.3   Uniform Nonstationary Gabor Systems

Nonstationary Gabor systems are uniform if $M_n =$ const. or $a_m =$ const. in the time and frequency adapted settings respectively. Such systems admit another way of computing the canonical dual systems by inverting a polyphase frame matrix [9]. Internally, the toolbox favors the painless algorithm over the uniform one if both are suitable.

5   Discrete Wavelet Transform

The Discrete Wavelet Transform (DWT) associated with a multiresolution analysis provides a dyadic decomposition of $f \in \mathbb{C}^L$ into J wavelet (detail) bands d_j and a single scaling (approximation) band a_J such that the coefficients are obtained by

$$d_j(n) = \sum_{l=0}^{L-1} f(l)\overline{g_j}(l - 2^j n), \text{ and } a_J(n) = \sum_{l=0}^{L-1} f(l)\overline{h_J}(l - 2^J n) \qquad (8)$$

for $n \in \{0, \ldots, N_j - 1\}$, where $N_j = \frac{L}{2^j}$ and $j \in \{1, \ldots, J\}$, assuming $L = 2^J N_J$ for some integer N_J and $N_J + \sum_j N_j = L$. Here $g_j, h_J \in \mathbb{C}^L$ are obtained from a pair of characteristic basic wavelet vectors, the scaling sequence h_1 and the wavelet sequence g_1 recursively such that

$$h_{j+1}(l) = \sum_{k=0}^{N_j-1} h_1(k)h_j(l - 2^j k), \qquad g_{j+1}(l) = \sum_{k=0}^{N_j-1} g_1(k)h_j(l - 2^j k). \qquad (9)$$

The formulas are sometimes referred to as a *discrete scaling*. In this dyadic setting, the DWT is non-redundant and the reconstruction from the coefficients is possible if h_1 and g_1 and the dual filters $\tilde{h}_1$ and $\tilde{g}_1$ form a perfect reconstruction orthogonal (paraunitary) or biorthogonal filterbank, such that h_1 ($\tilde{h}_1$) and g_1 ($\tilde{g}_1$) are half-band low-pass and high-pass filters, respectively. Such filters will be further referred to as the *basic wavelet* filters. The dual filters differ from the original ones only in the biorthogonal case. The reconstruction is given by

$$f(l) = \sum_{j=1}^{J} \sum_{n=0}^{N_j} d_j(n)\tilde{g}_j(l - 2^j n) + \sum_{n=0}^{N_J} a_J(n)\tilde{h}_J(l - 2^J n), \qquad (10)$$

where $\tilde{h}_J$ and $\tilde{g}_j$ are derived from the dual filters in the similar manner as in (9).

The commonly used basic wavelet filters are short FIR filters with smooth and slowly decaying frequency responses. This fact exhibits in a poor frequency selectivity. Combined with the octave-only frequency division coming from the dyadic structure, this makes the DWT seemingly not attractive from the audio signal processing point of view. Nevertheless, the DWT was used in a number of applications dealing with audio signals see e.g. the literature survey in [26]. Moreover, there is a body of wavelet filterbank-based transforms improving upon the DWT properties which are described in the rest of this section.

Fast Wavelet Transform – Mallat's algorithm (`fwt`, `ifwt`): The Eq. (9) are in fact an enabling factor for the well-known Mallat's algorithm (also known as the fast wavelet transform). The algorithm comprises of an iterative application of the involuted (time reversed and conjugated) elementary two-channel filterbank followed by subsampling by a factor of two

$$d_{j+1} = \left(a_j * \overline{g_1}(. - l)\right)_{\downarrow 2}, \qquad a_{j+1} = \left(a_j * \overline{h_1}(. - l)\right)_{\downarrow 2}, \qquad (11)$$

where $*$ is the convolution operation and $a_0 = f$. The iterative application of the elementary filterbank forms a tree-shaped filterbank, where just the low-pass output is iterated. The signal reconstruction from the coefficients is then done by applying a mirrored filterbank tree using the dual basic filters $\tilde{g}_1$ and $\tilde{h}_1$. An example of the discrete wavelet representation of a test signal using $J = 11$ levels is depicted in Fig. 3 on the left.

In addition, the routines are capable of working in a more general setting allowing arbitrary number of filters followed by arbitrary subsampling factors in the elementary filterbank as it is required by some generalized wavelet filters constructions e.g. M-band wavelets [38], dual-density wavelets [35], framelets [14] and others.

The toolbox contains an easily extendible collection of routines for generating a number of wavelet filters families (see functions with the `wfilt_` prefix).

Wavelet Filterbank Tree (`wfbt`, `iwfbt`): Wavelet filterbank trees generalize the DWT filter tree by allowing further recursive decomposition of the high-pass filter output and by allowing a direct definition of a basic filterbank in each of the tree nodes. A flexible frequency covering can be achieved this way. It can also be used to construct more involved wavelet tree filterbanks like the ones used in dual-tree (M-band) complex wavelet transforms [7,36]. An example of a depth 8 full tree decomposition is shown in Fig. 3 on the right.

Wavelet Packet Transform, Best Tree Selection (`wpfbt`, `iwpfbt`, `wpbest`): The wavelet packet transform coefficients are formed by outputs of each of the node in the wavelet filterbank tree. Such a representation is highly redundant but leafs of any admissible subtree form a non-redundant representation – a basis, assuming the basic wavelet filterbank in each node is critically subsampled. The best subtree (basis) search algorithm relies on comparing a cost function associated witch each wavelet packet coefficient subband. Both additive [43] and non-additive [42] measures are incorporated in the wavelet module. The search proceeds by pruning the full tree as follows: first, the depth J full wavelet packet decomposition of a signal is performed. Then, the nodes are traversed in the breadth-first order starting from the highest level. At each node, the input cost

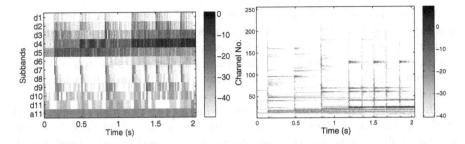

Fig. 3. On the left, the amplitude of DWT of an excerpt of the `gspi` test signal using $J = 11$ levels and the 16tap symlet basic wavelet filters (see help for `wfilt_sym`) is displayed. On the right, there is a representation obtained by a depth 8 full tree decomposition. Both representations are non-redundant. The figures can be reproduced by running `demo_wavelets`.

and the combined output costs are compared. If the input cost is less than the output cost, the current node and all possible descendant nodes are marked to be deleted, if not, the input is assigned the combined output cost. After traversing the whole tree, the marked nodes are removed and the resulting tree is considered to be the best tree (or near-best when using the non-additive cost functions) with respect to the chosen cost function. An example of such a representation is in Fig. 4 on the left. The right plot shows the depth of the node in the tree for the current channel. The lower this number is, the broader is the frequency band and the higher is the number of coefficients in the subband.

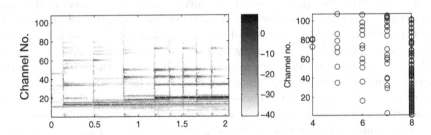

Fig. 4. The best basis representation starting from a full depth-8 wavelet packet tree using the Shannon entropy as the cost function. The figure can be reproduced by running the example in the help section of the `wpbest` function.

There have been several attempts to use wavelet filterbank trees and wavelet packets to process audio signals, mainly in the context of audio compression. The authors of [25] used M-band wavelet filterbanks in order to divide the frequency band into nonlinear frequency bands reminiscent of the tempered musical frequency scale or into an auditory frequency scale. See `demo_wfbt` from the toolbox.

All wavelet-type transformations mentioned so far are also available in undecimated versions in the toolbox (undecimated is sometimes referred to as stationary in the literature). These representations are very redundant, shift-invariant and the subbands are aliasing-free. The lack of aliasing makes the reconstruction more robust against coefficient modifications. A fast À-trous algorithm [23] is used when computing such transforms.

There are several boundary extension techniques available for wavelet based filterbanks implemented in the toolbox. Apart from the default periodic extension, the toolbox supports two types of symmetric extension and extension with zeros, which might lessen the effect of boundary conditions in some situations. Since the wavelet filters are exclusively short FIR filters, the information about the necessary samples beyond the boundaries can be stored in additional coefficients. The downside of this algorithmic approach is that the underlying frame abstraction becomes unclear.

6   Generalized Fourier Transform

The Generalized Goertzel algorithm (gga): The traditional Goertzel algorithm [19] (introduced in 1958) is a fast algorithm for evaluating individual samples of the DFT of $f \in \mathbb{C}^L$ i.e.

$$c(k) = \sum_{l=0}^{L-1} f(l)e^{-2\pi ikl/L}. \tag{12}$$

The number of real floating point operations required by the Goertzel algorithm is approximately three-quarters of the operations used in the direct evaluation. The Goertzel algorithm also does not require explicit evaluation of all the complex exponentials. A generalization of the Goertzel algorithm was presented in [41]. It allows obtaining individual values at an arbitrary position on the unit circle such that k in (12) does not have to be an integer, with no increase of the computational complexity. The algorithm can be useful for detecting the presence of harmonic signals with frequencies not being multiples of the fundamental frequency. An example in Fig. 5a shows regular DFT samples (solid lines) of a test signal consisting of a sum of harmonic components and samples obtained by the generalized Goertzel algorithm (bold dashed lines) selecting k to coincide with the known frequencies.

The chirp Z transform (chirpzt): The toolbox also contains an implementation of a similar purpose algorithm called the chirp Z transform [34], sometimes incorrectly called the fractional Fourier transform. The algorithm can be used for fast evaluation of K equispaced samples on the unit circle (or more generally on a spiral in the Z-domain) starting at an arbitrary (possibly non-integer) position such that $k = k_0 + nk_d$ in (12) for $n \in \{0, \ldots, K-1\}$ and $k_0, k_d \in \mathbb{R}$. The effective implementation of the algorithm is based on a fast convolution of the signal with a chirp and some pre- and post-processing operations. The algorithm can be used for "zooming" to a specific frequency range as is shown in Fig. 5b

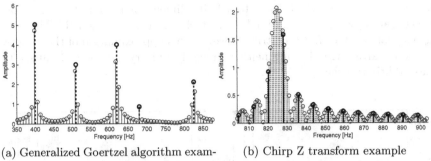

(a) Generalized Goertzel algorithm example

(b) Chirp Z transform example

Fig. 5. Frequency content of a test signal of length 1024 sampled at rate 8 kHz consisting of the sum of five real harmonic components at 400, 510, 620, 680, 825 Hz with amplitudes 5, 3, 4, 1, 2 respectively. The figures can be reproduced by the examples in the help section of the `gga` and `chirpzt` functions respectively.

where the bold solid lines represent the regular DFT samples and the dashed ones are obtained by the chirp Z transform.

Fractional Fourier transform (`dfracft`,`ffracft`): The *fractional Fourier transform* (FRFT) is a generalization of the classical Fourier transform and has received considerable attention in the literature, the most complete survey to date can be found in [28]. The FRFT of a function depends on the parameter α, for $\alpha = 1$ it coincides with the ordinary FT. We will denote the FRFT as $\mathcal{F}_\alpha$. The parameter α (or more precisely $\alpha\pi/2$) is also referred to as *angle* of the transform, since $\mathcal{F}_\alpha f$ can be regarded as a rotation of the signal f in the TF-plane by the angle $\alpha\pi/2$. The Fourier Transform is a special case and is a rotation by $\pi/2$. For a survey paper on computational aspects of the FRFT we refer to [10], we express our gratitude towards the authors of this paper for allowing us to integrate their code.

Currently there are two different methods available in LTFAT to compute the FRFT for a given angle. The first one is based on the computation of a discrete set of Hermite functions by diagonalizing a discretized version of the Hamiltonian operator (`dfracft`). The (quantum mechanical) Hamiltonian operator is the sum of the squares of the position and the momentum operators. The square of the continuous momentum operator $\mathcal{D}^2 = d^2/dt^2$ can be approximated by the second difference operator $\tilde{\mathcal{D}}^2$ acting on C^L. The square of the momentum operator can consequently be approximated by $\tilde{\mathcal{D}}^2$ on the Fourier side. This leads to an eigenvalue problem of size $L \times L$ for the computation of the discrete Hermite functions, the detailed construction can be found in [11]. Basing the computation of the FRFT on this set of discrete Hermite functions, the transform has all the desirable properties, such as unitarity and index additivity ($\mathcal{F}_\alpha \mathcal{F}_\beta = \mathcal{F}_{\alpha+\beta}$).

The continuous FRFT can be written in several different ways, one of them is through composition of a chirp multiplication followed by a chirp convolution and another chirp multiplication. The integrals can be approximated using

quadrature formulas, which leads to a finite dimensional computational procedure (`ffracft`) with complexity $L \log L$, which is faster than the FRFT based on
diagonalization of an $L \times L$ matrix. However, this approximation of the integrals
has the disadvantage of being neither precisely unitary, nor does it satisfy the
index additivity exactly (Fig. 6).

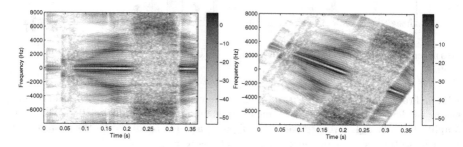

Fig. 6. DGT spectrograms of the **greasy** test signal before (left) and after (right)
applying the fractional Fourier transform with $\alpha = 0.3$ using the `ffracft` function.

7   Examples

7.1   Applying a Frame Multiplier

Frame multipliers are useful for separating, deleting and selective enhancement
of objects in the time-frequency plane and for approximating responses of linear
time-varying systems. Figure 7a shows a spectrogram of a result of applying a
frame multiplier using a tight Gabor frame ($a = 200$, $M = 1000$, 20 ms Hann
window) with the symbol depicted in Fig. 7b. The symbol approximates a band-
pass filter with varying center frequency over time.

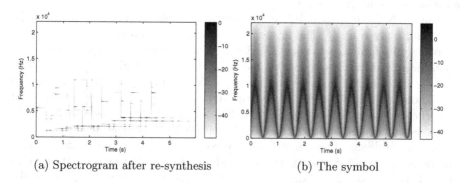

(a) Spectrogram after re-synthesis   (b) The symbol

Fig. 7. Simulating an audio effect using a frame multiplier applied to the **gspi** test
signal. The figures can be reproduced by running `demo_bpframemul`.

7.2 Enforcing Sparsity

Different signal characteristics like transients or the harmonic structure can be made more prominent by applying transforms with appropriate time-frequency resolutions combined with a procedure which enforces the representation to be *group* sparse in time or frequency. Figure 8a shows the transient part and Fig. 8b the tonal part of an excerpt of the gspi test signal. The tonal part is obtained using higher number of frequency channels and forcing the representation to be sparse in frequency and vice versa the transient part.

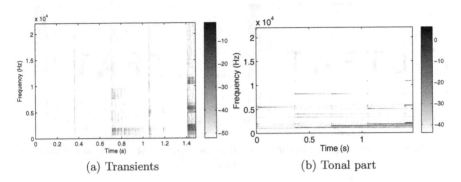

(a) Transients   (b) Tonal part

Fig. 8. Separation of the transient and the tonal components using group sparsity. The figures can be reproduced by running demo_audioshrink.

7.3 Reconstruction from Magnitude only

Figure 9a depicts the original DGT spectrogram (magnitude of the coefficients) of an excerpt of the gspi test signal, whereas Fig. 9b is a visualization of the phase difference between the original phase and the phase reconstructed iteratively using the Griffin-Lim algorithm. The difference is zeroed for coefficients

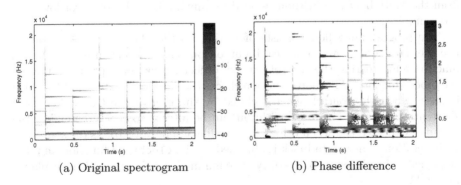

(a) Original spectrogram   (b) Phase difference

Fig. 9. Reconstructing a signal from the magnitude of the coefficients only. The figures can be reproduced by running demo_phaseret.

smaller than −50 dB. Clearly some regions of the phase in the spectrogram were reconstructed with a constant phase shift, other exhibit a periodically reoccurring patterns in the phase difference.

The reconstruction from the magnitude of the coefficients can be also used for synthetic spectrograms. Figure 10 shows an example of creating an audible sound from an image. The DGT (real) time-frequency grid was used with $a = 8$ and $M = 800$. The iterative algorithm gives a more pleasant sound than the mere direct reconstruction with phase set to zero.

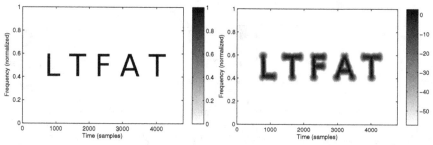

(a) Original spectrogram (linear scale) (b) Spectrogram of the signal with a new phase.

Fig. 10. The figures can be reproduced by running `demo_frsynabs`.

8   Block-Stream Processing Framework

Audio processing experiments become much more impressive when it is allowed to change parameters during the playback or when the data are obtained directly from a microphone, processed and immediately played. In such cases, it is necessary to process small chunks of data to keep the processing delay low. LTFAT provides a simple and unified framework for producing such streams of blocks in order to achieve the real-time data stream capture and the playback directly from the Matlab/Octave without a need for any additional toolbox or low-level programming.

The programming flow consists of setting up the block stream parameters like the data source, audio device, input/output channels etc. using the `block` function and creating the control window object `blockpanel` prior to entering the processing loop. The loop condition checks the value of a state variable, which is unset when the control panel is closed by the user or the Ctrl-C keyboard shortcut is pressed. The loop condition can be altered to check the end of the stream if expected e.g. when using an audio file or a data vector as the source. In each iteration, a new data block is obtained by the `blockread` function and it is enqueued to be played by `blockplay`. The minimal working example is displayed in Fig. 11.

The real-time processing capabilities of Matlab/Octave are quite limited when compared to the professional low-level solutions, therefore we cannot

```
block('playrec');
p = blockpanel({'GdB','Gain',-20,20,0,21});
while p.flag
    gain = blockpanelget(p,'GdB');
    f = blockread();
    blockplay(f*10^(gain/20));
end
blockdone(p);
```

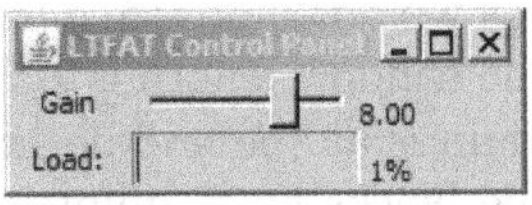

Fig. 11. A minimal block-stream processing example: take input from a microphone and route it trough the loop to the speakers allowing setting gain in the range from −20 to 20 dB during playback using the slider in the panel (on the right).

recommend using the block-processing framework in settings where glitch-less playback is required. Nevertheless, the block-stream framework allows quick prototyping of algorithms in a real-time setting with a minimal programming effort.

8.1 Transform Domain Processing

The block-stream processing framework was designed to be used in conjunction with the frames framework introduced in Sect. 2 in order to provide means for a real-time time-frequency analysis, visualization, modification and synthesis. There are two obstacles when considering applying transforms from the toolbox on a real-time stream of data blocks:

1. The computational complexity of the desired operation.
2. The processed signal periodicity assumption.

The fast execution is achieved by pre-computing all the fixed data by means of the `blockframeaccel` or `blockframepairacel` functions prior entering the processing loop complemented with an efficient C implementation of algorithms. The periodicity assumption goes against the way how data are actually obtained in a real-time setting. Therefore the direct naive application of the transform to individual blocks will produce "bad" coefficients not fit to be directly manipulated or plotted even though the block can be reconstructed perfectly. LTFAT supports two approaches for adapting the transforms to avoid or at least lessen the impact of the assumed periodicity: the combined *overlap-save/overlap-add* approach for transforms using FIR windows/filters and the *slicing window* approach for all other transforms.

(a) The combined overlap-save/overlap-add approach is conceptually similar to the one in [33], where it was used for developing an algorithm for an error-free block-wise discrete wavelet transform. The algorithm is based on a principle of overlap-save (also known as the overlap-discard) type block convolution for the analysis and overlap-add type block convolution for the synthesis. The necessary overlap lengths can be determined exactly from the finite windows/filter lengths the transform is based on.

The algorithm as described here holds for the following assumptions:

1. The window hop size a (or the subsampling factor) is uniform for all windows.
2. The window length is $L^w = k2a + 1$ for k being some positive integer and the origin is at the middle sample.
3. The blocks have uniform lengths $L^b = la$ for l being some positive integer.
4. $L^b > L^w$.

These assumptions are often too restrictive in practice, but more general settings require rather large number of additional operations the description of would obscure the principal idea of the algorithm. The current implementation requires the first assumption and uniform length (though arbitrary) FIR windows having the same position of the origin. Moreover, the implementation is able to handle blocks with varying lengths.

Analysis part:

1. Read a block of data, extend it from the left side by the $L^w - 1$ last samples form the previous block.
2. Apply the transform to the extended block.
3. From the resulting coefficients, keep only those at indexes $\{k, \ldots, l + k - 1\}$ starting counting from zero.

The last step discards coefficients which are time-aliased due to the implicit periodic boundary handling. The discarding is done from the both sides because the windows used in the LTFAT computation routines are not causal. The remaining coefficients are equal to the corresponding coefficients from a transform of a signal without dividing it into blocks. The cropped coefficients, possibly modified, form the input for the synthesis part of the algorithm.

Synthesis part:

1. Create zero arrays of length $2k + l$ for each channel and copy the coefficients obtained by the analysis procedure to time positions $\{k, \ldots, l + k - 1\}$.
2. Apply the inverse transformation to the extended coefficients.
3. Recall the $L^w - 1$ last samples from the previous block and add them to the first $L^w - 1$ samples of the current block.
4. Store the last $L^w - 1$ samples as the overlap used in the next block.

A toy example of applying the algorithm is depicted in Figs. 12 and 13 for the analysis and synthesis parts respectively.

(b) The Slicing window method was originally presented in [22]. In contrast to the previous approach, the slicing window method does not try to determine overlaps exactly, but instead employs a slicing window to weigh blocks of samples producing *slices*. After windowing, the slice is optionally symmetrically zero-padded to lessen the effect of the time aliasing. After reconstruction, the slice is weighted by a dual slicing window and the reconstructed signal assembled in an overlap-add manner. The same slicing window can be used for dividing the signal and for the assembly, if the squares of all it's time shifts form a partition

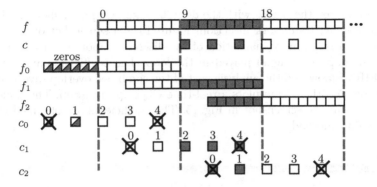

Fig. 12. An example of the analysis part of the combined overlap-save/overlap-add algorithm for $a = 3$, $L^b = 9$ and $L^w = 7$ ($l = 3$, $k = 1$). The figure shows the first three blocks of the signal f and the true time positions of coefficients c. Each of the blocks f_0, f_1 and f_2 is extended from the left side by $L^w - 1 = 6$ samples and transformed. The respective coefficients c_0, c_1, c_2 are obtained and only the ones with indexes $\{1, 2, 3\}$ are retained. Note the algorithm produces k additional coefficients at the beginning when compared to the true coefficients c.

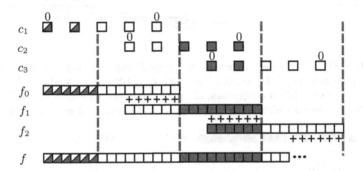

Fig. 13. An example of the synthesis part of the combined overlap-save/overlap-add algorithm. The coefficients c_0, c_1 and c_2 are extended with zeros and the reconstructed blocks f_0, f_1 and f_2 are overlapped. Note the overall delay of the algorithm is $L^w - 1 = 6$ samples.

of unity. More general combinations of windows are also possible, see [22] for the details. Note that the coefficients reflect the shape of the slicing window, so non-linear processing like thresholding applied directly to the coefficients may introduce blocking artifacts. In the toolbox, the method is implemented in such a way the slicing window is applied to a concatenation of the previous and the current block so the slicing window shift is L^b effectively. By default, a square-root of a peak-normalized Hann window is used but the programming interface allows specifying customized slicing windows.

In the toolbox, the demos with the `demo_blockproc_` prefix show the block-stream processing framework in action. Figure 14 is a screenshot of one of the demos doing a real-time visualization of the discrete Gabor transform spectrogram of the `gspi` test signal played in the loop. The coefficients are obtained using a FIR window and the analysis part of the combined overlap-save/overlap-add method. Another demo plots a real-time CQT spectrogram. The same test signal is used in the screenshot in Fig. 15. The coefficients are obtained by the slicing window method.

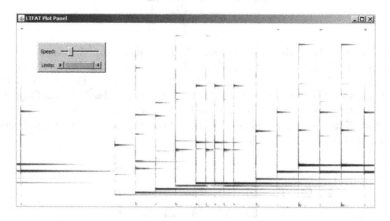

Fig. 14. Real-time DGT spectrogram of the (looped) `gspi` test signal (262144 samples, sampling frequency 44.1 kHz) using $L^b = 1024$, $a = 100$, $M = 3000$ and 20 ms Hann window. For the visualization purposes, absolute values of coefficients are limited to the range -70 dB ... 20 dB which is linearly mapped to the inverted grayscale colormap.

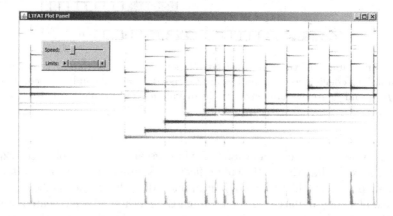

Fig. 15. Real-time CQT spectrogram of the `gspi` test signal. Only frequencies in the range 200 Hz ... 20 kHz are displayed using 48 bins per octave (320 bands), $L^b = 1024$, slicing window length $2L^b$ and additional L^b zeros of a symmetric zero padding. For visualization purposes, coefficients from consecutive blocks were overlapped to better approximate the true coefficients.

9 Design and Implementation

The toolbox is designed in such a way that the functions forming the programming interface in most cases only check and format the user defined inputs and pass them further to the routines with the comp_ prefix, that perform the actual computations. The majority of the comp_ functions can be replaced (shadowed) by compiling the MEX/OCT files with the identical name to speedup the computations. The MEX/OCT files themselves do not contain the computations, but again just format the inputs (unify data types, change complex numbers memory layout) and obtain data pointers and call the actual computational routine(s) from the separately compiled backend C library to which they link to. The backend library depends on the FFTW library and on the BLAS and LAPACK libraries, which are usually already contained in the Matlab/Octave installation. On Windows systems, a manual installation of the FFTW library is necessary at the moment when using Matlab. In order to minimize the code repetition, the backend library is built in such a way the actual code is independent of the desired data type (floating data types with different precision) and even of the real or the complex data type where possible.

The regular toolbox functionality can be used without the backend library and MEX/OCT interfaces. The block-stream processing framework however requires compiling the MEX interface playrec (http://www.playrec.co.uk, contained in LTFAT), which depends on the Portaudio library (http://www.portaudio.com), which is again distributed with recent versions of Matlab. The compilation process is automated via the ltfatmex command, but pre-built packages can be downloaded from the toolbox webpage. An additional possibility for Octave users is installing LTFAT directly trough the integrated package management system pkg, which takes care of compiling everything during the installation process.

10 Outlook

This section describes possible enhancements and features of the toolbox which might be included in the future versions.

Quadratic time-frequency distributions – Although the family of quadratic time-frequency distributions cannot be associated with frames because of their non-linear character, they offer yet another way of studying audio signal features [12]. Moreover, algorithms for synthesizing signals from their quadratic representations exist, so there is a possibility for doing modifications on the coefficients in a similar manner as with frame multipliers.

Modern algorithms for phase-less reconstruction – A reconstruction from only the magnitude of frame coefficients is currently a very active topic in research. We plan to implement some of the modern algorithms, see e.g. [15], to complement the Griffin-Lim algorithm.

Gabor dual windows using convex optimization – Explicit formulas for Gabor dual windows are known only for the canonical dual frame. If the frame system is redundant, infinitely many dual windows exists. Using results from [30,31] we will add an option to search for the optimal dual window given a prior criterion.

Algorithms for computation of optimal dual uniform FIR filterbank frames – The current algorithm for computing dual uniform FIR filterbank (based on [9]) frames in LTFAT suffers from two drawbacks. First, it is capable of computing the canonical dual frame only and it does not preserve the FIR property. The plan is to include results from [18] to allow more freedom in choosing the optimal FIR filterbank dual frames.

Acknowledgments. The authors would like to thank the people that made contributions to the toolbox: Remi Decorsiere, Monika Dörfler, Nina Engelputzeder, Hans Feichtinger, Thomas Hrycak, Florent Jaillet, A.J.E.M. Janssen, Norbert Kaiblinger, Matthieu Kowalski, Ewa Matusiak, Piotr Majdak, Nathanaël Perraudin, Pavel Rajmic, Thomas Strohmer, Bruno Torrésani, Jordy van Velthoven and Tobias Werther.

We would like to express our gratitude towards authors of the Uvi Wave toolbox [32], from which we have taken some wavelet filters generation routines.

The work on this paper was partly supported by the Austrian Science Fund (FWF) START-project FLAME ('Frames and Linear Operators for Acoustical Modeling and Parameter Estimation'; Y 551-N13).

References

1. Balan, R., Casazza, P., Edidin, D.: On signal reconstruction without phase. Appl. Comput. Harmon. Anal. **20**(3), 345–356 (2006)
2. Balazs, P.: Frames and finite dimensionality: frame transformation, classification and algorithms. Appl. Math. Sci. **2**(41–44), 2131–2144 (2008)
3. Balazs, P., Dörfler, M., Kowalski, M., Torrésani, B.: Adapted and adaptive linear time-frequency representations: a synthesis point of view. IEEE Signal Process. Mag. (Special Issue: Time-Freq. Anal. Appl.) **30**(6), 20–31 (2013)
4. Balazs, P.: Basic definition and properties of Bessel multipliers. J. Math. Anal. Appl. **325**(1), 571–585 (2007). http://dx.doi.org/10.1016/j.jmaa.2006.02.012
5. Balazs, P., Dörfler, M., Jaillet, F., Holighaus, N., Velasco, G.A.: Theory, implementation and applications of nonstationary Gabor frames. J. Comput. Appl. Math. **236**(6), 1481–1496 (2011). http://ltfat.sourceforge.net/notes/ltfatnote018.pdf
6. Balazs, P., Feichtinger, H.G., Hampejs, M., Kracher, G.: Double preconditioning for Gabor frames. IEEE Trans. Signal Process. **54**(12), 4597–4610 (2006). http://dx.doi.org/10.1109/TSP.2006.882100
7. Bayram, I., Selesnick, I.W.: On the dual-tree complex wavelet packet and M-band transforms. IEEE Trans. Signal Process. **56**(6), 2298–2310 (2008)
8. Beck, A., Teboulle, M.: A fast iterative shrinkage-thresholding algorithm for linear inverse problems. SIAM J. Imaging Sci. **2**(1), 183–202 (2009). http://dx.doi.org/10.1137/080716542
9. Bölcskei, H., Hlawatsch, F., Feichtinger, H.G.: Frame-theoretic analysis of oversampled filter banks. IEEE Trans. Signal Process. **46**(12), 3256–3268 (2002)
10. Bultheel, A., Martínez, S.: Computation of the fractional Fourier transform. Appl. Comput. Harmon. Anal. **16**(3), 182–202 (2004)

11. Candan, C., Kutay, M.A., Ozaktas, H.M.: The discrete fractional Fourier transform. IEEE Trans. Signal Process. **48**(5), 1329–1337 (2000)
12. Cohen, L.: Time-frequency distributions-a review. Proc. IEEE **77**(7), 941–981 (1989)
13. Daubechies, I., Defrise, M., De Mol, C.: An iterative thresholding algorithm for linear inverse problems with a sparsity constraint. Commun. Pure Appl. Math. **57**, 1413–1457 (2004)
14. Daubechies, I., Han, B., Ron, A., Shen, Z.: Framelets: MRA-based constructions of wavelet frames. Appl. Comput. Harmon. Anal. **14**(1), 1–46 (2003)
15. Decorsiere, R., Søndergaard, P.L., Buchholz, J., Dau, T.: Modulation filtering using an optimization approach to spectrogram reconstruction. In: Proceedings of Forum Acusticum 2011. European Acoustics Association (2011)
16. Feichtinger, H.G., Strohmer, T. (eds.): Gabor Analysis and Algorithms. Birkhäuser, Boston (1998)
17. Flandrin, P.: Time-Frequency/Time-Scale Analysis, Wavelet Analysis and its Applications, vol. 10. Academic Press Inc., San Diego (1999). (with a preface by Yves Meyer, Translated from the French by Joachim Stöckler)
18. Gauthier, J., Duval, L., Pesquet, J.: Optimization of synthesis oversampled complex filter banks. IEEE Trans. Signal Process. **57**(10), 3827–3843 (2009)
19. Goertzel, G.: An algorithm for the evaluation of finite trigonometric series. Am. Math. Mon. **65**(1), 34–35 (1958)
20. Griffin, D., Lim, J.: Signal estimation from modified short-time Fourier transform. IEEE Trans. Acoust. Speech Signal Process. **32**(2), 236–243 (1984)
21. Gröchenig, K.: Foundations of Time-Frequency Analysis. Birkhäuser, Boston (2001)
22. Holighaus, N., Dörfler, M., Velasco, G.A., Grill, T.: A framework for invertible, real-time constant-Q transforms. IEEE Trans. Audio Speech Lang. Process. **21**(4), 775–785 (2013)
23. Holschneider, M., Kronland-Martinet, R., Morlet, J., Tchamitchian, P.: A real-time algorithm for signal analysis with the help of the wavelet transform. In: Combes, J.M., Grossmann, A., Tchamitchian, P. (eds.) Wavelets. Time-Frequency Methods and Phase Space, pp. 286–297. Springer, Heidelberg (1989)
24. Kowalski, M.: Sparse regression using mixed norms. Appl. Comput. Harmon. Anal. **27**(3), 303–324 (2009). http://hal.archives-ouvertes.fr/hal-00202904/
25. Kurth, F., Clausen, M.: Filter bank tree and M-band wavelet packet algorithms in audio signal processing. IEEE Trans. Signal Process. **47**(2), 549–554 (1999)
26. Merry, R., Steinbuch, M., van de Molengraft, M.: Wavelet theory and applications, a literature study. DCT 2005.53 (2005). http://alexandria.tue.nl/repository/books/612762.pdf
27. Necciari, T., Balazs, P., Holighaus, N.: Søndergaard, P.L.: The ERBlet transform: an auditory-based time-frequency representation with perfect reconstruction. In: Proceedings of the 38th International Conference on Acoustics, Speech, and Signal Processing (ICASSP 2013), pp. 498–502. IEEE, Vancouver, May 2013
28. Ozaktas, H.M., Zalevsky, Z., Kutay, M.A.: The Fractional Fourier Transform with Applications in Optics and Signal Processing. Wiley, New York (2001)
29. Perraudin, N., Balazs, P., Sondergaard, P.: A fast Griffin-Lim algorithm. In: 2013 IEEE Workshop on Applications of Signal Processing to Audio and Acoustics (WASPAA), pp. 1–4, Oct 2013
30. Perraudin, N., Holighaus, N., Soendergaard, P., Balazs, P.: Gabor dual windows using convex optimization. In: Proceedings of the 10th International Conference on Sampling Theory and Applications (SAMPTA 2013) (2013)

31. Perraudin, N., Holighaus, N., Søndergaard, P.L., Balazs, P.: Designing Gabor windows using convex optimization (2014). arXiv:1401.6033
32. Prelcic, N.G., Márquez, O.W., González, S.: Uvi Wave, the ultimate toolbox for wavelet transforms and filter banks. In: Proceedings of the Fourth Bayona Workshop on Intelligent Methods in Signal Processing and Communications, Bayona, Spain, pp. 224–227 (1996)
33. Průša, Z.: Segmentwise discrete wavelet transform. Ph.D. thesis, Brno University of Technology, Brno (2012)
34. Rabiner, L., Schafer, R., Rader, C.: The chirp Z-transform algorithm. IEEE Trans. Audio Electroacoust. 17(2), 86–92 (1969)
35. Selesnick, I.W.: The double density DWT. In: Petrosian, A.A., Meyer, F.G. (eds.) Wavelets in Signal and Image Analysis, pp. 39–66. Springer, Amsterdam (2001)
36. Selesnick, I.W.: The double-density dual-tree DWT. IEEE Trans. Signal Process. 52(5), 1304–1314 (2004)
37. Søndergaard, P.L., Torrésani, B., Balazs, P.: The linear time frequency analysis toolbox. Int. J. Wavelets Multiresolut. Anal. Inf. Process. 10(4), 1250032-1–1250032-27 (2012)
38. Steffen, P., Heller, P., Gopinath, R., Burrus, C.: Theory of regular M-band wavelet bases. IEEE Trans. Signal Process. 41(12), 3497–3511 (1993)
39. Stoeva, D.T., Balazs, P.: Invertibility of multipliers. Appl. Comput. Harmon. Anal. 33(2), 292–299 (2012)
40. Stoeva, D.T., Balazs, P.: Canonical forms of unconditionally convergent multipliers. J. Math. Anal. Appl. 399, 252–259 (2013)
41. Sysel, P., Rajmic, P.: Goertzel algorithm generalized to non-integer multiples of fundamental frequency. EURASIP J. Adv. Signal Process. 2012(1), 56 (2012)
42. Taswell, C.: Near-best basis selection algorithms with non-additive information cost functions. In: Proceedings of the IEEE International Symposium on Time-Frequency and Time-Scale Analysis, pp. 13–16. IEEE Press (1994)
43. Wickerhauser, M.V.: Lectures on wavelet packet algorithms. In: Lecture notes, INRIA (1992)
44. Wiesmeyr, C., Holighaus, N., Søndergaard, P.L.: Efficient algorithms for discrete Gabor transforms on a nonseparable lattice. IEEE Trans. Signal Process. 61(20), 5131–5142 (2013)

Sparse Gabor Multiplier Estimation for Identification of Sound Objects in Texture Sound

Monika Dörfler[(✉)] and Ewa Matusiak

NuHAG, Faculty of Mathematics, University of Vienna, Vienna, Austria
{monika.doerfler,ewa.matusiak}@univie.ac.at

Abstract. In this contribution we present a novel method for identifying *novelty* and, more specifically, *sound objects* within *texture sounds*. We introduce the notion of texture sound and sound object and explain how the properties of a sound that is known to be textural may be exploited in order to detect deviations which suggest the presence of novelty or distinct sound event, which may then be called sound object. The suggested approach is based on Gabor multipliers, which map the Gabor coefficients corresponding to certain time-segments of the signal to each other. We present the results of simulations based on both synthetic and real audio signals.

Keywords: Gabor multiplier · Sound object · Texture sound

1 Introduction

Audio signals are central in everyday human life and the manner sound is perceived is highly sophisticated, complex and context-dependent. In some applications, one may be interested in identifying change in an ongoing audio scenario, related to a certain sound texture, or in distinguishing between what may be called a "sound object" and more textural sound components constituting an acoustical background. The notion of sound object ("objet sonore") was introduced by Pierre Schaeffer [17] as a generalization of the concept of a musical note, in particular their definition implies a time-limitation of sound objects.

Human listeners tend to perceive sound in a structured manner, with the ability to focus and de-focus. Whether a particular event is experienced as a relevant novelty as opposed to background, textural sound, seems to depend both on cultural and educational background, cp. [11], that may be shared by a group of listeners. From a certain point of view, the perception of sound components as background (textural) sound or object (compactly structured) sound, depends on the "zoom" the listener wishes to adopt or unconsciously assumes. In this contribution, we attempt to mimic these observations in a technical way,

This research was supported by the Vienna Science and Technology Fund (WWTF) through project VRG12-009 and the Austrian Science Fund (FWF):[V 312-N25].

M. Aramaki et al. (Eds.): CMMR 2013, LNCS 8905, pp. 443–462, 2014.
DOI: 10.1007/978-3-319-12976-1_26

by "defining" a sound to be textural if it does not change certain characteristics which are first to be determined from a certain amount of data. In that sense, we need the a priori knowledge that a particular part of a signal represents textural sound segments. Any signal components representing a significant change are then considered to contain novelty in the sense of not belonging to the previous texture sound or background. In an additional step, it is to be determined whether the identified novelty presents the transition to a texture sound of a new quality or marks the presence a sound object, which, by its original definition, is characterized by a certain time limitation or compactness.

Humans, due to the properties of their auditory system, perceive sound as represented in a coordinate system representing time and frequency (pitch). Thus the natural representation of sound signals tries to simultaneously represent the time- and frequency content of the signal, similar to the description of music by means of written music. A standard approach to obtain a time-frequency representation of a given signal is the *short-time Fourier transform* (STFT), defined in Sect. 2, which is closely related to Gabor analysis. We are going to rely on results from the latter in our work in order to obtain signals' time-frequency representations and to map the time-frequency characteristics of a given signal or class of signals to another one. The properties of the resulting mappings will then inform us about the variability in time-frequency characteristics between the different signals.

We are thus led to the following approach: given a signal which is known to present a texture sound, we observe its inherent characteristics. Using the obtained information, we can then look for significantly different, hence salient, signal components, which we define to represent either a change in the characteristic of texture or as the presence of a sound object, depending on the temporal extension and coherence of the observed novelty. Similarity is measured by the deviation of a Gabor multiplier mask from the constant 1 mask (no modification) under a rather strong sparsity constraint.

This article is organized as follows. The tools from time-frequency analysis involved in the proposed method and their application to the transformation of sounds are presented in the Sect. 2. Section 3 then introduces the technical tools for the identification of sound objects. Numerical results of simulations on real-life and synthetic data are presented in Sect. 4 and we conclude with a short discussion and perspectives.

2   Time-Frequency Analysis and Gabor Frames

We start by introducing the basic ideas of Gabor analysis and fix notation.

While computations are obviously exhibited on finite discrete signals, for theoretical considerations we work with square integrable functions for simplicity and in particular to avoid heavy notation. Thus, we consider functions f in $L^2(\mathbb{R})$, with norm $\|f\|_2^2 = \int_t |f(t)|^2 \, dt$.

The basic idea of time-frequency analysis is to extract the *local* frequency content of a given signal. The most popular transform associated with time-frequency analysis is thus the *short-time Fourier transform* (STFT), which consists of localizing the signal of interest f to a certain short time-interval by multiplication with a window function g and subsequent Fourier transform. We thus denote, for any signal $f \in L^2(\mathbb{R})$ and a window function $g \in L^2(\mathbb{R})$, the short-time Fourier transform of f with respect to g by $\mathcal{V}_g f$, defined as

$$\mathcal{V}_g f(\tau, \omega) = \int_{\mathbb{R}} f(t) g(t - \tau) e^{-2\pi i \omega t} dt. \tag{1}$$

The STFT can be conveniently inverted for any non-zero window, using the same window as synthesis window or a different window $h \in L^2(\mathbb{R})$, such that $\langle g, h \rangle_{L^2}$[1]:

$$f(t) = \frac{1}{\langle g, h \rangle} \int_{\mathbb{R}} \int_{\mathbb{R}} \mathcal{V}_g f(\tau, \omega) h(t - \tau) e^{2\pi i \omega t} d\tau d\omega. \tag{2}$$

It is convenient to introduce operators to describe the shift in time by τ and the modulation by ω, which can also be seen as a shift in frequency. We thus denote, for $f \in L^2(\mathbb{R})$ and $\omega, \tau \in \mathbb{R}$, the frequency shift operators by $M_\omega f(t) = e^{2\pi i \omega t} f(t)$ and the time shift operator by $T_\tau f(t) = f(t - \tau)$, respectively. The representation of f via its STFT can then, for the special case $g = h$ with $\|g\|_2 = 1$ concisely be written as

$$f = \int_{\mathbb{R}} \int_{\mathbb{R}} \langle f, M_\omega T_\tau g \rangle M_\omega T_\tau g \, d\tau d\omega. \tag{3}$$

With this notation, we see that the STFT analyses and reconstructs the signal f with the same family of building blocks, which localize the energy around a time-frequency point (τ, ω). However, the STFT is a very redundant representation.

2.1   Gabor Frames

In order to obtain a signal representation with a reasonable amount of redundancy, the time-shift variable τ and the frequency-shift variable ω of the STFT must be discretized. In other words, the analysis window g is shifted along a discrete lattice $k\tau_0$, $k \in \mathbb{Z}$ and the Fourier transform of the localized signals $f \cdot T_{k\tau_0} g$ is sub-sampled on the discrete lattice $l\omega_0$, $l \in \mathbb{Z}$. Then, the integrals in (2) and (3) are replaced by discrete sums and we obtain the following operator:

$$S_{g,h} f = \sum_{l \in \mathbb{Z}} \sum_{k \in \mathbb{Z}} \langle f, M_{l\omega_0} T_{k\tau_0} g \rangle M_{l\omega_0} T_{k\tau_0} h \tag{4}$$

As opposed to the continuous case, however, the operator S will usually not be equal to a multiple of the identity; in order to accurately reconstruct f from the *Gabor coefficients* $\langle f, M_{l\omega_0} T_{k\tau_0} g \rangle$, the set of time-frequency shifted versions of g needs to form a *Gabor frame* and a specific window must be chosen for reconstruction. These considerations lead to the following definition.

---

[1] $\langle g, h \rangle_{L^2}$ denotes the L^2-inner product, defined as $\langle g, h \rangle_{L^2} = \int_t g(t) \overline{h(t)}$.

Definition 1. *A collection* $\mathcal{G}(g, \tau_0, \omega_0) = \{g_{k,l} := M_{l\omega_0}T_{k\tau_0}g\}_{k,l\in\mathbb{Z}}$ *is called a* **Gabor frame** *for* $L^2(\mathbb{R})$ *if the operator* $S_{g,g}$ *is bounded and invertible on* $L^2(\mathbb{R})$.

Note that the coefficients $\langle f, g_{k,l}\rangle = \langle f, M_{l\omega_0}T_{k\tau_0}g\rangle$ in $S_{g,g}$ are samples of a short-time Fourier transform of f at sampling points $(k\tau_0, l\omega_0)$.

For every frame $\mathcal{G}(g, \tau_0, \omega_0)$ there exists a function γ, called (canonical) dual window, such that $\mathcal{G}(\gamma, \tau_0, \omega_0)$ is again a frame, called dual Gabor frame, and $f = S_{g,\gamma}f = S_{\gamma,g}f$ for all $f \in L^2(\mathbb{R})$. Using the invertibility of the frame operator, this can be seen as follows:

$$f = S_{g,g}^{-1}S_{g,g}f = \sum_{k\in\mathbb{Z}}\sum_{l\in\mathbb{Z}}\langle f, M_{l\omega_0}T_{k\tau_0}g\rangle S_{g,g}^{-1}(M_{l\omega_0}T_{k\tau_0}g).$$

Now it can be shown that $S_{g,g}^{-1}M_{l\omega_0}T_{k\tau_0} = M_{l\omega_0}T_{k\tau_0}S_{g,g}^{-1}$ and thus

$$f = \sum_{k,l}\langle f, g_{k,l}\rangle M_{l\omega_0}T_{k\tau_0}S_{g,g}^{-1}g = \sum_{k,l}\langle f, g_{k,l}\rangle M_{l\omega_0}T_{k\tau_0}\gamma = S_{g,\gamma}f \qquad (5)$$

with the dual window defined as $\gamma := S_{g,g}^{-1}g$.

Another convenient special case is the choice of a *tight Gabor frame*, which allows to use the same window in both analysis and reconstruction. Similar to the dual window, the canonical tight window can be obtained for any Gabor frame by $g^t = S_{g,g}^{-\frac{1}{2}}g$, and leads to the expansion

$$f = \sum_{k,l}\langle f, g_{k,l}^t\rangle M_{l\omega_0}T_{k\tau_0}g^t = S_{g^t,g^t}f. \qquad (6)$$

Due to the special structure of the Gabor frame operator, the inversion of the frame operator is easy and very efficient in certain cases, cf. [4,5]. Luckily, most settings relevant in applications can be treated using these methods. For a detailed introduction to Gabor frames, including all the above results an their proofs, we refer the interested reader to [5,9,10]. The reference software, based on MATLAB, containing all necessary files as well as excellent documentation, is freely available at http://ltfat.sourceforge.net, also cf. [19].

2.2 Time-Frequency Analysis of Sound Signals

In this section, we will show the modulus squared of the subsampled STFT or Gabor coefficients[2] of several audio signals, in order to motivate our approach for finding sound objects in texture sounds.

The first example, in Fig. 1, shows the Gabor coefficients of a prototypical, synthesized instrument sound. The sound consists of 15 harmonics, decaying in both time and frequency. The amplitude is encoded in darkness: darker pixels

---

[2] Note that the resulting visual representation is also known as spectrogram. However, for the reconstruction as discussed in the previous section, the phase factors of the coefficients are crucial and cannot be omitted.

mean a higher absolute value of the coefficient $\langle f, M_{l\omega_0} T_{k\tau_0} g \rangle$. The main characteristic of this sound, which qualifies as a "sound object", is that its energy is concentrated in few limited areas of the time-frequency plane. In other words, in the synthesis Eq. (5), only a few atoms will significantly contribute to the reconstructed signal; this implies, that the sound is *sparsely represented* by means of the Gabor frame.

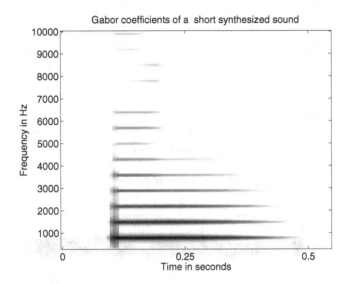

Fig. 1. Spectrogram of a sinusoidal sound object.

The second example, on the other hand, shows the Gabor coefficients of a rain sound in Fig. 2. Rain is a typical instance of a texture sound: while micro changes are clearly visible in the spectrogram, the overall impression is that the sound is characterized by a certain stationarity, no clear beginning or end and no truly significant changes. As opposed to the previous example, the energy of the signal is rather evenly distributed in time and frequency: we cannot expect to get along with few coefficients in the synthesis of such a signal by means of a Gabor frame.

Finally, we show in a third example the composition of a rain (texture) sound with two short sinusoidal sounds (sound objects), see Fig. 3. Here, we also plot the waveform itself, in which the two sinusoidal objects can hardly be distinguished, while in the Gabor coefficients they are clearly visible. It is thus clear, that for the sound events we wish to identify as sound objects, the energy is well-concentrated when the signal is represented using Gabor frames.

2.3 Gabor Multipliers

Gabor multipliers [6–8] describe the transition from a given signal f_1 to a signal f_2 with different time-frequency characteristics by multiplicative modification of the

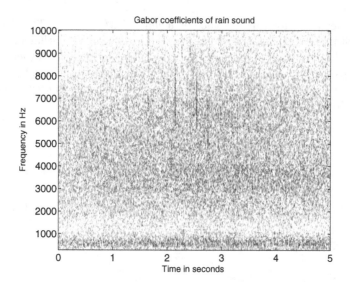

Fig. 2. Spectrogram of rain sound.

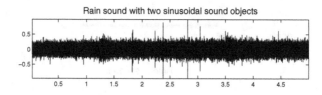

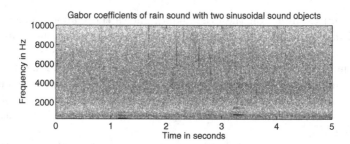

Fig. 3. Spectrogram of rain sound with two sinusoidal sound objects.

input signal's Gabor coefficients $\langle f_1, g_{k,l} \rangle$ in (5). More precisely, let $\mathcal{G}(g, \tau_0, \omega_0)$ be a Gabor frame, γ a dual window and $\mathbf{m} = \{m_{k,l}\}_{k,l \in \mathbb{Z}}$ a bounded complex-valued sequence. Then the Gabor multiplier associated to $(g, \gamma, \tau_0, \omega_0)$ with mask $\mathbf{m}$ is given by

$$G_{\mathbf{m}}f = \sum_{k,l \in \mathbb{Z}} m_{k,l} \langle f, g_{k,l} \rangle \gamma_{k,l}. \tag{7}$$

We see that, by encoding the transition between signals by means of time-frequency characteristics, Gabor multipliers give information about the time-frequency location of significant change and thus of potential novelty: whenever the signals are similar in certain time-frequency areas, e.g. around (τ, ω), we can expect the mask $\mathbf{m}$ to be close to 1 near (τ, ω).

Special Gabor Multipliers via Regularized Inverse Problems. In [15, 16] the authors addressed the problem of mapping a given signal into another one by means of Gabor multipliers to transform sounds. More precisely, for two signals f_1 and f_2, their objective was to find a mask $\mathbf{m}$ such that the Gabor multiplier $G_{\mathbf{m}}$ takes f_1 into f_2 subject to certain constraints on the mask $\mathbf{m}$. The constraints on the mask may be formulated as *sparsity priors* in time-frequency or total energy. For our problem, we want the mask to deviate from 1 in absolute value only if the encountered changes are sufficiently significant to pass as either a sound object or a change in texture. Small changes, inherent to texture itself, should be ignored. This is achieved by choosing an appropriate coefficient prior and tuning the parameter λ in the following minimization problem

$$\mathbf{m} = \arg\min_{\mathbf{m}} \| f_2 - G_{\mathbf{m}} f_1 \|_2^2 + \lambda d(\mathbf{m}). \tag{8}$$

The following choices of d will be considered: if d is given by $d(\mathbf{m}) = \|\,|\mathbf{m}| - 1\|_1$, sparsity of the deviations from absolute value 1 in the mask is enforced. Another popular choice is $d(\mathbf{m}) = \|\mathbf{m} - 1\|_2^2$ to control total energy; if the ℓ^1 is replaced by a mixed norm or weighted norm, cf. [12], structural consideration can be introduced. The parameter λ determines the influence of the regularization term in (8).

Solving the Optimization Problem. In [15, 16] different strategies for finding the solution to (8) for various regularization terms are presented. Here, we recall the solution for $d(\mathbf{m}) = \|\,|\mathbf{m}| - 1\|_1$ and $d(\mathbf{m}) = \|\mathbf{m} - 1\|_2^2$. It is, on the one hand, possible to obtain a solution to (8) by means of iterative shrinkage operators, cf. [1–3]. However, these iterative approaches can be quite computationally expensive. In our experiments, we found that obtaining a *diagonal approximation*, as suggested in [16] is usually sufficient in the context of our problem. It can be found by replacing the optimization problem (8) by the corresponding problem formulated directly in the Gabor (or time-frequency) domain. To see this, assume that we have a tight frame and note that

$$f_2 - G_{\mathbf{m}} f_1 = \sum_{k,l \in \mathbb{Z}} \langle f_2, g_{k,l} \rangle g_{k,l} - \sum_{k,l \in \mathbb{Z}} m_{k,l} \cdot \langle f_1, g_{k,l} \rangle g_{k,l}$$

Denoting the coefficient sequences by $c_{k,l}^1 = \langle f_1, g_{k,l} \rangle$ and $c_{k,l}^2 = \langle f_2, g_{k,l} \rangle$, we can thus replace (8) by its formulation directly in the Gabor domain:

$$\mathbf{m} = \arg\min_{\mathbf{m}} \sum_{k,l \in \mathbb{Z}} |c_{k,l}^2 - m_{k,l} c_{k,l}^1|^2 + \lambda d(\mathbf{m}). \tag{9}$$

The solution to this simplified problem is then given, for $d(\mathbf{m}) = \|\mathbf{m} - 1\|_2^2$, by

$$m_{k,l} = \frac{|\overline{c_{k,l}^1}c_{k,l}^2| + \lambda}{|c_{k,l}^1|^2 + \lambda} \cdot e^{i \arg[\overline{c_{k,l}^1}c_{k,l}^2]} \tag{10}$$

and for $d(\mathbf{m}) = \||\mathbf{m}| - 1\|_1$, by

$$m_{k,l} = \begin{cases} \frac{|\overline{c_{k,l}^1}c_{k,l}^2| - \frac{\lambda}{2}}{|c_{k,l}^1|^2} \cdot e^{i \arg[\overline{c_{k,l}^2}c_{k,l}^1]} & \text{if } \frac{|\overline{c_{k,l}^1}c_{k,l}^2|}{|c_{k,l}^1|^2} \geq 1 + \frac{\lambda}{2|c_{k,l}^1|^2} \\ \frac{|\overline{c_{k,l}^1}c_{k,l}^2| + \frac{\lambda}{2}}{|c_{k,l}^1|^2} \cdot e^{i \arg[\overline{c_{k,l}^2}c_{k,l}^1]} & \text{if } \frac{|\overline{c_{k,l}^1}c_{k,l}^2|}{|c_{k,l}^1|^2} \leq 1 - \frac{\lambda}{2|c_{k,l}^1|^2} \\ \equiv 1 & \text{else.} \end{cases} \tag{11}$$

For derivation and proofs, see [15,16].

3   Technical Tools for Identifying Novelty

We now explain how the typical characteristics of texture sounds can be exploited by means of the estimation of Gabor multiplier masks in order to identify sound objects. We assume, that we are given a part of signal which is known to contain a pure texture signal. This prior information is not based on specific signal properties but must be obtained from some kind of annotation: as explained in the introduction, certain sound events may be considered to be part of the texture (background) signal or a more independent sound event, depending on the "auditory zoom" the listener assumes.

Let $f \in L^2(\mathbb{R})$ be the background, texture signal or part of signal. We divide it into overlapping slices f_i, $i \in \mathbb{Z}$, in the following way:

$$f_i(t) = f(t) \text{ for } t \in [\alpha_i, \beta_i], \ \alpha_{i-1} < \alpha_i \leq \beta_{i-1}, \ \alpha_{i+1} \leq \beta_i < \beta_{i+1} \tag{12}$$

3.1   Identifying Novelty

Let us denote the set of indices corresponding to slices, defined in (12), which belong to the known textural part of a given signal by $\mathcal{J}_0$. Then the slices f_i, $i \in \mathcal{J}_0$, are similar by assumption, hence also their Gabor transforms. The grade of similarity is learned from the first part of the signal, which is known to be textural. In this situation, the modulus of the mask $\mathbf{m}_{i,j}$ of a Gabor multiplier transforming f_i into f_j for $i, j \in \mathcal{J}_0$, i.e. $f_j = G_{\mathbf{m}_{i,j}} f_i$, is close to constant 1 and $d(\mathbf{m}_{i,j})$ is close to zero.

During the learning phase, the parameter λ is tuned to only allow for small deviations from the constant mask $\mathbf{m} = 1$. In order to account for micro-changes typically found in textural sounds, we average the norm over N randomly picked slices f_i, $i \in \mathcal{J}_0$ for $1, \ldots N$ in the textural section of the signal. In other words, we compute $s_{i_0} = \sum_{j=1}^{N} d(\mathbf{m}_{j,i_0})$ for all $i_0 \in \mathcal{J}_0$ in order to determine a detection-threshold $\epsilon > 0$ for unknown data. Subsequently, any deviation substantially higher than the deviations found during the learning phase is considered a cue for the presence of novelty.

Thus, the problem of identifying novelty in a texture sound or background is based on studying the transition masks: for every new slice f_n in the unknown signal part, we pick N indices at random from $\mathcal{J}_0$ and compute $s_n = \sum_{j=1}^{N} d(\mathbf{m}_{j,n})$. Whenever $s_n > \epsilon$, for the ϵ determined from the deviations to be expected from the data observed in the textural part, then we may assume the presence of a sound object or novel texture in slice f_n.

3.2 Temporal Extension and Structured Sparsity

In order to distinguish between novel features of the texture sound, in particular, the transition to a modified texture, and an event which should be called sound object, the introduction of a time-limitation is necessary. As pointed out before, the particular length up to which novel characteristics should be understood as an object depends on the context, e.g., in the case of music, on the inherent tempo of the musical piece. In general, a fraction of a second to few seconds (<10) may be seen as a guideline to the possible length of a sound object. After that time limit, the value of s_k should drop back to the chosen ϵ and thus signify the return to the previously perceived texture sound. This notion of sound object can be manually applied to the resulting error curves.

More directly, the required *persistence* over time can be enforced by applying the principles of structured or social sparsity, cf. [12–14,18]. Here, the thresholding operators applied in order to achieve sparse multipliers, as in (11), is replaced by more complicated thresholding operator. In particular, the thresholding value, which determines, whether a particular coefficient in the mask is set to 1 or is only modified appropriately, will depend on a *neighborhood*, to be determined according to a priori knowledge, of every coefficient in consideration. For example, if we wish to identify sound object with a harmonic structure which is persistent over time (for a certain duration), we can shrink the coefficients $c_{k,l}$ according to a neighborhood in time. That means, that a coefficient is more likely to be considered as relevant, if an entire neighborhood has absolute values different from 1, rather than if only an isolated component is strong. In a similar manner, objects, which are persistent in frequency (e.g. percussive components) may be systematically search for by imposing persistence over all (or certain) frequencies. An example of this approach is presented in Sect. 4.3.

4   Simulations

We will now present results obtained with the introduced method, both on synthetic and natural sounds. In particular, in Sect. 4.1, we compare various classes of different textures, while Sect. 4.2 shows, how sound objects can be detected in texture sounds. Finally, in Sect. 4.3, we present an example of detection improvement by imposing structural considerations in the sparsity constraint.

4.1   Comparing Textures

In this section we compare three different texture sounds: rain, fire and wind. We take three synthetic and one natural signal from each texture and use different values for λ in order to find an optimal λ such that the signals within one category are most similar to one another. The signals are divided into overlapping slices, with 50 % overlap, and slices of 20480 samples. We work with a standard tight Gabor frame with a Hann window of length 1024 and 75 % overlap. The texture signals g_i, $i = 1,\ldots,12$, are compared against 10 random slices g_j^k, each of length L, of the signals g_j and the average of $\||\mathbf{m}_{i,(j,k)}| - 1\|_1$ is computed. More precisely, for a given textural signal g_{j_0}, we compare it against each g_j by choosing at random 10 slices of g_j, denoted by g_j^k, and evaluate

$$s_{i,j} = \frac{1}{10}\sum_{k=1}^{10} \||\mathbf{m}_{i,(j,k)}| - 1\|_1, \tag{13}$$

for each slice i of g_{j_0}, where $\mathbf{m}_{i,(j,k)}$ is the mask minimizing a transition from $i - th$ slice of g_{j_0} to the slice g_j^k. We then take the mean value $E(j_0,j)$ of $s_{.,j}$. The results, for $\lambda = 0.5, 0.8, 1.2, 1.5$, are depicted in Fig. 4. We can observe that different values of λ work better for different textures. We would like to find an optimal λ such that the algorithm ignores small differences between the signals form the given category and the masks taking one slice to another are close to 1. As expected, the smallest deviation occur when the signals are compared within their categories. In Fig. 4, it corresponds to diagonal squares.

4.2   Identifying Sound Objects in Sound Textures

In this section we present numerical results for two rather distinct texture sounds: heavy rain and an audio scene recorded in a jungle. Note that the sound-files corresponding to the examples as well as supplementary examples, codes and extensions are available at the website http://homepage.univie.ac.at/monika. doerfler/SoundObj.html.

Example 1: Rain. In order to give a proof of concept, we first apply the proposed method to finding synthetic signals s which unambiguously qualify as sound objects within the synthetic rain signal; we use damped sums of six different harmonics of 0.5 s length. The SNR[3] of the objects present in the texture sound is between -5 dB and -7.5 dB. The spectrogram of the concatenated sound is shown in Fig. 5. For this sound, we choose slices of approximately 250 ms length and 75 % overlap and work with the Gabor coefficients obtained from a standard tight Gabor frame with a Hann window of length 1024 and 75 % overlap. For the identification of the two sound objects, we pick $N = 8$ slices f_j from the initial texture part of the signal at random and compute the average s_k

---

[3] We define the signal to noise ratio (SNR) by $SNR_{dB} = 10\log_{10}(\|s\|_2^2/\|f\|_2^2)$, given in dB, by where f is the background signal, which can be seen as "noise" in which s, the sound object is to be traced.

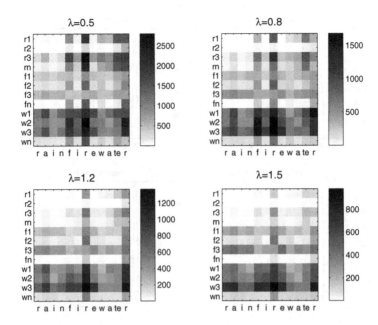

Fig. 4. Textures: the mean values of average deviations $s_{j_0,j}$ between different textures for different sparsity levels λ. Here $r1, r2, r3$ denote synthetic rains and rn a natural rain signal. Similarly $f1, f2, f3, fn$ are fire textures, while $w1, w2, w3, wn$ denote wind texture signals.

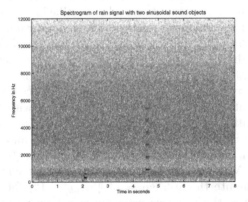

Fig. 5. Spectrogram of rain sound with two sinusoidal sound objects.

of $\|\,|\mathbf{m}_{j,k}| - 1\|_1$ for f_j, $j = 1, \ldots, 8$ and all k. We show the results for 4 different levels of sparsity, more precisely, for $\lambda = 0.2, 0.5, 2.5, 8$ in Fig. 6. Apparently, the sound objects are well identified by the proposed algorithm; it becomes clear from these first results, however, that the choice of λ may be subtle, in particular for more complex signals: if it is chosen too high, salient features may be lost.

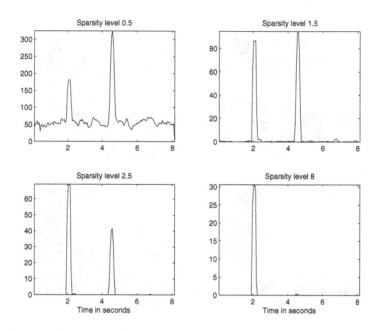

Fig. 6. Average deviation s_k from textural character for different sparsity levels for rain signal.

On the other hand, for too small λ, irrelevant signal components, which should be interpreted as part of the texture, may be identified as novelty.

We now consider the following setting: given the recording of a natural rain f we place randomly two objects, namely a washing machine sound and an industrial sound with SNR of the objects present in the texture between $-4\,\mathrm{dB}$ and $-7.5\,\mathrm{dB}$. We wish to recover the positions of the foreign sound events (sound objects). To do so, we choose slices f_k of the signal f, now containing the objects, of approximately half a second (20480 samples) length with 50 % overlap. As before, we work with the Gabor coefficients obtained from a standard tight Gabor frame with a Hann window of length 1024 samples and 75 % overlap. For the identification of the two sound objects, for each slice f_k we pick $N = 10$ slices g_j, $j = 1, \ldots, N$, from a fixed data set of 10 different synthetic rain signals at random and compute the average s_k of $\|\|\mathbf{m}_{j,k}| - 1\|_1$ for g_j, $j = 1, \ldots, 10$ and all k. For each λ, the resulting error curve is then normalized, such that the maximum value assumed is 1. We pick various thresholds values and decide that a sound object is present in slice k, whenever the value s_k is above that threshold. Note that the same threshold can simultaneously be applied to all values of λ due to the previous normalization step.

In comparing the resulting positions of the objects with the true positions, we analyze the receiver operating characteristic (ROC) curve and compute the following:

- accuracy $= \frac{TP+TN}{TP+TN+FP+FN}$
- specificity $= \frac{TN}{TN+FP}$
- sensitivity $= \frac{TP}{TP+FN}$

where TP, TN, FP, FN signify true positives, true negatives, false positives and false negatives, respectively. The corresponding graphs are plotted over varying threshold values, from 0.01 to 0.5 with step size 0.01, in Fig. 7. The simulations were performed for $\lambda = 0.5, 0.8, 1.2, 1.5$, and with an average of 20 trials per threshold.

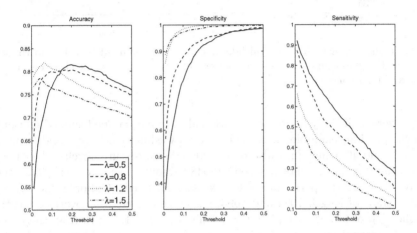

Fig. 7. Receiver Operating Characteristic (ROC) curves for different values of λ.

An ideal method for identifying the sources in the mixture would have both specificity and sensitivity equal to one. In more realistic settings it is necessary to find a threshold for which a good compromise between high specificity and high sensitivity is achieved. As can be seen from the rightmost plot in Fig. 7, for each λ: increasing threshold results in decreasing number of correctly detected positions of objects. On the other hand, as can be seen from the middle plot, the optimum value for specificity is reached earliest for $\lambda = 1.2$. This means that one can choose a threshold where specificity is optimal (i.e. no false positives) while still having acceptable sensitivity (i.e. amount of true positives). This also results in the highest value in terms of accuracy being reached earliest for $\lambda = 1.2$ (leftmost plot). Similarly good results are also achieved for $\lambda = 0.8$.

Example 2: Jungle. The second sound, of 58 s length, is more complex; its waveform and spectrogram are depicted in Fig. 8.

The jungle texture is dense and shows distinct periodic structures. Between second 14 and 22 a salient change in texture (and amplitude) takes place due to the appearance of a new animal sound (a cicada); this novelty (in texture) is expected to be identified by the proposed algorithm. On the other hand, two new

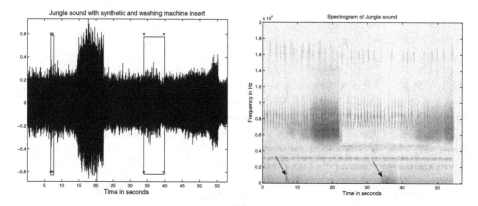

Fig. 8. Jungle sound with two artificially added sounds, marked by a box in the left display and by two arrows in the spectrogram. The appearance of the cicada is clearly visible around second 13.

objects were artificially added to the original sound: a damped sum of sinusoids as in the previous example, at second 7, and a washing machine sound between second 34 and 40, which may also be considered as a texture novelty. We choose slices of approximately half a second (20480 samples) length with 50 % overlap. We compare the performance for two standard tight Gabor frames with a Hann window of length 1024 and 4096, respectively, and 75 % overlap. For the identification of novelty, we pick $N = 10$ slices f_j, $j = 1, \ldots, 10$ from the initial part of the signal at random and compute the average s_k of $\||\mathbf{m}_{j,k}| - 1\|_1$ for f_j, $j = 1, \ldots, 10$ and all k. Based on the first, purely textural part of the signal, λ should be tuned in order to allow only negligible deviation of the absolute value of $\mathbf{m}$ from 1. Here, we show the results for 4 different levels of sparsity, more precisely, for $\lambda = 0.2, 0.5, 2.5, 4.5$. The results are shown in Figs. 9 and 10. The sinusoidal sound object has a clear local persistence and limitation in time which the texture part lacks, but which is typical for many instrument signals; this signal component is reliably identified even under strong sparsity constraints. A priori knowledge - or assumption - about the objects one may be interested in, can be further exploited in order to improve the method's success and reliability. On the other hand, the identification of the novelty introduced by the washing machine sound, which may be considered as a texture sound itself, is more subtle - also perceptually, cf. the sound signal available on the companion website. Here, we encounter a doubtful event which may or may not be considered as an object, rather extended in time, or a mere modification of texture. Furthermore, this novelty may easily be missed by an inappropriate choice of sparsity level. The cicada, on the other hand, is only correctly identified for rather low sparsity levels; this is all the more astonishing because its appearance introduces a strong increase in amplitude. However, its energy is sufficiently spread in timefrequency to disappear as soon as strong sparsity priors are used. We observe in this example, that the influence of the underlying Gabor frame is relatively

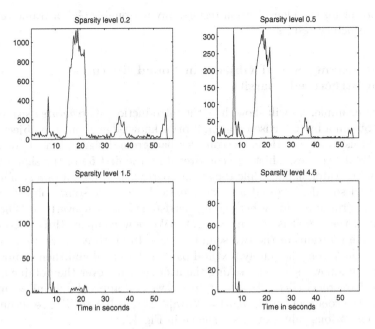

Fig. 9. Jungle sound: average deviation s_k from textural character for different sparsity levels, short window (1024 samples).

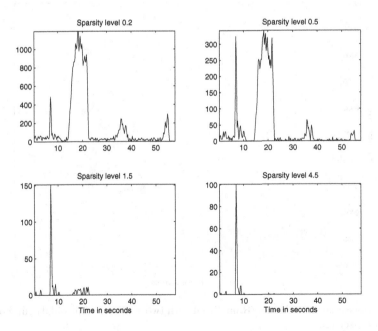

Fig. 10. Jungle sound: average deviation s_k from textural character for different sparsity levels, long window (4096 samples)

unimportant for the identification results; any reasonable Gabor framework will yield satisfactory results.

4.3 Identifying Sound Objects in Sound Textures by Structured Sparsity

As a last example, we will show, how the introduction of *structured sparsity* can help to obtain a more focused search, if prior knowledge about the objects to be identified, is available. Here, we consider background signal, which consists of two different textures, which are concatenated: the first 5 s of the signal consist of a running water signal, while the second part is, as before, a rain signal. Both are natural sounds. Inserted are two identical synthetic sound objects with a harmonic structure and rather strong persistence in each overtone. The spectrogram of the signal is shown in Fig. 11. We now compare three methods to identify the positions of the two sound objects. In all three cases, we randomly choose 5 slices from the purely textural part of the signal and then compare the incoming, unknown slices, by taking the average error over the obtained masks for these 5 reference slices. As sparsity prior, we first apply the shrinkage method based on the coefficient prior $d(\mathbf{m}) = \lambda \||\mathbf{m}| - 1\|_1$, as before. The resulting error curves, for various values of λ, are shown in Fig. 12.

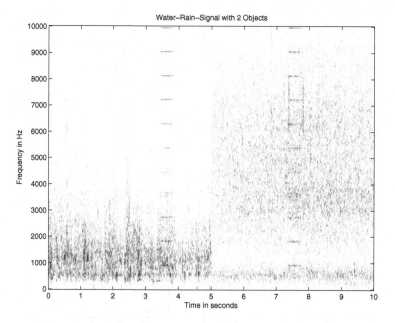

Fig. 11. Spectrogram of Water/Rain signal with two synthetic sinusoidal sound objects randomly inserted.

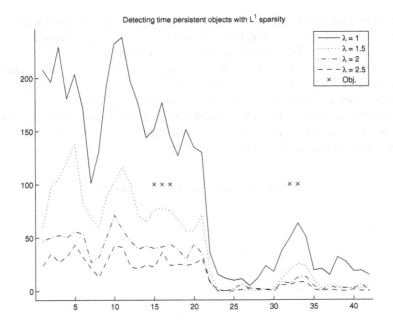

Fig. 12. Detection curves obtained by imposing L^1-sparsity constraints.

We then modify the shrinkage operators presented in (11) by making the shrinkage dependent on a frequency- or time-neighborhood. Here, since the single slices are time-limited (and frequency-limited due to the sampling), we simply used the entire slice-length as our neighborhood. Setting

$$\tilde{m}_{k,l} = \frac{\overline{c^1_{k,l}} c^2_{k,l}}{|c^1_{k,l}|^2},$$

we then replace the shrinkage in (11) by

$$m_{k,l} = \begin{cases} \tilde{m}_{k,l} \cdot \left(1 - \frac{\lambda}{2\sqrt{\sum_k |\tilde{m}_{k,l} - 1 + \frac{\lambda}{2}|^2}}\right) + 1 & \text{if } \sqrt{\sum_k |\tilde{m}_{k,l} - 1 + \frac{\lambda}{2}|^2} > \frac{\lambda}{2} \\ \tilde{m}_{k,l} \cdot \left(1 - \frac{\lambda}{2\sqrt{\sum_k |\tilde{m}_{k,l} - 1 - \frac{\lambda}{2}|^2}}\right) + 1 & \text{if } \sqrt{\sum_k |\tilde{m}_{k,l} - 1 - \frac{\lambda}{2}|^2} > \frac{\lambda}{2} \\ \equiv 1 & \text{else} \end{cases} \quad (14)$$

for obtaining time-persistence and by

$$m_{k,l} = \begin{cases} \tilde{m}_{k,l} \cdot \left(1 - \frac{\lambda}{2\sqrt{\sum_l |\tilde{m}_{k,l} - 1 + \frac{\lambda}{2}|^2}}\right) + 1 & \text{if } \sqrt{\sum_l |\tilde{m}_{k,l} - 1 + \frac{\lambda}{2}|^2} > \frac{\lambda}{2} \\ \tilde{m}_{k,l} \cdot \left(1 - \frac{\lambda}{2\sqrt{\sum_l |\tilde{m}_{k,l} - 1 - \frac{\lambda}{2}|^2}}\right) + 1 & \text{if } \sqrt{\sum_l |\tilde{m}_{k,l} - 1 - \frac{\lambda}{2}|^2} > \frac{\lambda}{2} \\ \equiv 1 & \text{else} \end{cases} \quad (15)$$

in order to impose frequency persistence.

The resulting error curves, for different values of λ, in both cases are shown in Figs. 13 and 14, respectively. It is obvious from this simple example, that the detection of objects with known time-frequency characteristics can be improved and stabilized by imposing the corresponding coefficient priors. Here, imposing time-persistence leads to a significantly improved accuracy (in the sense that either false positive are more likely to be avoided and/or more true positives are achieved) over all values of λ and for both background textures than the usage of pure sparsity (Fig. 12) or, even more impressively, than the usage of the incorrect orientation of persistence in Fig. 13.

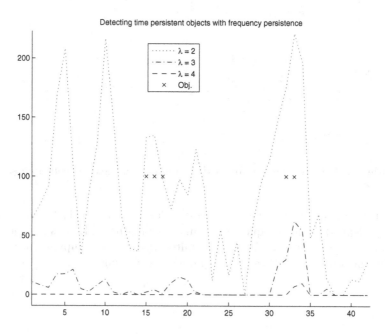

Fig. 13. Detection curves obtained by imposing frequency persistence.

5   Discussion and Perspectives

We presented results of ongoing work on a method for identifying novelty; the proposed approach exploits the assumed textural character of known signals and decides that 'foreign' sound components are present, if these characteristics are significantly violated. The masks computed during the evaluation process can be directly employed for the extraction of signal components of interest. This idea will be investigated in the framework of more extended numerical experiments to evaluate the performance of the proposed method on larger samples of both texture sounds and sound objects. Furthermore, first attempts to apply the idea of structured or social sparsity to the identification of novelty and sound objects

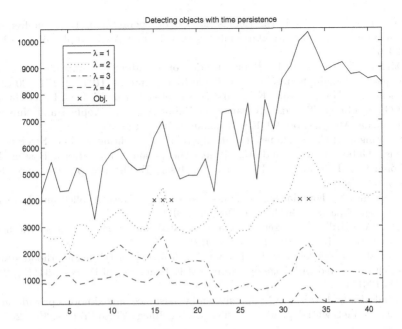

Fig. 14. Detection curves obtained by imposing time persistence.

show promising results and will be further exploited. These questions will be investigated in detail in ongoing work on the topic; software, sound examples and results are and will be presented on the companion website http://homepage. univie.ac.at/monika.doerfler/SoundObj.html.

Acknowledgments. We would like to thank Anaïk Olivero for sharing code for computing Gabor masks and Richard Kronland-Martinet and his team in LMA, CNRS Marseille, for giving us permission to use their software SPAD.

References

1. Beck, A., Teboulle, M.: A fast iterative shrinkage-thresholding algorithm for linear inverse problems. SIAM J. Imaging Sci. **2**(1), 183–202 (2009)
2. Beck, A., Teboulle, M.: Fast gradient-based algorithms for constrained total variation image denoising and deblurring problems. IEEE Trans. Image Process. **18**(11), 2419–2434 (2009)
3. Daubechies, I., Defrise, M., De Mol, C.: An iterative thresholding algorithm for linear inverse problems with a sparsity constraint. Comm. Pure Appl. Math. **57**(11), 1413–1457 (2004)
4. Daubechies, I., Grossmann, A., Meyer, Y.: Painless nonorthogonal expansions. J. Math. Phys. **27**(5), 1271–1283 (1986)
5. Dörfler, M.: Time-frequency analysis for music signals. a mathematical approach. J. New Music Res. **30**(1), 3–12 (2001)

6. Dörfler, M., Torrésani, B.: Representation of operators in the time-frequency domain and generalized Gabor multipliers. J. Fourier Anal. Appl. **16**(2), 261–293 (2010)
7. Dörfler, M., Torrésani, B.: Representation of operators by sampling in the time-frequency domain. Sampl. Theory Signal Image Process. **10**(1–2), 171–190 (2011)
8. Feichtinger, H.G., Nowak, K.: A first survey of Gabor multipliers. In: Feichtinger, H.G., Strohmer, T. (eds.) Advances in Gabor Analysis. Applied and Numerical Harmonic Analysis, pp. 99–128. Birkhäuser, Boston (2003)
9. Feichtinger, H.G., Strohmer, T. Introduction. In: Feichtinger, H.G., Strohmer, T. (eds.) Gabor Analysis and Algorithms Theory and Applications, Boston, MA, Applied and Numerical Harmonic Analysis. Birkhäuser, Boston, pp. 1–31, 453–488 (1998)
10. Gröchenig, K.: Foundations of Time-Frequency Analysis. Applied and Numerical Harmonic Analysis. Birkhäuser, Boston (2001)
11. Klien, V., Grill, T., Flexer, A.: On automated annotation of acousmatic music. J. New Music Res. **41**(2), 153–173 (2012)
12. Kowalski, M., Siedenburg, K., Dörfler, M.: Social sparsity! neighborhood systems enrich structured shrinkage operators. IEEE Trans. Signal Process. **61**(10), 2498–2511 (2013)
13. Kowalski, M., Torrésani, B.: Sparsity and persistence: mixed norms provide simple signals models with dependent coefficients. Sig. Image Video Process. **3**(3), 251–264 (2009)
14. Kowalski, M., Torrésani, B. Structured sparsity: from mixed norms to structured shrinkage. In: SPARS'09 - Signal Processing with Adaptive Sparse Structured Representations (2009)
15. Olivero, A. Les multiplicateurs temps-fréquence. Applications à l'analyse et à la synthèse de signaux sonores et musicaux. Ph.D. thesis (2012)
16. Olivero, A., Torresani, B., Kronland-Martinet, R.: A class of algorithms for time-frequency multiplier estimation. IEEE Trans. Audio, Speech Lang. Process. **21**(8), 1550–1559 (2013)
17. Schaeffer, P.: On Automated Annotation of Acousmatic Music. Editions du Seuil, Paris (2002)
18. Siedenburg, K., Dörfler, M.: Persistent time-frequency shrinkage for audio denoising. J. Audio Eng. Soc. **61**(1/2), 29–38 (2013)
19. Sondergaard, P., Torrésani, B., Balazs, P.: The linear time frequency analysis toolbox. Int. J. Wavelets Multiresolut. Inf. Process. **10**(4), 1250032 (2012)

Waveform-Aligned Adaptive Windows for Spectral Component Tracking and Noise Rejection

Yang Zhao and David Gerhard[✉]

Department of Computer Science, University of Regina, Regina, SK, Canada
{zhao224y,gerhard}@cs.uregina.ca

Abstract. A new Short-Time Fourier Transform (STFT) pipeline is presented which uses a two-pass method to adapt the size of the analysis window to the period of the signal, which is assumed in this case to be at least pseudo-periodic. The pipeline begins with pitch estimation, followed by upsampling, to construct a new analysis window that matches the length of a single period. This reduces or eliminates the spectral leakage problems which are typical of traditional STFT analysis techniques. The result is a discrete and accurate spectral representation that provides highly accurate location of partials from one analysis frame to the next. We have extended this method to allow noise cancellation by selecting an analysis window that contains a small whole number of complete cycles. We also present a new display method based on this pipeline which greatly improves the spectrogram through enhanced distinction among partials. Finally, validation is performed by signal restoration on 40 clips, showing the superiority of the pipeline for true periodic signals and comparability for pseudo-periodic signals.

Keywords: Spectrogram · Spectral leakage · Noise exclusion · Fundamental frequency alignment

1 Introduction

The Fourier Transform (FT) has been widely used in various fields. In signal processing, the typical usage of FT is to decompose a signal to measure the amplitude of individual frequency components therein. Most of the time, the Discrete Fourier Transform (DFT) is used to process digital signals, and the Fast Fourier Transform (FFT) algorithm has improved the computational efficiency to the point that FFT is a standard, unquestioned tool in most audio processing pipelines. Because the traditional Fourier Transform does not give any information on the time at which a frequency component occurs, the Short-Time Fourier Transform (STFT) is commonly used, which employs a moving FFT window to track the change in harmonic content of a nonstationary signal. The STFT defines a particularly useful class of time-frequency distributions which specify complex amplitude versus time versus frequency for any signal.

© Springer International Publishing Switzerland 2014
M. Aramaki et al. (Eds.): CMMR 2013, LNCS 8905, pp. 463–480, 2014.
DOI: 10.1007/978-3-319-12976-1_27

The framing of the STFT causes spectral leakage. The STFT represents a signal within a frame as a sum of sinusoids, and two characteristics of the technique contribute to spectral leakage. First, if the analysis frame is considered using a simple square window (called a "boxcar" window), the transform usually sees significant discontinuity at the frame boundaries, and these discontinuities (not being present in the original signal) cause new frequency components to be introduced in the signal. This problem is usually mediated by introducing a different window like a triangular window or a Hanning window, which reduces the signal to zero at the edges of the frame. This removes the discontinuity but also changes features of the signal, and does not completely mediate spectral leakage. The second characteristic that contributes to spectral leakage is the fact that the analysis window has a base frequency that is (most often) different from the fundamental frequency of the signal being analyzed. The true fundamental of the signal therefore falls between two available components of the base frequency of the window, and more commonly is spread over a few adjacent frequency bins. Most researchers have taken this to be a standard unfixable drawback of the FFT algorithm, since the major speed enhancements of the FFT come from the requirement that the analysis window be a power of two samples long (typical values are 256, 512 and 1024). Various methods have been proposed to mediate spectral leakage, such as coherent sampling [2], signal rounding [12] and hardware window correction [7], and similar techniques has been used in music- and speech-based applications [10,11].

As a common analysis method that reveals the microstructure of vocal, instrumental and synthetic sounds, the results of spectrum analysis are often valuable in pitch and rhythm recognition, as well as voice analysis applications. However, the spectrogram output of spectrum analysis has a significant shortcoming in that it involves an intrinsic trade-off between time resolution and frequency resolution. The reason for the time-frequency resolution trade-off is the Fourier domain property that a window and its spectrum cannot both be arbitrarily narrow. The implication is that improvements in the identification of spectral detail from a spectrogram can only be achieved at the expense of deterioration in temporal resolution. The question here becomes how to obtain a best balance between these two contradictory sides, or more specifically, when we would know that a best frequency resolution has already been reached and further deterioration in temporal resolution would not help at all. In fact, a wide range of off-the-shelf audio editing applications have incorporated the feature of spectrogram observation and analysis.

Among the four parameters of STFT (window type, window length L, FFT size N and frame offset/hop size I) L is of prime importance because the width of the windowing limits both the time and frequency resolution of the analysis. If L is too small, sinusoids are not resolved and we can only observe some energy fluctuations; if L is too large, time variation of sinusoids cannot also be observed correctly, and pseudo-periodic signals tend to blur the spectral content within a window. For harmonic (*i.e.* pitched) sounds, the ideal situation is that the width of the window should be equal to fundamental frequency (f_0). Usually, however, f_0 is unknown *a priori*, and in fact STFT itself is often used to extract f_0.

Fig. 1. WAAW pipeline combining pitch estimation and upsampling to obtain optimal frequency-based DFT length.

Modern computing allows us to have "fast enough" STFT without the power-of-two requirement, opening up the possibility of selecting a window size appropriate to the task. An adaptive model [8] that calculates a dynamic frame size would allow it to vary from one analysis frame to the next. A pitch-related window size has been used in separating harmonic sounds [9] and an optimal FFT window was proposed [4] by setting the FFT window to $1/f_0$. The idea has never been evaluated quantitatively, and improved performance and f_0 estimation (e.g. [5]), means that it is feasible to include such a dynamic STFT in a standard real-time workflow.

Our STFT system uses waveform-aligned adaptive windows (WAAW). This paper presents a verification of the resolution, speed, and representation, as well as the utility of this method in noise rejection and signal processing. The main target of this workflow is pitched monophonic sounds, $e.g.$ voice or musical instruments.

The remainder of the paper is organized as follows. In Sect. 2, we introduce the main steps in the pipeline, including pre-processing, pitch estimation and upsampling. Section 3 presents a novel approach to plot the spectrum based on the frequency information obtained from the pipeline. An application of this method for noise rejection in harmonic signals is described in Sect. 4. Afterwards, the performance tests are reported in Sect. 5, from the aspects of both visualization and ability to recover the original signals. Finally in Sect. 6, we discussed some remaining issues and possible improving directions about the work.

2   WAAW STFT Pipeline

The pipeline of the system is shown in Fig. 1. The sequence of operations is as follows:

1. The signal is framed with a large frame size.
2. The pitch of the signal is estimated for each frame.
3. The signal is up-sampled to reduce the inter-sample error for best window size selection.
4. The frame is windowed based on the best DFT length
5. The DFT is calculated on the new window
6. Partials are tracked from one frame to the next based on ordinal position.

A complete description of each step in the sequence is given below.

2.1   Pitch Estimation

There are three categories of pitch estimation algorithms [6]: time domain, frequency domain, and statistical methods. We opted to use the YIN [5] system, pitch estimation system based on quadratic interpolation of autocorrelation, because of its low error rate and low computational load. We avoided frequency-domain pitch estimation methods because they often assume the success of the STFT which we are attempting to improve. The pitch estimation produced by Yin is then used to align the analysis window to the signal being analysed. It should be noted that unhitched signals will not respond well to this algorithm, as the size of the analysis window will be unpredictable. If a signal contains pitched and unhitched segments, a simple existence-of-pitch system should be employed so that WAAW is applied only to pitched portions of the signal, and traditional STFT could be applied to non-pitched portions of the signal.

2.2   Upsampling

Only cycles which are exact multiples of the window size (in time) will begin and end on a sample. Generally, however, there is a large probability that a cycle will begin to repeat at a point between two samples. Choosing one or the other of these samples would produce a window size slightly larger or smaller than the period, causing spectral leakage. Upsampling is introduced to reduce the error. Assuming a band-limited signal, there exists an upsampling factor μ which allows a cycle to complete in a whole number of samples, but this is impractical. In practice we use a fixed μ (e.g. 10) to upsample the original signal and allow the signal to repeat closer to a discrete sample, which makes it possible for a more accurate window size matched to the period of the signal under analysis.

Because analysis frames are being matched to the extracted frequency of the signal, frames no longer have a power-of-2 number of samples, and the FFT is no longer "fast". Instead, we can specify the next highest power-of-two frame-size, and define μ as the ratio between the resulting sampling frequencies. Suppose there are l_c samples in a cycle before upsampling, we then choose $l'_c = 2^c$ (c is some integer making l'_c a power of 2 larger than l_c) samples as the number of samples in a cycle after the upsampling. The resampling factor μ would then be:

$$\mu = \frac{f_s}{f'_s} = \frac{f_s}{(l'_c - 1)/T} \tag{1}$$

where f_s and f'_s are the sampling rate (in Hz) before and after the upsampling process, respectively. T is the length of a cycle (in seconds). Figure 2 shows the result of upsampling.

Only the frequency bins for the original sampling rate are shown when plotting a spectrogram (Sect. 3), and downsampling should be used in the restoration task (Sect. 5.3).

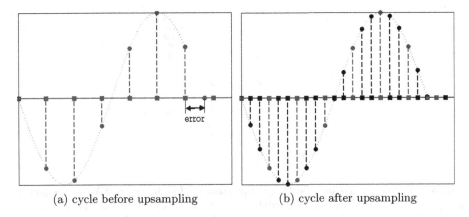

(a) cycle before upsampling   (b) cycle after upsampling

Fig. 2. Upsampling improves window alignment. (a) The cycle starts at a sample, but ends between two samples. (b) After a 3× upsampling, the cycle ends at a sample location.

2.3 Windowing

An often ignored feature of the FFT is that it assumes that the signal is periodic and that the domain of the transform is exactly one period (or an integer number of periods). Direct application of the FFT to signals that have a fractional period *i.e.*, not an integer number of cycles in the analysis domain (in practice, almost all signals) results in spectral leakage. Although this leakage cannot be eliminated, it can be reduced by applying an appropriate windowing function to reduce discontinuities at the analysis domain boundaries.

Typically, the user must choose the appropriate window function for the specific application, but in practice most users select a standard window function such as Hamming or Hanning. When windowing is not applied correctly, then errors may be introduced in the FFT amplitude, frequency or overall shape of the spectrum.

Spectral leakage results in incorrect approximations of the true harmonic content of the signal, and is due to the fact that in a particular analysis window, any given harmonic basis function will not complete a whole number of cycles. Take, for example, a single sinusoidal component. If the analysis window is not aligned, the infinite extension of the signal (required to perform the Fourier analysis) results in a sharp discontinuity. Scaling the analysis window by a windowing function resolves these issues by forcing the signal to zero at either end of the window, thus ensuring no discontinuities; however, this is done at the cost of modifying the spectral content of the signal, causing the familiar spectral blurring. Our approach is to solve the problem of misaligned cycles by modifying the size of the analysis window rather than by modifying the signal to be analyzed.

Because upsampling based on the analyzed pitch means that any cycle will start and stop (as close as possible) on a sample, the waveform will be aligned

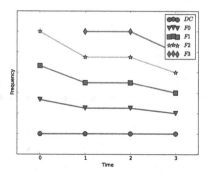

Fig. 3. An illustration of our spectrogram plotting method based on WAAW. Frequency samples belonging to the same partial are connected. Note that the spectrogram is plotted in a "per partial" manner and colour is first mapped to the power of frequency points on a single partial, and then updated as more partials are added.

and a "boxcar" window can be applied without concern for spectral leakage. Additionally, no window overlap ("hop") is needed, since the signal is not modified by a window. The concept, then, is that each cycle of the signal will be analyzed separately.

3   Spectrogram Display

The traditional FFT is visualized by plotting the amplitude of each spectral coefficient against the frequency of that coefficient and (for STFT) plotted against time. This is commonly displayed as a heat map, with x = time, y = frequency, and z = amplitude shown in colour or grayscale.

Since the period of natural signals is expected to vary over time, The WAAW system will use a different period for each frame and therefore a different frame size for each analysis frame, which results in a different number of frequency coefficients, spaced differently in the frequency spectrum. This variable frequency resolution makes a traditional STFT rendering impossible. If we were to draw the frequency components from the lowest frequency to the highest frequency for each window, with one frequency component per pixel (as is done in STFT visualizations), frames with the same or similar frequencies would not necessarily align, and it would be difficult to see from one frame to the next how the spectral content changes.

In the WAAW method, each frequency coefficient now represents a verified harmonic partial of the (pseudo)periodic signal (starting from f_0), rather than a frequency component of the analysis window. For this reason we must visualize the partials based on their relative frequency location as well as time location. We developed a method which we call *partial-ordinal alignment* which analyses each frame and ranks the partials based on their location in the harmonic sequence. (f_1, f_2, etc.). This allows us to connect time-adjacent samples in the visualization

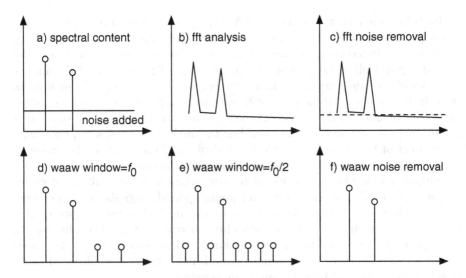

Fig. 4. A theoretical description of sub frequency window noise rejection. (a) shows a theoretical signal with noise added. In traditional FFT (b), the noise becomes part of the signal, traditional noise removal (c) may remove too much or not enough, because there is no assumption of which components may be noise or signal. In WAAW-based noise rejection, a larger window is used (e) thus all odd partials can be assumed to be noise, and be removed. A noise profile is constructed allowing analysis and removal of even (signal) partials that are also noise.

which belong to the same partial (Fig. 3). Finally, colour is added to indicate the amplitude of each partial track, similar to the traditional FFT spectrogram.

4   Noise Rejection Using Multiple Cycles per Analysis Window

One significant concern of the WAAW system as presented is that when attempting to reject noise for a harmonic signal, all of the energy (both signal and noise) is represented by the harmonic series represented by the size of the analysis window. Simply put, if we want to reject noise, there is nowhere else for the noise to be but the harmonic series produced by the WAAW method. In order to combat this problem, we modify the WAAW method as presented to allow a whole number of cycles within the analysis frame instead of allowing only a single cycle in the analysis frame. In other words, for a signal with fundamental frequency f_0, we use an analysis window aligned to some whole number ratio f_0/n (equivalent to a whole number multiple of the period nt. This results in a longer analysis window, but most importantly, it provides for off-pitch frequency analysis, with additional partials between the target partials that can be used to collect and extract some of the noise.

Each frequency partial in the WAAW display is a representation of the spectral content of a bin of frequencies centred at the frequency of the partial. Using a window size based on f_0, we assume all energy in the waveform relates to the desired signal itself, consisting of a harmonic series of partials at whole number multiples of the fundamental. If, however, there is energy at other frequencies in the original waveform, these will not be able to be represented except as energy within one or more of the partials of the harmonic series. By halving the fundamental frequency of analysis (*i.e.* doubling the analysis window size), we double the number of frequencies available for analysis, and the result is that noise at these frequencies is contained in these off-pitch harmonics.

Although it would be possible to use any whole number multiple of cycles for the analysis window, in practice, for pseudo-periodic signals, there is enough difference in the period from one cycle to the next that using more than a few cycles in the analysis window will also contribute to spectral blurring. In our experiments, we used two cycles per analysis frame with success. For more stationary signals, more cycles could be used and a tradeoff would need to be found between spectral blurring and noise rejection.

Figure 4 shows the traditional techniques of noise removal based on a single frame of the STFT, compared to the WAAW system with a multi-cycle analysis window. If the analysis window contains two cycles of the signal, we can assume that all even harmonic components correspond to the signal itself, and all odd harmonic components must therefore be noise. Half of the noise can therefore be rejected by simply deleting the odd harmonics of the two-cycle WAAW analysis before performing resynthesis.

4.1 Noise Profiling on Off-Pitch Harmonics

Since we know that the odd harmonics represent energy that is not in the signal, and is therefore noise, we can use these odd harmonics (also referred to as off-pitch harmonics) to do a second step of noise removal. By analyzing the noise characteristics of the odd harmonics, we can infer a general structure of the underlying noise, and use this noise profile to remove any even partials that match this profile.

For the trials described below, we have injected gaussian noise into the samples, and so the noise analysis consists of evaluating the components that we know are noise, calculating the mean and standard deviation of these off-pitch partials, and using this to make a noise floor threshold at $\mu + 2\sigma$ which should encompass approximately 95 % of the noise thus characterized. This simple noise-removal technique is very fast and reasonably accurate when compared to traditional noise-removal techniques applied to the STFT (Fig. 5).

4.2 Noise Rejection of a Square Wave

In order to prove that our noise removal technique is able to distinguish signal coefficients from noise coefficients, we consider a square wave, which consists of odd harmonics of a fundamental. If we apply our initial WAAW analysis system,

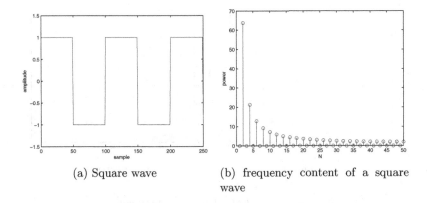

(a) Square wave

(b) frequency content of a square wave

Fig. 5. A square wave contains energy at odd harmonics only.

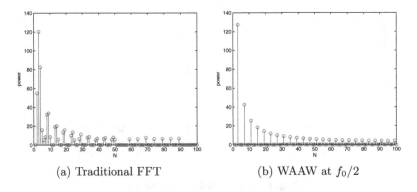

(a) Traditional FFT

(b) WAAW at $f_0/2$

Fig. 6. Frequency representation of a square wave.

we should see every other coefficient with a value of zero. Using two periods of the square wave, we get energy in every fourth coefficient, as shown in Fig. 6b. Figure 6a shows the spectral analysis of a square wave by the closest power-of-two traditional FFT, and it is clear that partials of the signal are spread out over two or more components of the representation.

If we then apply noise to the signal and repeat the analysis (Fig. 7), we will see that removing the noise using the traditional FFT methods results in spectral content removed or in noise left behind (Fig. 8), while extracting the noise profile on the off-pitch components and classifying the on-pitch harmonics as signal or noise based on the statistical similarity to the off-pitch harmonics results in a simple, robust, and effective noise removal system (Fig. 9).

It is clear from inspection that the WAAW method results in better noise rejection while maintaining signal integrity. Numerical measures presented in Sect. 5 also show that the WAAW noise rejection method is superior to traditional systems.

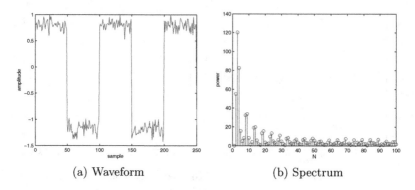

(a) Waveform   (b) Spectrum

Fig. 7. Square wave with 15 dB noise added

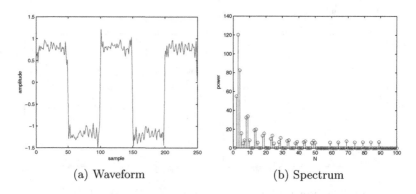

(a) Waveform   (b) Spectrum

Fig. 8. Traditional noise removal

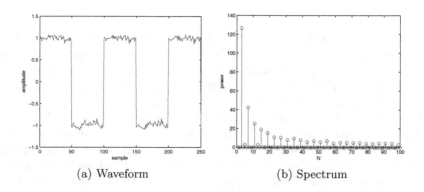

(a) Waveform   (b) Spectrum

Fig. 9. WAAW noise removal

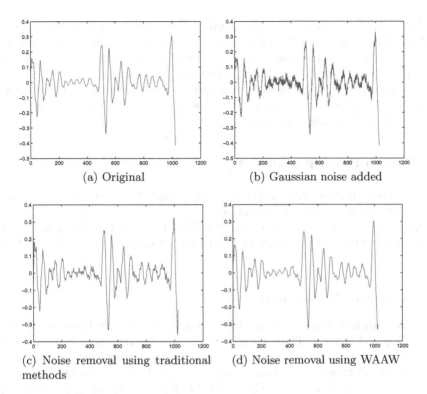

(a) Original   (b) Gaussian noise added

(c) Noise removal using traditional   (d) Noise removal using WAAW
methods

Fig. 10. Two periods of the voice waveform, used as a single analysis window for
WAAW noise removal

4.3 Noise Rejection of a Natural Signal

In this experiment, we took a natural signal (a human voicing a single "ah" vowel
at 90 Hz) and analyzed the signal using WAAW and FFT, both before and after
injecting 15 dB of white noise. The following figures inspect the waveform in
time to further expose the concepts of the algorithm and show the accuracy of
noise removal in the time domain. Figure 10a shows a single analysis frame of
the unaltered signal. Note that there are exactly two periods of the waveform
in the analysis window. Note also that the two periods are not identical—this
is typical for pseudoperiodic natural signals. Figure 10b shows the signal with
the addition of 15 dB white noise. Although white noise affects the signal at all
frequencies, we see more of the high frequency noise because there is less high
frequency content in the original signal.

Traditional noise removal techniques involve analyzing the high frequency
components (with the assumption that these will contain noise but not signal),
using these components to infer a noise floor, and using that noise floor to
subtract the white noise from the signal. Figure 10c shows the result of this
noise removal. Some noise is still present, and this is because the noise statistics
were inferred from a small range of frequencies.

The WAAW system was able to reproduce the original signal, minus the noise, with much more accuracy (Fig. 10d), because the noise floor threshold is inferred from the off-pitch components across all frequencies, giving a more accurate estimation of the noise floor. Further, since the on-pitch frequencies are aligned as closely as possible with the analysis frame, signal components are not blurred and noise can be rejected on a component-by-component basis. Numerical measures of this test are presented in Sect. 5.

5   Performance Evaluation

We use two evaluation metrics: (1) accurate frequency represented in a visually effective way; and (2) signal restoration.

All tests were conducted on a *Xeon 3.2 GHz* PC with a *CreativeLabs SB X-Fi* audio board. The audio excerpts for testing are all sampled at 44.1 kHz and last for about 3 s.

5.1   Spectrum Visualization

Using real-world signals, we show two examples of a single frame of analysis using FFT and WAAW. These visualizations show the frequency spreading that is inherent in the FFT, because the pitch of the partials in the signal does not line up with frequency bins available in the FFT. Figure 11a shows the spectrum calculated using a traditional FFT, for an artificial signal consisting of 6 sinusoidal components at various amplitudes and whole number multiples of $f_0 = 1$ kHz. The breakout box shows the frequency spread for each partial across between 5 and 10 components. Figure 11b shows that each sinusoidal partial of the original signal is recognized as a single component in the WAAW representation. Further, the original FFT takes 1024 samples while the WAAW-based spectrum can fully represent the same signal in 44 samples.

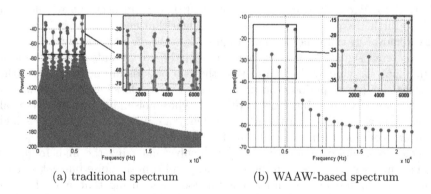

(a) traditional spectrum   (b) WAAW-based spectrum

Fig. 11. The spectrum of a single frame of a sinusoidal using two different FFT sizes. (a) has an FFT size of 1024 samples, while 44 samples are shown in (b).

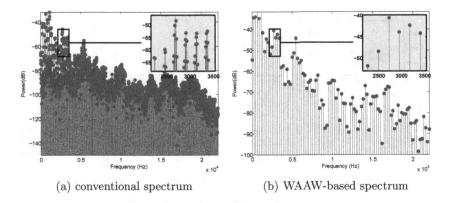

(a) conventional spectrum   (b) WAAW-based spectrum

Fig. 12. Spectrum of a frame of human voice. (a) window size = 4096 samples; (b) window size = $1/f_0$ = 196 samples.

Figure 12 shows the same test for a human voice with $f_0 \approx 225$ Hz. In the case of the FFT, each partial of the signal is again spread across multiple frequency components, while in the WAAW spectrum, each partial is represented by a single frequency component, giving a more compact and accurate representation. The window size of the FFT is 4096 samples and the window size of the WAAW is 196 samples. Fewer frequency bars are produced with WAAW because the period is shorter than the traditional FFT size; it is easier to find the harmonic structure from the WAAW; and each partial is represented as a single frequency rather than a cluster of closely-related frequencies.

5.2 Spectrogram Display

The previous section shows how the WAAW-based STFT excels the traditional one in presenting the structure of frequency components for a single frame of signal. The advantage of WAAW, however, lies more on its ability to show the variation of each partial over time. The spectrogram is used to reflect these changes over successive frames.

Figure 13 compares three spectrogram displays of a 3 s sweep sound using traditional STFT, time-frequency reassignment [1] and WAAW method. With a traditional spectrogram shown in Fig. 13a, it can be difficult to discern the individual partials, especially when the frequency changes fast within a short time or is at a low frequency. Figure 13b improves the discernability between partials by better localizing the instantaneous energy, but erroneous frequency components are still kept and the discrete re-localized energy points in the spectrogram breaks the continuity of partial trends. Figure 13c is simpler to view and avoids noisy or erroneous frequency components between harmonics. In addition, Fig. 13c shows more clearly how the partials change in amplitude over time especially at low frequencies and fast transitions, which is blurred and cannot be distinguished in Fig. 13a.

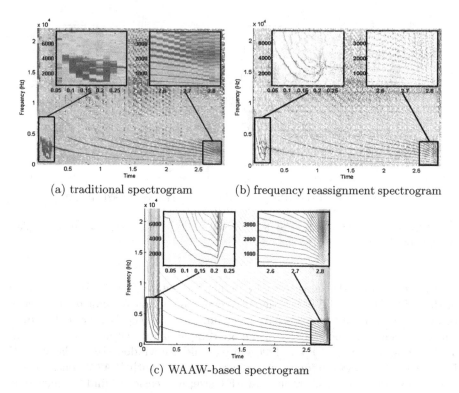

(a) traditional spectrogram   (b) frequency reassignment spectrogram

(c) WAAW-based spectrogram

Fig. 13. Spectrogram of a "sweep". (a) STFT; frame size = 2048 samples. (b) Reassignment; frame size = 2048 samples. (c) WAAW; frame size changing based on the pitch of the signal at each frame. Note how the WAAW method gives resolution of partials well below the frequency resolution of the traditional STFT.

5.3 Restoration Test

We use four sets of audio for testing: (1) sinusoidal waves with varying fundamental frequency ranging from 100 Hz to 1 kHz, (2) speech samples obtained from interviews with students, (3) vocal singing clips and (4) instrument sounds including piano, violin, accordion, flute *etc.* Each group has 10 clips, each 4 to 6 s at 44 kHz and each has been corrupted with white Gaussian noise at 10 dB and 15 dB.

Restoration Procedure. Regarding the re-synthesis procedure, the whole piece of audio is first framed with a frame size N_f. The conventional method has a 50 % overlap with or without a window applied, whereas our method does not have an overlap or a window. For the FFT spectrum, a simple denoising process (flat noise floor with fixed threshold followed by the inverse FFT) is used to restore the original signal for each frame.

$$\hat{X} = \hat{X} \cdot (|\hat{X}| \geq \delta) \tag{2}$$

The hard[1] thresholding here sets any frequency coefficient less than δ to zero. In our experiment, the threshold δ is set to be the maximum amplitude of the frequency samples within the highest quarter of the frequency band. For the conventional method, the FFT and IFFT length are a power of 2 larger than the frame size. In WAAW, the pitch is first detected for each short frame and a dynamic FFT size is then used. After upsampling, 2 cycles of samples starting from the beginning of the frame (or more cycles if the number of samples in 2 cycles is less than that in the frame) are used for FFT, in which some frequency components are removed according to the steps laid out in Sect. 4. Only the leading section of samples from the result of the IFFT is used to fill up the frame as a restoration. Finally the restored signal is downsampled to the original sampling rate after all frames have been processed.

After the signal is restored, we use three numeric indexes [3], to give an objective comparison between STFT and WAAW restoration: input signal-to-noise ratio SNR; a segmented SNR_{seg} (a 20 ms-averaged SNR); and a segmented spectral distance (SPD_{seg}), which is often employed in vocal signal coding and is defined as

$$\text{SPD}_{seg} = \frac{10}{\ln 10} \int_{-\pi}^{\pi} \left(\ln |S_o|^2 - \ln |S_r|^2 \right)^2 \frac{d\theta}{2\pi} \, , \tag{3}$$

where S_o and S_r stand for the periodograms of the original signal and the restored signal, respectively.

Evaluation Results. We first test the performances of the two methods on each of the four groups of corrupted signals. The frame size for the two methods are both 256 samples, with half overlapped hanning windows for STFT.

From Table 1 we can see that WAAW produces satisfactory results compared with conventional STFT. For sinusoidal signals (group 1), WAAW out-performs STFT. For real-world signals (group 2, 3 and 4), the difference gap narrows although WAAW still has a slight advantage over STFT. This is because real signals are typically pseudo-periodic, and the YIN algorithm chooses a single pitch per frame even though the pitch changes from cycle to cycle within the frame. Future work will address this issue by adaptively and iteratively reducing the frame size.

Figure 14 shows the gain trend for the two methods with varying frame size and window shape in the restoration of two pieces. Here, "gain" indicates the difference between the restored SNR and the input SNR. As frame size increases, both methods perform better. Also, the conventional method performs poor without a window, while our method remains competitive even without a window. This is due to spectral leakage in the conventional STFT, as well as removal of low-amplitude components in the threshold denoting process. This is why our

---

[1] The threshold is also subtracted from any coefficient that is greater than the threshold in a soft thresholding. This not only smooths the time series, but moves it toward zero, which is not desired.

Table 1. Evaluation of signal restoration using frequency-based denoising and different FFT size selection schemes (unit: dB).

G1: *sinusoidal*	SNR	SNR$_{seg}$	SPD$_{seg}$	**G2:** *speech*	SNR	SNR$_{seg}$	SPD$_{seg}$
noise = 10	10.00	10.00	851.23	noise = 10	10.14	6.87	689.25
WAAW	16.99	17.05	330.95	WAAW	14.96	11.95	299.52
STFT	14.65	14.70	406.10	STFT	14.18	11.13	301.56
noise = 15	15.00	15.00	605.52	noise = 15	15.14	11.88	491.95
WAAW	21.56	21.61	210.37	WAAW	18.77	16.09	196.33
STFT	18.42	18.47	304.20	STFT	18.01	15.04	219.56

G3: *singing*	SNR	SNR$_{seg}$	SPD$_{seg}$	**G4:** *instrument*	SNR	SNR$_{seg}$	SPD$_{seg}$
noise = 10	10.07	5.50	758.15	noise = 10	10.04	7.72	750.64
WAAW	15.60	11.21	332.63	WAAW	15.36	13.17	318.67
STFT	14.59	10.28	333.64	STFT	14.14	11.98	324.84
noise = 15	15.08	10.51	546.78	noise = 15	15.03	12.71	539.77
WAAW	19.73	15.46	221.02	WAAW	19.58	17.48	210.09
STFT	18.45	14.23	238.30	STFT	18.07	15.98	237.59

method has the highest performance in Fig. 14a. When we consider Fig. 14b, however, the problems of real-world signals re-emerge. While we can choose an exact period or multiple of a period for our analysis window, if the signal in the window is not perfectly aligned (since it is pseudo-periodic), there is some unavoidable spectral leakage representing the change in the spectral content of the signal over the course of a single period.

The frame size for WAAW corresponds directly to the number of cycles of the original signal used in the analysis window. In real world signals, the fundamental frequency changes from one cycle to the next, which is why a larger window is detrimental to the WAAW algorithm. However, the WAAW does not benefit from the larger window because the waveform alignment already makes available additional information that a larger window in a traditional system would make available. What is clear from Fig. 14 is that window size does not play a role in the quality of the reconstruction for WAAW as it does for FFT. This is a significant advantage because the selection of an appropriate window size is a critical but often overlooked part of the FFT process.

6   Discussion

Our method is vulnerable to the accuracy of the pitch estimation. A slight error in the pitch analysis will result in the introduction of spectral leakage. Future work will include investigating adaptive time-domain pitch analysis methods. The WAAW method only applies to monophonic signals. Polyphonic signals will be considered in the future.

The FFT size derived from pitch is usually not a power of two. Our upsampling method is tuned to produce a power of two number of samples within a

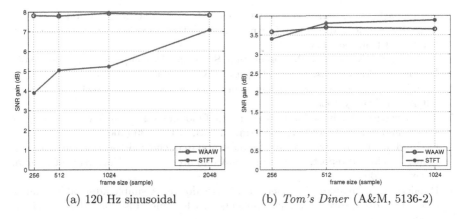

(a) 120 Hz sinusoidal   (b) *Tom's Diner* (A&M, 5136-2)

Fig. 14. SNR gain for WAAW and STFT from 10 dB corrupted signals, by frame size

period, but this often results in a very large up-sampling rate leading to a large number of samples and an increase in processing time.

While adding pitch estimation to a traditional STFT increases the time to produce a spectrogram, our method removes irrelevant information and makes pitch and partial information more visible than in the traditional FFT representation. We see the extra time as a tradeoff to make these new features possible.

7   Conclusion

This paper presents a new spectrogram representation method based on waveform-aligned windows for FFT. Instead of a traditional fixed FFT size, a new and dynamic FFT size is calculated based on the corresponding pitch of a signal frame. We choose an FFT size that exactly equals the smallest period (or a multiple of periods) so that the fundamental frequency along with all of its harmonically related information are shown, but the spectral leakage of the traditional FFT is completely removed. Like the traditional spectrogram, our new representation also consists of 3 dimensions: x = time, y = frequency and z = component amplitude, with a color scale that indicates the amplitude. The difference is that the harmonic information (partials) are emphasized and the inter-harmonic spectral leakage is eliminated, so that examiners can see the interplay of the true partials without being distracted by noise introduced by the transform. In the WAAW representation, one can not only see how the pitch fluctuates over time but also easily and clearly track the trends of other harmonics.

References

1. Auger, F., Flandrin, P.: Improving the readability of time-frequency and time-scale representations by the reassignment method. IEEE Trans. Signal Process. **43**, 1068–1089 (1995)

2. Breitenbach, A.: Against spectral leakage. Measurement **25**(2), 135–142 (1999). http://www.sciencedirect.com/science/article/B6V42-3X652TH-C/2/0e63c15ee62b1307b871d9463caa6438

3. Canazza, S.: Noise and Representation Systems: A Comparison among Audio Restoration Algorithms. Lulu Enterprise, USA (2007)

4. de Cheveigné, A.: Hearing science and speech recognition. Technical report, IRCAM, February 1998

5. de Cheveigné, A., Kawahara, H.: YIN, a fundamental frequency estimator for speech and music. J. Acoust. Soc. Am. **111**(4), 1917–1930 (2002)

6. Gerhard, D.: Pitch extraction and fundamental frequency: history and current techniques. Technical report, Department of Computer Science, University of Regina, November 2003

7. Hidalgo, R., Fernandez, J., Rivera, R., Larrondo, H.: A simple adjustable window algorithm to improve FFT measurements. IEEE Trans. Instrum. Measur. **51**(1), 31–36 (2002)

8. Liuni, M., Robel, A., Matusiak, E., Romito, M., Rodet, X.: Automatic adaptation of the time-frequency resolution for sound analysis and re-synthesis. IEEE Trans. Audio Speech Lang. Process. **21**(5), 959–970 (2013)

9. Min, K., Chien, D., Li, S., Jones, C.: Automated two speaker separation system. In: Proceedings of IEEE ICASSP, pp. 537–540 (1988)

10. Morise, M.: A method to estimate a temporally stable spectral envelope for periodic signals. In: Proceedings of Meetings on Acoustics, vol. 19, p. 060022. Acoustical Society of America (2013)

11. Vích, R., Vondra, M.: Pitch synchronous transform warping in voice conversion. In: Esposito, A., Esposito, A.M., Vinciarelli, A., Hoffmann, R., Müller, V.C. (eds.) COST 2102. LNCS, vol. 7403, pp. 280–289. Springer, Heidelberg (2012)

12. Xu, F.: Algorithm to remove spectral leakage, close-in noise, and its application to converter test. In: Proceedings of the IEEE Instrumentation and Measurement Technology Conference, pp. 1038–1042, April 2006

Image-Sound Interaction

Sound and Gesture

Daniel Deshays[(✉)]

ENSATT - École Nationale Supérieure des Arts et Techniques du Théâtre,
Lyon, France
daniel.deshays@sfr.fr
http://www.deshays.net

Abstract. The sound generated by bodily gesture holds in itself the
intention that preceded its production, and constitutes in some way the
evidence of an action that has occurred. The nature of the sound of an
object that is placed on a surface reveals the purpose that led to that
gesture: violence, for instance, or clumsiness. What is perceived and conveys meaning is the primary intent that is carried in the sound. This is -
such as the timbre of the voice - an important clue for the interpretation
of hidden meaning by the listener. These elements are at the heart of
sound itself. The desire to listen is born out of surprise, which in turn
originates from a sense of rupture and depends on the conditions under
which discontinuity operates. It is this lack of continuity that captures
our attention, and it is rupture that triggers the need to understand what
has just occurred. This is precisely one of the driving forces behind the
reactivation of our listening. Furthermore, what is really important in
terms of listening is not what is defined but rather what is uncertain.
It is the degree of uncertainty that triggers our attention. Our listening
is constructed in proportion to its incompleteness. If what is offered is
excessive, this will only arouse a fleeting interest. Any element that is
clearly perceived and understood is immediately superseded, owing to
our "survival instinct", which necessarily intervenes so as to engage any
subsequent event. Listening opts first for what is suggested rather than
what is offered. All this naturally complies with the safeguarding of our
libido, and indeed, how could it be otherwise? We all know that we no
longer desire, and quickly abandon, what we are too sure of possessing.

1 Experience: Drawing as Gesture

In 1994 I was invited to teach sound practice to visual artists at the Fine Arts
School in Paris (ENSBA - École Nationale Supérieure des Beaux-Arts de Paris).
I was asked to teach these students in the same way I used to at the Drama
School in Lyon (ENSATT - École Nationale Supérieure des Arts et Techniques
du Théâtre). I replied that it would be impossible for me to do it without taking
into account the specificity of the visual arts. Then I understood that what the
School Director was asking me was, like in theatre, to bring into focus the sound
mise-en-scène. I suppose that he must have been given this impression from what
he heard me saying about my teaching experience in theatre, in particular the
fact that I wasn't happy to use sound to simply underline the drama work.

© Springer International Publishing Switzerland 2014
M. Aramaki et al. (Eds.): CMMR 2013, LNCS 8905, pp. 483–493, 2014.
DOI: 10.1007/978-3-319-12976-1_28

In fact, what truly interested me was to be at the centre of the "plastic" experience. To be more precise, to be at the heart of the interrelation between material and artistic gesture, and make these students aware of an aspect that is, after all, at the essence of their own practice. This was an area that I didn't know well (the field of visual arts) but where I felt able of pursuing, alongside these students, an approach that aimed at grasping the aural dimension.

I was soon going to be confronted with an unexpected opportunity that would allow me to take further my intent. In 1995 a student came to see me and said "I would like to attend your sound workshop but the only thing that I am able to do is to draw". This appeared to me as the opportunity to seize. I replied that this seemed more than enough for me, and that it was indeed a chance to be able to start off from drawing, which is at the very core of the visual arts practice.

Drawing is the realm of trace - trace in the sense of, for example, a pencil stroke on paper - and I could not prevent myself of linking this to the fact that every sound is produced by impact or friction. Assuming that trace is based on friction, we developed the following experience: we began by listening to the sound made by various drawing tools such as pencil, charcoal, different brushes, and an inkless metal pen. Then we looked into aspects that were related to the quality of the paper, such as grain, texture or thickness, and compared it to canvas, plastic and glass. We quickly realised that the material on which we were working acted as a resonator or acoustic amplifier. At that point, we had the idea of working on large, well-stretched canvases, or on wooden or metallic tables that were reasonably heavy. The sound was recorded on multitracking (this was at the advent of computer recording software), and we used a quadraphonic recording system that I had put in place.

I suddenly realised that, despite the utensils that were used to draw, what was truly audible was the gesture itself. Even if we changed the drawing tool or the material on which the friction was being produced, the main aspect that remained was a repetition of the same gesture. Undeniably, sound is above all the sound of gesture. The student's movements were too simple and predictable, so I challenged him to draw with his left hand in order to overcome any automatisms. I asked him to draw small-sized figures that would be enlarged (amplified) - as it is frequently done with images - and this should allow for a new dimension to emerge, based on the thickness of the stroke.

We decided to play those sounds through the four speakers that had been placed on the floor, at each corner of the room where we were working. The amplification was particularly rewarding. I quickly realised that the visual image would slowly form itself by the overlaying of various strokes, and that one trace could continue another to create a figure. However, in what concerned the recording things did not work this way: the various strokes seemed to come in a succession, one after the other. This was obviously due to the fact that a recording is based on a temporal progression. I tried to imagine what would be to reassemble these sounds and be able to listen to all of them together within a defined time frame. As a result, I had to find the average time of mnemonic persistence that would be necessary to maintain a recollection of the start of the event. I understood that such duration depended mainly on the number of events that had occurred during that time lapse: the greater the profusion of events involved in the stroke, the shorter the time during which we would be able to recall it. After having defined a short duration frame, I tried to render more perceptible the sound of simultaneous strokes by placing another four speakers at the corners of the ceiling. We now had eight speakers positioned in a cubic layout. We worked on both these projection planes, the ceiling and the floor, which allowed us to easily differentiate the progression of two simultaneous strokes. I suddenly realised that eight speakers positioned in such a manner did not just determine two but rather ten projection planes, if we consider the rim plus the diagonals.

We had built, without being fully aware, a magnificent sound projection device: a machine for sketching virtual figures. Consequently, I understood that it was not necessary to draw using tools that produced visual traces, so we started to develop a panoply of tools that only produced aural traces. We started by sending a jet of air through a straw on sand or water, and created bubbles on thick liquids such as oil, jam or porridge. We increased the jet pressure and then we changed the movements made with those tools. This was followed by the sliding of objects on the ground, and the spillage of sand, liquid or waste. It became clear that there was a complementary nature involved in the choice of the material and the type of gesture, and between the capture distance and the motion of the capturing device.

I understood that the placement of sounds in space, by increasing the volume through multitracking - rather than by doing just a rough mixing - changed the facts: we were now facing a sense of monumentality, in a sculptural dimension, and going towards an architecture of sound. Still, we remained at the centre of the visual arts practice, and not collage. Even more than in the work of Tinguely, we were in control of an object that remained ontologically specific to the domain of the plastic arts. I believe that such a return to the essence of the factuality of the pair "gesture and tool" enabled me to discover the reason why sound should be brought into this realm. The student did not truly understand the scope of our approach but from that moment onwards I felt able to do anything. Sound had definitely a place in the visual arts and I had found the roots.

A second experience, with another student, made me progress somewhat further. She worked on video. She had filmed a sequence based on fluid motion and was in search of a sound counterpart to the flow of her visual material. The student worked hard, and every week we would listen to the result but this turned out to be always disappointing. To try solving this dilemma I decided to replace her but it was all in vain. Like her, I was unable to find a solution. All the sonic material that we created seemed inadequate, and the sound/image fusion we were wishing for would not materialise.

By pure chance, I picked up a cardboard pipe that I found in the room. It was about the same size as a scuba diving mask and could contain both my eyes. When I held it against the screen I was surprised to realise that, all of a sudden, the sounds became wonderfully connected to the images. At that point I understood that the issue was not coming from the image itself, or from the nature of the accompanying sound: a further dimension should be taken into account, and this implied finding the right connection between these two elements. It is the nature of this link that allows fusion to take place. We now had the feeling of being immersed, of "swimming" in this liquid matter that was coming in and out of our visual field. The sound became our environment and therefore provided an adequate ground for the partial viewing of our gaze.

The issue of installing sound and images, or other objects, in space became manifest through this experience. The link between sound and image was determined by the manner in which the perceiving bodies were placed. The listening conditions became for me an aspect that was closely related to the nature of the sound diffusion, the placement of the sound sources and the loudness. These elements were the variables that, through their interaction, determined and reorganised the viewing conditions.

The period I spent at the ENSBA - École Nationale Supérieure des Beaux-Arts de Paris was a time for countless discoveries that, at each time, drove me further towards the essence of the sound mise-en-scène.

2   Listening, A Sense of Touch

The sound generated by bodily gesture holds in itself the intention that preceded its production, and constitutes in some way the evidence of an action that has occurred. The nature of the sound of an object that is placed on a surface reveals the purpose that led to that gesture: violence, for instance, or clumsiness. What is perceived and conveys meaning is the primary intent that is carried in the sound. This is - such as the timbre of the voice - an important clue for the interpretation of hidden meaning by the listener.

These elements are at the heart of sound itself. They persist in it as a sort of internal movement that is intrinsic to sound's own materiality. The perception of such sounds unconsciously awakes in us memories of déjà-vu, and this often induces prompt bodily reactions. Gesture responds to what is heard; we do it unconsciously and without any delay - and even when the ensuing protective gesture is not produced, the neural network that could steer such a response is already connected and ready to react appropriately ([2], p. 65).

The notion of inner movement - a subjective representation - is both the result and the cause of an infinite number of particular situations. The inner movement can remain in us merely at a sensorial level and never transform itself onto a gesture taking the form of outward expression. This movement is a driving force and most often it is the result of a desire to act. Such desire is itself fostered by the external perception that preceded it. However, this movement can equally be a direct response; and by this I mean a "pure reflex" that is not the fruit of any type of analysis of the situation. For example, this is what the study of the function of mirror neurons has taught us. This movement can also be a place of sharing that brings together those who make the sound (musical or not) or the gesture, and those who receive it. The body emits flows. However, these flows initiate inner movements that do not always lead to specific actions; Berthoz tells us that to listen is to act but this does not necessarily mean that a response will take place ([2], p. 12).

An imaginary movement is like a catalyst that strives to reach its completion through a specific gesture. An orchestra conductor or a dancer, are typical examples of people who produce visible gestures which are part of a system of gestural impulses that emanate from a desire to produce meaning. All those who work with their own body - carpenters, ironware craftsmen, road workers and reapers - know what it is that drives the breadth of their gestures. This is equally true of dentists or surgeons whose gestures are smaller and finer. We all share this sense of inner movement which accompanies the desire to produce external motion outside of our body, and that is based on what has been conceived within us. This inner motion is developed from a desire that is often born out of an idea. Incidentally, could this be the physical essence of every movement - including the act of listening - that happens at an unconscious level? (I will come back to this later). I am thinking here that when we listen we are often unaware that we are doing it. It is also collectively, in festive gatherings, that this kind of motion seems to arise from these shared moments as a sort of necessity: the need to exhaust our bodies - and here I am referring to *The Accursed Share (La part maudite)* by Georges Bataille [1] - because gesture arises from pure expenditure. It can often be excessive and created by exaggerated emotions, rendering the resulting movement clearly approximate.

I would like to confront these considerations with the reality of the practices that are implemented by the industries dealing creatively with sound. This does not concern exclusively the film or the music industry, but all artistic fields.

3   The Components and Their Variability

Rather than approaching directly the topic of sound production, it seems interesting to focus on its basic components, the various elements on which every production is based: **material**, **gesture**, and **space**. I should add here that the production procedures dispute the vitality and richness of these elements, and their ability to induce sensorial stimulation.

By procedure (or protocol) I am referring to the successive stages in the evolution of a project that correspond to automatic steps, inferred developments, and operational means conceived by procedural agreements in order to reach a calibrated result in a more or less definite way.

This succession of operations prevents the access to a vast palette of sensorial possibilities that should be made available in any creative endeavour. The procedures themselves, which regulate all the operations involving sound, are not even apparent to those who use them, so ingrained have they become in their everyday habits. The primary reason for this, of course, is that production needs to be swift owing to financial considerations. The second reason is that in any creative process, there are so many variables on the gounds of artistic uncertainty that the daily routine mentioned above represents a welcome haven of certitude and reliability. This is why these procedures are very rarely questioned. Consequently, asking "how do we do this?" in view of the elaboration of new forms is hardly ever asked. The implementation of such production procedures concerns primarily the more technical sectors but they also tend to pervade the creative realm: we often hear people saying "we should use a certain type of loudspeaker", or "we should record sound in a certain way" not only in the theatre but also in recording studios and in sound design departments.

Contrary to what one might presume, such procedures do not concern exclusively technical operations. Each step leading to the production of a work of art - because it is art that we are talking about here - from preparation to completion must be questioned in this regard. To consider the act of creation from a historical viewpoint, by listening for example to old radio productions, would enable a better understanding of how practice has evolved. Looking retrospectively into history allows us put into perspective and to perceive things that are not so readily apparent in a contemporary context.

The history of practice in connection with that of technology would also unveil other aspects regarding the evolution of sound writing, although it would be necessary to take a closer look in order to obtain a clearer understanding of how the production style has progressed.

If both ends of the production chain seem important, the middle part is just as crucial. In what concerns radio drama for instance, what could be the cause for the apparent disenchantment, and hence the lack of interest, of the listeners? The type of staging/mise-en-scène? The small number of directors? The stagnation of the studios? Lifeless sound recordings? Writers who are no longer able to stir their actors?

How could we revive the desire to listen? I would like to return here to the fundamentals of sound writing and try to demonstrate that the points mentioned above represent variables that are not difficult to reinstate.

4   Restoring the Conditions for the Existence of Wealth and Diversity in Sound Assembling

The properties of sounds depend primarily on their production conditions and manipulation. I am using here the plural form to bring out the idea of diversity:

- The diversity of sound colour in the acoustic spaces of the mise-en-scène;
- The diversity of positioning for both the sound sources and the capture equipment used in these different spaces;
- The diversity of the movements made by the sound sources themselves: in film the gestures are really carried out, for example speaking while working, or walking, has an expressive effect on the voice that denotes a body at work or in movement.
- The variety of movements made by the sound recording equipment: the boom microphone, for example, makes it possible to hear acoustic variations that are due to the physical motion occurring in the spatial environment.

Cinema is always reminding us that the distance at which sound is captured is constantly varying, by adapting it to the framing of the image. The concept of cutting and editing during, and even before shooting is a variable that radio should adopt. Similarly, it is necessary to define the physical movements in order to allow the voices to be emitted. Behind each voice there is a body, and the body changes timbre depending on the positions it adopts. What we hear behind a voice is a body in motion, and behind these movements, feelings can be perceived - and it is because such sounds inevitably refer back to the body through our own memory, that just any recording cannot be acceptable.

The flat post-synchronization of television serials, done with motionless actors in front of a microphone, immediately reminds us of how boring such a set-up can be. Without the visuals, listening to these detached voices would be quite unbearable.

5 The Meaning of Sound Capture

Recording sound is generally considered to be a neutral act, a sort of protocol that captures objectively the sound being produced. However, we tend to forget that what the microphone picks up is not truly representative of what we hear. The recording offers us far more data than what is heard in reality. Through our sense of spatial listening we are able to filter out the sonic chaos of the world that we inhabit. We also tend to forget that the "sound image" reproduced by loudspeakers prevents our brain of making the selection that would have naturally been done in a real-life situation.

When we listen to recorded sound, there is a loss of that wonderful freedom that we enjoy when we are listening directly to the world around us, and which allows each listener to select from the environment what he or she wishes to hear. Instead, there is a sort of constructed continuity that makes our temporal perception resemble that of a clock. However, our perception is rather fragmented, and is produced by instantaneous samplings and withdrawals. It presupposes the freedom to let our listening wander around, taking and selecting at any given moment only what we wish to hear. Conversely, the recording of street sounds, for example, is a continual flow of fixed sonic events that reflects the choice dictated by the microphone's placement. Such a relentless flow of events bears no relationship to our subconscious way of listening, which is non-continuous and subjective, and is constantly selecting what it wants to hear and leaving out what it considers to be of no interest.

The recording appears thus as a whole, as an entire slice of reality that presents itself as an absolute and all-encompassing value, along with the obligation to listen to the whole "package". Consequently, and in order to be able to create with sound, it is necessary to discard the excess that is offered to the microphone. It is therefore crucial to select and organise the recorded material in order to strip down the sound continuum to what is truly essential.

Sound is meant to affect us, and not merely to communicate words that express a certain feeling. Sounds can produce sensations even before producing meaning, so it is through our senses that the meaning can reach us.

When we listen to sound, we can perceive a certain "plasticity" which is both related to the materiality of the sounding object and the nature of the event that makes it audible. This event can be a simple gesture, or the result of a natural element such as wind or rain. The sound of ripe wheat blown by the wind tells me as much about the malleability of the plant as it does about the flow of the wind. I can feel it in my body, conveyed through my ears, just as I would feel it on my skin if I were out in the field. Sometimes we say "your voice touches me", and this is because the senses of hearing and touch share a similar space of fleeting perception.

Let us come back to sound recording: this act implies the desire to be heard and to designate, and it certainly is related to the ability to make a voluntary choice. To record sound means to lay designated objects on a medium, and from this viewpoint we can say that it is equivalent to writing.

By its ability to capture a fleeting moment photography draws our attention to its variables: axis, distance, lighting, depth of field. Sound recording should use this as a model not only to make sounds "visible" but also to create a vocabulary of montage that could be adapted to each work. A lexicon of sound recording must be specific. Sound capture becomes lifeless if it claims to be "neutral". There is no such thing as a neutral presentation - it simply does not exist. Any approach that consists of rendering neutral an artistic production always harms it. Painting and photography, both figurative arts that can freeze time, made it possible for cinema to understand how to construct an image amidst a series of differing viewpoints.

In its early days, cinema found itself constrained to join end to end the excessively short reels of film which manufacturers were able to produce, making it impossible to film an entire theatrical act in continuity. In this way, film makers were forced to invent not only editing but also the continuity cut (axial cut) in order to bridge the transition from one reel to the next - in other words, this temporal ellipsis corresponded to the time required to change the reel. In this way, and due to the change of axis, the spectator could "forget" the position occupied by the characters in the preceding take.

The problem with sound is precisely the opposite: any gap can be bridged too easily. Even if editing takes place in the same axis, this will not be heard. Unlike image, there is no visible motion jumping in the characters' faces or bodies. Therefore sound does not have to worry about cuts in space or changes in axis, even if this could provide a good opportunity to invent new kinds of transitions that could contribute to revive listening.

Sound emerges in us in the form of homogeneous spaces. In compliance with our basic need to spare our energy, our imagination produces within us a continuous performance space. I would like to refer here to the recent work of Alain Berthoz, professor at the Collège de France, and in particular the book *La simplexité* [3].

The desire to listen is born out of surprise, which in turn originates from a sense of rupture and depends on the conditions under which discontinuity operates. It is this lack of continuity that captures our attention, and it is rupture that triggers the need to understand what has just occurred. This is precisely one of the driving forces behind the reactivation of our listening.

Furthermore, what is really important in terms of listening is not what is defined but rather what is uncertain. It is the degree of uncertainty that triggers our attention. Our listening is constructed in proportion to its incompleteness. If what is offered is excessive, this will only arouse a fleeting interest. Any element that is clearly perceived and understood is immediately superseded, owing to our "survival instinct", which necessarily intervenes so as to engage any subsequent event. Listening opts first for what is suggested rather than what is offered. All this naturally complies with the safeguarding of our libido, and indeed, how could it be otherwise? We all know that we no longer desire, and quickly abandon, what we are too sure of possessing.

What sound recording must do is to enact situations, to promote physical confontation. What I wish to hear in a recording - and in the details of the actions made available by sound production - is the quality of the desire to share that is brought into play. The slightest movement triggered by hesitation, or on the contrary by certainty, will nourish the quality of the sensation, regardless of coming from a voice, an object, or even the microphone that is capturing the sound. These seemingly minor details are at the heart of what is truly at stake when we listen.

6   Space and Staging

In the same way, the complexities and wealth of acoustic spaces are essential variables in terms of our listening tension. The plethora of diversity and detail conveyed by a physical movement that occurs in the intricacy of an acoustic space is one of the driving forces behind listening.

A sound that seems inadequate in relation to its normal environment can attract attention even if this is only an element of mise-en-scène. Placing sound events in unexpected spaces can be quite surprising, especially when the unsuitability of such spaces is not directly perceived. Even if there is a clear perception that something unusual is happening, the listener might not be able to attribute it to one particular element. For example, listening to the sound of a motor scooter within the acoustics of a church is certainly an association that will not go unnoticed. All of a sudden we feel the need to reinterpret each of the elements at play but, above all, we question the reason behind such a confrontation.

The acoustics of an indistinct space do not remain for long in our memory. Our listening aptitude will quickly fade away. If we choose to place the elements at play, or the sound capture device, at the threshold of two different spaces this will make them appear in direct juxtaposition, and thus persist in our consciousness. What is primarily perceived is the moment of rupture in space, the passage from one acoustic space to another. The most perceivable location is therefore at the threshold separating or uniting the two spaces. In this way, we become aware of the differences in quality between those two spaces, both in terms of volume and construction material. When bodies in motion, or any sound-producing objects, are confronted with a particular volume, the sound of their actions (or movements) is perceived differently and reinterpreted in relation to the acoustics of the space.

The neutralisation of acoustics is not devoid of interest but it will function better if it corresponds to a specific requirement to create a space depleted of sound as, for instance, in the plays of Samuel Beckett. The studio as a neutral space makes it possible to eliminate the intrusive background noise that we find too often in the real world. However its lack of presence as a sound space can be a limiting factor to the expression of sound creativity. We should therefore consider other quiet spaces that have a more vibrant acoustics than a studio, and that could provide a livelier sound environment. The complexity of such spaces, due to their architectural diversity, can enable a succession of flexible, vivid and ever-changing situations that can bring back a sense of surprise to the listener - for the time being, convolution reverb has not yet reached a standard of quality similar to reality.

We are all aware of this, at least intuitively. However, we must keep it in mind at all moments of our activity - and despite the job position that we occupy - in order to make available to the listener the most desirable element of all: the perception of liveliness.

7   The Tool Vs. the Hand

To what extent might new tools aid us in preserving the sense of touch that is essential to the sharing of our sensitivity? Few shortcuts are possible between thought and gesture: it is always the body, or that of another, that will execute - even by an indirect path - the gesture that is originated in thought. There is no shortcut between thought and action.

A trace, resulting from a specific desire, becomes apparent - just as a sound is the trace of the intention at the origin of the gesture that produced such sound. That gesture is deeply rooted in the materiality of sound. We have fully grasped it: what is really crucial in the perception of a sound is the intention being conveyed, and this is the foundation for any meaning carried by such event. If the sound-object seems to carry meaning, this derives from the intention of the gesture that drives it. The intonation in the human voice is a clear example of this.

When I hear an action, this has already been controlled by the ear of the person who produced it. A carpenter uses his hearing to measure the force needed to hammer a nail into a piece of wood. It is the sound that he produces, and which he hears, that enables him to measure his next gesture. His own ear is the regulator of this inner movement via feedback. It is by listening to the sound produced by the hammering of the nail that he is able to adjust the strength of his gesture.

This inner movement is not necessarily at the root of sound. The sound originates on the outside, the place that nurtures all desires, in the same way as the silence of another person impels me to respond. It is between perception and affect, together with a desire to reply that such response emerges - but it is always adjusted.

Regarding the order of priorities of our perception, when a glass is put on a table, at first we don't get the impression that the sound produced by the glass conveys the meaning of the object that it represents. This is equally true for the table that is hit by the glass. What becomes apparent in the first place, is the relationship created by the glass/table association that is perceived in the gesture. The only real sound is the sound that is born out of an inner movement. Anyway, it seems clear that the material existence of an intention is situated outside the body: this appears to be, in fact, the only place where such an event exists. Otherwise how could we deem, for example, clumsiness, a missed punch, stumbling and falling, or missing a target?

What kind of gesture has brought together the glass and the table in order to produce that sound, and what was the prevailing intention? The event that led to placing the glass on the table in a slightly violently manner will be the first aspect to be perceived behind the sound: a sound that will only secondarily appear as the sound of a glass because the gesture - which could have been made on any other object - expresses, in the first instance, anger. What is first heard is the sense of exasperation. However, for those of us who work in sound or are stage directors, it is at the moment of fracture that the sound becomes meaningful.

Therefore, it is exactly at this point that we should question the nature of the sounds that are juxtaposed to cinematic images - what kind of material should we choose: Foley sounds, an isolated sound event, or a sound library... since they do not contain the same gesture or, sometimes, even no gesture at all. I should listen carefully to the nature of the touch that is reaching me, since it's unbearable to be touched in just any way. It is at this stage that my connection to others starts to materialise. Gentleness, tenderness or violence begin here and will gain my body through gesture: via sound as air displacement, by traversing the ear. An initial inner pressure coming from a sound-producing body (emitter) will lead to a final inner pressure in another body (receiver).

To place oneself on the tactile realm is to dispose the conditions under which such a contact can occur. To establish a space of contact is to create an environment where bodies can be placed. We must question the function of a loudspeaker, and examine the scenography of space. The touching space is the place for body-to-body interaction, and it is exactly at this point that the sensorial is shared and art can emerge.

References

1. Bataille, G.: La part maudite. Édition de Minuit, Paris (2011)
2. Berthoz, A.: Le sens du mouvement. Éditions Odile Jacob, Paris (2008)
3. Berthoz, A.: La simplexité. Éditions Odile Jacob, Paris (2009)

Changing the Interval Content of Algorithmically Generated Music Changes the Emotional Interpretation of Visual Images

Fernando Bravo[✉]

Centre for Music and Science, University of Cambridge, Cambridge, UK
nanobravo@fulbrightmail.org

Abstract. The ability of music to influence the emotional interpretation of visual contexts has been supported in several psychological studies. However, we still lack a significant body of empirical studies examining the ways in which specific structural characteristics of music may alter the affective processing of visual information. The present study suggests a way to use algorithmically generated music to assess the effect of sensory dissonance on the emotional judgment of a visual scene. This was examined by presenting participants with the same abstract animated film paired with consonant, dissonant and no music. The level of sensory dissonance was controlled in this experiment by employing different interval sets for the two contrasting background music conditions. Immediately after viewing the clip, participants were asked to complete a series of bipolar adjective ratings representing the three connotative dimensions (valence, activity and potency). Results revealed that relative to the control group of no music, consonant background music significantly biased the affective impact by guiding participants toward positive valence ratings. This finding is discussed in terms of interval content theory within the general perspective of post-tonal music theory and David Temperley's probabilistic framework (model of tonalness).

Keywords: Sensory dissonance · Emotion · Audiovisual · Film-music · Interval vector/content · Tonalness · Algorithmic composition · MaxMSP · Cinema4D

1 Introduction

The amount of empirical research in psychology of film music has increased exponentially during the past two decades. However, very few studies have examined in detail the ways in which specific structural characteristics of music may alter the emotional processing of visual information. Mapping a systematic relationship between musical structural features and certain aspects of the audiovisual experience might be crucial for potential applications concerned with clinical psychology and affective neuroscience.

The present study builds on a previous empirical work by the author [12] that showed strong evidence in support of the effect of tonal dissonance level on interpretations regarding the emotional content of visual information. That experiment

© Springer International Publishing Switzerland 2014
M. Aramaki et al. (Eds.): CMMR 2013, LNCS 8905, pp. 494–508, 2014.
DOI: 10.1007/978-3-319-12976-1_29

stimulated the investigation of tonal and post-tonal interval theory, and the parallel design of interactive multimedia tools to examine these processes in a strictly controlled empirical setting.

The objective of the experiment reported in this article is to evaluate the affective impact of sensory dissonance (controlled by interval content) on an abstract animation. Sensory dissonance refers to a specific psychoacoustic sensory property used to qualify intervals, associated with the presence/absence of interactions between the harmonic spectra of two pitches. Tonal dissonance includes sensory dissonance but is also influenced by tonal function and melodic motion [8] and therefore, it captures a more conceptual meaning beyond psychoacoustic effects that is typically expressed with terms such as tension or instability [24]. The present study's experimental design made use of algorithmically generated music to test its research question, and to analyse audiovisual interaction effects in visual information reception.

2 Background

2.1 Psychology of Film Music

We often seem oblivious to the versatility of film sound. Randy Thom has described the theoretical functions that sound (in terms of music and sound design) performs in a movie [37]. Sound can set up the pace of a scene, describe an acoustic space or establish a geographical locale. An element of the plot can be clarified with sound or it can render it ambiguous. Sound can connect otherwise unconnected ideas, characters, places or moments. Sound can draw attention to a particular detail or draw attention away from it. Sound can heighten realism or it can diminish it.

Sound is also considered one of the key elements contributing to the emotional meaning of film. For example, in "2001: A Space Odyssey", Kubrick used four highly modernistic compositions by György Ligeti which employ micropolyphony (the use of sustained dissonant chords that shift slowly over time). In this film, dense vocal clusters and dissonant chords were employed to project an emotional atmosphere of horror and to symbolize an omnipresent but unseen malevolence [2].

This article will focus on the particular role of music as a source of emotion in film. During the last two decades several empirical studies have been conducted to clarify the relationship between film music and its emotional function in movies and other types of multimedia. Annabel Cohen [14, 15] has comprehensively examined these studies and also elaborated a theoretical framework for supporting future research in this field.

Marshall and Cohen's early work [26] investigated the effect of connotative and structural information dispensed by musical soundtracks upon the emotional judgments in an abstract animation created by Heider and Simmel [21]. Heider and Simmel developed the animation to show that people form stereotypes even of inanimate objects.

Marshall and Cohen studied the effects of two different soundtracks on the impressions about the three moving geometrical figures depicted in the film clip (a large triangle, a small triangle and a small circle). They measured viewers' responses using the semantic differential technique [29], and they demonstrated that the mood of the music can alter the affective impact of a visual scene. Several subsequent empirical studies have shown similar evidence for additivity of audio and visual meaning along specific emotional dimensions [4, 5, 9, 17, 25, 34].

Boltz et al. [10, 11] showed that music can not only affect perceptual judgments but also influence memory of filmed events. They suggested that film music may not only perform functions of mood influence, but that it may also contribute to the story's comprehension. In interpreting these results they made use of specific principles of schema theory.

According to schema theory [3, 13, 20, 28, 35] we constantly apply interpretative cognitive frameworks when trying to process complex information. People use schemata to make sense and understand the world. Through the use of schemata, most everyday situations do not require laborious processing. People can quickly organize new perceptions into a coherent and intelligible whole. For example, most people have a window schema and can apply it to open windows they have never seen before. In more complex situations, schemas allow one to make sense of people's behaviour at a specific moment and to anticipate what is likely to occur next.

In the context of film, music is often used to bias spectators towards an interpretative framework, which in turn affects the emotional processing of the visual scene [11].

2.2 Consonance, Dissonance and Interval Content

The source of musical influence is essentially the physical and structural characteristics of music. The experiment presented here aimed to control in detail these structural features, with the purpose of investigating how they could affect the emotional interpretation of visual information. In particular, the objective was to isolate sensory dissonance, while controlling for all other musical structure variables, and to examine the effect of this specific variable on the emotional judgments of an abstract animation.

In considering consonance and dissonance, it is important to distinguish between musical and sensory consonance/dissonance. Musical consonance/dissonance concerns the evaluation of a given sound within a musical context, and can be induced by many factors such as dynamics, gesture, rhythm, tempo and textural density. Sensory consonance/dissonance refers to specific qualities an interval can posses [6], and it is studied by the psychoacoustic literature.

This study focused on sensory consonance/dissonance. Helmholtz [22] proposed that sensory consonance was associated with the absence of interactions (sensation of "beats" or "roughness") between the harmonic spectra of two pitches, a theory that was also supported in the model of Plomp and Levelt [31]. According to this model, the most consonant intervals would be the ones that could be expressed with simple frequency ratios, which has been supported by psychological study [16, 33, 38]. Intervals such as the unison (1:1), the octave (2:1), perfect fifth (3:2), and perfect fourth (4:3) are regarded as the most consonant. Intermediate in consonance are the major third (5:4), minor third (6:5), major sixth (5:3), and minor sixth (8:5). The most acoustically dissonant intervals (composed of frequencies the ratio between which is not simple) are the major second (9:8), minor second (16:15), major seventh (15:8), minor seventh (16:9), and the tritone (45:32).

Melodic intervals (sequential tone pairs) do not produce roughness or beats due to their non-simultaneity; however, they are also judged along the dimension of consonance/dissonance according to their frequency ratios [1, 32].

Intervals that are pychoacoustically dissonant usually coincide with intervals that are musically dissonant. Within a tonal music-theoretic context, Paul Hindemith's work is especially noteworthy [23]. According to Hindemith, the overtone series system (Fig. 1) gives a complete proof of the natural basis of tonal relations. In general, as new intervals are introduced, the stability decreases and the two tones involved are considered more distant in their relation. All music theories have a general agreement on this model.

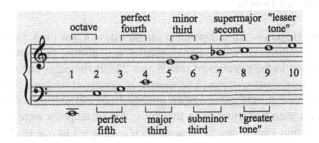

Fig. 1. Overtone series with intervals labelled.

The experiment reported here employed stochastically generated music within the general perspective of post-tonal music theory. The notion of interval-class content, introduced by Allen Forte [19] is of particular relevance for the present work. This concept, widely used in the analysis of atonal twentieth-century music, offers a valuable approach to qualifying sonorities. The interval-class content is usually presented as a string of six numbers (called interval vector) that summarizes the number of interval classes a sonority contains. This vector can act as a functional tool for portraying the general level of consonance/dissonance in a specific sonority.

2.3   The Present Study

The experiment was conducted to assess the effect of sensory dissonance on the emotional evaluation of a visual scene. The same abstract animated short film, which depicts a set of cubes moving around a static sphere, was presented to three independent groups. One group saw the film paired with consonant background music, a second group saw the film with dissonant background music, and a third control group saw the film with no music at all.

The level of sensory dissonance was controlled in this experiment by employing different intervals sets for the two contrasting background music conditions.

In order to examine if music could bias the emotional interpretation of the animated film, participants were asked to evaluate the actions and personality of the cubes on nine 7-point bipolar adjective scales. The work of Osgood [29] on the Semantic Differential technique showed that connotative meanings depend on three different dimensions: valence, activity and potency. In this experiment, adjective pairs representing each of the three connotative dimensions were used.

The question posed in this study was whether two contrasting background music materials, which only differed in terms of sensory dissonance level (controlled by interval content), would selectively bias observers' emotional interpretation of visual information.

3   Experimental Investigation

3.1   Experimental Design

Design and Participants. An independent samples design was used. One hundred and twenty healthy volunteers, with normal hearing and normal or corrected-to-normal vision, were tested in the experiment (mean age: 22). Participants were recruited from the Iowa State University campus. The study was approved by Iowa State University Ethics Committee. Subjects gave written informed consent and received no financial remuneration for their participation in the study. All participants were presented with the same visual film clip. Subjects were randomly assigned to one of three accompanying music-type conditions, which varied in terms of interval class content (consonant intervals, dissonant intervals, or no music). The between-subjects variable was the particular type of music paired with the film.

Stimulus Materials – Presentation Phase. The visual material used in this study was developed by the author using Maxon Cinema 4D Software. The film (90 s in duration) portrayed a set of cubes moving around a static sphere (Fig. 2).

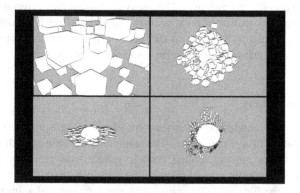

Fig. 2. Four screen shots from the animated film (the following link contains the video for further viewing: http://vimeo.com/nanobravo/cubescmmr).

The film was designed with the intention of portraying an ambiguous visual scenario, in which the actions and personality of the cubes were unclear and could be interpreted in either a positive or negative way. In a pre-test, four different render-styles of the same silent film (comprising different types of lines and colours) were presented to seven independent judges who were asked to rate each, on a 7-point scale, for its degree of ambiguity. A specific render-style (black & white format and thin sketched lines), which was judged to be the most ambiguous, was then used as stimuli for the proper experiment.

Two contrasting (in terms of consonance level) musical accompaniments were composed for this study, controlling for all the other musical structure variables. The scores were developed using an Interactive Intermedia tool created by the author with Max/MSP/Jitter visual programming software. The "Interval Vector" Max Patch, shown in Fig. 3, allows to test and analyse a wide variety of algorithmically-generated musical strategies, and further to explore cross-modal effects on visual information. The patch requires an initial pitch interval selection to create an interval set, then provides control over many coincident variables such as register, loudness, rhythm, timbre, melody, intensity and instrumentation.

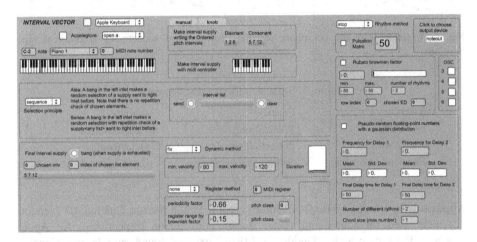

Fig. 3. Interval Vector Max Patch user interface.

In the present experiment the interest was centred on the effect of interval content exclusively. Thus, one background music condition was generated using a consonant interval content (the interval set [5-fourth-, 7-fifth-, 12-octave-]), while the other employed a dissonant interval content [1-minor second-, 2-major second-, 6-tritone-]. Musical stimuli (Fig. 4) were created as General MIDI files, played with the same sample-based instrument (Sibelius essentials – 035 Pick Bass) and attached to the visual clip.

Stimulus Materials – Testing Phase. In the testing phase of the experiment, a 9-item questionnaire was constructed that was designed to evaluate participants' emotional interpretations of the cubes' personality, actions and overall intentions in the film clip. The scaling instrument allowed a precise exploration of the effect on the valence, potency and activity dimensions. Each of the three dimensions was represented by three bipolar adjective scales, resulting in a 9-item scale shown in Table 1. The questionnaire used 7-point bipolar adjective scales, ranging from -3 to 0 to $+3$.

Consonant interval content [5, 7, 12]

Dissonant interval content [1, 2, 6]

Fig. 4. Excerpts from the consonant and dissonant musical soundtracks at different time positions.

Table 1. Semantic differential scale items.

Valence	Potency	Activity
Good/Bad	Weak/Strong	Passive/Active
Nice/Awful	Powerful/Powerless	Quiet/Restless
Pleasant/Unpleasant	Submissive/Aggressive	Calm/Agitated

Apparatus. Cycling 74 Max/MSP/Jitter (version 5) and Maxon Cinema 4D (version 12) were used for sound and visual stimuli construction respectively. An Apple Macbook Pro laptop with a Digidesign MBox2 external sound module, two Genelec 8030A active monitors, Pro Tools 8 LE system and Apple Quicktime Pro software were used for sound editing, film scoring and stimuli playback. The volume of the music was set to identical levels for the two audiovisual conditions. During the actual experiment, participants viewed the animated film that was played on a Laptop and projected via an LCD projector onto a screen. The sound was reproduced with two Genelec 8030A monitors interfaced with the Digidesign MBox2 external sound module.

Procedure. Participants were randomly assigned to one of the three conditions (Visual Alone, Audiovisual Dissonance and Audiovisual Consonance). They were informed that they would be watching an animated film clip and later asked some questions. Immediately after viewing the film clip, participants were administered the questionnaire where they had to complete the set of bipolar adjective ratings. The experimental session lasted approximately 20 min.

4 Experimental Results

A multivariate analysis of variance was conducted to assess whether there were differences between the three music type groups (Visual Alone, Audiovisual Dissonance and Audiovisual Consonance) on a linear combination of each three criterion-variables (adjective pairs) used per dimension (valence, potency and activity).

A Pillai's trace multivariate statistic was used for testing the global hypothesis and to correct for a possible parameter estimation bias due to the high intercorrelation between the criterion-variables within dimension.

No significant differences were found between the three conditions for the potency and activity dimensions. A significant difference was found for the valence dimension, Pillai's Trace = 0.133, F (115, 232) = 2.752, $p < 0.05$, multivariate $\eta^2 = 0.066$. Examination of the coefficients for the linear combinations distinguishing music type conditions indicated that adjective ratings for Nice-Awful and Pleasant-Unpleasant, contributed most to distinguishing the groups. In particular, adjective pair Nice-Awful (0.625) contributed significantly toward discriminating Visual alone group from the other two groups, and adjective pair Pleasant-Unpleasant (−0.85) contributed significantly toward distinguishing Audiovisual Consonance from the other two groups. The adjective pair Good-Bad did not contribute significantly to distinguishing any of the groups.

From the multivariate test statistic we can conclude that the type of music employed had a significant effect on the valence dimension. To determine the precise nature of this effect univariate tests were conducted.

A statistically significant difference was found amongst the three levels of music type (Visual alone, Audiovisual Dissonance and Audiovisual Consonance) on all three 7-point bipolar adjective scales of the valence emotional dimension. Bad-Good, $F_{2,117} = 5.037$, $p < 0.05$; Awful-Nice, $F_{2,117} = 5.089$, $p < 0.05$; Unpleasant-Pleasant, $F_{2,117} = 3.361$, $p < 0.05$.

With regard to the relatively small overall sample size, a Levene's Test for equality of error variances was conducted on each dependent variable. The Levene's Test was significant only for the criterion-variable Nice-Awful. Since the "robustness" of ANOVA methods against violations of central assumptions is not limitless, especially when small samples are involved, the results for this particular dependent variable should be viewed with caution.

Since Levene's Test was significant for the dependent variable Nice-Awful, and because of the uncertainty of knowing whether the population variances are equivalent, the Games-Howell procedure was utilized.

Post hoc Games-Howell tests indicated that the Visual Alone group and the Audiovisual Consonance group differed significantly in all three valence adjective pairs ratings: Good-Bad ($p < 0.05$, $d = 1.15$); Nice-Awful, ($p < 0.05$, $d = 0.97$); Pleasant-Unleasant, ($p < 0.05$, $d = 0.9$). No significant difference was found between the two audiovisual conditions, nor between the Audiovisual Dissonance condition and Visual-Alone condition.

Moreover, simple contrasts were carried out to compare each audiovisual group (Audiovisual Dissonance and Audiovisual Consonance) to the Visual Alone control group. These contrasts represent AV-Diss vs. V-Alone and AV-Cons vs. V-Alone. Each contrast is performed on each dependent variable separately and so they are identical to the contrasts that have been obtained from the univariate ANOVA. 95 % confidence intervals were produced for the estimated difference. When comparing AV-Diss vs. V-Alone, these boundaries cross zero, therefore we cannot be confident that the observed group difference is meaningful. However, for the contrast AV-Cons vs. V-Alone the confidence intervals do not cross zero: Good-Bad, 95 % CI [−1.87, −0.43]; Nice-Awful, 95 % CI [−1.59, −0.36]; Pleasant-Unpleasant, 95 % CI [−1.67, −0.13]. As such, we can be confident that genuine group differences exist between AV-Cons and V-Alone conditions. These results are consistent with those reported for the Games-Howell procedure.

After converting all of the negative adjective ratings to negative numbers, and the positive adjective ratings to positive numbers, the set of ratings for a given adjective pair are shown in Fig. 5 as a function of the type of accompanying music (Visual Alone, Audiovisual with dissonant interval content and Audiovisual with consonant interval content). Table 2 shows group means and standard deviations for each dependent variable.

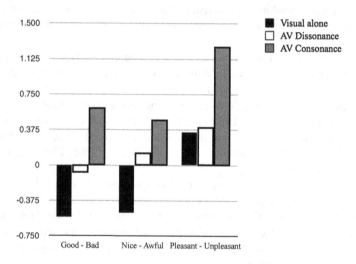

Fig. 5. Adjective pair ratings as a function of the type of accompanying music (visual alone, consonant interval content and dissonant interval content).

Table 2. Means and standard deviations comparing the three types of accompanying music (valence dimension).

Music type	n	Good-Bad		Nice-Awful		Pleasant-Unpleasant	
		M	SD	M	SD	M	SD
Visual alone	40	−0.55	1.6	−0.5	1.15	0.35	1.79
AV dissonance	40	−0.07	1.50	0.12	1.78	0.4	1.89
AV consonance	40	0.6	1.76	0.47	1.10	1.25	1.53

5 Discussion

The main finding of this experiment is that there were differences concerning the evaluation of the clip on the valence dimension due to the music condition. The statistical analysis evidenced a significant difference between the visual alone condition and the audiovisual consonant condition on all three adjective pairs representing the valence dimension. Interval content seems to have influenced the emotional evaluation of the animation since all the other musical structure variables were strictly controlled.

Due to the fact that only one visual scene was used and because no significant difference was found between the consonant and the dissonant conditions, no general conclusion can be made. Further studies should work with more than one visual scene and also explore how the level of sensory consonance/dissonance may interact with other musical structure features (e.g. timbre) when influencing the emotional processing of visual information.

In relating the alteration in emotional meaning of film to different background music, Marshall and Cohen [26] postulated a Congruence-Associationist Theoretical Framework. They stated that an interaction of the temporal structure of the film and music can influence visual attention. The connotative attributes of music may then be ascribed to the visual attentional focus. In the present experiment, the movement, position and size of the cubes were synchronously mapped to the triggered sounds. Therefore, it can be argued that music directed attention to the cubes through temporal-structural congruence, and the particular connotation of consonant intervals became associated with the attended visual feature. The gradual change in the valence dimension may be simply interpreted as the music increasing the interest of the very abstract visual materials. However, it is important to note that the difference in the valence ratings only reached statistical significance with the consonant interval content as background music.

In the Western music cultural convention dissonant intervals have historically been linked to "oppressive", "scary" and "evil" connotative meanings. On the other hand, consonant intervals usually elicit pleasant feelings to most people [7, 31, 33]. As Meyer expressed "certain musical relationships appear to be well-nigh universal. In almost all cultures, for example, the octave and the fifth or fourth are treated as stable, focal tones toward which other terms of the system tend to move" [27]. In this experiment, consonant intervals biased participants' judgments toward positive valence ratings. These results are consistent with those of others who found evidence for additivity of audio and visual meaning along the valence dimension [9, 26].

Music theory provides technical descriptions of how styles organize musical sounds and offers insights about musical structures that might underlie listeners' interpretations. Allen Forte has described that the quality of a sonority can be characterized by listing the intervals it contains [19]. Forte introduced the basic concept of 'interval vector' to analyse the properties of pitch class sets and the interactions of the components of a set in terms of intervals. The model he proposed only considers interval classes (i.e. unordered pitch-intervals measured in semitones). An interval vector is an array of numbers that expresses the intervallic content of a certain sonority. It has six digits, with each digit standing for the number of times an interval class appears in the set. According to Forte, such interval vector conveys the essential sound (colour, quality) of a sonority.

Table 3 summarizes interval class content for each background music condition. In this study, the contrasting conditions were obtained by employing two distinct interval contents, by means of which a uniform level of consonance/dissonance was attained throughout a given version. The analysis provided can therefore represent the comparative level of dissonance across the specified categories.

Table 3. Interval Vector for the two music conditions.

Interval set/ Prime form	Unordered pitch-intervals					
	1	2	3	4	5	6
Cons. [5, 7, 12] /(0 ,2 ,7)	0	1	0	0	2	0
Diss. [1, 2, 6] /(0,1, 2, 6)	2	1	0	1	1	1

The consonant condition is generally governed by collections of intervals considered to be consonant: fourths, fifths and octaves (octaves are not reflected by interval vectors). Fourths and fifths are summarized as 2 occurrences within the unordered pitch-interval 5. It is important to note that sporadic major seconds may occur in the consonant condition when some of the triggered pitches overlap (e.g. measure 77 in the consonant excerpt shown in Fig. 4). In contrast, the use of dissonant intervals (minor second, major second, and tritone) is characteristic of the dissonant version.

The term tonalness refers to "the degree to which a sonority evokes the sensation of a single pitched tone" [30], in the sense that sonorities with high tonalness evoke a clear perception of pitch. As a component of consonance, tonalness has been defined as the "ease with which the ear/brain system can resolve the fundamental" [18], being the easier, the more consonant.

David Temperley [36] proposed a method to measure both tonalness and tonal ambiguity of pitch-class sets. Tonal ambiguity can be captured by Temperley's Bayesian key-finding model. The ambiguity of a passage may be defined as the degree to which it clearly implies a key. Table 4 shows, for the two pitch-class sets used in this experiment: sets (0, 2, 7) and (0, 1, 2, 6), the probability of each key given the set. Figure 6 plots Table 4, a quick glance shows that the distribution of values is much more even in the case of the pitch-class set (0, 1, 2, 6) than in (0, 2, 7). For the pitch-class set (0, 2, 7) four keys' values (C Mayor/minor and G Mayor/minor) are far higher than any other. For the set (0, 1, 2, 6) the probability mass is more evenly divided.

Following the key-finding model and the Bayesian "structure–and-surface" approach, Temperley suggests a way to calculate the overall probability (Tonalness) of a pitch-class set occurring in a tonal piece. Table 5 shows this quantity for the two pitch-class sets that were used in the experiment. This overall probability describes how characteristic each pitch-class set is of the language of common practice tonality (i.e. how tonal the set is). It can be seen that the pitch-class set (0, 2, 7) is somewhat more probable than the pitch-class set (0, 1, 2, 6). As Temperley himself points "there

Table 4. The probability of each key given the two pitch-class sets, (0, 2, 7) and (0, 1, 2, 6), used in the experiment (Calculations were done in Max/MSP following Temperley's Bayesian key-finding model).

Key	Cons [5, 7, 12]/(0, 2, 7)		Diss [1, 2, 6]/(0, 1, 2, 6)	
	Mayor Key	minor Key	Mayor Key	minor Key
C	0.00048587	0.00054569	0.00000131	0.00000199
C#/Db	0.00000031	0.00000044	0.00000737	0.00000789
D	0.00001046	0.00002680	0.00001662	0.00000080
D#/Eb	0.00005349	0.00000015	0.00000014	0.00000073
E	0.00000004	0.00001396	0.00000026	0.00000056
F	0.00009450	0.00001585	0.00000073	0.00000109
F#/Gb	0.00000005	0.00000060	0.00000628	0.00004816
G	0.00043425	0.00051584	0.00001036	0.00001206
G#/Ab	0.00000984	0.00000025	0.00000076	0.00000007
A	0.00000031	0.00001754	0.00000611	0.00000042
A#/Bb	0.00007647	0.00000028	0.00000137	0.00000422
B	0.00000005	0.00000834	0.00000093	0.00003275

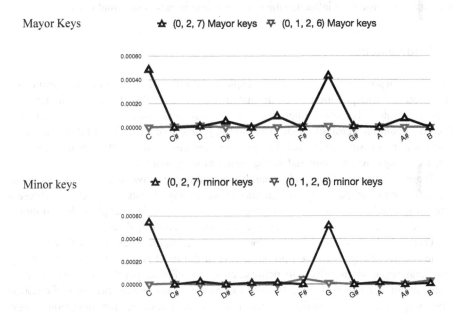

Fig. 6. Plotted probability of each key (in Mayor and minor modes) given the two pitch-class sets, (0, 2, 7) and (0, 1, 2, 6).

is more to tonality, and judgments of tonality, than sheer pitch-class content" [36]. However, there is no doubt that the pitch-class content strongly contributes to the tonalness of a passage. The Bayesian model presented by Temperley captures this aspect of tonality and therefore portrays an indirect tool to quantify consonance level.

Table 5. Tonalness of the two music conditions (using the Koska-Payne key-profiles).

Interval set/Prime form	Tonalness
Consonance [5, 7, 12]/(0, 2, 7)	0.002311
Dissonance [1, 2, 6]/(0, 1, 2, 6)	0.000163

The presented analysis seems to reflect that tonalness might be a helpful quantifiable consonance component for predicting valence associations. Additional research is needed to further assess this hypothesis using more levels of tonalness, and to examine the ways in which these sonorities may interact with formal characteristics of images that are different from the ones utilized in this experiment. Moreover, it would be interesting to explore if subtle adjustments in tonalness level (e.g. the diminished triad - tonalness = 0.00032 vs. the harmonic minor scale - tonalness = 0.00028) could still lead to biases in the emotional judgements.

This paper examined the role of consonance/dissonance in the relatively abstract domain of pitch-class sets. While more research is required to further analyse this issue in more complex situations of real music, it is hoped that the work developed here will contribute to stimulate new questions aimed towards understanding the ways in which structural characteristics of music may influence the emotional interpretation of visual contexts.

6   Conclusions

The main purpose of the study was to explore the influence of sensory dissonance on the emotional interpretation of an animated film. The results of the experiment indicated that interval content altered the emotional evaluation of visual information. The consonant background music condition appeared to exert a direct influence on the emotional processing of visual imagery by guiding participants towards positive valence ratings, when compared to the visual alone condition.

There is a lack of empirical research examining the ways in which specific characteristics of music may shape the emotional processing of visual contexts. The present study suggested a way to use algorithmically generated music to explore the emotional effect of interval content in a systematic and strictly controlled setting.

These results have implications for a variety of fields, such as multimedia, film music or advertising. However, probably one of the most constructive and potentially beneficial applications relates to neuroscience and clinical psychology. Strictly controlled audiovisual stimuli could be used to investigate the neural correlates of emotion processing, and these studies might have direct relevance for developing new approaches to characterize and diagnose complex mental health disorders.

Acknowledgments. Thanks to Prof. Ian Cross, Prof. Sarah Hawkins, Dr. Emmanuel A. Stamatakis, and to all the researchers at the Centre for Music and Science (Cambridge University). Thanks to Andrew Goldman for his very constructive comments on this paper. Thanks to Dr. Christopher Hopkins, Prof. Anson Call and Prof. Steve Herrnstadt (ISU). Thank you to the anonymous reviewers for their suggestions that improved the article considerably. This work was conducted at Cambridge University and is supported by a Queens' College Walker Studentship.

References

1. Ayres, T., Aeschbach, S., Walker, E.L.: Psychoacoustic and experiential determinants of tonal consonance. J Aud. Res. **20**, 31–42 (1980)
2. Barham, J.: Incorporating monsters: music as context, character and construction in Kubrick's the shining. In: Hayward, Philip (ed.) Terror Tracks: Music, Sound and Horror Cinema. Equinox, London (2009)
3. Bartlett, F.C.: Remembering. Cambridge University Press, London (1932)
4. Baumgartner, T., Esslen, M., Jäncke, L.: From emotion perception to emotion experience: emotions evoked by pictures and classical music. Int. J. Psychophysiol. **60**, 34–43 (2006)
5. Baumgartner, T., Lutz, K., Schmidt, C.F., Jäncke, L.: The emotional power of music: how music enhances the feeling of affective pictures. Brain Res. **1075**, 151–164 (2006)
6. Bharucha, J.J.: Anchoring effects in music: The resolution of dissonance. Cogn. Psychol. **16**, 485–518 (1984)
7. Blood, A.J., Zatorre, R.J., Bermudez, P., Evans, A.C.: Emotional responses to pleasant and unpleasant music correlate with activity in paralimbic brain regions. Nat. Neurosci. **2**, 382–387 (1999)
8. Bigand, E., Parncutt, R., Lerdahl, F.: Perception of musical tension in short chord sequences: The influence of harmonic function, sensory dissonance, horizontal motion, and musical training. Percept. Psychophys. **58**, 124–141 (1996)
9. Bolivar, V.J., Cohen, A.J., Fentress, J.: Semantic and formal congruency in music and motion pictures: Effects on the interpretation of visual action. Psychomusicology **13**, 28–59 (1994)
10. Boltz, M.G., Schulkind, M., Kantra, S.: Effects of background music on the remembering of filmed events. Mem. Cognit. **19**, 593–606 (1991)
11. Boltz, M.G.: Musical soundtracks as a schematic influence on the cognitive processing of filmed events. Music Percept. **18**, 427–454 (2001)
12. Bravo, F.: The influence of music on the emotional interpretation of visual contexts. In: Aramaki, M., Barthet, M., Kronland-Martinet, R., Ystad, S. (eds.) CMMR 2012. LNCS, vol. 7900, pp. 366–377. Springer, Heidelberg (2013)
13. Brewer, W.F.: Literacy, theory, and rhetoric: implications for psychology. In: Spiro, R.J., Bruce, B.C., Brewer, W.F. (eds.) Theoretical Issues in Reading Comprehension: Perspectives from Cognitive Psychology, Linguistics, Artificial Intelligence, and Education, pp. 221–239. Erlbaum, Hillsdale (1980)
14. Cohen, A.J.: Music as a source of emotion in film. In: Juslin, P., Sloboda, J. (eds.) Music and Emotion, pp. 249–272. Oxford University Press, Oxford (2001)
15. Cohen, A.J.: How music influences the interpretation of film and video: approaches from experimental psychology. In: Kendall, R.A., Savage, R.W. (eds.) Selected Reports in Ethnomusicology: Perspectives in Systematic Musicology, vol. 12, pp. 15–36. University of California, Los Angeles (2005)
16. DeWitt, L.A., Crowder, R.G.: Tonal fusion of consonant musical intervals. Percept. Psychophys. **41**, 73–84 (1987)
17. Eldar, E., Ganor, O., Admon, R., Bleich, A., Hendler, T.: Feeling the real world: limbic response to music depends on related content. Cereb. Cortex **17**, 2828–2840 (2007)
18. Erlich, P.: On harmonic entropy. Mills College Tuning Digest (1997)
19. Forte, A.: The Structure of Atonal Music. University Press, Yale (1973)
20. Hastie, R.: Schematic principles in human memory. In: Higgins, E.T., Herman, C.P., Zanna, M.P. (eds.) Social Cognition: The Ontario Symposium, vol. 1, pp. 39–88. Erlbaum, Hillsdale (1981)

21. Heider, F., Simmel, M.: An experimental study of apparent behaviour. Am. J. Psychol. **57**, 243–259 (1944)
22. Helmholtz, H.L.F.: On the Sensation of Tone as a Physiological Basis for the Theory of Music. Dover, New York (1954). (Original German work published 1863)
23. Hindemith, P.: Unterweisung im Tonsatz, 3 vols. (Mainz: Schott, 1937–70) (The Craft of Musical Composition, vol. 1: Theoretical Part, translaed by Mendel, A). Associated Music Publishers, London, New York (1942)
24. Lerdahl, F., Krumhansl, C.L.: Modeling tonal tension. Music Percept. **24**, 329–366 (2007)
25. Lipscomb, S.D., Kendall, R.A.: Perceptual judgment of the relationship between music and visual components in film. Psychomusicology **13**, 60–98 (1994)
26. Marshall, S.K., Cohen, A.J.: Effects of musical soundtracks on attitudes toward animated geometric figures. Music Percept. **6**, 95–112 (1988)
27. Meyer, L.B.: Emotion and Meaning in Music. University of Chicago Press, Chicago (1956)
28. Neisser, U.: Cognition and Reality. W. H. Freeman, San Francisco (1976)
29. Osgood, C.E., Succi, G.J., Tannenbaum, P.H.: The Measurement of Meaning. University of Illinois Press, Urbana (1957)
30. Parncutt, R.: Harmony: A Psychoacoustical Approach. Springer, Berlin (1989). ISBN 0-387-51279-9
31. Plomp, R., Levelt, W.J.M.: Tonal consonance and the critical bandwidth. J. Acoust. Soc. Am. **38**, 548–560 (1965)
32. Schellenberg, E.G., Trehub, S.E.: Frequency ratios and the discrimination of pure tone sequences. Percept. Psychophys. **56**, 472–478 (1994)
33. Schellenberg, E.G., Trainor, L.J.: Sensory consonance and the perceptual similarity of complex-tone harmonic intervals: tests of adult and infant listeners. J. Acoust. Soc. Am. **100**, 3321–3328 (1996)
34. Sirius, G., Clarke, E.F.: The perception of audiovisual relationships: a preliminary study. Psychomusicology **13**, 119–132 (1994)
35. Taylor, S.E., Crocker, J.: Schematic bases of social information processing. In: Higgins, E.T., Herman, C.P., Zanna, M.P. (eds.) Social Cognition: The Ontario Symposium, vol. 1, 27, pp. 89–134. Erlbaum, Hillsdale (1981)
36. Temperley, D.: Music and probability. MIT Press, Cambridge (2007)
37. Thom, R., Crocker, J.: Designing a movie for sound. In: Sider, L., Freeman, D., Sider, J. (eds.) Soundscapes: The School of Sound Lectures 1998–2001, vol. 1, 27, pp. 121–137. Wallflower Press, Great Britain (1998)
38. Vos, J., Vianen, B.G.: Thresholds for discrimination between pure and tempered intervals: the relevance of nearly coinciding harmonics. J. Acoust. Soc. Am. **77**, 76–187 (1984)

The Perception of Sound Movements as Expressive Gestures

Amalia de Götzen$^{(\boxtimes)}$, Erik Sikström, Dannie Korsgaard,
Stefania Serafin, and Francesco Grani

Aalborg University Copenhagen, Copenhagen, Denmark
{ago,es,dmk,sts,fg}@create.aau.dk

Abstract. This paper is a preliminary attempt to investigate the perception of sound movements as expressive gestures. The idea is that if sound movement is used as a musical parameter, a listener (or a subject) should be able to distinguish among different movements and she/he should be able to group them also according to the expressive intention that a given sound movement is supposed to convey. A couple of experiments have been carried out in this direction: first the subjects had to group the stimuli according to the perceived expressive intention, then they had to reproduce the sound movement by drawing it on a tablet. Preliminary results show that subjects could consistently group the stimuli, and that they primarily used paths and *legato–staccato* patterns to discriminate among different sound movements/expressive intention.

Keywords: Sound movements · Gestures · Spatialization · Expressiveness

1 Introduction

The location of sound in space has always been a parameter taken into some consideration by music composers and creators. This consideration has often appeared implicitly, for example in the disposition of instruments on stage or their positioning in a church; however, it has also made its way explicitly in composers' scores throughout history – the tradition of the renaissance *"cori battenti"* in the San Marco church in Venice and their use by Andrea and Giovanni Gabrieli in the sixteen century, or the *"lontano"*[1] indication in many scores of romantic and impressionistic music are but a few cases in point of this desire of incorporating space explicitly in the compositional process. Also, since the end of WW II space has emancipated its status in music as a compositional device while incorporating movement of sound in space; and after the seminal *Kontakte* (1959–60) by Karlheinz Stockhausen [13] it has become a regular feature in musical orchestration and scoring. Space location and movement are also widely used today in entertainment to enhance immersion and engagement in motion pictures etc.

---

[1] lontano: as from far away.

© Springer International Publishing Switzerland 2014
M. Aramaki et al. (Eds.): CMMR 2013, LNCS 8905, pp. 509–517, 2014.
DOI: 10.1007/978-3-319-12976-1_30

The studies on musical expressiveness are indeed more recent (cf. [9]) but their development has been so strong and pervasive that this topic has become a full track in itself in the past twenty years or so (cf. [6,7,10]).

However, analyses of the perceptual aspects of the expressiveness of motion of musical sounds through space are still quite scarce (cf. [8]). This is due, perhaps, to the subtlety of the percepts of sound positioning and to the difficulty of assessing the expressiveness of movement of sound in space. Recent studies in musical gestures come in handy in this context (cf. [1,12,14]) while current technology readily allows to design and setup some initial experimental assessment on this subject.

2 Sound Movement as a Musical Parameter

In this paper the term "sound movement" must be intended as "the real or virtual movement of a sound source in space". The perception of sound movement presents some specifically musical issues which must be taken in consideration when designing experiments. These issues can be summarized as follows:

1. while the location of sound is distinctly three-dimensional, humans perceive the position along the horizontal plane with much greater precision than that on the vertical plane (elevation – cf. [5,11]); when precision is at stake expressiveness is much more difficult to assess, and therefore the experiments proposed in this paper take in consideration the expressiveness of movements happening exclusively on the horizontal plane. The fragility of elevation perception is also widely acknowledged in music, where composers are undoubtedly attracted by the strong metaphors that lie behind "elevation" but they are seldom able to actually use this parameter effectively;
2. there is a dependence between movement, agogic and sound envelope: contemporary composers know well that short staccato sounds or fast percussive articulation allow for much stronger perception even of very fast movements, while slow attacks and decays are harder to locate in space; thus, the expressiveness of sound motion must be tested with opposed agogic and global envelopes to assess the actual contribution of motion itself.

These were the main considerations behind the selection and combination of tasks in the experiments described in this paper.

3 Experimental Setup

Both tests were performed in the Multimodal Experience lab at the Aalborg University in Copenhagen.

3.1 Material

12 examples were synthesized in order to reproduce different kinds of sound movements. Colored noise was used as a test sound. The parameters that could

be controlled were the following ones: speed (*slow* – *fast*), movement (*circular*, *discontinuous1* or *discontinuous2*), agogic (*legato* – *staccato*). *Discontinuous1* performed a rectangular shape motion around the listener, while *discontinuous2* performed a triangle "8"–shape motion with the listener in its center. This investigation stems from a musical perspective and from musical practice: the parameters mentioned above were chosen because they are the ones most frequently used by composers when defining the electronic scores of their compositions [2,3]. However, colored noise was used as sound source rather than musical excerpts to avoid biases that could derive from the intrinsic expressiveness of music which could be possibly perceived also without virtually moving the sound in space.

Fast movements lasted for about 3 s, while slow movements lasted for about 6 s. This is the list of the 12 stimuli:

1. *fast circular staccato*
2. *slow discontinuous1 legato*
3. *fast discontinuous1 legato*
4. *slow circular staccato*
5. *fast discontinuous2 legato*
6. *fast circular legato*
7. *slow circular legato*
8. *slow discontinuous2 staccato*
9. *fast discontinuous2 staccato*
10. *fast discontinuous1 staccato*
11. *slow discontinuous2 legato*
12. *slow discontinuous1 staccato*

In the second experiment the subjects had to draw the sound movement that they could perceive. The main idea in this experiment was to assess the subjects ability to discriminate between different movement gestures rather than analyzing the exact path of the sound. A second expected outcome was to assess if they used different signs to represent different parameters, for instance the "legato" and "staccato" one.

3.2   Apparatus

The auditory stimuli as well as the pre-defined sound movement patterns for each condition were generated and scripted using a patch made with Max/Msp 5.1.5. The externals VBAP[2] and Ambimonitor[3] externals for sound spatialization and management of azimuth and Cartesian coordinates were used to ease the panning the sound around in the speaker setup. The sounds used were generated by a noise object connected to a `lores~` object (resonant low-pass filter) with the cutoff frequency set to 1300 Hz and resonance argument set to 0.1. When the *legato* condition was active the sound was played constantly during the whole pattern with fade-in and fade out ramps 30 ms long. When the *staccato* condition

---

[2] http://www.acoustics.hut.fi/~ville/.
[3] http://www.icst.net/research/downloads/.

was active, the sounds were played in short bursts upon reaching each point along the path. Each sound burst lasted for 50 ms plus fade-in and a fade-out ramps of 10 ms each.

3.3 Procedure

Subjects were asked to sit on a high chair in the middle of a room with a surround audio system made of 16 loudspeakers. A little round table standing in front of them carried an iPad. In order to listen to the different sound movements they had to push 12 different icons drawn on the iPad screen; then they had to group them focusing their attention on the perceived expressive intention of each sound movement (nothing more precise than that was told to them). The chosen procedure is derived from a paper by Bigand [4] where subjects were asked to group together different musical excerpts according to the perceived expressive intention. In the second experiment subjects were asked to listen to a given sound movement and to try to write it on the iPad focusing on the reproduction of the expressive intention of each movement. They could listen to the sound stimuli as many time as they wished to and they could cancel–rewrite their drawing.

At the end of each test subjects were asked to answer a questionnaire: for the first test we asked to describe their grouping strategy (if any) and if they could fine any form of expressiveness in the stimuli they were listening to. After the second test they were asked to comment on the task they were assigned - basically to see if they were satisfied with the instrument they had to represent the sound movement.

3.4 Participants

A total of 23 subjects performed both tests. The subjects average age was 25.5, the youngest subject being 19 years old while the oldest was 46. There were a total of 13 male and 10 female participants, and just 6 among them had some musical background and/or were studying an instrument. Each test lasted around 20 min.

4 Data Analysis

The collected data has been processed and visualized. In the following subsections the main results will be discussed.

4.1 Grouping Task

The collected data was first analyzed in order to see if there were any outlier that had to be removed from the data set. Out of the 23 participants just one of them did not perform any of the required tasks, just listening to the stimuli without grouping them. So this subject's data was removed: 22 subjects correctly performed the test.

The data was then processed through hierarchical cluster analysis in order to detect the groups formed by each subject. The results of the grouping task of each subject was displayed with a dendrogram accompanied by the representation on a two-dimensional plane. Figure 1 represent the grouped data of "subject 4", while Fig. 2 shows the averaged dendrogram, taking in to account the grouping performed by all subjects.

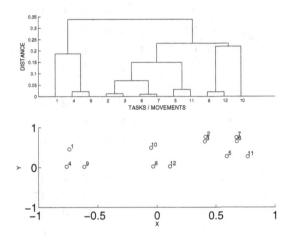

Fig. 1. The top figure shows the clusterization of the data that is visualized in a normalized bi-dimensional space on the bottom figure.

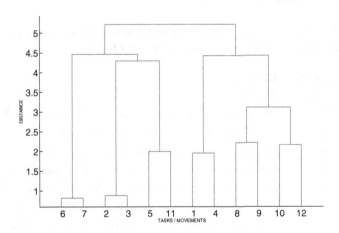

Fig. 2. The averaged dendrogram

The first part of the analysis concerned the number of groups produced by participants. They distinguished an average of 5 groups (5.1818) and there was no difference between musicians and non musicians or male and female. Then the grouping of the participants were converted to a 12×12 matrix of co-occurrence. Each cell of the matrix in Table 1 indicates the number of times that two stimuli were grouped together.

Table 1. Grouping results by task

	1	2	3	4	5	6	7	8	9	10	11	12
1	0	0	0	21	1	2	2	4	6	3	0	4
2		0	22	0	4	0	0	0	0	1	4	1
3			0	0	3	0	0	0	0	1	4	1
4				0	0	2	2	6	4	3	0	6
5					0	1	1	0	1	1	20	0
6						0	22	0	0	0	0	0
7							0	0	0	0	0	0
8								0	15	7	1	11
9									0	9	2	4
10										0	0	17
11											0	0
12												0

The numbers in bold indicate the most grouped pair of stimuli, some of them were grouped together by all the participants. The most frequently coupled movements are then reported in Table 2.

Table 2. This table shows the most important Pairwise Results, summarizing what kind of tasks/sound movements were mostly grouped together.

Paired tasks	Number of times	Tasks description
2 with 3	22	*slow discontinuous1 legato* and *fast discontinuous1 legato*
6 with 7	22	*fast circular legato* and *slow circular legato*
1 with 4	21	*fast circular staccato* and *slow circular staccato*
5 with 11	20	*fast discontinuous2 legato* and *slow discontinuous2 legato*
10 with 12	17	*fast discontinuous1 staccato* and *slow discontinuous1 staccato*
8 with 9	15	*slow discontinuous2 staccato* and *fast discontinuous2 staccato*
9 with 12	11	*fast discontinuous2 staccato* and *slow discontinuous1 staccato*

It can be observed that the subjects were able to actually distinguish among *legato* and *staccato* movements and between the 3 different movements (*circular, discontinuous1* and *discontinuous2*) while they did not used the speed at all in order to perform the grouping task. They got confused about the two different discontinuous patterns just in the last group (movement 9 with movement 12).

Most of the participants reported in the questionnaire that they filled up after the test that the motion of sound was reminiscent of different expressive intentions: the circular motion was connected to a calm and pleasant sound (something related to water and sea) while the discontinuous movements made them more anxious or nervous, notwithstanding the speed used. The difference between *legato* and *staccato* was also mentioned by most of the participants.

4.2 Drawing Test

The aim of this second test was to verify if the same subjects that did the grouping task were then able to reproduce graphically the movements that they perceived and what aspects were then emphasized. 23 subjects participated to this test. Many subjects actually complained about some technical issues, like the difficulty to have a good representation of the movement's speed, while others would have liked to have different colors or pens and in general they were asking for more freedom. At any rate, the drawings produced a wealth of additional information. The drawings were initially analyzed for every single participant, trying to see if he/she could produce a representation of legato–staccato, fast–slow and the path/gesture parameters in a consistent way and with good approximation. 96 % of the subjects could represent with a good level of precision the circular movements, while the 84 % of the participants could recognize the "8-shape" movement. This was something expected since the main difference between the two movements was that in the 8 shape the sound is actually "running through" the listener and this should be a strong expressive aspect of the performed sound.

92 % of the subjects represented also the "legato-staccato" parameter and 66 % of the subjects represented (with an expected tolerance) two different speeds, even if quite far from the actual speeds used. The rectangular shape was most of the time confused with the circular one. In Figs. 3 and 4 is it possible to see a couple of drawings.

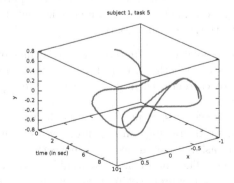

Fig. 3. Subject n. 1, Task n. 5: 8 shape legato movement

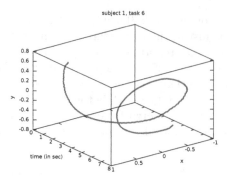

Fig. 4. Subject n. 1, Task n. 6: circular shape legato movement

An interesting aspect is that they were no able to distinguish their path while trying to draw them, even if they grouped the stimuli also according to the different discontinuous movements. This is particularly true for the "rectangular" movement, that was mostly confused with the circular one.

5   Conclusions and Future Work

It is interesting to notice that the results presented in this paper closely match those of an earlier paper (cf. [8]) with the notable exception of the role of speed. The important point was in the experiment carried out in [8] the subjects were asked to evaluate a specific motion within a valence–arousal Russell circumplex while in the present experiment no such metaphoric canvas was used; however, since the grouping results are quite similar in both experiments, it is possible to draw stronger conclusions concerning the perception of expressiveness related to sound motion in space. The role of speed remains to be further assessed: [8] used strongly contrasting speeds while the current experiment had opted for smaller speed differences to try to assess the strength of speed as a parameter. Surprisingly, the perception of the speed parameter turned out to be quite fragile (i.e.: smaller speed differences eliminate the dissimilarity perception altogether), thus requiring further experimental work to be carried out. Other developments that are connected to these experiments concern:

- movement drawing re-synthesis: after collecting drawings by subjects it would be interesting to assess whether the latter are able to recognize their own drawings, that is to correlate their gesture to the perception of the actual movement drawn;
- real–time expressive gestures: if previous tests demonstrate that there is a correspondence between drawings and sound movement, a "performing" test can be carried out asking the subjects to move the sound as if they were happy–sad–angry–etc. The aim of this test would be to see whether subjects, being free to choose an expressive intention, would be consistent with the grouping results presented in the current paper.

References

1. Andersen, T.H., Zhai, S.: "writing with music": Exploring the use of auditory feedback in gesture interfaces. ACM Trans. Appl. Percept. **7**(3), 17:1–17:24 (2008). http://doi.acm.org/10.1145/1773965.1773968

2. Bernardini, N., Vidolin, A.: Recording *orfeo cantando... tolse* by Adriano Guarnieri: sound motion and space parameters on a stereo cd. In: Proceedings of the XII Colloquio di Informatica Musicale - Gorizia 1998, Gorizia, pp. 262–265 (1998)

3. Bernardini, N., Vidolin, A.: Note di Live Electronics, pp. 157–161. Edizioni del Teatro La Fenice, Venezia (2002)

4. Bigand, E., Vieillard, S., Madurell, F., Marozeau, J., Dacquet, A.: Multidimensional scaling of emotional responses to music: the effect of musical expertise and of the duration of the excerpts. Cogn. Emot. **19**(8), 1113–1139 (2005). http://dx.doi.org/10.1080/02699930500204250

5. Blauert, J.: Spatial Hearing: The Psychophysics of Human Sound Localization. MIT Press, Cambridge (1983)

6. Bresin, R., Friberg, A.: Evaluation of computer systems for expressive music performance. In: Kirke, A., Miranda, E.R. (eds.) Guide to Computing for Expressive Music Performance, pp. 181–203. Springer, London (2013). http://dx.doi.org/10.1007/978-1-4471-4123-5_7

7. Camurri, A., Volpe, G., Poli, G.D., Leman, M.: Communicating expressiveness and affect in multimodal interactive systems. IEEE MultiMedia **12**(1), 43–53 (2005). http://dx.doi.org/10.1109/MMUL.2005.2

8. de Götzen, A.: Enhancing engagement in multimodality environments by sound movements in a virtual space. IEEE MultiMedia **11**(2), 4–8 (2004). http://dx.doi.org/10.1109/MMUL.2004.1289034

9. Imberty, M.: Entendre la musique. Sémantique psychologique de la musique. Dunod (1979)

10. Juslin, P., Sloboda, J.: Psychological Perspectives on Music and Emotion, Music and Emotion-Theory and Research. Oxford University Press, Oxford (2001)

11. Kendall, G., Martens, W.: Simulating the cues of spatial hearing in natural environments. In: Proceedings of the International Computer Music Conference 1984, pp. 111–125. International Computer Music Association, San Francisco (1984)

12. Rocchesso, D., Delle Monache, S.: Perception and replication of planar sonic gestures. ACM Trans. Appl. Percept. **9**(4), 18:1–18:21 (2012). http://doi.acm.org/10.1145/2355598.2355601

13. Stockhausen, K.: Musik in Raum. Dumont-Verlag, Köln (1958)

14. Thoret, E., Aramaki, M., Kronland-Martinet, R., Velay, J.L., Ystad, S.: From sound to shape: auditory perception of drawing movements. J. Exp. Psychol. Hum. Percept. Perform. (2014). http://www.biomedsearch.com/nih/From-Sound-to-Shape-Auditory/24446717.html

Musical Sonification of Avatar Physiologies, Virtual Flight and Gesture

Robert Hamilton[✉]

Center for Computer Research in Music and Acoustics,
Stanford University, Stanford, USA
rob@ccrma.stanford.edu

Abstract. Virtual actors moving through interactive game-space environments create rich streams of data that serve as drivers for real-time musical sonification. The paradigms of avian flight, biologically-inspired kinesthetic motion and manually-controlled avatar skeletal mesh components through inverse kinematics are used in the musical performance work *ECHO::Canyon* to control real-time synthesis-based instruments within a multi-channel sound engine. This paper discusses gestural and control methodologies as well as specific mapping schemata used to link virtual actors with musical characteristics.

Keywords: Musical sonification · Procedural music · Video games · Virtual gesture

1 Introduction

From a creative musical standpoint, there have traditionally been necessary synergies between motion and action in space and the production and manipulation of musical sound. And for most pre-digital musical systems, physical gesture was an inherent component of instrumental performance practice. From the sweep of a bow across strings, to the swing of a drumstick, to the arc of a conductor's baton, action and motion in space were directly coupled as physical or intentional drivers to the mechanical production of sound and music [6].

The introduction of computer-based musical systems has removed the necessity of such direct couplings, allowing abstract data-analysis or algorithmic process to both instigate and manipulate parameters driving musical output. However artists seeking to retain some level of human-directed control within the digital context often develop and employ mapping schemata linking control data to musical form and function. Such mappings provide an interface between human intention and digital process and can range from the simple to the complex, from the distinct to the abstract.

All environment and character modeling, custom animations and art direction for *ECHO::Canyon* were created by artist Chris Platz.

© Springer International Publishing Switzerland 2014
M. Aramaki et al. (Eds.): CMMR 2013, LNCS 8905, pp. 518–532, 2014.
DOI: 10.1007/978-3-319-12976-1_31

1.1   Reactive Mapping and Gesture

Choreographies of music and action found in dance and film commonly make use of a reactive association between gesture and sound. Dancers' reactions - spontaneous or choreographed - to a musical event or sequence of events often form physical motions or gestures with direct temporal correspondence to the onset, duration or contour of a sounding event [12]. Similarly, events in static visual media such as film, music video and some computer games are often punctuated by the synchronization of visual elements with unrelated auditory or musical cues, linking the audio and visual in our perception of the event without any causal relationship existing between the two modalities.

1.2   Causal Mapping in Virtual Space

Interactive virtual environments and the tracking of actor motion and action within those environments affords yet another approach to the mapping of physiological gesture to parameters of sound and music for multimodal presentation. As avatars within three-dimensional space are wholly-digital constructs, there exists a massive amount of data readily available that represents their internal and external state, their ongoing relationship to other objects in the surrounding environment, and the state of the environment itself. This data can drive complex dynamic musical and sound-generating systems while preserving a causal link between the visual gesture and the resultant audio gesture.

1.3   Multimodal Gesture and Motion

With virtual actors, the contours of motion in virtual space - both macro, such as a three-dimensional Cartesian vector, or micro, such as the relative articulation of individual bones within an avatar skeletal mesh - can be tracked and used as control data for computer-based musical systems. In this manner, the gesture or motion itself drives and controls the sound-generating process, an inversion of a more common reactive model and very much in line with traditional models of instrumental performance.

By pairing macro and micro avatar motions with real-time musical sonification, composers and designers repurpose elements of model physiology and structure, as well as the topographies of virtual space itself, into components of musical gesture. Multiple modalities of interaction can then be combined to create performance works wherein the interactions between virtual actor and virtual environment drive any number of parameters of computer mediated musical sound, structure and space.

2   Musical Sonification in *ECHO::Canyon*

ECHO::Canyon (2013) by Robert Hamilton and Chris Platz is an interactive musical performance piece built within UDKOSC [10], a modified version of

Fig. 1. In *ECHO::Canyon* interactions between player-controlled flying avatars and the environment itself drive procedural sound and music generation using UDKOSC.

the Unreal Development Kit or UDK, a free-to-use version of the commercial Unreal 3 gaming engine[1]. Premiered on April 25, 2013 at Stanford University's Center for Computer Research in Music and Acoustics, *ECHO::Canyon* creates a reactive musical environment within which the idiomatic gestures and motions of flight are mapped to musical sound-producing processes.

During the piece performers control virtual actors moving through a fully-rendered outdoor landscape using a computer keyboard and mouse or commercial game-pad controller. Each actors' location and rotation in game-space, as well as other parameters describing their interactions with objects within the environment are streamed in real-time to sound-servers using the Open Sound Control (OSC) protocol [20]. The environment itself is sculpted in such a way as to allow performers the freedom to perform musical interactions by moving above, around and through the topography. In this way the process of environment design takes on the role of composition, with sections of virtual hills, canyons and valleys acting as musical pathways through the environment.

While *ECHO::Canyon* is built within a gaming engine, unlike many commercial games where audio and music play a supporting role to displays of rich visual content [21], the role of music and sound within the work are intended to occupy a perceptual role equal to the presented visual modality. Sonifications used in *ECHO::Canyon* are designed to be musical and performative in nature, and are fundamentally presented as foreground constructs, rather than as background or more associative "sound-effect" constructs. To that end traditional approaches for game sound design are replaced instead by sets of composed interactions.

---

[1] Unreal Development Kit by Epic Software. http://www.udk.com.

3   Prior Work

The use of video game engines for music and sound generation has become increasingly common as generations of musicians who have grown up with readily accessible home video game systems, internet access and personal computers seek to bring together visually immersive graphical game-worlds, wide-area networks, interactive control methodologies and musical performance systems.

Though its graphical display is rendered in 2-dimensions, *small_fish* by] Furukawa, Fujihata and Muench [8] is a game-like musical interface which allows players to create musical tapestries based on the interaction of dynamic components within the environment. Similarly playful in scope, *LUSH* by Choi and Wang uses models of organic interaction and gameplay within an OpenGL framework to represent and control sound generating and organizing processes [5].

Commercial gaming environments have been repurposed as dynamic music-producing systems in *Soundcraft* [4], *q3apd* [16] and *q3osc* [9]. Multi-modal musical performances built within an earlier version of UDKOSC, as well as within a customized implementation of the open-source Sirikata [18] virtual environment produced a series of immersive and interactive musical works [11]. And the mapping of game-play interactions to real-time sound generating process has been pursued as a prototyping methodology by sound designers like Leonard Paul [17], and as an immersive creative interface and display by Florent Berthaut [3] (Fig. 2).

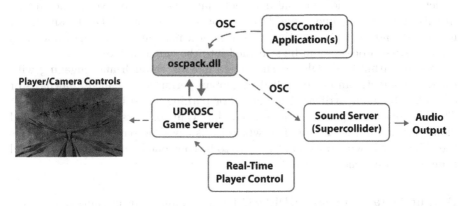

Fig. 2. UDKOSC processes OSC input to control avatar and camera motion while generating OSC output representing avatar and skeletal mesh location, rotation and action/state data.

4   System Overview

To produce musical works such as *ECHO::Canyon*, multiple software and hardware systems must efficiently share large amounts of real-time data with low latency and a high success-rate of packet delivery. At the same time, the sound generation and three-dimensional graphics rendering are extremely taxing for even higher-end personal computer systems. To optimize both sound and video production, multiple machines are used in any one performance, connected over a local gigabit ethernet network. A sound server running SuperCollider typically runs on one computer (OS X, Linux or Windows) while the UDKOSC game-server and individual game-clients each run on their own Windows machine.

4.1   UDKOSC

UDKOSC was designed to bring together real-time procedural sound synthesis, spatialization and processing techniques from the realm of computer music with the visually immersive networked multi-player environments of commercial-grade gaming engines. Gestures, motions and actions generated by actors in game-space are analyzed and transformed in real-time into control messages for complex audio and musical software systems. UDKOSC was developed to support the creation of immersive mixed-reality performance spaces as well as to serve as a rapid prototyping tool for procedural game audio professionals [19].

While the UDK explicitly restricts developers from accessing the Unreal Engine's core C++ engine, it exposes a higher-level scripting language known as UnrealScript. UnrealScript allows developers to bind Windows Win32.dll's to UnrealScript classes, enabling external blocks of code to interact with the scripting layer. Using this DllBind functionality, UDKOSC binds a customized version of OSCPack [2] to a series of Unrealscript classes and mirrored data structures, passing bidirectional data both into and out from the game engine. In this manner real-time game data can be streamed over UDP to any given ip-address and port combination at the same time control messages and data from external processes can be streamed into the game engine.

Actors within the UDK, or characters moving through and engaging with the environment, can be controlled by human performers - called "Pawns" - or controlled by game artificial-intelligence or pathing algorithms - called "Bots". These actors are separate entities from the "Camera", essentially a projected viewpoint within the environment which is displayed on screen. UDKOSC adds the ability for Pawns, Bots and Cameras to be controlled via commands received from externally-generated OSC messages.

Output Data. Currently, UDKOSC tracks a number of in-game parameters for each actor and exports them using OSC including:

- Pawn and Bot unique identifier within the UDK
- Pawn and Bot Cartesian location (X, Y and Z coordinates) and rotation (pitch, yaw and roll)
- Camera view rotation
- Projectile Cartesian location and collision event (triggered when the projectile touches a solid entity within the environment)
- Interp Actor, Trigger and Static mesh Cartesian location and collision events
- Location and rotation for individual bones from a Pawn's Skeletal Mesh.

Input Data. UDKOSC can receive commands over OSC including:

- Pawn and Bot movement speed, direction vector and rotation
- Projectile target location
- Camera cartesian location, rotation and speed
- Camera mode: fixed location, manual rotation, first and third-person modes.

4.2 Music and Sound Server

On the receiving end of the UDKOSC output stream is a music and sound server capable of interpreting OSC messages and mapping game parameters to musical generation and control processes. While any OSC-capable system can be used as the interpreter for UDKOSC output, for most UDKOSC projects, our preference has been to use Supercollider [15] running numerous synthesis processes and spatialized across multiple channels using ambisonics [14].

Within Supercollider, data representing avatar positioning, rotation and action is mapped to specific parameters within instances of synthesized instruments. In *ECHO::Canyon*, the flight of a player-controlled "Valkordia" pawn through the environment is sonified in real-time. At any given moment of the piece each pawn's speed, rotation, absolute Z-location, height relative to the "ground", side proximity to solid environment structures and a Euclidean distance to a series of "crystal" objects in the environment all serve as parameters driving real-time synthesis. Alongside one or multiple human-controlled pawns, flocks of OSC-controlled Valkordia bots, themselves driving separate synthesis processes, are controlled with pre-composed OSC-emitting scripts. During flight as well as during a specially-designed "posing state", the location of bones in the bird-skeleton's wings are tracked and mapped to their own synthesis algorithms.

Musical output for *ECHO::Canyon* is currently spatialized across multi-channel speaker systems by a Supercollider-based sound server making use of stereo output, simple 4-channel panning or first-order ambisonics as the performance space allows. When ambisonic output is used events are placed in the soundfield in a mapping schema uncommon in standard video-game audio where coordinate locations in the environment are mapped to static corrolary locations within the listeners' soundfield. When stereo or 4-channel panning is employed, location-based sound events are placed in a more conventional actor-centric perspective, with their amplitudes scaled proportionally to the distance between actor and sound-emitting location.

5 Macro and Micro Scale Gestures

While acknowledging that conversations attempting to define gesture and how that term pertains to music can engender fierce debate, for the scope of this project, gestures can perhaps be initially defined as intended actor motion or action created within game-space for the purpose of instigating or controlling visual or auditory response. Using UDKOSC, this kind of actor motion can be tracked on a *macro* scale – essentially the gross contours of 3D motion within the environment – as well as on a *micro* scale – the location and rotation of specific bones within and around an actor skeleton. From a compositional standpoint, such an approach allows for great flexibility in the investigation of wholly different types of sounds, mapping schemata and controlled musical interactions.

For example, a dance-like series of motions ("actor sprints up a ramp, jumps, twirls and lands") or a direct mapping of human-physical gesture via a Kinect controller ("actor's skeletal mesh mimicks user swinging an arm side-to-side") can each be considered a gesture in this context. The user-directed intention of each motion, controlled or generated, combined with the sound, itself generated in real-time during the creation of the motion, becomes a significant component of the multi-modal gesture.

5.1 Macro-scale Gesture

Interactions between user-controlled actors and some other entity, either part of the environment or another moving actor, can be categorized as macro-scale gestures. For macro-scale gestures, the scope of a given gesture generally involves the entire actor itself taken as a single-entity, tracking its location in three-dimensional space over a window of time.

Perceptually speaking, macro-scale gestures can occupy the same attentional space as routines or phrases in dance, wherein an actor performs a series of linked motions or actions to convey an intention. Gestures in this vein can encompass multiple actors, interacting with each other either as individual components of a dynamic gesture or as grain-like instances within a singular cloud or mass.

Fig. 3. Valkordia Skeletal Mesh with highlighted right wing-tip bone

Flight-Based Gesture. For *ECHO::Canyon*, the theme of avian flight is central to the musical sonification, animation and control schemata created and used for the piece. A character model called a "Valkordia" was created, fusing physical characteristics and idiomatic movements from both bird and insect-like creatures. Articulated motion of the Valkordia wings and its torso during flight can be seen in Fig. 3. Bones found in the model's front right wing (visible as a

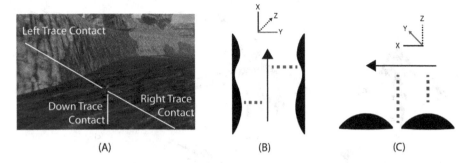

Fig. 4. Ray traces visualized as vertical and horizontal lines in (A) track the distance between the Skeletal Mesh and objects and contours of the environment, both to its right and left sides (B), as well as directly below (C).

white vertical line through the first pose's middle feather) were tracked to drive a noise-generating process when the avatar was in flight.

The relation of a flying Valkordia actor to the environment was a key gestural component in the shaping of *ECHO::Canyon* both literally and figuratively. Valleys, mountains and caves were sculpted with articulated shapes to accentuate specific features of synthesis processes. Figure 4 shows vertical and horizontal ray traces tracking the relative distance between a flying actor, the ground, and the walls of a valley. In this example, the ray trace distances were used to control amplitude and filter frequencies of separate synthesis processes, as well as panning for the horizontal traces.

Flocking Pawns. Our cognitive abilities to group and associate like motions of active objects into single cohesive units can bring disparate dynamic elements together into one unified mass gesture [13]. The sonification of such behaviors with simple sound sources can create dynamic musical textures through similar motion and position of each source [7]. *ECHO::Canyon* makes use of flocks of OSC-controlled Valkordia pawns with a relatively simple mapping of their Z-coordinate to a simple oscillator and their distance from the player actor to the oscillator's amplitude. Each bird in the flock tracks a target position which is moved in pre-composed patterns through the game-space by an OSC-generating script. The sonic result is a shifting grain-like cloud of pitched oscillators.

5.2 Micro-scale Gesture

With the intention of drawing audience and performer attention to the actor itself and away from the environment, micro-scale gestures are comprised of motions and articulations of a given avatar's virtual physiology. By mapping the subtle motions of bones within an actor's skeletal mesh to both dynamic control systems and evocative musical processes, the micro-scale gestures within *ECHO::Canyon* provide a vastly different viewing and listening experience than the work's macro-scale gestures.

Fig. 5. Valkordia model with manual wing positioning during "Posing" state

Posing State. Performers in *ECHO::Canyon* enter the posing state by toggling a key on the game-pad. Upon entering the state, actors no longer fly through the environment; instead each avatar interpolates into a nearly vertical pose and control over the actor's front two wings are directly mapped to each of the gamepad's two-dimensional analog joystick controls. Users control the forward, side and back rotation of each wing independently by rolling the analog joysticks around in circular patterns, mimicking the rotation of arms or wings in shoulder sockets. A series of wing poses can be seen in Fig. 5, examples (A) through (F).

Rather than mapping pre-composed wing animations to output from the joystick controllers, each wing instead tracks an end effector, using inverse kinematics [1]. The location of each effector is itself controlled in 3D space by the joystick output, scaled and acting upon a Cyclic-Coordinate Descent or CCD Skeletal Controller, itself a component of the UDK. In Fig. 6, the effectors for each wing are visualized as globes towards which the chain of bones from the tip of each wing to the shoulder socket are reaching.

Tracking Bone Location. The tracking of individual bone locations relative to a central point on the actor's skeletal mesh changes the focus and scale of gestures to reside firmly in the micro-scale. In this manner, the extension of a wing to its full length can be mapped to a "larger" sounding sonic response than a "smaller" gesture, closer to the central point. Each bone that comprises a model's skeletal mesh can be tracked in UDKOSC, though due to the high number of individual bones used in many well-articulated skeletal meshes, it is

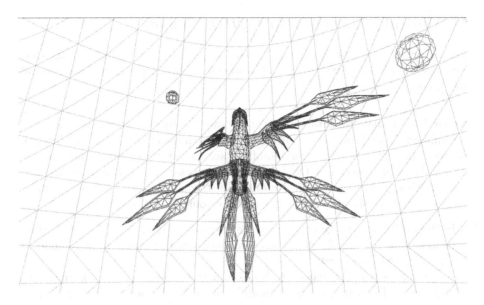

Fig. 6. Using inverse kinematics controlled by a dual-joystick gamepad, players can dynamically control Valkordia wing poses.

generally a good idea to track a few key bones to reduce the amount of data tracked and output in real-time.

In the posing state, the relative X, Y and Z positions of one single bone located at the tip of each wing is tracked and output with OSC. In Fig. 7 data from a right wing bone is shown, first in a flying state, and then during manual control over the wing position. The peaks showing manual arm gestures are clearly visible on the right half of each plot. By comparison, the oscillating wing motion during flight shows clearly as a fairly continuous signal on the left half of each plot. It should be noted that coordinates in the Unreal Engine are measured in "Unreal Units", a unit of virtual measure where one UU corresponds roughly to 0.75 in., or one foot = 16 UU and 1 m = 52.5 UU.

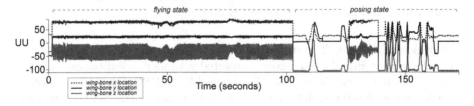

Fig. 7. Wing X,Y,Z Coordinate data in a flying state and during manually controlled wing gestures

6   Musical Sonification in *ECHO::Canyon*

The following list defines an example set of control events and actions that have been explored within *ECHO::Canyon* and a description of their musical analogues:

Actor Proximity. An actor's relative distance to objects in the environment is determined through the use of horizontal and downward ray traces. The distance between the center of an actor's bounding-box and an object with which the ray trace collides is output over OSC. From a design standpoint, traces are used to drive musical processes when an actor moves through a space such as a tunnel, cave or chasm, or simply swoops down above some part of the terrain.

- In SuperCollider, horizontal ray trace distance and global location is used to modulate the amplitude, central frequency and grain count of a cloud of granulated SinOsc bursts.
- Amplitude is scaled inversely to horizontal trace distance, while grain count and central frequency are both modulated by the actor's current height, or Z-location.
- Vertical trace distance shapes both the amplitude and the chaotic oscillations of a "screetch"-like sine feedback FM oscillator with phase modulation feedback using the SinOscFB UGen.

Actor Speed and Motion. As user avatars move through three-dimensional coordinate space, each avatar's X, Y and Z location data is streamed over OSC to a sound-server (see Fig. 8). The speed of motion is calculated and used to scale the speed of the flight animation, itself driving parameters of a noise-based synthesis instrument.

- Actor speed is indirectly sonified as the speed of oscillation of the right and left wing bones drives each bone's position in the Z-plane (relative to the actor's central coordinate location).
- Location data controls simple amplitude and ambisonic spatialization of continuous sound-sources for each osc-controlled Valkordia flocking pawn.
- Actor speed also modulates the frequency of a filter shaping the output from each actor's downward trace SinOscFB process.

Actor Bone Motion. The structural core of each actor's character model is a skeletal mesh comprised of numerous connected-yet-independent bones, each one with a coordinate location and rotation accessible via OSC. By tracking motion of each bone within the skeletal mesh, complex control signals can be generated through the use of simple avatar motions.

- During flight, the relative z-location of each wing bone is sonified with a simple sine oscillator, with subtle beating frequencies made audible through a slight frequency offset between each wing's synth.

- During the manual posing state, the same mapping continues, however the manual extension of each wing causes the pitch of each oscillator to modulate within a range of approximately four-semitones.
- The frequency of an actor's manually-triggered "call" sound is mapped to the combined distance between right and left wing tip bones.

Actor-Group Motion and Density. While individual actor avatars each communicate their positions through individual OSC streams, actors moving in concert together – in flocks, swarms or herds - can be tracked and sonified as a group. For fast moving particle-based objects, like projectiles generated by an actor or actors, granular synthesis-based instruments have proven an interesting mapping. Similarly, flocks of flying avatars tracked as simple sine-waves have been used to create a shifting field of additive signals.

- Flocks of OSC or AI controlled Valkordia pawns are represented with simple sine oscillators which can be spatialized in an ambisonic soundfield.
- Projectiles "fired" by an actor generate an inexpensive pitched collision sound – a burst of noise passed through a tuned filter – when the projectile bounces off a surface in the environment. The filter frequency is mapped to the distance of the collision point from the coordinate center of the environment. As high numbers of projectiles can be quickly generated by performers, all synthesis processes used with projectiles in UDKOSC are relatively computationally cheap.
- Projectile location can also be spatialized in an ambisonic soundfield. In this case each projectile is represented by a simple sine oscillator with its freqency mapped to the calculated distance from the environment center.

Spatio-Centric Spatialization. In contrast to traditional gaming concepts of user-centric audio, a spatio-centric presentation superimposes a virtual space onto a physical multi-channel listening space, spatializing sound events around a physical space to correlated coordinates in the virtual space. The goal of such presentations are to immerse an audience in an imposed sound world, creating a perceptual superimposition of virtual and physical environments.

Figure 8 traces a simple Valkordia flight path in three-dimensions. If this were presented in a rectangular concert space, the position of the displayed sound source would move along the shown trajectory.

- When ambisonic spatialization is used, each sound generated is positioned in the soundfield according to its position in game-space. Unlike traditional gaming presentations, where sounds are generally positioned relative to the player's head location, such a presentation can represent the location of multiple users and objects to an audience watching without a decided "first-person" viewpoint.

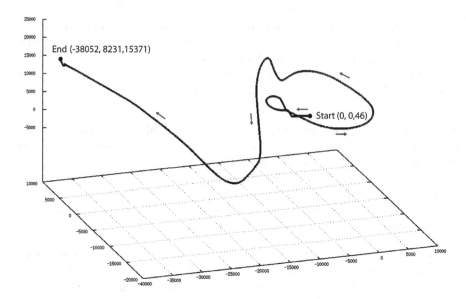

Fig. 8. Actor flight path in 3D coordinate space.

Location-Based Triggers. Specific locations in coordinate space are stored on the sound server and users' relative Cartesian distance from each location can be used as a synthesis parameter. For instance, by mapping amplitude of a sound source to such a distance measurement, an instrument's volume will fluctuate as a factor of a user's distance from a particular location.

- In Fig. 1, a number of large crystal-like structures are visible, each of which serves as a location-based sound source.
- Each crystal location drives a separate instance of the Gendy1 dynamic stochastic synthesis UGen.
- An actor's distance from each of these crystals controls both the Gendy1's amplitude as well as the frequency of a ResonZ two pole filter.

Active Triggers. For sound events or processes that require simple mode/context switching control or triggering, users can actively interact with a trigger in the form of a button or key-press. When a user fires a "use" event the trigger sends an OSC message with its name, location and trigger state.

- The most commonly used trigger of this sort in *ECHO::Canyon* is the Valkordia's "call": a layered cloud of granular pitches with frequencies randomized within a narrow range.
- The central frequency of each call is set by the actor's Z-coordinate which is itself mapped into the note range of a semitone/chromatic scale.

7   Conclusions

Advances in technology have made the creation and exploration of computer generated audio-visual spaces not only possible but increasingly common. In the realms of sound design and music, real-time data generated by actors and their interactions in virtual space can be used to procedurally generate sound and music, creating a tight coupling between visual and auditory modalities. For composers and sound designers, procedural systems such as UDKOSC allow for a great deal of flexibility in how mappings between visual stimuli, control devices and generated audio and music can be defined. And while the mapping choices made for *ECHO::Canyon* represent but one possible artistic approach towards the sonification of real-time data streams, they demonstrate a number of potential mapping schemata for the cross-modal combination of visual and auditory events.

References

1. Aristidou, A., Lasenby, J.: Inverse kinematics: a review of existing techniques and introduction of a new fast iterative solver. Technical Report, Cambridge (2009)
2. Bencina, R.: Oscpack (2006). http://code.google.com/p/oscpack
3. Berthaut, F., Hachet, M., Desainte-Catherine, M.: Interacting with the 3D reactive widgets for musical performance. J. New Music Res. **40**(3), 253–263 (2011)
4. Cerqueira, M., Salazar, S., Wang, G.: Soundcraft: transducing starcraft. In: Proceedings of the New Interfaces for Musical Expression Conference, Daiejon, pp. 243–247 (2013)
5. Choi, H., Wang, G.: LUSH : an organic eco + music system. In: Proceedings of the New Interfaces for Musical Expression Conference, Sydney, pp. 112–115 (2010)
6. Dahl, S., Bevilacqua, F., Bresin, R., Clayton, M., Leante, L., Poggi, I., Rasamimanana, N.: Gestures in performance. In: Godøy, R., Leman, M. (eds.) Musical Gestures: Sound, Movement, and Meaning, pp. 36–68. Routledge, New York (2010)
7. Davis, T., Karamanlis, O.: Gestural control of sonic swarms: composing with grouped sound Objects. In: The Proceedings of the 4th Sound and Music Computing Conference, Lefkada, Greece, pp. 192–195 (2007)
8. Furukawa, K., Fujihata, M., Muench, W.: small_fish (2000). http://hosting.zkm.de/wmuench/small_fish
9. Hamilton, R.: Q3OSC: or how I learned to stop worrying and love the game. In: Proceedings of the International Computer Music Conference, Copenhagen (2008)
10. Hamilton, R.: Sonifying game-space choreographies with UDKOSC. In: Proceedings of the New Interfaces for Musical Expression Conference, Daiejon, pp. 446–449 (2013)
11. Hamilton, R., Caceres, J., Nanou, C., Platz, C.: Multi-modal musical environments for mixed-reality performance. JMUI **4**(3–4), 147–156 (2011)
12. Jensenius, A., Wanderley, M., Godøy, R., Leman, M.: Musical gestures: concepts and methods of research. In: Godøy, R., Leman, M. (eds.) Musical Gestures: Sound, Movement, and Meaning, p. 13. Routledge, New York (2010)
13. Lehar, S.: Gestalt Isomorphism and the primacy of subjective conscious experience: a gestalt bubble model. Behav. Brain Sci. **26**(4), 375–444 (2004). Cambridge University Press

14. Malham, D., Myatt, A.: 3-D sound spatialization using ambisonic techniques. Comput. Music J. **19**(4), 58–70 (1995). Winter
15. McCarthy, J.: SuperCollider. http://supercollider.sourceforge.net
16. Oliver, J.: q3apd (2008). http://www.selectparks.net/archive/q3apd.htm
17. Paul, L.J.: Video game audio prototyping with half life 2. Transdisciplinary Digital Art. Sound, Vision and the New Screen. Communications in Computer and Information Science, vol. 7, pp. 187–198. Springer, Heidelberg (2008)
18. Sirikata (2009). http://www.sirikata.com
19. Verron, C., Drettakis, G.: Procedural audio modeling for particle-based environmental effects. In: Proceedings of the 133rd AES Convention, San Francisco (2012)
20. Wright, M., Freed, A.: Open sound control: a new protocol for communicating with sound synthesizers. In: Proceedings of the International Computer Music Conference, Thessaloniki (1997)
21. Zehnder, S., Lipscomb, S.: The role of music In video games. In: Vorderer, P., Bryant, J. (eds.) Playing Video Games: Motives, Responses, and Consequences, pp. 282–303. Lawrence Erlbaum Associates, Routledge, New York (2009)

Auditory Perception and Cognitive Inspiration

Understanding Coarticulation
in Musical Experience

Rolf Inge Godøy[✉]

Department of Musicology, University of Oslo, Oslo, Norway
`r.i.godoy@imv.uio.no`

Abstract. The term *coarticulation* designates the fusion of small-scale events, such as single sounds and single sound-producing actions, into larger units of combined sound and body motion, resulting in qualitative new features at what we call the *chunk timescale* in music, typically in the 0.5.–5 s duration range. Coarticulation has been extensively studied in linguistics and to a certain extent in other domains of human body motion as well as in robotics, but so far not so much in music, so the main aim of this paper is to provide a background for how we can explore coarticulation in both the production and perception of music. The contention is that coarticulation in music should be understood as based on a number of physical, biomechanical and cognitive constraints, and that coarticulation is an essential factor in the shaping of several perceptually salient features of music.

Keywords: Coarticulation · Chunking · Context · Music perception · Motor control · Performance

1 Introduction

This paper is about how perceptually salient units in musical experience emerge by principles of coarticulation. The term *coarticulation* designates the fusion of small-scale events such as single sounds and single sound-producing actions into phrase level segments, or what we prefer to call *chunks*, very approximately in the 0.5–5 s duration range. Such fusions into chunks are ubiquitous in music, for instance in the fusion of a rapid succession of tones and finger motion into what we perceive holistically as an ornament, or in the fusion of drum sounds and associated mallets/hand/arm motion into a rhythmical groove pattern.

Although musical experience can be considered continuous in time, it is also clear that what we perceive as salient features of music, e.g. rhythmical and textural patterns, melodic contours, expressive nuances, etc. are all based on holistic perceptions of a certain length of musical sound and music-related body motion: we need to hear and keep in short-term memory a certain stretch of music in order to decide what it is and to assess what are the salient features of this excerpt. This segmenting and evaluation of continuous sensory information we refer to as *chunking*. We use the term 'chunking' because this term not only signifies a segmentation or parsing of continuous sensory streams, but also a transformation to something more solid in our minds, to something that does not exist at the timescale of continuous sensory streams.

© Springer International Publishing Switzerland 2014
M. Aramaki et al. (Eds.): CMMR 2013, LNCS 8905, pp. 535–547, 2014.
DOI: 10.1007/978-3-319-12976-1_32

As coarticulation is basically about the fusion of smaller elements into larger units, understanding coarticulation may be very useful for understanding chunking in music, and could also be useful for a number of other music-related domains such as music psychology, music theory, and music information retrieval, as well as in advancing our understanding of the relationships between sound and body motion in music, i.e. in research on so-called *embodied music cognition* [9, 14, 21].

In presenting the main ideas of coarticulation in music, we first need to look at what are the significant timescales at work in musical experience, because coarticulation is mostly a local phenomenon, typically in the mentioned 0.5–5 s duration range. We also need to look at some issues of continuity, discontinuity, and chunking in music, before we go on to the main principles of coarticulation, followed by an overview of ongoing and possible future work in this area.

2   Timescale Considerations

Needless to say, we have musical sound at timescales ranging from the very small to the very large, i.e. from that of single vibrations or spikes lasting less than a millisecond to that of minutes and hours for whole works of music. The point here is that each timescale has distinct perceptual features, and to take this into account, we have in our research postulated three main timescales for musical sound. An almost identical classification scheme of timescales applies to music-related body motion, however with the significant difference that the maximum speed possible in human motion is of course much less than that typically found in audible vibrations:

- *Micro timescale*, meaning the timescale of audible vibrations, thus including perceptual phenomena such as pitch, loudness, stationary timbre, and also fast but sub-audio rate fluctuations (i.e. below the rate of approximately 20 events per second) in the sound such as tremolo, trill, and various rapid timbral fluctuations. At this micro timescale, we typically perceive continuity in both sound and motion, and we keep whatever we perceive in so-called *echoic memory*, memory that forms the basis for perceiving more extended segments of sound and motion at the *meso timescale* (see next point). Interestingly, there also seems to be a limitation on motor control at this timescale by the phenomenon of the so-called *Psychological Refractory Period*, which among other things, suggests that below the (very approximate) 0.5 s duration limit, body motion trajectories will often run their course without feedback control [20, 22, 33], something that is one of the constraints linked to coarticulation (see Sect. 6 below).
- *Meso timescale*, or what we call the *chunk timescale*, similar in duration to what Pierre Schaeffer and co-workers called the *sonic object* [28, 29], typically in the very approximately 0.5–5 s duration range. The crucial feature of the meso timescale is the holistic perception of sound and body motion chunks, much due to the fusion effect of coarticulation. As suggested by Schaeffer, meso timescale chunks are probably also the most significant for various salient perceptual features such as the shapes (or envelopes) for pitch, dynamics, timbre, various fluctuations, various rhythmical and textural patterns, something that has been confirmed by listeners'

identification of musical features in short fragments [8]. Also other important elements converge in making the meso timescale significant, such as the assumed limits of short-term memory [31], the average duration of everyday human actions [30], and importantly, theories of the perceptual present [24].

- *Macro timescale*, meaning longer than the typical duration range of the meso timescale, usually consisting of concatenations of meso timescale chunks in succession, and typically extending over whole sections and even whole works of music.

What is essential for coarticulation is that it is found on the meso timescale (but based on continuous, micro timescale elements), and that it concerns both the perception and the sound-producing (and also the sound-accompanying) body motion at this timescale (see [14] for a discussion of sound-related body motion categories). It is in fact the *contextual smearing* of micro timescale elements at the meso timescale that is the hallmark of coarticulation in general, and so we claim, also of musical sound and music-related body motion, something that we should first see in relation to some notions of continuity and discontinuity in music.

3 Continuity vs. Discontinuity

Western music theory has traditionally regarded the tone (or in cases of non-pitched percussion instruments, the sound event) as the basic ingredient of music, i.e. as represented by the symbols of Western common practice music notation. Although we may think of musical experience as a continuous stream of sound, there is then at the core of Western musical practice a 'discretization' of music into discontinuous tone (or sound) events, represented by notation symbols. This notation paradigm has had as one consequence the concept of music as something that is made by putting notes together, and furthermore, followed by adding some kind of expressivity to these concatenations of notes in performance. One further consequence of this has been a certain abstraction of musical features from their origin in sound-producing body motion, hence often leading to a more 'disembodied' view of music as a phenomenon.

Shifting our perspective to the sound-producing body motion of music, we realize that any musical sound (or group of sounds) is included in some kind of action trajectory, e.g. to play a single tone on a marimba, the mallet/hand has to make a trajectory from the starting (equilibrium) position out towards the impact point on the instrument, followed by a rebound and a trajectory back to the initial position. This means that we have continuity in musical practice in the sense of continuity in sound-producing body motion, but we also have continuity in the resultant musical sound: in spite of a symbolic representation of a tone (or non-pitched sound), it will always have a temporal extension as well as various internal time-dependent features such as its dynamic, pitch and timbre related evolution in the course of the sound, and additionally, very often also be contextually smeared by neighboring sounds. In this sense, we can speak of *temporal coherence* of both sound-producing body motion and the resultant sound, meaning a contextual smearing of that which Western music notation designates by discrete symbols. In the case of *Music Information Retrieval*, the task is obviously the opposite, i.e. to try to reconstruct the discrete symbolic notation from the continuous stream of contextually smeared musical sound (se e.g. [23]).

This temporal coherence and resultant contextual smearing of both body motion and sound is the very basis for the emergence of coarticulation in music (as well as in language and other domains). What we have then is the emergence of new and somehow meaningful meso timescale chunks, chunks that in turn may be regarded as 'discrete' in the sense that they are holistically perceived (and conceived), i.e. that segments of the continuous streams of sound and motion sensations are perceived 'all-at-once' as fused and coherent entities, and not primarily as note-level discrete events.

4 Chunking Theories

Attempts to understand chunking have variably looked at features in the sensory input, i.e. in what we could call the *signal*, and for mechanisms in the human mind for segmenting the continuous signal into chunks by the use of various *mental schemas*. We have thus *exogenous* (signal based) and *endogenous* (mental schema based) elements variably at work in chunking in music [10]. As this has consequences for our understanding of coarticulation, we should have a brief look at exogenous and endogenous elements in chunking, noting that in practice there may be an overlap between these two. As for the typically exogenous sources for chunking, we have the following:

- Auditory qualitative discontinuities of various kinds: sound-silence transitions, register changes, timbral changes, etc., partly following experimental findings, partly inspired by classical gestalt theories [2], theories also applied to note level chunking [32]. Although auditory (and notation based) chunking can work well in cases with salient qualitative discontinuities, this becomes problematic when these discontinuities are weak or even non-existent such as in sequences of equal duration and/or equal sounding tones, sequences that most listeners may still subjectively segment into chunks based on various mental schemas (e.g. of meter).
- In human motion research, looking for shifts between motion and stillness as a source for chunking, however with the difficulty that humans (and other living organisms) are never completely still, necessitating some kind of thresholding or other motion signal cues such as peaks of acceleration and/or jerk for finding the start and stop points of action chunks [18]. And as is the case for auditory signals, subjective perception may very well segment streams of body motion into chunks based on various mental schemas, in particular schemas of goal-directed body motion.

Given the various difficulties with purely exogenous sources of chunking, there has been a long-standing and extensive effort in the cognitive sciences to search for more endogenous sources for chunking. This was a central topic in phenomenological philosophy at the end of the 19th century, in particular for Edmund Husserl with his idea that experience spontaneously proceeds by a series of chunks that each contain a cumulative image of the recent past, the present moment, and also of future expectations [11, 19]. The inclusion of future expectations in Husserl's model is quite remarkable in view of recent theories of motor control, i.e. that at any point in time, we are not only having the effects of the recent past body motion, but just as much preparing the coming body motion. This inclusion of the recent past and the near future in chunking are as we shall see one of the hallmarks of coarticulation in the form of so-called *carryover* and *anticipatory* effects. Additionally, there are some more recent research findings on endogenous elements in chunking that we have found useful for understanding coarticulation:

- *Goal-directed motion* [27], meaning that human motion is planned and controlled in view of arriving at certain goal postures at what we in our context have chosen to call *goal points*, meaning effector (i.e. fingers, hands, arms, torso, vocal apparatus) postures and positions at certain salient points in time such as downbeats and other accents in the music.
- *Action hierarchies* [15], also suggesting that human motion is controlled by goals, but that sub-motions (i.e. small-scale effector motions) are recruited as needed, and importantly, are then fused by coarticulation.
- *Action gestalts* [20], documenting that human motion is pre-planned as holistic chunks.
- *Intermittent control* [22], suggesting that continuous control of human motion is neither well documented nor would be particularly effective as there would invariably be delays in any feedback system, hence that a more discontinuous, 'point-by-point' or 'chunk-by-chunk' kind of motor control scheme would be more efficient.
- *Psychological Refractory Period* mentioned above [20, 22, 33], suggesting that there is a minimal duration for intervening in motor control, hence yet another indication that motor control proceeds in a chunk-by-chunk manner.

Chunking in perception and cognition could be summarized as the cutting up of continuous streams into somehow meaningful units and *the transformation of the sequential to the simultaneous in our minds*. All the details of how this works seems not yet to be well understood, however chunking seems to be based on a combination of exogenous and endogenous elements. This is actually one of the main points of the so-called motor theory of perception [7], namely that we perceive sound largely also with the help of mental images of how we believe the sound is produced, and it seems that this also applies to the perception of coarticulation.

5 Principles of Coarticulation

Coarticulation, understood as the fusion of small-scale events into larger chunks, is a general feature of most human (and animal) body motion, and can be understood as a 'natural' or emergent phenomenon given various biomechanical and cognitive constraints of the organism, as well as some physical constraints of musical instruments and even room acoustics (i.e. smearing of the acoustical signals by reverberation). Given these various constraints, coarticulation concerns not only the production of body motion and sound, but also the features of the sensory output, and the perception of these features, as has been extensively studied in linguistics [17].

Basically, coarticulation can be seen in a broader context as an advantageous element: "…it is a blessing for us as behaving organisms. Think about a typist who could move only one finger at a time. Lacking the capacity for finger coarticulation, the person's typing speed would be very slow. Simultaneous movements of the fingers allow for rapid responding, just as concurrent movements of the tongue, lips and velum allow for rapid speech. Coarticulation is an effective method for increasing response speed given that individual effectors (body parts used for movement) may move relatively slowly." ([26], p. 15). Thus, coarticulation concerns both temporal unfolding of motion and the degree of effector activation in motion:

- *Temporal coarticulation*: otherwise singular events embedded in a context, meaning that past events influence present events, i.e. that the position and shape of effectors are determined by recent actions, by *spillover* or *carryover* effects. But also future events influence present events, i.e. the positions and shapes of effectors are determined by the preparations for future actions, showing *anticipatory* effects.
- *Spatial coarticulation*: motion in one effector (e.g. hand) recruits motion in other effectors (e.g. arm, shoulder, torso).

And furthermore:

- Coarticulation seems to be a biomechanical necessity, i.e. is based on constraints of our bodies' capacity to move.
- Coarticulation seems to be a motor control necessity, i.e. is based on our need for anticipatory programing of motion in order to be fast and efficient.
- Coarticulation results in contextual smearing of the perceptual output, i.e. of both sound and body motion.

As to the last point, we could speculate that there has been an evolutionary 'attunement' of production and perception here in the sense that various linguistic, musical, and other expressions are based on the combined biomechanical and motor control constraints that lead to coarticulation, and that the ensuing perceptions of these expressions are well adapted to coarticulation, i.e. that our perceptual system actually expects coarticulation to take place.

6 Constraint Based Coarticulation

Coarticulation can be understood as an emergent phenomenon, given various constraints of the human body and our cognitive apparatus, but also of musical instruments and even of room acoustics:

- Sound-producing actions, both instrumental and vocal, include (variably so) a preparatory motion phase, e.g. positioning of the effector such as the bow above the strings on a violin ready for a downstroke, or the shaping of the vocal apparatus and inhaling before a voice onset.
- Body motion takes time: needless to say, there are speed limitations on all kinds of human body motion, meaning that there is always a travel time for an effector from one position or shape to another position or shape, implying in turn that there is a

contextual smearing by continuous body motion between the temporally more discrete postures.

- Another feature related to speed limitations is the emergence of changes known as *phase transitions* [16], meaning switching to a different grouping and/or motion pattern due to changes in speed, e.g. as in the transition from walking to running. This can be observed in music as a transitions from discrete motion to more continuous motion e.g. in tremolo as can be seen in Fig. 1. To what extent such phase transitions are due to biomechanical or motor control constraints is not clear, but once the threshold from discrete individual hitting motion to continuous oscillating motion is crossed, we do in fact have a constraint based case of coarticulatory fusion.

- Control theory, both in machines and in human motion, has often distinguished between so-called *open loop* (meaning no feedback) and *closed loop* (meaning having feedback) control schemes. The dominant view has been that closed loop is at work in human motor control, however, one problem with this view is that feedback control takes time and thus cannot be continuous, and rather has to be intermittent as suggested by the abovementioned theories of the Psychological Refractory Period. This would result in motion trajectories that, once initiated, run their course, fusing all micro motions within such trajectories by coarticulation.

- Lastly, we also have the physical phenomenon of incomplete damping, both in instruments and in rooms, meaning that there is a contextual smearing due to reverberation in the source as well as in the rooms where the musical performances take place. Coarticulation is then actually also related to the physics of energy dissipation, and furthermore, not just regarding rate of damping in instruments and rooms, but also to the physics of body motion, e.g. as in the rebound of mallets in percussion performance.

In a sense, coarticulation is an attempt to live with, or even exploit, these various constraints, for the purpose of human expression, including music: besides coarticulation as a result of constraints, we of course also have volitional, or intended,

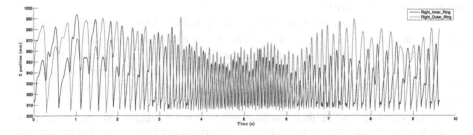

Fig. 1. The motion trajectories of two mallets held by the right hand alternating between two tones, E4 and C5, on a marimba, initially slow, then accelerating to a fast tremolo and then decelerating back to slow alternations. Notice the bumps due to the recoil for slow motions, their disappearance with acceleration, and reappearance with deceleration, signifying a phase transition from discrete to continuous and back to discrete motions as a function of speed (The plotting in this figure and Figs. 2 and 3 are all based on marker data from a Qualisys infrared motion capture camera system recording the musicians' body motion at 100 Hz).

coarticulation, meaning that musicians have the capacity to produce expressive musical sound *with* these features of coarticulation.

7 Coarticulation in Practice

Although coarticulation has been most studied in linguistics and partly also in other domains concerned with human body motion, there have been some studies of coarticulation and/or coarticulation related phenomena in music:

- In piano playing: fingers move to optimal position before hitting keys [5].
- In string playing: left hand fingers in place in position well before playing of tones [34] and contextual smearing of bowing movements [25].
- In drumming, a drummer may in some cases start to prepare an accented stoke several strokes in advance [3].
- In trumpet performance, there are different articulations that (variably so) exhibit coarticulation between successive tones [1].

In our own research, we are presently studying coarticulation in performance on string instruments, as well as percussion instruments and piano. Coarticulation is perhaps most eminently present in non-keyboard instruments as these allow more control over articulatory details, and we are planning to move on to studying coarticulation in woodwind and brass instruments, and later on also in singing. Although coarticulation in the human vocal apparatus has probably been the most studied field of coarticulation [17], we envisage several challenges of correlating sound features and production features in singing.

We have in our own previous work on coarticulation focused on hand-wrist-elbow motion in piano performance (see [13] for details), but more recently focused on shorter passages and ornaments in piano, percussion and violin performance, in view of ornaments as prime cases of coarticulation by the constraints of high speed and assumed need for anticipatory motor control, as well as the resultant smearing of sound and motion. In Fig. 2, we see the motion of the five fingers of the right hand embedded in the motion of the wrist.

We have also studied coarticulation as motion trajectories to and from goal points, what we have called *prefix* and *suffix* trajectories to goal points (see [10] for more on goal points). An example of this can be seen in Fig. 3 where there is a rapid, burst-like cascade of tones leading up to the goal point of the Bb5, and with the marimba player's right hand continuing after hitting this Bb5 with a 'follow through' motion similar to what can be seen e.g. in golf or tennis.

We hypothesize that the focus on goal points in coarticulation may be related both to the abovementioned Psychological Refractory Period [20, 22, 33] and to findings on 'intermittent control' of body motion [22], suggesting a more 'point-by-point', rather than a continuous feedback, scheme in motor control. The idea of intermittent control is not new (although the labeling may be new), and the debate on continuous vs. intermittent control has in fact been going on for more than 100 years [4, 27].

As suggested in [12], partly inspired by some models of coarticulation in linguistics [6], the phenomenon of intermittent control by goal points could be schematically

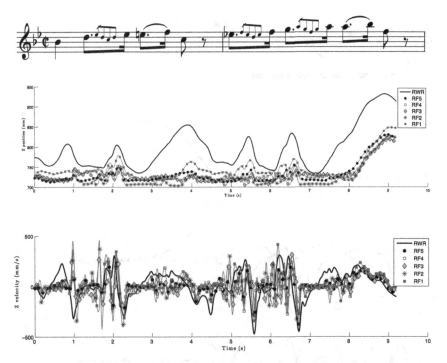

Fig. 2. The right hand fingers and wrist motions in performing the ornaments form the opening of the second movement of W. A. Mozart's Piano Sonata KV 332, the two graphs showing position (top), velocity (bottom). Notice in particular the motion of the wrist in relation to the finger motions, demonstrating both temporal and spatial coarticulation.

understood as illustrated as in Fig. 4. This illustration shows first a series of singular and separate goal points with the trajectories to and from these goal points (i.e. their prefixes and suffixes), then this series of goal points and their corresponding to and from trajectories closer together. In the latter case, with the overlapping prefix and suffix trajectories, the result is actually a more undulating motion curve, appearing to be continuous in spite of the singular goal points being intermittent as shown in the bottom part of this figure. In more general terms, this resembles the relation between a series of impulses and the impulse response of a system, something we are now developing further as a general model of goal points and coarticulation in music [12].

The basis for coarticulation is then that there are continuous sound and motion trajectories, effectively creating continuity and coherence in the perceived sound and body motion, however the control of these continuous trajectories may be based on discontinuous impulses. One interesting aspect of coarticulation is that it could be a supplement to more traditional bottom-up, signal based modeling of gestalt coherence in music. The saying that 'the whole is more than the sum of the parts' often encountered in connection with gestalt theory, acquires a new meaning when we take the coarticulatory contextual smearing into account: coarticulation is actually a transformation of the parts into something new by contextual smearing, so yes, the whole is more than a sum of the parts. In this perspective, most musical features can be

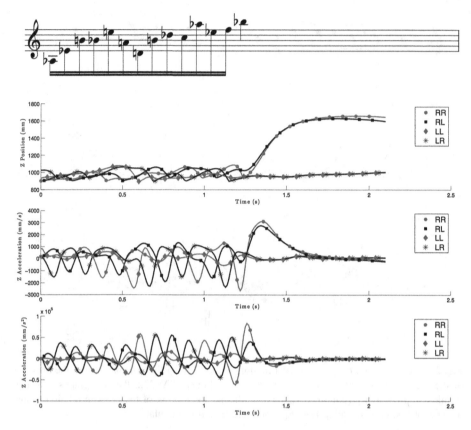

Fig. 3. The marimba performance with four mallets of a rapid prefix trajectory leading up to the goal point of the Bb5. The position, velocity and acceleration of the four mallets are displayed below the notation of this passage.

considered in view of being coarticulated gestalts: melodic, rhythmic, textural, metrical, etc. patterns could all be seen to owe their coherence to coarticulatory contextual smearing.

8   Summary and Further Work

Coarticulation, understood as the fusion of small-scale events into more superordinate chunks, clearly seems to be at work in music. Furthermore, in making a survey of various physical, biomechanical, and motor control constraints involved in sound-producing actions, it seems that coarticulation is an emergent phenomenon from these constraints. Additionally, it could be speculated that our perceptual apparatus is so attuned to coarticulation that without coarticulation, music would sound 'unnatural', something which is often the opinion of people listening to sampled instruments that are not capable of coarticulation like real acoustic instruments are.

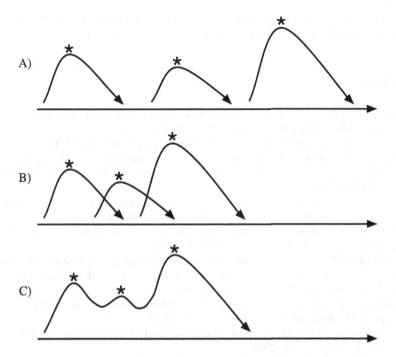

Fig. 4. A schematic illustration of motion in relation to goal points. If we consider a series of separate goal points (indicated with asterisks) with their respective prefixes and suffixes positioned along the temporal axis as in (A), there is a discontinuity between these goal point centered chunks. When we have several goal points more closely together as in (B), we have prefixes and suffixes that overlap, and we end up with continuous and undulating trajectories like in (C).

In relation to our Western musical concepts of discretized tones and notation, coarticulation may appear as something 'added' to the notes in performance. Yet, as is the case for coarticulation in language, this is turning things on the head, in forgetting that discretization into units both in music (pitches, durations) and in language (phonemes, syllables) are probably secondary to more primordial musical and speech practices where coarticulation would be intrinsic.

One task in future research will thus also be to take a critical look at notions of continuity and discontinuity in Western musical thought, in view of recognizing the continuous body motion and resultant contextual smearing as not something added to music, but as something intrinsic to music as a phenomenon. Needless to say, there are also substantial challenges of method, of finding out more in detail of what goes on in sound-producing body motion as well as the many details of coarticulation in perceived sound and body motion. Fortunately, we now have the methods (including the technologies) to explore the details of such real-life contextual smearing in music, and thus hopefully contribute to our understanding of music as a phenomenon.

Acknowledgments. Many thanks to the participating musicians in our recording sessions over the years, and many thanks to my colleagues in our team for helping with recording and processing of data, in particular to Alexander Refsum Jensenius and Minho Song for developing Matlab scripts used in the analysis and display of the motion capture data.

References

1. Bianco, T.: Gestural control in trumpet performance: experiments and modeling. Ph.D. thesis. Université Pierre et Marie Curie, Paris (2012)
2. Bregman, A.: Auditory Scene Analysis. The MIT Press, Cambridge (1990)
3. Dahl, S.: Movements and analysis of drumming. In: Altenmüller, E., Wiesendanger, M., Kesselring, J. (eds.) Music, Motor Control and the Brain, pp. 125–138. Oxford University Press, Oxford (2006)
4. Elliott, D., Helsen, W., Chua, R.: A century later: woodworth's (1899) two-component model of goal-directed aiming. Psychol. Bull. **127**(3), 342–357 (2001)
5. Engel, K.C., Flanders, M., Soechting, J.F.: Anticipatory and sequential motor control in piano playing. Exp. Brain Res. **113**, 189–199 (1997)
6. Farentani, E., Recasens, D.: Coarticulation models in recent speech production theories. In: Hardcastle, W., Hewlett, N. (eds.) Coarticulation: Theory, Data and Techniques, pp. 31–65. Cambridge University Press, Cambridge (1999)
7. Galantucci, B., Fowler, C.A., Turvey, M.T.: The motor theory of speech perception reviewed. Psychon. Bull. Rev. **13**(3), 361–377 (2006)
8. Gjerdingen, R., Perrott, D.: Scanning the dial: the rapid recognition of music genres. J New Music Res **37**(2), 93–100 (2008)
9. Godøy, R.I.: Motor-mimetic music cognition. Leonardo **36**(4), 317–319 (2003)
10. Godøy, R.I.: Reflections on chunking in music. In: Schneider, A. (ed.) Systematic and Comparative Musicology: Concepts, Methods, Findings, pp. 117–132. Peter Lang, Frankfurt (2008)
11. Godøy, R.I.: Thinking now-points in music-related movement. In: Bader, R., Neuhaus, C., Morgenstern, U. (eds.) Concepts, Experiments, and Fieldwork. Studies in Systematic Musicology and Ethnomusicology, pp. 245–260. Peter Lang, Frankfurt (2010)
12. Godøy, R.I.: Quantal elements in musical experience. In: Bader, R. (ed.) Sound—Perception—Performance. Current Research in Systematic Musicology, vol. 1, pp. 113–128. Springer, Berlin/Heidelberg (2013)
13. Godøy, R.I., Jensenius, A.R., Nymoen, K.: Chunking in music by coarticulation. Acta Acustica United Acustica **96**(4), 690–700 (2010)
14. Godøy, R.I., Leman, M. (eds.): Musical Gestures: Sound, Movement, and Meaning. Routledge, New York (2010)
15. Grafton, S.T., Hamilton, A.F.: Evidence for a distributed hierarchy of action representation in the brain. Hum. Mov. Sci. **26**, 590–616 (2007)
16. Haken, H., Kelso, J.A.S., Bunz, H.: A theoretical model of phase transitions in human hand movements. Biol. Cybern. **51**(5), 347–356 (1985)
17. Hardcastle, W., Hewlett, N. (eds.): Coarticulation: theory, data and techniques. Cambridge University Press, Cambridge (1999)
18. Hogan, N., Sternad, D.: On rhythmic and discrete movements: reflections, definitions and implications for motor control. Exp. Brain Res. **181**, 13–30 (2007)
19. Husserl, E.: On the phenomenology of the consciousness of internal time, 1893–1917 (English translation by Brough, J.B.). Kluwer Academic Publishers, Doredrecht/Boston/London (1991)

20. Klapp, S.T., Jagacinski, R.J.: Gestalt principles in the control of motor action. Psychol. Bull. **137**(3), 443–462 (2011)
21. Leman, M.: Embodied Music Cognition and Mediation Technology. The MIT Press, Cambridge (2008)
22. Loram, I.D., Gollee, H., Lakie, M., Gawthrop, P.J.: Human control of an inverted pendulum: is continuous control necessary? Is intermittent control effective? is intermittent control physiological? J. Physiol. **589**(2), 307–324 (2011)
23. Müller, M.: Information Retrieval for Music and Motion. Springer, Berlin (2007)
24. Pöppel, E.: A hierarchical model of time perception. Trends Cogn. Sci. **1**(2), 56–61 (1997)
25. Rasamimanana, N., Bevilacqua, F.: Effort-based analysis of bowing movements: evidence of anticipation effects. J. New Music Res. **37**(4), 339–351 (2008)
26. Rosenbaum, D.A.: Human Motor Control. Academic Press Inc, San Diego (1991)
27. Rosenbaum, D., Cohen, R.G., Jax, S.A., Weiss, D.J., van der Wel, R.: The problem of serial order in behavior: Lashley's legacy. Hum. Mov. Sci. **26**(4), 525–554 (2007)
28. Schaeffer, P.: Traité des Objets Musicaux. Éditions du Seuil, Paris (1966)
29. Schaeffer, P. (with sound examples by Reibel, G., and Ferreyra, B.): Solfège de L'Objet Sonore. INA/GRM, Paris (1998, first published in 1967)
30. Schleidt, M., Kien, J.: Segmentation in behavior and what it can tell us about brain function. Hum. Nat. **8**(1), 77–111 (1997)
31. Snyder, B.: Music and Memory: An Introduction. The MIT Press, Cambridge, Mass (2000)
32. Tenny, J., Polansky, L.: Temporal gestalt perception in music. J. Music Theory **24**(2), 205–241 (1980)
33. van de Kamp, C., Gawthrop, P.J., Gollee, H., Loram, I.D.: Refractoriness in sustained visuo-manual control: is the refractory duration intrinsic or does it depend on external system properties? PLoS Comput. Biol. **9**(1), e1002843 (2013). doi:10.1371/journal.pcbi.1002843
34. Wiesendanger, M., Baader, A., Kazennikov, O.: Fingering and bowing in violinists: a motor control approach. In: Altenmüller, E., Wiesendanger, M., Kesselring, J. (eds.) Music, Motor Control and the Brain, pp. 109–123. Oxford University Press, Oxford (2006)

Symbolic Segmentation: A Corpus-Based Analysis of Melodic Phrases

Marcelo Rodríguez-López[✉] and Anja Volk

Department of Information and Computing Sciences, Utrecht University,
Utrecht, The Netherlands
{m.e.rodriguezlopez,a.volk}@uu.nl

Abstract. Gestalt-based segmentation models constitute the current
state of the art in automatic segmentation of melodies. These models
commonly assume that segment boundary perception is mainly triggered
by local discontinuities, i.e. by abrupt changes in pitch and/or duration
between neighbouring notes. This paper presents a statistical study of a
large corpus of boundary-annotated vocal melodies to test this assumption. The study focuses on analysing the statistical behaviour of pitch
and duration in the neighbourhood of annotated phrase boundaries. Our
analysis shows duration discontinuities to be statistically regular and
homogeneous, and contrarily pitch discontinuities to be irregular and
heterogeneous. We conclude that pitch discontinuities, when modelled as
a local and idiom-independent phenomenon, can only serve as a weak
predictor of segment boundary perception in vocal melodies.

1 Introduction

Music segmentation is a basic problem in research fields concerned with automated music description and processing. Segmenting musical input is concerned
with modelling the formation of temporal units holding musical content. Historically, the tasks of music segmentation that have received more attention within
music content research fall into three groups: (*a*) the segmentation of musical
audio into notes, as part of transcription systems [2], (*b*) the segmentation of
symbolic encodings of music into phrases [18,19], and (*c*) the segmentation of
audio/symbolic music files into sections [16]. In this paper we focus on the study
on units of the second kind, i.e. those resembling the musicological concept of
the *phrase*. Given that phrase-level segmentation deals mainly with monophonic
music, this area is commonly referred to as *melodic segmentation*. In this paper
we address the problem of melodic segmentation from the perspective of Music
Information Retrieval (MIR), as part of the MUSIVA project [25].[1]

In MIR the task of melodic segmentation consist in identifying segment
boundaries, i.e. the transition points between cognitively-plausible segments.
Melodic segmentation has commonly been modelled from three perspectives.

---

[1] In the project we pay special attention to the role that segments play in assessing
the variation and similarity between melodies.

© Springer International Publishing Switzerland 2014
M. Aramaki et al. (Eds.): CMMR 2013, LNCS 8905, pp. 548–557, 2014.
DOI: 10.1007/978-3-319-12976-1_33

The first assumes that boundary perception is mostly related to self-organizing principles in the brain, so that the process is mainly idiom independent and that the information needed can be found in the immediate neighbourhood of the boundary [6,23]. The second assumes that the main cue for boundary detection is related to melodic self-similarity [7,11], also assuming that boundary perception is idiom independent, yet noting that access to information over the large sections of the melody is needed. The last perspective defends the view of exposure [1,20], which assumes that idiom-related factors, such as tonal/melodic/form-level prototypical patterns are important cues for segmentation.

Recent comparative studies of melody segmentation models [18,19,24,26] report results of only modest success, with F-scores [13] peaking at 0.60–0.66 when models are evaluated using large melodic corpora. Two models that have consistently ranked higher in these studies are LBDM [6] and Grouper [23]. Both models are based on heuristics inspired by Gestalt principles, i.e. idiom independent rules based on local information. Gestalt-based models commonly search for discontinuities in pitch and rhythmic parametrisations of melodies. In respect to rhythm this usually corresponds to relatively long durations or extended silences, and in respect to pitch to relatively large intervals. In this paper we report on a statistical analysis of local pitch and duration information surrounding human annotated segment boundaries. We aim to provide empirical evidence that supports/refutes the assumptions of locality and universality of discontinuity made by Gestalt-based segmentation models. In this paper we refer to this type of analysis as 'corpus-based', to distinguish it from listening studies [5,8,21] which have similar goals but follow a different experimental design.[2]

The remainder of this paper is organized as follows. In Sect. 2 we summarize work in corpus analysis of melodies and melodic phrase structure. In Sect. 3 we present our statistical analysis of phrase boundary neighbourhoods and discuss our results. Finally, in Sect. 4 we draw conclusions and outline future work.

2   Previous Work in Corpus Analysis of Melodic Phrases

In general, statistical analyses of melodic corpora with annotated phrases have focused on characterising within-phrase regularities, such as prototypical contours [10] and pitch-interval-size-shrinking [22]. Studies have also assessed the effect of within-phrase information in other musical processes, such as pulse induction [15] and melodic similarity [9].

Conversely, studies focusing on the immediate vicinity of annotated boundaries or considering successive phrases are scarcer. Here we review two. In [4] Brown et al. examined if the conditions of closure proposed by Narmour [14] could be observed in phrase and score endings of the Essen Folk Song Collection (EFSC). They found strong evidence for the occurrence of 2 (out of 6) conditions at phrase/score ends when compared to the total population of notes, namely for durational expansion and tonal resolution. Similarly, in [3] Bod analysed the

---

[2] Listening studies have commonly focused on testing segmentation theories using small datasets annotated by a high number of human listeners.

EFSC looking for phrase joints that challenge the assumptions of Gestalt-based segmentation models. Bod observed a class of phrase joints that he labelled "jump-phrases", which referred to phrases that contained a pitch interval jump at the beginning/end of a phrase (or in both) rather than at the joint. Bod reports that more than 32 % of the subset of the EFSC used in the study (1000 songs) contained at least one jump-phrase.

3   Corpus Analysis of Annotated Phrases

Aims and Contribution: In this paper we take as our working hypothesis that pitch and duration discontinuities (defined here as "jumps" in respect to a local context) can be considered relatively strong, universal cues for segment boundary perception. We aim to test this hypothesis based on empirical evidence provided by corpus statistics. To this end, we carry out a statistical analysis of pitch and duration *interval sizes* measured at phrase joints, and compare these interval sizes to interval sizes found in a local context around the boundary. The characterization of interval sizes resulting from this analysis contributes both to the deepening of the understanding of boundary perception, presenting an alternative to the previously mentioned listening studies, and also contributes to the development of more robust models of melodic segmentation.

Scope: The analysis presented here considers only pitch and duration information, and focuses on vocal folk melodies sampled from the EFSC. Our choice of melodic representation is taken so that it agrees with the information used by most Gestalt-based segmentation models. Likewise, our choice of melodic corpus is motivated by its widespread use in the testing of segmentation models, as it can be considered the de facto benchmark.

Practical Considerations: The EFSC is mainly comprised of vocal music. Hence, the influence of instrumental tessitura in the distributional properties of interval sizes cannot be directly attested. Moreover, EFSC melodies are limited to a single genre, and despite the EFSC's large size, the cultural traditions included are not equally well represented. Thus, if the entire corpus is used, a characterization of interval size in respect to stylistic traits is also difficult to measure. For these reasons, we focus on the two most distinct and well represented cultural traditions within the corpus, namely German and Chinese. In this study we assume that these two traditions are distinct enough so that the evidence of regularities (or lack thereof) can be used as an indicator (albeit modest) to assess the universality and locality of discontinuity-related boundary cues.

3.1   About the Essen Folk Song Collection (EFSC)

The Essen Folk Song Collection contains over 20,000 songs, of which 6,251 are at present publicly available. The EFSC data was compiled and encoded from notated sources by a team of ethnomusicologists and folklorists lead by Helmuth Schaffrath. The songs are available both in EsAC and **kern formats, and include information on pitch, duration, meter, barlines, rests, and phrase markings. Text accompanying the songs is not available in the encodings.

3.2   Melodic Representation and Pre-processing

The most common melodic parametrisation used in segmentation models consists of pitch and duration intervals. In this paper we measure pitch intervals (PIs) in semitones, and measure duration using inter-onset-intervals (IOIs) in seconds.

For the analysis of pitch and duration intervals, first PIs and IOIs of different melodies have to be made comparable. PIs are a relative, transposition-invariant measure, so no further processing is needed. IOIs, on the other hand, are an absolute measure. Thus, to achieve invariance to tempo, we simply normalized the durations of each IOI collected for a local context by the total duration of the context. We abbreviate normalized IOIs as NIOIs.

3.3   Experimental Procedure and Terminology

The subsets of the EFSC used for our analysis were obtained processing the **kern encodings with a combination of Python and Matlab scripting. We used the entire 'Germany' and 'China' sets for our experiments. Following [22], we filtered out songs which contained rests, and also excluded songs with just one phrase. The filtering resulted in 1,268 German folk songs, ranging in length from 13 to 184 notes. In total, this accounted for 5289 phrase-pairs, with phrases ranging from 2 to 21 notes. Similarly, we obtained 1416 Chinese songs, ranging from 17 to 270 notes. From this subset 4624 phrase-pairs were extracted, with phrases ranging from 2 to 28 notes.

We denote the extracted sequential phrase-pairs as $ph_{a,b}$ (with a, b denoting the left- and right- most phrases of the phrase pair). We collected statistics for intervals occurring within a local context established around the boundary of $ph_{a,b}$. The local context for analysis spans an interval of $[-2, 2]$, i.e. two notes to the left and two notes to the right of the boundary bisecting $ph_{a,b}$[3]. Here we consider a joint as the last note belonging to ph_a and the first note belonging to ph_b, and denote the interval computed at the joint as $j(ph_{a,b})$. Similarly, we denote the contextual intervals surrounding the joint as $c(ph_a)$ and $c(ph_b)$, when referring to them individually, and $c(ph_{a,b})$ when referring to both.

3.4   Results

From our working hypothesis we can derive three main assumptions used by Gestalt models: 1. discontinuities in pitch and/or duration are strong cues for segmentation, 2. discontinuities can be modelled as a local phenomenon, 3. discontinuity cues are universal. In the following we describe three experiments, using simple descriptive statistics and statistical hypothesis testing, to investigate the validity of these assumptions.

---

[3] We take a context size of $[-2, 2]$ as it commonly constitutes the upper limit for context sizes in comparative studies of melodic segmentation models [18, 19, 24, 26] (beyond this value the performance of Gestalt based models either drops or does not seems to result in significant improvements).

Experiment 1. First we sought to assess the level of strength of pitch and duration discontinuities, by testing the intuition that a higher strength should correlate with a strong presence of discontinuities at phrase joints. To this end we simply computed the proportion of phrase-pairs having a local discontinuity in respect to all phrase-pairs of each (German and Chinese) subset. We also computed the number of discontinuities that can be observed as a proportion of the phrase-pairs of each song. Table 1 lists the observed proportions.

In Table 1 we can observe a fairly weak presence of pitch discontinuities, both when compared to the total amount of phrase-pairs of each subset and to individual songs. Duration discontinuities, on the other hand, have a higher presence, especially for the Chinese subset ($\approx 73\%$ of all phrase-pairs, $\approx 58\%$ of songs have duration discontinuities in all boundaries of each song, and only $\approx 9\%$ of songs have no presence of duration discontinuities in the boundaries of each song).

We can also observe a general tendency of pitch and duration discontinuity to have higher presence in the Chinese subset (the relative increase in respect to the German subset varying between ≈ 12–18% for pitch and ≈ 13–34% for duration).

Table 1. Proportion of discontinuities observed in German and Chinese subsets. On the upper section a discontinuity d refers to the case: $j(ph_{a,b}) > c(ph_{a,b})$ for every $ph_{a,b}$ in *each subset*. On the lower section a discontinuity d refers to the case: $j(ph_{a,b}) > c(ph_{a,b})$ for every $ph_{a,b}$ in a song, and not-discontinuity nd refers to the case: $j(ph_{a,b}) < c(ph_{a,b})$ for every $ph_{a,b}$ in a song.

pitch	duration	Germany	China
d	-	32.41%	43.73%
-	d	49.57%	72.56%
d	-	04.51%	22.53%
-	d	24.13%	57.70%
nd	-	31.49%	28.53%
-	nd	23.26%	09.04%

Experiment 2. In our second experiment, we once more assessed the level of strength of pitch and duration discontinuities, this time by testing the intuition that higher strength should be reflected in low (or preferable no) overlap between the interval distributions of $j(ph_{a,b})$ and $c(ph_{a,b})$. To this end we give a visual depiction of the quartile spread of pitch and duration intervals in Fig. 1.

Figure 1 shows that pitch interval distributions *do* overlap (however slightly) in both subsets. The overlap is notably higher for the German subset, where not only box sizes and medians are close, but also the fact that $j(ph_{a,b})$ and $c(ph_b)$ present inverse skewness patterns suggests that phrase joints tend to have intervals of comparable or smaller size than their surrounding context. On the contrary, in the case of duration we can observe a clear dominance

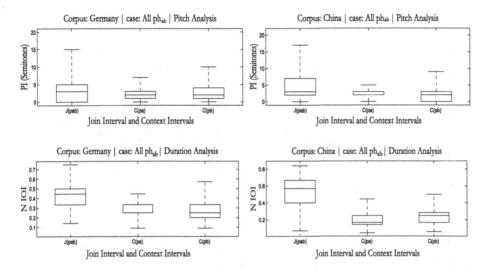

Fig. 1. Box plots of pitch and duration intervals of German and Chinese folk songs.

of larger intervals at the joint, which results in marginally overlapping inter-quartile ranges (depicted by the boxes) for German songs, and completely non-overlapping inter-quartile ranges for Chinese songs.

Experiment 3. In this experiment we investigated discontinuity strength from a third perspective and also examined if variations on the statistical behaviour of interval sizes could be attributed to non-local factors. To test a possible influence of non-local factors, we examined the influence of phrase-size by grouping all intervals according to the sizes of phrase-pairs $ph_{a,b}$. We investigated discontinuity strength by testing the statistical significance of central tendencies, i.e. a t-test comparison between the average size of all $j(ph_{a,b})$ per size-group and the average size of all $c(ph_{a,b})$ per size-group. Our results are presented in Fig. 2.

In the x-axis of Fig. 2 we present only size groups for which the differences between joints and contextual intervals are statistically significant.[4] In respect to pitch intervals, we can observe a higher number of statistically significant differences of intervals per size-group in the Chinese subset (19 out of 26) when compared to the German Subset (6 out of 19). This once again points to a higher degree of strength of pitch discontinuity in the Chinese subset. In pitch intervals we can also observe a clear influence of phrase length in the size of the interval: a progressive increase in the separation between the means of $j(ph_{a,b})$ and $c(ph_{a,b})$ for Chinese songs, and, on the contrary, a decrease between means in German songs. The last observation suggests once again than in German songs local pitch discontinuities are relatively weak predictors of phrase boundaries.

---

[4] To avoid a bias of subset size and phrase-group size on the statistical significance testing, we created equal size groups of both subsets and of all size-groups using random sampling.

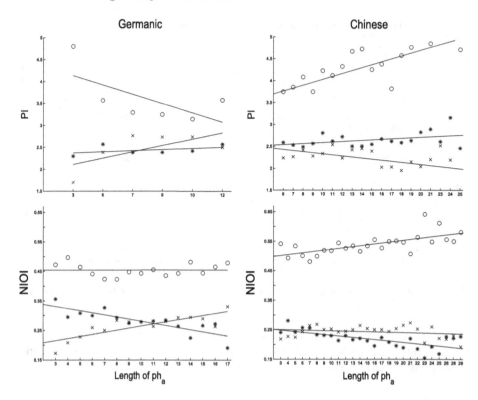

Fig. 2. Averages of $j(ph_{a,b})$ (circles), $c(ph_a)$ (crosses) and $c(ph_b)$ (asterisks), when grouped according to $ph_{a,b}$ size. Solid lines indicate corresponding regression slopes. We carried out a pairwise t-test between means at joints $j(ph_{a,b})$ and means at $c(ph_{a,b})$. The x-axis shows only size groups with statistically significant differences (at the 5 % level). Total # of $ph_{a,b}$ size groups are: Chinese = 26, German = 19.

In respect to duration, the high number of statistically significant differences and the steady (German) and divergent (Chinese) $j(ph_{a,b})$ tendencies shown by the regression lines support the findings of our previous experiments. That is, local leaps in duration make for a relatively strong predictor of phrase boundaries. This observation agrees with comparative studies [12,18,19,26]. We cannot, however, generalize this finding to all music, as our study only investigated two musical traditions, and more importantly may contain biases introduced by the boundary annotation process used in the EFSC.

4   Conclusion

In this paper we have presented a statistical study of melodic phrase boundaries. The aim of the study has been to test the assumptions of 'Gestalt-based' computer models of segmentation, which are currently at the state of the art of melody segmentation. In the study, we analysed the presence of pitch/duration 'discontinuities' in human-annotated phrase boundaries. The annotated phrases used for the study were extracted from a large corpus of vocal folk melodies, and separated in two subsets representing distinct geographical and cultural origins (German and Chinese).

Our analyses reveal that discontinuities in duration show statistical regularity and homogeneity in respect to melodic origin. Moreover, duration-related discontinuities seem to be unperturbed by non-local factors such as variations in phrase-length. These observations can be then taken as supporting evidence of the importance of duration-related discontinuities in the perception of melodic phrase boundaries of vocal folk music. However, our results (particularly those presented in Table 1), suggest that duration-related discontinuities on their own would not able to ensure high boundary prediction performance. Contrarily to discontinuities in duration, pitch-related discontinuities show far less regularity and homogeneity (their presence at annotated phrase boundaries shows dependencies on both cultural origin and phrase-length). We thus conclude that discontinuities in pitch, when modelled assuming locality and universality, can only be considered a weak predictor of phrase boundaries in folk vocal melodies. These finding suggests that the modelling of pitch discontinuities needs to be addressed from a different perspective. Perhaps a good alternative is to think of pitch-related discontinuities as disruptions in the expectation of pitch continuation. In this way the notion of an 'abrupt change' in pitch moves from a purely geometrical to a probabilistic ground. To test this intuition a model similar to the one proposed in [17] can be used.

In future work we will study how the statistical regularity and homogeneity of pitch and rhythm related local discontinuities varies in respect to factors such as musical style and instrumental tessitura, aiming to provide more conclusive proof of the insights given in this paper. We will also attempt to characterise the performance of known computer models of segmentation according to corpora of different characteristics (tradition, and again, style and instrumentation). To this end, we are currently working on the production of Jazz and Rock melodic corpora with phrase annotations.

Acknowledgments. We thank F. Wiering and the anonymous reviewers for the useful comments on earlier drafts of this document. M.E. Rodríguez-López and A. Volk are supported by the Netherlands Organization for Scientific Research, NWO-VIDI grant 276-35-001.

References

1. Abdallah, S., Plumbley, M.: Information dynamics: patterns of expectation and surprise in the perception of music. Connect. Sci. **21**(2–3), 89–117 (2009)
2. Benetos, E., Dixon, S.: Polyphonic music transcription using note onset and offset detection. In: 2011 IEEE International Conference on Acoustics, Speech and Signal Processing (ICASSP), pp. 37–40. IEEE (2011)
3. Bod, R.: Probabilistic grammars for music. In: Belgian-Dutch Conference on Artificial Intelligence (BNAIC) (2001)

4. Brown, A.R., Gifford, T., Davidson, R.: Tracking levels of closure in melodies. In: Proceedings of the 12th International Conference on Music Perception and Cognition, pp. 149–152 (2012)

5. Bruderer, M.J., Mckinney, M.F., Kohlrausch, A.: The perception of structural boundaries in melody lines of western popular music. Musicae Sci. **13**(2), 273–313 (2009)

6. Cambouropoulos, E.: The local boundary detection model (lbdm) and its application in the study of expressive timing. In: Proceedings of the International Computer Music Conference (ICMC01), pp. 232–235 (2001)

7. Cambouropoulos, E.: Musical parallelism and melodic segmentation. Music Percept. **23**(3), 249–268 (2006)

8. Deliège, I.: Grouping conditions in listening to music: an approach to lerdahl & jackendoff's grouping preference rules. Music Percept. **4**, 325–359 (1987)

9. Eerola, T., Bregman, M.: Melodic and contextual similarity of folk song phrases. Musicae Sci. **11**(1 suppl.), 211–233 (2007)

10. Huron, D.: The melodic arch in western folksongs. Comput. Musicology **10**, 3–23 (1996)

11. Lartillot, O.: Reflections towards a generative theory of musical parallelism. Musicae Sci. Discuss. Forum **5**, 195–229 (2010)

12. Lartillot, O., Mungan, E.: A more informative segmentation model, empirically compared with state of the art on traditional turkish music. In: Proceedings of the Third International Workshop on Folk Music Analysis (FMA2013), p. 63 (2013)

13. Manning, C.D., Schütze, H.: Foundations of Statistical Natural Language Processing, vol. 999. MIT Press, Cambridge (1999)

14. Narmur, E.: The Analysis and Cognition of Basic Melodic Structures: The Implication-realisation Model. University of Chicago Press, Chicago (1990)

15. Nettheim, N.: The pulse in german folksong: a statistical investigation. Musikometrika **20**(1), 94–106 (1997)

16. Paulus, J., Müller, M., Klapuri, A.: State of the art report: audio-based music structure analysis. In: Proceedings of the 11th International Society for Music Information Retrieval Conference, pp. 625–636 (2010)

17. Pearce, M., Müllensiefen, D., Wiggins, G.: A comparison of statistical and rule-based models of melodic segmentation. In: Proceedings of the Ninth International Conference on Music Information Retrieval, pp. 89–94 (2008)

18. Pearce, M.T., Müllensiefen, D., Wiggins, G.A.: Melodic grouping in music information retrieval: new methods and applications. In: Raś, Z.W., Wieczorkowska, A.A. (eds.) Advances in Music Information Retrieval. SCI, vol. 274, pp. 364–388. Springer, Heidelberg (2010)

19. Pearce, M., Müllensiefen, D., Wiggins, G.: The role of expectation and probabilistic learning in auditory boundary perception: a model comparison. Perception **39**(10), 1365 (2010)

20. Pearce, M.T., Wiggins, G.A.: The information dynamics of melodic boundary detection. In: Proceedings of the Ninth International Conference on Music Perception and Cognition, pp. 860–865 (2006)

21. Schaefer, R., Murre, J., Bod, R.: Limits to universality in segmentation of simple melodies (2004)

22. Shanahan, D., Huron, D.: Interval size and phrase position: a comparison between german and chinese folksongs (2011)

23. Temperley, D.: The Cognition of Basic Musical Structures. MIT Press, Cambridge (2004)

24. Thom, B., Spevak, C., Höthker, K.: Melodic segmentation: evaluating the performance of algorithms and musical experts. In: Proceedings of the International Computer Music Conference (ICMC), pp. 65–72 (2002)
25. Volk, A., de Haas, W.B., van Kranenburg, P.: Towards modelling variation in music as foundation for similarity. In: Proceedings of ICMPC, pp. 1085–1094 (2012)
26. Wiering, F., de Nooijer, J., Volk, A., Tabachneck-Schijf, H.: Cognition-based segmentation for music information retrieval systems. J. New Music Res. 38(2), 139–154 (2009)

Non-Verbal Imitations as a Sketching Tool for Sound Design

Guillaume Lemaitre[1,2,3]([✉]), Patrick Susini[2], Davide Rocchesso[3],
Christophe Lambourg[1], and Patrick Boussard[1]

[1] Genesis Acoustics, Aix-en-Provence, France
GuillaumeJLemaitre@gmail.com,
{chistophe.lambourg,patrick.boussard}@genesis.fr
[2] STMS-Ircam-CNRS-UPMC, Paris, France
susini@ircam.fr
[3] Università Iuav di Venezia, Venice, Italy
roc@iuav.it

Abstract. The article reports initial data supporting the idea of using non-verbal vocal imitations as a sketching and communication tool for sound design. First, a case study observed participants trying to communicate a referent sound to another person. Analysis of the videos of the conversations showed that participants spontaneously used descriptive and imitative vocalizations in more than half of the conversations. Second, an experiment compared recognition accuracy for different types of referent sounds when they were communicated either by a verbalization or a non-verbal vocal imitation. Results showed that recognition was always accurate with vocal imitations, even for sounds that were otherwise very difficult to verbally communicate. Recognition with verbalizations was accurate only for identifiable sounds. Altogether, these data confirm that vocal imitations are an effective communication device for sounds. We finally describe a recently-launched European project whose objective is precisely to use non-verbal imitations as a sketching tool for sound design.

Keywords: Vocal imitations · Imitations · Perception · Cognition · Recognition · Sound design

1 Introduction

For a long time, industry practitioners have struggled to reduce the loudness of products. But reducing loudness has a paradox: a noise can be less loud, but more annoying, or make a product less effective or less attractive (see [14] for compelling example in trains). Similarly, two sounds can be equally loud but differently annoying [2]. Practitioners in industry have therefore began to *design* sounds. The most notable example is probably that of quiet vehicles (electric and hybrid), that designers are embedding with artificial sounds for concerns of pedestrian safety, product aesthetic, and brand image. In interaction and product

© Springer International Publishing Switzerland 2014
M. Aramaki et al. (Eds.): CMMR 2013, LNCS 8905, pp. 558–574, 2014.
DOI: 10.1007/978-3-319-12976-1_34

design[1], designers and theorists are becoming aware that the sonic manifestations of objects can afford natural, powerful, and useful interactions, and participate in the aesthetic appraisal of a product [31]. The goal of the current study is to examine the potential use of non-verbal vocal imitations as a sketching tool for sound design and sonic interaction design.

Non-verbal vocalizations and manual gestures, more than speech, are naturally and spontaneously used in everyday life to describe and imitate sonic events. In fact, we have experimentally shown that naïve listeners, lacking a specialized vocabulary, categorize and describe sounds based on what they identify as the sound source [10,20]. When they cannot identify the source of the sounds, they rely on synesthetic metaphors to describe the timbre ("the sound is rough, cold, bitter") or try to vocally imitate the sounds. Vocal imitations therefore seem to be a convenient means of communicating sounds. In practice, they have been used in a few technical applications [8,11,12,24,25,34–36]. For instance, controlling sound synthesis with vocal imitations is a promising approach [4].

There are two different types of vocal imitations: imitations standardized in a language (onomatopoeias) and non-conventional and creative vocalizations. Onomatopoeias are very similar to words. Their meaning results from a symbolic relationship: "a word that is *considered by convention* to be *acoustically similar* to the sound, or the sound produced by the *thing* to which it refers" ([29] cited by [32]). They have probably been the most extensively studied type of vocal imitations [9,13,27,28,30,32,37,38,40].

In comparison, non-conventional vocal imitations have been rarely studied. Such an imitation is a non-conventional, creative utterance intended to be acoustically similar to the sound, or the sound produced by the thing to which it refers. Therefore, a non-conventional vocal imitation is only constrained by the vocal ability of the speakers and does not use symbolic conventions. For instance, [16] showed that human-imitated animal sounds were well recognized by listeners, even better than the actual animal sounds [15], yet the listeners did not have any problem discriminating between the two categories [17]. Our study focuses only on these non-conventional vocal imitations. In the following, the expression "vocal imitation" refers to *non-conventional non-verbal* vocal imitations, unless when specified.

But is every kind of sound vocalizable? The main limitation to what the voice can do probably comes from the glottal signal. The glottal signal is produced by a single vibrational system (the vocal folds), which implies that vocal signals are most often periodic (even though, chaotic, a-periodic or double-periodic oscillations can also happen), and essentially monophonic (even though some singing techniques can produce the illusion of multiple pitches). Furthermore, the pitch range of the human voice extends overall from about 80 Hz to 1100 Hz, and a single individual's vocal range usually covers less than two octaves. Another kind of limitation comes from speakers's native language. Speakers have a better ability to produce the speech sounds of their native language, and usually encounter

---

[1] Interaction design is the branch of design that focuses on how users interact with products and services [3,26].

utter difficulties when attempting to produce the sounds of a foreign language [33,39]. Finally, some speakers may be better able to invent successful vocal imitations of a sound than other ones.

The current study aimed at examining the potential use of non-verbal vocal imitations as a sketching tool for sound design. It had two goals. First, we set up a case study to observe whether speakers spontaneously use non-verbal vocal imitations to communicate sounds. The second goal was to assess how effectively vocal imitations communicate a referent sound, in comparison to a verbal description. In a preliminary study, we compared listeners' categorizations of a set of mechanical sounds and vocal imitations of these sounds [18]. Listeners recovered the broad categories of sound sources by listening to the vocal imitations. Here, we conducted an experiment in which participants recognized *sounds* based on vocal imitations and verbal descriptions. The goal was to assess whether vocal imitations conveyed enough information to communicate not only the broad categories of sounds but also the sounds themselves.

2 Case Study: Vocal Imitations in Conversations

We first conducted a case study to observe if and how French speakers use vocalizations in conversations[2]. During the case study, one participant listened to different series of sounds and had to communicate one target sound in the series to another participant. The task of the second participant was to recover the target sound. The participants could use any communication device that they felt appropriate and effective. The goal was to observe whether they would spontaneously use vocalizations and onomatopoeias in such an unscripted setting.

2.1 Method

Participants. Twelve participants (5 male and 7 female), between 26 and 45 years of age (mean 35 years old) volunteered as participants. All reported normal hearing and were French native speakers. They were screened on the basis of a questionnaire concerning their musical practice and their experience with sounds, and with a short interview with the experimenter. We selected only participants with limited musical or audio expertise to ensure homogeneous listening strategies [20]. Participants participated in couples. Three couples consisted of participants who already knew each other, and three couples of participants who had never met before.

Stimuli. The stimuli consisted of 30 sounds divided into 3 sets of 10 sounds. The first set (Set 1) consisted of sounds recorded in a kitchen, and for which identification data are available [10,20]. They were easily recognizable and could be easily named (e.g. the "beeps of a microwave oven"). The second set (Set 2) consisted also of kitchen sounds but they were more difficult to identify and name. They could still be described by the type of mechanical event causing the

---

[2] The vocabulary specific to sound is rather limited in French [5].

sounds (e.g. "some liquid in a vessel"). The level of these sounds was ecologically adjusted: in a preliminary experiment participants adjusted the level of each sound according to what it would sound like in the kitchen, compared to a fixed reference. The third set (Set 3) consisted of car horn sounds [22,23]. These sounds can all be described by the same expression ("a car horn") and are therefore more difficult to distinguish. These sounds were equalized in loudness in a preliminary experiment. The stimuli were all monophonic with a 16-bit resolution and a sampling rate of 44.1 kHz. Three target sounds were initially selected by the experimenter in each set (totaling nine target sounds). The three sets of sounds and the nine target sounds were selected so as to create different situations where sounds were more or less identifiable and the task more or less difficult. Table 1 lists these sounds.

Apparatus. The sounds were played with Cycling'74's Max/MSP version 4.6 on an Apple Macintosh Mac Pro 2 × 2.5 GHz PPC G5 (Mac OS X v10.4 Tiger) workstation with a RME Fireface 400 sound card, and were amplified by a Yamaha P2075 amplifier diotically over a pair of Sennheiser HD250 linear II headphones. Participants were seated in a double-walled IAC sound-isolation booth when listening to the sounds and during the conversations.

Procedure. Two participants were invited in each session. They each had a different role (Participant 1 or 2) that was randomly attributed at the beginning of the session. The experiment was divided into nine blocks. Each block corresponded to one of the nine target sounds (three sets times three target sounds). The order of the blocks was randomized for each couple of participants. For each block, Participant 1 was first isolated in a sound-attenuated booth and listened to all the sounds. Then, the interface highlighted a target sound. Participant 1 heard this sound three times. Afterwards, she or he joined Participant 2 and was required to communicate the target to her or him. The participants could freely talk, and were not specified how to communicate. Particularly, the possibility to use vocal imitations was not mentioned. The conversation was filmed. Once the conversation finished, participant 2 was isolated in the sound booth. She or he listened to the ten sounds, and selected the target sound. The order of the sounds in the interface was different for the two participants.

2.2   Results

For each series three indices were collected: the number of correct identifications of the target sound by Participant 2 (accuracy of identification), the presence or absence of vocal imitations during the conversation, and the duration of the vocal imitations. In addition, we also tallied the presence of gestures. Three experimenters measured the second index a-posteriori, by independently analyzing and annotating the video recordings of the conversations. Their annotations were completely identical.

Accuracy of recognition. Accuracy was 94.4 % in Set 1 and 83.3 % in Set 2. For these two groups of sounds, identification of the communicated sound was

Table 1. The three groups of ten sounds used in the case study. For the kitchen sounds (Sets 1 and 2), *identification confidence* was measured in [20]. Set 2 includes sounds with low confidence values. Identification confidence was not measured for the car horns. A car horn consist of a driver and a resonator The different devices are here described by the type of driver and resonator they were made of. The indexes in the left column are those used in the original studies, and are reported here to facilitate the comparison with the referent articles. The sounds in bold had were those that Participants 1 communicated to Participant 2 during the case study.

Sound	Description	Confidence value
Set 1 (easy-to-identify kitchen sounds)		
001	Ice cubes in an empty glass	7.26
010	Hitting a champagne cup	6.79
016	**Bips of a microwave oven**	7.37
017	Agitating hands in water	7.42
030	Putting a bowl on a table	7.95
040	Cutting bread	6.68
079	**Beating eggs inside a container**	7.00
080	Pouring cereals into a bowl	7.63
084	**Cutting vegetables with a knife**	7.05
097	Drops in a container	7.42
Set 2 (difficult-to-identify kitchen sounds)		
015	Ejection of a toaster compartment	4.89
051	Crushing a paper bag	2.95
054	Banging a wooden chair	2.89
058	Closing a door	3.95
074	**Removing the cover of a plastic container**	2.21
085	Tearing up vegetable leaves	3.21
089	Grinding salt	1.95
082	**Cracking open an egg**	3.53
094	**Unrolling absorbing paper, detaching a sheet**	2.74
095	Switching light on	3.10
Set 3 (car horn sounds)		
201	**Double electrodynamic driver + plate resonator**	n.a
202	**Pneumatic driver + horn resonator**	n.a
203	**Electrodynamic driver + plate resonator**	n.a
204	Electrodynamic driver + horn	n.a
205	Double electrodynamic driver + plate resonator	n.a
206	Electrodynamic driver + horn resonator	n.a
207	Double electrodynamic driver + horn resonator	n.a
208	Triple electrodynamic driver + horn resonator	n.a
209	Double electrodynamic driver + horn resonator	n.a
210	Pneumatic driver + horn resonator	n.a

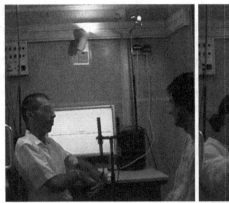

Fig. 1. Two extracts of videos taken of participants of the case study. In the left panel, Participant 1 (on the left of the picture) makes the gestures of whipping eggs in a bowl. In the right panel, Participant 1 uses gestures to describe the envelope of the sound.

equivalently accurate (t(4) = 1.000, p = 0.374). Accuracy was much smaller for Set 3 (27.8 %) and significantly different from Set 1 (t(4) = 4.811, p < .01). As assumed, the task was more difficult for the car horn sounds.

Vocal imitations. Vocal imitations were present in 59.3 % of the conversations (we define here a conversation as each interaction between the two participants to describe each sound). Vocal imitations were therefore spontaneously used to communicate the sounds. During post-experimental interviews, some participants reported a positive effect of vocal imitations. Some others reported that they thought vocal imitations were prohibited, yet they actually did a few vocal imitations. In fact, there were large discrepancies between the couples. One couple used vocal imitations in only 22 % of the conversations, whereas another used vocal imitations in every conversation. The distributions of vocal imitations in the three sets (50 %, 72.2 %, and 55.6 %) were not statistically different ($\chi^2(1,N = 18) = 1.87$, 0.115, 1.08, and p = 0.17, 0.78 and 0.3 respectively, when contrasting Set 1 vs. Set 2, Set 1 vs. Set 3, and Set 2 vs. Set 3).

Duration of vocal imitations during each conversation. Experimenters listened to the tapes of the conversations, isolated the vocal imitations and reported the duration. We divided this number by the duration of each referent sound to get an approximate value of how many times each sound was imitated during the conversations. On average, participants used 2.0 vocal imitations of the referent sound during the conversations (we manually verified that the duration of the vocal imitations was of the order of magnitude of the referent sound). Again, there were large differences between the couples, with one couple using 0.4 vocal imitations on average and one couple using 6.3 vocal imitations on average.

Imitative gestures. The conversations also included a number of imitative gestures. Experimenters watched the video recordings of the conversations, and isolated gestures that were either describing an action producing the sound (see the left panel of Fig. 1) or the sound itself (see the right panel of Fig. 1, though the distinction with gesture accompanying prosody is sometimes not clear). Overall, participants used imitative gestures in 79.6 % of the conversations. Most of the gestures imitated the action that produced the sounds: chopping carrots, pouring milk on cereals, etc. Twenty-three of the gestures used during case study also described the sound itself: the rhythm, the temporal envelope, the evolution of pitch, the volume, etc.

2.3   Discussion

The goal of this case study was to observe how speakers manage to communicate a sound one to another. The framework did not impose any restriction or specification on what participants could do. In this respect, the results clearly showed that vocal imitations and imitative gestures are spontaneous and common.

The next step was to test whether vocal imitations can effectively communicate the referent sounds and compare vocal imitations and verbal descriptions of sounds. The results of the case study showed that the social interaction between participants may also influence communication. Post-experimental interviews and informal analyses of the video recordings of the conversations suggested that the use of vocal imitations depended on the participants and on their mutual understanding. The experiment reported in the next paragraph therefore planned to involve no interactions between the participants producing the vocal imitationsand those identifying the referent sounds. This also prevented the potential influence of descriptive or imitative gestures.

The case study also showed a non-significant trend in the data that suggested that the type of referent sounds may influence the use of vocal imitations (vocal imitations were used more often in Set 2 than in Set 1). The experimental study described in Sect. 3 thus used different types of sounds, more or less identifiable.

3   Experimental Study: Vocal Imitations and Recognition

The experiment aimed to measure how well listeners recognize referent sounds when using two types of description: vocal imitations and verbalizations. We measured the accuracy of participants using each type of description to recognize the referent sounds among a set of distractor sounds, as they would do if someone was trying to communicate a sound just heard, remembered or imagined. Here, participants did not interact directly: descriptions were recorded in a preliminary session, and participants could only hear the descriptions (to prevent the influence of gestures). The experiment also used sets of sounds, more or less identifiable.

3.1   Method

Referent Sounds. We used 36 referent sounds, divided into four sets (identifiable complex events, elementary mechanical interactions, artificial sound effects, and unidentifiable mechanical sounds). The 36 sounds were selected from a total of 58 sounds. A preliminary experiment measured identification confidence for the 58 sounds [21]. The 36 sounds in the four categories were selected so as to minimize the overlap of identification confidence in the four distributions.

- *Identifiable complex events* were meant to correspond to sounds typically found in a household or office environment. They were sequences of sounds that could be recognized unambiguously as a common everyday scenario (e.g., "coins dropped in a jar"). We purposely used different instances of similar events (e.g., different guitar samples, different ways of dropping coins, etc.) so as to create a recognition task that was difficult;
- *Elementary mechanical interactions* were identifiable without eliciting the recognition of a particular object, context, or scenario (e.g., "a drip", without specifying any other information). We conceived the elementary interactions based on the taxonomy proposed by [6] and empirically studied by [19]. They correspond to the simplest interactions between two objects that produce sounds (e.g., tapping, scraping etc.). These interactions can be easily described (usually by a verb) but no cue is provided concerning the context in which the action takes place. For instance, the sound of drip could originate from a faucet leaking, a pebble falling in a pond, a rain drop, etc. As such we assumed that they should be slightly less identifiable than the identifiable complex events;
- **Artificial sound effects** were created by using simple signal-based synthesis techniques (FM synthesis, etc.), with a specific goal of not mimicking any real mechanical event. Even though these sounds are not produced by any easily describable mechanical interactions, they could possibly be associated with everyday interfaces using beeps and tones as feedbacks sounds. We expected them to be difficult to recognize but not completely impossible to describe;
- *Unidentifiable mechanical sounds* were generated with mechanical objects and interactions that turned out to be really difficult to identify in blind informal listening tests. Even the type of mechanical interaction generating the sounds could not be successfully identified.

Confidence values ranged from 2.5 to 6.7. The value of confidence in identification measures the number of different sources that participants can list for a given sound [1,21]. The mean confidence values were 6.1 for the identifiable complex events, 5.2 for the set of elementary mechanical interactions, 4.1 for the artificial sound effects, and 3.3 for the unidentifiable mechanical sounds. This shows that the categories corresponded to their definitions of identifiability.

Note the two former sets of sounds should elicit *everyday listening* (listeners focusing on the source of the sounds) whereas the two latter should elicit *musical listening* (focusing on the features of the sound signals) in the listeners [7,20].

Descriptions. We used vocal imitations and verbalizations selected from a preliminary experiment [21]. Descriptions were first produced in a preliminary session by ten Italian speakers (7 male and 7 female), between 20 to 64 years of age (median 26 years old), with no musical expertise. They were instructed to verbally describe or vocalize the referent sounds so as to communicate them to someone who will have to recover the referent sound. In another session, a set of listeners compared the referent sounds and the two types of descriptions, and rated the adequacy of each description to communicate the referent sound. We selected the three most adequate vocal imitations and the three most adequate verbal description for each referent sound (for instance: "It is the sound of a guitar that follows the rhythm note, note, pause"). This resulted in 54 descriptions in each set (nine referent sounds times six descriptions), totaling 216 descriptions.

Participants. Fifteen participants (8 male and 7 female), between 18 to 60 years of age (median 29 years old) volunteered as participants. All reported normal hearing and were Italian native speakers. They had a minimal musical expertise, ranging from no musical expertise or practice at all, to intermittent amateur practice.

Apparatus. Stimulus presentation and response collection were programmed on an Apple Macintosh MacBook with Matlab 7.1.0.584 and Psychtoolbox version 3.0.10. The digital files were played through Beyerdynamic DT 770, DT 880 pro, or AKG K518 LE headphones.

Procedure. Participants were presented with one set of nine referent sounds at a time. A set of nine numbers was presented on a custom interface, with each number corresponding to one sound. The association of numbers and referent sounds was randomized for each subject. Subjects could listen to each referent sound by hitting the corresponding number on a keyboard. They could listen to every sound as many times as they wished. Before each set, they were presented with the nine sounds played in a row with the corresponding number highlighted to facilitate memorization of the sound/number association.

For each set, the 54 descriptions (27 vocal imitations and 27 verbalizations) were presented to the participants in random order. Subjects could listen to each description as many time as they wished. They selected the referent sound that corresponded to each description from the list of the nine referent sounds (9-alternative forced choice).

3.2 Results

Recognition accuracy was computed for each set of referent sounds and each type of description (recognition accuracy) and submitted to a repeated-measure analysis of variance (ANOVA), with the four sets and the two types of description as within-subject factors. All statistics are reported after Geisser-Greenhouse correction for potential violations of the sphericity assumption.

The main effect of the sets was significant ($F(3,42) = 12.877$, $p < .001$, $\eta^2 = 13.2\%$). Planned contrasts showed that the only significant contrast between the sets was between the elementary mechanical interactions (83.3 %) and the unidentifiable mechanical sounds(72.2 %, $F(1,14) = 67.496$, $p < .001$). The main effect of the description was also significant ($F(1,14) = 47.803$, $p < .001$, $\eta^2 = 17.5\%$), indicating that accuracy was overall better for the vocal imitations than the verbalizations(81.5 % vs. 71.5 %). The interaction between the sets and the type of description was also significant ($F(3,42) = 46.334$, $p < .001$) and was the largest experimental effect ($\eta^2 = 38.4\%$).

We used ten paired-samples t-tests to investigate the details of the interaction (alpha values were corrected with the Bonferroni procedure). The results first showed no significant difference of accuracy between vocal imitations and verbalizations neither for the identifiable complex events (74.6 % vs. 79.5 %, $t(14) = -1.726$, $p = .106$) nor for the elementary mechanical interactions (81.0 % VS. 85.7 %, $t(14) = -1.629$, $p = 0.126$). Accuracy for vocal imitations was better than for verbalizations for artificial sound effects (85.9 % vs. 60.7 %, $t(14) = 9.83$, $p < .000$) and unidentifiable mechanical sounds (84.4 % vs. 60.0 %, $t(14) = 11.8$, $p < .000$).

Additional t-tests were used to analyze the scores for *vocal imitations only*. They showed no significant difference of accuracy between identifiable complex events and elementary mechanical interactions (74.6 % vs. 80.1 %, $t(14) = -2.146$, $p = .05$), but accuracy was worst for identifiable complex events than for artificial sound effects (74.6 % vs. 85.9 %, $t(14) = -3.77$, $p < 0.05/10$) and the unidentifiable mechanical sounds (74.6 % vs. 84.4 %, $t(14) = -3.42$, $p < .05/10$). Similarly, for the *verbalizations only*, accuracy was not significantly different between identifiable complex events and elementary mechanical interactions (79.5 % vs. 85.7 %, $t(14) = -2.046$, $p = .06$), but accuracy was better for identifiable complex eventsthan artificial sound effects (79.5 % vs. 60.7 %, $t(14) = 7.70$, $p < .000$). It was also better than the unidentifiable mechanical sounds(79.5 % vs. 60.0 %, $t(14) = 5.674$, $p < .000$). These results are graphically represented on Fig. 2.

3.3   Discussion

Overall, the results distinguished two groups of sounds. On the one hand, there was no difference in accuracy between the vocal imitations and the verbalizations for the identifiable complex events and elementary mechanical interactions. On the other hand, vocal imitations were significantly more effective than verbalizations for the artificial sound effects and the unidentifiable mechanical sounds. Sounds that could be easily described by citing a unique mechanical source (i.e., a high confidence score) were recognized equivalently well with both types of descriptions. Recognition of sounds that cannot be easily described was worse for verbalizations than for vocal imitations.

In short, the experiment showed that while recognition based on verbalizations depended on how easily sounds were identifiable and describable, this was not the case for recognition based on vocal imitations: Vocal imitations proved to be an effective communication tool for the four sets of sounds tested here.

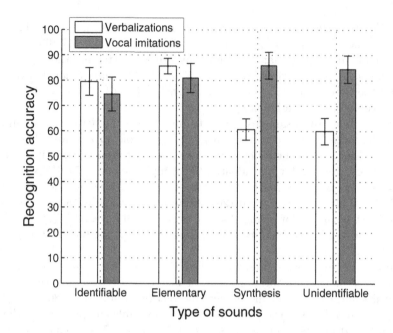

Fig. 2. Recognition accuracy. Vertical bars represent the 95 % confidence interval.

4   Using Vocal Imitations and Gestures for Sound Design

The two previous studies reported two results: (i) non-verbal vocal imitations are spontaneously used in conversations when speakers try to communicate a sound they have heard, and (ii) vocal imitations are as effective as verbal descriptions for identifiable sounds, and more effective than verbal sounds for non-identifiable sounds. These results confirm our initial idea than non-verbal vocal imitations may be a potent tool for sound design and sonic interaction design.

4.1   Vocal Imitations and Sound Synthesis

Practically, vocal imitations may be used for the control of sound synthesis. Various sound models are available that allow parametric exploration of a wide sound space. These models are however difficult to control and often require expertise in signal processing and acoustics. Using vocal imitations and gestures as an input to these models could bypass the necessity for the users to master hundreds of parameters. Controlling sound synthesis by simply vocalizing the sound a designer has in mind could become as easy as sketching a graphical idea with a pen and a sheet of paper.

The results of the case study have highlighted two potential kinds of non-verbal vocal imitations: those that describe the *event* creating the sounds (e.g. chopping carrots, crunching a soda can, etc.) and those that describe the *sound* itself (rhythm, time envelope). These suggests two potential ways of controlling sound synthesis: controlling *mechanical* properties of the sound source (type of interaction, material, shape, size of interacting objects, etc.) and controlling *acoustic* properties of the sounds (pitch, timbre, temporal evolution, etc.). The former idea is probably better-suited for physically-based sound synthesis, where the synthesis parameters actually correspond to the physics of a mechanical event producing the sounds (Young modulus, mode density, etc.). But it would also be interesting to use such imitations to control artificial sounds with no mechanical basis. The latter idea (vocalizing signal-based parameters) seems a priori well-suited for controlling signal-based synthesis (FM, additive, granular synthesis, etc.), where the mapping between properties of the vocal imitations and synthesis parameters is more straightforward.

Another idea is to *combine* different types of algorithms and different types of vocal controls. In one potential scenario, a user may first vocalize a rough idea of a sound. This first sketch could be used to select different options corresponding to different types of synthesis algorithms. Then the user could further specify the idea by tweaking the temporal evolution, fine timbral aspects, etc. Such a scenario is particularly appealing if the system can adapt itself to different users. Such a system would enable fast collaborative and interactive sound sketching. The same pipeline could be applied to sound retrieval in large data bases and combined to the control of audio post-processing. Potential applications are Foley effects for the movie and video game industries.

4.2 Sketching Audio Technologies with Vocalizations and Gestures: The SkAT-VG Project

Reaching the aforementioned goals requires to address important scientific and technological issues. For instance, whereas speech recognition techniques are now massively effective, little is known about "non-speech" sound analysis, processing, and recognition. The problem is probably non trivial since, by definition, creative vocal imitations are not embedded in a linguistic context that may bootstrap processing. Multidisciplinary research is thus required before designers can sketch ideas with their voice as easily as they sketch an idea on pad.

The European project SkAT-VG (sketching audio technologies with vocalizations and gestures[3]) has the objective to carry out such multidisciplinary research. SkAT-VG is aiming at exploiting non-verbal vocalizations and manual gestures to sketch sonic interaction. As shown before, vocal imitations and gestures are easily the most natural analogues to hand and pencil, having the innate capacity of conveying straightforward information on several attributes of a given sound. Non-verbal vocalizations, intermixed with ordinary verbal items, are used to communicate emotional states, to integrate the rhetoric of a sentence, or to imitate non-human sounds. The latter use is particularly close to the idea of sketching. Similarly, hands are commonly used to emphasize, supplement, or substitute part of the information conveyed by the voice. For instance, one would raise or lower his hand to indicate, respectively, increasing or decreasing pitch

---

[3] www.skatvg.eu.

or amplitude of a sound. The SkAT-VG project aims at extending the use of non-verbal vocalizations and manual gestures to the early stages of the design process, wherever the sonic behavior of objects is relevant for their use and aesthetics. Including vocal sketching in the design process will allow the designer to rapidly specify a sonic behavior by directly acting on an object mockup.

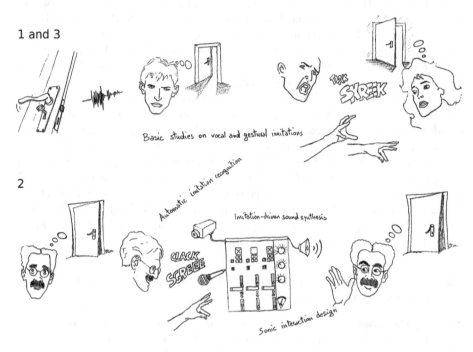

Fig. 3. Framework of the SkAT-VG project. The project has three main components. 1. Basic studies explore how human speakers use their voice and gestures to communicate about sounds and how listeners associate these productions with mental representations of sounds. 2. The project develops specific signal processing and automatic classification tools to automatically associate vocal and gestural inputs to control sound synthesis models. 3. Case studies and workshops allow developments empowering sound and interaction designers with new tools and methodologies.

Figure 3 represents the framework of the SkAT-VG project. The project has three main components: **Production and perception; Automatic classification; Sonic Interaction Design**.

Production and perception of vocalizations and expressive gestures. A person imitates a sounding object to let an interlocutor identify what she has in mind. Through an original mixture of psychology, phonetics, and gesture analysis SkAT-VG studies two hypotheses: first, that the articulatory mechanisms used to imitate sounds are related to the mechanical characteristics and behavior of the source; second, that expressive gestures communicate the temporal evolution of fine timbral properties.

Production and perception of vocal imitations are inextricably connected, as humans often tune their listening to the constraints of human vocal production (phonetic listening). Expertise in phonetics helps understanding how the physical dynamics of an event is mimicked by the voice. By adopting an analytical approach to the craft of vocal imitation, SkAT-VG aims at clearly characterizing how humans vocally imitate sounds. From the cognition side sound source identification is still an open issue. SkAT-VG focuses on relevant elementary auditory phenomena to understand which sound features allow identification. Similarly, studying expressive gestures helps understanding when and how humans mimic the causes or the effects of sounding actions and their temporal evolution.

Automatic identification of vocalizations and expressive gestures. Transforming imitations into synthetic sounds has two parts: automatic recognition of the sound source and estimation of the sound features. Automatic recognition requires three functions: (i) providing a relevant representation of the signals (acoustical features, articulatory mechanisms, gestural features) (ii) segmenting signals into meaningful elements, (iii) Predicting the category of the imitated sound. SkAT-VG will embody the results of the basic studies into state-of-the-art machine-learning techniques (classifiers), different from conventional speech recognition in that there is here no linguistic context. As regards estimation of the sound features novel techniques of adaptation and estimation of gesture characteristics allow to exploit the expressiveness of vocal and manual gestures for continuous interaction. In this context, this means that the recognizer is able to adapt to user-controlled variations, in such a way that continuous classification and early estimation of variations will be possible while performing the recognition task.

Sonic interaction design. From the beginning of the project user studies precisely specify the resulting sketching tools. Technically, these tools process vocalizations and gestures and transform them into synthetic sounds, further molded and included in actual prototypes. Various sound models are already available that allow parametric exploration of a wide sound space. This is extended in SkAT-VG by inclusion of vocal and gestural sketching in the design process, thus allowing the designer to rapidly specify a sonic behavior by directly acting on an object mockup. Basic articulatory mechanisms recognized from the vocalizations are therefore used to select appropriate synthesis methods. The selected synthesis models are driven so as to adaptively fine tune their parameters to match the target sound and the evolution of the expressive gestures as closely as they can. Manual gestures, already exploited as a source of expressive information at the imitation stage, are also used for real-time continuous control of sound synthesis.

5   Conclusion

This article first reported a case study in which a participant tried to communicate a sound that she or he had just heard. Participants were free to use any means they felt appropriate to communicate the sounds. Observation of the conversations showed that they spontaneously used vocal imitations and gestures. This suggested that these types of production may somehow improve the effectiveness of the communication. To test this idea, an experimental study was designed in which participants recognized target sounds on the basis of either a verbal description or a vocal imitation. The results showed that participants recognized the target sounds with vocal imitations at least as good as with verbalizations. In particular, when target sounds were not identifiable, recognition accuracy dropped with verbalizations but was always at ceiling level with verbalizations.

These results show that verbalizations are an intuitive and effective device to communicate about sounds. We finally described the rationale and the structure of a recently-launched European project (Sketching Audio Technologies with Vocalizations and Gestures: SkAT-VG) that aims at developing tools that let sound and interaction designers intuitively and rapidly sketch sounds using vocal imitations by and gestures.

Acknowledgments. The authors would like to thank Karine Aura, Arnaud Dessein, Massimo Grassi, and Daniele Galante for assistance while running the experiments and Nicole Navolio for proofreading the manuscript. This research was instrumental in preparation of the SkAT-VG project (2014–2016), retained for financial support of the Future and Emerging Technologies (FET) programme within the Seventh Framework Programme for Research of the European Commission, under FET-Open grant number: 618067.

References

1. Ballas, J.A.: Common factors in the identification of an assortment of brief everyday sounds. J. Exp. Psychol. Hum. Percept. Perform. **19**(2), 250–267 (1993)
2. Blommer, M., Amman, S., Abhyankar, S., Dedecker, B.: Sound quality metric development for wind buffetting and gusting noise. In: Proceedings of the Noise and Vibration Conference and Exhibition, Traverse City, MI. Society of Automotive Engineers International, Warrendale, PA (2003). SAE Technical paper series 2003-01-1509
3. Buxton, B.: Sketching the User Experience. Morgan Kaufman as an imprint of Elsevier, San Francisco (2007)
4. Ekman, I., Rinott, M.: Using vocal sketching for designing sonic interactions. In: DIS '10: Proceedings of the 8th ACM Conference on Designing Interactive Systems, pp. 123–131. Association for Computing Machinery, New York (2010)
5. Faure, A.: Des sons aux mots: comment parle-t-on du timbre musical? Unpublished doctoral dissertation, École de Hautes Études en Sciences Sociales, Paris, France (2000)
6. Gaver, W.W.: How do we hear in the world? Explorations in ecological acoustics. Ecol. Psychol. **5**(4), 285–313 (1993)
7. Gaver, W.W.: What do we hear in the world? An ecological approach to auditory event perception. Ecol. Psychol. **5**(1), 1–29 (1993)
8. Gillet, O., Richard, G.: Drum loops retrieval from spoken queries. J. Intell. Inf. Syst. **24**(2/3), 160–177 (2005)

9. Hashimoto, T., Usui, N., Taira, M., Nose, I., Haji, T., Kojima, S.: The neural mechanism associated with the processing of onomatopoeic sounds. Neuroimage **31**, 1762–1170 (2006)
10. Houix, O., Lemaitre, G., Misdariis, N., Susini, P., Urdapilleta, I.: A lexical analysis of environmental sound categories. J. Exp. Psychol. Appl. **18**(1), 52–80 (2012)
11. Ishihara, K., Nakatani, T., Ogata, T., Okuno, H.G.: Automatic sound-imitation word recognition from environmental sounds focusing on ambiguity problem in determining phonemes. In: Zhang, C., W. Guesgen, H., Yeap, W.-K. (eds.) PRICAI 2004. LNCS (LNAI), vol. 3157, pp. 909–918. Springer, Heidelberg (2004)
12. Ishihara, K., Tsubota, Y., Okuno, H.G.: Automatic transcription of environmental sounds into sound-imitation words based on japanese syllable structure. In: Proceedings of Eurospeech 2003, pp. 3185–3188. International Speech Communication Association, Geneva (2003)
13. Iwasaki, N., Vinson, D.P., Vigliocco, G.: What do English speakers know about gera-gera and yota-yota? A cross-linguistic investigation of mimetic words for laughing and walking. Japanese-language Educ. Around Globe **17**, 53–78 (2007)
14. Kahn, M.S., Högström, C.: Determination of sound quality of HVAC systems on trains using multivariate analysis. Noise Control Eng. J. **49**(6), 276–283 (2001)
15. Lass, N.J., Eastham, S.K., Parrish, W.C., Sherbick, K.A., Ralph, D.M.: Listener's identification of environnmental sounds. Percept. Mot. Skills **55**, 75–78 (1982)
16. Lass, N.J., Eastham, S.K., Wright, T.L., Hinzman, A.H., Mills, K.J., Hefferin, A.L.: Listener's identification of human-imitated sounds. Percept. Mot. Skills **57**, 995–998 (1983)
17. Lass, N.J., Hinzman, A.H., Eastham, S.K., Wright, T.L., Mills, K.J., Bartlett, B.S., Summers, P.A.: Listener's discrimination of real and human-imitated sounds. Percept. Mot. Skills **58**, 453–454 (1984)
18. Lemaitre, G., Dessein, A., Susini, P., Aura, K.: Vocal imitations and the identification of sound events. Ecol. Psychol. **23**, 267–307 (2011)
19. Lemaitre, G., Heller, L.M.: Auditory perception of material is fragile, while action is strikingly robust. J. Acoust. Soc. Am. **131**(2), 1337–1348 (2012)
20. Lemaitre, G., Houix, O., Misdariis, N., Susini, P.: Listener expertise and sound identification influence the categorization of environmental sounds. J. Exp. Psychol. Appl. **16**(1), 16–32 (2010)
21. Lemaitre, G., Rocchesso, D.: On the effectiveness of vocal imitation and ver- bal descriptions of sounds. J. Acoust. Soc. Am. **135**(2), 862–873 (2014)
22. Lemaitre, G., Susini, P., Winsberg, S., Letinturier, B., McAdams, S.: The sound quality of car horns: a psychoacoustical study of timbre. Acta Acust. United Acust. **93**(3), 457–468 (2007)
23. Lemaitre, G., Susini, P., Winsberg, S., Letinturier, B., McAdams, S.: The sound quality of car horns: designing new representative sounds. Acta Acust. United Acust. **95**(2), 356–372 (2009)
24. Nakano, T., Goto, M.: Vocalistener: a singing-to-singing synthesis system based on iterative parameter estimation. In: Proceedings of the Sound and Music Computing (SMC) Conference 2009, pp. 343–348. The Sound and Music Computing Network, Porto (2009)
25. Nakano, T., Ogata, J., Goto, M., Hiraga, Y.: A drum pattern retrieval method by voice percussion. In: Proceedings of the 5th International Conference on Music Information Retrieval (ISMIR 2004), pp. 550–553. The International Society for Music Information Retrieval, Barcelona (2004)
26. Norman, D.: The Design of Everyday Things. Basic Books, New York (2002)

27. Oswalt, R.L.: Inanimate imitatives. In: Hinton, L., Nichols, J., Ohala, J. (eds.) Sound Symbolism, pp. 293–306. Cambridge University Press, Cambridge (1994)
28. Patel, A., Iversen, J.: Acoustical and perceptual comparison of speech and drum sounds in the North India tabla tradition: an empirical study of sound symbolism. In: Proceedings of the 15th International Congress of Phonetic Sciences, pp. 925–928. Universita Autònoma de Barcelona, Barcelona (2003)
29. Pharies, D.A.: Sound symbolism in the Romance languages. Ph.D. thesis, University of California, Berkeley (1979)
30. Rhodes, R.: Aural images. In: Hinton, L., Nichols, J., Ohala, J. (eds.) Sound Symbolism, pp. 276–291. Cambridge University Press, Cambridge (1994)
31. Serafin, S., Franinović, K., Hermann, T., Lemaitre, G., Rinott, M., Rocchesso, D.: Sonic interaction design. In: Hermann, T., Hunt, A., Neuhoff, J.G. (eds.) Sonification Handbook, chap. 5, pp. 87–110. Logos Verlag, Berlin (2011)
32. Sobkowiak, W.: On the phonostatistics of English onomatopoeia. Studia Anglica Posnaniensia **23**, 15–30 (1990)
33. Strange, W., Shafer, V.: Speech perception in second language learners: the re-education of selective perception. In: Hansen Edwards, J.G., Zampini, M.L. (eds.) Phonology and Second Language Acquisition, chap. 6, pp. 153–192. John Benjamin Publishing Company, Philapelphia (2008)
34. Sundaram, S., Narayanan, S.: Vector-based representation and clustering of audio using onomatopoeia words. In: Proceedings of the American Association for Artificial Intelligence (AAAI) Symposium Series, pp. 55–58. American Association for Artificial Intelligence, Arlington (2006)
35. Sundaram, S., Narayanan, S.: Classification of sound clips by two schemes: using onomatopeia and semantic labels. In: Proceedings of the IEEE Conference on Multimedia and Exposition (ICME), pp. 1341–1344. Institute of Electrical and Electronics Engineers, Hanover (2008)
36. Takada, M., Tanaka, K., Iwamiya, S., Kawahara, K., Takanashi, A., Mori, A.: Onomatopeic features of sounds emitted from laser printers and copy machines and their contributions to product image. In: Proceedings of the International Conference on Acoustics ICA 2001. International Commission for acoustics, Rome, Italy (2001). CD-ROM available from http://www.icacommission.org/Proceedings/ICA2001Rome/. date last viewed 08 Sep 2013, paper ID: 3C.16.01
37. Takada, M., Fujisawa, N., Obata, F., Iwamiya, S.: Comparisons of auditory impressions and auditory imagery associated with onomatopoeic representations for environmental sounds. EURASIP J. Audio, Speech, Music Process. **2010**, Article ID 674248, 8p (2010)
38. Takada, M., Tanaka, K., Iwamiya, S.: Relationships between auditory impressions and onomatopoeic features for environmental sounds. Acoust. Sci. Technol. **27**(2), 67–79 (2006)
39. Troubetzkoy, N.S.: Principe de Phonologie. Librairie Klincksieck, Paris (1949)
40. Żuchowski, R.: Stops and other sound-symbolic devices expressing the relative length of referent sounds in onomatopoeia. Stud. Anglica Posnaniensia **33**, 475–485 (1998)

Influence of Rehearsal in an Auditory Memory Model for Audio Feature Estimation

Kristoffer Jensen[(✉)]

ad:mt, Aalborg University Esbjerg, Niels Bohrvej 6, 6700 Esbjerg, Denmark
krist@create.aau.dk

Abstract. Audio feature estimation involves measuring key characteristics from audio. This paper demonstrates the improvement of a feature estimation method using an auditory memory model with rehearsal included. The auditory memory model is achieved using onset detection to identify new audio components for insertion into the auditory memory, and an algorithm that then combines the characteristics of the current interval with those of the audio components in the auditory memory. The auditory memory model mimics the storing, retrieval and forgetting processes of the short-term memory, and in this work the rehearsal as well. The feature estimation using the auditory memory model has been successfully applied to the estimation of sensory dissonance, and the characteristics of the memory model has been shown to be of interest in music categorization. The rehearsal step in the memory model is an important step in the understanding of the model. In addition, the dissonance estimation correlation with human ratings is tested with or without including rehearsal in the auditory memory model.

Keywords: Feature estimation · Onset detection · Auditory memory · Rehearsal · Dissonance

1 Introduction

Audio feature estimation has many potential uses, of which music information retrieval (MIR) is an important one. In MIR, features are used to categorize, segment, or otherwise gain knowledge about the music. While audio feature estimation is not the only option for music recommendation, it presents a promising possibility. However, in order to use audio features in MIR, it is necessary to obtain robust, noise-free and informative features. The computational auditory memory model [7] that has been shown to be of use in categorization tasks [8], is here improved by the inclusion of rehearsal, i.e. the activation strength of elements in the memory model is increased when similar elements are introduced.

Human memory [5] is today divided into three stages; a sensory store, the short-term (working) memory, and the long-term memory (Atkinson and Shiffrin [2]). The short-term memory has different modalities [3]. Of these, the phonological loop is of interest here. The phonological loop consists of two parts, the articulatory store and loop. The store part is subject to rapid decay, unless the loop revives the trace, by continually repeating the current auditory events. This last part is supposedly a voluntary effect, controlled by the central executive. Opposed to this model that increases

© Springer International Publishing Switzerland 2014
M. Aramaki et al. (Eds.): CMMR 2013, LNCS 8905, pp. 575–585, 2014.
DOI: 10.1007/978-3-319-12976-1_35

the strength of the auditory trace by repeating the same trace internally [2, 3] is the more popular notion of rehearsal [14] when repeating the stimuli several times, either by rote rehearsal, in which the stimuli is repeated without changes, or by elaborative learning, by making inferences and elaborating on the learning. In this paper, when rehearsal is mentioned, rote rehearsal should be understood.

This paper first presents the auditory memory model in Sect. 2 with particular emphasis on the introduction of rehearsal and similarity measures and the behavior of these components, and then it shows how the auditory memory model can be integrated into the estimation of dissonance in Sect. 3, where the introduction of rehearsal in the auditory memory model is shown to improve the dissonance measure.

2 An Auditory Memory Model

Humans use memory to encode, store and retrieve information. Auditory information enters the brain through the auditory system and reaches the sensory store first. If the information is not reinforced it fades. Gross [5] gives three main causes of the mechanisms that causes fading: decay, which indicates a breakdown of the mental representation over time; displacement, which indicates that the memory has limited capacity, components in the auditory memory may be discarded when new components enter; and interference, the strength of the information in the auditory memory is affected by the context.

While Miller [12] gives the capacity of the short-term memory (STM) to be 7 ± 2 elements, the knowledge of the capacity of the STM is compromised by complications due to separating the STM from the LTM. Thus, Cowan [4] decreases the capacity of

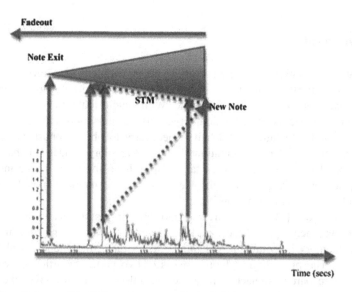

Fig. 1. The auditory model consists of an onset detector (below), and a store with a fading and exit mechanism (above).

the STM to 4 ± 1, and gives information about how to observe the pure storage capacity. There are reasons to believe that the short-term storage capacity is higher in practice, because of uses of other memory mechanisms. For instance, the echoic memory [14], responsible for storing auditory information in the STM, is capable of storing large amounts of auditory information for 3–4 s.

The model of the STM used here is shown in Fig. 1. It has two main components, the onset detector that identifies new auditory components, and the store that retains the components until it is purged. This model was first introduced in [7]. It has been shown to estimate the dissonance better than sensory dissonance without the use of a memory model when compared to human ratings [9].

2.1   Onset Detection

The onset detection is a modified spectral flux, called perceptual spectral flux (*psf*) [10], and is calculated as the sum of the magnitudes of all bins that are rising, scaled with the frequency weight. A peak detector algorithm is used that identifies onsets when the instantaneous value of the *psf* is above a weighted mean and maximum of the *psf* over a frame of a few seconds. The detector algorithm captures many of the features used by humans to separate auditory streams, including fundamental frequency, onset times, contrast to previous sounds and correlated changes in amplitude or frequency.

For each onset detected, an estimate of the new spectral content is inserted into the auditory model. This estimation, called the added spectrum, is calculated as the difference between the spectrums 0.04 s after and 0.1 s before. The post-element was 0.2 s in the previous studies involving the auditory memory model [7–9]. Other improvements to the auditory memory model include better onset detection, and speed-up optimizations. These changes affect the behavior and the characteristics of the auditory memory model, so the results presented here cannot be directly compared with earlier results.

2.2   Auditory Memory Model

The auditory memory model (AMM) has three functions; inserting new auditory components into the memory (storing), extracting this auditory component for further processing (remembering), and finally purging the auditory component when it has a low strength (forgetting). The actual activation strength of the auditory components in the memory model is calculated in a homogenous manner inspired by the activation model of Anderson and Lebiere [1]. In their model of memory decay, the activation strength of an element in the memory is weakened logarithmically with the duration. The displacement is modeled in the AMM in a similar manner, where the time is replaced with the number of auditory components currently in the auditory memory. The total activation strength is finally a sum of the two. As long as the total activation strength of an auditory component in the memory model is positive, this component is retained to further processing. When the activation strength is zero or below, the auditory component is purged from the memory. This model was first presented in [7]. The activation strength for an element k in the auditory memory is estimated as

$$A_k = A_t + A_N = 1 - 0.5 \ln(t_k + 1) + 1 - 0.5 \ln(N_k + 1). \tag{1}$$

Where t_k is the time of the current element (k) in the auditory model, and N_k is the number of elements in the memory model. A feature to be estimated will be given a value from the current audio element and the interaction between this element and the previous audio elements, multiplied by the activation strengths of the previous elements. In this way, the decay and displacement of the auditory elements are taken into account when calculating the activation strength.

The auditory elements interact and affect the activation strength because of the similarity or interference of the elements. This is integrated into the total activation strength in three steps; first, the similarity between the current element and the previous elements is calculated using the cosine distance

$$\text{sim}_k = S_c(sp, asp_k), \tag{2}$$

where S_c is the cosine distance, sp is the spectrum of the current auditory element, and asp_k is the added spectrum of the kth element in the auditory memory model. For each new auditory element, the similarities between this element and all the elements in the auditory memory are calculated and the rehearsal strength r_k of each auditory element is increased by the similarity between this element and the current element

$$r_k = r_k + sim_k, \tag{3}$$

and finally, the updated activation strength, taking into account the rehearsal strength

$$A_r = 0.1\ln(r_k + 1) \tag{4}$$

is

$$A_k = 1 - 0.5\ln(t_k + 1) + 1 - 0.5\ln(N_k + 1) + 0.1\ln(r_k + 1). \tag{5}$$

Contrary to the decay and displacement, where the activation strength is decreasing with the duration and number of elements, the rehearsal is increasing the activation strength, when more similar elements are arriving. This enables the recurrent auditory element to stay in the memory for a longer duration. As an example of the added activation strength caused by the rehearsal, Fig. 2 shows the similarity for seven contemporary classical music pieces (left), and the A_r influence to the total activation strength (right).

It is important to remember that the similarity and rehearsal values are calculated for each element in the auditory memory model, and every time a new element is detected by the onset detection method. The similarity has a skewed 'u' shape, with many dissimilar auditory elements, but also quite a large percentage of very similar values. The total rehearsal values have a peak around zero and another peak around one.

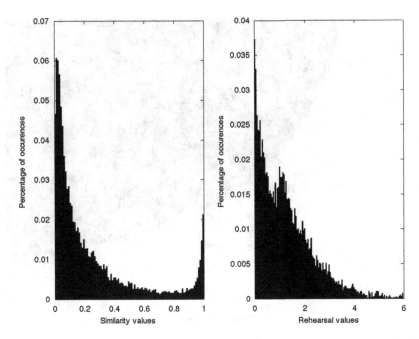

Fig. 2. Histograms of similarity (left), and rehearsal activation strength (right) for seven contemporary classical music pieces.

2.3   Content and Behavior of AM

The auditory model encodes and stores auditory components in the form of the added spectrum at the time of each onset. These components are retained for a certain time in the auditory memory until the component is purged. The characteristics of the memory model consist of the number of concurrent auditory components, and the duration of the memory. In Fig. 3 is shown the range of possible auditory memory model duration and number of components. In the figure, the color indicates the activation strength of one element that had been in the memory at the indicated duration at the same time as the indicated number of elements. White corresponds to activation strengths from 1.5 to 2 (when few elements occurres for a short time), and black corresponds to negative activation strength, corresponding to too many elements occurring for too long. Thus, the high activation strengths are found when few components are present in the auditory memory for a short time. Typically, the auditory memory content will be found in the upper left side, i.e. with relatively many auditory components, and relatively short memory duration.

In order to show the behavior of the auditory memory, two songs (*Whenever, Wherever* by Shakira and *All of Me* by Billie Holiday) have been processed. The resulting behavior with respect to duration and number of components of the auditory memory are shown in Fig. 4. The duration is the time of the element that has been the longest in the memory, calculated at every new onset.

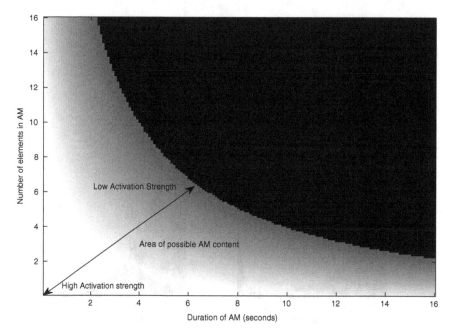

Fig. 3. Activation strength as a function of duration and number of elements. When an auditory component reaches the black area, it is forgotten.

The memory model characteristics with regards to duration and number of components are shown in Fig. 4 for two songs. It is clear that the songs have a stable behavior with respect to the auditory memory, resulting without rehearsal component (left), in a duration from 3 to 6 s and a number of components which varies between 6 and 11. The introduction of the rehearsal component increases the duration (from mean 4.26 s. to 4.96 s) and the number of components (from mean 8.07 to 9.25). The actual values fluctuate systematically, seemingly with the complexity of the music, and with negative correlation, i.e. when the number of components rises the duration falls and vice versa. *Whenever, Wherever* has a mean duration of 4.92 s (4.67 without rehearsal), and a mean number of components of 9.79 (9.39), *All of Me* has a mean duration of 5.01 s (4.97) and a mean number of components of 8.69 (8.75). The pop song thus seems to increase the mean duration and number of components, while the jazz song is less affected by the introduction of the rehearsal component. This is due to the more varied style of the latter and it effectively lowers the rehearsal values from mean 1.7 for the pop song to mean 1.0 for the jazz song).

The reason for this can be seen in Fig. 5. *Whenever, Wherever* (left) has much higher similarity (mean 0.31), and no totally dissimilar elements (similarity equal to zero), while *All of Me* (right) has an exponentially decreasing histogram, with many totally dissimilar auditory elements in the memory (mean 0.19), These changes in similarity is naturally translated into higher rehearsal values for *Whenever, Wherever*.

The general improvements mentioned above and the introduction of the rehearsal component have lowered the number of elements from between 12 and 14 to around 9.

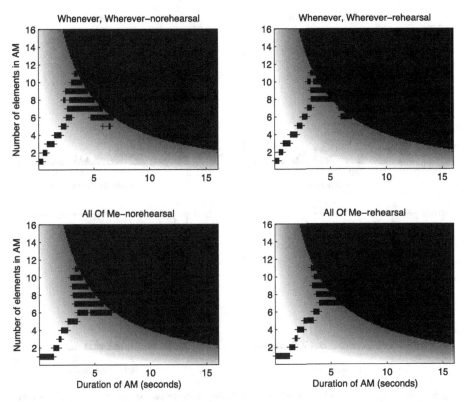

Fig. 4. Auditory memory duration and number of components without (left) and with (right) the rehearsal component for two songs. *Whenever, Wherever* (top), *All of Me* (bottom).

While this number is still above that of Miller [12], much of the content in the auditory memory has low activation strength, and the effective number of components is closer to the Miller number.

Snyder [16] gives the STM span of 3–5 s, which corresponds well to the numbers found here for the auditory memory model, again, in particular taking into account the weak activation strength of the components that has been in the auditory memory a long time.

All in all, the behavior of the model is reasonable when compared with knowledge of human short-term memory. The auditory memory model is closer to the theory after the improvements, speed-ups and the introduction of the rehearsal component.

3 Dissonance Measure

Dissonance is the first feature that has been subjected to processing through the auditory memory model. Sensory dissonance is related to the beatings between sinusoids over different auditory filters. There can be many beatings within the same sound, and the influence of the resulting sensory dissonance is additive [13]. The beatings will

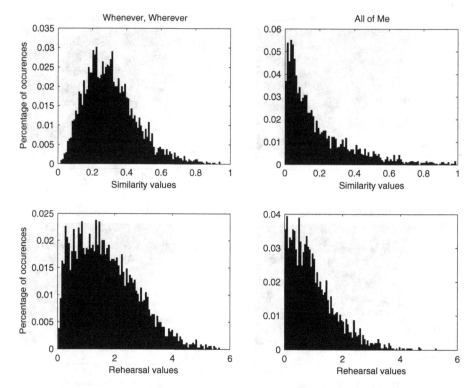

Fig. 5. Similarity (top) and Rehearsal (bottom) histograms for two songs, Whenever, Wherever (left), and All of Me (right).

be maximum at approximately one quarter of the critical band, and zero for low frequency beatings and for frequency differences above a critical band. In this work, the Plomb and Levelt model [13] is used, using the algorithms of [15]. In addition, the power law introduced in [11] is also used now, with β = 0.3.

In order to calculate the total sensory dissonance for one frame, all individual sensory dissonance values are added together. This is done for all spectral peaks within one critical band in the current frame. Because of the additive nature of the sensory dissonance, it is further hypothesized here that the influences of the spectral peaks in the auditory memory contribute to the sensory dissonance in the same additive manner, i.e. each spectral peak in the memory beats with the peaks in the current frame and the corresponding sensory dissonance is added to the total dissonance, scaled by the activation strength of the auditory memory components.

The total sensory dissonance has now been calculated with and without the memory model and the rehearsal component for seven contemporary classical music pieces. These are the same songs used in [9], and the goal is to see if the inclusion of the rehearsal component in the memory model improves the correlation with the human assessment of dissonance that has been made for the same songs. The results cannot be directly compared to earlier studies, because of the improvement and speed-up done to the algorithms.

In the experiment, 21 music listeners were asked to rate the tension of the music (9 pieces) by adjusting a slider [9]. These ratings were first introduced in [6]. The ratings were then compared to the different sensory dissonance measures, the one without the memory model and the one using the memory model according to [7], with all improvements and speed-up optimizations, and finally the one also including the rehearsal component. The maximum correlation values between the sensory dissonance and the human ratings are shown in Table 1.

Table 1. Results showing the correlation (ρ) between mean human tension rating and sensory dissonance with out and with memory model, and with and without rehearsal when using the memory model.

Genre	Composer	Duration	P (w/o) mm	ρ (w) mm	ρ (w) mm + r
Tonal	Mozart	7'24"	0.11	0.23	0.26
Tonal	Mozart MIDI	5'55"	0.20	0.15	0.24
Atonal	Webern	2'03"	0.50	0.60	0.62
Atonal	Webern MIDI	1'53"	0.07	0.13	0.14
Electronic	Stockhausen	0'28"	0.56	0.52	0.60
Electronic	Stockhausen	0'27"	0.64	0.74	0.77
Electronic	Stockhausen	1'00"	0.45	0.50	0.45
Electronic	Alva Noto	0'47"	0.19	0.30	0.36
Tonal	Debussy	0'39"	0.19	0.28	0.35

Most of the music available here does not give a strong rehearsal value like music with repeating notes would. The main improvement of the rehearsal is in popular music, as for instance seen in the higher similarities between auditory elements and the stronger rehearsal activation strength in the pop song (*Whenever, Wherever*), as compared to the jazz song (*All of Me*). Still, an improvement is observed for most of the songs and while a larger improvement is found for the introduction of the memory model compared to the sensory dissonance without a memory model, the introduction of the rehearsal component is also improving the correlation. In order to assess the validity of this observation, Friedman's non-parametric test is used. The memory model and the rehearsal component are correlating significantly differently ($\chi^2(2) = 9.56$, $p < 0.05$). However, further analysis shows that the rehearsal component is not significantly different to the memory model. The memory model relative mean improvement is 30 %, and the rehearsal component mean improvement is 10 %.

4   Conclusion

The feature estimation using the auditory memory model [7] predicts human tension ratings better [9], and it is of interest for music information retrieval [8]. The auditory memory model is comprised of two parts; the onset detection can be compared with the attention with which human beings focus on the sound, and the memory model is based on the knowledge retained within short-term memory, and contains a homogenous decay and displacement mechanism that calculates the activation strength of the components in the auditory memory as a function of the number of components in the memory model, and the total duration of the model. The memory model mimics the storing, retrieval and forgetting of the human auditory short-term memory. In this paper, an improvement to the memory model is introduced. The rehearsal gives more activation strength to audio components that are repeated, or similar to new auditory elements. It has been shown here that the selected pop music has more similar auditory elements, and thus has a higher mean rehearsal activation strength component, as compared to jazz.

The rehearsal component also seems to improve the memory model, so that its characteristics, with regards to the number of elements and durations, behaves in a manner that is better compatible with that of the human auditory short-term memory.

The auditory memory model has been used to improve the calculation of sensory dissonance. Sensory dissonance is additive for partials within the same time frame. Sensory dissonance is also modeled as being additive for the partials that belong to the auditory components in the memory. These partials are thus modeled as giving rise to beats together with the partials in the current time frame. The resulting sensory dissonance is shown to be smoother, and to have a larger magnitude. In addition, the improved memory model, with rehearsal activation strength is shown to perform better than the auditory model without rehearsal in a correlation study comparing sensory dissonance calculated with and without the memory models and the rehearsal component.

Both the characteristics of the auditory memory model, with regards to the duration and number of components, and the sensory dissonance calculated using the model, are shown to be informative about music. The auditory memory model with rehearsal and the associated sensory dissonance calculation process provide a promising technology for music information retrieval.

References

1. Anderson, J.R., Lebiere, C.: Atomic Components of Thought. LEA, Hillsdale (1998)
2. Atkinson, R.C., Shiffrin, R.M.: Human memory: a proposed system and its control processes. In: Spence, K.W., Spence, J.T. (eds.) The Psychology of Learning and Motivation, vol. 2, pp. 89–195. Academic Press, New York (1968)
3. Baddeley, A.D., Hitch, G.: Working memory. In: Bower, G.H. (ed.) The Psychology of Learning and Motivation: Advances in Research and Theory, vol. 8, pp. 47–89. Academic Press, New York (1974)
4. Cowan, N.: The magical number 4 in short-term memory: a reconsideration of mental storage capacity. Behav. Brain Sci. **24**, 87–185 (2000)
5. Gross, R.: Psychology: the science of mind and behaviour. Hodder Arnold Publication, London (2005)
6. Hjortkjær, J.: Toward a cognitive theory of musical tension. Ph.D. thesis, University of Copenhagen (2011)

7. Jensen, K.: On the use of memory models in audio features. In: Symposium of Frontiers of Research on Speech and Computer Music Modeling and retrieval (FRSM/CMMR - 2011), pp. 100–107. Bhubaneswar, India, 9–12 Mar 2011

8. Jensen, Kristoffer: Music genre classification using an auditory memory model. In: Ystad, Sølvi, Aramaki, Mitsuko, Kronland-Martinet, Richard, Jensen, Kristoffer, Mohanty, Sanghamitra (eds.) CMMR and FRSM 2011. LNCS, vol. 7172, pp. 79–88. Springer, Heidelberg (2012)

9. Jensen, K., Hjortkjær, J.: An improved dissonance measure using auditory memory. J. Acoust. Soc. Am. **60**(5), 350–354 (2012)

10. Jensen, K.: Multiple scale music segmentation using rhythm, timbre and harmony. EURASIP Journal on Applied Signal Processing, Special issue on Music Information Retrieval Based on Signal Processing **2007**, 11 (2007)

11. Kameoka, A., Kurivagawa, M.: Consonance theory part 1-2. J. Acoust. Soc. Am. **45**(6), 1451–1469 (1969)

12. Miller, G.A.: The magical number seven plus or minus two: some limits on our capacity for processing information. Psychol. Rev. **63**(2), 81–97 (1956)

13. Plomp, R., Levelt, W.J.M.: Tonal consonance and critical bandwidth. J. Acoust. Soc. Am. **38**(4), 548–560 (1965)

14. Radvansky, G.: Human Memory. Allyn and Bacon, Boston (2005)

15. Sethares, W.: Local consonance and the relationship between timbre and scale. J. Acoust. Soc. Am. **94**(3), 1218–1228 (1993)

16. Snyder, B.: Music and Memory. An Introduction. The MIT Press, Cambridge (2000)

Modeling of Sound
and Music - Computational Musicology

Cognitive Similarity Grounded by Tree Distance from the Analysis of K.265/300e

Keiji Hirata[1]([✉]), Satoshi Tojo[2], and Masatoshi Hamanaka[3]

[1] Future University Hakodate, 116-2 Kamedanakano-cho,
Hakodate, Hokkaido 041-8655, Japan
hirata@fun.ac.jp
[2] Japan Advanced Institute of Science and Technology,
1-1 Asahidai, Nomi, Ishikawa 923-1292, Japan
tojo@jaist.ac.jp
[3] Kyoto University, 46-29 Yoshida-Shimoadachicho, Sakyo, Kyoto 606-8501, Japan
masatosh@kuhp.kyoto-u.ac.jp

Abstract. Lerdahl and Jackendoff's theory employed a tree in a representation of internal structure of music. In order for us to claim that such a tree is a consistent and stable representation, we argue that the difference of trees should correctly reflect our cognitive distance of music. We report our experimental result concerning the comparison of similarity among variations on *Ah vous dirai-je, maman*, K. 265/300e by Mozart. First we measure the distance in trees between two variations by the sum of the lengths of time-spans, and then we compare the result with the human psychological similarity. We show a statistical analysis of the distance and discuss the adequacy of it as a criteria of similarity.

Keywords: Time-span tree · Generative theory of tonal music · Join/meet operations · Cognitive similarity

1 Introduction

Music theory gives us methodology to analyze music written on scores, and clarifies their inherent features in a comprehensive way. There have been many attempts to embody a music theory onto a computer system and to build a music analyzer. In particular, some music theories employ trees to represent the deep structure of a musical piece [1,6,10,11,15], and such a tree representation seems a promising way to automatize the analyzing process. It is, however, widely recognized that there are intrinsic difficulties in this; (i) how we can formalize ambiguous or missing concepts and (ii) how we can assess the consistency and stability of a fomalized music theory.

For (i), the approaches include the externalization of those hidden features of music. For example, Lerdahl and Jackendoff [10] (the generative theory of tonal music; GTTM hereafter) specified many rules to retrieve such information in music to obtain a time-span tree, though they proposed only heuristics

© Springer International Publishing Switzerland 2014
M. Aramaki et al. (Eds.): CMMR 2013, LNCS 8905, pp. 589–605, 2014.
DOI: 10.1007/978-3-319-12976-1_36

and missed fully explicit algorithms. Thus, to formalize this theory, we have complemented necessary parameters to clarify the process of time-span reduction [8]. Pearce and Wiggins [14] have built a model to derive as many features as possible from the scores; these features contain the properties of potentially non-contiguous events.

For (ii), we do not think there is an agreeable solution yet, but we propose to assess the consistency and the stability of a formalized music theory based on our cognitive reality. If the tree representation derived by a formalized music theory is sufficiently stable and consistent, the distance between those representations must reflect our human intuition on difference in music. Hence, if we are to compare the tree distance and our psychological difference and/or similarity, we can evaluate the consistency and the stability of a formalized music theory.

Here, we look back at the studies on similarity in music. In music information research, the similarity has been drawing attention of many researchers [9,19]. Some of the researchers are motivated by engineering demands such as music retrieval, classification, and recommendation, [7,13,16] and others by modeling the cognitive processes of musical similarity [4,5]. Several types of similarity have been proposed, including melodic similarity, e.g., van Kranenburg (2010) [18] and harmonic similarity, e.g., de Haas (2012) [3]. The song similarity in MIREX is widely recognized as an important category in the contest [12]. All these viewpoints suggest the importance of quantitative comparison, and thus we employ a numeric distance in measuring the cognitive similarity.

We have proposed a notion of distance among the time-span trees [17], however, in that research there lacked the discussion on the perception of similarity. As a result, it was difficult for us to explain that the distance could be a metric of similarity [3,9,13,18]. The contribution of this paper is that we have actually conducted a psychological experiment on the similarity among 12 variations on *Ah vous dirai-je, maman*, K. 265/300e by Wolfgang Amadeus Mozart, in comparison with the corresponding time-span distance.

This paper is organized as follows: in Sect. 2 we briefly summarize the notion of time-span tree and reduction. In Sect. 3, we introduce our notion of distance in time-span trees. Then, to apply the notion to arbitrary two music pieces, we generalize the distance in Sect. 4. In Sect. 5, we report our experimental result. First we measure the distance between two variations by the tree distance, and then we compare the result with the human psychological resemblance. We show the statistical analysis, and discuss the adequacy of our measure as a metric of similarity in Sect. 6. Finally we conclude in Sect. 7.

2   Time-Span Tree and Reduction

Time-span reduction in Lerdahl and Jackendoff's Generative Theory of Tonal Music (GTTM; hereafter) [10] assigns structural importance to each pitch events in the hierarchical way. The structural importance is derived from the *grouping analysis*, in which multiple notes compose a short phrase called a group, and from the *metrical analysis*, where strong and weak beats are properly assigned on each pitch event. As a result, a time-span tree becomes a binary tree constructed in bottom-up and top-down manners by comparison between the structural importance of adjacent pitch events at each hierarchical level. Although a pitch event means a single note or a chord, we restrict our interest to monophonic analysis in this paper, as the method of chord recognition is not included in the original theory. Figure 1 shows an excerpt from [10] demonstrating the concept of reduction. In the sequence of reductions, each reduction should sound like a simplification of the previous one. In other words, the more reductions proceed, each sounds dissimilar to the original. Reduction can be regarded as abstraction, but if we could find a proper way of reduction, we can retrieve a basic melody line of the original music piece. The key idea of our framework is that reduction is

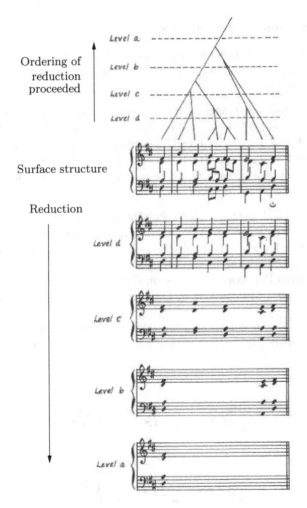

Fig. 1. Reduction hierarchy of chorale 'O Haupt voll Blut und Wunden' in St. Matthew's Passion by J.S. Bach [10, p. 115]

identified with the subsumption relation, which is the most fundamental relation in knowledge representation.

3   Strict Distance in Time-Span Reduction

In the section, the basic formalization of time-span trees is given as a prerequisite for extending our framework to be described later. Since the contents presented in the section overlap some of those in [17] and contain rather mathematical stuff, the readers who first want to comprehend an outline of the contributions could move onto the experimental section. Then, the readers would come back here afterward.

3.1   Subsumption, *Join*, and *Meet*

First we define the notion of *subsumption*. Let σ_1 and σ_2 be tree structures. σ_2 subsumes σ_1, that is, $\sigma_1 \sqsubseteq \sigma_2$ if and only if for any branch in σ_1 there is a corresponding branch in σ_2.

Definition 1 (*Join* and *Meet*). *Let σ_A and σ_B be tree structures for music A and B, respectively. If we can fix the least upper bound of σ_A and σ_B, that is, the least y such that $\sigma_A \sqsubseteq y$ and $\sigma_B \sqsubseteq y$ is unique, we call such y the join of σ_A and σ_B, denoted as $\sigma_A \sqcup \sigma_B$. If we can fix the greatest lower bound of σ_A and σ_B, that is, the greatest x such that $x \sqsubseteq \sigma_A$ and $x \sqsubseteq \sigma_B$ is unique, we call such x the meet of σ_A and σ_B, denoted as $\sigma_A \sqcap \sigma_B$.*

We illustrate *join* and *meet* in a simple example in Fig. 2. The '$\sqcup$' (*join*) operation takes quavers in the scores, so that missing note in one side is complemented. On the other hand, the '$\sqcap$' (*meet*) operation takes $\bot$ for mismatching features [2], and thus only the common notes appear as a result.

Obviously from Definition 1, we obtain the absorption laws: $\sigma_A \sqcup x = \sigma_A$ and $\sigma_A \sqcap x = x$ if $x \sqsubseteq \sigma_A$. Moreover, if $\sigma_A \sqsubseteq \sigma_B$, $x \sqcup \sigma_A \sqsubseteq x \sqcup \sigma_B$ and $x \sqcap \sigma_A \sqsubseteq x \sqcap \sigma_B$ for any x.

We can define $\sigma_A \sqcup \sigma_B$ and $\sigma_A \sqcap \sigma_B$ in recursive functions. In the process of unification between σ_A and σ_B, when a single branch is unifiable with a tree,

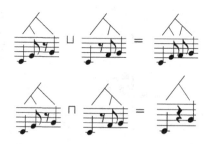

Fig. 2. *Join* and *meet*

$\sigma_A \sqcup \sigma_B$ chooses the tree while $\sigma_A \sqcap \sigma_B$ chooses the branch, in a recursive way. Because there is no alternative action in these procedures, $\sigma_A \sqcup \sigma_B$ and $\sigma_A \sqcap \sigma_B$ exist uniquely. Thus, the partially ordered set of time-span trees becomes a *lattice*.

3.2   Maximal Time-Span and Reduction Distance

In GTTM, a listener is supposed to construct mentally pitch hierarchies (reductions) that express maximal importance among pitch relations [10, p. 118]. We here observe a time-span becomes longer as the level of time-span hierarchy goes higher. Then, we can suppose that a longer time-span contains more information, and it is therefore regarded more important.

Based on the above consideration, we hypothesize:

If a branch with a single pitch event is reduced, the amount of information corresponding to the length of its time-span is lost.

We call a sequence of reductions of a music piece *reduction path*. We regard the sum of the length of such lost time-spans as the distance of two trees, in the reduction path. Thereafter, we generalize the notion to be feasible, not only in a reduction path but in any direction in the lattice.

We presuppose that branches are reduced only one by one, for the convenience to sum up distances. A branch is *reducible* only in the bottom-up way, i.e., a reducible branch possesses no other sub-branches except a single pitch event at its leaf. In the similar way, we call the reverse operation *elaboration*; we can attach a new sub-branch when the original branch consists only of a single event.

The *head* pitch event of a tree structure is the most salient event of the whole tree. Though the event itself retains its original duration, we may regard its saliency is extended to the whole tree. The situation is the same as each subtree. Thus, we consider that each pitch event has the maximal length of saliency.

Definition 2 (Maximal Time-Span). *Each pitch event has the maximal time-span within which the event becomes most salient, and outside the time-span the salience is lost.*

In Fig. 3(a), there are four contiguous pitch events, e1, e2, e3, and e4; each has its own temporal span (duration on surface), s1, s2, s3, and s4, denoted thin lines. Figure 3(b) depicts time-span trees and corresponding maximal time-span hierarchies, denoted gray thick lines. The relationships between spans in (a) and maximal time-spans in (b) as follows. At the lowest level in the hierarchy, the length of a span is equal to that of a maximal time-span; mt2 = s2, mt3 = s3. At the higher levels, mt1 = s1 + mt2, and mt4 = mt1 + mt3 + s4 = s1 + s2 + s3 + s4. That is, every span extends itself by concatenating the span at a lower level along the configuration of a time-span tree. When all subordinate spans are concatenated up into a span, the span reaches the maximal time-span.

Only the events at the lowest level in the hierarchy are reducible; the other events cannot be reduced. In Fig. 3(b), for the leftmost time-span tree $\sigma 1$, either

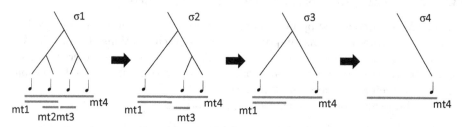

(a) Sequence of pitch events and their spans

(b) Reduction proceeds by removing a reducible maximal time-span

Fig. 3. Reduction of time-span tree and maximal time-span hierarchy; gray thick lines denote maximal time-spans while thin ones pitch durations

e2 or e3 is reducible; e2 is first reduced then e3. For $\sigma 2$, e3 is only reducible, not e1 because e1 is not at the lowest level in the maximal time-span hierarchy.

Let $\varsigma(\sigma)$ be a set of pitch events in σ, $\sharp\varsigma(\sigma)$ be its cardinality, and s_e be the maximal time-span of event e. Since reduction is made by one reducible branch at a time, a reduction path $\sigma^n, \sigma^{n-1}, \ldots, \sigma^2, \sigma^1, \sigma^0$, such that $\sigma^n \sqsupseteq \sigma^{n-1} \sqsupseteq \cdots \sqsupseteq \sigma^2 \sqsupseteq \sigma^1 \sqsupseteq \sigma^0$, suffices $\sharp\varsigma(\sigma^{i+1}) = \sharp\varsigma(\sigma^i) + 1$. If we put $\sigma_A = \sigma^0$ and $\sigma_B = \sigma^n$, $\sigma_A \sqsubseteq \sigma_B$ holds by transitivity. For each reduction step, when a reducible branch on event e disappears, its maximal time-span s_e is accumulated as distance.

Definition 3 (Reduction Distance). *The distance $d_\sqsubseteq$ of two time-span trees such that $\sigma_A \sqsubseteq \sigma_B$ in a reduction path is defined by*

$$d_\sqsubseteq(\sigma_A, \sigma_B) = \sum_{e \in \varsigma(\sigma_B) \setminus \varsigma(\sigma_A)} s_e.$$

For example in Fig. 3, the distance between $\sigma 1$ and $\sigma 4$ becomes $mt1 + mt2 + mt3$. Note that if e3 is first reduced and e2 is subsequently reduced, the distance is the same. Although the distance is a simple summation of maximal time-spans at a glance, there is a latent order in the addition, for reducible branches are different in each reduction step. In order to give a constructive procedure on this summation, we introduce the notion of total sum of maximal time-spans.

Definition 4 (Total Maximal Time-Span). *Given tree structure σ,*

$$tmt(\sigma) = \sum_{e \in \varsigma(\sigma)} s_e.$$

When $\sigma_A \sqsubseteq \sigma_B$, from Definitions 3 and 4, $d_\sqsubseteq(\sigma_A, \sigma_B) = tmt(\sigma_B) - tmt(\sigma_A)$. As a special case of the above, $d_\sqsubseteq(\bot, \sigma) = tmt(\sigma)$.

3.3 Properties of Distance

Uniqueness of Reduction Distance: First, as there is a reduction path between $\sigma_A \sqcap \sigma_B$ and $\sigma_A \sqcup \sigma_B$, and $\sigma_A \sqcap \sigma_B \sqsubseteq \sigma_A \sqcup \sigma_B$, $d_\sqsubseteq(\sigma_A \sqcap \sigma_B, \sigma_A \sqcup \sigma_B)$ is computed by the difference of total maximal time-span. Because the algorithm returns a unique value, for any reduction path from $\sigma_A \sqcup \sigma_B$ to $\sigma_A \sqcap \sigma_B$, $d_\sqsubseteq(\sigma_A \sqcap \sigma_B, \sigma_A \sqcup \sigma_B)$ is unique. This implies the uniqueness of reduction distance: if there exist reduction paths from σ_A to σ_B, $d_\sqsubseteq(\sigma_A, \sigma_B)$ is unique.

Next, from set-theoretical calculus, $\varsigma(\sigma_A \sqcup \sigma_B) \backslash \varsigma(\sigma_A) = \varsigma(\sigma_B) \backslash \varsigma(\sigma_A \sqcap \sigma_B)$. Then, $d_\sqsubseteq(\sigma_A, \sigma_A \sqcup \sigma_B) = \sum_{e \in \varsigma(\sigma_A \sqcup \sigma_B) \backslash \varsigma(\sigma_A)} s_e = \sum_{e \in \varsigma(\sigma_B) \backslash \varsigma(\sigma_A \sqcap \sigma_B)} s_e = d_\sqsubseteq(\sigma_A \sqcap \sigma_B, \sigma_B)$. Therefore, $d_\sqsubseteq(\sigma_A, \sigma_A \sqcup \sigma_B) = d_\sqsubseteq(\sigma_A \sqcap \sigma_B, \sigma_B)$ and $d_\sqsubseteq(\sigma_B, \sigma_A \sqcup \sigma_B) = d_\sqsubseteq(\sigma_A \sqcap \sigma_B, \sigma_A)$.

Here let us define two ways of distances.

$$d_\sqcap(\sigma_A, \sigma_B) = d_\sqsubseteq(\sigma_A \sqcap \sigma_B, \sigma_A) + d_\sqsubseteq(\sigma_A \sqcap \sigma_B, \sigma_B)$$
$$d_\sqcup(\sigma_A, \sigma_B) = d_\sqsubseteq(\sigma_A, \sigma_A \sqcup \sigma_B) + d_\sqsubseteq(\sigma_B, \sigma_A \sqcup \sigma_B)$$

Then, we immediately obtain $d_\sqcup(\sigma_A, \sigma_B) = d_\sqcap(\sigma_A, \sigma_B)$ by the uniqueness of reduction distance.

For any σ', σ'' such that $\sigma_A \sqsubseteq \sigma' \sqsubseteq \sigma_A \sqcup \sigma_B, \sigma_B \sqsubseteq \sigma'' \sqsubseteq \sigma_A \sqcup \sigma_B, d_\sqcup(\sigma_A, \sigma') + d_\sqcap(\sigma', \sigma'') + d_\sqcup(\sigma'', \sigma_B) = d_\sqcup(\sigma_A, \sigma_B)$. Ditto for the meet distance. Now the notion of distance, which was initially defined in the reduction path as $d_\sqsubseteq$ is now generalized to $d_{\{\sqcap, \sqcup\}}$, and in addition we have shown they have the same values. From now on, we omit $\{\sqcap, \sqcup\}$ from $d_{\{\sqcap, \sqcup\}}$, simply denoting 'd'. Here, $d(\sigma_A, \sigma_B)$ is unique among shortest paths between σ_A and σ_B. Note that shortest paths can be found in ordinary graph-search methods, such as *branch and bound*, Dijkstra's algorithm, best-first search, and so on. As a corollary, we also obtain $d(\sigma_A, \sigma_B) = d(\sigma_A \sqcup \sigma_B, \sigma_A \sqcap \sigma_B)$.

Triangle Inequality: Finally, as $d(\sigma_A, \sigma_B) + d(\sigma_B, \sigma_C)$ becomes the sum of maximal time-spans in $\varsigma(\sigma_A \sqcup \sigma_B) \backslash \varsigma(\sigma_A \sqcap \sigma_B)$ plus those in $\varsigma(\sigma_B \sqcup \sigma_C) \backslash \varsigma(\sigma_B \sqcap \sigma_C)$ while $d(\sigma_A, \sigma_C)$ becomes $\varsigma(\sigma_A \sqcup \sigma_C) \backslash \varsigma(\sigma_A \sqcap \sigma_C)$, we obtain $d(\sigma_A, \sigma_B) + d(\sigma_B, \sigma_C) \geq d(\sigma_A, \sigma_C)$: the triangle inequality. For more details on the theoretical stuff, see [17].

In Fig. 4, we have laid out various reductions originated from a piece. As we can find three reducible branches in A there are three different reductions: B, C, and D. In the figure, C (shown diluted) lies behind the lattice where three backside edges meet. The distances, represented by the length of edges, from A to B, D to F, C to E, and G to H are the same, since the reduced branch is common. Namely, the reduction lattice becomes parallelepiped,[1] and the distances from A to H becomes uniquely $2 + 2 + 2 = 6$. We exemplify the triangle inequality; from A through B to F, the distance becomes $2+2 = 4$, and that from F through D to G is $2 + 2 = 4$, thus the total path length becomes $4 + 4 = 8$. But, we can find a shorter path from A to G via either C or D, in which case the distance

---

[1] In the case of Fig. 4, as all the edges have the length of 2, the lattice becomes equilateral.

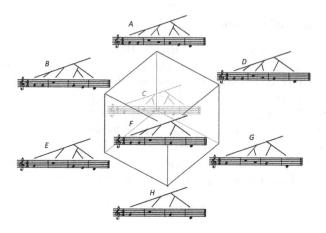

Fig. 4. Reduction lattice

becomes $2 + 2 = 4$. Notice that the lattice represents the operations of *join* and *meet*; e.g., $F = B \sqcap D$, $D = F \sqcup G$, $H = E \sqcap F$, and so on. In addition, the lattice is locally Boolean, being A and H regarded to be $\top$ and $\bot$, respectively. That is, there exists a complement,[2] and $E^c = D$, $C^c = F$, $B^c = G$, and so on.

Notice that time-span tree includes more information than a real score, as head and grouping hierarchy is added. On the other hand, a real score contains the information of each note and rest (e.g., onset and duration), which is lost in the time-span tree. In this sense, for a time-span tree, *rendering* procedure[3] needs to be compensated, to be an audible music. For example, let us consider level c in Fig. 1 which contains five pitch events (chords), the second of which is made of notes F♯5 A5 D6 and A6 drawn at the second beat of the first bar as if they would sound at the position. However, the maximal time-span of the chord begins at the first beat of the first bar and sustains for the duration of a half note. Therefore, we need to take care not to confuse the position of time-spans from those of rendered pitch events. Actually, in [10] the authors have avoided to add stems to note heads upon drawing individual notes in the reduction process in Fig. 1.

4   Generalized Distance in Trees

In this section, we extend the notion of strict distance, to be applicable to two different music pieces, which may not necessarily share a common-ancestor music piece in terms of reduction. To this purpose, we need to relax the condition of distance calculation.

---

[2] For any member X of a set, there exists X^c and $X \sqcup X^c = \top$ and $X \sqcap X^c = \bot$.

[3] Rendering was originally introduced in computer graphics, which means the operation of creating images from a model, such as a photorealistic image from a wireframe model.

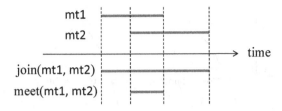

Fig. 5. Generalized join and meet operations to maximal time-spans

4.1 Interval Semantics on Absolute Time Axis

In order to compare two different melodies, we need to place those at proper places in a common temporal axis. Two arbitrary music pieces are possibly different from each other with a large variety; for example, a music piece beginning with auftakt or syncopation, containing hemiola, and being at a double tempo with the same pitch sequence. To handle such cases, we may need various types of adjustments of two music pieces for comparison; for example, alignment by the endpoints of music pieces and/or bar lines, and by stretching or compressing to make the two of same length.

At present, we take the simplest approach to the adjustment in which two music pieces are aligned only at the beginning bar line. Then, the join/meet operations are applied to maximal time-spans without stretching or compressing them. That is, when two temporal intervals have a common length, the result of a join operation encompasses the temporal union of the two intervals, and that of meet operation is exactly the temporal intersection (Fig. 5), where $mt\{1, 2\}$ means a maximal time-span, respectively. The decision is underlain by the following assumption: the longer a time-span is, the more informative it is, as the interval semantics of temporal logic [21].

4.2 Meet-Oriented Distance

In Sect. 3.3, we have shown that the distance via the meet and that via the join become the same in the lattice of strict descendents of one common music piece. However, when we are to apply two music pieces without a common ancestor, one serious problem is that such equality of join/meet distance may not be promised. First of all, we cannot calculate the join operation for all cases at present; for example, if the supremacy of the heads of two trees do not match, the result of the join operation is not defined (Fig. 6). In contrast, the result of meet operation can be calculated in any case. Therefore, in this paper, we decide to calculate the distance using the path via the meet $d_\sqcap$ in Sect. 3.3.

Figure 7 shows the excerpt from the Prolog program implementing the generalized join and meet operations. The join/meet operations are recursively applied in the top-down manner. In the Prolog program, a node in a time-span tree is represented by data structure $(T_p > T_s)$ or $(T_s > T_p)$, where T_p and T_s denote subtrees (Fig. 8). Subscripts 'p' and 's' represent that a branch is primary or secondary, and the temporal order between them is shown by '<' or '>'.

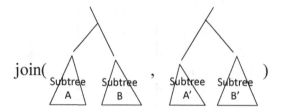

Fig. 6. Case of undefined result in join operation

```
join(X,Y,Join) :-          meet(X,Y,Meet) :-
X = (Xp > Xs),             X = (Xp > Xs),
Y = (Yp > Ys),!,           Y = (Yp > Ys),!,
join(Xp,Yp,Mp),            meet(Xp,Yp,Mp),
join(Xs,Ys,Ms),            meet(Xs,Ys,Ms),
Join = (Mp > Ms).          Meet = (Mp > Ms).
join(X,Y,Join) :-          meet(X,Y,Meet) :-
X = (Xs < Xp),             X = (Xs < Xp),
Y = (Ys < Yp),!,           Y = (Ys < Yp),!,
join(Xp,Yp,Mp),            meet(Xp,Yp,Mp),
join(Xs,Ys,Ms),            meet(Xs,Ys,Ms),
Join = (Ms < Mp).          Meet = (Ms < Mp).
join(X,Y,Join) :-          meet(X,Y,Meet) :-
X = (_ > _),               X = (Xp > _),
Y = (_ < _),!,             Y = (_ < Yp),!,
Join = undefined.          meet(Xp,Yp,Meet).
join(X,Y,Join) :-          meet(X,Y,Meet) :-
X = (_ < _),               X = (_ < Xp),
Y = (_ > _),!,             Y = (Yp > _),!,
Join = undefined.          meet(Xp,Yp,Meet).
```

Fig. 7. Prolog implementation of generalized join and meet operations (recursion part)

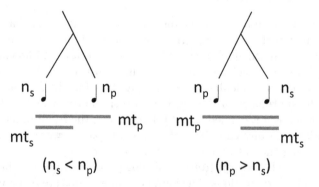

Fig. 8. Representation of time-span tree node in Prolog program

For treating the unmatched supremacy of the heads of two trees, the result of join is set to undefined in the third and fourth clauses of join in Fig. 7, and that of meet is calculated by the further meet of primary branches, Xp and Yp, ignoring secondary branches, in the third and fourth clauses of meet.

5 Experiment

We conduct two experiments using the same set of pieces: a similarity assessment by human listeners and the calculation by the proposed framework. Set piece is the Mozart's variations K.265/300e '*Ah, vous dirai-je, maman*', also known as '*Twinkle, twinkle little star*'. The piece consists of the famous theme and twelve variations of it. In our experiment, we excerpt the first eight bars (Fig. 9). Although the original piece includes multiple voices, our framework can only treat monophony; therefore, the original piece is arranged into a monophony. We extract salient pitch events from each one of two voices, choosing a prominent note from a chord, and disregard the difference of octave so that the resultant melody is heard smoothly. In total, we have the theme and twelve variations (eight bars long) and obtain 78 pairs to be compared ($_{13}C_2 = 78$).

For the similarity assessment by human listeners, eleven university students participate in our study, seven out of whom have experiences in playing music instruments more or less. An examinee listens to all pairs $\langle m_1, m_2 \rangle$ in the random order without duplication, where $m_{\{1, 2\}}$ is either theme or variations No. 1–12. Every time he/she listens to it, he/she is asked "how similar is m_1 to m_2?", and ranks it in one of five grades among *quite similar* = 2, *similar* = 1, *neutral* = 0, *not similar* = −1, and *quite different* = −2. At the very beginning, for cancelling the cold start bias, every examinee hears the theme and twelve variations (eight bars long) through without ranking them. In addition, when an examinee listens to and rank pair $\langle m_1, m_2 \rangle$, he/she should try the same pair later to avoid the order effect. Finally, the average rakings are calculated within an examinee and then for all the examinees.

For the calculation by the proposed framework, we use the meet-oriented distance introduced in Sect. 4.2. From Definitions 3 and 4, the distance is measured by a note duration, we set the unit of distance to one third of the sixteenth note duration so that a music piece not only in quadruple time but also in triple time can be represented. The correct time-span trees of the theme and twelve variations are first created by the authors and are next cross-checked to each other. Note that the meet operation takes into account only the configuration of a time-span tree, not pitch events; it is obvious from Definitions 3 and 4.

6 Results and Analysis

The experimental results are shown in the distance-matrix (Table 1). The theoretical estimation (a) means the results of calculation by the meet operation, and the human listeners (b) means the psychological resemblance by examinees. In (a), since the values of $meet(m_1, m_2)$ and $meet(m_2, m_1)$ are exactly the same,

Fig. 9. Monophonic melodies arranged for experiment

only the upper triangle is shown. In (b), if an examinee, for instance, listen to Theme and variation No. 1 in this order, the ranking made by an examinee is found at the first row, the second column cell (−0.73). The values in (b) are the averages over all the examinees.

Table 1. Calculation by meet operation and psychological resemblance

(a) Theoretical estimation

	No.1	No.2	No.3	No.4	No.5	No.6	No.7	No.8	No.9	No.10	No.11	No.12
Theme	183	177	195	183	117	249	162	15	21	363	262.5	246
No.1	–	228	332	326	264	360	219	174	204	456	409.5	421
No.2	–	–	264	216	246	282	105	168	186	438	391.5	423
No.3	–	–	–	252	262	320	259	188	198	462	334.5	379
No.4	–	–	–	–	238	246	213	176	186	424	387.5	399
No.5	–	–	–	–	–	276	243	114	108	414	298.5	325
No.6	–	–	–	–	–	–	291	234	264	378	409.5	449
No.7	–	–	–	–	–	–	–	153	171	429	376.5	400
No.8	–	–	–	–	–	–	–	–	30	348	259.4	255
No.9	–	–	–	–	–	–	–	–	–	378	277.5	261
No.10	–	–	–	–	–	–	–	–	–	–	406.5	403
No.11	–	–	–	–	–	–	–	–	–	–	–	298.5

(b) Rankings by human listeners (listening in row→column order)

	Theme	No.1	No.2	No.3	No.4	No.5	No.6	No.7	No.8	No.9	No.10	No.11	No.12
Theme	–	-0.73	-0.91	-1.09	-0.82	1.18	-1.00	-1.45	-0.64	1.36	0.64	0.73	1.00
No.1	-1.00	–	-0.82	-0.73	-0.91	-0.64	0.36	-0.64	-1.45	-0.82	-0.82	-1.00	-0.64
No.2	-0.91	-0.36	–	-0.64	-0.27	-0.82	-0.45	-0.55	-1.55	-0.91	-0.09	-0.64	-0.91
No.3	-0.82	-0.45	-0.82	–	0	-0.91	-1.00	-0.36	-1.36	-0.73	-0.64	-0.73	-0.91
No.4	-1.00	-0.82	-0.73	0.18	–	-0.73	-0.82	-0.82	-1.73	-0.91	-0.45	-1.27	-1.00
No.5	1.27	-1.18	-0.91	-0.91	-0.64	–	-0.82	-1.09	-1.00	0.73	0.55	0.36	0.73
No.6	-1.18	0.27	-0.27	-0.45	-0.82	-0.64	–	-0.36	-1.64	-0.91	-0.55	-0.64	-0.91
No.7	-1.18	-0.64	-0.45	-0.18	-0.82	-0.73	-0.64	–	-1.18	-0.73	-0.36	-0.64	-0.73
No.8	-0.73	-1.27	-1.36	-1.55	-1.27	-0.73	-1.00	-1.36	–	-0.09	-1.09	-0.64	-0.91
No.9	1.27	-0.91	-0.91	-0.73	-1.09	0.91	-1.27	-0.82	-0.18	–	0.55	0.45	1.00
No.10	0.55	-0.82	-0.27	-0.64	-0.36	0.73	-0.45	-0.82	-1.00	0.73	–	0.18	0.45
No.11	0.64	-0.82	-0.91	-0.73	-0.91	0.55	-0.91	-1.09	-0.73	0.64	0.27	–	1.00
No.12	1.09	-1.18	-1.09	-1.00	-1.00	0.91	-1.00	-1.18	-0.91	1.09	0.36	0.82	–

It is difficult to examine the correspondence between the results of calculated by the meet operation (a) and the psychological resemblance by examinees (b) in this distance-matrix. Then, we employ multidimensional scaling (MDS) [20] to visualize the correspondence. MDS takes a distance matrix containing dissimilarity values or distances among items, identifies the axes to discriminate items most prominently, and plots items on the coordinate system of such axes [20]. Putting it simply, the more similar items are, the closer they are plotted on a coordinate plane.

First, we use the Torgerson scaling of MDS to plot the proximity among the 13 melodies (Fig. 10), however, it is still difficult to find a clear correspondence. Therefore, we restrict plotting melodies to the theme and variations No. 1–9 (Fig. 11). Theme and No. i in the figure correspond to those in Fig. 9, respectively ($i = 1..9$). The contributions in MDS are as follows: (a) Theoretical estimation: first axis (horizontal) = 0.23, second = 0.21; (b) Human listeners: first axis (horizontal) = 0.33, second = 0.17.

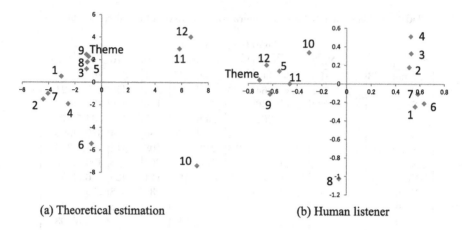

Fig. 10. Relative distances among theme and all variations in mutidimensional scaling

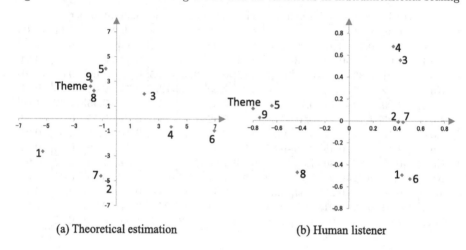

Fig. 11. Relative distances among theme and restricted melodies in MDS

In the figure, we can find an interesting correspondence between (a) and (b) in terms of positional relationships among 10 melodies. In both (a) and (b), we find that Theme, No. 5, No. 8, and No. 9 make a cluster; so No. 3 and No. 4 do; so No. 2 and No. 7 do. The positional relationship among the cluster of Theme, No. 5, No. 8 and No. 9, that of No. 2 and No. 7, and that of No. 3 and No. 4 resembles each other. The positional relationship between No. 1 and the others, except for No. 6, resembles, too. Since the contributions in the first axis of (a) are considered close to the second, by rotating the axes of (a) −90° (counter clockwise), a more intuitive correspondence may be obtained. On the other hand, the discrepancy between (a) and (b) is seen, too; the positional relationship between No. 6 and the others is significantly different. From the above, we argue that the operations on time-span trees of our framework are viable to a certain extent.

At present, our framework disregards matching of pitch events; the meet/join operations take only the information of the configuration of time-spans. Even without matching of pitch events, however, the result of meet/join operation more or less reflects the relationship among pitches indirectly. This intuition is justified as follows. Firstly, the relationship among pitches within a music piece influences the configuration of a time-span tree construction; in fact, some of preference rules for a time-span tree are involved with the pitch and/or duration of a pitch event. Secondly, since all melodies listed in Fig. 9 are a theme and the variations derived from it, we can assume that the chord progressions of them are basically the same with each other. Thus, join/meet operations do not need to take into account the difference between chords of the two inputs.

In the sense of the second justification, it is noteworthy that Theme (or No. 5, No. 9) and No. 8 are positioned close to each other in Fig. 11 (a) Theoretical estimation, while they are not in (b) Human listener. Because No. 8 has the almost the same rhythmic structure as Theme but is in the C minor key, the time-span trees are similar while the superficial impression to human listeners are not. On the other hand, the surface structures of the No. 1 and No. 6 are almost made of 16th notes and the both are chromatic (Fig. 9). Thus, the impressions of No. 1 and No. 6 to human listeners are similar as in Fig. 11 (b), and they are positioned close to each other. However, these two variations have fairly different chord progressions; No. $1 = I \rightarrow V \rightarrow IV \rightarrow I \rightarrow IV \rightarrow I \rightarrow II$ $V \rightarrow I$, and No. $6 = I \rightarrow I \rightarrow IV \rightarrow I \rightarrow V \rightarrow I \rightarrow II$ $V \rightarrow I$. Accordingly, the time-span trees of No. 1 and No. 6 become distinctive in theoretical estimation, and thus they locates at the two extremes in Fig. 11(a).

7 Concluding Remarks

We assumed that cognitive similarity should reside in the similarity of time-span trees, that is, the reduction ordering in time-span trees were heard similarly in the order of resemblance to human ears. Based on this assumption, we proposed a framework for representing time-span trees and processing them in the algebraic manner. In this paper, we examined the validity of the framework through the experiments to investigate the correspondence of theoretical similarity with psychological similarity. The experimental results supported the convincing correspondence to some extent.

Here we have three open problems. Firstly, we exclude variations No. 10–12 for visualization in Fig. 11. Here, we need to consider why variations No. 10–12 could not achieve a higher correspondence. As possible reasons, we speculate No. 10 contains reharmonization, No. 11 features ornamental 32nd notes and No. 12 is a music piece in triple time. Thus, we are interested in an even more generalized distance that is robust to these variations.

Secondly, in terms of the contributions in MDS, the third axis in theoretical estimation which is not depicted in Fig. 11 is 0.17, and that in human listeners 0.16. Since the third axis is still relatively significant, the dimension may reveal another hidden grouping among 13 music pieces.

Thirdly, in several cases, the join operation could not be calculated as was pointed out in Fig. 6. Besides, polyphonic melodies could not be handled by our framework. Since these limitations degrade the applicability of our framework, we should extend the representation method of a music piece and tolerate the condition of the join operation, preserving the consistency with the meet operation and vice versa.

Furthermore, future work includes building a large corpus that contains more diverse melodies and conducting experiments for us to investigate the correspondence of theoretical similarity with psychological similarity in more detail. In addition, to achieve the similarity that truly coincides with our cognition, we should formalize the operations on pitch events.

Acknowledgments. This work was supported by JSPS KAKENHI Grant Numbers 23500145 and 25330434. The authors would like to thank the anonymous reviewers of CMMR2013 for their constructive comments to improve the quality of the paper.

References

1. Bod, R.: A unified model of structural organization in language and music. J. Artif. Intell. Res. **17**, 289–308 (2002)
2. Carpenter, B.: The Logic of Typed Feature Structures. Cambridge University Press, Cambridge (1992)
3. de Haas, W.B.: Music information retrieval based on tonal harmony. Ph.D. thesis, Utrecht University (2012)
4. ESCOM: Discussion Forum 4A. Similarity Perception in Listening to Music, MusicæScientiæ (2007)
5. ESCOM: 2009 Discussion Forum 4B. Musical Similarity. Musicae Scientiae
6. Forte, A., Gilbert, S.E.: Introduction to Schenkerian Analysis. Norton, New York (1982)
7. Grachten, M., Arcos, J.-L., de Mantaras, R.L.: Melody retrieval using the Implication/Realization model. 2005 MIREX. http://www.music-ir.org/evaluation/mirexresults/articles/similarity/grachten.pdf. Accessed 25 June 2013
8. Hamanaka, M., Hirata, K., Tojo, S.: Implementing "A Generative Theory of Tonal Music". J. New Music Res. **35**(4), 249–277 (2007)
9. Hewlett, W.B., Selfridge-Field, E. (eds.): Melodic Similarity - Concepts, Procedures, and Applications. Computing in Musicology, vol. 11. The MIT Press, Cambridge (1998)
10. Lerdahl, F., Jackendoff, R.: A Generative Theory of Tonal Music. The MIT Press, Cambridge (1983)
11. Marsden, A.: Generative structural representation of tonal music. J. New Music Res. **34**(4), 409–428 (2005)
12. Mirex, HOME. http://www.music-ir.org/mirex/wiki/MIREX_HOME. Accessed 25 June (2013)
13. Pampalk, E.: Computational models of music similarity and their application in music information retrieval. Ph.D. thesis, Vienna University of Technology, March 2006
14. Pearce, M.T., Wiggins, G.A.: Expectation in melody: the influence of context and learning. Music Percept. **23**(5), 377–405 (2006)

15. Rizo-Valero, D.: Symbolic music comparison with tree data structure. Ph.D. thesis, Departamento de Lenguajes y Sistemas Informatícos, Universitat d' Alacant (2010)
16. Schedl, M., Knees, P., Böck, S.: Investigating the similarity space of music artists on the micro-blogosphere. In: Proceedings of ISMIR 2011, pp. 323–328 (2011)
17. Tojo, S., Hirata, K.: Structural similarity based on time-span tree. In: 10th International Symposium on Computer Music Multidisciplinary Research (CMMR), pp. 645–660 (2012)
18. van Kranenburg, P.: A computational approach to content-based retrieval of folk song melodies. Ph.D. thesis. Utrecht University (2010)
19. Volk, A., Wiering, F.: Tutorial musicology, Part 3: music similarity. In: 12th International Society for Music Information Retrieval Conference, ISMIR 2011 (2011). http://ismir2011.ismir.net/tutorials/ISMIR2011-Tutorial-Musicology.pdf. Accessed 15 June 2013
20. Wikipedia, Multidimensional scaling. http://en.wikipedia.org/wiki/Multidimensional_scaling. Accessed 15 June 2013
21. Wikipedia, Temporal Logic. http://en.wikipedia.org/wiki/Temporal_logic. Accessed 25 June 2013

Group Delay Function from All-Pole Models for Musical Instrument Recognition

Aleksandr Diment[1]([✉]), Padmanabhan Rajan[2],
Toni Heittola[1], and Tuomas Virtanen[1]

[1] Department of Signal Processing, Tampere University of Technology,
Tampere, Finland
{aleksandr.diment,toni.heittola,tuomas.virtanen}@tut.fi
[2] School of Computing and Electrical Engineering,
Indian Institute of Technology, Mandi, Himachal Pradesh, India
padman@iitmandi.ac.in

Abstract. In this work, the feature based on the group delay function from all-pole models (APGD) is proposed for pitched musical instrument recognition. Conventionally, the spectrum-related features take into account merely the magnitude information, whereas the phase is often overlooked due to the complications related to its interpretation. However, there is often additional information concealed in the phase, which could be beneficial for recognition. The APGD is an elegant approach to inferring phase information, which lacks of the issues related to interpreting the phase and does not require extensive parameter adjustment. Having shown applicability for speech-related problems, it is now explored in terms of instrument recognition. The evaluation is performed with various instrument sets and shows noteworthy absolute accuracy gains of up to 7 % compared to the baseline mel-frequency cepstral coefficients (MFCCs) case. Combined with the MFCCs and with feature selection, APGD demonstrates superiority over the baseline with all the evaluated sets.

Keywords: Musical instrument recognition · Music information retrieval · All-pole group delay feature · Phase spectrum

1 Introduction

Musical instrument recognition is one example of the subtopics of music information retrieval, and it has been most actively explored since the 1990s when the systems aimed at handling small numbers of instruments represented by isolated notes were already reaching impressive performance scores of 98 % [17] and 100 % [16]. During the following years, various systems realising numerous methods and applied for different numbers of instruments have been developed.

This research has been funded by the Academy of Finland, project numbers 258708, 253120 and 265024.

M. Aramaki et al. (Eds.): CMMR 2013, LNCS 8905, pp. 606–618, 2014.
DOI: 10.1007/978-3-319-12976-1_37

The recent works on the subject utilise existing classification methods, which are novel in terms of the given problem (e.g., semi-supervised learning [5] and applying missing feature approach for polyphonic instrument recognition [11]), as well as introduce new features (e.g., multiscale MFCCs [26] and amplitude envelopes of wavelet coefficients [13]). There exists an established set of features commonly applied for instrument recognition. Depending on whether they treat audio from the temporal or spectral point of view, these are subcategorised accordingly.

The temporal features address instrument recognition under the assumption that the relevant information is within the transient properties of a signal. Such assumption is perceptually motivated: the attack characteristics are believed to play crucial role in human recognition of musical instruments [7].

The spectral features employ a different approach. Particularly, those that are related to the harmonic properties of a sound (e.g., inharmonicity and harmonic energy skewness) do preserve the important properties of the musical instrument timbre [1]. The same applies to other spectrum-related features as well, such as mel-frequency cepstral coefficients (MFCCs). However, being spectrum-based, these features tend to concentrate only on the magnitude part of the spectrum.

Spectral information is complete only if both magnitude and phase spectra are specified. Signal processing difficulties, such as wrapping of the phase and dependency of the phase on the window position, make direct processing of the phase spectra challenging. A popular solution is to use the *group delay function*, which is defined as the negative derivative of the phase spectrum. The group delay function is well-behaved only if the zeros of the system transfer function are not close to the unit circle.

One example of overcoming the latter difficulty is by computing the so-called *modified group delay function* [24], which has been applied for speech recognition [15,24], as well as recently for musical instrument recognition [6]. It has shown in the case of instrument recognition a comparable performance with such established features as MFCCs and an up to 5.1 % recognition accuracy improvement in combination with MFCCs. However, the parameters of the function need to be adjusted to the specific application scenario, which is computationally expensive, so a simpler approach is desirable.

This work proposes utilising a more elegant method of acquiring a well-behaved group delay feature, which is novel in instrument recognition and does not require as much adjustment of parameters to an application scenario. The main aspect of this method is to calculate the group delay function from all-pole models of a signal, formed by linear predictive analysis (later referred to as APGD, all-pole group delay). While achieving the same goal of overcoming the irrelevant high amplitude spurious peaks in the group delay function, it appears more universally applicable and, therefore, beneficial. Previously, this method has shown to be successful in formant extraction [27] and speaker recognition [25].

The calculation of the APGD feature is proposed for pitched instrument recognition, either primarily or as a complement to the established MFCCs, motivated by the fact that additional information relevant in terms of musical instrument classification is concealed in phase. Its performance is evaluated in separate note classification scenarios with instrument sets of different sizes.

The paper is organised according to the following structure. Section 2 presents the motivation for computing group delay as a feature in general and the APGD version in particular, as well as its calculation procedure. Subsequently, Sect. 3 introduces the implemented instrument recognition system, which incorporates APGD calculation as its feature extraction block. Its performance is consecutively evaluated in Sect. 4. Finally, the conclusions about the applicability of the feature are drawn along with the future research suggestions in Sect. 5.

2   Group Delay Function

In this section, firstly, a motivation for utilising phase information for musical instrument recognition is stated along with the reasoning for computing APGD in particular. Subsequently, the details of calculation of the group delay function and its APGD extension are presented.

2.1   Motivation for Musical Instrument Recognition

Phase is often overlooked in many audio processing solutions due to the complications related to the unwrapping of the phase spectrum. In spite of that, phase could be highly informative due to its high resolution and ability of indicating peaks in the magnitude spectrum envelope. In terms of speech-related problems, these correspond to formants, useful for extracting speech content. There has been studies [2] showing that phase contributes significantly to speech intelligibility, contrary to the common notion of its perceptual negligibility.

In the musical instrument signals, however, the presence of formants in the spectrum is not as strong [16], or they are not a factor independent from fundamental frequency, in contrast to speech signals. For example, in the spectra of trombone or clarinet, due to the acoustical change of active volume of their body during the sound production, the resonances depend on pitch [9, 20].

Nevertheless, a phase-based feature is applicable for instrument recognition as well. Broadly speaking, while the commonly applied MFCCs feature is capable of modelling the resonances introduced by the filter of the instrument body, it neglects the spectral characteristics of the vibrating source, which also play their role in human perception of musical sounds [10]. Incorporating phase information attempts to preserve this neglected component.

Furthermore, considering instruments with such resonators as stretched strings and air columns in pipes, their natural resonances are not perfectly harmonic. However, due to such phenomenon as *mode locking*, individual modes of such instruments are locked into the precise frequency and phase relationships, leading to repeating waveforms of sustained tones of these instruments. This phenomenon occurs in case certain conditions favouring the effect are met [9]. A phase-related feature could aid in capturing the presence of this effect.

2.2   Group Delay Function

The *group delay function* is of a signal $x[n]$ obtained as [3]

$$\tau_g(\omega) = -\text{Im}\left(\frac{d}{d\omega}\log(X(\omega))\right) \tag{1}$$

$$= \frac{X_R(\omega)Y_R(\omega) + X_I(\omega)Y_I(\omega)}{|X(\omega)|^2}, \tag{2}$$

where $X(\omega)$ and $Y(\omega)$ are the Fourier transforms of $x[n]$ and $y[n]$, and $y[n] = nx[n]$. The advantage of Eq. (2) over the conventional way to obtain phase information is that no explicit unwrapping is needed.

The group delay function is well-behaved only if the zeros of the system transfer function are not close to the unit circle. The zeros may be introduced by the excitation source or as a result of short time processing [4,15]. When zeros of the transfer function are close to the unit circle, the magnitude spectrum exhibits dips at the corresponding frequency bins. Due to this, the denominator term in Eq. (2) tends to a small value, resulting in a large value of the group delay function $\tau_g(\omega)$. This manifests itself in spurious high amplitude spikes at these frequencies, masking out the resonance structure in the group delay function.

One way of addressing this issue is by introducing a modification [24] of the group delay function (MODGDF), which suppresses the zeros of the transfer function. This is done by replacing the magnitude spectrum $X(\omega)$ by its cepstrally smoothed version $S(\omega)$. Two additional parameters are introduced to control the dynamic range.

Although this has shown to be a reasonable approach, applicable among others for musical instrument recognition [6], the presence of the three parameters that need to be adjusted to an environment does not necessary appear desirable due to the computational requirements such parameter tuning imposes. Another way of obtaining a group delay function, which lacks of this complication, is the group delay function of all-pole models.

2.3   Group Delay Function of All-Pole Models

By modelling a musical instrument with a a source-filter model [19] and assuming the filter all-pole, the spectrum of the such filter may be approximated with aid of linear prediction. The latter has been shown to be an efficient tool for the analysis of sounds of musical instruments, whose transient part is significant in terms of tone quality, such as piano [23]. Another example where all-pole modelling has been used for analysis of musical instrument sounds is the modelling of the guitar body response [18].

Linear prediction is formulated as [21]

$$H(\omega) = \frac{G}{1 - \sum_{k=1}^{p} a(k)e^{-j\omega k}}. \tag{3}$$

The coefficients $a(k)$ are determined by the method of least squares in such a way that the power spectrum of $H(\omega)$ matches the power spectrum of the signal

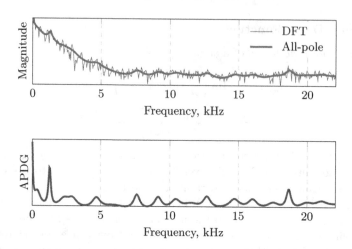

Fig. 1. A frame of a piano note "A0" (MIDI note 21) played in normal playing style with dynamics forte: its magnitude spectra (DFT and all-pole, upper panel) and a group delay function, model order 40 (lower panel).

$|X(\omega)|^2$. The all-pole group delay function is computed from the phase response of this filter formed by $H(\omega)$.

Figure 1 shows the magnitude spectra and corresponding all-pole group delay of one frame of a one note produced by piano. One of the fundamental properties of the group delay function is its high resolution, which makes the formants visible and contributes additional information to the magnitude spectrum. Indeed, in the figure, one may observe the clearly emphasised formants in the APGD plot, not as easily seen in magnitude spectrum, which makes the function helpful for an instrument classification problem.

To convert the all-pole group delay function into a feature, a discrete cosine transform (DCT) is applied. This performs decorrelation, and a certain number of coefficients are retained, excluding the zeroth. The feature is calculated in short frames under the assumption of spectral stationariness within their length, and the Fourier analysis is performed with the aid of DFT. The overal calculation procedure of APGD, illustrated by a block-diagram in Fig. 2, is the following.

1. Perform all-pole modeling on the frame. Obtain the filter coefficients $a(k)$.
2. From the $a(k)$, form the frequency response $H(\omega)$ using Eq. (3) with $G = 1$ (for a simplified representation capturing formant locations).
3. Compute the group delay function by taking the negative derivative of the phase response of $H(\omega)$. In practice, the derivative is computed using the sample-wise difference.
4. Take DCT on the group delay function and keep a certain number of coefficients, excluding the zeroth.
5. Delta coefficients are appended to the feature in a conventional manner.

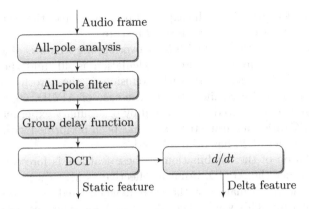

Fig. 2. A block diagram of the calculation of APGD.

3 System Description

The details of the developed musical instrument recognition system that incorporates APGD as one of its features are addressed in this section. The simplified block diagram of the system is presented in Fig. 3, and the upcoming subsections are following the implementation of its building blocks.

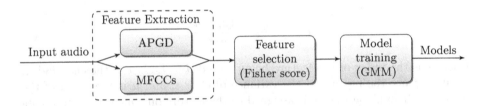

Fig. 3. A block diagram of the feature extraction and training phases.

3.1 Feature Extraction

As primarily explored features, APGD, as well as its first derivative, are incorporated in the calculation. Additionally, a baseline scenario is included, i.e., the calculation of the static and delta MFCCs. Those are currently quite commonly applied for musical instrument recognition, proven to be amongst the most effective features [8] due to their ability to parametrise the rough shape of the spectrum, which is different for each instrument. The mel transformation, which is included in the calculation of MFCCs, is based on human perception experiments and has been demonstrated to effectively represent perceptually important information in terms of instrument recognition [22]. The classification results produced by recognisers based on MFCCs have been shown to resemble human classifications in terms of the similar confusions [8]. This baseline MFCCs scenario is intended to indicate the expected performance of the system with the given data when utilising such established feature.

Frame-blocking is performed with 50 %-overlapping windows of length 20 ms. The number of mel filters in MFCCs calculation is 40, and the number of extracted coefficients is set to 16 with exclusion of the zeroth (i.e., resulting in 15 static and 15 delta coefficients). In the case of APGD, 60 static and 60 delta coefficients are extracted as suggested by preliminary experiments. For the value of the LPC order, a parameter search has been performed within the range 20–70, and the order of 40 has been selected.

The calculation of the combination of these features is foreseen in order to investigate whether the APGD, if not as effective as MFCCs *per se*, is capable of enhancing the performance of the system when used as a complement to the baseline feature. This way, a feature set that incorporates both amplitude and phase information is acquired. The combined features of dimension 150 are obtained by concatenating the values of MFCCs and APGD.

3.2   Feature Selection

Generally, feature selection is applied in order to keep those features that are more relevant for the separability of classes. In this study, one of the goals is to demonstrate the effectiveness of the combined method when the dimensionality is reduced down to the size of the baseline MFCCs feature vectors.

The chosen approach for feature selection is the Fisher score [14]:

$$F_r = \frac{\sum_{i=1}^{c} n_i (\mu_i - \mu)^2}{\sum_{i=1}^{c} n_i \sigma_i^2}, \qquad (4)$$

where r is the index of the feature being scored, $i = 1, \ldots, c$ is the class index, μ_i and σ_i^2 are the mean and the variance of class i, and μ is the mean of the whole set. The highest score is assigned to the feature on which the data points of different classes are far from each other, and the points of the same class are close to each other. A fixed number of features having the highest score are selected.

3.3   Training and Recognition

The training and recognition phases are performed by employing Gaussian mixture models (GMM). For each class, the feature vectors from the training data are used to train the GMM, i.e., to estimate the parameters of such model that best explains these features. The expectation-maximisation (EM) algorithm is used for this purpose, and each class is represented by a GMM of 16 components.

In recognition, the trained models of each class are fit into each frame of the test instances, producing log-likelihoods. Log-likelihoods are accumulated over the frames of the test instance. Thereupon, the label of the class whose model has produced the highest log-likelihood is assigned to that instance.

4 Evaluation

The performance of the proposed approach is evaluated in a separate note-wise instrument classification scenario. Several instrument sets grouped by the level of complexity of the resulting problem are considered. The instrument content of these sets is presented below, followed by the obtained evaluation results.

4.1 Acoustic Material

The recordings (sampling frequency 44.1 kHz) used in evaluation originate from the RWC Music Database [12]. Each of the instruments is represented in most cases by three instances, which stand for different instrument manufacturers and musicians. These are subdivided into subsets according to the playing styles (e.g., bowed vs plucked strings), and only one playing style per instrument is taken into account. In total, three instruments sets (Table 1) are considered, consisting of 4, 9 and 22 instruments. The choice of instruments in the first two sets is influenced by the requirement of a sufficiently high number of notes per instrument for its consistent representation. The largest set, composed of diverse instruments and even vocals, not necessary sufficiently represented in the database, is intended to demonstrate a highly complex classification scenario.

Table 1. Instrument sets used in evaluation.

Set	List of instruments
4-set	Acoustic Guitar, Electric Guitar, Tuba, Bassoon
9-set	Piano, Acoustic Guitar, Electric Guitar, Electric Bass, Trombone, Tuba, Bassoon, Clarinet, Banjo
22-set	"4-set" + "9-set" + "woodwinds" (Oboe, Clarinet, Piccolo, Flute, Recorder) + "strings" (Violin, Viola, Cello, Contrabass) + vocals (Soprano, Alto, Tenor, Baritone, Bass)

The dataset, where each instrument is represented by several hundred recordings, is randomly divided into the training and test subsets. The subsets are acquired from different instrument instances in order to resemble a real-life application scenario. The ratio between the sizes of the training and test subsets is roughly 70 %/30 %.

4.2 Results

The evaluation results obtained with each of the instrument sets are summarised in Table 2. The values of the accuracy of MFCCs are somewhat different (within the range of 1 %) from the previously reported [6], although the same database and the same instruments were used. This is due to the fact that the corresponding tests needed to be repeated in order to report additional, more detailed

Table 2. Evaluation results, where the performance of APGD is compared to the performance of MODGDF [6]. FeatSel 30 and 120 stand for applying the feature selection and selecting 30 and 120 features, respectively.

Method	Recognition accuracy, %		
	4-set	9-set	22-set
MFCCs	90.9	83.7	68.8
MODGDF	84.4	59.9	41.7
APGD	97.9	84.8	63.3
MODGDF + MFCCs	96.0	84.9	70.7
APGD + MFCCs	93.7	87.0	68.3
APGD + MFCCs + FeatSel 30	95.5	84.2	66.2
APGD + MFCCs + FeatSel 120	94.4	**85.7**	**70.0**

results. The randomisation of the separate note recordings that occurs during the division of the dataset into training and test sets, as well as randomisation during the initialisation of the EM algorithm are the reasons for such behaviour. The overall trend of accuracy improvements along the evaluated scenarios, however, is the same, and the differences between the performance of presented methods are of the same character.

The results include among others applying feature selection methodology with selecting 30 and 120 features. In the first case, the idea is to demonstrate the effectiveness of the combined approach when the data dimensionality is reduced down to the size of MFCCs vectors. In the case of 120 selected features, shown to be an optimal parameter during preliminary tests, the goal is to maximise accuracy gains.

By examining the obtained results, one may observe that APGD, used as such, is capable of serving as a reliable feature. The improvement over the baseline MFCCs scenario is apparent with both 4- and 9-instrument sets. The more real-life application case, namely, the set of 22 instruments, has shown to be somewhat complicated for the APGD feature, showing a decrease in accuracy of 5.5 %. However, by combining both features and applying feature selection, the accuracy improvement compared to the baseline case is, nevertheless, achieved. The combined method with feature selection has demonstrated to be effective even when the dimensionality of the feature space is reduced down to the size of the baseline MFCCs vectors, i.e., when no more degrees of freedom is introduced. This shows that APGD does indeed provide new information in terms of musical instrument classification, which is explained both by the relevance of LPC analysis of musical instrument sounds and its capability of capturing phase information, which the conventional features tend to neglect.

A somewhat more specific comparison of the features can be performed by observing the instrument-wise accuracies. As seen in Fig. 4, obtained with the set of nine instruments, the accuracy improvement introduced by APGD-based methods compared to MFCCs is mostly pronounced in the cases of string

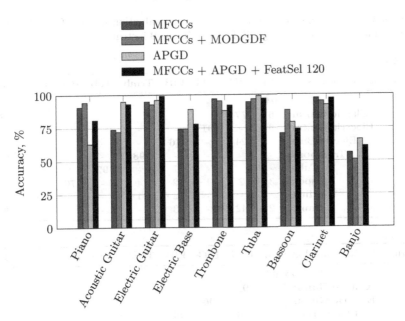

Fig. 4. Instrument-wise accuracies in selected evaluation scenarios with the 9 instruments set.

instruments (Acoustic Guitar, Electric Guitar, Electric Bass and Banjo), which is in agreement with the reported applicability of all-pole modelling of guitar body response [18]. Additionally, some improvement is noticeable in the cases of instruments Tuba and Bassoon, which may be interpreted by phase-based nature of APGD, since the improvement in these instruments is also apparent in the case of MODGDF.

Even more thorough analysis of the results may be performed by addressing the confusion matrices, presented in Table 3. Amongst the most obvious observations one may mention how the APGD-based method missclassifies the instrument Piano for Banjo, whereas MFCCs tend to classify Piano correctly in most of the cases. However, by applying a combined method with feature selection, this erroneous behaviour is suppressed to some degree.

Another observation is that the instrument Classic Guitar appears for the MFCCs-based method somewhat confusable with other string instruments. On the other hand, the APGD and combined methods make such confusions significantly less often, which corresponds to the previously made conclusion on the applicability of LPC-based methods for string instruments.

Additional observations can be drawn from the presented data, however, it is not always as straightforward to find a meaningful explanation to the observed phenomena. For instance, it remains unclear why MFCCs sometimes confuse Tuba with Electric Bass. However, this is overcome by the APGD-based methods, which show an almost 100 % accuracy on Tuba, presumably, due to the importance of the phase characteristics of the sound of this instrument.

Table 3. Confusion matrices obtained with the evaluation of MFCCs, APGD and combined method with selecting 120 features in the 9 instrument case.

MFCCs

Instrument \ Recognised as	Pn	ClG	ElG	ElB	Trmb	Tub	Bsn	Clrn	Bnj
Piano	94	-	-	-	-	-	-	-	6
Classic Guitar	6	77	-	9	-	-	-	-	8
Electric Guitar	9	-	91	-	-	-	-	-	-
Electic Bass	-	24	-	76	-	-	-	-	-
Trombone	-	-	-	-	98	-	-	1	1
Tuba	-	-	-	7	-	92	1	-	-
Bassoon	3	2	1	2	4	-	76	2	10
Clarinet	-	-	-	2	1	-	-	97	1
Banjo	2	42	-	3	-	-	1	-	52

APGD

Instrument \ Recognised as	Pn	ClG	ElG	ElB	Trmb	Tub	Bsn	Clrn	Bnj
Piano	63	2	-	-	-	-	-	2	34
Classic Guitar	3	95	-	-	-	-	-	-	2
Electric Guitar	-	-	96	-	-	-	-	1	3
Electic Bass	1	10	-	89	-	-	-	-	-
Trombone	-	-	-	-	88	-	1	2	8
Tuba	-	-	-	1	-	99	-	-	-
Bassoon	-	-	-	-	4	-	79	13	3
Clarinet	-	3	-	1	-	-	-	92	5
Banjo	1	21	-	11	1	-	-	-	66

APGD + MFCCs + FeatSel 120

Instrument \ Recognised as	Pn	ClG	ElG	ElB	Trmb	Tub	Bsn	Clrn	Bnj
Piano	81	2	-	-	-	-	-	-	17
Classic Guitar	4	93	-	2	-	-	-	-	1
Electric Guitar	-	-	99	-	-	-	-	-	-
Electic Bass	1	21	-	78	-	-	-	-	-
Trombone	-	-	-	-	92	-	4	1	4
Tuba	-	-	-	3	-	97	-	-	-
Bassoon	-	-	-	1	2	-	74	9	14
Clarinet	-	2	-	2	-	-	-	97	-
Banjo	1	30	-	8	-	-	-	-	61

5   Conclusions

This paper studies the use of all-pole group delay features for musical instrument recognition. The proposed method of utilising the APGD feature for the given problem has shown to be valid, with its performance on the comparable levels with the commonly used MFCCs. The absolute recognition accuracy gain has shown to be up to 7 % in the simpler classification scenario. In the complex classification scenario, APGD on its own shows somewhat lower performance, however, by incorporating the combined features with feature selection, accuracy gains are present in all of the evaluated cases. The work has shown that by combining the relevance of linear predictive analysis for instrument recognition with the significance of the phase information, often neglected by the commonly used features, APGD demonstrates its effectiveness and a promising potential for musical instrument recognition.

As a future research suggestion, it is worthwhile to study the performance of the proposed method in a group-wise classification scenario, as opposed to the currently presented instrument-wise case. Namely, training models of groups, composed of instruments, similar in terms of the physics of their sound production, could reveal interesting dependencies and enable a more thorough investigation of the importance of the phase for musical instrument recognition.

References

1. Agostini, G., Longari, M., Pollastri, E.: Musical instrument timbres classification with spectral features. In: IEEE Fourth Workshop on Multimedia Signal Processing, pp. 97–102 (2001)
2. Alsteris, L.D., Paliwal, K.K.: Short-time phase spectrum in speech processing: a review and some experimental results. Digital Signal Proc. **17**(3), 578–616 (2007)
3. Banno, H., Lu, J., Nakamura, S., Shikano, K., Kawahara, H.: Efficient representation of short-time phase based on group delay. In: Proceedings of the 1998 IEEE International Conference on Acoustics, Speech and Signal Processing, vol. 2, pp. 861–864, May 1998
4. Bozkurt, B., Couvreur, L., Dutoit, T.: Chirp group delay analysis of speech signals. Speech Commun. **49**, 159–176 (2007)
5. Diment, A., Heittola, T., Virtanen, T.: Semi-supervised learning for musical instrument recognition. In: 21st European Signal Processing Conference 2013 (EUSIPCO 2013). Marrakech, Morocco, Sep 2013
6. Diment, A., Padmanabhan, R., Heittola, T., Virtanen, T.: Modified group delay feature for musical instrument recognition. In: 10th International Symposium on Computer Music Multidisciplinary Research (CMMR). Marseille, France, Oct 2013
7. Duxbury, C., Davies, M., Sandler, M.: Separation of transient information in musical audio using multiresolution analysis techniques. In: Proceedings of the COST G-6 Conference on Digital Audio Effects (DAFX-01). Limerick, Ireland (2001)
8. Eronen, A.: Comparison of features for musical instrument recognition. In: 2001 IEEE Workshop on the Applications of Signal Processing to Audio and Acoustics, pp. 19–22 (2001)
9. Fletcher, N.H., Rossing, T.D.: The Physics of Musical Instruments. Springer, New York (1998)
10. Fuhrmann, F.: Automatic musical instrument recognition from polyphonic music audio signals. Ph.D. thesis, Universitat Pompeu Fabra (2012)
11. Giannoulis, D., Klapuri, A.: Musical instrument recognition in polyphonic audio using missing feature approach. IEEE Trans. Audio Speech Lang. Process. **21**(9), 1805–1817 (2013)
12. Goto, M., Hashiguchi, H., Nishimura, T., Oka, R.: RWC music database: music genre database and musical instrument sound database. In: Proceedings of the 4th International Conference on Music Information Retrieval (ISMIR), pp. 229–230 (2003)

13. Hacihabiboglu, H., Canagarajah, N.: Musical instrument recognition with wavelet envelopes. In: Proceedings of Forum Acusticum Sevilla (CD-ROM) (2002)

14. He, X., Cai, D., Niyogi, P.: Laplacian score for feature selection. In: NIPS, vol. 186, p. 189 (2005)

15. Hegde, R., Murthy, H., Gadde, V.: Significance of the modified group delay feature in speech recognition. IEEE Trans. Audio Speech Lang. Process. **15**(1), 190–202 (2007)

16. Jensen, K.: Timbre models of musical sounds: from the model of one sound to the model of one instrument. Report, Københavns Universitet (1999)

17. Kaminsky, I., Materka, A.: Automatic source identification of monophonic musical instrument sounds. In: Proceedings of IEEE International Conference on Neural Networks, IEEE, vol. 1, pp. 189–194 (1995)

18. Karjalainen, M., Hrm, A., Laine, U.K., Huopaniemi, J.: Warped filters and their audio applications. In: 1997 IEEE ASSP Workshop on Applications of Signal Processing to Audio and Acoustics, IEEE, pp. 4 (1997)

19. Klapuri, A.: Analysis of musical instrument sounds by source-filter-decay model. In: IEEE International Conference on Acoustics, Speech and Signal Processing. vol. 1, pp. I-53–I-56 (2007)

20. Kostek, B., Czyzewski, A.: Representing musical instrument sounds for their automatic classification. J. Audio Eng. Soc. **49**(9), 768–785 (2001)

21. Makhoul, J.: Linear prediction: a tutorial review. Proc. IEEE **63**(4), 561–580 (1975)

22. Marques, J., Moreno, P.J.: A study of musical instrument classification using gaussian mixture models and support vector machines. Cambridge Research Laboratory Technical Report Series CRL 4 (1999)

23. Meillier, J.L., Chaigne, A.: AR modeling of musical transients. In: 1991 International Conference on Acoustics, Speech, and Signal Processing. ICASSP-91, IEEE, pp. 3649–3652 (1991)

24. Murthy, H., Gadde, V.: The modified group delay function and its application to phoneme recognition. In: 2003 IEEE International Conference on Acoustics, Speech, and Signal Processing. Proceedings (ICASSP '03), vol. 1, pp. I-68-71 (2003)

25. Rajan, P., Kinnunen, T., Hanili, C., Pohjalainen, J., Alku, P.: Using group delay functions from all-pole models for speaker recognition. Proc. Interspeech **2013**, 2489–2493 (2013)

26. Sturm, B., Morvidone, M., Daudet, L.: Musical instrument identification using multiscale mel-frequency cepstral coefficients. In: Proceedings of the European Signal Processing Conference (EUSIPCO), pp. 477–481 (2010)

27. Yegnanarayana, B.: Formant extraction from linear-prediction phase spectra. J. Acoust. Soc. Am. **63**(5), 1638–1640 (1978)

A Multiple-Expert Framework for Instrument Recognition

Mikus Grasis, Jakob Abeßer[✉], Christian Dittmar, and Hanna Lukashevich

Semantic Music Technologies Group, Fraunhofer IDMT, Ilmenau, Germany
{mikus.grasis,jakob.abesser,christian.dittmar,
hanna.lukashevich}@idmt.fraunhofer.de

Abstract. Instrument recognition is an important task in music information retrieval (MIR). Whereas the recognition of musical instruments in monophonic recordings has been studied widely, the polyphonic case still is far from being solved. A new approach towards feature-based instrument recognition is presented that makes use of redundancies in the harmonic structure and temporal development of a note. The structure of the proposed method is targeted at transferability towards use on polyphonic material. Multiple feature categories are extracted and classified separately with SVM models. In a further step, class probabilities are aggregated in a two-step combination scheme. The presented system was evaluated on a dataset of 3300 isolated single notes. Different aggregation methods are compared. As the results of the joined classification outperform individual categories, further development of the presented technique is motivated.

Keywords: Instrument recognition · Partial tracking · Partial-wise features · Overtones · Classifier ensemble · Decision fusion

1 Introduction

Each music genre is characterized by a typical range of music instruments, which have a major influence on the timbre of musical pieces. Algorithms for automatic instrument recognition are useful for a wide range of application scenarios. First, these algorithms allow for an efficient search, indexing, and recommendation of music pieces based on timbral similarity. Second, genre classification algorithms are likely to perform better if the presence of instruments and instrument groups can be applied as audio features. Third, the automatic recognition of instruments allows to select instrument-adaptive algorithms for source separation and automatic music transcription. Finally, the temporal progression of instrumentation and instrument density often correlates with perceptual time-continuous properties such as dynamic and tension.

Musical Redundancy Towards Instrumentation. In terms of instrumentation, music pieces show different levels of redundancies:

© Springer International Publishing Switzerland 2014
M. Aramaki et al. (Eds.): CMMR 2013, LNCS 8905, pp. 619–634, 2014.
DOI: 10.1007/978-3-319-12976-1_38

1. **Global redundancy:** If a particular instrument plays throughout a segment (e.g., the chorus), multiple note events can be detected and assigned towards that instrument.
2. **Local redundancy concerning partial envelopes:** Notes played on harmonic instruments consist of a fundamental frequency component and multiple overtones. Both the magnitude and the frequency envelopes of the harmonic component show a similar progression over time.
3. **Local redundancy concerning spectral frames:** Notes played on harmonic instruments usually show a very similar spectral distribution in adjacent spectral frames (e.g. in the beginning of the note decay part).

In this paper we propose an instrument-recognition framework that combines classification results from different feature categories—*note-wise, partial-wise* and *frame-wise* features. Although we only evaluated the framework with isolated note recordings so far, the approach is targeted towards the use on polyphonic material.

2   Previous Work

A number of solutions have been presented for the identification of musical instruments from a given audio signal. Aside from early experiments [12] many works have initially focused on the identification of monophonic sound sources. These concepts regard spectral properties of fixed-length segments [3], or take into account the temporal properties of isolated notes [5]. Later contributions cover aspects such as the pitch dependency of timbre [13] or the temporal integration of spectral features over time [11].

Over the latest years identification of instruments in polyphonic music recordings has received an increasing attention. Recognition of polyphonic sources is often performed as identification of dominant solo instruments. This has been done with feature-based approaches and an extensive training on real-world polyphonic training data [7]. Also the application of source separation techniques has been beneficially applied in this context [2]. Other approaches aim at a decomposition of the musical signal. For instance, Itoyama et al. presented a system for simultaneous separation and classification of sounds [10]. However, these algorithms tend to show heavy computational requirements. Another approach is the *selective* classification of signal-portions that show no interference from spectral overlaps. This concept has been applied by classifying instruments based on individual partials by Barbedo & Tzanetakis in [1].

We propose to extend the concept of partial classification proposed by Barbedo & Tzanetakis to a *multiple-expert instrument classification* scheme. The separate classification of observations from different feature categories allows the selective processing of unimpaired signal components. This strategy could ensure a robust classification that is applicable to polyphonic and multi-instrumental music signals, which are characterized by spectral overlap of different sound sources.

3   Proposed System

The proposed system operates on the basis of individual single notes. For that purpose, automatic music transcription algorithms must be applied. Classification of single notes bears the advantage that multiple notes can be evaluated in order to derive a final instrument class label for a given music segment (e.g. in case of a dominant main instrument). The transcription algorithms return a list of note events, which are characterized by the parameters *onset* (note start), *offset* (note end) and *pitch*. In the pre-processing stage of the framework (Sect. 3.2), the Short-time Fourier transform (STFT) of the analyzed signal is computed. In the partial tracking step (Sect. 3.3), the fundamental frequency and the first 9 overtones of each note events are tracked in the magnitude spectrogram. This results in a magnitude and frequency track for each harmonic component. As shown in Sects. 3.4 and 3.5 audio features are calculated from multiple categories and classified separately using Support Vector Machine (SVM) models. Finally, Sect. 3.6 describes a two-stage aggregation process that assigns a class of instrument labels for each note event.

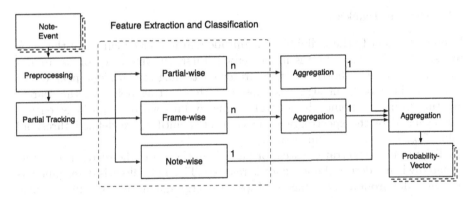

Fig. 1. Proposed Multiple-Expert System for Instrument Recognition. Each feature group results in one (1) or multiple (n) class probability vectors.

3.1   Note Event Detection (Music Transcription)

The proposed algorithm is eventually to be applied on real-world polyphonic and multi-instrumental signals. In this case a prior detection of fundamental frequencies and note boundaries of individual note events must be performed. Current automatic transcription algorithms still yield typical detection error (note boundaries, pitch). In the case of defective note boundaries the presented approach can represent an improvement compared to a solely note-based feature extraction system: the classification of frame-wise features remains unaffected. However, pitch detection errors show their effect on the systems' partial tracking procedure. The effects of the common *octave error*, where a pitch is detected an octave above or below the actual pitch, are limited to the number of correct partials detected, though. Let's say the given f_0 is an octave too high, in this case every other partial envelope is missed, the remaining are of undiminished quality. On the other hand, if the detected f_0 has been an octave below the true f_0, the system will try to find partial envelopes where none can be found. As will be explained in Sect. 3.3, such would be discarded due to low energy.

3.2   Pre-processing

The incoming samples are expected to be at a sampling rate of 44.1 kHz. All samples are normalized to their maximum value. Although this neglects dynamic information, we found in our experiments that normalization improves classification results slightly. Next, a 2048 point STFT with an overlap of 512 samples and a four-time zero-padding is performed, resulting in a time resolution of 86.13 frames per second and a window length of about 46.4 ms. The individual time frames have been weighted by a Hamming window function before transformation.

3.3   Partial Tracking

In order to identify the individual magnitude and frequency curves of the overtones, a tracking procedure is implemented. First, the frequency of the fundamental f_0 at a time shortly after the frame containing the envelope peak of the time-domain note event signal is chosen as the starting point for the search. Starting from this point, the loudest frequency bins within a pre-selected frequency band of the spectrogram are connected until a pre defined threshold value $L_{abort} = -39$ dB is undershot.

To prevent from erratic search for partials in the noise, the search is also terminated when a detected noise floor is reached. This noise floor is determined as a mean value from a percentage n of lowest energy magnitude bins in the spectrogram of the given note. In our experiments, we found $n = 15\%$ to work best.

For statistical recognition systems it is of great importance to obtain the best possible representations of the classes to be selected. Thus all partials that are to be classified are selected by means of a required minimum energy and length. Successive overtones in the harmonic series show increasing variance in their temporal development. We limited the number of partials to the fundamental frequency and 9 overtones, as this yielded the best performance in a conducted cross-validation experiment (see Fig. 2).

Figure 3 illustrates the tracked partials for two different instruments. Individual partials of the piano note exhibit irregularities in magnitude progression due to *string beating* phenomena[1].

---

[1] The so-called *string beating* occurs with string instruments (e.g., guitar or piano) and is caused through superimpositions of closely pitched oscillation modes.

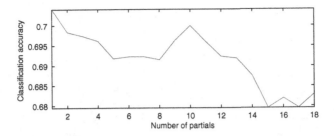

Fig. 2. Classification accuracy for partial-wise classification in dependence of the number of partials extracted.

3.4 Feature Extraction

The audio features that are extracted for each note are categorized into three groups:

1. *Note-wise features* - These global features are extracted once for each note event.
2. *Partial-wise features* - These features characterize the frequency course and the magnitude envelope of each detected partial of a note.
3. *Frame-wise features* - Theses features can be extracted in individual time frames both on spectrogram frames as well as on partial magnitude and frequency values.

Figure 1 illustrates the different feature categories. In the following three sections, examples for all feature categories are explained in detail.

Note-wise Features

Aggregated timbre-features. The first group of note-wise features is based on a simple two-stage envelope model that is used to partition the duration of a note event into an attack part and a decay part. Frame-wise timbre features such as spectral centroid, spectral crest factor, spectral decrease, spectral roll-off, and spectral slope are aggregated over both envelope parts by computing the statistical measures minimum, maximum, mean, median, and variance which are then used as features.

Subharmonic energy. The second group of note-wise features characterizes the energy distribution in subharmonic regions, i.e., the spectral regions between the partials. First, a general measure of noisiness is computed by removing the harmonic components from the spectrum using a comb filter that is aligned to the f_0 curve. The aggregated energy in the remaining spectrogram is divided to the original spectrogram energy. Second, the presence of subharmonics[2] is

---

[2] Subharmonics can for instance be observed in flageolet tones from string instruments as well as in brass instrument notes.

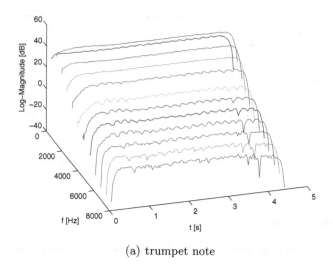

(a) trumpet note

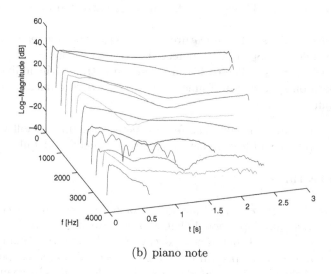

(b) piano note

Fig. 3. Two examples for the tracked partials in the logarithmic magnitude spectrum: a trumpet note and a piano note.

investigated in a similar way, only that additional comb filters are applied at different fractional positions between the note partials.

Partial-wise Features. These features capture characteristics of the individual frequency and magnitude envelopes that have been detected in the spectrum of a single note. A first group of features is derived from the magnitude function $a_k(t)$ of an individual partial:

Temporal centroid. The temporal centroid of a magnitude envelope is a powerful feature to separate sounds with transient excitation from such with a continuous excitation. For plucked string instruments the temporal centroid is very close to the start of the note (because, after an initial displacement of the string a note will just fade). For bowed string instruments, and also for notes that are played by wind instruments, the centroid will tend to be placed in the middle of the note, as energy is supplied to the sound over the duration of the note.

Envelope energy. The energy is determined as the integral of the envelope function and is well suited to distinguish between short and long notes played.

Fluctuation of magnitude. To calculate a measure of the local fluctuation of magnitude, the moving average of the given envelope function is withdrawn by means of a moving average filter. Variance as well as the zero crossing rate are then determined from the remaining envelope and used as features.

Duration of attack and decay parts. For many instruments magnitude envelopes can be approximated with a simple, two-stage model consisting of attack and decay parts. As suggested in [15] the logarithmic time durations of both parts are used as features. In addition, the ratio between the durations of both parts is calculated.

Polynomial approximation of the magnitude envelopes. A linear function of the magnitude envelope is approximated by linear regression (linear magnitude in the attack and logarithmic magnitude of the decay part). The coefficients of this function are then used as features.

The following features can be calculated for a frequency course $f_k(t)$ as well as a magnitude function $a_k(t)$ of an individual partial:

Modulation of frequency & magnitude. Different physical phenomena such as can

- frequency modulations (Vibrato) and
- magnitude modulations (Tremolo, string beating)

be approximated with a number of periods of a sinusoid function. This function is retrieved from the modulation spectrum of the current frequency or magnitude envelope $f_k(t)$ or $a_k(t)$ by searching for salient peaks in a range from $2-20\,\mathrm{Hz}$. The following features are then calculated:

- Modulation frequency in Hz
- Modulation lift in cents (for frequency modulation) respectively without unit (for magnitude modulation)
- Dominance measure for strength of modulation (normalized value between 0 and 1)
- Number of oscillation periods

Frame-wise Features. The frame-based features are calculated either over the entire spectral frame or on the magnitudes and frequencies of the harmonics within a frame. As feature extraction showed to be more robust for the entire spectral frame as for the individual harmonics this feature group was divided into two categories to be classified separately: *frames spectral* and *frames harmonic*.

The first group of frame-wise features (*frames spectral*) consists of timbre features such as spectral centroid, spectral crest factor, spectral decrease, spectral roll-off, and spectral slope.

The second group (*frames harmonic*) regard the frequency positions and magnitudes of individual partials in a given spectral frame. Features of this category include the harmonic relative magnitudes, inharmonicity and tristimulus.

3.5   Classification

SVM Classifiers have proven to show good performance in instrument recognition tasks, as in [8]. Since the focus of this work is to evaluate the multiple–classification approach, we use SVM's to classify the observations of all three categories of extracted features for reasons of simplicity[3]. Before classification a normalization of the feature vectors to zero mean and unit variance is performed. The RBF function (radial basis function) is applied as the kernel function for the SVM classifier.

For an unknown note event, which is to be classified, first all features are calculated. Using the trained classifiers, vectors of class probabilities are determined for each feature group. As indicated in Fig. 1 the number of vectors from the classifiers for the frames and overtones depend on the number of detected frames or overtones. The classifier, which is based on note-wise features returns exactly one probability vector.

3.6   Result Aggregation

The aim of the framework is to end up having a single vector of class probabilities from which the most likely instrument can be derived. This aggregation is performed in a two-stage combination scheme.

First, during the *within-ensemble* aggregation, the class probabilities within the feature categories are aggregated, so that from all classifiers ultimately one single vector is returned. Second, in the *between-ensemble* aggregation these vectors from the different feature categories are fused to a single vector, which is then returned by the framework. Additionally in this second stage of the aggregation process, *classifier weighting* is applied, in order to mirror relevance as supplied by the classifier accuracies.

The following methods of combination were examined for the two levels of aggregation:

Mean. The aggregation result is formed by the mean values of the individual class probabilities.

---

[3] The LIBSVM implementation, as described in [4] was used.

Highest Maximum. From the given observations the vector containing the highest single class probability is chosen.

Best-to-Second. From the given observations the vector with the best difference between highest and second class probability is chosen.

Majority Voting Hard. A majority voting scheme is conducted. A voice by weight of 1 is awarded to the class with highest probability in each probability vector.

Majority Voting Soft. A majority voting scheme is conducted. A voice by weight of the highest probability is awarded for each probability vector.

For the combination of the final class probability vectors of the individual categories *classifier weighting* was applied. Each classifier was given a weight previously obtained from the cross-validation accuracies in the individual categories. Using this weight relevant decisions are given more significance during the aggregation process and the final classification result can be improved, as will be discussed in the results section. The final output of the aggregation framework is a vector of class probabilities that has the length of the number of instrument classes.

4 Evaluation

For evaluation experiments a dataset consisting of 3300 isolated single note recordings of the 11 instruments shown in Table 1 was compiled. The samples were chosen randomly from three publicly available large-scale databases of instrument sounds: RWC Musical Instrument Sound Database [9], McGill University Master Samples [14] and IOWA Musical Instrument Samples [6]. The selected notes cover the entire pitch ranges of the instruments above a MIDI-pitch of 45 (A2). This constraint was made for spectral resolution to be ensured as sufficient for the partial tracking procedure. In order to obtain maximum variance of the training data, all dynamic levels and a wide range of playing styles found in the individual databases were used in the dataset. For example, the flute samples cover the playing styles *normal, staccato, vibrato,* and *flutter* and the violin samples cover the playing styles *normal, staccato, ponticello,* and *vibrato.*

The prepared data was used to perform a 10-fold cross validation over all the included samples. Particular attention was paid to keep the partitions of the individual cross-validation folds alike for the different classification categories.

5 Results

5.1 Aggregation Experiments

For the prepared dataset all combinations of methods for the two levels of aggregation were evaluated. For this procedure, all class probabilities of the different

Table 1. Instruments used in the evaluation experiments.

Instrument	RWC	Iowa	McGill
Piano	X		X
Violin	X	X	X
Flute	X	X	X
Trumpet	X	X	X
Sax	X		X
Ac.-Guitar	X		
El.-Guitar	X		
B3-Organ	X		
Vocal	X		
Cello	X	X	X
Clarinet	X	X	X

classification categories were stored for each fold of the cross-validation. Then, aggregation was performed and the accuracies of the individual folds were averaged.

Table 2 shows the accuracies obtained for the tested combination schemes. As we can see combination of class probabilities using the mean value in both aggregation stages led to the highest mean class accuracy of 91.2 %. The aggregation methods *Highest Maximum* and *Best-to-Second* scored very similar results, whereas hard majority voting between the individual feature categories brought less accurate classifications.

Table 2. Aggregated mean class accuracy values in percent for different combinations of result aggregation methods.

Inbetween-ensemble: Within-ensemble:	Mean	Highest Max	Best to Second	Majority Hard	Majority Soft
Mean	**91.2**	88.3	88.6	87.8	89.5
Highest Max	90.5	88.6	88.4	87.1	88.7
Best-to-Second	90.7	88.8	88.5	87.3	88.9
Majority Hard	89.8	87.2	85.7	87.8	88.5
Majority Soft	89.9	87.6	85.8	87.8	88.8

5.2   Results for the Individual Features Categories

As shown in Table 3 note-wise classification obtained the best accuracy of .85. The applied spectral features and their statistical evaluation for the attack and decay segments therefore capture characteristic properties of the instruments well. The classification of individual harmonics has surprisingly achieved an accuracy which exceeds the detection performance of individual spectral frames (accuracy of .68 for the overtones in comparison to an accuracy .60 for the frame-wise classification). This underlines the importance of the temporal information of instrument sounds. Furthermore, it appears that a classification can be successfully performed on the basis of isolated overtones for several instruments.

Table 3. Accuracies for individual classification categories.

Aggregated	Note	Partials	Frames spectral	Frames harmonic
.91	.85	.68	.60	.32

5.3   Results for the Aggregated Classification

Figure 4 shows the confusion matrix for the best configuration of the aggregated classification. For each line, the classified samples of an instrument distribute to the available range of instruments, which are applied from left to right. A number of corresponding confusions can be found within the result. These include instruments with similar mechanisms of sound production. For example piano, acoustic guitar and electric guitar are all instruments with a transient sound excitation (piano notes are *struck* and guitar notes are *plucked* or *picked*), and are therefore confused more likely. The representatives of the woodwind family, flute, saxophone, and clarinet also form such a corresponding confusion group. If we have a closer look at the row for the violin, clarinet or saxophone it can be inferred that virtually no confusion is made between these instruments and such with a transient excitation. A rather unexpected result however, occurs with the (mostly) bowed instruments: violin and cello. On the one hand these show mutual confusions as could be expected, but also a noticeable tendency towards the woodwind-family instruments can be observed. This may be explained by the fact that both instrument families show considerable amounts of noise in their respective spectral distributions.

An examination of the individual classification categories reveals insights towards beneficial effects of the combined classification process:

1. *Improvements towards the best classification category.* As we can see in Fig. 4, 2.0 % of the violin samples have been misclassified as flute. For the individual feature categories the misclassification rates for this particular confusion were 2.7|8.3|1.9|14.4 % respectively[4]. The results of the best classification category (frame-wise spectral classification) have made a positive effect for the combined classification result.

2. *Improvements through synergistic effects.* An ideal constellation for *classifier fusion* is to have classifiers that make different mistakes on a given sample. It is presumed that in this case correct results from an ensemble can overrule

---

[4] note|partials|frames spectral|frames harmonic.

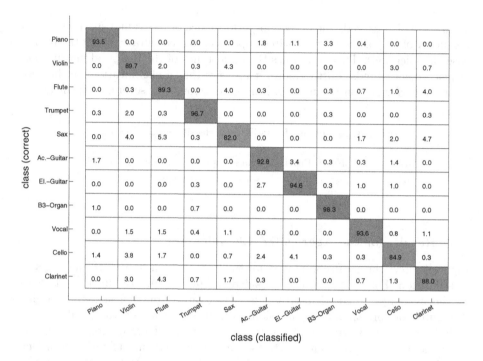

Fig. 4. Confusion matrix for the best configuration of the presented system.

the mistakes of a single classifier. Final classification result for the Hammond B3 organ was 98.3 % (Fig. 4) compared to 92.9|80.0|54.0|40.2 % for the individual feature categories. The frame-wise spectral classification showed strong confusions towards the trumpet (20.3 %), and the partial-wise classification tended towards cello (8.1 %) and the piano (6.7 %). As we see the combined result has been improved significantly, when compared with the best feature category.

These examples acknowledge for the effectiveness of the multiple expert classification approach on the instrument recognition task.

5.4 Comparison Against Other Musical Instrument Recognition Systems for Isolated Notes

The comparison to other state-of-the-art instrument recognition systems poses some difficulties, as taxonomies vary in terms of instruments and playing styles employed. A benchmark score has been reported by Tjoa and Liu in 2010 [16]. On a taxonomy of 24 instruments, including drum sounds, a mean class accuracy of 92.3 % was achieved. The average number of items per class is similar to the system presented in this paper, although it has to be pointed out that the number of items per class strongly varied.

6 Preliminary Experiment for Polyphonic Evaluation

A system for instrument recognition is of most use if it can be applied to a polyphonic data in the real-world case. Therefore we perform an additional evaluation experiment on artificial mixtures in this section. A set of training and test segments in two voices is assembled by which the classifiers for the individual feature categories are trained and evaluated. All individual single notes used in the training pieces are stored separately and then used to compare classifier performance on the basis of different training sets. Finally, we perform the aggregation of results with the winner method obtained from a prediction on the polyphonic training set.

Selected Instruments. We selected seven classical orchestra instruments that are available in all three of the before mentioned publicly available large scale instrument databases: piano, violin, flute, cello, trumpet, saxophone, and clarinet. In RWC database selected instruments are present in three different instances, i.e. different manufacturer, recording studio, and executing musician. Together with the representations from IOWA, and McGill database we get a number of five individual instances for each instrument in total.

Preparation of Artificial Mixtures. For the preparation of training and test mixtures we first divide the set of available samples by individual instrument instances. Selected samples for the experiment have the following origin:

- Training: IOWA, RWC1, and RWC2
- Test: McGill and RWC3

We avoid combining all samples for either training or test from only RWC database to beware of biassing effects. The individual audio mixtures are then synthesized by placing an individual tone sample with required pitch at the time position of the notes that are played. All selected samples are normalized to their maximum absolute value.

Melodic Material. The melodic material is based on midi-files of two-part inventions from J. S. Bach that are available for public download[5]. For each midi-file we consider all possible permutations of the instruments that were selected for the experiment, resulting in 49 different instrument combinations. This way every instrument happens to be playing either the left or right hand of the selected piano piece with every other instrument in combination. The midi-file segments are limited to a playing length of 12 s total and the first bar is omitted as it presents the theme of either composition for one hand only. BPM count of the selected midi-files was reduced by 50 % to ensure less problematic minimum note length.

Experimental Setup. Figure 5 shows an overview for the setup of the conducted experiment.

---

[5] http://www.bachcentral.com/midiindexcomplete.html.

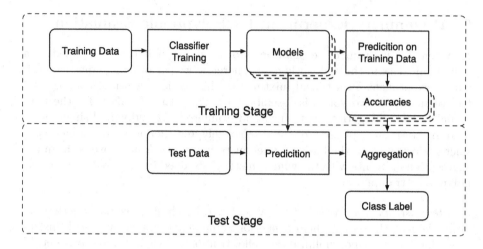

Fig. 5. Setup for polyphonic evaluation.

Results for individual feature categories and aggregated classification are shown in Table 4. We can see that also for classification on harmonically overlapped material the aggregated classification process can outperform the classifiers from single feature categories.

Table 4. Classification accuracies depending on training base for model training.

	isolated and poly	polyphonic	isolated
Note	.37	.38	.25
Frames spectral	.33	.34	.28
Frames harmonic	.41	.41	**.36**
Partials	.33	.39	.22
Aggregated	**.44**	**.45**	.28

7   Conclusions

We have presented a new approach towards instrument recognition making use of redundancies in harmonic structure and temporal development of a note. Features from multiple categories have been extracted and classified separately with SVM models. In a two-step combination scheme, class probabilities have been fused *within* and also *in-between* individual feature categories. As we have seen in the discussed results (Sects. 5, 6) the aggregated classification outperforms the best classification result of the individual categories. Relevant decisions are obviously given more authority during the combination and classifier weighting process.

8   Outlook

Further development of the system shall include development of confidence measures for the individual observations of each classification category. This approach seems very beneficial for instrument recognition in polyphonic, multi-timbral music. In this case unaffected signal portions, i.e. frames, that suffer from no temporal overlapping, or overtones, that are not spectrally overlapped, could be assigned with a high relevance in the classification process. Also, classification techniques such as source separation, training with real world data or the combination of adjacent single note decisions could be successfully combined with the presented strategy.

Acknowledgments. This research work is a part of the SyncGlobal project. It is a 2-year collaborative research project between piranha womex AG from Berlin and Bach Technology GmbH, 4FriendsOnly AG, and Fraunhofer IDMT in Ilmenau, Germany. The project is co-financed by the German Ministry of Education and Research within the framework of an SME innovation program (FKZ 01/S11007).

References

1. Barbedo, J.G.A., Tzanetakis, G.: Instrument identification in polyphonic music signals based on individual partials. In: Proceedings of the 2010 IEEE International Conference on Acoustics, Speech, and Signal Processing (ICASSP), Dallas, Texas, USA, pp. 401–404 (2010). http://ieeexplore.ieee.org/xpls/abs_all.jsp?arnumber=5495794, http://ieeexplore.ieee.org/lpdocs/epic03/wrapper.htm?arnumber=5495794
2. Bosch, J.J., Janer, J., Fuhrmann, F., Herrera, P.: A comparison of sound segregation techniques for predominant instrument recognition in musical audio signals. In: Proceedings of the 13th International Society for Music Information Retrieval Conference (ISMIR), Porto, Portugal, pp. 559–564 (2012). http://ismir2012.ismir.net/event/papers/559-ismir-2012.pdf
3. Brown, J.C., Houix, O., McAdams, S.: Feature dependence in the automatic identification of musical woodwind instruments. J. Acoust. Soc. Am. **109**(3), 1064–1071 (2001). http://link.aip.org/link/JASMAN/v109/i3/p1064/s1&Agg=doi
4. Chang, C.C., Lin, C.J.: LIBSVM: a library for support vector machines. Technical report, Department of Computer Science, National Taiwan University, Taipei, Taiwan (2013)
5. Eronen, A.: Comparison of features for musical instrument recognition. In: Proceedings of the 2001 IEEE Workshop on the Applications of Signal Processing to Audio and Acoustics (WASPAA), Mohonk, New York, USA, pp. 19–22 (2001). http://ieeexplore.ieee.org/xpls/abs_all.jsp?arnumber=969532, http://ieeexplore.ieee.org/lpdocs/epic03/wrapper.htm?arnumber=969532
6. Fritts, L.: University of Iowa musical instrument sample database (1997). http://theremin.music.uiowa.edu/MIS.html
7. Fuhrmann, F., Haro, M., Herrera, P.: Scalability, generality and temporal aspects in automatic recognition of predominant musical instruments in polyphonic music. In: Proceedings of the 10th International Society for Music Information Retrieval Conference (ISMIR), Kobe, Japan, pp. 321–326 (2009). http://ismir2009.ismir.net/proceedings/OS3-1.pdf

8. Fuhrmann, F., Herrera, P.: Polyphonic instrument recognition for exploring semantic similarities in music. In: Proceedings of the 13th International Conference on Digital Audio Effects (DAFx), Graz, Austria (2010). http://mtg.upf.es/system/files/publications/ffuhrmann_dafx10_final.pdf

9. Goto, M., Hashiguchi, H., Nishimura, T., Oka, R.: RWC music database. In: Proceedings of the 4th International Society for Music Information Retrieval Conference (ISMIR), Baltimore, Maryland, USA, pp. 229–230 (2003). http://ukpmc.ac.uk/abstract/CIT/688685

10. Itoyama, K., Goto, M., Komatani, K., Ogata, T., Okuno, H.G.: Simultaneous processing of sound source separation and musical instrument identification using Bayesian spectral modeling. In: Proceedings of the 2011 IEEE International Conference on Acoustics, Speech, and Signal Processing (ICASSP), No. 3, Prague, Czech Republic, pp. 3816–3819 (2011). http://ieeexplore.ieee.org/xpls/abs_all.jsp?arnumber=5947183, http://ieeexplore.ieee.org/lpdocs/epic03/wrapper.htm?arnumber=5947183

11. Joder, C., Essid, S., Richard, G.: Temporal integration for audio classification with application to musical instrument classification. IEEE Trans. Audio Speech Lang. Process. 17(1), 174–186 (2009). http://ieeexplore.ieee.org/xpls/abs_all.jsp?arnumber=4740151, http://ieeexplore.ieee.org/lpdocs/epic03/wrapper.htm?arnumber=4740151

12. Kinoshita, T., Sakai, S., Tanaka, H.: Musical sound source identification based on frequency component adaptation. In: Proceedings of the Workshop on Computational Auditory Scene Analysis (IJCAI-CASA), Stockholm, Sweden, pp. 18–24 (1999). http://lab.iisec.ac.jp/~tanaka_lab/publications/pdf/conference/conference-99-04.pdf

13. Kitahara, T., Goto, M., Okuno, H.G.: Musical instrument identification based on F0-dependent multivariate normal distribution. In: Proceedings of the 2003 IEEE International Conference on Acoustics, Speech, and Signal Processing (ICASSP), Hong Kong, China, vol. 5, pp. 421–424 (2003). http://ieeexplore.ieee.org/xpls/abs_all.jsp?arnumber=1199996, http://ieeexplore.ieee.org/lpdocs/epic03/wrapper.htm?arnumber=1199996

14. Opolko, F., Wapnick, J.: The McGill University Master Samples Collection on DVD (3 DVDs) (2006)

15. Peeters, G.: A large set of audio features for sound description (similarity and classification) in the CUIDADO project. Technical report, IRCAM, Paris, France (2004). http://www.citeulike.org/group/1854/article/1562527

16. Tjoa, S., Liu, K.J.R.: Musical instrument recognition using biologically inspired filtering of temporal dictionary atoms. In: Proceedings of the 11th International Society for Music Information Retrieval Conference (ISMIR), Utrecht, The Netherlands, pp. 435–440 (2010). http://www.mirlab.org/conference_papers/International_Conference/ISMIR2010/ISMIR_2010_papers/ismir2010-74.pdf

Syncopation as Transformation

George Sioros[1](✉) and Carlos Guedes[2]

[1] Faculdade de Engenharia da Universidade do Porto,
Rua Doutor Roberto Frias s/n, 4200-465 Porto, Portugal
gsioros@gmail.com
[2] NYU Abu Dhabi, 5th St., Abu Dhabi, United Arab Emirates
cag204@nyu.edu

Abstract. Syncopation is a rhythmic phenomenon present in various musical styles and cultures. We present here a set of simple rhythmic transformations that can serve as a formalized model for syncopation. The transformations are based on fundamental features of the musical meter and syncopation, as seen from a cognitive and a musical perspective. Based on this model, rhythmic patterns can be organized in tree structures where patterns are interconnected through simple transformations. A Max4Live device is presented as a creative application of the model. It manipulates the syncopation of midi "clips" by automatically de-syncopating and syncopating the midi notes.

Keywords: Syncopation · Transformations · Meter · Rhythm · Generation · Analysis

1 Introduction

Syncopation is an essential musical phenomenon found in several and diverse styles of western music, as well as in certain non-western music. It is commonly related to rhythmic complexity and music tension [4, 5, 7]. It is well understood among musicians and it has been the subject of research in several fields such as computational musicology and music cognition. Definitions of syncopation often relate syncopation to the musical meter, describing it, for example, as a contradiction to the prevailing meter [18]. Musicological definitions of syncopation focus on its conceptual aspects or describe it as a technique [11, 18]. More formalized definitions approach syncopation as a matter of magnitude [3, 6, 8, 10, 16] and the subject of comparison between rhythmic patterns: patterns are considered to be more syncopated or less syncopated than others. Other studies are limited to specific cases [23] or music styles [8, 24]. However, there has been no formalized model that analyzes and generates syncopation.

Recently we presented an algorithm that allows for the manipulation of syncopation, i.e. a computer algorithm that is able to remove or introduce syncopation in a certain rhythmic pattern in a controlled way [20]. Here, we extend the algorithm to a set of formalized generic transformations that can analyze, generate and manipulate the syncopation in binary patterns. The transformations are derived by the definition of syncopation as a cognitive mechanism related to metrical expectations [7].

We introduce the concept of the syncopation tree as a way of organizing and interconnecting patterns. A syncopation tree is essentially a web of patterns, where

M. Aramaki et al. (Eds.): CMMR 2013, LNCS 8905, pp. 635–658, 2014.
DOI: 10.1007/978-3-319-12976-1_39

each pattern is connected to other patterns through the application of series of simple transformations. Patterns belonging in the same tree originate from the same root, i.e. they originate from the same non syncopating pattern. The tree structure can be useful in developing models for clustering rhythms together or in defining measures of rhythmic similarity and distance.

The syncopation transformations are accompanied by a method for enhancing the metrical and syncopation feel through dynamic accents. We assign dynamic accents to the onsets on the beat (thus enhancing the metrical feel) and then shift them to off the beat positions (thus enhancing the syncopation feel).

A software application in the form of a Max4Live device is also presented. The software is intended to be used as a tool to explore syncopation both in live performance and in off-line composition. It takes a midi clip and generates different versions of it that range from no syncopation to maximum syncopation. The device can read midi clips and transform them in real time. Transformations are controlled through a simple "syncopation slider".

In Sect. 2, we provide a brief description of the main syncopation definitions and measures related to our model of syncopation. In Sect. 3, we describe a way of automatically constructing a metrical template and how it must be adapted for modeling syncopation. In Sect. 4, we describe the syncopation transformations for binary patterns and we present the concept a syncopation tree as a structure for organizing rhythmic patterns. In Sect. 5, we extend the transformations to include dynamic accents. In Sect. 6, we present a software application as an example for the creative exploration of syncopation. Finally, in Sect. 7, we present the main conclusions of this study.

2   On Measuring Syncopation

Complex music, even when it is not repetitive, it often evokes the sensation of a regular pulse in listeners that becomes evident when they tap in synchrony with the music. Often those pulses feature accents so that some of them are perceived as stronger than the rest. These structured, accented pulses are the basis for a definition of meter as a cognitive mechanism that expresses our expectations about when music events will occur [9]. Syncopation has been described as the feeling of surprise that arises when a rhythmic event that was anticipated at a particular moment did not actually occur [7].

Longuet-Higgins and Lee presented a syncopation model that identifies the syncopation in the pairs of notes and the rests or the tied notes that follow them [14]. Accordingly, a rest or tied note in a strong metrical position preceded by an event in a weaker metrical position constitutes a syncopation. David Huron, in his study of the American popular music [8], used a similar definition using the term "Lacuna" to describe syncopation. Behind both definitions lies the same expectation principle: an event in a weak metrical position is bound to an event in the following strong metrical position and when the expected strong note does not occur the weak one is left hanging [2, p. 295].

Longuet-Higgins and Lee defined syncopation with the aid of metrical weights. The metrical weights correspond directly to the metrical level that each metrical position in a bar initiates (see Sect. 3 for a more detailed description). The slower the metrical level the higher the metrical weight. In Fig. 1, the metrical levels of a 4/4 m are numbered from 0 to 4. The metrical weights are the negative of those indexes (i.e. from −4 to 0). Syncopations are found when the metrical position of a rest or a tied note has a higher weight than that of the position of the preceding note onset.

W.T. Fitch and A.J. Rosenfeld derived a syncopation measure [3] from the Longuet-Higgins and Lee definition (hereafter LHL). The LHL measure attributes to each syncopation a score that is the difference between the two metrical weights described above. The total syncopation in a rhythmic pattern is the sum of all the syncopation scores. In this paper, when a rhythmic pattern consists of more than one bar, we divide the sum by the number of bars in order for all the results to have comparable scales.

David Temperley explored the uses of syncopation in rock [23], using a definition of syncopation that bears strong resemblance to the Longuet-Higgins and Lee definition and Huron's expectation principle. In his study, syncopation is defined as the displacement of events from metrically strong positions to preceding weaker ones. The syncopation transformations that we describe in this paper are inspired by this study.

As the above definitions of syncopation suggest, we need a formalized way of describing the underlying meter in order to be able to manipulate the syncopation in a rhythmic pattern. We need to construct a metrical template according to the time signature. In the next section we describe such a template, and an automatic way of constructing it. It will serve as the basis for all syncopation manipulations that follow.

3   Metrical Template for Syncopation

The meter determines a hierarchical structure like the one found in the Generative Theory of Tonal Music by Lerdahl and Jackendoff [12]. Such a structure consists of pulses with different metrical strength values that represent the alternating strong and weak beats commonly found in a musical meter (Fig. 1). Similarly to the metrical structure used by Longuet-Higgins and Lee in their syncopation definition [14], each pulse initiates a metrical level and its metrical strength is proportional to that level. The metrical hierarchy can be thought of as a superposition of layers of pulses with different periods, in which the period of one layer is an integer multiple of all faster ones [17, 25]. Each pulse belongs to the various metrical levels according to the time signature, e.g. the quarter notes or the sixteenth notes found in a 4/4 bar. The pulses constitute a metrical grid which quantizes the time positions of the onsets of the events in a rhythmic pattern resulting into the binary representation of Fig. 1.

The metrical template is constructed automatically for each meter and tempo in which the rhythmic patterns are heard. It is constructed by successively subdividing the bar into faster metrical levels. For example, the 4/4 m can be subdivided first into two half notes, then each half note into two quarter notes, each quarter note into two eight notes and so on, until the fastest metrical subdivision is reached. That way, the hierarchical character of the template is ensured. The metrical levels are indexed by numbers, referred to as metrical indexes for easy reference, starting with the number 0 for the slower one and increasing as one goes to faster levels. The process of successively subdividing the bar results in alternating weak and strong pulses, forming a pattern characteristic of each time signature. The stronger a pulse is, the slower the metrical level it belongs to (lower index), so that weak pulses belong to faster metrical levels (higher indexes). In Fig. 1 an example of such a metrical template is given. A detailed description of an automatic way of generating a metrical template for any given time signature can be found in [21].

The duration of each metrical subdivision depends on the tempo, e.g. the quarter note at 100 bpm has duration of 600 ms. The lower threshold for the duration of a metrical subdivision has been estimated in several studies to be roughly around 100 ms [13, 17, 19]. The fastest metrical subdivision that we included in the metrical template is the fastest subdivision above that threshold.

An upper threshold for the duration of the metrical levels needs also to be determined. Before determining the upper threshold, we need to define the duration of a syncopation and examine its relation to the metrical levels. The definition of syncopation, as originally formulated by Longuet-Higgins and Lee [14] or Huron [2, p. 295] and also adopted here, attributes syncopation to the pair of an onset on a weak pulse with the following silent strong pulse. One can, therefore, talk about and define the duration of the syncopation as the duration between those two pulses. The duration of the syncopation depends, on one hand, on the metrical levels of the corresponding pulses, and on the other hand, on the tempo. One question that arises is: how does the duration of the syncopation affect the feeling of syncopation?

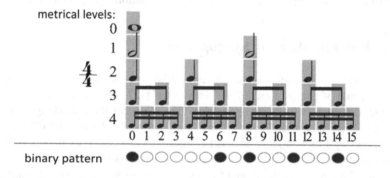

Fig. 1. Top: Example of the construction of a metrical template for a 4/4 m. The meter is successively subdivided generating the 5 metrical levels. The metrical strength (*grey rectangles*) of each metrical position corresponds to the metrical levels it belongs to. *Bottom*: A binary pattern.

The effect of the duration of syncopation on the feeling of syncopation becomes apparent when one tries to de-syncopate a rhythmic pattern. If one tries to de-syncopate the patterns of Fig. 2, he will follow different approaches for pattern A and B. In pattern A, the tied eighth note should clearly be moved to the following quarter note. When it comes to pattern B, the tied quarter note falls on the beat and therefore, intuitively, does not need to be de-syncopated. However, the two cases are identical with respect to the definition of syncopation. The difference between the two is their relation to what is considered to be the beat level (or tactus).

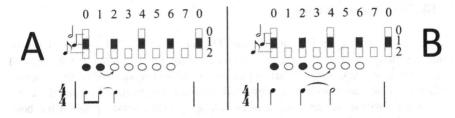

Fig. 2. Syncopation at slow metrical levels. A: a pattern syncopating at the eighth note metrical level. B: The same pattern at half speed. Above the two patterns the corresponding metrical template is shown.

During the performance, the listener does not have the score or the notated meter in his mind. He can only tell the difference based on the duration; *A* is performed twice as fast as *B*. For example, if *B* is performed at 100 BPM the duration of the quarter note (q.n.) will be 600 ms. Performing the same pattern twice as fast, i.e. accelerating the q.n. duration to 300 ms, is equivalent to converting the q.n. to eighth notes (*A*). The perceived meter and beat do not change between the two performances. The metrical salience of each level depends predominantly by its period, with a peak salience in the region between 500 ms–1 s [13, 17]. The perceived beat—the most salient metrical level—will be the one with the duration of 600 ms in both performances. The eighth note of pattern *A* falls on the faster metrical level of 300 ms which is significantly less salient. Therefore it is perceived as off the beat and as strongly syncopating.

This aspect of syncopation and its relation to pulse salience has not been thoroughly studied. However, based on our experience, we understand that syncopation involving only slower metrical levels is not felt as strong. In other words, instances of syncopation with duration longer than that of the most salient level seem to be felt significantly less strong. The LHL syncopation measure [14] takes this effect into account indirectly, by giving to the syncopation that involves adjacent metrical levels a relatively small weight. Other syncopation measures, such as the weight-note-to-beat distance (WNBD) [6], relate syncopation directly to the beat level, ignoring all slower metrical levels.

In order to take the above effect of tempo into consideration in the construction of the template, we employ a similar approach to the WNBD by essentially "chopping off" the slower metrical levels. We chose the level that falls in the range between 500 ms and 1 s as the slowest metrical level represented in our structure. For example, in the case of a 4/4 m at 160 bpm (q.n. = 375 ms), the metrical template of Fig. 1 will become as in Fig. 3. At this tempo, only 3 metrical levels survive with corresponding durations of 750 ms (0), 375 ms (1) and 187.5 ms (2).

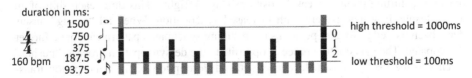

Fig. 3. Example of a metrical template in which very fast metrical levels (below 100 ms duration) and very slow ones (above 1 s duration) are disregarded.

4 Shifting Onset Positions

According to the Longuet-Higgins and Lee [14] or Huron's [7] definition of syncopation, a syncopating event is an event at a weak metrical position that is not followed
by an event in the next strong metrical position. If this event was shifted to the strong
position the syncopation would be eliminated. With this observation in mind, the event
at the weak position can be thought of as belonging to the strong position but been
anticipated at an earlier position. Therefore, one can imagine the inverse shift as a way
of generating syncopation at a strong metrical position, i.e. by shifting an event found
at a strong position to an earlier, weaker pulse (Fig. 4). The transformations described
in Sect. 4.1 are such simple shifts of onsets in a binary pattern. The following formalization of the transformations consists of defining the conditions under which such
shifts remove the syncopation or generate syncopation in a given binary rhythmic
pattern. Applying the formalized transformation on a binary pattern gives rise to the
syncopation tree, a network of interconnected patterns, described in Sect. 4.2. In
Sect. 4.3 we provide recursive algorithms for automatically generate specific branches.
Finally, in Sect. 4.4, we make a preliminary evaluation of the transformations.

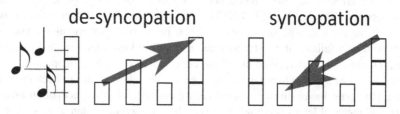

Fig. 4. The de-syncopation transformation shift events forward to slower metrical levels. The
syncopation transformation shifts events backwards to faster metrical levels.

4.1 The Transformations

Removing the syncopation is a process of forward shifting of the onsets that syncopate
to stronger metrical positions (Fig. 4, left). Each shift of an event results in a new
pattern with decreased syncopation. When all events have been shifted to their non-
syncopating positions the resulting de-syncopated pattern has no syncopation. We call
such a pattern a root. Pulses that belong to slower metrical levels are considered to
be stronger, so that the de-syncopation process moves events from fast metrical levels
to slower ones.

New syncopation is generated by anticipating the onsets found in strong metrical
positions, shifting them to weaker positions (Fig. 4, right). This time, each shift of an
event results in a new pattern with increased syncopation. When all "strong" onsets
have been moved to weaker positions the resulting syncopated pattern cannot be further
syncopated. The syncopation process, opposite to the de-syncopation process, "pushes"
events to the faster metrical levels. A detailed description of the syncopation transformation and its inverse—the de-syncopation transformation—follows.

Syncopation. The syncopation transformation takes a binary pattern and generates syncopation by anticipating the events found in strong metrical positions. Onsets in pulses that belong to strong metrical positions (slow metrical levels, low metrical indexes) are shifted to preceding pulses belonging to weaker metrical positions (faster metrical levels, higher level indexes).

When syncopating, there might be more than one pulse to shift an onset to. In other words, there might be more than one way to syncopate at a certain metrical position. A strong pulse might be preceded by more than one weak pulses, e.g. a pulse that belongs to the quarter note level is preceded by a pulse at the eighth note level and another one at the sixteenth note level, both belonging in faster metrical levels than the initial one (Fig. 5). We define as the type of syncopation the value of the difference of the metrical levels of the two pulses: the pulse that the onset belongs to originally and the one that it is shifted to[1]. An event is then shifted according to the chosen type to the first pulse that precedes the original position and belongs to the corresponding metrical level. Encoding the syncopation shifts into types of metrical level differences provides the freedom to associate them to metrical positions, to metrical levels or to specific onsets.

For example, if the type is set to 1 (the difference of the metrical indexes = 1), a quarter note is shifted to the preceding eighth note since the eighth note level is one metrical subdivision faster than the quarter note level; while, if the type is set to 2, the same quarter note is shifted to the preceding sixteenth note (Fig. 5). In general, the larger the type value (the difference of the metrical indexes), the shorter it is the duration of the generated syncopation. This is a direct consequence of the alternating character of strong and weak pulses of the metrical template. The number of syncopation types that is available for each pulse depends on how many faster metrical levels exist in the template.

Each syncopation shift is described by a pair of numbers: the pulse that originally carries the onset and the type of syncopation shift that the onset undergoes. They can be thought of as the "coordinates" of the transformation. The pulse index directly corresponds to the "horizontal" coordinate. The type value corresponds to the vertical length of the arrow that represents the shift.

An onset cannot be shifted if one or more onsets block its way. This rule ensures that the order that the events are performed is preserved. In the example of Fig. 5, we cannot apply the syncopation transformation (8, 1) if an onset is found in any of the pulses 5, 6 or 7. The transformation is forbidden.

The above rule might seem at first glance as having no purpose. After all, the onsets in the binary string are indistinguishable from one another and the order in which they are played back is unimportant. Nevertheless, we will later attribute dynamic accents to the onsets. Each one will receive a specific amplitude value and it will carry it in all the generated variations. Thus, onsets will be eventually distinct and therefore their order must be preserved. Moreover, this way the process is more general and can be

---

[1] Alternatively we could have encoded the transformation as the pair of pulses, the initial pulse of the onset and the pulse it is shifted to. This way of encoding correctly describes the particular transformation. However, as it will become apparent in the following, using the level differences is a more general and more flexible representation.

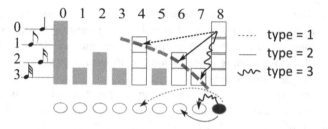

Fig. 5. An example of the types of syncopation transformations available for an onset at a specific pulse (pulse 8). White square represent the preceding pulses of faster metrical levels that are available for syncopating pulse 8. The rest of the pulses have been greyed out. The corresponding de-syncopation transformation is obtained by reversing the direction of the arrows.

expanded to include other types of phenomenal accents, such as pitch or timbre changes, or other properties of the events that can make them distinct.

De-syncopation. The de-syncopation transformation is a direct consequence of the operational definition of syncopation followed in this article [2, p. 295, 4]: syncopation in the binary patterns is found in those events that are placed in a relatively weak metrical position (faster metrical levels, higher metrical indexes) and are not followed by an event in the following stronger position (slow metrical level, low metrical index). In order to de-syncopate such an event, we shift its onset to a position where it no longer syncopates, i.e. to the following strong metrical position that was initially empty, thus evoking the feeling of syncopation.

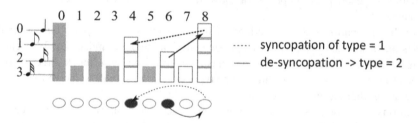

Fig. 6. If the order of onsets was not preserved during the transformations, the 1-1 correspondence of the two transformations would be lost.

The de-syncopation transformation is essentially the inverse of the syncopation transformation. In Fig. 5, onsets that might be found in pulses 4, 6, or 7, can be de-syncopated by reversing the direction of the arrows. As an onset gets de-syncopated, it reveals the type of the syncopation transformation that it had previously undergone. The de-syncopation can be thought of as the analysis process yielding the type of syncopation that was previously generated by a syncopation transformation. An event might need to be shifted more than once in order to be completely de-syncopated. For example, an event found in pulse 5 in Fig. 5 needs to be shifted first to pulse 6 and then to pulse 8 yielding the corresponding syncopation transformations (6, 1) and (8, 1) expressed as pairs of pulses and types.

The above definition of syncopation attributes the syncopation to the event being anticipated. However, the syncopation is only felt at the moment of the following silent pulse and is retrospectively attributed to the event being heard. The following alternative phrasing of the syncopation definition attributes syncopation to the silent pulse where the syncopation is actually felt instead of the onset that initiates it: "syncopation is found in the silent pulses that belong in strong metrical positions (slower levels, lower indexes) and that are preceded by onsets in one of the immediately preceding weaker metrical positions". Thus, de-syncopation must be applied to the silent pulse by shifting the preceding onset. In Fig. 6, de-syncopating pulse 8 is done by shifting the onset of pulse 6 to pulse 8 (solid arrow), yielding the corresponding syncopation type and completing the syncopation pair (8, 2).

The de-syncopation transformations reveal a deeper reason for preserving the order of onsets when syncopating and forbidding certain transformations. If one could jump over an existing onset when syncopating, then the transformations could not have a 1-1 correspondence. Imagine an onset originally existing in pulse 8 of Fig. 6 and apply the (8, 1) syncopation transformation (dashed arrow). The de-syncopation of pulse 8 would result in a different pattern than the one we started with. Moreover, it would return a different syncopation transformation—of type 2, as we already saw. Thus, the two transformations would not be reversible if two onsets could reverse their order.

The described transformation guarantees that the resulting pattern will not syncopate. This is not true for other similar transformations. In some cases, one could de-syncopate off-beat events by shifting them to the preceding on-beat position instead of the following one. However, the two directions are not equivalent. The operational definition of syncopation attributes the syncopation feel to the lack of an event in the following strong position. The forward shifting of events always guarantees the resulting pattern will not syncopate, as the "empty" strong pulse that was causing previously the syncopation will now receive an onset.

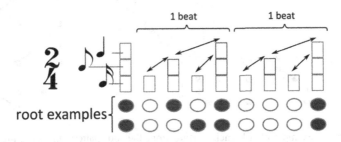

Fig. 7. The syncopation shifts can only move onsets in the duration of a single beat.

An important property of the transformations comes about the structure of the metrical template of alternating strong and weak pulses and the prominent role given to the beat—the most salient of the metrical levels. As we have seen, the transformations can shift events either forward to slower metrical levels or backwards to faster metrical levels. Since the beat level is the slowest metrical level included in the template, each transformation has local character; it displaces events within the duration of a single beat[2] (see Fig. 7). Thus, any pattern longer than a beat can be considered a concatenation of shorter and independent—with regard to the syncopation transformations—single beat patterns.

4.2   The Syncopation Tree

The two transformations described above can be used to generate paths of syncopation transformations, i.e. a sequence of specific transformation steps, each of which represents the displacement of a single event. To be consistent with our nomenclature, we call such a path a "branch"; for example, the branch that connects a syncopated pattern to its non-syncopating root or to some other syncopated pattern. The branches that connect all possible patterns that originate from the same root form a syncopation tree. In this section we are providing with an overview of the generation of syncopation trees and some of their properties.

On the left side of Fig. 8, we present an example of how a branch is generated starting from the root pattern and applying a series of transformations until we reach the end of the branch where no onset can be syncopated further. However, one could start from any pattern and apply syncopation and de-syncopation transformations to reach another pattern of the same tree. The root pattern of the example has 3 events and is considered to be a repeating loop (the first event is repeated at the end). The branch consists of a set of transformations of specific types indicated by the two numbers next to each pattern. The specific branch is generated by applying the transformations in a particular order. The pairs of numbers form two arrays: (i) one contains the indexes of the pulses in the particular order of the transformations and (ii) the second contains the

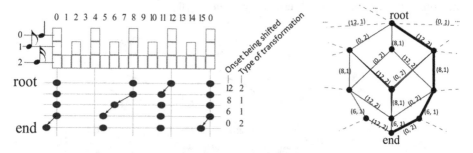

Fig. 8. Left: An example of a branch starting from the root pattern and finishing to an end pattern that cannot be further syncopated. Right: Example of a syncopation tree (partially shown). The patterns are shown as dots and the lines connecting them correspond to the indicated transformations. The thick line corresponds to the branch shown on the left. The patterns shown are connected with the same set of syncopation transformations applied in a different order.

---

[2] The duration of the beat is offset by a single pulse to what commonly is considered the duration of the beat (Fig. 7). The beat duration here ends ON the beat and includes all preceding pulses between the current and the previous beat.

type of each transformation. The two arrays completely describe the branch. We refer to such coupled arrays as the branch arrays.

The order of the transformations can change to generate a different branch. As long as the type of each syncopation is kept the same, the end pattern will always be the same. In other words, as long as we include the same transformations but apply them in a different order, we will reach the same end pattern[3]. However, it must be noted that not all permutations are possible. Here, the transformation (8, 1) must always be applied before the (6, 1) otherwise there will be no onset in pulse 6 to be shifted. Some intermediate patterns will also be shared among the branches. In the right side of Fig. 8, we show the branches of the corresponding syncopation tree that include all possible permutations of the transformations in the left (solid lines, the thick solid line is the branch shown in detail at the left).

Each dot in the right part of the figure represents a specific pattern and is connected to the root pattern with a specific number of steps, independently of the exact branch that one might follow. This is a general property of all syncopation trees and not of this particular example. The root pattern as well as the number of de-syncopation steps for a given syncopated pattern is independent of the order in which the pulses are de-syncopated. Only the intermediate patterns differ.

The entire tree is formed by several branches like the ones shown in Fig. 8. These branches form a network that begins at the root and has several ends. The number of ends depends on the number of possible transformations that can be performed within each beat duration. In our example, the 3 onsets belong to different beats and can undergo 2 different transformations each: either the $(i, 1)$ or the $(i, 2)$ followed by the $(i - 2, 1)$, where i is the index of the pulse. Therefore, we have $2^3 = 8$ different ends in this tree. In Fig. 8, we show only the branches that lead to the end pattern shown on the left. The branches that lead to the rest of the ends are connected to the patterns of the figure through the dashed lines.

The complexity of the tree depends on the root pattern and the metrical template used. Visualization of the tree can become challenging as the number of the connections of each pattern can be large. One can imagine the tree as a three dimensional structure with the root pattern in the center of a sphere and the end patterns on its surface. The intermediate patterns form a web in the interior of the sphere.

Any two patterns in the tree have at least one branch that connects them, passing through several other patterns. Generating such branches is equivalent to analyzing the relations of the generated patterns.

Since events cannot be shifted from one beat to another, each beat must contain the same number of events in all patterns of the same tree. As a consequence, patterns with different distribution of events in the beats will have different roots and therefore belong in different trees. However, more than one root patterns exist that have the same number of events in each of their beats (Fig. 7). As consequence, the distribution of events in beats is not the only criterion for two patterns to belong in the same tree.

---

[3] In order for the end pattern to be the same, all transformations in a given permutation must result in the shift of an event, i.e. the permutation should not result in forbidden or blocked transformations.

4.3   Recursive Algorithms

De-syncopation. The generation of a branch consists in determining the corresponding series of syncopation transformations expressed as a branch array, i.e. an order array coupled to a type array. Such arrays can be generated by a de-syncopation process, i.e. by recursively applying a de-syncopation transformation for each pulse that is found to syncopate until there is no syncopating pulse. Using the de-syncopation output for a given rhythmic pattern, one can generate all intermediate patterns from the corresponding root pattern to the original input pattern. As we already saw, the root pattern is independent of the order in which the pattern is de-syncopated.

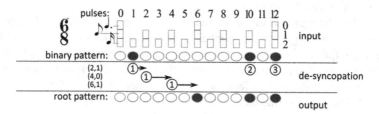

Fig. 9. Illustration of a recursive de-syncopation process. The metrical template shown corresponds to a 6/8 m at 180 bpm (q.n.d. = 1000 ms). Each onset of the binary pattern is numbered in a circle. The de-syncopated process is shown as arrows.

Figure 9 illustrates the process through an example. Pulses are examined in a certain order and when a silent pulse is preceded by an onset in a faster metrical level, the onset is shifted as described in Sect. 4.1. In this example, the pattern is scanned from right to left. However, the order in which the pulses are examined can be, in principle, freely chosen. The first pulse examined is pulse 12, which carries an onset and therefore does not syncopate. Pulse 11 as well as all pulses of the fastest metrical level cannot syncopate. Pulse 10 is also ignored, as it carries an onset. Pulse 8, 6 and 4 do not syncopate since they are not preceded by an onset in a faster metrical level. The first silent pulse found to syncopate is pulse 2 that belongs to the eight note level. Event ① precedes it in pulse 1 (sixteenth note level). Therefore it is shifted to pulse 2 yielding the undergone syncopation transformation (2, 1).

The process restarts from pulse 12 and now the first syncopating pulse is 4. This is a special case of syncopation where the preceding event is in a pulse of the same metrical level as the pulse in question. However, they both belong in a subdivision of the beat, i.e. they do not belong in the slowest metrical level included in the template. In that case, the event needs to be shifted and the type of syncopation is 0 yielding the (4, 0) transformation. This special case can occur in meters with a ternary subdivision of the beat such as the 6/8. In the final round, pulse 6 needs to be de-syncopated resulting in the (6, 1) transformation.

The following pseudo code illustrates the basic steps in the de-syncopation algorithm:

```
##inputs
bool PATTERN = {O1, O2, ..., On}
int LEVELS = {L1, L2, ..., Ln}
int ORDER = {P1, P2, ..., Pm}
##outputs
int outORDER = {empty array}
int outTYPE = {empty array}
## DE-SYNCOPAION LOOP
Repeat
    For each position p in ORDER
        if (PATTERN[p]==FALSE AND LEVELS[p]<=max(LEVELS))
            r = Find_Preceding_Pulse(p)
            if (PATTERN [r to p-1 r]==FALSE)
            PATTERN[r]=FALSE;
            PATTERN[p]=TRUE//Shift onset r->p
            Output PATTERN
            Append p in outORDER
            Append (LEVELS[p]- LEVELS[r])in outTYPE
    end
Until no onsets can be shifted
Output outORDER, outTYPE
```

The above code makes use of a subroutine for finding the preceding onset, if any:

```
Find_Preceding_Pulse(p)
LMIN = LEVELS[p]
p--; CurrentML = LEVELS[p]
While (LEVELS[p] > LMIN AND PATTERN[i]==FALSE)
    p--; CurrentML = min(LEVELS[p], CurrentML)
End
If (PATTERN[p]==TRUE AND LEVELS[p]==CurrentML AND
                                    L[p]>LMIN)
    Return p
Else Return -1
End
```

The above code receives as input three arrays: (i) the pattern as a binary string (PATTERN), (ii) the metrical template as an array of the metrical indexes (LEVELS) and (iii) the ORDER array which represents the order in which the pulses should be scanned and the found syncopations should eliminated. The algorithm outputs the new binary pattern with each shift of an event. At the same time it stores the details of each shift in two arrays. The outORDER array contains the pulse of the shift and the outTYPE array contains the metrical level difference. The two arrays together comprise the branch arrays generated by the de-syncopation and describe the transformations applied to the input pattern. They are output at the end of the de-syncopation loop. In the example of Fig. 9 the two arrays would be:

```
outORDER  = 2,  4,  6
outTYPE   = 1,  0,  1
```

A couple of examples of default values for the input order array would be the pulses in their natural order, from left to right (0, 1, 2, etc.), or in their order of importance, e.g. according to their metrical level, de-syncopating first the faster metrical levels, or according to the indispensability values of Clarence Barlow [1, 2]. Not all pulses need to be contained in the order array, since not all pulses carry onsets that need to be de-syncopated. However, it is important to ensure that all pulses that will syncopate in any of the intermediate steps of the de-syncopation process will be included in the input order array. As long as this is ensured, the order of transformations only affects the intermediate steps. The root pattern and the instances of syncopation found are the same for any order. The number of elements in the output branch arrays, as well as the values of each pair in the arrays, is unaffected by the input order. Only their position in the arrays could in certain cases change, depending on the pattern. In the example of Fig. 9, the result is always the same; all output arrays and patterns will be exactly the same, independently of the input order.

Syncopation. In order to automatically syncopate an input pattern, one can apply repeatedly a series of syncopation transformations until no onsets can be further shifted. The branch arrays for the syncopation process need to include all pulses that carry onsets in any of the output patterns of the applied transformations. That will ensure that when the transformations are applied recursively all onsets will be shifted in syncopating positions and the end of the branch will be reached.

The process is similar to the one shown on the left side of Fig. 8. However, in that example, the transformations were applied once and were particular to the generated branch. In a recursive syncopation process, the branch arrays can be generic and can automatically generate a complete branch from root to end pattern. For example, a default order of transformations can be generated by starting from the pulses in the slowest metrical level and continue to the faster ones until all pulses are included (the fastest metrical level can be ignored). After applying the possible transformations to all the pulses in the array, the process repeats until no onset can be displaced.

For each pulse, a type of transformation should also be assigned. Several options for default values are available. The simplest is a constant value for all pulses. The types can also be chosen according the metrical level of each pulse. For example, all notes could be shifted to the preceding sixteenth note. That would be a type 2 for the quarter notes and a type 1 for the eight notes.

In cases where the level difference expressed in the type of syncopation results in a metrical level faster than the fastest metrical subdivision included in the metrical template, then this fastest metrical subdivision is used disregarding the type. For example, if the type is set to 2 for an onset at the eight note level, it should be shifted to the preceding thirty-second note. If the metrical template only goes as fast as the sixteenth note level, then the onset should be shifted to the preceding sixteenth note, disregarding the type value found in the array.

If one wishes to reverse the transformations generated by the de-syncopation algorithm, he only needs to reverse the two branch arrays, outORDER and outTYPE, produced by the recursive de-syncopation process. Performing the transformation once on the root pattern generates the exact steps of the de-syncopation.

Moreover, one can use the arrays produced during the de-syncopation of a pattern as a point of departure for creatively generating transformations for another pattern. Transformations can even be mapped across different meters, by mapping the order and types to the metrical levels instead of the pulses. For example, during a de-syncopation process, the events found at the eight note metrical level were shifted to the quarter note level (type 1). They were also shifted before any other events at faster levels. Those transformations can be mapped and used when syncopating another pattern with a different metrical template. Pulses at the same metrical level could be put last in the order array and receive the same value of type transformation, i.e. shifts to the preceding pulses of the next faster subdivision. The values for the type array can also be "learned", e.g. by analyzing a collection of rhythms instead of a single pattern and then generating appropriate order and type values. Of course such mappings are not always meaningful.

The following pseudo code illustrates the basic steps in the syncopation algorithm:

```
##inputs
bool PATTERN = {O1, O2, ..., On}
int LEVELS = {L1, L2, ..., Ln}
int ORDER = {P1, P2, ..., Pk}
int TYPE = {T1, T2, ..., Tk}
int MAXrepeat = maximum number of repetitions
int step = 0;
##outputs
int outORDER = {empty array}
int outTYPE = {empty array}
## SYNCOPATION LOOP
Repeat
    For each position p[i] in ORDER //at index i of ORDER
        if PATTERN[p[i]]==TRUE AND
                                LEVELS[p[i]]!=maximum[LEVELS]
            Find preceding position r:
                    (LEVELS[r] = LEVELS[p[i]] + TYPE[i])
            if PATTERN[p[i]-1 to r]==FALSE
                PATTERN[p[i]]=FALSE;
                PATTERN[r]=TRUE//Shift p[i]-> r
                Output PATTERN
                Append p[i]in outORDER
                Append (LEVELS[r]- LEVELS[p[i]])in outTYPE
    end
step += 1
Until no onsets can be shifted OR step >= MAXrepeat
Output outORDER, outTYPE
```

A "*find preceding position*" subroutine is used to find the preceding pulse that belongs to the faster metrical level. The subroutine is similar to the one used in the de-syncopation algorithm with the difference that it is looking for a silent pulse and that the pulse belongs to specific metrical level determined by the type of transformation.

At the end of the algorithm shown above, a pair of branch arrays results as output. These arrays may differ from the input ones. As the pattern is scanned according to the input order, some transformations might be blocked or skipped when an onset is not found resulting in a different final order. The two arrays, outORDER and outTYPE, contain the actual transformations that were performed.

Figure 10 presents a schematic overview of the entire process of generating a complete branch that passes through a particular pattern. The process is divided in an analysis and a generation stage. First, the de-syncopation of the input pattern to its root provides a detailed analysis of the syncopation of the given pattern. Second, a complete branch is generated, starting with the root pattern, reaching the input pattern and expanding to the other end, to a maximally syncopated pattern. The first part is performed by the de-syncopation algorithm and the second by the syncopation algorithm.

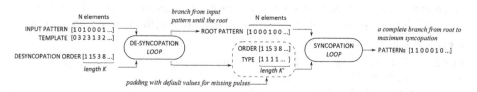

Fig. 10. Overview of the generation of a branch of syncopation transformations that passes through a given input rhythmic pattern

It is important to note that the de-syncopation process functions as an analysis stage, even though it actually generates all the intermediates between the root and the input pattern as part of the analysis. The root pattern together with the branch arrays of order and types gives a complete picture of the generated patterns and their relations in a compressed form. The mere collection of the actual intermediate patterns can be thought of as a "by-product" of the process.

The second part of the process generates the entire branch beginning with the root. By altering the order of elements in the syncopation arrays, one can generate a different branch that might not pass by the given input pattern but it will end at the same end pattern. The patterns found in that branch will share the same types of syncopations, although the patterns in their entirety would not be identical. However, altering the type values leads to a completely different branch.

4.4 Preliminary Evaluation of Transformations

In this section we evaluate the syncopation transformations described in Sects. 4.1 and 4.3 in practice, i.e. with actual musical material and not just theoretical binary patterns. We applied the transformations on a collection of MIDI drum loops. Then, we used the LHL syncopation metric described in Sect. 3 to measure the syncopation in the original loops and in three more versions that have undergone the syncopation transformations: (1) the root pattern, (2) a syncopated version with 30 % of the total transformations applied, and (3) a syncopated version with 70 % of the total transformations applied. The two syncopated versions were automatically syncopated with a default branch array. Therefore, they belong to different branches than the corresponding original patterns.

The MIDI collection was taken from [15] and consists of 160 drum loops of different music styles. The MIDI files were segregated into three separate MIDI streams according to the MIDI note numbers that correspond to the kick drums, snare drums and hi-hats. All 480 loops (3 × 160) were in a 4/4 m and quantized to the 16th note grid and they were converted to binary patterns before applying any transformation. In all cases we used a metrical template that corresponds to a 4/4 m at 100 bpm.

First, they were de-syncopated according to the process described in Sect. 4.3. Second, the resulted de-syncopated patterns were re-syncopated with 30 % and 70 % of total of the possible syncopations applied. The order array was generated by shuffling the indexes of all pulses. The type of the syncopation process was set to 2, forcing the syncopation shifts always to two metrical subdivisions faster. We used the LHL metric to measure the syncopation in all versions of each of the 480 loops. An overview of the results is shown in Fig. 11.

The de-syncopation and re-syncopation algorithms performed as expected. The de-syncopation algorithm removed completely the syncopation in all 480 binary patterns (syncopation score = 0). This was expected as the de-syncopation process directly corresponds to the way onsets are matched to following silent pulses in the definition of syncopation in the LHL algorithm.

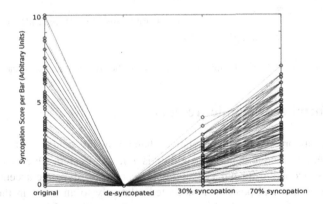

Fig. 11. Syncopation measurements using the LHL algorithm on 4 different versions of the patterns found in the 480 binary patterns. Each circle represents a single measurement. The grey lines connect the measurements for the 4 different versions of each pattern. As the number of measurements is large, several lines naturally overlap. The darker the line is, the more the overlaps.

The re-syncopated process increased gradually the syncopation. The 30 % transformation increased the syncopation in the majority of the patterns (in 469 out of 480 patterns). The 70 % transformation increased further the syncopation for the majority of the patterns (in 445 out of 480 patterns). No pattern had less syncopation in the 70 % than in the 30 % transformations. In a few exceptions, the patterns had the same syncopation score for the de-syncopated and 30 % transformation (11 patterns), or for the 30 % and 70 % transformations (35 patterns) (horizontal lines in Fig. 11). In 6 patterns out of the total 480 the re-syncopation transformations did not create any syncopation.

The exact relation between the syncopation scores and the percentage of the applied transformations depends on two factors: (1) the number of onsets per bar in the pattern that can actually be shifted and are not blocked by other onsets and (2) their metrical positions. When only a small number of events can be shifted there are accordingly few steps between the de-syncopated version and the fully syncopated version (100 % of the transformations applied). The number of events that can be shifted in the pattern strongly depends on the density of events per bar. For very low density (e.g. only a couple of events per bar) or very high density (when almost all metrical positions are occupied) the onsets available for syncopation are very few. The evaluation shows that the syncopation transformations increase the syncopation with each step, even when the available steps are very few.

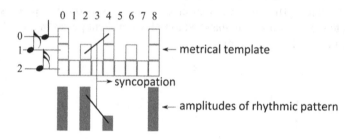

Fig. 12. An example of a temporary mismatch of the dynamic and metrical accents.

5   Transforming Dynamic Accents

Dynamic accents are produced by relative changes in the loudness of serial events. When an event is louder than its neighbor is felt as stressed. One can extend the definition of syncopation for binary patterns to account for dynamic accents. When an event at a weak metrical position is accented relatively to an event in the following strong position, syncopation is felt. The syncopation will be felt stronger when the onset in the weak position is more stressed and when the metrical levels of the two pulses are further apart. The syncopation measure proposed by Sioros and Guedes [22] uses this principle to measure syncopation in accented patterns.

Loudness changes are distinguished from metrical accents [12]. They are part of larger group of physical accents that arise from changes in some dimension of the sounding events. They are often referred to as phenomenal accents. With this distinction in mind, syncopation can be described as "*a temporary mismatch of the phenomenal and metrical accents*".

In Fig. 12, an example of a syncopation arising from dynamic accents is shown. A loud event in pulse 0 is followed by an equally loud event in pulse 2. Although pulse 2 belongs in a weak metrical position, it is not against our metrical expectations to hear an onset there. However, the loud event in pulse 2 will raise our expectations for a loud event in pulse 4. When a much quitter event actually follows, the previous event sounds relatively stressed. This stress is against our metrical expectations and the feeling of syncopation is evoked. As the difference in loudness gets greater the feeling is more intense. In the extreme case that no onset is heard on the strong pulse, our definition of syncopation is equivalent to the definitions for binary patterns (see Sect. 2).

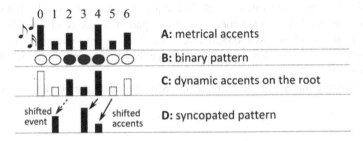

Fig. 13. Example illustrating the process of assigning and manipulating dynamic accents. *A*: Metrical accents calculated based on the metrical template. *B*: A binary, de-syncopated pattern. *C*: Dynamic accents on the events in their de-syncopated positions. *D*: Syncopated pattern. The event on pulse 2 is now shifted to pulse 1 (*dashed arrow*). The events on pulses 3 and 4 cannot be shifted. Instead, the accents on pulse 3 and 4 are shifted (*solid arrows*).

We introduce dynamic accents to the binary patterns for two reasons: (i) to enhance the metrical feel by accenting the onsets on strong pulses and (ii) to generate syncopation on onsets that could not be shifted by a syncopation transformation such as the ones described in Sect. 4.

Each onset is assigned a specific dynamic accent in the range between 0 (a silent onset) and 1 (loudest possible) relative to the metrical strength of its position. In that way, a binary pattern becomes a sequence of amplitude values. In Sect. 5.1, the accents are assigned to the onsets according their de-syncopated positions enhancing that way the metrical feel (phenomenal accents matching the metrical accents). In Sect. 5.2, the accents are "shifted" to onsets in weaker metrical position generating syncopation (mismatch of phenomenal and metrical accents).

5.1 Generating Accents

The metrical feel is enhanced when phenomenal accents coincide with the metrical accents, i.e. when changes in the loudness, pitch etc. coincide with the alternation of strong and weak pulses characteristic of the meter. Based on this principle, each onset is assigned an amplitude value relative to the metrical strength of the pulse that the onset belongs to.

The amplitudes are assigned to the root pattern and the onsets carry the accents to all syncopating positions. This is because a syncopating onset can be found in weak metrical positions. If we were to assign the amplitude according to this weak position, we would weaken the syncopation without necessary enhancing the metrical feel since the onset will still be syncopating. Furthermore, if the onset is shifted to its de-syncopated position carrying a weak accent, the syncopation might not be completely eliminated.

The amplitudes are assigned to the onsets themselves and not to the pulses, so that when the onsets are shifted to different positions in the various syncopated versions, they still carry their accents from the root pattern (Fig. 13). For example, an onset found at the beat or quarter note level in the root pattern will still be a loud onset with a high amplitude value even when it is shifted to a faster metrical level. In that way, the feeling of syncopation is intensified. The syncopating event is distinct from other events that are found in fast metrical levels but that do not syncopate. Those non-syncopating events receive lower amplitudes since they belong in fast metrical levels in the root pattern.

The following mathematical formula is used to calculate the amplitudes of onsets:

$$A(i) = C^{L(p_i)} \tag{1}$$

where $A(i)$ (range: 0–1) is the amplitude of event i, C is a parameter that controls the "contrast" between strong and weak metrical positions, p_i is the pulse that event i belongs to (in the root pattern) and $L(p_i)$ is the metrical level of that position. The parameter C ranges between 0 (only the slowest metrical level survives) and 1 (all metrical levels receive the same amplitude).

5.2　Generating Syncopation

Dynamic accents can generate syncopation when the actual displacement of onsets is not possible. Imagine the extreme case where all pulses, even at the fastest metrical subdivision, carry an onset. That would be, for example, the case of drum rolls. In such cases, onsets cannot be shifted since there are no empty pulses available and the only way to reveal the meter or contradict it is through the use of accents. In order to introduce syncopation to such a pattern, we stress certain off-beat onsets while atten-uating the ones that follow them on the beat. For those onsets, the phenomenal accents would not coincide with the metrical accents, and that mismatch of phenomenal to metrical accents would be felt as syncopation.

The accents of the onsets in their de-syncopated positions are proportional to the metrical strength of the positions. Instead of shifting the onsets, the accents can receive an equivalent shift, while the onsets themselves are kept in their initial positions. In that way, the accent of a loud event in a strong position will be anticipated and will be shifted to a preceding event in a weaker metrical position.

In order for the shift to be effective, the amplitude of the onset in the strong position must be attenuated. Looking closer at the metrical template and the way it is constructed, one observes that strong and weak pulses are always alternating. Strong pulses, which belong to slow metrical levels, are always followed by weak pulses, which belong to faster metrical levels. Shifting the metrical template to the left by one pulse provides us the attenuated amplitude for the strong event (Fig. 13D, solid arrows).

The generation of syncopation based on dynamic accents is a secondary mechanism that is needed only when the onsets themselves cannot be shifted. Otherwise, the onsets carry with them the dynamic accents, so that onsets and accents are anticipated together.

The example in Fig. 13 illustrates how dynamic accents are used. Metrical accents are calculated according to the metrical template (A). They are, then, assigned to the onsets of a de-syncopated pattern (B and C). Finally, syncopation is generated in two ways (D): (1) by shifting the onsets that also carry their accents, and (2) by shifting the metrical accents instead of the onsets themselves.

6 Max4Live Device

Our MIDI device manipulates effectively and in real time the syncopation in midi clips. It systematically removes the syncopation and creates new syncopation in the clip according to the transformations described in Sects. 4 and 5.

The device constructs automatically a metrical template that corresponds to the time signature and tempo settings of the Ableton Live Set. The template defines the fastest metrical subdivision, i.e. a quantization grid, and the number of pulses or steps in the pattern as described in Sect. 3.

The user interface of the device is shown in Fig. 14. When a midi clip is playing in the same track as the device, its contents are automatically "loaded" in the Max4Live device. The midi notes are grouped together according to the pulse they belong. In the center of the device, a display area presents a rough representation of the midi contents to the user. Pulses containing note events are shown as red squares. Grey bars represent the "beat", i.e. the pulses that belong to the slowest metrical level of the template.

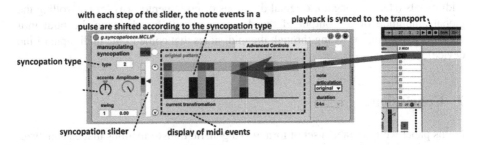

Fig. 14. The MIDI Max4Live device that manipulates the syncopation in midi clips.

The syncopation transformations are applied on each pulse as if it was a binary pattern. Pulses containing note events are treated as the onsets of the binary pattern. When an onset is displaced to another pulse, all the note events of the respective pulse are shifted together. The transformations are applied automatically according to the algorithms described in Sect. 4.3. The pattern is first de-syncopated and its root is determined. Then a branch is generated starting from the root and reaching an end pattern. The type of the "extra" transformations needed to syncopate the midi notes beyond the original syncopation can be set on the left side of the device through a number box named "type".

A syncopation slider on the left of the display area controls which pattern in the generated branch is selected for playback. At the lower end of the slider, the root pattern is found. As one raises the slider, he will pass by the original midi clip that is marked as a red square on the slider. Raising the slider further will lead to further syncopation until the end of the branch is reached at the upper end of the slider.

A different branch can be generated that does not pass by the original pattern in the midi clip and does not necessarily end at the same end pattern. By de-activating the red button named "orig" right above the slider, a branch is generated based on a default order and the user input type value. The order is chosen according to the indispensability values of Barlow's algorithm [1, 2].

For the onsets that cannot be shifted, their dynamic accents are shifted as described in Sect. 5. First, dynamic accents are imposed on the note events, substituting their original velocity values with velocity values that match the metrical template. Second, when a specific transformation in the branch array cannot be applied (because a note event "blocks" it), the velocities are shifted instead. A dial at the left side of the device controls the dynamic accents applied. When the dial is turned to the left, no accents are applied and all onsets have maximum velocity. When the dial is turned fully right, only the slower metrical level survives. In the center position, the velocity of the events is relative to the metrical strength of their positions.

In the display area and just below the red squares denoting the midi clip contents, a representation of the currently selected pattern is shown. As one moves the syncopation slider, the pattern that is selected changes and it is displayed as black bars that represent the pulses containing note events. The height of each bar is relative to the midi velocity assigned to the note events in the pulse.

A few other secondary controls are available: (i) for choosing the articulation of the midi events (staccato, legato, original durations or portamento), (ii) for controlling the global amplitude of the output of the device, and (iii) for choosing the midi thru operation (blocking or letting through the midi notes that come in the midi input of the device).

7   Conclusions

In this paper we presented a set of formalized generic transformations that can analyze, generate and manipulate the syncopation in binary patterns. The transformations are based on the cognitive definition of syncopation as a violation of metrical expectancies. The transformations serve as a tool for analyzing and generating syncopation in rhythmic patterns. In fact the two processes are combined under the concept of a syncopation transformation; the transformation describes the syncopation in a pattern at the same time that it generates the pattern itself. We extended the main transformations to include dynamic accents that can be applied on binary patterns to enhance the metrical feel or generate syncopation.

We introduce the concept of the syncopation tree. The rhythmic patterns found on the branches of the tree are interconnected through specific sequences of transformations. Any two patterns on a tree can be transformed from one to the other following a branch of single-step transformations. One can navigate from one pattern to another unveiling the relations between the patterns. In each tree, it exists only one pattern with no syncopation, called the root pattern. The particular branch that connects a pattern to its root provides with a detailed description of the syncopation in the pattern, such as the number of syncopating events, the position of the syncopations and the metrical levels involved. The transformations and syncopation tree can serve as the basis for rhythmic similarity or distance measures.

The way syncopation is encoded and described in this model helps in creatively exploring its uses. For example, one can think of modeling the syncopation of one particular music style as specific transformations on certain root patterns. These transformations could then be applied on root patterns that do not belong to the modeled styled. The modeling of a musical style can be done by automatically de-syncopating a number of patterns characteristic of that style, e.g. rhythmic patterns performed simultaneously by different instruments. The resulted transformations could then be combined and applied to the root of any other pattern effectively "copying" the syncopation style.

The applications of the syncopation transformations to music and syncopation styles are left to be explored in the future work of our group. However, we developed a software application as a small example of a creative application of the syncopation transformations. It has the form of a Max4Live midi device that manipulates the syncopation of midi clips.

The Max4Live devices and related externals are available for download at our website: http://smc.inescporto.pt/shakeit/.

Acknowledgments. This research was partly funded by the Media Arts and Technologies project (MAT), NORTE-07-0124-FEDER-000061, financed by the North Portugal Regional Operational Programme (ON.2 – O Novo Norte), under the National Strategic Reference Framework (NSRF), through the European Regional Development Fund (ERDF), and by national funds, through the Portuguese funding agency, Fundação para a Ciência e a Tecnologia (FCT).

References

1. Barlow, C.: Corrections for Clarence Barlow's article: two essays on theory. Comput. Music J. **11**(4), 10 (1987)
2. Barlow, C., Lohner, H.: Two essays on theory. Comput. Music J. **11**(1), 44–60 (1987)
3. Fitch, W.T., Rosenfeld, A.J.: Perception and production of syncopated rhythms. Music Percept. **25**(1), 43–58 (2007)

4. Gabrielsson, A.: Adjective ratings and dimension analyses of auditory rhythm patterns. Scand. J. Psychol. **14**(4), 244–260 (1973)
5. Gómez, F., Thul, E., Toussaint, G.: An experimental comparison of formal measures of rhythmic syncopation. In: Proceedings of the International Computer Music Conference, pp. 101–104 (2007)
6. Gómez, F., Melvin, A., Escuela, U.: Mathematical measures of syncopation. In: Proceedings of BRIDGES: Mathematical Connections in Art, Music and Science, pp. 73–84 (2005)
7. Huron, D.: Sweet Anticipation: Music and the Psychology of Expectation. The MIT Press, Cambridge (2006)
8. Huron, D., Ommen, A.: An empirical study of syncopation in American popular music, 1890–1939. Music Theory Spectr. **28**(2), 211–231 (2006)
9. Jones, M.R.: Musical time. In: Hallam, S., et al. (eds.) The Oxford Handbook of Music Psychology, pp. 81–92. Oxford University Press, Oxford (2009)
10. Keith, M.: From Polychords to Polya: Adventures in Musical Combinatorics. Vinculum Press, Princeton (1991)
11. Kennedy, M., Bourne, J. (eds.): Oxford Dictionary of Music. Oxford University Press, New York (1994)
12. Lerdahl, F., Jackendoff, R.: A Generative Theory of Tonal Music. The MIT Press, Cambridge (1983)
13. London, J.: Hearing in Time. Oxford University Press, Oxford (2012)
14. Longuet-Higgins, H.C., Lee, C.S.: The rhythmic interpretation of monophonic music. Music Percept. **1**(4), 424–441 (1984)
15. Miron, M., Davies, M., Gouyon, F.: An open-source drum transcription system for pure data and max MSP. In: The 38th International Conference on Acoustics, Speech, and Signal Processing, Vancouver, Canada (2013)
16. Palmer, C., Krumhansl, C.L.: Mental representations for musical meter. J. Exp. Psychol. **16**(4), 728–741 (1990)
17. Parncutt, R.: A perceptual model of pulse salience and metrical accent in musical rhythms. Music Percept. **11**(4), 409–464 (1994)
18. Randel, D.M.: The Harvard Dictionary of Music. Belknap Press of Harvard University Press, Cambridge (1986)
19. Repp, B.H.: Rate limits of sensorimotor synchronization. Adv. Cogn. Psychol. **2**(2–3), 163–181 (2006)
20. Sioros, G., Miron, M., Cocharro, D., Guedes, G., Gouyon, F.: Syncopalooza: manipulating the syncopation in rhythmic performances. In: Proceedings of the 10th International Symposium on Computer Music Multidisciplinary Research, pp. 454–469. Laboratoire de Mécanique et d'Acoustique, Marseille (2013)
21. Sioros, G., Guedes, C.: A formal approach for high-level automatic rhythm generation. In: Proceedings of the BRIDGES 2011 – Mathematics, Music, Art, Architecture, Culture Conference, Coimbra, Portugal (2011)
22. Sioros, G., Guedes, C.: Complexity driven recombination of MIDI loops. In: Proceedings of the 12th International Society for Music Information Retrieval Conference, Miami, Florida, USA, pp. 381–386 (2011)
23. Temperley, D.: Syncopation in rock: a perceptual perspective. Pop. Music. **18**(1), 19–40 (1999)
24. Volk, A., de Haas, W.: A corpus-based study on ragtime syncopation. In: 14th International Society for Music Information Retrieval Conference, Curitiba, Brazil (2013)
25. Yeston, M.: The Stratification of Musical Rhythm. Yale University Press, New Haven (1976)

Cent Filter-Banks and its Relevance to Identifying the Main Song in Carnatic Music

Padi Sarala$^{(\boxtimes)}$ and Hema A. Murthy

Indian Institute of Technology, Madras 600036, India
padi.sarala@gmail.com, hema@cse.iitm.ac.in

Abstract. Carnatic music is a classical music tradition from Southern India. It is primarily based on vocal music, where the lead performer is a singer. A typical Carnatic music concert is made up of several items. Each item can be made up of a number of segments, namely, monophonic *vocal solo*, monophonic *violin solo*, polyphonic (vocal and accompanying instruments) *composition* (or *song*) and monophonic percussion (*thaniavarthanam*). The *composition* (or *song*) segment is mandatory in every item. The identification of composition segments is necessary to determine the different items in a concert. Owing to the improvisation possibilities in a composition, the compositional segments can further consist of monophonic segments. The objective of this paper is to determine the location of *song* segments in a concert. The improvisational aspects of a concert lead to the number of applauses being much larger than the number of items. The concert is first segmented using the applauses. Next, inter-applause segments are classified as *vocal solo*, *violin solo*, *composition* and *thaniavarthanam* segments. Unlike Western music, the key used for different items in the concert is fixed by the performer. The key also referred to as tonic can vary from musician to musician and can also vary across concerts by the same musician. In order to classify different inter-applause segments across musicians, the features must be normalised with respect to the tonic. A new feature called Cent Filter-bank based Cepstral Coefficients (CFCC) that is tonic invariant is proposed. *Song* identification is performed on 50 live recordings of Carnatic music. The results are compared with that of the Mel Frequency Cepstral Coefficients (MFCC), and Chroma based Filter-bank Cepstral Coefficients (ChromaFCC). The *song* identification accuracy with MFCC is 80%, with CFCC features is 95% and with ChromaFCC features is 75%. The results show that CFCC features give promising results for Carnatic music processing tasks.

Keywords: Cent filter-banks · Segmentation of carnatic music concert · Applause identification

1 Introduction

Music Information Retrieval (MIR) has become a very challenging task owing to huge audio repositories that are available on the Internet. Significant research

© Springer International Publishing Switzerland 2014
M. Aramaki et al. (Eds.): CMMR 2013, LNCS 8905, pp. 659–681, 2014.
DOI: 10.1007/978-3-319-12976-1_40

has been done on Western music like tempo estimation [39], beat estimation [2], instruments identification [20], and transcription of Western music [29]. Indian music is hardly analysed or subjected to many of the recent technologies in music information retrieval. Indian music includes both Carnatic music and Hindustani music. Carnatic music is prominent in the Southern parts of India and Hindustani music is prominent in the Northern part of India. Unlike Western music, in Carnatic music, a *song* that is composed in a specific melody (*rāga*) and rhythm can be rendered differently by different musicians. This is primarily because Carnatic music has been handed over from the teacher to the student and taught orally. This has resulted in a number of different schools of learning with renderings being identified with the specific school. Archival of Carnatic music is therefore a difficult task.

Owing to the CompMusic project[1], Indian, Chinese, Turkish, and Andulasian music have received significant attention over the last five years [8,44,45]. A number of different research efforts have resulted in significant progress in processing Carnatic music [5,19,21,23,34,36,43,46]. As the tonic that is likely to be used by a musician is not known apriori, this task was first addressed [5,19] and tonic can be identified very accurately using 90 seconds of audio [6]. A *rāga* in Carnatic music is identified by its typical motifs. Efforts on motif recognition and spotting have gained impetus over the last two years [19,22,35]. In Carnatic music, the percussion instruments are pitch instruments. Some efforts on rhythm analysis in Carnatic music can be found in [3,4,14].

Carnatic music concerts are generally continuous unsegmented recordings that are replete with applauses[2]. Applauses have been successfully used to segment these recordings [36–38]. The applause locations in a concert are identified and the concert is segmented at applause locations. The objective of this paper is to further classify inter-applause segments as monophonic vocal, monophonic violin, polyphonic composition and monophonic percussion, which are referred to as *vocal solo, violin solo, song (composition)*[3], and *thaniavarthanam* in this paper. Locations of these segments in a three hour continuous recording are useful for aspiring musicians. A finer segmentation of the concert into *vocal solo, violin solo, song,* and *thaniavarthanam*, vocal-violin tandem, different percussion instruments in tandem, can be useful to a keen learner, listener or researcher. These segments can be automatically detected within a concert instead of the listener manually searching for these events in the audio.

Mel Frequency Cepstral Coefficients (MFCC) features are seldom used for music modeling tasks, while ChromaFCC [16,31] are preferred. The basic issue in using MFCCs for music processing is the key that is used to render a given item. To address this issue, a chroma filter-bank is suggested[4]. In this filter-bank, the frequency spectrum is folded on to a single octave and a variant of MFCC

---

[1] http://compmusic.upf.edu/.

[2] http://www.sangeethapriya.org.

[3] *composition* can also be referred as *song* (*composition* and *song* are interchangeably used in this paper).

[4] www.ee.columbia.edu/~dpwe/resources/Matlab/chroma-ansyn.

based on the chroma filter-bank are designed. In Western music, the tunings are predefined. Therefore, this approach may be adequate. Further, the inflection of notes is significantly less in Western music. In Carnatic music on the other hand, the inflection of a note can span two adjacent semitones. A singer also performs the concert with respect to a reference called tonic (Shadja) [5]. Any melodic analysis of Indian music therefore requires a normalisation with respect to the tonic. Although the segmentation of a concert and locating the main *song* is primarily associated with timbre, the spectrum must be normalised by the tonic because the pitches seen in a musical item depend on the tonic chosen by the musician. Table 1 reinforces this conjecture given that even for the same melody, the range of pitches can be significantly different. The melodic atoms and the timbre associated with the voice change with the octave in which the *composition* is rendered. To address this, a new feature called Cent Filter-bank based Cepstral Coefficients (CFCC) is proposed in this paper.

Several methods have been developed for audio segmentation. These methods can be metric-based or model-based methods. In [12], segmentation of audio stream into homogeneous regions using Bayesian Information Criterion(BIC) is discussed. The paper [1] discusses speech/music segmentation using Hidden Markov Model (HMM) with entropy as a feature. In both metric-based and model-based methods, MFCCs are the most frequently used features. Logan et. al [27] have discussed MFCC features for music modeling. The paper [47] discusses the importance of MFCC features for identifying the Erhu instrument by building GMM models. Roisin et.al [28] use MFCC features to identify musical instruments like Piano, Violin, Flute. Principal Component Analysis (PCA) is used to determine the coefficients that are suitable for identifying musical instruments. In the paper [17], a wide range of spectral and temporal properties like spectral centroid, RMS value, fundamental frequency of sounds are used in a K-NN classifier for musical instrument identification. Sheng et.al [18] uses LPC, LPCC and MFCC features for segmentation and identification of vocal music, instrumental music and a combination of both vocal and violin music. Hidden Markov Models are built for three classes and the segmentation accuracy is obtained by testing segments of length 1–2 s. Moreno et.al [30] have discussed instrument classification using LPC and MFCC features with Gaussian Mixture Model (GMM) and Support Vector Machine (SVM) based classifiers. While the problem of segmentation has been researched in the literature, most of the work is on Western or middle-Eastern music. There is very little serious work on Indian music and in particular Carnatic music. Owing to nature of Western music, significant progress has been made. In Indian music, the primary issue is the tonic.

The purpose of this paper is to segment the three hour concert into different segments like *vocal solo*, *violin solo*, *song*, and *thaniavarthanam*. A concert is generally replete with applauses and these applause locations are identified using spectral domain features as described in a previous work [36]. Using applauses as cue, a concert can be segmented into different segments. These segments are labelled as *vocal solo*, *violin solo*, *song*, and *thaniavarthanam* by building

Gaussian Mixture Models (GMM) with CFCC features. Finally, *song* segments are highlighted for archival purposes.

The paper is organised as follows. Section 2 gives the overview of a Carnatic music concert and importance of tonic with respect to Carnatic music. Section 3 discusses details of CFCC feature extraction and its importance compared with other features like MFCC, ChromaFCC, Constant Q transform (CQT) based features. Segmentation of a concert and *Main song* detection is discussed in Sect. 4. Section 5 discusses the database used for evaluation and experiments performed on Carnatic music concerts for the identification of the *Main song*. Finally, Sect. 6 concludes the work.

2   Background

2.1   A Carnatic Music Concert

Carnatic music is primarily a South Indian music tradition and Hindustani spans most of the country in India. Carnatic music concert is said to have a specific format introduced by Ariyakkudi Ramanuja Ayyangar [24]. A typical Carnatic music concert can be two to three hours long and it can have 10–12 items or pieces. A concert can have three different phases namely, the opening phase with *compositions* rendered in medium and fast tempo, the second phase introduces some of the major *rāgas* of Carnatic music, and the third phase called concluding phase focuses on a number of smaller or lighter *compositions* (tukkadas) [33]. A concert in Carnatic music is replete with applauses. As most Indian music is improvisational, the audience applauds the artist spontaneously.

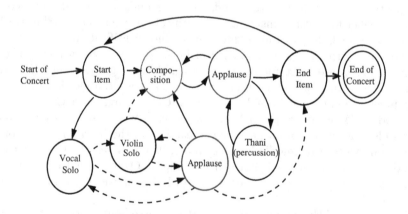

Fig. 1. General structure of a Carnatic music concert.

The general structure of a concert in Carnatic music is illustrated in Fig. 1. As shown in Fig. 1, a concert is made up of a number of different items. Each item can optionally have a *vocal solo* or a *violin solo* or a percussion solo (referred to as Thani in the Figure) but a *composition* is mandatory. Generally, the audience applauds the artist at the end of every item. Owing to the spontaneity that can be leveraged by an artist in a Carnatic music concert, the concert is more like a dialogue between the artist and the audience [32]. From Fig. 1, we can observe that each item can have a *vocal solo, violin solo, composition)*, and *thaniavarthanam* segments[5].

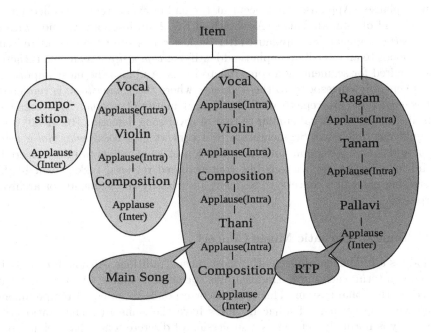

Fig. 2. General structure of an Item in Carnatic music concert. In Figure applauses after every segment are indicated by intra-applauses and applauses after end of an item are indicated by inter-applauses.

There are many segments in an item in Carnatic music that lend themselves to improvisation. *Alāpanā* in Carnatic music, also called as *vocal solo*, denotes one such branch. It is characterised by the absence of a definable and recurring rhythmic pattern or metre (tala) [33]. Thaniavarthanam is a segment where mridangam solo is performed as most important percussion instrument. Violin *alāpanā* is similar to the vocal *alāpanā*, where the violinist explores the *rāga*. A good violinist generally attempts to give a sketch that is more or less similar to that of the vocalist. This is generally about half the duration of the *alāpanā* by the vocalist. *Composition* is an important segment in a concert and it can be thought of as an ensemble where the *vocal solo*, the *violin solo* and the *percussion* are present simultaneously[6]. An item in a vocal Carnatic music concert can have

---

[5] Carnatic Music terms are explained in the Appendix.

[6] Hereafter we refer to this as (main) song.

different structures and it generally ends with the *composition* segment. In fact, an item can occasionally have no *composition* segment. Although this is indicated in Fig. 1, in this paper we assume that a *composition* segment is present in every item.

Figure 2 shows different types of items in a concert. As shown in Fig. 2, applauses can occur after every segment namely *vocal solo*, *violin solo*, *composition*, and *thaniavarthanam*. These applauses are called intra-item or within item applauses. Applauses that occur at the end of every item are called inter-item or end of item applauses. As shown in Fig. 2, an item always ends with a *composition* segment. The applause after the last *composition* segment in an item corresponds to an inter-item applause. Identifying *composition* segments is therefore required for segmenting a concert into items. And also the most important items generally correspond to the segments where the *composition* is rendered. All *compositions* are replete with the typical motifs of a *rāga*. *Song* segment identification is somewhat similar to that of cover song detection [16,31,40] with a significant difference. Segmentation of a concert into *vocal solo*, *violin solo*, *song*, and *thaniavarthanam* and identification of *song* segments in a concert is useful for different applications like content-based retrieval tasks, to highlight interesting parts of a concert, to segment and classify the segments for archival purposes.

2.2   Tonic in Carnatic Music Concert

Melody is a fundamental element in most music traditions. Although melody is a common term, each music tradition has specific differences. Western music is based on the tonal system. This system corresponds to an equal temperament scale where every pair of adjacent notes have the same frequency ratio [41]. A melody is normally defined as a succession of discrete tones that belong to a given scale and tonality context. Most melodic studies use the symbolic representation of music and use concepts like notes, scales, octaves, tonality and key signatures. Melodic analysis of a Western piece of music is normally based on a quantised representation of pitches and durations within a well defined framework of possible relationships [42]. Melody in Indian classical music relates to the concept of *rāga*. A *rāga* also prescribes the way a set of notes are to be inflected and ordered. Western Music is based on a Harmonic scale, while Indian Music is based on the natural scale. Most Indian music does not correspond to a specific tuning, and if any, it is more related to just intonation than to equal temperament [41]. The key for a *song* in a Western music item is generally defined by the composer, while the key for a *song* in Indian music is defined by the performer.

Melody in Indian music is defined with respect to the key chosen. In a Carnatic music concert, the tonic is chosen by the performer and accompaniments are tuned to the same tonic. Tonic chosen for a concert is maintained throughout the concert using an instrument called "tambura" which provides the drone [7]. The chosen key depends on the vocal range of the performer. Carnatic music is based on the twelve semitone scales and frequencies of semitones depends on the tonic. Table 1 shows the svaras which are very basic in Carnatic music.

Table 1. Carnatic music svaras and their frequency ratios. Table also shows the twelve semitone scale for four different musicians.

Sno	Carnatic music svara	Label	Frequency ratio	Semitone scale for different tonics			
				138	156	198	210
1	Shadja (Tonic)	S	1.0	138	156	198	210
2	Shuddha rishaba	R1	(16/15)	147.20	166.40	211.20	224
3	Chatushruthi rishaba	R2	(9/8)	155.250	175.50	222.75	236.25
4	Shatshruthi rishaba	R3	(6/5)	165.250	187.20	237.60	252
3	Shuddha gAndhara	G1	(9/8)	155.250	175.50	222.75	236.25
4	ShAdhArana gAndhara	G2	(6/5)	165.60	187.20	237.60	252
5	Anthara gAndhara	G3	(5/4)	172.50	195.0	247.5	262.5
6	Shuddha madhyama	M1	(4/3)	184.0	208.0	264.0	280
7	Prati madhyama	M2	(17/12)	195.50	221.0	280.5	297.5
8	Panchama	P	(3/2)	207.00	234.0	297.0	315
9	Shuddha daivatha	D1	(8/5)	220.80	249.60	316.8	336
10	Chatushruthi daivatha	D2	(5/3)	230.00	260.0	330.0	350
11	Shatshruthi daivatha	D3	(9/5)	248.40	280.80	356.4	378
10	Shuddha nishAdha	N1	(5/3)	230.0	260.0	330.0	350
11	Kaisika nishAdha	N2	(9/5)	248.40	280.80	356.4	378
12	KAkali nishAdha	N3	(15/8)	258.75	292.50	371.25	393.75

Any melody is defined with respect to these svaras. Table 1 shows frequencies corresponding to the twelve semitones for four singers, each with a different tonic. From Table 1, we can see that frequencies of semitones vary with respect to the tonic. Therefore, modeling or processing of Carnatic music requires normalisation with respect to the tonic.

3   Cent Filter-Bank Feature Extraction

As explained in Sect. 1, notes that make up a melody in Carnatic music are defined with respect to a reference called tonic. Thus, the analysis of a concert therefore depends on the tonic. The tonic values for male and female singers has a particular range. Tonic range for female singers is 160 Hz to 250 Hz and for male singers is 100 Hz to 175 Hz.

A number of different variants of MFCC [15] features are used both in speech and music processing. When MFCCs are used to model music, a common frequency range is used for all musicians. To address this issue, chroma filter-banks were suggested and is extensively used in music, especially Western classical music [16,31]. This is still not adequate for Indian music as the folding over to a single octave is not appropriate as the characteristic traits of the musician/melody may be observed in a particular octave or across octaves. In this paper, we propose a new filter-bank structure called cent filter-bank that seems to show promise for segmentation of Indian music.

In our initial attempts at determining *song* location, 3–5 min of each type segment was manually labelled in a concert and MFCC based GMM models were trained for *song, violin solo, vocal solo,* and *thani (percussion)*. These models were then used to determine the location of *song*s in the entire 3 h concert. To avoid training for every concert, segments were manually labeled for concerts of different musicians. MFCC based GMMs were once again trained using this data. Although the segmentation performance was accurate for concerts of musicians used in training, the performance on unseen musicians was poor. On the other hand, the segments that correspond to Thani (percussion) were easily detected owing to the timbral characteristic being significantly different. The poor performance on segments other than percussion suggests that cent filter-bank based coefficients, which are normalised with respect to tonic, are required to capture the note positions. To create cent filter-banks, the power spectrum of the music signal is first normalised with respect to the tonic using the definition of the cent defined in Eq. (1). Figure 3 shows the extraction of CFCC features for a concert.

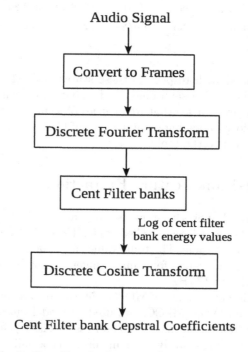

Fig. 3. Cent filter-bank energy feature extraction.

Extraction of cent filter-bank based cepstral coefficients is detailed below

1. The audio signal is divided into frames.
2. The short-time Discrete Fourier Transform (DFT) is computed for each frame.
3. The power spectrum is then multiplied by a bank of filters that are spaced uniformly in the tonic normalised scale called as cent scale. The cent scale is defined as:

$$cent = 1200 \cdot \log_2 \left(\frac{f}{tonic} \right) \tag{1}$$

4. The energy in each filter is computed. The logarithm of filter-bank energies is computed.
5. Discrete Cosine Transform (DCT-II) of log filter-bank energies is computed.
6. The cepstral coefficients obtained after DCT computation are used as features for building the GMM models.

3.1   Tonic Identification

A number of different approaches to tonic identification ranging from simple processing of pitch histograms on entire concert to sophisticated signal processing [5,7] and machine learning algorithms [6,19] on short segments of music have been proposed in the literature. The objective here is to obtain the tonic of a concert. Therefore, simple pitch histogram based method is employed.

The tonic does not change across various items in a concert. As a result, each concert is simply segmented into 6 parts. For each part, pitch is extracted using Yin [13] algorithm. All the histograms are multiplied to get a single final histogram. In this histogram, the location of the maximum peak corresponds to the tonic used by the musician for the concert. Figure 4 shows a pitch histogram for a female and a male singer. The frequency location of the maximum peak is the tonic. The tonic for the female singer in Fig. 4 is 200 Hz and male singer tonic is around 100 Hz. The tonic identification accuracy using pitch histograms and different tonic values for each singer is discussed in Sect. 5.

3.2   Importance of CFCC Feature

In this paper, we have compared cent filter-banks with mel filter-banks, chroma filter-banks and constant Q transform (CQT) based filter-banks. CQT filter-banks are proposed in [10] for music instrument identification. In CQT, the filter-banks are placed on the "$\log_2$" frequency scale whereas in cent filter-banks, filter-banks are placed on the $\log_2$ frequency scale, where the frequency is normalised with respect to the tonic. Figure 5(a) and (b) show cent filter-bank and CQT filter-bank energies (as a function of time) on a motif of *rāga Kambhoji* in Carnatic music sung by a male and a female musician. The filters are placed

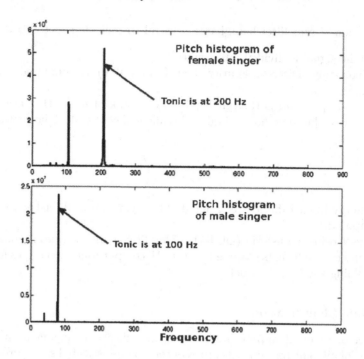

Fig. 4. Composite pitch histogram for a female and male singer.

uniformly on the cent scale. The range of cents for both approaches is set to six octaves from −1200 to 6000 cents.

From Fig. 5(a) and (b), it is observed that while Fig. 5(b) shows no structure, in Fig. 5(a), the pitch trajectory corresponding to the motif is clearly visible. This is primarily because in Fig. 5(b), the filter-bank does not correspond to the range of the musician. The range of frequencies are then changed to 0-10800 cents for the constant Q filter-bank. Figure 5(c) shows the time frequency representation for the modified CQT filter-bank. Although the motif is clearly visible, there is a linear shift of the frequencies along the Y-Axis in Fig. 5(c) between the male and female musician. This is primarily due to the tonic. It is also observed that the lower octaves hardly contain any information. While it was quite trivial to choose the frequency range in cents for the cent filter-bank scale, the frequency range for the CQT based filter-bank scale had to be carefully chosen to ensure that both musicians' motifs are visible. This is the primary reason for choosing the filter-banks normalised with respect to tonic. Henceforth, only CFCC, ChromaFCC and MFCC based features are compared and used to build the GMM models.

Figure 6 shows the mel filter-bank, cent filter-bank energies, and chroma filter-bank energies for short segments of Carnatic music, corresponding to that of *song*, *violin solo*, and *vocal solo* respectively. Since Carnatic music is replete with inflections or *gamakas* [25,26], in the chroma filter-bank implementation

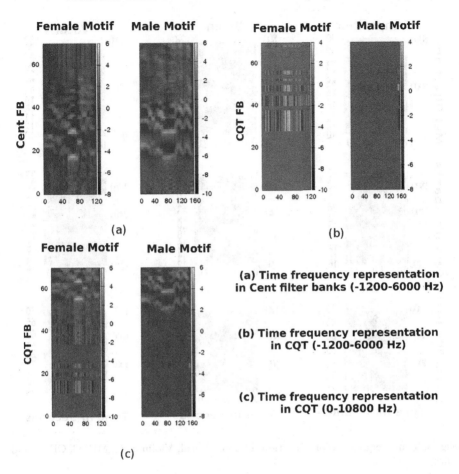

Fig. 5. Time frequency representations using tonic normalised cent filter-banks and CQT filter-banks.

the filters overlap. The width of a filter may be as large as 2 semitones. From Fig. 6, it can be seen that while in the chroma filter-bank the note is emphasised, in the mel filter-bank, the prominent pitch is completely masked. On the other hand, in the cent filter-bank, the prominent pitch is still emphasised. The timbral characteristics of the segment are also emphasised in the vicinity of the prominent pitch. These filter-bank energies are then converted to cepstral coefficients using DCT. To maintain consistency across the three approaches, the range of frequencies was set to 8000 Hz for mel filter-bank, and 6 octaves were chosen for both chroma and cent filter-banks in the figure. The choice of 6 octaves is based on the fact that the range of a voice is at most 3 octaves. The chroma filter-bank was also normalised with the tonic of the performer.

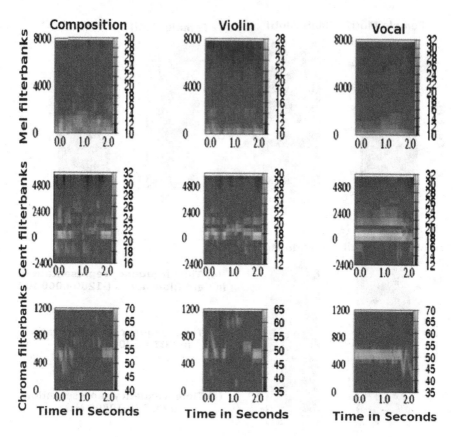

Fig. 6. Time frequency representations of Song, Vocal, Violin using MFCC, CFCC and ChromaFCC.

Figure 7 shows time-filter-bank energy plots for both the Mel scale and Cent scale for different musicians. The time-filter-bank energies are shown for the same motif of the *rāga* sung by two male[7] and one female musician[8]. Filter-bank energies are plotted for three different musicians (ALB Motif with 160 tonic, Sanjay Motif with 155 tonic and DKP Motif with 161 tonic) with different tonic values. In case of mel scale, filters are placed uniformly for every concert irrespective of tonic values where as, in case of cent scale, the filter-banks are normalised with respect to tonic. From Fig. 7, it is clear that the motifs across musicians are comparable in the cent scale rather than the mel scale.

---

[7] ALB-Alathur Brothers and Sanjay- Sanjay Subramanian.
[8] DKP-DK Pattamal.

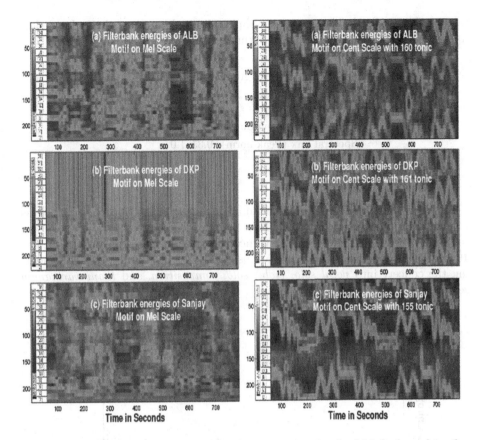

Fig. 7. Filter-bank Energies of a Composition segment in the Mel Scale and in the Cent scale with different tonic values.(In Figure DKP-DK Pattamal female musician, ALB-Alathur Brothers, Sanjay are male musicians).

4   Segmentation of Carnatic Music Concert

4.1   Applause Analysis

As explained in Sect. 2, a Carnatic music concert is a dialogue between the audience and the artist. Applauses can occur anywhere in the concert. Figure 1 shows possible applauses in a concert. Paper [36] discusses applause identification in a Carnatic music concert and its application to archival of a Carnatic music. The paper also discusses the use of Cumulative Sum (CUSUM) [9] to highlight the important aspects of a concert. A concert is segmented using applauses, where spectral domain features with appropriate thresholds are used. Paper [36] have discussed the details about spectral domain features for applause detection in a concert. As these features are single dimensional, a simple threshold is used to discriminate music and applause. Table 2 shows the threshold ranges for every feature. These thresholds are chosen empirically and based on these thresholds, applause and music segments are determined.

Table 2. Decision Thresholds for Applause and Music discrimination.

Feature	Threshold range
Spectral flux (Nonorm)	0.2–1.0
Spectral flux (Peak norm)	0.35–1.0
Spectral entropy	0.79–1.0

Figure 8 shows applause locations in a 3 h concert using Spectral Entropy as a feature. Figure 8 shows the CUSUM of Spectral Entropy values and peaks correspond to applause locations. The Concert has 22 applauses in total and it has 10 items. These applause locations are used as segment boundaries for segmenting the concert into *vocal solo*, *violin solo*, *composition*, and *thaniavarthanam* segments.

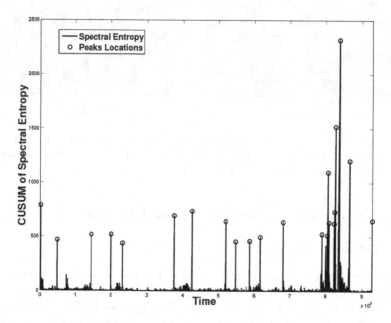

Fig. 8. Applause locations for a concert using spectral entropy as a feature.

4.2 Identifying the Main Song in Carnatic Music Concert

A Carnatic music concert can have 8–10 *composition* segments. Identifying *composition* segments helps to find number of items in a concert [38]. In order to find the *composition* segments in a concert, GMMs are built for four classes, namely, a *vocal solo*, a *violin solo*, a *composition* ensemble and *thaniavarthanam* using CFCC features. Figure 9 shows the framework for segmenting the concert into *vocal solo, violin solo, song,* and *thaniavarthanam* using GMMs.

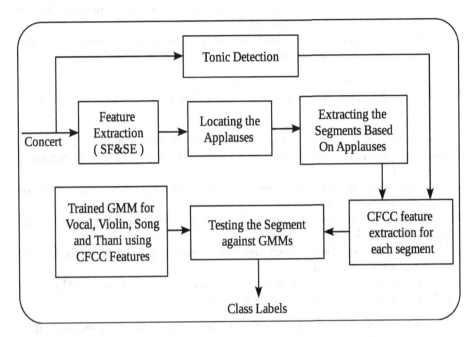

Fig. 9. Framework of segmenting the concert into vocal solo, violin solo, song and thaniavarthanam using GMMs.

To build the GMMs for the segmentation of the concert, *vocal solo, violin solo, thaniavarthanam,* and *composition* segments are manually segmented from the database. From male/female recordings, three segments are chosen for training the GMM for each class. MFCC, ChromaFCC, and CFCC features of 20 dimensions are extracted. GMMs with 32 mixtures are built for each of the four classes. The training process is discussed later in this Section. All 50 recordings are segmented based on applause locations and all these segments are manually labeled as *vocal solo, violin solo, thaniavarthanam,* and *composition.* Labeled data is used as the ground truth for finding the segmentation performance[9]. After segmenting the concerts based on the applauses, there are 990 segments in total and these segments are tested against the GMMs. All these segments are labeled using 1-best result. The GMM training and testing details are as follows:

---

[9] Labeling was done by the first author and verified by a professional musician.

Training the Models: During training, the following steps are performed.

1. Models are built separately for male and female musicians. From male/female recordings, 3 segments are randomly chosen for each class
2. 20 dimensional MFCC, ChromaFCC, and CFCC features are extracted with a frame size of 100 ms and hop size is 10 ms. CFCC and ChromaFCC are extracted after tonic normalisation.
3. 32 mixture GMM models are built for the 4 classes namely *vocal solo, violin solo, song,* and *thaniavarthanam.*

Testing the Models: During testing, the following steps are performed for every concert.

1. Tonic is identified for each concert using the pitch histograms.
2. Applause locations are identified in a concert using the approach discussed in Sect. 4.1.
3. Once the applause locations are identified, segments between a pair of applauses is used for testing.
4. These segments are tested against the trained GMM models that are built for the forementioned classes.
5. The segments are labeled using the 1-best result and the location of *song* segments are highlighted.
6. The recordings of male and female singers are tested against the GMM models built for male and female singers separately.

Figure 10 shows the overall procedure for identifying the *song* segments in a concert. In this Figure, the first row corresponds to the audio with the applause locations marked. The second row indicates the different segments between pair of applauses. The third row corresponds to the labeling of all the segments into *vocal solo, violin solo, song,* and *thaniavarthanam.* In the last row, *song* segments are highlighted.

5   Experimental Evaluation

In this section, we first give a brief introduction to the database used for experimental study and then describe the experimental setup. The performance of the given approach is discussed in Sect. 5.3.

5.1   Database Used

For evaluation purpose, 50 live recordings of male and female singers are taken[10]. All recordings correspond to vocal concerts where the lead performer is a vocalist. Each concert is about 2–3 h long. The total number of applauses across all the

---

[10] These live recordings were obtained from a personal collection of audience, musicians. These were made available for research purposes only.

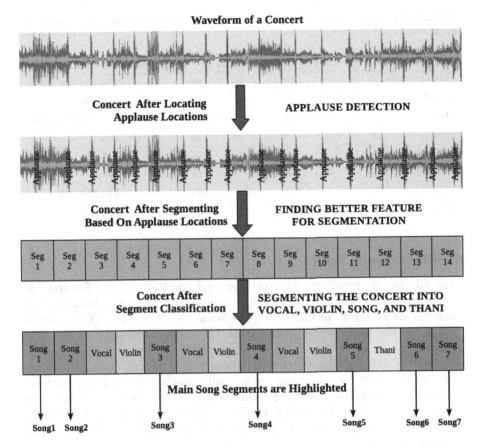

Fig. 10. Overall procedure for segmenting the concert into vocal solo, violin solo, composition and thaniavarthanam.

concerts is 990. There are 990 segments in total in which 175 segments are *vocal solo*, 133 segments are *violin solo*, 576 segments are *song* and 106 segments are *thaniavarthanam*. All recordings are sampled at 44.1 KHz sampling frequency with 16 bit resolution. For feature extraction, the analysis window of size 100 ms is chosen and hop size (overlap) is set to 10 ms.

Table 3 gives the details of the database used. Table 3 gives the statistics about the concerts with respect to musicians and number of applauses. Tonic values for each concert is computed using pitch histograms as explained in Sect. 3.1. These are tabulated in Table 3. Observe that the tonic value is not constant across different concerts by the same musician. There are 4 concerts for *Male* 1 musician and each concert is performed with different tonic like 158, 148, 146, 138 respectively. Tonic identification using pitch histograms gives 100 % accuracy for 50 recordings.

Table 3. Database used for study, different tonic values identified for each singer using pitch histograms.

Singer name	No. of concerts	Duration (Hrs)	No. of applause	Different tonic
Male 1	4	12	89	158,148,146,138
Female 1	4	11	81	210, 208
Male 2	5	14	69	145, 148,150,156
Female 2	1	3	16	198
Male 3	4	12	113	145,148
Female 3	1	3	15	199
Male 4	26	71	525	140,138,145
Male 5	5	14	62	138,140

5.2 Experimental Setup

1. For all the 50 recordings, spectral flux and spectral entropy features are extracted with a window size of 100 ms and overlap of 10 ms. Applauses are marked for all the recordings using the Sonic-Visualizer [11]. These marked applauses are used as the ground truth for finding the applause detection accuracy.
2. To build GMMs for segmentation of the concert, *vocal solo*, *violin solo*, *thaniavarthanam*, and *song* segments are manually segmented from the database. From male and female recordings, three segments are chosen for training the GMM for each class. MFCC, ChromaFCC, and CFCC features of 20 dimensions are extracted. GMMs with 32 mixtures are built for each of the four classes.
3. All 50 recordings are segmented based on applause locations and all these segments are manually labeled as *vocal solo*, *violin solo*, *thaniavarthanam*, and *song*. Labeled data is used as the ground truth for finding the segmentation performance[11]. After segmenting the concerts based on the applauses, there are 990 segments in total and these segments are tested against the GMMs.
4. The performance measure used for evaluating the applause detection and segmentation algorithm is

$$\text{Accuracy} = \frac{\text{Correctly Identified Segments}}{\text{Total Number of Segments}} \times 100\,\%$$

5.3 Experimental Results

The analysis of locating the *song (composition)* segment locations for all the concerts is done in the following two stages.

1. As explained in Sect. 4.1, applauses are located using spectral domain features like spectral entropy and spectral flux. Table 4 shows the applause detection

---
[11] Labeling was done by the first author and verified by a professional musician.

accuracy based on the thresholds. The applause detection accuracy is calculated at the frame level. From Table 4, we can see that a simple threshold is sufficient for identifying the applause locations.

Table 4. Applause and music detection accuracy.

Feature	Accuracy (%)
Spectral flux (Nonorm)	85 %
Spectral flux (Peaknorm)	96 %
Spectral entropy	95 %

2. Secondly, based on applause locations, all concerts are segmented. The segments are labeled using GMMs with CFCC features. Table 5 gives the performance for locating the *Main songs* using mel filter-banks, cent filter-banks, and chroma filter-banks based cepstral coefficients. Cent filter-banks based cepstral coefficients seem to perform significantly better than the other two approaches for Carnatic music. Perhaps the performance on the chroma filter-bank is poor as only five of the useful octaves with respect to tonic are used. This filter-bank needs to be re-engineered for Indian music.

Table 5. Main song identification performance using MFCC, ChromaFCC and CFCC.

Feature name/Model	Male singers	Female singers	Average accuracy
MFCC	78 %	92 %	80 %
ChromaFCC	60 %	70 %	75 %
CFCC	90 %	97 %	95 %

6   Conclusion and Future Work

This paper discusses the importance of cent filter-bank energy feature for locating the *song* segments in a Carnatic music concert. CFCC feature is compared with MFCC and ChromaFCC features. The results show that CFCC features outperform MFCC and ChromaFCC features for segmenting the concert and locating the *song* segments. *Song* identification in a concert is very important for new musicians. In particular, *Main songs* are replete with motifs that make up a melody. Also, a number of variants of the *songs* are available based on the tutelage. Indexing segments of a concert enables automatic archival. Further, *song* segments can be used for identifying the number of items in a concert. The segmentation algorithm fails when there is no applause between segments. The next step in the direction of segmentation would be to determine segment boundaries without applauses. A *composition* is also made of a number of segments, namely, pallavi, anupallavi, charanam, chittai svarams, each with possibilities for exploration and improvisation. Segmentation of a *composition* into its components would be another useful task that must be pursued.

Acknowledgments. This research was partly funded by the European Research Council under the European Unions Seventh Framework Program, as part of the CompMusic project (ERC grant agreement 267583).

Appendix: Carnatic Music Terms

- *Rāga alāpanā* : *Rāga alāpanā* is an impromptu elaboration of the *rāga* at hand. There are no lyrics in an *alāpanā*.
- Composition or Song: Song is a rendition of precomposed lyrics in a specific *rāga* and *tala*. It is set to predefined tune and elaborates the *rāga*.
- Thanam: Thanam is another form of improvisation of the *rāga* using the syllables "Tha Nam". Thanam has an intrinsic rhythm but does not follow any cyclic rhythmic structure.
- Kalpana Svaram: In this kind of improvisation, the svaras/musical notes of that *rāga* are sung/played.
- Niraval: A meaningful line from a composition is taken up for improvisation. The structure of the line is kept intact and the melody is improvised in the *rāga* in which the composition is set.
- Thaniavarthanam: It is the term used for the mridangam solo performance in the concert.
- Main Song: This terminology is used for the song which is chosen for extensive elaboration in the concert. It contains all the improvisational elements such as *alāpanā*, niraval, kalpana svaras. The main song always ends with the Thaniavarthanam.
- Pallavi: A pallavi is a single line of music set to a thala. The pallavi has two parts, divided by an aridhi which is a pause between the two parts. The first part is called the purvanga and the second part after the aridhi is called the uttaranga. niraval is performed on the pallavi.
- Ragam Thanam Pallavi: This piece is a combination of *Rāga alāpanā*, Thanam and the Pallavi. Hence the name, Ragam Thanam Pallavi(RTP).
- Ragamalika: The performer, within a piece (for e.g.: RTP) performs many ragas at a stretch one after the other. This is known as a ragamalika. Literally it means, "A Chain of Ragas".
- Viruttham/slokha is an extempore free flow enunciation of a poem without rhythmic accompaniment. This poem if in the language sanskrit is called a slokha. The viruttham/slokha is rendered in a single *rāga* sometimes in multiple ragas.
- Mangalam: Mangalam is the conclusive piece of every Carnatic music performance.

References

1. Ajmera, J., McCowan, I., Bourlard, H.: Speech/music segmentation using entropy and dynamism features in a HMM classification framework. Speech Commun. **40**, 351–363 (2003)
2. Alonso, M.A., Richard, G., David, B.: Tempo and beat estimation of musical signals. In: ISMIR (2004). http://dblp.uni-trier.de/db/conf/ismir/ismir2004.html# AlonsoRD04
3. Anantapadmanabhan, A., Bello, J.P., Krishnan, R., Murthy, H.A.: Tonic-independent stroke transcription of the mridangam. In: AES 53rd International Conference on Semantic Audio. AES, London, 27 January 2014
4. Ananthapadmanabhan, A., Bellur, A., Murthy, H.A.: Modal analysis and transcription of strokes of the mridangam using non-negative matrix factorisation. In: Proceedings of IEEE Interntional Conference on Acoustics, Speech, and Signal Processing, Vancouver, Canada, May 2013
5. Bellur, A., Ishwar, V., Serra, X., Murthy, H.A.: A knowledge based signal processing approach to tonic identification in indian classical music. In: International CompMusic Wokshop, Instanbul, Turkey (2012)
6. Bellur, A., Murthy, H.A.: A cepstrum based approach for identifying tonic pitch in Indian classical music. In: National Conference on Communication, February 2013
7. Bellur, A., Murthy, H.A.: A novel application of group delay function for identifying tonic in Carnatic music. In: Proceedings of European Conference on Signal Processing, September 2013
8. Bozkurt, B.: Features for analysis of Makam music. In: Workshop on Computer Music, Instanbul, Turkey, July 2012
9. Brodsky, B.E., Darkhovsky, B.S.: Non-parametric Methods in Change-Point Problems. Kluwer Academic Publishers, New York (1993)
10. Brown, J., Puckette, M.S.: An efficient algorithm for the calculation of a constant q transform. J. Acoust. Soc. Am. **92**(5), 2698–2701 (1992)
11. Cannam, C., Landone, C., Sandler, M., Bello, J.: The sonic visualiser: a visualisation platform for semantic descriptors from musical signals. In: 7th International Conference on Music Information Retrieval (ISMIR-06), Victoria, Canada (2006)
12. Chen, S., Gopalakrishnan, P.: Speaker, environment and channel change detection and clustering via the Bayesian Information Criterion. In: Proceedings of the DARPA Broadcast News Transcription and Understanding Workshop (1998). http://www.nist.gov/speech/publications/darpa98/pdf/bn20.pdf
13. Cheveigne, A.D., Kawahara, H.: Yin, a fundamental frequency estimator for speech and music. J. Acoust. Soc. Am. **111**(4), 1917–1930 (2002)
14. Chordia, P.: Segmentation and recognition of tabla strokes. In: Proceedings of International Society for Music Information Retrieval (ISMIR) (2005)
15. Davis, S., Mermelstein, P.: Comparison of parametric representations for monosyllabic word recognition in continuously spoken sentences. IEEE Trans. Acoust. Speech Signal Process. **28**, 357–366 (1980)
16. Ellis, D.: Chroma feature analysis and synthesis (2007). http://www.ee.columbia. edu/~dpwe/resources/Matlab/chroma-ansyn
17. Eronen, A., Klapuri, A.: Musical instrument recognition using cepstral coefficients and temporal features. In: Proceedings of IEEE International Conference on Acoustics, Speech, and Signal Processing, vol. 2, pp. II753-II756 (2000)
18. Gao, S., Maddage, N.C., Lee, C.H.: A hidden markov model based approach to music segmentation and identification. Technical report, International Conference on Information, Communications and Signal Processing (2003)

19. Gulati, S., Salamon, J., Serra, X.: A two-stage approach for tonic identification in indian art music. In: Workshop on Computer Music, Istanbul, Turkey, July 2012
20. Herrera, P., Peeters, G., Dubnov, S.: Automatic classification of musical instrument sounds. J. New Music Res. **32**(1), 3–21 (2003)
21. Ishwar, V., Bellur, A., Murthy, H.A.: Motivic analysis and its relevance to raga identification in carnatic music. In: Proceedings of the 2nd Computer Music Workshop, Istanbul, Turkey, July 2012
22. Ishwar, V., Dutta, S., Bellur, A., Murthy, H.A.: Motif spotting in an alapana in carnatic music. In: Proceedings of International Society for Music Information Retrieval (ISMIR), Curitiba, Brazil, November 2013
23. Koduri, G.K., Serra, J., Serra, X.: Characterization of Intonation in Karṇāṭaka Music by Parametrizing Context-based Svara Distributions. In: Workshop on Computer Music, Instanbul, Turkey, July 2012
24. Krishna, T.: A Southern Music: The Karnatik Story, 1st edn. HarperCollins Publishers in India, New Delhi (2013)
25. Krishnaswamy, A.: Inflexions and microtonality in south indian classical music. In: Frontiers of Research on Speech and Music (2004)
26. Krishnaswamy, A.: Multi-dimensional musical atoms in south-indian classical music. In: International Conference on Music Perception and Cognition (2004)
27. Logan, B.: Mel frequency cepstral coefficients for music modeling. In: International Symposium on Music Information Retrieval (2011)
28. Loughran, R., Walker, J., O'Neill, M., O'Farrell, M.: The use of mel-frequency cepstral coefficients in musical instrument identification. In: International Computer Music Conference, Ireland (2008)
29. Marolt, M.: Trancription of polyphonic piano music with neural networks. In: 10th Mediterranean Electrotechnical Conference, vol. 2, pp. 512–515 (2000).
30. Marques, J., Moreno, P.J.: A study of musical instrument classification using gaussian mixture models and support vector machines. Technical report, Compaq Corporation, Cambridge Research laboratory (1999)
31. Muller, M., Kurth, F., Clausen, M.: Audio matching via chroma-based statistical features. In: ISMIR (2005)
32. Murthy, M.V.N.: Applause and aesthetic experience (2012). http://compmusic.upf.edu/zh-hans/node/151
33. Pesch, L.: The Oxford Illustrated Companion to South Indian Classical Music. Oxford University Press, Oxford (2009)
34. Ross, J.C., Rao, P.: Detection of Raga-characteristic phrases from Hindustani Classical Music Audio. In: Workshop on Computer Music, Instanbul, Turkey, July 2012
35. Ross, J.C., Vinutha, T., Rao, P.: Detecting melodic motifs from audio for hindustani classical music. In: Proceedings of International Society for Music Information Retrieval (ISMIR), Portugal, October 2012
36. Sarala, P., Ishwar, V., Bellur, A., Murthy, H.A.: Applause identification and its relevance to archival of carnatic music. In: Workshop on Computer Music, Instanbul, Turkey, July 2011
37. Sarala, P., Murthy, H.A.: Cent filter banks and its relevance to identifying the main song in carnatic music. In: Proceedings of Computer Music Multidsciplinary Research (CMMR), Marseille, France, October 2013
38. Sarala, P., Murthy, H.A.: Inter and intra item segmentation of continuous audio recordings of carnatic music for archival. In: Proceedings of International Society for Music Information Retrieval (ISMIR), Curitiba, Brazil, November 2013
39. Scheirer, E.D.: Tempo and beat analysis of acoustic musical signals. J. Acoust. Soc. Am. **103**(1), 588–601 (1998). http://dx.doi.org/10.1121/1.421129

40. Serra, J., Gomez, E., Herrera, P., Serra, X.: Chroma binary similarity and local alignment applied to cover song identification. IEEE Trans. Audio Speech Lang. Process. **16**(6), 1138–1151 (2008)
41. Serra, J., Koduri, G.K., Miron, M., Serra, X.: Tuning of sung indian classical music. In: Proceedings of ISMIR, pp. 157–162 (2011)
42. Serra, X.: Opportunities for a cultural specific approach in the computational description of music. In: Workshop on Computer Music, Istanbul, Turkey, July 2012
43. Srinivasamurthy, A., Subramanian, S., Tronel, G., Chordia, P.: A beat tracking approach to complete description of rhythm in indian classical music. In: Workshop on Computer Music, Instanbul, Turkey, July 2012
44. Srinivasasmurthy, A., Serra, X.: A supervised approach to hierarchical metrical cycle tracking from audio music recordings. In: Proceedings of IEEE International Conference Acoustics, Speech, and Signal Processing, May 2014
45. Tian, M., Srinivasasmurthy, A., Sandler, M., Serra, X.: A study of instrument-wise onset detection in beijing opera percussion ensembles. In: Proceedings of IEEE International Conference Acoustics, Speech, and Signal Processing, May 2014
46. Vidwans, A., Ganguli, K.K., Rao, P.: Classification of indian classical vocal styles from melodic contours. In: Workshop on Computer Music, Instanbul, Turkey, July 2012
47. Weng, C.W., Lin, C.Y., Jang, J.S.R.: Music instrument identification using mfcc: Erhu as an example. In: Proceedings of the 9th International Conference of the Asia Pacific Society for Ethnomusicology (Phnom Penh, Cambodia, 2004), Cambodia, pp. 42–43 (2004)

Author Index

Printed in the United States
By Bookmasters